A COMMENTARY ON THE
BOOK OF THE TWELVE

KREGEL EXEGETICAL LIBRARY

A COMMENTARY ON THE
BOOK OF THE TWELVE

The Minor Prophets

MICHAEL B. SHEPHERD

Kregel
Academic

A Commentary on the Book of the Twelve: The Minor Prophets

© 2018 by Michael B. Shepherd

Published by Kregel Publications, a division of Kregel Inc., 2450 Oak Industrial Dr. NE, Grand Rapids, MI 49505-6020.

The English translations of the original Greek or Hebrew texts of the Bible are the author's own.

The Hebrew font used in this book is NewJerusalemU and the Greek font is GraecaU; both are available from www.linguisticsoftware.com/lgku.htm, +1-425-775-1130.

ISBN 978–0–8254–4459–3

Printed in the United States of America
18 19 20 21 22 / 5 4 3 2 1

Dedicated to my Mom, Janice D. Shepherd,
who encouraged me to read the Bible at a young age

CONTENTS

COMMON ABBREVIATIONS

BDB	The Brown-Driver-Briggs Hebrew and English Lexicon
BHS	*Biblia Hebraica Stuttgartensia*
DCH	*Dictionary of Classical Hebrew*
GKC	*Gesenius' Hebrew Grammar*
HALOT	*The Hebrew and Aramaic Lexicon of the Old Testament*
LXX	*Septuagint*
MT	*Masoretic Text*
Syr.	*Syriac Peshitta*
Tg. Jon.	*Targum Jonathan*
TLOT	*Theological Lexicon of the Old Testament*
Vulg.	*Latin Vulgate*[1]

---

1. Abbreviations in footnotes can be found in the Bibliography. See also the second edition of *The SBL Handbook of Style*.

INTRODUCTION

This volume offers something unique when compared to other commentaries on the so-called Minor Prophets. Numerous works have been published on Hosea–Malachi in either single-volume or multi-volume format that treat these prophetic books as twelve separate compositions, often rearranging them in chronological order. This approach is largely due to the lasting effects of the rise of historical criticism in the eighteenth and nineteenth centuries.[1] More recent biblical scholarship has sought to give an account of the transmission of the Book of the Twelve as a single composition in antiquity by highlighting the historical evidence for its unity and by tracing the internal clues to the work of a final composer. The present volume is an effort to bring that scholarship into a commentary setting that will be accessible to students, pastors, and scholars alike.[2] It is hoped that a better

---

1. See Hans W. Frei, *The Eclipse of Biblical Narrative: A Study in Eighteenth and Nineteenth Century Hermeneutics* (New Haven, CT: Yale University Press, 1974). It may be helpful to think of the analogy of commentaries on the Pentateuch. It is quite rare to see a single volume commentary on Genesis–Deuteronomy (e.g., John H. Sailhamer, *The Pentateuch as Narrative* [Grand Rapids: Zondervan, 1992]), even though the book of Moses was considered a single work in antiquity.
2. Marvin Sweeney (Berit Olam: Studies in Hebrew Narrative and Poetry [Collegeville, MN: Liturgical, 2000]) and James Nogalski (Smyth and Helwys Bible Commentary series [2011]) have published multivolume commentaries (Hos.–Jon. and Mic.–Mal.) on the Twelve. The present commentary differs in approach and presentation. Sweeney highlights common themes among the Twelve (cf., the work of Paul House on the Twelve). Nogalski traces the historical development of the Twelve through

understanding of the compositional unity of the Twelve will remove the sense of disconnectedness that readers initially experience with the Prophets and lead to a greater appreciation of the ongoing relevance of the Twelve as Christian Scripture.

THE PLACE OF THE TWELVE IN THE HEBREW CANON

The threefold shape of the Hebrew Canon features the Torah, the Prophets, and the Writings (Prol. Sir.; 4QMMT; Luke 24:44; *Contempl.* 1f., 25).[3] The Book of Twelve falls within the second of these three divisions, although the exact location of the Twelve in the Prophets varies among the witnesses. The Former Prophets (Joshua, Judges, Samuel, and Kings) provide the narrative context for the Latter Prophets, whose writings display the form and style that readers of the Bible typically associate with prophecy.[4] The earliest attestation (c. 200 BC) to the arrangement of the Latter Prophets occurs in Sirach 48–49, which mentions them in the order of Isaiah, Jeremiah, Ezekiel, and "the Twelve Prophets" (Sir. 49:10). This order of the Latter Prophets is what appears in the major codices of the Prophets and the Hebrew Bible from the medieval period.[5]

The Babylonian Talmud (c. AD 600), however, bears witness to a different arrangement of the Latter Prophets: Jeremiah, Ezekiel, Isaiah, and the Twelve Prophets (*b. B. Bat.* 14b).[6] This order does

---

various hypothetical stages of redaction. The present work, however, follows the compositional strategy of a single author.

3. See Roger T. Beckwith, "Formation of the Hebrew Bible," in *Mikra: Text, Translation, Reading & Interpretation of the Hebrew Bible in Ancient Judaism & Early Christianity*, ed. Martin Jan Mulder and Harry Sysling (Philadelphia: Fortress, 1988; reprint, Peabody, MA: Hendrickson, 2004), 39–88. The terminology is variable. "Torah" alone or "Prophets" alone can refer to the entire canon (John 10:34; Rom. 1:2). "The Torah (or, Moses) and the Prophets" can refer to the entire canon (Luke 24:27; cf., Luke 24:44).

4. See Claus Westermann, *Basic Forms of Prophetic Speech*, trans. Hugh Clayton White (Louisville: Westminster John Knox, 1991). See also John H. Sailhamer, *Biblical Prophecy* (Grand Rapids: Zondervan, 1998).

5. See Ernst Würthwein, *The Text of the Old Testament*, 2d ed., trans. Erroll F. Rhodes (Grand Rapids: Eerdmans, 1994), 35–37.

6. It is possible that Matt. 27:9–10—a citation from Zech. 11:13 attributed to Jeremiah—reflects the understanding that Jeremiah was the head of the Prophets (but see Mark 1:2–3 where citations from Exodus 23:20; Malachi 3:1, and Isaiah 40:3 are attributed to Isaiah, presumably as the head of the Prophets [textual witnesses to Mark 1:2 vary]). See Michael B. Shepherd, *The Twelve Prophets in the New Testament* (New York: Peter Lang, 2011), 59.

not find any support from the manuscript witnesses. But the Talmud does raise an interesting question about why Hosea does not come first among the eighth-century prophets Hosea, Isaiah, Amos, and Micah.[7] The initial response is that Hosea is written with Haggai, Zechariah, and Malachi who conclude prophecy. The Talmud then asks why Hosea cannot be separated and placed first. The response is that the scroll would be too small and might be lost. This issue apparently affected the arrangement of the Latter Prophets in the early Septuagint codices (c. fourth century AD). Both Codex Vaticanus and Codex Alexandrinus place the Book of the Twelve prior to Isaiah, Jeremiah, and Ezekiel. Codex Sinaiticus, on the other hand, has Isaiah, Jeremiah (Ezekiel is missing), and the Book of the Twelve (missing Hosea–Micah). All three codices group Lamentations with Jeremiah—presumably because of the reference to Jeremiah in the Greek superscription to Lamentations. Vaticanus and Alexandrinus also group Daniel with Ezekiel, due to Daniel's reputation as a prophet (Matt. 24:15).[8]

Codex Vaticanus departs from the threefold shape of the Hebrew Bible—Torah, Prophets, Writings—when it puts the Prophets section last. This Christian tradition, which is usually assumed to be based on the relationship between the Prophets and the New Testament documents, has had a lasting influence on Latin, German, and English translations. Nevertheless, it is a secondary tradition with no foundation in witnesses to the Hebrew canon. One of the earliest references to Greek translation of the Hebrew Bible occurs in the Prologue to Sirach, which speaks of translation of "the Law and the Prophets and the rest of the books."[9] Furthermore, Sinaiticus and Alexandrinus both follow the general order of the Hebrew canon.

If the intended order of the Latter Prophets is Isaiah, Jeremiah, Ezekiel, and the Twelve, then it stands to reason that these books

---

7. Modern scholarship typically considers Amos to be the first of the "writing" prophets (e.g., Bernhard W. Anderson, *Understanding the Old Testament*, 4th ed. [Englewood Cliffs: Prentice-Hall, 1986], 292).

8. See Michael B. Shepherd, *Daniel in the Context of the Hebrew Bible* (New York: Peter Lang, 2009), 4.

9. Incidentally, the Prologue to Sirach and the conclusion to the book in Sirach 48–50 make it clear that Sirach and his grandson did not see their book as part of the Tanakh. The apocryphal and pseudepigraphal books, while valuable for the early history of interpretation, never found a place in the composition of the Hebrew canon. The inclusion of apocryphal books in later Septuagint codices has no bearing on this.

bear some meaningful relationship to one another.[10] Isaiah comes first, sharing a substantial section of material with the book of Kings (2 Kgs. 18–20; Isa. 36–39). Then follow Jeremiah and Ezekiel in chronological order. The Book of the Twelve shares the same scope (preexilic, exilic, and postexilic) and the same interest in the nations as the book of Isaiah. It is also evident from the composition of the Twelve that the final composer of the book was a careful student of the book of Jeremiah (see below, The Composition of the Twelve). The Babylonian Talmud even claims that Ezekiel and the Twelve were produced by the same group—the Men of the Great Assembly (*b. B. Bat.* 15a). At the very least, these books all share the same interest in judgment resulting from the broken Sinai covenant, as well as the hope of future restoration in a new covenant relationship.

If the Book of the Twelve appears at the end of the Prophets section, there is some question about what connection it might have to what stands at the beginning of the Writings division. According to Luke 24:44 (cf., 4QMMT; *Contempl.* 1f., 25), the book of Psalms heads the third division of the Hebrew Bible. The Babylonian Talmud (*b. B. Bat.* 14b) has the book of Ruth prior to the book of Psalms, but this separates Ruth from the Megilloth (the festival scrolls) with which the book would normally circulate (i.e., Ruth, Song of Songs, Ecclesiastes, Lamentations, and Esther).[11] The Leningrad Codex places Chronicles

---

10. See Odil Hannes Steck, *The Prophetic Books and Their Theological Witness*, trans. James D. Nogalski (St. Louis: Chalice, 2000); Benjamin D. Sommer, *A Prophet Reads Scripture: Allusion in Isaiah 40–66* (Stanford, CA: Stanford University Press, 1998); Christopher R. Seitz, *The Goodly Fellowship of the Prophets: The Achievement of Association in Canon Formation* (Grand Rapids: Baker, 2009); Michael B. Shepherd, *The Text in the Middle* (New York: Peter Lang, 2014).

11. The Megilloth circulated in this arrangement for compositional reasons prior to their rearrangement in Rabbinic Bibles according to the order of the festivals for liturgical purposes (see Julius Steinberg and Timothy J. Stone, "The Historical Formation of the Writings in Antiquity," in *The Shape of the Writings*, ed. Julius Steinberg and Timothy J. Stone [Winona Lake, IN: Eisenbrauns, 2015], 49–51; see also Shepherd, *Daniel in the Context of the Hebrew Bible*, 59–61). The argument that this placement of Ruth somehow introduces the book of Psalms (see Stephen Dempster, "A Wandering Moabite: Ruth—A Book in Search of a Canonical Home," in *The Shape of the Writings*, 87–118) is not very strong, nor is the argument that the placement of Ruth prior to Samuel (e.g., Vaticanus and Alexandrinus) introduces the reader to David (Ruth 4:22). The inclusion of the genealogy at the end of the story of Ruth presupposes that the reader

ahead of Psalms (cf., the Aleppo Codex), but a good case can be made for the placement of Chronicles at the conclusion of the Hebrew canon (Matt. 23:35; *b. B. Bat.* 14b). The book of Chronicles itself presupposes a canon that begins with Genesis (1 Chr. 1:1) and ends with the decree of Cyrus (Ezra 1:1–4) in the book of Ezra-Nehemiah (2 Chr. 36:22–23), which corresponds to the arrangement of the Tanakh.

Assuming for a moment that the book of Psalms follows the Twelve, it is worth noting that this order more than the others shows evidence of an awareness of canon formation.[12] The first division of the canon—the Pentateuch—ends with the expectation of a prophet like Moses (Deut. 18:15, 18; 34:10). The beginning of the second division of the canon—the Prophets—instructs Joshua to murmur in the Torah day and night (Josh. 1:8). At the end of the Prophets section, the Book of the Twelve concludes with the expectation of a prophet like Elijah (Mal. 3:1, 23 [Eng., 3:1; 4:5]). The beginning of the third division—the Writings—then commends to the reader the practice of murmuring in the Torah day and night (Ps. 1:2). This use of such unique language at these strategic locations can hardly be a coincidence.[13]

There is good evidence for the prophetic shaping of the entire canon of Hebrew Scripture.[14] The Torah itself is ultimately the product of Moses and the Prophets (2 Kgs. 17:13; Dan. 9:10; Ezra 9:10–11), and already within the Hebrew Bible there are references to the Torah and the Prophets together (Isa. 1:10; 2:3; 8:16, 20; Zech. 7:12).[15] Several passages are conscious of a corpus of prophetic literature that serves

---

already knows David. Furthermore, David's name does not appear in the book of Samuel until 1 Samuel 16. With all due respect to the historical note in Ruth 1:1 that connects the story to the period of the Judges, it is Ruth's position after Proverbs in the Leningrad Codex that bears the marks of compositional intentionality (e.g., Prov. 31:10, 31; Ruth 3:11).

12. See John H. Sailhamer, *Introduction to Old Testament Theology* (Grand Rapids: Zondervan, 1995), 239–49.

13. What this reflects is not a single scroll with all the books in a particular arrangement (but see *b. B. Bat.* 13b). Rather, it reflects the shaping of the individual books in light of one another and with a specific order of the books in mind. Thus, it is possible to speak of the Hebrew Bible as a book made of many books. Both are the product of authorship. In many ways, the Book of the Twelve is a microcosm of this phenomenon.

14. See Joseph Blenkinsopp, *Prophecy and Canon: A Contribution to the Study of Jewish Origins* (Notre Dame, IN: University of Notre Dame Press).

15. See Hans-Christoph Schmitt, "Redaktion des Pentateuch im Geiste der Prophetie," *VT* 32 (1982): 170–89; Stephen B. Chapman, *The Law and the Prophets*, FAT 27 (Tübingen: Mohr Siebeck, 2000); John H. Sailhamer, *The*

as the object of study for later prophets (e.g., Ezek. 38:17; Zech. 1:4; Dan. 9:2). Thus, later prophets play the role of scribe (i.e., sage or biblical scholar) in relation to a collection of prophetic writings in much the same way that earlier prophets played such a role in relationship to the Pentateuch (see Prov. 29:18 LXX; Ezra 7:6, 10; b. B. Bat. 12).[16] Even the Writings section shows signs of prophetic shaping. Of course, the book of Daniel falls within this division, but another key example would be the book of Psalms, which both the Chronicler (e.g., 1 Chr. 25:1) and the New Testament authors (e.g., Acts 2:30) interpret as a prophetic composition rather than as a hymnbook.

AUTHORSHIP AND DATE

It is possible to talk about authorship of the Twelve on two different levels. On the one hand, there are twelve separate works, each marked by its own superscription (Hos. 1:1; Joel 1:1; Amos 1:1; Obad. 1; Jon. 1:1; Mic. 1:1; Nah. 1:1; Hab. 1:1; Zeph. 1:1; Hag. 1:1; Zech. 1:1; Mal. 1:1). The superscriptions identify the contents of each book as the word(s), prophetic vision, or burden/oracle that a particular prophet received. In several cases, there is an indication of the dates that the prophet's ministry spanned. These dates range from the eighth century down to the postexilic period. On the other hand, there is internal evidence that an unnamed final composer (cf., Hebrews) brought these twelve works together to form a single composition.[17] This evidence primarily appears in the seams that connect the end of one book to the beginning of another (see below, The Composition of the Twelve).[18] Since the material of the twelve individual prophets takes the reader at least into the fifth century

---

Meaning of the Pentateuch: Revelation, Composition, and Interpretation (Downers Grove, IL: InterVarsity, 2009).

16. See Karel van der Toorn, *Scribal Culture and the Making of the Hebrew Bible* (Cambridge: Harvard University Press, 2007), 2. Ezra's involvement in the shaping of the canon is a good example of how someone from priestly circles with scribal training and access to texts could acknowledge indebtedness to prophetic tradition (Ezra 9:10–11). See Michael Fishbane, *Biblical Interpretation in Ancient Israel* (Oxford: Clarendon, 1985), 36. Of course, several of the "writing" prophets had priestly backgrounds themselves (Jeremiah, Ezekiel, and Zechariah).

17. The Babylonian Talmud (b. B. Bat. 15a) attributes the book to the Men of the Great Assembly. These scholars were associated with the reforms and compositional efforts of Ezra (Ezra 7:6, 10; Neh. 8–9).

18. It is not in the interest of the present commentary to entertain the possibility of reconstructing hypothetical previous stages in the composition of the Twelve. Current research on this suggests that the enterprise is

BC, and since Sirach refers to "the Twelve Prophets" circa 200 B.C., it is most likely that the composer of the Twelve completed his work either in the fourth or the third century BC. The work of this biblical author was designed to give the Book of the Twelve a message for future generations of believers beyond the lifetime of the historical prophets.

Lest the reader think that the final composer of the Twelve was an editor, it is important to recognize that biblical authors (and authors from the ancient Near East in general) were those who put together (i.e., composed) larger and smaller pieces of material from different times and places.[19] This was their normal mode of operation. These authors gave the resulting literary works their essential theological message. Furthermore, the biblical authors openly cited their sources.[20] Perhaps an appropriate analogy for the Book of the Twelve would be the book of Psalms. Recent scholarship has come to recognize that the book of Psalms is more than a collection of individual psalms. The book as a whole is the product of anonymous authorship/composition.[21] Much like the Book of the Twelve, the individual parts have superscriptions associated with particular figures (e.g., Ps. 3), but the seams of the five books of the larger Psalter betray an effort to organize the psalms in a meaningful way (Pss. 41:14 [Eng., 41:13]; 72:18–20; 89:53 [89:52]; 106:48).

It is not the goal of the present commentary to give a biographical account of the historical prophets by reconstructing the life setting of their words and actions as if the texts were nothing more than transcripts of sermons designed only for ancient audiences and now in need of updating for contemporary readers.[22] The textualization of

---

dubious at best. The extant form of the Twelve reflects the work of a single ordering mind. It is not the product of conflict or compromise.

19. See S. R. Driver, *An Introduction to the Literature of the Old Testament* (New York: Charles Scribner's Sons, 1891), xi; Jeffrey H. Tigay, *The Evolution of the Gilgamesh Epic* (Philadelphia: University of Pennsylvania Press, 1982; reprint, Wauconda, IL: Bolchazy-Carducci, 2002), 42.

20. E.g., Num. 21:14; Josh. 10:13; 2 Sam. 1:18; 1 Kgs. 11:41; 14:19, 29; Jer. 25:13; 30:2; 36; 51:60; Isa. 2:1; 13:1; Prov. 10:1; 22:17; 24:23; 25:1; 30:1; 31:1; 1 Chr. 4:22; 9:1; 28:12, 19; 29:29; 2 Chr. 9:29; 12:15; 13:22; 16:11; 20:34; 24:27; 25:26; 26:22; 27:7; 28:26; 32:32; 33:18–19; 35:26–27; 36:8.

21. See, e.g., Gerald H. Wilson, "Psalms and Psalter: Paradigm for Biblical Theology," in *Biblical Theology: Retrospect and Prospect*, ed. Scott J. Hafemann (Downers Grove, IL: InterVarsity, 2002), 100–110.

22. "The moments that passed in their lives are not now available and cannot become the object of scientific analysis. All we have is the consciousness of those moments as preserved in words" (Abraham J. Heschel, *The Prophets* [New York: HarperCollins, 1969; reprint, Peabody, MA: Prince, 2001], vii).

the prophets means that the literary work—the verbal meaning of the composer—becomes the object of study.[23] This literary work refers to real events, but it now has a life of its own and creates a world of its own.[24] That is, it is not a question of the book's historicity. Rather, it is a matter of the book's unique and revelatory depiction of things, in distinction from the events themselves.[25] Furthermore, the Book of the Twelve is not designed for any one particular audience. It is intended for whoever reads it.

> We should not concern ourselves with the question of how one can read a prophetic book from then to now (the possibilities are legion). We should instead concern ourselves with how a prophetic book should be read according to the desire of those who shaped it during its formative period. This reading determines the formation as a historical process in its time. It is a question of the signals placed in the book itself and a question of

---

"Prophecy, then, may be described as *exegesis of existence from a divine perspective*. Understanding prophecy is an understanding of an understanding rather than an understanding of knowledge; it is exegesis of exegesis" (ibid., xii). Cf., 2 Tim. 3:16; 2 Pet. 1:19–21.

23. See William M. Schniedewind, *How the Bible Became a Book: The Textualization of Ancient Israel* (Cambridge: Cambridge University Press, 2004). Schniedewind makes the case that the textualization process was transformative. It is not so much the story of how the Bible became a book as it is the story of how it became bookish. That is, the Bible became authoritative and spoke on its own terms.

24. "The term *figural* entails a *literary dimension*, that is, the way that prophetic materials have been intentionally related to one another by known and unknown authors, editors, and tradents—terms that within the context of the Old and New Testaments have their own distinctive character, as over against modern analogues. Original utterances, in literary form, have occasioned cross-references and a wider field of association, to which they now belong and within which meaning is generated" (Christopher R. Seitz, *Prophecy and Hermeneutics: Toward a New Introduction to the Prophets* [Grand Rapids: Baker, 2007], 8.) "*History* is the term we frequently use to describe, by appeal to an external grid of association, how the biblical materials can be rearranged, so as to reconstruct their movement from earliest to latest developmental moments. But understood by attention to the figural character of prophetic speech, the term *history* will here refer to the achievement of the biblical witness in its final literary form, as the temporal dimension" (ibid.).

25. This relationship of works of art to the world is captured beautifully in the famous painting of the pipe by Rene Magritte whose caption reads: *Ceci n'est pas une pipe* ("This is not a pipe").

the processes of reworking that were conducted and received in the book itself. Hence, in our method the only observations of indicators and inter-relationships that play a role are those in which the text of the book itself (as a historical entity at the time of its formation) signals how it wants to be received using the configuration and assertions of its vocabulary.[26]

THE TEXT OF THE TWELVE

The original text of the Book of the Twelve must be established on a case-by-case basis from all the available textual witnesses. The following commentary does not favor or give priority to any one textual tradition over the others. At the same time, the plurality of witnesses should not discourage the reader from seeking a text that stood at the beginning of transmission.[27] Textual difficulties and complexities have led many modern scholars to abandon the pursuit of original texts in favor of theories of multiple pristine texts or multiple manifestations of the same oral tradition. While it would be an infinitely easier task to bail out in this fashion, the bulk of the evidence suggests that in most cases it is possible to trace linear development.[28] Having said this, it is not the desire of this commentary simply to discard anything not considered original. On the contrary, non-original texts often provide valuable insight into the early history of interpretation.

The Masoretic Text (MT) and the Septuagint (LXX) feature different arrangements of the first six books of the Twelve (MT: Hosea, Joel, Amos, Obadiah, Jonah, and Micah; LXX: Hosea, Amos, Micah, Joel, Obadiah, and Jonah). One Hebrew manuscript of the Twelve from the Dead Sea Scrolls ends with Zechariah, Malachi, and Jonah (4QXII[a]). Because these witnesses represent variant literary editions of the Book

---

26. Steck, *The Prophetic Books*, 16.
27. "Rather, we focus on the written text or edition (or a number of consecutive editions) that contained the finished literary product (or one of its earlier stages) that stood at the beginning of the textual transmission process. This formulation gives a certain twist to the assumption of an original text as often described in the scholarly literature. Our definition does not refer to the original text in the usual sense of the word, since the copy described here as the final literary product could have been preceded by earlier literary crystallizations" (Emanuel Tov, *Textual Criticism of the Hebrew Bible*, 3d ed. [Minneapolis: Fortress, 2012], 165).
28. "Even if one is unable to decide between two or more readings, the possibility that one of them was nevertheless original and that the other(s) was (were) secondary cannot be rejected. One's inability to decide between different readings should not be confused with the question of the original form of the biblical text" (ibid., 164).

of the Twelve, it is necessary to make a decision about which composition of the Twelve to translate and interpret.[29] The MT order has much to commend it. On the surface, it is the strange or "difficult" arrangement that likely gave rise to the others. It is not arranged according to length or date or any other obvious ordering principle. There is very little reason to think that someone would have changed something like the order of the LXX to that of the MT. The arrangement of the MT also has support from the Dead Sea Scrolls: (1) 4QXII[a–c, e] (Hebrew), (2) MurXII (Hebrew) with parts of Joel–Zechariah, and (3) the Greek Minor Prophets Scroll found at Naḥal Ḥever (8ḤevXII gr, c. 50 BC–AD 50), which has parts of Jonah, Micah, Nahum, Habakkuk, Zephaniah, and Habakkuk.[30]

The order of the first six books in the LXX arrangement of the Twelve is roughly according to length and date when compared to the MT (cf., *Lives of the Prophets* 5–10: Hosea, Micah, Amos, Joel, Obadiah, and Jonah). This arrangement appears to be a purely editorial decision and does not show sufficient signs of original authorial/compositional intent. Furthermore, there is no Hebrew manuscript evidence to support the LXX. Even the earliest extant Greek scroll of the Twelve (8ḤevXII gr) follows the order of the MT. But perhaps the most telling indication of the secondary nature of the LXX order is the fact that the Greek text itself seems to presuppose the MT arrangement in several places. For example, the Greek rendering of Amos 9:12 appears to have the Amos-Obadiah sequence in view (cf., Acts 15:17), which would only be the case in the MT (see below, The Composition of the Twelve).

Barry Alan Jones has made a case for the priority of the LXX order and the 4QXII[a] order.[31] That is, he argues for the arrangement of the

---

29. See Eugene Ulrich, *The Dead Scrolls and the Origins of the Bible* (Grand Rapids: Eerdmans, 1999); Tov, *Textual Criticism*, 283–326; Shepherd, *The Twelve Prophets*, 69–78.
30. It is well known that the text of the Greek Minor Prophets Scroll is a revision of the Old Greek translation toward the proto-Masoretic text. This revision is known as proto-Theodotion or *kaige*-Theodotion. Nevertheless, a decision about the secondary nature of this translation is not necessarily a decision about the order of the books. It is quite possible that the Greek Minor Prophets Scroll has a revised translation whose order of books has the priority. It is then equally possible that the LXX Book of the Twelve has a more original translation but a secondary arrangement of the books. See Aaron Schart, "Zur Redaktionsgeschichte des Zwölfprophetenbuchs," *VF* 43 (1998): 13–33.
31. Barry Alan Jones, *The Formation of the Book of the Twelve: A Study in Text and Canon* (Atlanta: Scholars, 1995). See also Mika S. Pajunen and Hanne

first six books of the Twelve in the LXX with the exception of Jonah, which he places at the end of the Twelve according to 4QXII[a]. Not only does this position carry with it the problems of the LXX mentioned above, but also it involves an anomalous witness (4QXII[a]) that has no support anywhere. As intriguing as it might be to speculate about the meaning of the placement of Jonah at the end of the Twelve, the paucity of evidence for this reading is overwhelming.[32] This hypothetical proposal by Jones does not appear in any extant manuscript witness.

THE COMPOSITION OF THE TWELVE

Perhaps the most compelling case for the priority of the MT order comes from the internal clues to the work of a final composer deliberately connecting the books so that they occur in a particular arrangement in order to communicate the intended theological message. Scholarly interest in this phenomenon has reached an all-time high in the last thirty years.[33] The present section will review the historical evidence

---

von Weissenberg, "The Book of Malachi, Manuscript 4Q76 (4QXII[a]), and the Formation of the 'Book of the Twelve,'" *JBL* 134 (2015): 731–51.

32. This is not to mention the fact that such an order would disrupt the canonical relationship between Malachi and Psalms noted above (see the earlier section, The Place of the Twelve in the Hebrew Canon).

33. E.g., Paul House, *The Unity of the Twelve* (Sheffield: Almond, 1990); James D. Nogalski, *Literary Precursors to the Book of the Twelve*, BZAW 217 (Berlin: de Gruyter, 1993); idem, *Redactional Processes in the Book of the Twelve*, BZAW 218 (Berlin: de Gruyter, 1993); Jones, *The Formation of the Book of the Twelve*; James Nogalski and Marvin Sweeney, eds., *Reading and Hearing the Book of the Twelve* (Atlanta: SBL, 2000); Rolf Rendtorff, *The Canonical Hebrew Bible: A Theology of the Old Testament*, trans. David E. Orton (Leiden: Deo, 2005) 264–66; Seitz, *Prophecy and Hermeneutics*; Michael B. Shepherd, "Compositional Analysis of the Twelve," *ZAW* 120 (2008): 184–93; idem, "The New Exodus in the Composition of the Twelve," in *Text and Canon: Essays in Honor of John H. Sailhamer*, ed., Robert L. Cole and Paul J. Kissling (Eugene, OR: Pickwick, 2017), 120–36; Ehud Ben Zvi and James D. Nogalski, *Two Sides of a Coin: Juxtaposing Views on Interpreting the Book of the Twelve / the Twelve Prophetic Books* (Piscataway, NJ: Gorgias, 2009). See also K. Budde, "Eine folgenschwere Redaktion des Zwölfprophetenbuchs," *ZAW* 39 (1922): 218–29; R. E. Wolfe, "The Editing of the Book of the Twelve," *ZAW* 53 (1935): 90–129; D. Schneider, "The Unity of the Book of the Twelve" (Ph.D. diss., Yale University, 1979). Andersen and Forbes have even suggested that the orthography of the Twelve is an important piece of evidence for unity: "The Minor Prophets are . . . remarkably homogeneous in their spelling. The Book of the Twelve was evidently edited and transmitted as a single scroll"

for the unity of the Twelve and then provide an overview of the internal evidence for the composition of the Twelve. Detailed explanation of the internal evidence will appear at the appropriate points in the commentary. Also, the interpretive framework provided by the composer's work will inform exposition at lower levels of the text.

Historical Evidence for the Unity of the Twelve

As mentioned above (see The Place of the Twelve in the Hebrew Canon), the earliest reference (c. 200 BC) to the Book of the Twelve as a unit occurs in Sirach 49:10. After the references to Isaiah, Jeremiah, and Ezekiel (Sir. 48–49) the reader might expect a list of the twelve prophets from Hosea to Malachi, but Sirach simply refers to "the Twelve Prophets." This is similar to the practice in the New Testament documents (first century AD) where the authors typically cite Isaiah (e.g., Matt. 3:3; 4:14) and Jeremiah (Matt. 2:17) by name, but in Acts 7:42 Stephen introduces a quote from Amos as that which is "written in the Book of the Prophets." Paul introduces a quote from Habakkuk as that which is "said in the Prophets" (Acts 13:40). James introduces a quote from Amos as "the words of the Prophets" (Acts 15:15).[34]

The Dead Scrolls also bear witness to the unity of the Twelve. Several fragmentary scrolls from Qumran combine more than one book of the Twelve on a single scroll (4QXII[a–c, e], c. 150–25 BC). This is comparable to the practice of combining more than one book of the Pentateuch on a single scroll (e.g., 4QGen-Exod[a]; 4QPaleoGen-Exod[l]). That is, the combination of more than one book of the Twelve was not simply due to their short length. There were other short books like the Megilloth that could have been included, but the Scrolls witness to the combination of the same books of the Twelve in the same order (with the exception of the oldest fragment, 4QXII[a], which ends with Jonah). The Greek Minor Prophets Scroll from Naḥal Ḥever (8ḤevXII gr, c. 50 BC–AD 50) and the Hebrew scroll of the Twelve from Murabba'at (Mur XII, c. AD 75–100) also testify to the combination of the Twelve on a single scroll in the traditional Hebrew order (see above, The Text of the Twelve).

(Francis I. Andersen and A. Dean Forbes, *Spelling in the Hebrew Bible*, BibOr 41 [Rome: Biblical Institute, 1986], 315–16).

34. Of course, it is also possible to introduce a citation from Mic. 5:1 (Eng., 5:2) as that which was "written by the prophet" (Matt. 2:5; cf., Matt. 2:15; 21:4; textual witnesses vary for Acts 2:16) or to quote from Hosea by name (Rom. 9:25; cf., Tob. 2:6), but more often there is no reference to a name or individual prophet.

Jewish (e.g., *b. B. Bat.* 14b) and Christian (e.g., Jerome: *unum librum esse duodecim Prophetarum*) lists of canonical books from the first century to the medieval period count the Twelve Prophets as one book.[35] The traditional number of twenty-two or twenty-four books in the Hebrew Bible cannot be achieved without counting the Twelve as one (not to mention the combination of other "books" now separated in modern English translations). Furthermore, the Masoretic Text marks the middle verse of every biblical book with a note in the margin (e.g., Isa. 33:21; Jer. 28:11; Ezek. 26:1),[36] but the Masoretes did not mark the middle verse of each of the twelve prophets from Hosea to Malachi. Rather, there is an indication in the margin of Mic. 3:12 that this is the middle of "the book" in verses. The masora at the end of Malachi clarifies that "the book" is the Book of the Twelve, showing that the Masoretes thought of Hosea–Malachi as a single composition that was to be transmitted as a whole.

Internal Evidence for the Composition of the Twelve
There are essentially three criteria for identification of the activity of the final composer of the Twelve. The first and most obvious is the way in which the content of the "seams" (pieces of text that connect the end of one book to the beginning of the next) stands apart from the material that precedes and follows. The second criterion is the development of the author's programmatic text in Hosea 3:4–5. When each of the seams picks up the message of these verses and develops their language and theme, it is a sign of intelligent design. The author uses this technique to unify the theological message of the Twelve. The final criterion is dependence upon the book of Jeremiah. Wherever the first two criteria are met (seam and message), there is a citation from the book of Jeremiah. It is evident that the book of Jeremiah had a

---

35. See E. Earle Ellis, "The Old Testament Canon in the Early Church," in *Mikra*, 653–90. See also Calvin: "the Twelve Minor Prophets form but one volume" (*Commentaries on the Twelve Minor Prophets*, vol. 1, *Hosea*, trans. John Owen, Calvin's Commentaries XIII [reprint, Grand Rapids: Baker, 2005], 35).
36. The MT also marks the middle of the Prophets (Isa. 17:2), the middle of the Writings (Ps. 130:2), and the middle letter of the Tanakh (Jer. 6:7). For the Pentateuch, the Masoretes marked the middle word (Lev. 11:16) and the middle letter (Lev. 11:42) of the whole book as well as the middle verse for each of the five parts (Gen. 27:40; Exod. 22:27; Lev. 15:7; Num. 17:20; Deut. 17:10). This was a way to safeguard the accuracy of the Bible's transmission.

profound influence on the composer and informed the way the Book of the Twelve was put together. No effort is made here to reconstruct hypothetical stages in the development of the Twelve. The primary focus will be the final form of the text.

The program in Hosea 3:4–5 sets forth the themes of judgment and messianic salvation in the last days (cf., Isa. 2:1–5; Mic. 4:1–5).[37] This text stands out from its surroundings not only because it introduces material that the seams of the Twelve will develop but also because it is not directed to the northern kingdom of Israel as the reader might expect from the prophet Hosea. It is also not part of the so-called Judean redaction of the book that made Hosea's prophecies applicable to the southern kingdom.[38] Rather, the text of Hosea 3:5 envisions a reunited kingdom under the rule of the future ideal Davidic king (cf., Jer. 3:14–18). This is the trajectory of the final composer's work. It is then consistent with this composer's work elsewhere in the Twelve that Hosea 3:5 is a citation from the book of Jeremiah:[39]

> Afterwards the sons of Israel will return and seek the LORD their God and David their king and fear to the LORD and to his goodness at the end of the days (Hos. 3:5).

> In that day . . . they will serve the LORD their God and David their king whom I will raise up for them (Jer. 30:8–9 [see *Tg. Jon.*]; Jer. 23:5–6; cf., 2 Sam. 7:12).

---

37. See the rendering of Hosea 3:5 in *Targum Jonathan*: "After thus the sons of Israel will return and seek the fear of the LORD their God, and they will obey the Messiah the son of David their king, and they will follow eagerly the worship of the LORD and the abundance of his goodness that will come to them at the end of the days." See also W. Staerk, "Der Begrauch der Wendung בְּאַחֲרִית הַיָּמִים im alttestamentliche Kanon," *ZAW* 11 (1891): 247–53.

38. Hos. 1:7; 2:2 (Eng., 1:11); 4:15; 5:5, 10, 12–14; 6:4, 11; 8:14; 10:11; 12:1, 3 (Eng., 12:2, 4).

39. The pattern and wording of Hosea 3:4–5 is also very close to 2 Chronicles 15:3–4 where the prophet Azariah tells Asa the story of how Israel went for many days without a true God, a teaching priest, or the Torah (cf., Hos. 3:4), but the people returned to the LORD and sought him, and he allowed himself to be found by them (cf., Hos. 3:5; see also Jer. 29:12–14). This account lacks the eschatology and messianism of Jer. 31:8 and Hos. 3:5, but it does provide the general framework for the prophecy of both judgment (Hos. 3:4) and restoration (Hos. 3:5). The Chronicles story does not appear in the presentation of Asa in the book of Kings, but the Chronicler does cite an earlier written source for his Asa material (2 Chr. 16:11).

This text from Jeremiah occurs at the beginning of a "book" (Jer. 30:2) that speaks of restoration (Jer. 30:3; cf., Deut. 30:3) "at the end of the days" (Jer. 30:24; cf., Hos. 3:5) in a new exodus (Jer. 31:2–6; cf., Exod. 15:20) and in a new covenant relationship (Jer. 31:31–34). Both Hosea and the rest of the Twelve will employ this imagery of a new act of divine deliverance (e.g., Hos. 2:16–25; Eng., 2:14–23).

Hosea-Joel
The first compositional seam of the Twelve occurs at Hosea 14:10 (Eng., 14:9) and Joel 1:2–3, connecting the end of Hosea to the beginning of Joel. This material meets the first criterion of a seam in that it stands apart from what precedes and follows. The contrast of the righteous and the wicked (Hos. 14:10 [Eng., 14:9]; cf., Prov. 10:1–22:16) and the passing of instruction from the older generation to the younger generation (Joel 1:2–3; cf., Prov. 1–9) are the hallmarks of the wisdom literature, not the Prophets. This guides the reader to seek wisdom about the future work of God (Hos. 3:4–5) in the Book of the Twelve, meeting the second criterion of a seam (cf., Deut. 34:5–Josh. 1:9 ["Spirit of wisdom" (Deut. 34:9)]).[40] It is also the way the Book of the Twelve ends and connects to the following book of Psalms (Mal. 3:22 [Eng., 4:4]–Ps. 1 [righteous and wicked]). And lastly, this seam meets the third criterion when it quotes from the book of Jeremiah:

Who is wise? (or, Whoever is wise,) Let him understand these things. [Who] has understanding? (or, [Whoever] has understanding,) Let him know them (Hos. 14:10a [14:9a]).

Who is the wise man? Let him understand this. And to whom has the mouth of the LORD spoken? Let him declare it (Jer. 9:11a [9:12a]).[41]

According to the Jeremiah context, the people have abandoned the LORD's instruction. The LORD will scatter the people among the nations (Jer. 9:12–15 [9:13–16])—the cause of a sound of wailing (Jer. 9:18 [9:19]; cf., 31:15). The wise man should not boast in his wisdom

---

40. According to Brevard Childs, Hos. 14:10 (Eng., 14:9) "functions as an explicit directive to the reader to instruct him in the proper understanding of the collection" (*Introduction to the Old Testament Scripture* [Philadelphia: Fortress, 1979], 382). Childs, however, is only referring to the collection of Hosea's oracles. The suggestion here is that the verse has this function for the entirety of the Twelve.

41. See also Ps. 107:43; Eccl. 8:1; Jas. 3:13.

but in his knowledge of the LORD (Jer. 9:22, 23 [9:23, 24]). The LORD will judge those who are uncircumcised of heart (Jer. 9:24, 25 [9:25, 26]; cf., Jer 4:4), directing the reader to the hope of the circumcised heart in the new covenant beyond exile (Deut. 30:6; Jer 31:31–34).

Joel-Amos
The next "seam" has a slightly different character to it, involving a text inserted at the end of Joel (Joel 4:16a [Eng., 3:16a]) and at the beginning of Amos (Amos 1:2a): "The LORD from Zion roars, and from Jerusalem gives his voice."[42] The text of Amos 1:2 is sandwiched between the superscription (Amos 1:1) and the opening address to the nations (Amos 1:3–2:16). The context of the Joel insertion is the Day of the LORD (Joel 4:14–15, 17 [Eng., 3:14–15, 17]),[43] a time in which there will be both judgment (Joel 1:15; 2:1, 11) and restoration (Joel 3:1–5 [Eng., 2:28–32]) in accordance with the program of the Twelve (Hos. 3:4–5). According to Rolf Rendtorff, "the theme of the Day of YHWH which dominates the book of Joel also occurs in Amos 5.18–20, with echoes of Joel 2.2."[44] Also, the text of Joel 4:16a (Eng., 3:16a) and Amos 1:2a comes from the book of Jeremiah: "The LORD from on high roars, and from his holy habitation gives his voice" (Jer. 25:30a). The context there is the cup of judgment (Jer. 25:15) that passes to all the nations. Thus, the Joel-Amos seam meets all the qualifications: distinct language, the message of Hos. 3:4–5, and citation from Jeremiah.

Amos-Obadiah
After nine chapters of words of judgment directed primarily to the northern kingdom of Israel, the book of Amos concludes with one of the most glorious pictures of restoration for the fallen booth of David anywhere in Scripture (Amos 9:11–15). This striking contrast has not gone unnoticed by critical scholars who typically assign this conclusion to someone living at a much later time than that of Amos.[45] This often

---

42. There is also a text in Joel 4:18 (Eng., 3:18) that finds its way into the seam at the end of Amos (Amos 9:13b). Moreover, the reference to Edom in Joel 4:19 (Eng., 3:19) anticipates the key role of Edom at the beginning and the end of Amos (Amos 1:6, 9, 11; 9:12).
43. The third person reference to the LORD in Joel 4:16 (Eng., 3:16) interrupts the LORD's discourse in the preceding and following verses.
44. Rolf Rendtorff, *The Old Testament: An Introduction*, trans. John Bowden (Philadelphia: Fortress, 1986), 220.
45. E.g., William R. Harper, *A Critical and Exegetical Commentary on Amos and Hosea*, ICC (New York: Charles Scribner's Sons, 1905), 195–200.

gives the impression that the passage is secondary and not original to the words of the prophet, and is therefore to be discarded. But such a decision would miss the fact that the text is primary to the prophetic composer of the Twelve. It is precisely this small piece of text at the end of Amos that links the book to the following work of Obadiah.

According to Amos 9:11–12, the restoration of the Davidic kingdom will take place in order that the people of God may "possess (יירשו) the remnant of Edom (אדום)" and all the nations on whom the LORD's name is called. Edom here represents all the nations to be possessed in God's kingdom (cf., Isa. 34). This is the way the Greek text of Codex Alexandrinus interprets the passage: "that the remnant of mankind (= אדם) may seek (= ידרשו) the Lord (= את)."[46] That is, the believing remnant from the nations will seek the Lord in the last days along with the believing remnant of Israel in accordance with Hosea 3:5 (cf., Acts 15:17). The following book of Obadiah then focuses on the judgment of Edom for the first two-thirds of the text before shifting to the Day of the LORD (Obad. 15) and the list of those to be "possessed" in God's kingdom (Obad. 16–21), a list that includes Edom—the mountain of Esau (Obad. 19).[47]

And so, the content of this seam that connects Amos to Obadiah stands apart from the material that precedes it, and the message develops the program of Hosea 3:4–5, informing the reader that the believing Gentiles will also take part in God's kingdom. It is not for ethnic Israel alone (Gen. 12:1–3; Isa. 2:1–5; 66:18–25)—a theme that will continue in Jonah. But does this seam also quote from the book of Jeremiah and thus fulfill the third criterion for the work of the final composer of the Twelve? As it turns out, the first part of Obadiah (Obad. 1–5) cites extensively from the oracle against Edom in Jeremiah 49:7–22,

---

46. "Israel's enemies are collectivized here in the form of the nation of Edom, not only because Edom was historically a perennial enemy of Israel, but more importantly because the Hebrew name *Edom* can also be read as 'humanity'" (Sailhamer, *Introduction to Old Testament Theology*, 251). Cf., Ezek. 34:31; 35; 36:37–38. The difference between the verbs "possess" and "seek" would only be a single consonant in the Hebrew text. It is possible that the translator had a different Hebrew text, but it is also possible that the translator chose to introduce his interpretation of the original text on this basis of this slight alteration. As for the object marker (את), there is good evidence that this stood for the Lord himself in some cases (e.g., Zech. 12:10), the first and last letters of the alphabet representing the one who is the beginning and the end (Isa. 41:4; 44:6; Rev. 1:8; 22:13).

47. The root ירש ("possess") from Amos 9:12 occurs five times in Obadiah 17–21. The possession of the nations involves dispossession of the enemies of God's people and inclusion of those who desire to be part of his kingdom.

particularly Jeremiah 49:9, 14–16. Obadiah's text consistently has the longer version, suggesting that the direction of dependence was from Jeremiah to Obadiah.[48] The composer's inclusion of Obadiah between Amos and Jonah has breathed new, long-lasting life into the little book that it likely would not have had on its own. The book now contributes greatly to what the Prophets want to say about the nations.

Obadiah-Jonah

The decision to juxtapose Obadiah and Jonah creates a meaning of its own.[49] The initial oddness of the Amos-Obadiah-Jonah sequence is what catches the reader's eye, almost as if the short text of Obadiah itself were in its entirety functioning as a seam. The use of Jeremiah there has already been noted (Obad. 1–5). So, in what way does the book of Jonah continue from Amos-Obadiah the message of the inclusion of the Gentiles in God's plan according to Hosea 3:5? In short, what Edom was to Amos and Obadiah (i.e., a representative of the nations to be included in God's kingdom), Nineveh is to the book of Jonah. Nineveh is "the great city" (Jon. 1:2; 3:2; 4:11) in the book of Jonah in the sense that it has great importance in the Gentile world (Gen. 10:11–12).[50] It thus serves well to represent those from the nations who believe and thus stand in stark contrast to the prophet Jonah (Jon. 1:16; 3:5).[51] It is God's prerogative to include them (Jon. 4:11).

Jonah-Micah

In terms of genre, the book of Jonah stands apart from the book of Micah as much as it does from Obadiah or any other book of the

---

48. Also, the text of Amos 9:14 uses deuteronomic language of restoration (Deut. 30:3) that is common to the book of Jeremiah (e.g., Jer. 29:14; 30:3; 31:23; 32:44; 33:7).

49. This phenomenon is familiar from other art forms in addition to literature: *"two film pieces of any kind, placed together, inevitably combine into a new concept, a new quality, arising out of that juxtaposition"* (Sergei M. Eisenstein, *The Film Sense*, trans. and ed. Jay Leyda [San Diego: Harcourt Brace & Company, 1942], 4).

50. C. F. Keil, *The Pentateuch*, trans. James Martin, Keil & Delitzsch Commentary on the Old Testament 1 (Edinburgh: T. & T. Clark, 1866–91; reprint, Peabody, MA: Hendrickson, 2001), 106.

51. Because the city of Nineveh represents the Gentile world so well, the Book of the Twelve can also use it or the nation of Assyria in a negative way for those who do not believe among the nations (e.g., Nahum). Note how Jonah and Nahum both end with very different rhetorical questions about Nineveh (Jon. 4:11; Nah. 3:19).

Twelve. But the language of the final chapter of Jonah, which cites from Exod. 34:6–7 (Jon. 4:2b; cf., Joel 2:13–14),[52] already anticipates the language of the final composer's seam work that connects the end of Micah (Mic. 7:18–20) to the beginning of Nahum (Nah. 1:2b–3a). This language from God's revelation of himself to Moses highlights the two themes of judgment and restoration from the programmatic passage in Hosea 3:4–5.[53] The two books do share an interest in the inclusion of Assyria and the nations (e.g., Mic. 4:1–5; 5:1–5 [Eng., 5:2–6]; cf., Isa. 2:1–5; 19:24–25). One passage in particular (Mic. 4:1–5) occurs directly after the middle verse of the Twelve in Micah 3:12. The text of this verse also appears in Jer. 26:18 as part of the advice from the elders to the people not to execute Jeremiah for the harshness of his temple gate speech (Jer. 7:1–15). According to this advice, Hezekiah did not kill Micah for his prophecy about Jerusalem being turned into ruins, therefore, the people should not kill Jeremiah for his words of judgment. This prophecy of Micah obviously preceded the lifetime of Jeremiah, but that does not mean it occupied its current place in the book of Micah before the completion of Jeremiah's book. The clue in the text of Micah 3:12 is the Aramaic plural spelling of "ruins" (עִיִּין) in contrast to the usual Hebrew plural spelling in Jer. 26:18 (עִיִּים). The Aramaic masculine plural ending on Hebrew words is a feature of later Hebrew texts in the Bible (e.g., הִמִּין in Dan. 12:13b). It appears that the composer of the Twelve has left his mark at this central location in the makeup of his final product.

Micah-Nahum
The hymn in the final three verses of the book of Micah (Mic. 7:18–20) stands apart from the content of the prayer that precedes it (Mic. 7:14–17). These verses borrow extensively from the language of God's revelation of himself to Moses in Exodus 34:6–7. Likewise, the beginning of the following book of Nahum has a piece of text (Nah. 1:2b–3a) that stands apart from its surroundings and cites from Exod. 34:6–7. Verses 2b–3a of Nahum 1 interrupt the partial Hebrew acrostic poem in Nah. 1:2–8 between the *aleph* (Nah. 1:2a) and *beth* (Nah. 1:3b) lines.[54]

Who is a God like you, forgiving iniquity,[55]

---

52. Note how it is possible to read directly from Jonah 4:2a to Jonah 4:3.
53. See Fishbane, *Biblical Interpretation*, 335–50.
54. See Michael B. Shepherd, "Hebrew Acrostic Poems and Their Vocabulary Stock," *JNSL* 36/2 (2010): 95–108.
55. See Exod. 34:7a.

And passing over transgression for the remnant of his inheritance?
(He does not hold forever on to his anger,
For delighting in covenant loyalty [חֶסֶד] is he.
He will have compassion [from רחם] on us again,
He will subdue our iniquities;)
And you will cast into sea's depths all their sins.
You will give faithfulness to Jacob,
Covenant loyalty (חֶסֶד) to Abraham,
Which you swore to our fathers long ago
(Mic. 7:18–20).

The LORD takes vengeance against his foes,
And he keeps wrath for his enemies.
The LORD is slow to anger (אֶרֶךְ אַפִּים) and great of strength,
But the LORD will by no means leave the guilty unpunished[56]
(Nah. 1:2b–3a).

This seam harkens back to the themes of judgment and restoration in Hosea 3:4–5 by using the language of Exodus 34:6–7. And while it is possible to identify some of Jeremiah's language here (e.g., Jer. 3:5; 31:34), it is perhaps best to be content with the influence of Jeremiah at Micah 3:12.

Nahum-Habakkuk
The historical oracles of the prophets Nahum and Habakkuk have now been framed by two poems (Nah. 1:2–8; Hab. 3:3–15) that reflect the eschatological interests of the composer of the Twelve (Hos. 3:4–5). They recast the prophecies of the past as images of future and final judgment of the wicked and deliverance of the righteous. Nahum's vision was primarily about the historical deliverance of Judah, the downfall of Assyria, and the demise of the city of Nineveh (Nah. 1:9– 3:19). The partial acrostic poem in Nahum 1:2–8 (which was likely excerpted from a larger, complete acrostic), however, mentions none of those things, speaking instead about God's judgment of the world and his deliverance of those who take refuge in him in terms drawn from the exodus story and from biblical theophanies like Psalm 18:8–16 (Eng., 18:7–15). Likewise, the poem in Habakkuk 3:3–15 talks not about Habakkuk's immediate circumstances but about God coming to judge the wicked and deliver the righteous using images from the biblical narrative such as the exodus, the flood, and the conquest of the land. The poem was probably taken from a larger collection of poetry.

---

56. See Exod. 34:7b.

We know this because the superscription to the following psalm was included in Habakkuk 3:19b.[57]

The two poems in Nahum and Habakkuk share the language of the "day of distress" (Nah. 1:7; Hab. 3:16). What they lack is any direct citation from the book of Jeremiah. In this case, the composer has included his quote from Jeremiah slightly prior to the poem in Habakkuk 3. The text of Habakkuk 2:13–14 does not fit into the pattern of the woe oracles in Habakkuk 2:5–20. These two verses are citations from Jeremiah 51:58b and Isaiah 11:9. It is likely that Habakkuk prophesied earlier than Jeremiah (see commentary), but it is also true that the text of Jeremiah 51:58b; Habakkuk 2:13b is more at home in the Jeremiah context. Thus, in Habakkuk 2:13b the text does not come from the prophet Habakkuk, but from the prophetic composer of the Twelve who has studied the book of Jeremiah.

Habakkuk-Zephaniah
The phrase "day of distress" (Nah. 1:7; Hab. 3:16) that links the two poems in Nah. 1:2–8 and Hab. 3:3–15 surfaces at the beginning of the following book of Zephaniah with reference to the Day of the LORD (Zeph. 1:14–16). The theme of the Day of the LORD, which was so crucial to Joel, Amos, and Obadiah, now returns in the latter part of the Twelve in the books of Zephaniah, Zechariah, and Malachi. As mentioned above, this theme develops the two parts of the program of the Twelve in Hosea 3:4–5: judgment (Zeph. 1:2–3:8) and restoration (Zeph. 3:9–20). Zephaniah even uses Habakkuk's language to say that the Day of the LORD is near (Hab. 2:20b; Zeph. 1:7a).

---

57. The superscription in Habakkuk 3:1 refers to Habakkuk 3:2, 16–19a. The superscription in Habakkuk 3:19b is usually rendered, "For the director on my stringed instruments." This makes little sense in context and often gives the impression that its inclusion was an accidental oversight. But the translation, "For the director," assumes that the Hebrew phrase refers to the one who is preeminent in the musical setting. It is also possible, however, to render the phrase as "For the one who endures [to the end]." See BDB, 663–64. This understanding is perhaps behind the translation of this phrase in a number of superscriptions in LXX Psalms: *eis to telos* ("to/ for the end"). As for the phrase, "on my stringed instruments," it is possible to render it as "in my afflictions" (see A. E. Cowley, *Aramaic Papyri of the Fifth Century B.C.* [Oxford: Clarendon, 1923; reprint, Eugene: Wipf & Stock, 2005], 100). Thus, the translation of Habakkuk 3:18b would be, "For the one who endures to the end, in my afflictions." This matches the situation of Habakkuk who must hope in the future work of God in the midst of troublesome times (cf., Isa. 8:16–20; Dan. 12:13).

Zephaniah was a contemporary of Jeremiah (Jer. 1:1–3; Zeph. 1:1). The first and last words of the book that bears Zephaniah's name contain material very close to that of the book of Jeremiah. In a reversal of Genesis 1:1–2:3, the opening words announce that the LORD will make an "end" (אָסֹף אָסֵף) of everything on the surface of "the earth" (הָאֲדָמָה), including "people" (אָדָם), "animals" (בְהֵמָה), "birds" (עוֹף הַשָּׁמַיִם), and "fish" (דְּגֵי הַיָּם) (Zeph. 1:2–3; cf., Ezek. 38:20; Hos. 4:3). Very similar terminology appears in Jeremiah 7:20; 8:13; 9:9 (Eng., 9:10); 15:3. The last words of Zephaniah include the statement in Zephaniah 3:17b, "He will rejoice over you" (יָשִׂישׂ עָלַיִךְ). This is similar to Deuteromony 28:63; 30:9; and Isaiah 62:5b; 65:19a. But it is also close to Jeremiah 32:41: "And I will rejoice over them" (וְשַׂשְׂתִּי עֲלֵיהֶם).

Zephaniah-Haggai

The concluding section in Zephaniah 3:9–20 stands apart from the predominant judgment language of the book and uses the language of restoration, remnant, and gathering known to the reader of other prophets, including the book of Jeremiah. This message of restoration provides an eschatological context for reading the following prophecies of Haggai—prophecies that were initially limited to events surrounding the construction of the Second Temple. Now within the context of the Twelve the book of Haggai has new life and ongoing relevance, speaking not only of the past but also of the last days (Hos. 3:5). This is analogous to the placement of Ezekiel 33–39 and Ezekiel 40–48 next to one another. Ezekiel 33–39 is the prophet's restoration section (cf., Zeph. 3:9–20). Ezekiel 40–48 is his vision of the new temple (cf., Hag.). The vision thus becomes a priestly prophet's way to illustrate what future and final restoration will look like.

Haggai-Zechariah

The Haggai-Zechariah sequence is a natural one given the fact that these prophets were contemporaries who prophesied together in support of the rebuilding project led by Zerubbabel and Joshua (Ezra 5:1–2; see the date formulae in Haggai 1:1, 15; 2:1, 10, 20; Zech. 1:1, 7: 7:1). But it is the small piece of text at the end of Haggai (Hag. 2:20–23) that serves to connect the two books most closely in terms of composition and content. The text of Haggai 2:23 is a citation and a reversal of Jeremiah 22:24. The LORD announced in Jeremiah 22:24 that he would tear Jehoiachin off his right hand as a seal/signet-ring. But now in Haggai 2:23 Zerubbabel, a descendant of the Davidic king Jehoiachin (1 Chr. 3:17–19), is the chosen seal/signet-ring. The messianic implications are hard to miss, especially when the LORD refers to Zerubbabel as "my servant" (cf., Isa. 42:1–7; 49:1–9; 50:4–11; 52:13–53:12). It will be up to the following book of Zechariah to clarify that Zerubbabel is only a prefiguration of the real servant of the LORD. Zechariah uses the language of Haggai 2:23 in Zechariah 3:8; 6:12–13 to indicate that the servant is not a contemporary of Joshua. Rather, he is the messianic Branch from Jeremiah 23:5–6 who will build the temple in accordance with the Davidic covenant (2 Sam. 7:13) and occupy the offices of priest and king. This corresponds to the eschatological messianism of Hosea 3:5. Furthermore, in light of the dependence upon Jeremiah 22:24; 23:5–6 in the connection between Haggai and Zechariah, it is also worth noting that the opening verses of Zechariah (Zech. 1:2–6), which stand apart from the visions of the first six chapters, also quote from the book of Jeremiah (Jer. 25:4–7; 31:18; Zech. 1:3, 4).

Zechariah-Malachi
The final two sections of the book of Zechariah both have the same heading: "The oracle of the word of the LORD" (Zech. 9:1; 12:1). The only other place where this heading occurs in the entire Hebrew Bible is at the beginning of the following book of Malachi (Mal. 1:1). Such a distinctive use of section markers serves to join the two books. Furthermore, the eschatology and messianism of these sections are well known (e.g., Zech. 9:9–10; 12; 14; Mal. 3:1) and fit nicely with the program of the Twelve (Hos. 3:4–5). Matthew cites this latter part of Zechariah as if it were from the prophet Jeremiah (Zech. 11:13; Matt. 27:9–10). There are several plausible suggestions to explain this phenomenon, but one possibility is that Zechariah or the composer of the Twelve has borrowed from material of Jeremiah that never made it into Jeremiah's book. At the very least, we know that both Zechariah (e.g., Zech. 1:12; 7:5; see Jer. 25:11; 29:10) and the composer of the Twelve read Jeremiah faithfully.

Malachi-Psalms
This last seam suggests that the Book of the Twelve has been fitted to the context of the larger canon in a manner that is consistent with the composer's work elsewhere. The book of Malachi consists of six disputations designed to show that the postexilic community is still in a broken covenant relationship and in need of a new covenant (Mal. 1:2–5; 1:6–2:9; 2:10–16; 2:17–3:5; 3:6–12; 3:13–21 [Eng., 4:3]). The last three verses, however, are almost universally recognized as an appendix (or two appendices) that stands outside of the main content of the book.[58] This piece of text connects the end of the Twelve to the following Psalm

---

58. See Ralph L. Smith, *Micah–Malachi*, WBC 32 (Nashville: Thomas Nelson, 1984), 340–42.

1 in a manner similar to the way the end of the book of Moses connects to the beginning of Joshua (see above, The Place of the Twelve in the Hebrew Canon).[59] It highlights the Day of the LORD theme so important to the development of Hosea 3:4–5 elsewhere in the Twelve (Mal. 3:23 [Eng., 4:5]). Furthermore, there is a citation from Jeremiah in Psalm 1. The psalm in its entirety is modeled on the contrast of the righteous and the wicked in Jeremiah 17:5–8, but the wording is most closely aligned in the description of the righteous person:[60]

> Blessed is the man who trusts in the LORD (Jer 17:7a).
> Blessed is the man who . . . murmurs in his Torah (Ps 1:1a, 2b).
> He will be like a tree planted by water (Jer 17:8a1).
> He will be like a tree planted by streams of water (Ps 1:3a1).

Summary
This section is designed to bring together the preceding discussion on the composition of the Twelve in a way that the reader can see at a quick glance the author's seams and how those seams meet the criteria.

I.   The Program of the Twelve (Hos. 3:4–5)
    A.   Distinctiveness: not directed to the northern kingdom and not part of Judean redaction
    B.   Message: judgment and messianic salvation in the last days
    C.   Citation of Jeremiah: Hosea 3:5 cites Jeremiah 30:9

II.   Hosea-Joel Seam (Hos. 14:10 [Eng., 14:9]; Joel 1:2–3)
    A.   Distinctiveness: wisdom language in prophetic books
    B.   Message: reading strategy for the Twelve
    C.   Citation of Jeremiah: Hos. 14:10a (Eng., 14:9a) cites Jeremiah 9:11a (Eng., 9:12a)

III.   Joel-Amos Seam (Joel 4:16a [Eng., 3:16a]; Amos 1:2a)
    A.   Distinctiveness: same text inserted at end of Joel and beginning of Amos
    B.   Message: the Day of the LORD (Joel 4:14 [Eng., 3:14])

---

59. Psalms 1 and 2 form a separate introduction to the book (*b. Ber.* 9b–10a).
60. William Holladay argues for the priority of Psalm 1 (*Jeremiah 1: A Commentary on the Book of the Prophet Jeremiah Chapters 1–25*, Hermeneia [Philadelphia: Fortress, 1986], 489–90), but it appears more likely that the psalmist has taken something abstract ("trusts") and given it concrete expression ("murmurs in his Torah").

C. Citation of Jeremiah: Joel 4:16a (Eng., 3:16a) and Amos 1:2a cite Jeremiah 25:30b

IV. Amos-Obadiah Seam (Amos 9:11–15; Obad. 1–5; 17–21)
  A. Distinctiveness: restoration for fallen booth of David (Amos 9:11–15)
  B. Message: Edom represents nations included in God's kingdom (Amos 9:12; Obad. 19)
  C. Citation of Jeremiah: Obadiah 1–5 cites from Jeremiah 49:9, 14–16

V. Obadiah-Jonah Sequence[61]
  A. Distinctiveness: juxtaposition
  B. Message: Nineveh is to Jonah what Edom was to Amos-Obadiah (Jon 1:2; 3:2; 4:11)
  C. Citation of Jeremiah: Obadiah 1–5

VI. Jonah-Micah Sequence
  A. Distinctiveness: quote from Exodus 34:6–7 (Jon. 4:2b; Mic. 7:18–20)[62]
  B. Message: judgment and restoration
  C. Citation of Jeremiah: Micah 3:12 cites Jeremiah 26:18 in a later form[63]

VII. Micah-Nahum Seam (Mic. 7:18–20; Nah. 1:2b–3a)
  A. Distinctiveness: separate hymn (Mic 7:18–20) and insertion to acrostic (Nah. 1:2b–3a)
  B. Message: quotation from Exodus 34:6–7 (judgment and restoration)
  C. Citation of Jeremiah: Micah 3:12

VIII. Nahum-Habakkuk Frame (Nah. 1:2–8; Hab. 3:3–15)
  A. Distinctiveness: poems at the beginning and the end serve as bookends
  B. Message: judgment of the wicked and deliverance of the righteous in the last days
  C. Citation of Jeremiah: Habakkuk 2:13–14 cites Jeremiah 51:58 and Isaiah 11:9

---

61. The small book of Obadiah functions like a seam between Amos and Jonah.
62. This practice of using material from the end of one book in the seam at the end of the following book is also attested in Joel 4:18a (Eng., 3:18a); Amos 9:13b.
63. Remember, this is the middle verse of the Twelve.

IX. Habakkuk-Zephaniah Sequence/Seam (Hab. 2:20b; 3:16b; Zeph. 1:2–3, 7a, 15)
  A. Distinctiveness: distinctive language ("Hush"; "day of distress")
  B. Message: the Day of the LORD
  C. Citation from Jeremiah: Zephaniah 1:2–3 cites from Jeremiah 7:20; 8:13; 15:3

X. Zephaniah-Haggai Sequence/Seam (Zeph. 3:9–20)
  A. Distinctiveness: restoration section
  B. Message: temple project in Haggai is now a picture of future restoration
  C. Citation of Jeremiah: Zeph. 3:17b cites Jeremiah 32:41a

XI. Haggai-Zechariah Seam (Hag. 2:20–23; Zech. 1:2–6)
  A. Distinctiveness:
    1. separate ending on Zerubbabel (Hag. 2:20–23)
    2. separate introduction to the visions (Zech. 1:2–6)
  B. Message: Zerubbabel prefigures the Messiah (Zech. 3:8; 6:12–13)[64]
  C. Citation of Jeremiah:
    1. Haggai 2:23 cites Jeremiah 22:24
    2. Zechariah 1:4 cites Jeremiah 25:4–7[65]

XII. Zechariah-Malachi Combination (Zech. 9:1; 12:1; Mal. 1:1)
  A. Distinctiveness: the only three occurrences of this heading
  B. Message: eschatology and messianism (Zech. 9:9–10; 12; 14; Mal. 3:1)
  C. Citation of Jeremiah: Zech. 11:13; Matt. 27:9–10

XIII. Malachi-Psalms (Canonical) Seam (Mal. 3:22–24 [Eng., 4:4–6]; Ps. 1)[66]
  A. Distinctiveness:
    1. Malachi 3:22–24 is not part of the six disputations in the book
    2. Psalms 1 and 2 form a separate introduction (b. Ber. 9b–10a)
  B. Message: the Day of the LORD
  C. Citation of Jeremiah: Psalm 1 cites Jeremiah 17:5–8

---

64. Cf., 2 Sam. 7:13; Isa. 52:13–53:12; Jer. 23:5–6; Zech. 9:9–10; 12:10.
65. See also Jer. 31:18 and Zech. 1:3.
66. Cf., Deut. 34:5–Josh. 1:9.

BOOK OF THE TWELVE

HOSEA

HOSEA 1:1

1:1 The word of the LORD that came to Hosea the son of Beeri in the days of Uzziah, Jotham, Ahaz, Hezekiah the kings of Judah and in the days of Jeroboam the son of Joash the king of Israel.

The superscription to the book of Hosea is comparable in form and function to other superscriptions in the Latter Prophets (e.g., Isa. 1:1; Joel 1:1; Amos 1:1; Mic. 1:1). The "word of the LORD" here does not refer to one specific prophecy of Hosea but to the entirety of what the reader encounters in the book that bears Hosea's name. It encompasses the full span of Hosea's prophetic ministry. The text does not explain how the word of the LORD came to Hosea (e.g., visions, dreams, etc.). It only indicates that Hosea's message is in fact divine revelation and not merely the prophet's own assessment of things (see 2 Pet. 1:19–21). Furthermore, this revelation is rooted in real time and space. When the superscription says that Hosea was the son of Beeri, it is not because Beeri is well known from elsewhere. Rather, it is because Hosea was a historical prophet and not a figment of the writer's imagination. This is confirmed by the temporal reference to the days of four eighth-century Judean kings and the days of Jeroboam II. Such a reference provides a narrative context for the prophecies in the book (2 Kgs. 12–20) much like the way the stories of David and Solomon provide context for the psalms and the wisdom literature. But the arrangement of this temporal reference raises an important question. Why are the kings of Judah listed first even though Hosea was primarily a prophet to the northern kingdom of Israel? This follows the pattern of the book of Kings, which normally correlates the reign of kings in the north with that of those in the south (e.g., 2 Kgs. 14:23). Hosea's ministry is now correlated with his prophetic contemporaries in the south (Isa. 1:1; Mic. 1:1). In addition, it will be evident that the content of the book ultimately reaches beyond the northern kingdom of Israel to include not only Judah but also the nations, especially when read within the larger context of the Book of the Twelve.

HOSEA 1:2–9[1]

1:2a The first part of the word of the LORD through Hosea.[2]

1:2b And the LORD said to Hosea, "Go, take for yourself a wife of fornication and children of fornication, for the land certainly fornicates away from the LORD."[3] 1:3 And he went and took Gomer the daughter of Diblaim, and she conceived and bore to him a son.[4]

The text of Hosea 1:2a is the superscription for the first subsection of the book in Hosea 1:2b–9. The Hebrew word תחלה ("first part") does not simply mean "beginning" in the sense of "an initial point in time" (ראשון) or "an initial indefinite duration" (ראשית). It is the first stage in a series of equal stages, and so it is a fitting way to refer to the first section of many that make up "the word of the LORD" from Hosea 1:1. The message came to Hosea, and now it comes to the audience through

---

1. See *b. Pesaḥ.* 87.
2. The Masoretic vocalization of Hosea 1:2a, which requires a finite verb after a noun in the construct state ("The first part of the LORD spoke"), is unusual although not unprecedented (cf., Num. 3:1b; Isa. 29:1a; see also GKC §130d). The Septuagint, the Syriac, and *Targum Jonathan*, however, reflect a vocalization of the same consonantal text (תחלת דבר יהוה) that would be more in accordance with the ordinary use of the construct state, involving a chain of nominal elements ("The first part of the word of the LORD"). This is not really a text-critical issue, in which case the more difficult reading might be preferable. It is more a matter of interpretation of the same text, in which case the option with the least attendant problems is preferable.
3. *Targum Jonathan*: "Go, prophesy against the inhabitants of the idolatrous city who continue to sin. For the inhabitants of the land surely go astray from the worship of the Lord."
4. *Targum Jonathan*: And he went and prophesied concerning them that if they repented, they would be forgiven. If not, they would fall as the leaves of a fig tree fall. But they continued to do evil deeds.

Hosea. There is some question about whether this section and subsequent sections in Hosea constitute poetry. This is more likely the case where there is sustained use of parallelism, figurative language, and terseness of expression. It is perhaps better to speak of the prophetic literature in terms of a heightened style.[5]

When the LORD instructs the prophet to take "a wife of fornication" (אשׁת זנונים), there is no indication in the present context of the exact nature of this woman's sexual promiscuity.[6] There is also no indication of whether she is engaged in this activity at the time of the marriage or simply inclined to be engaged in it at some later point, although the analogy with the LORD's relationship to Israel would seem to suggest the latter.[7] The "children of fornication" are not necessarily those who are the product of illegitimate relationships. Rather, they are those who, like their mother, are inclined to a certain type of unfaithful behavior. The LORD wants the prophet to do this because generations of the people of the land have been engaged in this activity in a spiritual sense. That is, Hosea's marriage to Gomer will be a sign act (cf., Ezek. 24:15–27) that illustrates how the LORD made a covenant with Israel, but Israel became unfaithful (cf., Jer. 3; Ezek. 16). It is important for the reader to remember that these words are not here primarily to teach lessons about marriage.[8] They are here to communicate a message about human infidelity toward God and about divine faithfulness toward humanity.

1:4 And the LORD said to him, "Call his name Jezreel, for in yet a little while I will visit the bloodshed of Jezreel upon the house of Jehu and cause the kingdom of the house of Israel to cease.[9] 1:5 And so, in that day I will break the bow of Israel in the valley of Jezreel."

---

5. See James L. Kugel, *The Idea of Biblical Poetry: Parallelism and Its History* (New Haven, CT: Yale University Press, 1981; reprint, Baltimore: Johns Hopkins University Press, 1998).
6. The law against this kind of marriage in Leviticus 21:7 applies specifically to priests and refers to women who are currently engaged in fornication of some kind.
7. See Douglas Stuart, *Hosea–Jonah*, WBC 31 (Nashville: Thomas Nelson, 1987), 26–27.
8. Note the absence of any indication of Hosea's emotion or concern (cf., Gen. 22).
9. *Targum Jonathan*: And the Lord said to him, "Call their name 'Scattered Ones,' for in yet a little while I will avenge the blood of the idol worshipers that Jehu shed in Jezreel when he killed them because they worshiped Baal. They turned to go astray after the calves at Bethel. Thus, I will

The meanings of the names of Hosea's children all contribute to his prophecy in some way (cf., Isa. 7:3; 8:1–4, 18; 10:21). These names initially have a negative connotation, but this changes in chapter 2 (Hos. 2:1–3, 25 [Eng., 1:10–2:1, 23]). In the present context, there is a sound play between "Jezreel" and "Israel." It is only later in Hosea 2:25 (Eng., 2:23) that the meaning of "Jezreel" ("God sows") becomes significant. Here the idea is that what happened at Jezreel is somehow a microcosm of the ongoing problems everywhere in Israel. According to the narrative in 2 Kings 9–10, Jehu was God's chosen instrument to bring the Omride dynasty and its Baal worship to an end. Jehu successfully fulfilled this task in the blood bath at Jezreel (2 Kgs. 10:11), but he did not subsequently keep the Torah of the LORD (2 Kgs. 10:30–31). Rather, he followed in the sins of Jeroboam (1 Kgs. 12:25–33) like all the other kings of the north. Thus, the cycle of rebellion continued unabated.

1:6 And she conceived again and gave birth to a daughter. And he said to him, "Call her name Lo Ruhamah, for I will never again have compassion on the house of Israel that I should in any way forgive them.[10] *1:7 But on the house of Judah I will have compassion and deliver them by the LORD their God. And I will not deliver them by bow or by sword or by warfare, by horses or by horsemen."*

The daughter's name, "Lo Ruhamah," means "she has not received compassion," decisively marking the broken covenant relationship and the ensuing consequences of such a fracture (cf., Hos. 2:6 [Eng., 2:4]; Amos 8:2). Verse 7, however, introduces the house of Judah in a positive light. This text is usually considered to be part of a Judean redaction designed to make Hosea's oracles to the north applicable to the south (Hos. 1:7; 2:2 [Eng., 1:11]; 4:15; 5:5, 10, 12–14; 6:4, 11; 8:14; 10:11; 12:1, 3 [Eng., 11:12; 12:2]). But this does not mean that the reader can simply peel back this layer. It is present in all textual witnesses to the book. The deliverance of Judah will not take place by human means (cf., Hos. 2:20 [Eng., 2:18]). It will be a divine deliverance.

---

reckon it innocent blood upon the house of Jehu, and I will cause the kingdom to cease from the house of Israel."

10. The latter part of this verse is rendered differently by the early versions. The LXX says, "But I will surely oppose them." *Targum Jonathan* reads, "If they return, I will surely forgive them." Hans Walter Wolff suggests, "instead, I will withdraw it from them" (*Hosea*, trans. Gary Stansell, Hermeneia [Philadelphia: Fortress, 1974], 8–9). For the above translation, see GKC §120c and BDB, 671.

1:8 And she weaned Lo Ruhamah and conceived and bore a son. 1:9 And he said, "Call his name Lo Ammi, for you are not my people, and I am not 'I AM' to you."

The name of the third child, Lo Ammi, means "not my people" (cf., Deut. 32:21). Israel is no longer God's covenant people until he restores them in a new covenant relationship. Therefore, he is no longer their covenant God. He refers to himself here by his covenant name (יהוה) in the first-person form (אהיה) in which he explained it to Moses in Exodus 3:14. There he indicated that he was the God who would be present with his people (cf., Exod. 3:12).[11] Here he says that he will not be that God to them anymore. Unfortunately, most English versions do not pick up this feature of the Hebrew text (e.g., NRSV).

HOSEA 2:1–3 (ENG., 1:10–2:1)

2:1 (Eng., 1:10) And the number of the sons of Israel will be like the sand of the sea, which cannot be measured or counted. And then, in place of which it is said to them, "You are not my people," it will be said to them, "Sons of a living God." 2:2 (Eng., 1:11) And the sons of Judah and the sons of Israel will be gathered together, and they will appoint for themselves one head and go up from the land, for great will be the day of Jezreel. 2:3 (Eng., 2:1) Say to your brothers, "Ammi," and to your sisters, "Ruhamah."

This passage does not have a separate introductory formula. Nevertheless, the form and content of the text suggest that it is a new unit. The use of a series of *weqatal* forms in the Hebrew text marks a shift from the words of judgment in Hosea 1:2–9 to words of hope in the future.[12] Already the prophet anticipates a reversal of the negative connotation of his children's names. Furthermore, it is precisely this future hope that contributes to the overall purpose of the making of the Twelve (Hos. 3:4–5). Verse 1 (Eng., 1:10) begins where Hosea 1:9 ended in the sense that it cites from the Pentateuch (Gen. 22:17; cf., Isa. 10:22–23).[13] The words of the covenant with Abraham (Gen. 15) anticipate not only a plurality of descendants but also an individual

---

11. See Rolf Rendtorff, *The Canonical Hebrew Bible: A Theology of the Old Testament*, trans. David E. Orton (Leiden: Deo, 2005), 40.
12. Wolff, *Hosea*, 24–25.
13. Those who wish to see the opposite direction of dependence must nevertheless reckon with the presentation of the biblical texts themselves.

seed from the tribe of Judah (Gen. 12:3; 27:29; 49:8–12; Num. 24:7–9; Jer. 4:2; Ps. 72:17; Gal. 3:16, 29; cf., 2 Sam. 7:1–17).[14] The present text in Hosea has both in view.

Some translations give the impression that the second half of Hosea 2:1 (Eng., 1:10) refers to a specific place such as the land of Israel or the land of exile (e.g., *Tg. Jon.*) where it was said that Israel was no longer God's people. But it is more likely that the phrase "in place of which" means "instead of" (BDB, 880; cf., Isa. 33:21). Instead of being called "Lo Ammi" ("not my people") they will be called "sons of a living God" (cf., Josh. 3:10).[15] Verse 2 (Eng., 1:11) presupposes the exile of both Judah and Israel and envisions their return (cf., Deut. 29–30). The language of appointing a head comes from Numbers 14:4 (Neh. 9:17) where the Israelites wanted to replace Moses and return to Egypt. But now the language takes on a positive connotation in that a new Moses will lead a new exodus not from Egypt but from Assyria and Babylon (see Deut. 18:15, 18; 34:10; Isa. 11:16; 43:16–21; Hos. 2:17 [Eng., 2:15]; 11:1, 5, 11 [cf., Num. 24:7–9]; Mic. 7:15).[16] According to *Targum Jonathan* this head will be from the house of David (cf., Ezek. 34:23; 37:24; see also Rashi).

The day of Jezreel (i.e., Israel) will no longer be a time of judgment as in Hosea 1:4–5. It will be "great" in the sense that the people will be able to say to their brothers, "Ammi" ("my people"), and to their sisters, "Ruhamah" ("she has received compassion"). This is the language of the covenant formula, "I will be their God, and they will be my people" (Jer. 31:33). The apostle Paul picks up the wording of Hosea 2:1–3, 25 (Eng., 1:10–2:1, 23) and applies it to the Jewish-Gentile church (Rom. 9:25–26; cf., 2 Pet. 1:10).[17] This is in part due to the fact that the church is the new covenant community, but there is also textual warrant for

---

14. See Michael B. Shepherd, *The Text in the Middle* (New York: Peter Lang, 2014), 21–24, 122–29.

15. Note how the MT of Deuteronomy 32:8 interprets the phrase "sons of God" (4QDeutʲ) to mean "the sons of Israel," whereas the LXX interprets it to mean "angels of God."

16. It is from the context of Babylonian exile that Jesus understands his role as the servant of the Lord (Isa. 61; Luke 4:16–30; cf., Matt. 2:15).

17. "Through its apostasy from God, Israel had become like the Gentiles, and had fallen from the covenant of grace with the Lord. Consequently, the re-adoption of the Israelites as children of God was a practical proof that God had also adopted the Gentile world as His children" (C. F. Keil, *The Minor Prophets*, Keil & Delitzsch Commentary on the Old Testament 10 [Edinburgh: T. & T. Clark, 1866–91; reprint, Peabody, MA: Hendrickson, 2001], 34).

Paul's reading. Within the larger context of the Twelve, the Gentiles are included in God's kingdom in accordance with the program set forth in Hosea 3:5 (e.g., Amos 9:12; Acts 15:17).[18] Paul also cites Deut. 32:21 and Isaiah 65:1 to make his case (Rom. 10:19–20). It is important to remember that from the very beginning the covenant relationship was intended to restore the lost blessing to all the nations through Abraham and his seed (Gen. 12:1–3). It was not to make distinctions according to ethnicity but according to faith.

HOSEA 2:4–15 (ENG., 2:2–13)

2:4 (Eng., 2:2) "Contend with your mother, contend, for she is not my wife, (and I am not her husband), so that she might remove her fornication from before her,[19] and her adultery from between her breasts, 2:5 (Eng., 2:3) lest I strip her naked and exhibit her like the day when she was born, and make her like the wilderness, and set her like a dry land, (and kill her with thirst). 2:6 (Eng., 2:4) And on her sons I will not have compassion, for they are sons of fornication. 2:7 (Eng., 2:5) For their mother fornicated, she who conceived them acted shamefully, for she said, 'I will go after my lovers, the providers of my food and my water, my wool and my flax, my olive oil and my drinks.'"

In this section, the Hebrew parallelism is more sustained, making it possible to identify features like parenthetical comments as noted in the translation. Here God has a point of contention (cf., Hos. 4:1; Mic. 6:2b) with his wife (Israel), so he calls on her children (the people) to contend with her, essentially asking the nation to indict itself (cf., Hos. 5:5; 7:10).[20] This obviously translates the metaphor of Hosea 1:2. The language of Hosea 2:4a (Eng., 2:2a) seems to suggest divorce (i.e., the broken covenant; cf., Hos. 1:9), but Hos. 2:4b–5 (Eng., 2:2b–3) apparently has a preventative, if not redemptive, purpose in mind for the contention. This is consistent with Jeremiah's citation of the divorce law (Deut. 24:1–4; Jer. 3:1; cf., Isa. 50:1). The law forbids a man (the LORD) to remarry a woman (Israel) whom he divorced if another man

---

18. See Michael B. Shepherd, *The Twelve Prophets in the New Testament* (New York: Peter Lang, 2011), 7–13.
19. LXX Hos. 2:4b1 (Eng., 2:2b1): "and I will remove her sexual immorality from before my face." For the syntax of the Hebrew jussive in this clause, see GKC §109f.
20. According to Rashi, the mother is the nation of today, and the children are the future generations. See also Ezekiel 23:2.

(Baal) has since married and divorced her. But the LORD intends to override this law by his grace in a new covenant relationship.

Failure to heed this contention and to remove the figurative sexual immorality and adultery from the place where those acts occur will result in a reversal of the covenant relationship, stripping Israel naked like the day she was born (cf., Ezek. 16). Israel will go back to the wilderness (exile),[21] the place to which the LORD brought her when he redeemed her from Egypt and the place where he provided for her and sustained her (Exod. 16–17; Num. 11–20; Jer. 2:6). It will now be a place of judgment from which a new deliverance will be necessary (cf., Num. 13–14; Ezek. 20:33–44). Israel's children, of course, are included in this, and so they have the same accusation and announcement of judgment against them (Hos. 2:6 [Eng., 2:4]). Like their mother who conceived them, they have acted shamefully. Verse 7 (Eng., v. 5) even gives insight into Israel's thought process. She considered her lovers (i.e., the Canaanite gods such as Baal), not her husband (the LORD), to be the providers of her food, water, and other products. She gave Baal the credit for the LORD's blessings.[22] Thus, Israel's worship had become syncretistic at best and, at worst, false and idolatrous.

2:8 (Eng., 2:6) "Therefore, look, I am about to hedge your path[23] with thorns,[24] and I will build her wall, so that her paths she will not find.[25] 2:9 (Eng., 2:7) And she will pursue her lovers, but she will not reach them; and she will seek them, but she will not find. And she will say, 'I will go and return to my former husband, for it was better for me then than now.' 2:10 (Eng., 2:8) But she, she has not acknowledged that I am the one who gave to her the grain and the new wine and the fresh olive oil. And silver, I increased it for her; and gold, they made it into the Baal idol. 2:11 (Eng., 2:9) Therefore, I will turn and take my grain in its time and my new wine in its season; and I will take my wool and my flax, which were to cover her nakedness."

---

21. The parenthetical comment at the end of Hosea 2:5 (Eng., 2:3) makes it clear that this is not talking about barrenness as much as it is about a wilderness experience.
22. It does not seem helpful to see in this a reference to real sexual acts with cultic prostitutes in the Baal fertility cult (see James L. Mays, *Hosea*, OTL [Philadelphia: Westminster, 1969], 38–39). At the very most, this sort of thing remains in the background of the text, but see Hos. 4:14.
23. 4QpHos[a], LXX, and Syr. read: "her path" (cf, Hos. 2:8b [Eng., 2:6b]).
24. See GKC §116p.
25. See Diethelm Michel, *Tempora und Satzstellung in den Psalmen* (Bonn: H. Bouvier u. Co., 1960), 129–30.

The announcement of judgment is marked in this passage by the two occurrences of לכן ("Therefore") in Hosea 2:8, 11 (Eng., 2:6, 9). The LORD will block the way to Israel's religious practices, preventing her from reaching her lovers and finding what she seeks (cf., Hos. 3:3). This will create a situation in which the thought process of Hosea 2:7b (Eng., 2:5b) will be transformed so that Israel will return to the LORD, her former husband, realizing that he was much better all along (Hos. 2:9b [Eng., 2:7b]; cf., Deut. 30:3; Hos. 3:5). Israel had not "acknowledged" (ידע) the LORD or what he had done for her (Hos. 2:10 [Eng., 2:8]; see Deut. 7:13).[26] She had even taken his gifts of gold (e.g., Exod. 12:35) and made them into Baal idols (see *Tg. Jon.*; cf., Hos. 8:4; 13:2), possibly referring to the two golden calves that Jeroboam set up at Dan and Bethel (cf., Hos. 10:5; 13:2; see 1 Kgs. 12:28–29; see also Exod. 32; Deut. 9).[27] So, the LORD will take away his blessings (Hos. 2:11 [Eng., 2:9]; cf., Lev. 26; Deut. 28; Joel 1:10; Hag. 1:11) so that Israel might learn to appreciate them and to recognize the LORD rather than Baal for them.[28]

2:12 (Eng., 2:10) "And now, I will uncover her senselessness to the eyes of her lovers, and no one will rescue her from my hand. 2:13 (Eng., 2:11) And I will cause all her rejoicing to cease—her festival, her new moon, her Sabbath [or, mid-month], and all her appointed time. 2:14 (Eng., 2:12) And I will destroy her grapevine and her fig tree of which she said, 'A prostitute's pay is what they are to me, which my lovers gave to me.' And I will make them into a forest, and the creature of the field will devour them. 2:15 (Eng., 2:13) And I will visit upon her the days of the Baals to whom she makes sacrifices smoke. And she adorned herself with her ring and her jewelry and went after her lovers, but me she forgot," the prophetic utterance of the LORD.

---

26. The root ידע often has this sense in Hosea (e.g., Hos. 4:6; 6:6; 11:3; see BDB, 394–95).

27. Given the wording of Hosea 8:4 and 13:2, it is possible to render Hosea 2:10b (Eng., 2:8b): "And silver I increased for her, and gold, which they made into the Baal idol." Some translations understand this to mean that they offered silver and gold to Baal or in some way used it in worship of Baal (e.g., NRSV).

28. The reference to removing the covering for her nakedness in Hosea 2:11b (Eng., 2:9b) goes back to the wording of Hosea 2:5a (Eng., 2:3a), but there may also be a subtle allusion to the law in Exodus 21:10, indicating that it is not the LORD who has taken another woman. Rather, it is Israel who has taken another man, thereby dissolving the covenant relationship. See also Gen. 3:7; Deut. 28:48; Ezek. 16:8, 39.

The macrosyntactic marker ועתה ("And now") at the beginning of Hos. 2:12 (Eng., 2:10) sets apart this new subunit.[29] The LORD will expose Israel's "senselessness" or "foolishness" (נבלות) to the very ones with whom she committed her acts of infidelity (cf., Ezek. 16:37).[30] This judgment will be inescapable. The LORD will bring Israel's festivals and appointed times to a halt (Hos. 2:13 [Eng., 2:11]; see Lev. 23) precisely because she had made these into occasions to worship Baal rather than the LORD (cf., 1 Kgs. 12:25–33).[31] He will also destroy his blessings (Hos. 2:14 [Eng., 2:12]; cf., Hos. 2:7, 11 [Eng., 2:5, 9]), which Israel considered to be the gifts of her lovers as pay for her services as a prostitute (cf., Hos. 9:1; Mic. 1:7). Her grapevines and fig trees will become an overgrown forest to be devoured by wild creatures (cf., Isa. 7:23–25).

The language at the beginning of Hosea 2:15 (Eng., 2:13) is reminiscent of Hosea 1:4b. The idiom "to visit upon" (פקד על) means in this context to bring the consequences or punishment of an action upon the responsible party (BDB, 823). Here the judgment is for "the days of the Baals," which likely refers to the festivals and appointed times in Hosea 2:13 (Eng., 2:11) that had been used to honor Baal.[32] The use of "Baals" in the plural refers to multiple local manifestations and places of worship (e.g., Baal of Peor [Num. 25]; see BDB, 127). It is to these Baals that Israel offers sacrifices. The syntax of Hosea 2:15 (Eng., 2:13) following the relative clause ("to whom she makes sacrifices smoke") features two *wayyiqtol* clauses and one "*waw* + x + *qatal*" clause. English translations usually render these last three clauses as if they were a continuation of the *yiqtol* verb (often translated as a past tense), for which the reader might expect *weqatal* forms. It seems better to understand the *wayyiqtol* clauses separately as a telling of the story of

---

29. See Alviero Niccacci, *Syntax of the Verb in Classical Hebrew Prose*, trans. W. G. E. Watson (Sheffield: JSOT, 1990), 96, 101; Christo H. J. van der Merwe, Jackie A. Naudé, and Jan H. Kroeze, *A Biblical Hebrew Reference Grammar* (Sheffield: Sheffield Academic, 1999), 333.

30. The term נבלות is sometimes rendered "lewdness" or "shame" (e.g., NET, NRSV). This is a case of confusion between meaning and referent. The word means "folly," but it can refer to shameful acts. Thus, Israel's fornication is described as foolishness. See BDB, 614–15; Stuart, *Hosea–Jonah*, 51.

31. Michael Fishbane makes a good case for the rendering of שבת ("Sabbath") in this verse as "mid-month" on the basis of Leviticus 23:10–16; 2 Kings 4:23; Isaiah 1:13; Amos 8:5; and Psalm 81:4 (Eng., 81:3) (*Biblical Interpretation in Ancient Israel* [Oxford: Clarendon, 1985], 145–51). See also Colossians 2:16.

32. Keil, *The Minor Prophets*, 40.

how Israel adorned herself for her lovers. The *"waw* + x + *qatal"* clause would then mark the contrast: "But as for me, they forgot."[33]

HOSEA 2:16–25 (ENG., 2:14–23)

2:16 (Eng., 2:14) "Therefore, look, I am about to make her simple [LXX: "deceive her"; Evv.: "allure" or "entice" her], and I will walk her into the wilderness and speak to her heart,[34] 2:17 (Eng., 2:15) and I will give to her her vineyards [LXX: "possessions"] from there, and the valley of Achor for an opening of hope; and she will answer [LXX: "be afflicted"; NET: "sing") thither like the days of her youth and like the day of her going up from the land of Egypt."

Once again לכן ("Therefore") marks a unit as it did in Hosea 2:8, 11 (Eng., 2:6, 9), but this time the inference drawn brings words of hope rather than judgment.[35] The *piel* participle of פתה ("make simple") in this context likely has the sense of persuading or seducing (e.g., Exod. 22:15; Judg. 14:15; 16:5; Prov. 1:10; 16:29) rather than deceiving (e.g., 2 Sam. 3:25; Prov. 24:28). The wilderness is now a place where the LORD will speak to Israel's heart (cf., Gen. 34:3; 50:21; Judg. 19:3; Isa. 40:2; see also Deut. 32:10; Hos. 9:10) rather than a place where he strips her and kills her with thirst (Hos. 2:5 [Eng., 2:3]).

The description is typical throughout. What took place in the olden time is to be repeated, in all that is essential, in the time to come. Egypt, the Arabian desert, and Canaan are types. Egypt is a type of the land of captivity, in which Israel had been oppressed in its fathers by the heathen power of the world. The Arabian desert, as the intervening stage between Egypt and Canaan, is introduced here, in accordance with the importance which attached to the march of Israel through this desert under the guidance of Moses, as a period or state of probation and trial, as described in Deuteronomy 8:2–6, in which the Lord humbled his people, training it on the one hand by want and privation to the knowledge of its need of help,

---

33. See Niccacci, *Syntax of the Verb*, 35–109.
34. *Targum Jonathan*: "Then, look, I am about to make her subservient to the Torah, and I will perform for her signs and powers just as I did for her in the wilderness. And by the hand of my servants the prophets I will speak comforts to her heart."
35. For the use of לכן in biblical Hebrew, see Christo H. J. van der Merwe, "The Challenge of Better Understanding Discourse Particles: The Case of לכן," *JNSL* 40/2 (2014): 127–57.

and on the other hand by miraculous deliverance in the time of need (e.g., the manna, the stream of water, and the preservation of their clothing) to trust to His omnipotence, that He might awaken within it a heartfelt love to the fulfilment of His commandments and a faithful attachment to Himself. Canaan, the land promised to the fathers as an everlasting possession, with its costly productions, is a type of the inheritance bestowed by the Lord upon His church, and of blessedness in the enjoyment of the gifts of the Lord which refresh both body and soul.[36]

The LORD will restore from the context of the wilderness the very vineyards he once destroyed (Hos. 2:17 [Eng., 2:15]; see Hos. 2:14 [Eng., 2:12]). He will give the valley of Achor to Israel for an opening (or, doorway/entrance) of hope. According to the story in Joshua 7, the valley of Achor (עכור) was the place where Achan (עכן) "transgressed" (עבר) and "troubled" (עכר) the people of Israel. The fact that Achor is now a figurative doorway of hope speaks volumes about God's redemptive power (cf., Isa. 65:10). Israel will "respond" (ענה) in the direction of the wilderness like the days of her youth. It is possible that this is the homonym "sing" (ענה), especially given the fact that this will be like the original exodus. After the account of the exodus in Exodus 14 and the Song of Moses in Exod. 15:1–18, Miriam and the women come out and "sing" (ענה) (Exod. 15:20–21). This hope of a new exodus will remain prominent throughout Hosea (Hos. 8:13; 9:3; 11:1, 5, 11) and the Book of the Twelve.[37]

2:18 (Eng., 2:16) "And so, in that day," the prophetic utterance of the LORD, "you will call, 'My husband,' and never again call to me, 'My Baal' [LXX: Baalim]. 2:19 (Eng., 2:17) And I will remove the names of the Baals from her mouth, and they will never again be remembered by their name. 2:20 (Eng., 2:18) And I will make with them a covenant in that day—with the creatures of the field and with the birds of the sky and the creeping things of the ground. And bow and sword and warfare are what I will break from the land, and I will cause them to lie down in security. 2:21 (Eng., 2:19) And I will betroth you to me forever, and I will betroth you to me with righteousness and with justice and with covenant loyalty and with compassion. 2:22 (Eng., 2:20) And I will betroth you to me with faithfulness, and you will acknowledge the LORD. 2:23 (Eng., 2:21) And then, in that day, I will answer [> LXX, Syr.]," the

---

36. Keil, *The Minor Prophets*, 41. It is important to recognize that this is not typological interpretation. It is identification of figuration in the intent (i.e., verbal meaning) of the biblical author.

37. See Shepherd, *The Twelve Prophets*, 22–24.

prophetic utterance of the LORD, "I will answer the heavens, and they will be the ones that answer the land, 2:24 (Eng., 2:22) and the land will be the one that answers the grain and the new wine and the fresh olive oil, and they are the ones that will answer Jezreel. 2:25 (Eng., 2:23) And I will sow her for myself in the land, and I will have compassion on Lo Ruhamah, and I will say to Lo Ammi, 'You are my people,' and as for him, he will say, 'My God.'"

The repeated use of the phrase "in that day" (ביום ההוא) in this section (Hos. 2:18, 20, 23 [Eng., 2:16, 18, 21]) refers to the day of the new exodus from Hosea 2:16–17 (Eng., 2:14–15).[38] The MT of Hosea 2:18 (Eng., 2:16) uses the second feminine singular verb תקראי ("you will call"). The LXX, however, uses a third singular verb, presumably reflecting the third feminine singular Hebrew תקרא ("she will call"). This latter reading is probably a secondary adjustment by a scribe or by the translator designed to harmonize the text with the third person references to Israel in the following verses. Israel will no longer confuse Baal with the LORD by crediting the LORD's blessings to Baal or by using the LORD's festivals and appointed times to worship Baal. She will acknowledge the LORD as her true husband and not as her Baal. It is somewhat ironic that the Hebrew word בעל (*baal*) can mean "husband" without reference to the Canaanite deity (e.g., Gen. 20:3; see also Jer. 3:14; 31:32).[39]

The LORD will remove (cf., Hos. 2:4b [Eng., 2:2b]) the names of the Baals (e.g., Baal of Peor [Num. 25]; see Hos. 2:15 [Eng., 2:13]) so that they will no longer be mentioned or invoked.[40] He will also make a new covenant (Hos. 2:20 [Eng., 2:18]; cf., Jer. 31:31–34).[41] The language of

---

38. See Mays, *Hosea*, 47.

39. The term בעל (*baal*) in the sense "Lord" was once used like אל ("El" or "God") and יה ("Yah," short for יהוה "Yahweh" or "the LORD") as a theophoric element in Hebrew names, but it was later changed to בשת (*bosheth* ["shame"]) because of its association with the Canaanite fertility/storm god Baal. Thus, Greek witnesses to the Hebrew text of 2 Samuel 2:8 reflect the name "Ishbaal" ("man of the Lord"), which became understood as "man of Baal" and was thus changed to "Ishbosheth" ("man of shame"). Cf., Mephibaal/Mephibosheth (2 Sam. 4:4).

40. Mays, *Hosea*, 49.

41. This is not a covenant renewal. The old covenant is broken. The passage in Jeremiah 31:31–34 describes the new covenant first of all by saying that it is not the old covenant (cf., Deut. 28:69 [Eng., 29:1]). It will be an unconditional covenant rather than a conditional one, and the Torah will be on the heart (effective) rather than on the tablets (ineffective). From a grammatical standpoint, in order to say, "renewed covenant," the text of

this covenant—wild creatures, birds, creeping things—is similar to the covenant with Noah (Gen. 9:9–10). Like the unconditional terms of the Noahic covenant, which sought to restore the lost blessing of life and dominion in the land (Gen. 1:26–28; 9:1–2) and to instill confidence that judgment by flood waters would never occur again (Gen. 9:11), this new covenant will unconditionally ensure that the people will dwell in security from the ravages of wild beasts (Hos. 2:14b [Eng., 2:12b]; 4:3) and warfare (cf., Hos. 1:7b).[42] Lest the reader think that this is too much of an earthly hope for it to be the new covenant established in Christ's blood (Luke 22:20; Heb. 8), it is important to remember that the messianic kingdom (Isa. 11:1–10) and the new creation (Isa. 65:17–25) are both physical and spiritual, rendering the bodily resurrection (Dan. 12:2) an essential feature of the believer's future.

The repeated use of "betroth" (ארשׂ) in Hosea 2:21–22 (Eng., 2:19–20; cf., Jer. 2:2) is an extension of the marital metaphor from that of marriage-infidelity-divorce to that of remarriage (i.e., new covenant). Marriage itself is more of a unity than a covenant (Gen. 2:24), but certain features of the marriage relationship lend themselves to illustrations of divine-human covenants. It is worth noting then that the marriage metaphor with reference to the old covenant is primarily negative, highlighting infidelity and divorce. The same metaphor with reference to the new covenant is primarily positive, illustrating the unity of the body with Christ (e.g., Eph. 5:15–33).[43] Here the threefold use of "betroth" is perhaps intended to counteract the negative connotation of the names of Hosea's three children (cf., John 18:15–18, 25–27; 21:15–19). The LORD will betroth his people to himself indefinitely in justice and righteousness and covenant loyalty and compassion (Hos. 2:25 [Eng., 2:23]) and faithfulness. There is some question about whether this means to say that the LORD or the people will have these qualities.[44] These are certainly qualities that the LORD desires from his people (Deut. 10:12; Mic. 6:8), qualities that they will in fact have in the new marriage (Isa. 62:1–5), but the LORD is the

---

Jeremiah 31:31 would need an attributive feminine singular *pual* participle of חדשׁ to modify ברית ("covenant"): ברית מחדשׁה. But the text has ברית חדשׁה. The *piel* verb of חדשׁ does occur in biblical Hebrew with the meaning "renew" (e.g., 1 Sam. 11:14) but never with ברית ("covenant") as its object. This only happens in post-biblical literature (1Q28b 5:21; 1Q34 2:6). Cf., Hebrews 8.

42. See Isa. 2:4; Jer. 23:6; Ezek. 34:25; Mic. 4:3; Zech. 9:10; 14:11.
43. See Mays, *Hosea*, 50–52.
44. See Stuart, *Hosea–Jonah*, 59.

grammatical subject of the main verbs in these verses, so the prepositional phrases are likely intended to modify his action (Ps. 33:4–5). It
is no accident then that these qualities are the hallmarks of the messianic kingdom (Isa. 9:5–6 [Eng., 9:6–7]; 11:3–5; Jer. 23:5–6; Ps. 72). In
that context, the people will "know" (ידע) the LORD in the sense that
they will recognize and acknowledge him for who he really is (cf., Hos.
2:10 [Eng., 2:8]).[45]

In that day, the LORD will answer (Hos. 2:23–24 [Eng., 2:21–22];
cf., Jer. 33:3). His answer makes its way down as if through a chain of
command. The personified sky asks for clouds so that it can respond
to the land's request for rain. The land in turn can then answer the
demand for nutrients from the grain, the new wine, and the fresh
olive oil (see Hos. 2:10 [Eng., 2:8]; Joel 2:19; Zech. 8:12). And finally,
those products can answer Jezreel's (i.e., Israel's) prayer for food. Verse
25 (Eng., v. 23) picks up the name Jezreel ("God sows") and removes
the negative connotation it had in Hosea 1:4–5 (cf., Jacob/Israel [Gen
32:29; 35:10]): "And I will sow her for myself in the land" (cf., Jer. 31:27;
Hos. 10:12; Zech. 10:9). It then does the same for the names of Hosea's
other two children. The LORD will have compassion on Lo Ruhamah
("she has not received compassion"), and Lo Ammi ("not my people")
will be Ammi ("my people") (see Hos. 1:6–2:3 [Eng., 1:6–2:1]; cf., Isa.
51:16; Hos. 14:4 [Eng., 14:3]; Zech. 13:9).[46]

HOSEA 3

*3:1 And the LORD said to me, "Again go, love a woman loved by a male
companion [LXX: a woman loving evil][47] and practicing adultery as
the LORD loves the sons of Israel, and they turn to other gods and are
lovers of raisin cakes." 3:2 And I acquired her by trade for myself for
fifteen pieces of silver and a homer of barley and a lethech of barley.[48]*

---

45. It is also possible that this is "know" (ידע) in the carnal sense (BDB, 394),
    the consummation of the marital relationship as a continuation of the be-
    trothal metaphor. See Stuart, *Hosea–Jonah*, 60.
46. See John Chrysostom's comment on this passage about believing Jews
    and Gentiles (Alberto Ferreiro, ed., *The Twelve Prophets*, ACCS OT XIV
    [Downers Grove, IL: InterVarsity, 2003], 13).
47. The LXX does not reflect a different Hebrew text, only a different vocal-
    ization/interpretation of the same consonants. The MT has אֲהֻבַת רֵעַ. The
    LXX reflects אֹהֶבֶת רַע.
48. For the use of *daghesh forte* in the first two words of this verse, see GKC
    §120c, h.

*3:3 And I said to her, "For many days you will live to me [i.e., as mine].
You will not fornicate and you will not belong to a man, and also I to
you." 3:4 Because for many days the sons of Israel will live without a
king and without a prince and without sacrifice and without a pillar
and without ephod and teraphim.*[49] *3:5 Afterward, the sons of Israel
will return and seek the LORD their God and David their king and fear
to the LORD and to his goodness at the end of the days.*

In this passage, Hosea becomes the narrator. The key word at the beginning of Hosea 3:1 is עוֹד ("again"). Does this belong with what precedes
("And the LORD said to me again") or with what follows ("Again go,
love") (cf., Zech. 11:15)? If it belongs with what follows, is the LORD
commanding Hosea to love Gomer again, or is he commanding him to
love another sexually immoral woman?[50] The situation is complicated
by the lack of Gomer's name in the text. The woman in Hosea 3:1 is not
merely someone who is inclined toward sexual promiscuity. She has been
"loved" by another man and has committed adultery. The exact nature
of her relationship to this other man is not delineated. It is not impossible that this woman is Gomer, unless the reader's view of marriage and
the LORD's relationship with Israel precludes such an understanding.
It is also possible that this is a different woman. The interpreter must
not press the analogy too far. It is not the purpose of the text to tell
Hosea's story. It is the text's purpose to use certain features of Hosea's
marriage(s) to illustrate the LORD's relationship with his people. Thus,
the reader must allow the text to draw the appropriate analogy and to
leave other details untouched. In this case, the analogy drawn says that
the LORD loves Israel even though the people turn to other gods and are
lovers of raisin cakes. Here the term "love" (אהב) may very well have the
sense of "devotion/commitment" rather than pure emotion. God's love in
this context is an act of election on the basis of a covenant relationship
(cf., Deut. 7:7–11). The reference to "other gods" is likely an allusion to
the Decalogue (Exod. 20:3). The raisin cakes are perhaps a way to describe the love relationship (Song 2:5).

The reader's view of the woman in Hosea 3:1 will affect interpretation of Hosea 3:2. If the woman is Gomer, then Hosea is buying her
back, although the text does not say from where he is buying her back
(e.g., the slave trade, prostitution, etc.; cf., Exod. 21:32). If this is another woman, then Hosea is acquiring her with a bride price (cf., Exod.

---

49. For the use of אִין in the sense "without," see BDB, 34–35.
50. For the former view, see Wolff, *Hosea*, 60. For the latter, see Stuart, *Hosea–
Jonah*, 66.

22:15). Again, the reader must not allow the uncertainties of Hosea's life to distract from the point of the text. Furthermore, it is not the role of the interpreter to write a narrative around the scrap of information in Hosea 3:2 in order to make Hosea into some sort of romantic and heroic model for troubled husbands everywhere to follow. The analogy that the text wants to make is very clear from the parallel wording in verses 3 and 4. For "many days" (ימים רבים) Hosea will sequester his wife to live (ישב) with him alone. She will be deprived of things both good and bad. She will not fornicate (לא תזני; cf., לא תנאף Exod. 20:14) or belong to another man, but Hosea also indicates by saying "and also I" (וגם אני) that not even he will go in to her or have sexual relations with her (Luther: *und auch ich will nicht zu dir eingehen*).[51] Likewise, Israel will live (ישב) for "many days" (ימים רבים) without things both good and bad (see Hos. 10:2–3). This speaks of exile. She will not have things given to her by the LORD such as a king, a prince, or sacrifice (c.f., CD 20:16). She will also not have those things that expressed her spiritual infidelity: pillar (Deut. 16:22), ephod (Judg. 8:27), and teraphim (2 Kgs. 23:24).

This creates the perfect opportunity for the composer of the Twelve to introduce his program from Jeremiah 30:9 in Hosea 3:5 (see Introduction, The Composition of the Twelve). This program looks beyond any return of the northern kingdom of Israel from Assyria or even the return of Judah from Babylon. It envisions the restoration of the lost blessing of life and dominion in the land (Gen. 1:26–28) to all the nations (Gen. 12:1–3; Amos 9:12). The people will seek the LORD and David their king. This is not the historical David or a resurrected David but the Davidic king who will build the temple and reign over an everlasting kingdom (*Tg. Jon.*; cf., 2 Sam. 7:12–14; Isa. 9:5–6 [Eng., 9:6–7]; Jer. 23:5–6; Ezek. 34:23; 37:24; Zech. 6:12–13). It is in this sense that the composer of the Twelve is Christ-centered.[52] The people will also fear "to the LORD" (אל יהוה) and "to his goodness" (אל טובו). This is the opposite of fearing away from him (cf., Mic. 7:17b). It is a healthy fear. The term "goodness" refers to the blessings of the land and perhaps also spiritual blessings (BDB, 375; Exod. 33:19; Eph. 1:3). The eschatological phrase "at the end of the days" (באחרית הימים) does not merely refer to days to come (contra E. Jenni, *TLOT*, 1:87–88). Its

---

51. For this use of גם, see Francis I. Andersen, *The Sentence in Biblical Hebrew* (The Hague: Mouton, 1974), 157. For the idiom "to go in to" meaning "to have sex with" implied by אליך, see BDB, 98.

52. See Augustine (Ferreiro, ed., *The Twelve Prophets*, 15–16) and John Calvin, *Hosea*, Calvin's Commentaries XIII (reprint, Grand Rapids: Baker, 2005), 133.

sparse and strategic use always occurs in passages that speak of the messianic kingdom: in the poems of the Pentateuch that interpret the preceding narratives (Gen. 49:1, 8–12; Num. 24:7–9, 14, 17; Deut. 4:30; 31:29; 33:5, 7), in the programmatic and restoration passages of the Prophets (Isa. 2:1–5; Jer. 23:30; 30:24; 48:47; 49:39; Ezek. 38:14–17; Hos. 3:5; Mic. 4:1–5), and in the visions of Daniel (Dan. 2:28; 10:14).

HOSEA 4

4:1 Hear the word of the LORD, O sons of Israel, for the LORD has a point of contention with the inhabitants of the land, for there is no faithfulness, and there is no covenant loyalty, and there is no acknowledgement of God in the land. 4:2 Taking oaths falsely and murdering and stealing and committing adultery, they break through [LXX: are poured out on the land], and bloodshed touches bloodshed. 4:3 Therefore, the land will mourn, and all the inhabitants therein will languish with the creatures of the field [LXX adds: and with the creeping things of the ground] and with the birds of the sky, and also/even the fish of the sea will be gathered.

This unit follows the typical pattern of a prophetic judgment oracle: introduction (Hos. 4:1), accusation (Hos. 4:2), and announcement of judgment (Hos. 4:3). The opening call to "hear" is well known from Deuteronomy (Deut. 4:1; 5:1; 6:4) and the Prophets (Amos 3:1; 4:1; 5:1; Mic. 1:2; 3:1; 6:1) and also occurs in Hosea 5:1. The LORD has a point of contention (cf., Hos. 2:4 [Eng., 2:2]; 12:3 [Eng., 12:1]; Mic. 6:2) with the people for their lack of faithfulness to the covenant relationship. They do not acknowledge or recognize the LORD (cf., Hos. 2:10 [Eng., 2:8]; 4:6; 5:4; 6:6).[53] Rather, they acknowledge Baal. But the text no longer uses Hosea's marriage to illustrate the broken covenant relationship. It now speaks directly about the specific terms of the covenant.

Verse 2 cites from the Decalogue precisely because the ten words on the two tablets of stone represent the covenant in its entirety (Deut. 4:13; Hos. 8:12). The number, order, and wording of the ten words here differ from what occurs in Exodus 20 and Deuteronomy 5, but this is not necessarily an indication that the prophet is working independently of those textual sources. The prophet seeks not merely to reproduce the ten words but to interpret and apply them. His selection and arrangement of them are ways to introduce his interpretation and application. Furthermore, citations of the Decalogue elsewhere are

---

53. *Targum Jonathan* calls this acknowledgement "the fear of the Lord."

typically not simple repetitions (e.g., Exod. 34:10–26; Lev. 19:11–12; Deut. 5; Jer. 7:9; Zech. 5:4; Mal. 3:5; Ps. 24:4; Matt. 19:18; Mark 10:19; Luke 18:20; Rom. 13:9).[54]

Hosea's אלה וכחש ("taking an oath and lying") is a figure of speech known as hendiadys ("one meaning through two words") and essentially means the same thing as Jeremiah's השבע לשקר ("swearing falsely") (Jer. 7:9).[55] This terminology derives from two different yet related prohibitions in the Decalogue. The prohibition against "false testimony" (עד שקר) in Exodus 20:16 is worded as "empty testimony" (עד שוא) in Deuteronomy 5:20. By means of this latter reference the reader is able to make the connection to the prohibition against taking the LORD's name "in vain" (לשוא) (Exod. 20:7; Deut. 5:11). Thus, the prohibitions are specifically directed against misuse of the LORD's name in the context of the taking of an oath to support false testimony in a court of law (Lev. 19:11–12; Deut. 19:18; Zech. 5:4; Ps. 24:4).

"Murdering" (רצח), "stealing" (גנב), and "adultery" (נאף) are also in Jeremiah's list but in a different order (Jer. 7:9). These are the same Hebrew roots from Exod. 20:13–15—again in a different order. רצח is specifically "murdering" rather than "killing" in general. גנב is initially defined as "kidnapping" in the Covenant Code (Exod. 21:16), but it can also be used more broadly. נאף is a particular act of sexual immorality that involves the taking of another man's wife in some way (e.g., 2 Sam. 11). This is perhaps the most poignant of the list in the present context given the fact that the same term has been used to describe the infidelity of Hosea's wife (Hos. 3:1) and the spiritual infidelity of Israel who forsook her husband (the LORD) for another man (Baal). Such behavior is now compounded by literal acts of adultery in the land. All of these things spread abroad and increase among the people in the land (BDB, 829).[56]

---

54. Both Hosea and Jeremiah use a series of infinitives absolute. See Shepherd, *Text in the Middle*, 77–78. See also the Nash Papyrus (Gary D. Martin, *Multiple Originals: New Approaches to Hebrew Bible Textual Criticism* [Atlanta: SBL, 2010], 205–248). For a helpful treatment of Exodus 20, see Brevard S. Childs, *The Book of Exodus: A Critical, Theological Commentary*, OTL (Louisville: Westminster John Knox, 1974), 385–439.

55. See E. W. Bullinger, *Figures of Speech Used in the Bible* (London: Spottiswoode, 1898; reprint, Grand Rapids: Baker, 1968), 657–72. See also Hos. 7:1; 10:4; 12:1–2 (Eng., 11:12–12:1).

56. It does not appear to be the case that Hosea or Jeremiah (Jer. 7:9) intended to leave out other commands/prohibitions or to isolate in some way these that receive mention. They both select the prohibitions that only require the mention of a single verbal root (Exod. 20:13–15) in order to represent the law in its entirety in a concise manner.

"Bloodshed touches bloodshed" in the sense that one murderous act is added to another before the previous one is even finished (cf., Isa. 5:8). The announcement of judgment in Hosea 4:3 amounts to a reversal of the preparation of the land of the covenant (Gen. 1:3–2:3, 11–14; 15:18; cf., Hos. 2:20 [Eng., 2:18]; Zeph. 1:2–3).[57] It is even more severe than the flood (Gen. 6–7) in that it includes the gathering of the fish. Jeremiah describes what the land will look like after the exile of Judah in terms of a similar reversal (Jer. 4:23–29; cf., Gen. 1:2).

4:4 But do not let anyone contend, and do not let anyone reprove (and your people are like those who would contend with a priest). 4:5 And you will stumble by day, and also a prophet will stumble with you by night. And I will destroy your mother, 4:6 my people are destroyed for the lack of acknowledgment. Because you rejected the acknowledgment, I will reject you from serving as priest. And because you forgot the instruction of your God, also I will forget your children. 4:7 As they increased so they sinned against me. Their glory for disgrace will I exchange. 4:8 The sin offering of my people they eat, and to their iniquity each one lifts up his soul/desire. 4:9 And so, like the people like the priest. And I will visit upon him his ways, and his deeds I will cause to return to him. 4:10 And they will eat, but they will not be satisfied. They will fornicate, but they will not break through. For it is the LORD they have forsaken by maintaining fornication.

The above translation and the present commentary work under the assumption that the Masoretic Text is intelligible the way it stands. Many other translations and commentaries assume that the Hebrew text is corrupt and in need of revocalization and/or conjectural emendation.[58] These adjustments are not on the basis of the available textual witnesses. Rather, they are driven in large part by the concern to have the passage directed primarily against the priests. But the extant text has a message both for the people and for the priests. The opening אַךְ ("But") sets up a contrast between the LORD's contention in Hosea 4:1–3 and the expression of the prophet's will that no "one" (אִישׁ) should contend with the LORD (Hos. 4:4a).[59] To this is added the comment that

---

57. See John H. Sailhamer, *Genesis Unbound* (Sisters: Multnomah, 1996).
58. E.g., Wolff, *Hosea*, 70–72; Stuart, *Hosea–Jonah*, 70–72.
59. Note the chiastic structuring of the Hebrew parallelism in Hos. 4:4a. See Wilfred G. E. Watson, *Classical Hebrew Poetry: A Guide to Its Techniques* (Sheffield: Sheffield Academic, 1984; reprint, London: T&T Clark, 2006), 201–208.

the people are like those who would contend with a priest—someone who represents the LORD himself (see Rashi).[60] The *BHS* apparatus changes this to mean, "And with you I contend [or, is my contention], O priest."

The usual assumption is that Hosea 4:5a speaks of priests and prophets stumbling together by day and by night, but the Masoretic Text suggests that the subject of the second masculine singular verb at the beginning of the verse is anyone from among the people. This would fit well with the description of the people's stumbling in Hosea 5:5. They stumble even when they should be able to see well. Hosea does not have as much to say about false prophets as others do (e.g., Jer. 23:9–40; Ezek. 13), but here he includes them with the general populace as those who will stumble by night, perhaps indicating that there has been a setting of the sun on their reception of prophetic visions (cf., Mic. 3:6).

The parallelism suggests that the last clause of Hosea 4:5b is the first half of a line that continues in Hosea 4:6a. Here the prophet acts in his role as messenger as if his voice were that of the LORD himself, speaking in the first person: "I will destroy your mother (cf., Hos. 2:4 [Eng., 2:2]), and my people are destroyed for the lack of acknowledgment" (Hos. 4:1; cf., Isa. 5:13). That is, the people have failed to acknowledge the LORD as their true husband and the giver of all things. Because they refuse to grant such recognition, the LORD will reject them as priests (Hos. 4:6b; cf., Exod. 19:6; Isa. 61:6; 66:21).[61] The *wayy-iqtol* at the beginning of the last line of Hos. 4:6 signals a continuation of the "Because you do . . . I do" pattern. The nation has forgotten the LORD's instruction (cf., Hos. 8:1). Therefore, he will forget its people and its future generations.

According to the measure of the LORD's blessings the people's sins have increased (Hos. 4:7a; 10:1; cf., Deut. 32:15). The *tiqqune soferim* ("corrections of scribes") reads,[62] "Their glory for disgrace will I exchange" (Hos. 4:7b; cf., Hab. 2:16). The original reading says, "My glory for disgrace they exchanged" (cf., Jer. 2:11). The people exchanged their glory (God) for the worship of Baal (disgrace), resulting in divine judgment.

---

60. The masculine singular pronoun "your" in "your people" probably refers to "anyone" from Hos. 4:4a.
61. Keil, *The Minor Prophets*, 52–53. Cf., 1 Sam. 2:11–3:21; 1 Kgs. 12:31–33; 2 Chr. 11:13–17.
62. Ernst Würthwein, *The Text of the Old Testament*, 2d ed., trans. Erroll F. Rhodes (Grand Rapids: Eerdmans, 1994), 17–18.

In verse 8 the priests are the grammatical subject of the verbs. This sets up the comparison between the people and the priests in verses 9 and 10. The priests have abused their privilege of partaking in the sin offering (Lev. 6:17–23). It has now become an occasion to indulge their sinful desires. Therefore, the people and the priests alike will bear the consequences of their actions (Hos. 4:9), eating without satisfaction and fornicating without spreading abroad (Hos. 4:10a; cf., Hos. 3:3–4; 4:2b). They both have forsaken the LORD in their own way—the people by consuming the LORD's blessings and worshiping Baal, and the priests by facilitating the worship of Baal and abusing the LORD's offerings (Hos. 4:10b).

4:11 And new wine [lit., wine and new wine] is what takes the heart of my people. 4:12 His wooden idol is what he [i.e., the people] consults, and his rod is what declares to him. For a spirit of fornication has led astray, and they fornicate from under their God. 4:13 On the tops of the mountains is where they sacrifice, and on the hills is where they make sacrifices smoke—under oak and poplar and terebinth, for its shade is good. Therefore, your daughters will fornicate, and your daughters-in-law will commit adultery. 4:14 Will I not [or, I will not] visit upon your daughters when they fornicate and upon your daughters-in-law when they commit adultery, when they [masc. pl.] with the female prostitutes make a separation and with the temple prostitutes sacrifice? (And a people without understanding will be thrown down.) 4:15 If you fornicate, O Israel, let not Judah be guilty. And do not go to Gilgal, and do not go up to Beth Aven, and do not swear, "As the LORD lives." 4:16 Indeed, like a stubborn heifer Israel has been stubborn, now will the LORD tend them like a lamb in the broad place? 4:17 Ephraim is joined to idols. Leave him to himself. 4:18 Their strong drink turns aside. They continually fornicate. They most certainly love disgrace, her shields [or, the disgrace of her shields]. 4:19 Wind has bound her in its wings, and they will be ashamed of their sacrifices [LXX: altars].

The verse divisions for Hosea 4:10–12 are neither original nor particularly helpful. Most translators and commentators will make some sort of adjustment here. The "wine and new wine" in Hosea 4:11 is perhaps another example of hendiadys given the use of a singular verb, but in what way does the new wine take the heart of the people? It is possible that this is a reference to the loss of mental faculties due to drunkenness (Prov. 23:29–35), but the preceding and following context suggests that this has something to do with spiritual fornication. According to Hosea 2:10 (Eng., 2:8), Israel did not acknowledge that the new wine was from the LORD. The fact that she credited this to Baal was an indication of her spiritual infidelity. She thought that her grapevine was her harlot's wage (Hos. 2:14 [Eng., 2:12]).

Israel does not consult God (Judg. 18:5; 20:18; 1 Sam. 14:37) but a wooden idol (Hos. 4:12a; cf., Isa. 44:9–20).[63] A rod is what guides the people, although it is not clear if this branch or stick is a diviner's rod (BDB, 596) or a synonymous parallel to the wooden idol. In any case, Israel has the same spirit of fornication that plagued Hosea's wife Gomer (Hos. 1:2), albeit in a metaphorical sense rather than a literal one (Hos. 4:12b; cf., Hos. 5:3–4). Wolff suggests that to fornicate "from under" God is an indication of rebellion in comparison to the break of relationship described by doing so "from after" God as in Hosea 1:2 (cf., 2 Kgs. 8:20, 22; Ezek. 23:5).[64] Given the sexual metaphor, however, it seems possible that this is a picture of a woman who moves from the place of intercourse with her husband in order to assume the position with another man. The problem with this interpretation is that there is very little, if any, clear usage of "from under" with this meaning in the language.

The description of alternative worship on high places in Hosea 4:13a is a familiar one to the reader of the book of Kings. In direct violation of the centralization of worship prescribed by Deuteromony 12:1–7 and contrary to the establishment of Solomon's temple (1 Kgs. 6–8), it is the hallmark of Jeroboam and the kings who followed in his sins (1 Kgs. 12:31). Jeroboam wanted to maintain political allegiance in the north, so he created religious alternatives to what the south had in Jerusalem. Unfortunately, the once innocuous high places (1 Sam. 9:12) resulted in the downfall of both the north and the south (Jer. 2:20; 3:6). The inference drawn in Hosea 4:13b is that the daughters of the men of Israel will fornicate, and their daughters-in-law will commit adultery. This is quite possibly a reference to the sexual acts of cult prostitutes designed to prompt the activity of the fertility god(s) (cf., Hos. 4:14). At the very least it would seem that literal acts of sexual immorality and the spiritual infidelity that such acts often symbolize have coalesced here (cf., Num. 25:1–3). Another possibility, however, is that the term "daughters" does not refer to actual women but to the daughter villages of the land (i.e., satellites around the larger cities; see BDB, 123).

---

63. Note the use of fronting in the Hebrew text of Hosea 4:11–13. See Adina Moshavi, *Word Order in the Biblical Hebrew Finite Clause*, LSAWS 4 (Winona Lake, IN: Eisenbrauns, 2010).
64. Wolff, *Hosea*, 85. Numbers 5 speaks of a woman being "under" her husband, that is, under his authority (Num. 5:19, 20, 29).

Some translations render the first part of Hosea 4:14 as a statement that the LORD will not punish (lit., "visit upon") the daughters. According to this, the LORD will simply give them over to the depravity of their ways (cf., Rom. 1:18–32), but contextually it seems more appropriate to understand this as a rhetorical question, given the fact that Assyrian captivity is on the horizon. The above translation renders all three occurrences of כִּי as "when," although most render the first two as such and then switch the last one to a causal conjunction. Not only does consistency favor "when" for the third כִּי, but also the latter part of the verse appears to be yet another way of describing the sexually immoral and adulterous actions of the people. The use of the third masculine pronoun "they" (הֵם) initially seems odd since the presumed antecedent would be the daughters, unless the reader is to assume a new subject here (e.g., the priests). But if the daughters actually represent daughter villages, then these would be the men of those villages who go off with the cult prostitutes to perform their religious rites (cf., Deut. 23:18). The extra comment in Hosea 4:14b about the people's lack of understanding says it all (cf., Deut. 32:6; Hos. 13:13; 14:10 [Eng., 14:9]; Prov. 10:8, 10).

The irony of the concern for Judah in Hosea 4:15a is that Judah eventually became far worse in the offense of which Israel is guilty (Jer. 3; Ezek. 23). Gilgal was well known as a place of illicit sacrifice (Hos. 9:15; 12:12 [Eng., 12:11]; Amos. 4:4; 5:5). A comparison with several other texts (Hos. 5:8; 10:5, 8; Amos 5:5) suggests that "Beth Aven" ("house of trouble/idolatry") is a derogatory name for "Bethel" ("house of God"; see *Tg. Jon.*), one of the locations along with Dan where Jeroboam set up a golden calf (1 Kgs. 12:29; cf., Amos 5:5; 8:14). Once known as the place where God appeared to Jacob (Gen. 28; 35), it was now notorious for idolatry on a scale comparable to what happened at Sinai (Exod. 32). The final prohibition—"and do not swear, 'As the LORD lives'"— implies the misuse of the LORD's name in an oath formula (BDB, 311; Exod. 20:7; Lev. 19:12; Hos. 4:2). According to the use of this language in Jeremiah, this involved swearing in his name falsely (or disingenuously) and swearing in the name of Baal (Jer. 4:2; 5:2; 12:16).

The comparison of Israel to a stubborn animal in Hosea 4:16a is a familiar one (cf., Deut. 32:15; Isa. 1:3), but less certain is the interpretation of Hosea 4:16b. Those who take it as a statement that the LORD will now shepherd the people like a lamb in a broad place differ widely in their understanding of the metaphor. Rashi suggests that the LORD will now feed Israel in a limited way. Calvin takes it to mean that the people will be driven to solitude. Keil says they will be left exposed to wild beasts. In other words, these commentators all attempt to explain in a negative fashion what on the surface appears to be a positive image. Stuart, on the other hand, says that the LORD will only tend the people as their shepherd when he is finished judging them. The above translation understands this to be a rhetorical question that assumes a negative answer. In light of Israel's stubborn behavior, the LORD cannot be expected to continue to lead them as their shepherd, can he? There must be consequences for such behavior.

Ephraim (i.e., the northern kingdom of Israel) is now joined to idols rather than the LORD, therefore, the people are to be left to their own devices (Hos. 4:17). The reference to strong drink turning aside in Hosea 4:18a is appropriate given the relationship between new wine and spiritual fornication mentioned in Hosea 4:11–12. The turning aside of the strong drink likely stands by association for the turning aside of the people from the way of the LORD as the remainder of the verse seems to suggest. It is most probable that Hosea 4:18b involves two infinitive absolute constructions (see *BHS* apparatus), the first to indicate what the people continually do (i.e., fornicate) and the second to show what they most prefer—disgrace rather than glory (cf., Hos. 4:7). The term קלון ("disgrace") is in apposition to מגניה ("her shields"), or else it should be revocalized to the construct state. The third feminine singular pronominal suffix on מגניה is somewhat unexpected here, but it does set up the use in Hosea 4:19. It likely refers to the "land" (ארץ [fem.]) of Israel, that is, by metonymy the inhabitants of the land. The land's shields would then be her corrupt leaders (cf., Ps. 47:10 [Eng., 47:9]). What does it mean that wind has bound her in its wings (Hos. 4:19)? This is perhaps an instance of double entendre. The "wind" (רוח) is the "spirit" (רוח) of fornication (Hos. 4:12b) that has led the people astray and will ultimately result in exile. At that time, they will be ashamed of their sacrifices (cf., Ezek. 16:61).[65]

A Short Note on Teaching and Preaching Hosea 4
It seems fitting to offer at this juncture a caveat on handling passages from the Prophets like Hosea 4 in the context of the church. It is not the task of the preacher to adopt the persona of the prophet Hosea and deliver a moralistic message to the congregation as if they were ancient Israel living under the terms of the Sinai covenant. Such an approach requires little reflection on the meaning of these texts within the larger context of the Twelve. The intent of the prophetic composer of the Book of the Twelve is to highlight the failure of the people to

---

65. The LXX reading "altars" instead of "sacrifices" is likely the preferable one here (cf., Hos. 10:1).

keep the old covenant in order to anticipate the necessity of the new covenant. The message of the Prophets is not simply to do better. It is to look forward to the future transformative work of God in the human heart. The Book of the Twelve is new covenant Scripture and should be delivered as such to the new covenant community. The Hebrew Bible is Christian Scripture not in the sense that Christians living in the first century AD wrote it but in the sense that Christianity stands in continuity with the message of the Prophets who not only rebuked the general populace and their leaders for their infidelity but also looked beyond the old covenant relationship to a new work of God in Christ.

HOSEA 5

5:1 Hear this, O priests, and pay attention, O house of Israel, and O house of the king, give ear, for to you is the judgment/justice, for a trap is what you are to Mizpah, and a net spread upon Tabor. 5:2 And as for slaughter, those who swerve cause to be deep. But as for me, I am discipline to all of them. 5:3 I am the one who knows Ephraim, and as for Israel, he is not hidden from me. Indeed, now you have committed fornication, O Ephraim, Israel is unclean. 5:4 Their deeds do not allow them to return to their God, for a spirit of fornication is in their midst, and the LORD they do not acknowledge. 5:5 And the pride of Israel will testify against him, and Israel and Ephraim will stumble over their iniquity. (Also Judah stumbles with them.) 5:6 With their sheep and with their cattle they will go to seek the LORD, but they will not find. He has withdrawn from them. 5:7 It is against the LORD that they have acted treacherously, for strange sons have they born. Now a new moon [LXX: mildew] will devour them with their fields.

The call to hear at the beginning of Hosea 5:1 marks a new section (cf., Hos. 4:1). This call goes out to the priests, the general populace of the northern kingdom (cf., Hos. 4:4–10), and the royal house because the responsibility of "justice" (מִשְׁפָּט) belongs to them and because the words of "judgment" (מִשְׁפָּט) apply to them (Hos. 5:11). They are a trap in the south (Mizpah) and a net in the north (Tabor) in the sense that they promote the alternatives to the centralization of worship in Jerusalem in accordance with Jeroboam's program (1 Kgs. 12:25–33; see Rashi). Many commentators abandon the MT in Hosea 5:2 in favor of continuing the hunting metaphor from Hosea 5:1 (cf., LXX), but the MT is in fact intelligible and similar in language to other passages in the Prophets. Those who swerve are the people who fall away or revolt (Pss. 40:5 [Eng., 40:4]; 101:3). To cause to be deep means to attempt to hide something from the

LORD (Isa. 29:15; 31:6; Hos. 9:8–9). In this case, the people think that they can slaughter and sacrifice animals to Baal without the LORD noticing (Hos. 2:15 [Eng., 2:13]; 4:13), but according to Hosea 5:3 the LORD knows it all. Thus, he will be the one to discipline them (cf., Deut. 8:5).[66]

The spiritual fornication and infidelity of Ephraim/Israel is not hidden from the LORD at all (Hos. 5:3; cf., Hos. 6:10). He is very much aware of their impurity, which prevents them from coming into his presence (cf., Num. 5:13, 14, 20, 27–29; Jer. 2:23; Ezek. 20:30, 31, 43; 23:7, 13, 30). The people are bound by their own sin from returning to their God, for they have a spirit of fornication and have failed to acknowledge the LORD (Hos. 5:4; cf., Hos. 4:1, 6, 12). Such theology requires a divine initiative for a new covenant relationship (Hos. 2:16–25 [Eng., 2:14–23]; 6:1, 3; cf., Jer. 31:18). The people's pride testifies against them (Hos. 5:5; cf., Isa. 3:9; 59:12; Jer. 14:7; Hos. 7:10) and will lead to their downfall (Hos. 4:5; Prov. 16:18). The parenthetical comment at the end of Hosea 5:5 adds that this will also apply to Judah (Hos. 4:15; 5:10; cf., 2 Kgs. 17:19).

The syncretistic worship of Israel will do them no good (Hos. 5:6). This is not the way the LORD wants to be sought (cf., Isa. 1:10–17; Jer. 29:13; Hos. 3:5; 5:15; 6:6). He has in fact withdrawn from them. The nation has acted unfaithfully against the LORD because it has born for Baal children estranged from the worship of the one true God (Hos. 5:7; Deut. 32:16; Isa. 1:4; Hos. 1:2; 2:4 [Eng., 2:2]; 7:9).[67] The judgment for this will be the way in which the very festivals such as the new moon festival that the people dedicate to Baal in an effort to obtain his blessing will actually result in the consumption and loss of the people and their land (cf., Jer. 3:24). The early versions and modern commentators are divided on how to understand Hosea 5:7b, but a comparison with Hosea 2:13–15 (Eng., 2:11–13) helps to clarify things. When Israel has finished offering all their produce and livestock to Baal at the festivals intended for the LORD, there will be no one to replenish their supplies, and they themselves will go into exile.

5:8 Blast a shofar in Gibeah, a clarion in Ramah. Shout, Beth Aven, behind you, Benjamin [LXX: Benjamin is amazed/confused].[68] 5:9

---

66. Note again how the prophet assumes the voice of the LORD here (Hos. 5:2–3) and then later in the same passage refers to him in the third person (Hos. 5:6–7).
67. Rashi takes this to be a reference to intermarriage among the nations (Ezra 9–10; Neh. 13), which would lead to idolatry (Deut. 7; 23).
68. *"O prophets! Raise your voices like* a horn; *prophesy that murderous nations will come against them because they made Saul of* Gibeah *king over*

Ephraim, a desolation is what she will become in a day of rebuke; it is among the tribes of Israel that I have made known what is reliable. 5:10 The princes of Judah are like movers of a boundary. Upon them I will pour out like water my fury. 5:11 Oppressed is Ephraim about to be, crushed in judgment [LXX: Ephraim oppressed his adversary, he trampled judgment], for he undertook/persisted, he walked after command [LXX: empty things]. 5:12 And as for me, I will be like a moth to Ephraim and like rottenness to the house of Judah. 5:13 And Ephraim saw his sickness, and Judah his wound. And Ephraim went to Assyria and sent to king Yarev ["contentious king"; or, מלכי רב "great king" or "my king is great"]. But as for him, he will not be able to heal you, and from you a wound will not depart. 5:14 For I will be like a lion to Ephraim, and like a young lion to the house of Judah. I, I am the one who will tear and go. I will take, and there will not be a rescuer. 5:15 I will go, I will return to my place [Tg. Jon.: my holy dwelling which is in heaven] until they are guilty [Tg. Jon.: until they acknowledge that they sinned] and seek my face. In their distress, they will look eagerly for me.

To blast a shofar or a trumpet is to sound an alarm (BDB, 1075; cf., Jer. 4:5; 6:1; Hos. 8:1; Joel 2:1, 15). In this case, it is a warning in the land of the north of coming divine judgment by means of an attack at the hands of a foreign enemy. The place names in Hosea 5:8 attracted the attention of *Targum Jonathan*, which linked them to key figures in biblical narrative: the failed king Saul (Gibeah), Samuel (Ramah) whose words the people did not heed, and the temple (Benjamin) that the people neglected. Gibeah is also mentioned in Hosea 9:9; 10:9 where the reference is most likely to Judges 19–21, the story of how Israel as represented by the tribe of Benjamin became the new Sodom and Gomorrah (cf., Gen. 19).[69] Beth Aven has already been used as a derogatory name for Bethel (Hos. 4:15).

---

them. Cry aloud as though you sound the trumpet; say that kings and their armies will come against them, because they did not listen to the words of Samuel, the prophet from Ramah. *Announce to them the alarms of the warriors because they acted faithlessly with my Memra, and they turned backwards from my worship and did not worship before me in the Sanctuary which is in the land of the tribe of* Benjamin" (Kevin J. Cathcart and Robert P. Gordon, *The Targum of the Minor Prophets: Translated, with a Critical Introduction, Apparatus, and Notes*, The Aramaic Bible 14 [Collegeville: Liturgical, 1989], 39–40).

69. See Shepherd, *Text in the Middle*, 19–20.

Ephraim will become a desolate place "in a day of rebuke" (ביום תוכחה)—a unique phrase for the time of judgment—largely because of the Assyrian invasion, exile, and captivity that will decimate and reconfigure the population (2 Kgs. 17; cf., Isa. 13:9). This judgment is a sure thing according to the word of the LORD through the prophet in Hosea 5:9b. Although the downfall of the northern kingdom of Israel initially benefited Judah economically, the south would eventually meet the same fate for the same reasons. The princes or leaders/rulers/officials of Judah were like those who moved a boundary marker (Hos. 5:10)—a proverbial way of saying that they were corrupt in the way they handled the ancient traditions (Deut. 19:14; 27:17; Prov. 22:28). So, God will pour out his wrath like water (cf., Isa. 8:5–8; CD 19:15–16).

Ephraim is about to be oppressed, that is, crushed in judgment (Hos. 5:11). This is because the people have walked after צו ("command"). The difficulty with rendering this word as "command" is that it is not clear what command or whose command is in view. It certainly cannot be said that Ephraim has walked after God's command. The LXX here reads "empty things," perhaps reflecting a Hebrew *Vorlage* of שוא (cf., Jer. 2:5; see also Vulg.: "filth" [= צו or צאָה?]; Isa. 28:8). The only other passage where צו occurs in the Hebrew Bible is Isaiah 28:10–13, and it may provide a clue to its meaning in Hosea 5:11. Some render the occurrences in Isaiah as "command," but it seems best in context to understand Isaiah 28:10 to be the people's mockery of Isaiah's prophecy as babbling: *tsav latsav tsav latsav qav laqav qav laqav.* Then, in dramatic irony, the same sounds represent the unintelligible speech of the people's foreign captors (Isa. 28:13). Thus, in the Hosea context the idea would be that the people have gone after what is foreign (i.e., the worship of Baal; Hos. 2:15 [Eng., 2:13]).

Verses 12–14 of Hosea 5 include both Ephraim and Judah. The LORD himself will be like a moth and rottenness to them, eating away at their very existence (Hos. 5:12). Verse 13a employs *wayyiqtol* forms in order to imitate storytelling and to recount the people's failed efforts to remedy their situation (cf., 4QpHos[b]). Ephraim saw its sickness (and Judah its wound), but they did not turn to the LORD (Hos. 5:4; cf., Isa. 53:4–6). Instead they sought refuge and political alliance in Assyria (2 Kgs. 17:3; Hos. 7:11; 10:6). Since Yarev is not the name of any known Assyrian king, "contentious king" or "great king" (מלכי רב) is likely a title for the Assyrian king in general and not a reference to any particular king. Nevertheless, Assyria would not be able to heal them and in fact would become God's chosen instrument of judgment. God himself will be like a lion to Ephraim and Judah (cf., Hos. 13:7–8; Lam. 3:10), tearing them as a predator would its prey without anyone to rescue them (cf., Hos. 6:1). The bitter irony of this image is that Israel, and Judah in particular, had been compared to a lion (Gen. 49:8–12; Num. 23:24; see also Ezek. 19).[70]

When the LORD says that he will return to his place in Hosea 5:15, it may be a continuation of the simile in Hosea 5:14. That is, the image may be that of a lion returning to its lair. *Targum Jonathan*, however, understands this to be a return to God's holy dwelling place in heaven (Ps. 11:4; cf., Hos. 5:6). This withdrawal will last until the people acknowledge their guilt (see *Tg. Jon.*; cf., Hos. 10:2) and seek the LORD, something that will not happen until the last days according to Hos. 3:5 (cf., Hos. 7:10). Only in their distress will they look for the LORD with genuine eagerness (cf., Neh. 9:26–31). The LXX may very well be correct in understanding the last clause of Hos. 5:15 to be an introduction to the discourse in Hosea 6:1–3. If that is in fact the case, then the speech should probably be taken as a genuine expression of repentance, however hypothetical or idealistic it may be.

HOSEA 6:1–11A

6:1 "Come and let us return [or, that we may return] to the LORD. Though he is the one who tore us like prey, he will heal us. Though he struck, he will bind us.[71] 6:2 He will make us alive after two days, on the third day he will cause us to rise, (and we will live before him).[72] 6:3 And we will acknowledge [or, let us acknowledge], we will pursue [or, let us pursue] acknowledgment of the LORD.[73] Like dawn his going forth is established. And he will come like the rain to us, like latter spring rain he will shower [or, early fall rain; or, he will teach] the land." 6:4 What will I do with you, Ephraim? What will I do with you, Judah? And your covenant loyalty is like a morning cloud, and like the dew that passes

---

70. The choice of two different Hebrew words for lion in Hosea 5:14—the first a poetic term and the second meaning "young lion"—is probably for stylistic variation.

71. This translation is based on the understanding that כִּי is concessive rather than causal (BDB, 473) and is implied at the beginning of Hosea 6:1b. Also, the verb יָךְ should be וְיָךְ. The initial *waw* was lost due to haplography (see the *waw* at the end of the preceding word). The use of *wayyiqtol* signals a continuation of the pattern from Hos. 6:1a.

72. *Targum Jonathan*: "He will make us alive in the days of comfort, which are about to come in the day of the resurrection of the dead. He will raise us, and we will live before him."

73. The cohortatives here likely express resolve or determination (GKC §108).

away early. 6:5 Therefore, I cut by the prophets, I slay them by the words of my mouth. (And your judgments are like the dawn that goes forth [LXX: And my judgment like light goes forth].) 6:6 For it is covenant loyalty in which I delight and not sacrifice, and acknowledgment of God rather than burnt offerings.[74] 6:7 But as for them, it is like mankind [LXX: anthropos; Tg. Jon.: former generations; Vulg., Rashi: like Adam; Luther: at Adam] that they transgress covenant. There [i.e., in Israel; cf., v. 10] they act treacherously against me. 6:8 Gilead is a city of troublemakers, foot-tracked with blood. 6:9 And as those who wait for a man in gangs [but see GKC §231], a band of priests [LXX: priests hide the way of the Lord], on the way they commit murder to Shechem. Indeed, evil is what they commit [or, an evil plan is what they make]. 6:10 It is in the house of Israel that I have seen a horrible thing. There Ephraim has fornication, Israel is unclean. 6:11 (Also Judah, he has appointed a harvest for you).[75]

The speech in Hosea 6:1–3 is likely not the actual voice of the people (cf., Hos. 6:4–11), unless what they are saying is in fact disingenuous. Otherwise there would be no need for the prophet to continue with words of judgment. It is most probable that this is an example of the kind of repentance that the LORD would like to hear from the people. The text of Jeremiah 3:22b–25 provides another instance of such a model prayer. The return to the LORD must be initiated by the LORD himself (Hos. 5:4; 6:11), but when that happens the people will recognize that the very one who tore them like a lion tears its prey will be the one to heal them (Hos. 5:14; cf., Deut. 32:39; Isa. 12:1; Hos. 14:5 [Eng., 14:9]; Ps. 85:7 [Eng., 85:6]). Their healing will not come from foreign aid (Hos. 5:13).

The language of Hosea 6:2 appears to draw on the story of the binding of Isaac in which Abraham expresses a hope in a resurrection on the third day (Gen. 22:4–5; Heb. 11:17–19; see also 2 Kgs. 20:5).

It is possible to understand the expression "after two days, on the third day" (Hos 6:2) as a numerical device (cf., Amos 1–2; Prov. 30) or to mean "in a little while," but elsewhere significant events in the Bible do take place

---

74. See GKC §119w.
75. The *BHS* format puts Hosea 6:11b with Hosea 7:1 contra the MT. This is preferable for several reasons. Because Hosea 6:11a is an added comment with a third-person verb, it does not seem appropriate to modify it with a temporal infinitive construction that uses a first-person suffix. Also, the semantic and syntactic similarities of Hosea 6:11b to the first part of Hosea 7:1 are very strong.

on a literal third day (e.g., Exod. 19:16; Josh. 1:11; Jon. 3:4; Esth. 5:1). Modern critical scholarship understands the revival in Hos 6:2 to be a national and political restoration of Israel, but this was not the way the text was read in antiquity. *Targum Jonathan*, for example takes this revival to be the resurrection from the dead. The description of the coming of YHWH in Hosea 6:3 is similar to prophetic depictions of the messianic kingdom (e.g., Ezek. 34:26). In the New Testament, it is Jesus's resurrection that takes place on the third day (Matt. 16:21), but because he is the firstborn from the dead (Col. 1:18), this is also the beginning of the resurrection of the people of God.[76]

---

76. Shepherd, *Text in the Middle*, 44. Cf., Calvin's commentary on the passage and Paul's reference to the Scriptures in 1 Cor. 15:3–5. See also Ferreiro, *The Twelve Prophets*, 26–28. "For such a hope, however, focused as it was on the consummation of history, it was essential that in the establishment of the divine community those also should have their part who in the decisive crisis had fought in the front line. As they had witnessed to the living God right to the end, without thought for their own mortal danger, so that same God would not complete his kingdom without them. The conviction, amid the seemingly hopeless distresses of the time of persecution, that one was set in the last decisive moments before the final victory of the cause of God, and would receive from him the reward of either eternal acceptance or rejection, filled the historical moment with a final, absolute importance, and gave each individual combatant the sense of taking part with his whole existence in the world process now hastening to its goal. *Here the prophetic view of history at last finds its full application to the life of the individual.*" (Walther Eichrodt, *Theology of the Old Testament*, vol. 2, trans. J. A. Baker [Philadelphia: Westminster, 1967], 514–15). Other passages that have historically figured prominently in the Tanakh's doctrine of the resurrection include but are not limited to Isaiah 26:19; Ezekiel 37; Hosea 13:14; Psalms 16:10; 17:15; 49:16 (Eng., 49:15); Job 14:14; 19:26; Daniel 12:2. Gerhard von Rad's comment on Psalm 49:16 (Eng., 49:15) is particularly insightful: "This statement can hardly be referred to anything other than a life after death, for the thought of the whole psalm revolves, in the sense of the problem of theodicy, around the question of the grace of Jahweh in the life of the individual, and comes to the conclusion that the proud rich must remain in death" (*Old Testament Theology*, vol. 1, *The Theology of Israel's Historical Traditons*, trans. D. M. G. Stalker [New York: Harper & Row, 1962], 406). The Job 14 passage is often taken to mean that because people do not regrow like trees after they have been cut they therefore do not have a hope in a resurrection. But the point is quite the opposite. Resurrection is not like the regrowth of trees at all. People do not grow back like trees. They receive new life and new bodies altogether. See LXX, Job 14:14.

To object that life after death was not part of the consciousness of ancient Israel fails to reckon with two important details. First, the prophet or the biblical author is not necessarily a representative of the mainstream institutions and beliefs of his day. And second, it is by no means an unrealistic assumption that someone in history prior to the book of Daniel gave some thought to what happens to a person after death. It is at the very least circular to argue that the Hebrew Scriptures do not reveal a resurrection because ancient Israel could not have understood or believed it and vice versa.

The ideal voice of the people confidently expresses the hope that they themselves and not merely a future generation will in fact live before the LORD, that is, in his presence (Hos. 6:2). In the messianic kingdom, the resurrected people of God will finally acknowledge the LORD (and not Baal) for who he is (Hos. 6:3). The above translation understands Hosea 6:3a1 to be parallel to the end of Hosea 6:2. *BHS* puts Hosea 6:3a1 parallel to what follows. It is possible to take the text both ways depending on the interpretation of the pronominal suffix on מוֹצָאוֹ ("his going forth"). If it refers to the LORD, then Hosea 6:3a2 likely goes with Hosea 6:3b. His coming is as sure as a morning sunrise. If it refers to the dawn ("like dawn whose going forth is established"), then it probably belongs with what precedes and describes the way in which the people will pursue right recognition of the LORD. The deciding factor may very well be the use of messianic imagery that links Hosea 6:3a2 to Hosea 6:3b (2 Sam. 23:4; Ezek. 34:26; Joel 2:23; Mal. 3:20; Ps. 72:6).[77] He will come as sure as the rains that nourish the ground (cf., Isa. 55:10–11; Hos. 14:6 [Eng., 14:5]).[78]

In Hosea 6:4a there is no formal introduction to the LORD's discourse (cf., Hos. 4:1), but it is the voice of the LORD through the prophet expressing by means of the force of rhetorical questions the futility of working with both Ephraim and Judah in a covenant relationship.[79] Their covenant loyalty is as reliable as a cloud or as the fog that dissipates at the very beginning of the day and does not last. It is like the dew that evaporates early without a trace. Thus, the confession of Hosea 6:1–3 is by no means a present reality. The people are at best fickle. Therefore, the LORD announces that he cuts them by means of the prophets (like Hosea), slaying them with the words of his mouth

---

77. See Keil, *Minor Prophets*, 64.
78. The word יוֹרֶה is either a masculine singular *qal* active participle, a third masculine singular *hiphil yiqtol*, or a noun ("early rain") from the root ירה ("throw, shoot") (see BDB, 434–35). Cf., Hos. 10:12.
79. See Watson, *Classical Hebrew Poetry*, 338–42.

(Hos. 6:5). That is, the accusations and announcements of judgment that come through the prophets metaphorically cut the people like a sword. The LORD's word is as good as done. In fact, the last clause of Hosea 6:5b appears to be an additional comment intended to make this very point. Just as the LORD will come as surely as the dawn (Hos. 6:3), so his judgment is as certain as the light of a morning sunrise (cf., Mic. 7:8–13; see BDB, 21). The difference between the MT and the LXX of Hos. 6:5b is a difference in dividing the letters of the Hebrew text (see *BHS* apparatus). The MT probably preserves the original intent since the text is a parenthetical authorial comment that refers to the LORD in the third person. The translator or scribe for the LXX or its *Vorlage* likely did not follow this and adjusted the text so that the LORD remains the first-person speaker.

The text of Hosea 6:6 stresses that it is covenant loyalty and acknowledgment of God that the LORD desires, not sacrifices or burnt offerings. This implies that the people were in fact offering their sacrifices, but for the wrong reasons (Hos. 2:15 [Eng., 2:13]), perpetuating a false sense of security that their religious rituals and institutions were sufficient for their well-being. Such concern for what is primary and essential to the covenant relationship is an important feature of the message of the Prophets and the Psalms (1 Sam. 15:22; Isa. 1:10–17; 57:19; 58; Jer. 7:21–23; Hos. 14:3 [Eng., 14:2]; Amos 5:21–24; Mic. 6:6–8; Zech. 7; Ps. 4:6 [Eng., 4:5]; 27:6; 40:7–9 [Eng., 40:6–8]; 50:14, 23; 51:18–21 [Eng., 51:16–19]; 54:8 [Eng., 54:7]; 107:22 [Eng., 107:21]; 116:17 [Eng., 116:16]; 141:2; Prov. 21:3; *Let. Aris.* 234; Mark 12:33; Heb. 10:5–10; 13:15; *b. Meg.* 3b).[80] It is important to note the force of the wording of this verse. It does not say that the LORD desires covenant loyalty and acknowledgment with sacrifices and burnt offerings, but "not sacrifice" and "rather than burnt offerings." Of course, there is a way to use sacrifices and burnt offerings rightly in the expression of worship (Ps. 51:18–21 [Eng., 51:16–19]), but that is not the point that the Prophets are trying to stress. The laws regarding sacrifices were added secondarily because of transgression (Jer. 7:21–23; Gal. 3:19) and do not form the heart of the covenant relationship. The LORD desires spiritual sacrifices (Hos. 14:3 [Eng., 14:2]; Mic. 6:8).[81]

---

80. See Shepherd, *Text in the Middle*, 120–22.
81. For a discussion of Jesus's reference to Hosea 6:6, see Shepherd, *The Twelve Prophets*, 14–15. With regard to the use of ἔλεος ("mercy") in the LXX (and NT) to translate חסד ("covenant loyalty"), the Greek term does not capture the meaning of the Hebrew, which is often parallel to אמונה ("faithfulness"), and so should be taken as a mere symbol for the Hebrew

Israel, "like mankind" (כאדם) in general, transgresses covenant relationships (Hos. 6:7). Israel is no different than the rest of fallen humanity in this regard (1 Kgs. 8:46). But not everyone understands the text this way (see above translation). Some take אדם to be a place name—"Adam" (Josh. 3:16)—requiring an adjustment of the prefixed preposition from a *kaph* ("like") to a *beth* ("at"), two letters commonly confused in textual transmission, resulting in the reading באדם ("at Adam"). Proponents of this view point to the use of שם ("there") in the second half of the verse, which refers to a place. Against this view is the lack of any account of a special breaking of the covenant at Adam as opposed to any other location in the land of Israel. Transgression of the covenant was widespread in the land. Furthermore, the reader would expect a reference to a more prominent and notorious location like Bethel to represent the entire land (Hos. 4:15). The adverb שם likely refers to the land of Israel as it does in Hosea 6:10.

Others suggest that "Adam" is a reference to the man in the Garden of Eden who supposedly transgressed the first covenant (a so-called covenant of works). The term ברית ("covenant") does not appear in Genesis 1–3 or in any other biblical passage that refers to those chapters. All other accounts of biblical covenants either use the term ברית or have other passages that refer to them as such.[82] Advocates of this view argue that the opening chapters of Genesis contain the components of a covenant,[83] but they must still explain why the term is absent and why other biblical authors do not refer to the account clearly and repeatedly as a covenant. Of course, this is inevitably part of the reason some want to see a reference to a covenant with Adam in Hosea 6:7. Covenant theologians need such a reference in order to complete their system, unless they are willing to posit the only covenant in the

---

original (i.e., ἔλεος = "covenant loyalty" where it stands for חסד). "We believe that if a certain Greek word represents a given Hebrew word in most of its occurrences, it has become almost by implication a mere symbol for that Hebrew word in the translation" (Emanuel Tov, *The Greek and Hebrew Bible: Collected Essays on the Septuagint* [Atlanta: SBL, 2006], 90).

82. E.g., the covenant with David (2 Sam. 7) does not use the term, but other passages refer to it as a covenant (2 Sam. 23:5; Ps. 89:4 [Eng., 89:3]; 132:12; 2 Chr. 13:5; 21:7).

83. The mere presence of a prohibition in Genesis 2:17 is not enough to sustain this view. If every occurrence of a prohibition in the Bible constitutes a stipulation in the making of a covenant, then there are many unidentified covenants—many more than proponents of this view would care to concede. Divine-human covenants in the Bible are designed to restore the lost blessing. There was not yet a need for such restoration in the garden.

Bible that is never called a covenant.[84] But this is not an exegetical reason for interpreting Hosea 6:7 the way they have.

The reference to Gilead as a city in Hosea 6:8 is unusual. Gilead is the land or territory east of the Jordan where Reuben, Gad, and the half tribe of Manasseh settled (Num. 32; Josh. 22). To call it a city is perhaps a way to group it with other cities mentioned thus far in Hosea (e.g., Hos. 4:15). Like Beth Aven (= Bethel), Gilead is a "city" full of those who commit *aven* ("trouble" or "idolatry"; cf., Ps. 5:6 [Eng., 5:5]). Contrary to their promise to remain faithful to the LORD, those who settled in Gilead committed spiritual fornication by the eighth century BC and were subject to exile at the hands of the Assyrians (1 Chr. 5:25–26). "Foot-tracked with blood" suggests the murderous nature of their religious apostasy, which is made explicit in the following verse.

The text of Hosea 6:9 turns again to the priests (cf., Hos. 4:9). Those who were responsible for mediating the covenant relationship and teaching the people were the very ones leading the rebellion. The image is that of a gang of bandits lying in wait to ambush the innocent along the road to Shechem, which along with other locations such as Shiloh, Bethel, and Samaria had become an important center in the north (Gen. 12:6; 33:18–20; Josh. 24:1, 25). It is not necessarily the case that the priests were literally committing murder in this way (although, see Hos. 4:2). It is perhaps a graphic way of depicting the fatal effects of supporting and facilitating Baal worship. Thus, the horrible thing that the LORD has seen is the spiritual fornication of Ephraim, rendering them unfit for public worship (Hos. 6:10; cf., Hos. 5:3). The added parenthetical comment in Hosea 6:11a includes Judah in this negative assessment as indicated by גַּם ("also"). The harvest in this context is thus not a good thing but a figure of punishment (see Jer. 50:16; Joel 4:13 [Eng., 3:13]; BDB, 894).[85]

---

84. Wayne Grudem, *Systematic Theology* (Grand Rapids: Zondervan, 1994), 516–18. Of course, it is possible to conceptualize something without the use of a specific term, but the point here is that this never happens in the case of making covenants. Grudem argues that "there is no single well-known transgression of a covenant by *man*" to which "like mankind" could refer. But this is precisely the point. Israel is unfaithful like the rest of mankind (the nations/Gentiles) in general. It is not a reference to a specific transgression. Grudem also misunderstands the phrase "like mankind" to compare Israelites to what they already are (i.e., men), which has nothing to do with the explanation offered here.

85. It is worth noting that the references to Judah in Hosea are not exclusively positive or negative, thus adding a balanced layer that parallels the words of judgment and restoration to Israel. As for Hosea 6:11b, see the note to the above translation. Commentary on this verse will appear in the next section.

HOSEA 6:11B–7:16

When I restore the fortunes [LXX: captivity] of my people,[86] *7:1 as soon as I heal Israel, the iniquity of Ephraim will be exposed, and the evils of Samaria, for they practice deception. And a robber, he enters. A band / gang raids in the street. 7:2 And they do not say in their heart [or, think to themselves] that all their evil is what I remember. Now their evil deeds surround them. Before my face is where they are. 7:3 With their evil they make the king happy, and with their lies princes. 7:4 All of them are adulterers, like a burning oven [see GKC §80k] without a baker. He ceases stirring up [the fire] from kneading dough until it is leavened [cf., Tg. Jon.]. 7:5 On the day of our king princes become sick [LXX: begin] with heat from wine. He / It draws his / its hand with scoffers [or, His / Its hand draws scoffers]. 7:6 For they draw near [LXX: light up = קדחו] like the oven, their heart is in their ambush. The whole of the night their baker [LXX: Ephraim; Syr.: their anger] sleeps, in the morning it burns like a fire of flame. 7:7 All of them are hot like the oven, and they devour their judges. As for all their kings, they have fallen, and there is no one who calls among them to me.*

The language of restoration (cf., Deut. 30:3; Jer. 29:10–14; 30:2–3, 18; 31:23; 32:44; 33:7, 11) and healing (Hos. 6:1; cf., Hos. 5:4) at the beginning of this unit anticipates a new covenant relationship necessarily initiated by the LORD himself.[87] But the present context does not paint the picture of restoration commonly known from other prophetic texts. Rather, it speaks of the exposure of the people's sin, something akin to what Ezekiel 20:43 says the people will remember when the LORD restores them: "And you will remember there your ways and all your evil deeds by which you made yourselves unclean, and you will loathe yourselves because of all your evils that you committed." The capital city of Samaria receives mention here for the first time in Hosea. Such a reference is fitting due to the fact that the "deception" (שקר) that

---

86. The translation "fortunes" understands שבות to be a noun from שוב and thus a cognate of the preceding infinitive. The LXX understands the noun from שבה ("take captive"). While this latter rendering does fit many contexts well, it has clear difficulties with others (e.g., Job 42:10). See *TLOT* 3.1314–1315.

87. For a discussion of the syntax of Deuteronomy 30:1–7 and all other texts with the expression "restore the fortunes of," see Shepherd, *Text in the Middle*, 96–99. Other occurrences in the Book of the Twelve include Joel 4:1 (Eng., 3:1); Amos 9:14; and Zephaniah 2:7; 3:20.

the people practiced was the false religion of Baal worship (cf., Jer. 3:10; 5:2) for which Ahab established an altar and built a temple in Samaria (1 Kgs. 16:32). The text of Hosea 7:1b reiterates what has already been said about the people's behavior—the stealing (Hos. 4:2) and the raiding bandits (Hos. 6:9). The people do not think that the LORD remembers their evil, but their deeds surround them to such an extent that they are all that the LORD sees when he looks at the people (Hos. 7:2; cf., Hos. 5:2–4).

Verses 3–7 are some of the most challenging textually and exegetically in the entire book. The above translation is an attempt to make sense of the MT in the absence of any viable extant textual alternatives. Contrary to the confidence of some commentators, the exact setting of what this passage describes is not clear from the context (royal anointing, royal birthday, or some other festive occasion) and fortunately not necessary to obtain the sense of the text. The pronominal suffixes in Hosea 7:3 apparently refer back to the people of Ephraim in the first two verses of the chapter. It is a sad commentary on the state of affairs in Israel that the evil of the people (i.e., their idolatry and breaking of the Decalogue) is what makes their king and his princes/officials happy. They (i.e., the people of Ephraim) are all adulterers (Hos. 7:4), which could be literal (Hos. 4:2) or figurative (Hos. 3:1). They are like a burning oven left untended by a baker. This metaphor extends through verse 7 and is apparently intended to depict the ongoing and unextinguished nature of their adulterous actions.

Again, the referent for "the day of our king" is not stated (Hos. 7:5), but it is obviously an occasion for princes and/or officials to become drunk (cf., Isa. 28:1). Some commentators see an indication of court conspiracy in this passage (e.g., Mays, Stuart), but such a situation is veiled beyond clear recognition at best. The second half of Hosea 7:5 is either a reference to the king making some sort of agreement with scoffers (cf., Prov. 6:1; 17:18) or a reference to what wine does with scoffers (Prov. 1:22; 23:29–35). The LXX of Hos. 7:6a has the preferable reading, "light up," as indicated in the above translation, continuing the metaphor of the burning oven. The MT's "their heart is in their ambush" is difficult but understandable in light of Hosea 6:9; 7:1. Once again the baker is absent, but this time it is because of sleep (Hos. 7:6b). In the morning, however, the fire is stoked just like the adulterous/idolatrous passions of the people whose ways seem to be renewed with each day. Thus, not only do they burn continuously, but also they are repeatedly inflamed. The people like a hot oven consume their own judges (Hos. 7:7a; cf., Hos. 8:4a), which may be a term for those attempting to correct them (cf., Isa. 29:21; Amos 5:10), but it could also be a term for kings (BDB, 1047). All their kings have fallen (Hos. 7:7b; cf., Hos. 10:3, 15). This is not only because of the history of assassination in the northern kingdom (1 Kgs. 12–2 Kgs. 17). It is also because of the apostasy of the persistent sins of Jeroboam, resulting in divine judgment and Assyrian captivity. No one calls to the LORD (cf., Isa. 64:6 [Eng., 64:7]; Hos. 7:11b).

7:8 Ephraim, among the peoples he mixes himself. Ephraim is a cake not turned. 7:9 Strangers devour his strength, but he does not know it. Also gray hair, it scatters in him, but he does not know it. 7:10 (And the pride of Israel testifies against him.) And they do not return to the LORD their God, and they do not seek him in all this. 7:11 And Ephraim is like a simple, mindless dove. To Egypt they call, to Assyria they go. 7:12 When they go I will spread my net over them. Like the birds of the sky I will bring them down. I will discipline them as listening to their congregation.[88]

The oven metaphor shifts in Hosea 7:8. The people of Ephraim are no longer the hot oven consuming their leaders (Hos. 7:3–7). Now the people are the cake in the oven being consumed by foreigners (Hos. 7:8–9; cf., Isa. 1:7; Ezek. 11:2–13; Hos. 8:7–8). Ephraim has brought this upon himself, mixing himself like flour with oil among the peoples and engaging in the religious practices of the surrounding Gentiles (see BDB, 117). But Ephraim receives no favors for this unholy union. The nations are all too happy to take advantage of them. The cake is unturned and left to be burned on one side with the other side undone. Ephraim, however, is unaware of this. Like an old man oblivious to the effects of stress and aging, the people persist in their ignorance and denial.

The first part of Hosea 7:10 comes from Hosea 5:5a. Israel's own prideful actions against the LORD are self-condemning. They refuse to turn to the LORD or seek him (cf., Hos. 5:4). Like a dumb animal, they fall into a trap when they think they are fleeing to safety in Egypt or Assyria (Hos. 7:11; cf., Isa. 31; Jer. 2:18; Hos. 5:13; 8:9). The LORD himself will spread his net over them in those places. That is, Assyria in particular will be his instrument of judgment and the place of exile

---

88. For the correct vocalization of אֲיַסְּרֵם ("I will discipline them"), see BDB, 416. The *BHS* apparatus suggests that the text stands for אַאַסְרֵם ("I will bind them"). It is also possible to emend the text slightly to אָסֵר ("I will remove them"). The proposal in the *BHS* apparatus for כְּשֹׁמֵעַ לְעֵדָתָם ("as listening to their congregation") is מִשָּׁם עַל רָעָתָם ("from there for their evil").

and captivity for unwitting Ephraim. Of course, the people of Ephraim are fully responsible for their actions, but there is also a sense in which they are bound by their sin and in need of changed hearts. Like a flock of birds the LORD will bring them down as soon as he hears them (Hos. 7:12).

7:13 Woe to them, for they flee from me. Destruction to them, for they transgress against me. And as for me, will I redeem them? [or, I will redeem them] And as for them, they speak to me lies. 7:14 And they do not cry out to me in their heart, for they wail upon their beds. It is for grain and new wine that they cut themselves [read יתגודדו*]. They turn [Tg. Jon.: rebel] against me. 7:15 And as for me, I discipline, I strengthen their arms, but it is against me that they plan evil. 7:16 They turn not upwards [or, to Most High; see BDB, 752; cf., 2 Sam 23:1 MT, 4QSamᵃ, LXX; see also Hos 11:7].[89] They are like a deceitful [i.e., unreliable; or, slack] bow. Their princes will fall by the sword because of the indignation of their tongue [NET: because their prayers to Baal have made me angry]. This will be their mocking in the land of Egypt.*

This unit takes the form of a typical prophetic woe oracle: introduction (Hos. 7:13), accusation (Hos. 7:14–16a1), and announcement of judgment (Hos. 7:16a2–b). The reference to the flight of the people in Hosea 7:13a1 picks up the thread of the image in Hosea 7:11–12. Some commentators understand Hosea 7:13b1 to mean either that the LORD redeemed Israel in the past, making their present lies about their faithfulness to him appear especially egregious (cf., Jer. 2:23), or that he will redeem them in the future in spite of their failures. But contextually it seems preferable to take this as a rhetorical question requiring a negative response. Verse 14 speaks of the disingenuous way that the people cry out to the LORD (cf., Hos. 8:2–3), wailing upon their beds not because of their sin but because they find themselves in trouble or in need (cf., Judg. 10:11–16). It is really from Baal that they expect their grain and new wine to come (Hos. 2:10 [Eng. 2:8]), so, according to pagan ritual they cut themselves in an effort to prompt him into action (cf., 1 Kgs. 18:28).[90]

---

89. The LXX says they turn "to nothing" (= לבליעל). The *BHS* apparatus suggests that they turn "to Baal" (לבעל). See also Jer. 2:8b2, 11b.

90. NET: "This reflects the pagan Canaanite cultic practice of priests cutting themselves and draining their blood on the ground to elicit agricultural fertility by resurrecting the slain fertility god Baal from the underworld." The reading יתגררו in L is due to common confusion of ר and ד.

In spite of the LORD's discipline (Hos. 7:12, 15), which was intended to be beneficial to the people (Deut. 8:5), they plot evil against him. That is, the LORD takes Israel's worship of Baal as something directed against him personally. The MT of the first part of Hosea 7:16 appears to be another way to say what was said in Hosea 7:10b (see the above translation for other options). Ephraim is like an unreliable bow. The archer attempts to shoot an arrow only to discover that his weapon is out of commission. This text bears some sort of relationship to Psalm 78:9, 57, where Ephraim is cast as the unfaithful throughout the biblical history of the nation of Israel in contrast to the chosen tribe of Judah.[91] Thus, the announcement of judgment is that their princes (and therefore all those associated with them) will fall by the sword (cf., Hos. 7:3, 5, 7b). It is not clear what "the indignation of their tongue" is. זעם ("indignation") is normally of God, not of humans (BDB, 276–77). The only other exception would be Jeremiah 15:17, but even there it seems to be that Jeremiah is filled with divine indignation. It appears likely that the indignation in Hosea 7:16 is not that of the princes but that of God directed against their words. Ironically, this will be "their mocking," that is, the words of derision and reproach directed toward them in a foreign land ("Egypt," literally and/or metaphorically; cf., Hos. 7:11), which will likely be heard in a foreign language (Isa. 28:11; see BDB, 541).

HOSEA 8

8:1 To your palate [LXX: bosom = חק] a shofar! Like the eagle [he comes] against the house of the LORD [cf., Tg. Jon.; Deut 28:49], because they have transgressed my covenant, and it is against my instruction that they have rebelled. 8:2 To me they cry out, "My God, we Israel acknowledge you." 8:3 Israel rejects what is good [Tg. Jon.: worship of me]. An enemy will pursue him. 8:4 They install kings, but not from me. They remove kings [or, They install officials], but I do not acknowledge it. With their silver and their gold they make for themselves idols / shapes so that he is cut off [LXX, Syr., Tg. Jon.: they are cut off]. 8:5 He has rejected [LXX has imperative] your calf, O Samaria. My nostril flares against them [i.e., My anger burns against them]. How long will they be incapable of innocence? 8:6 For it is from Israel, and it is something that a craftsman made, but a non-god is what it is. For pieces is what the calf of Samaria will be. 8:7 For wind is what they sow, and storm wind is what they harvest. Standing grain does not have a sprout. It

---

91. See Shepherd, *The Textual World of the Bible*, 48–52.

[i.e., a sprout] does not produce flour. If it were to produce, strangers / foreigners would swallow it. 8:8 Israel is swallowed. Now they are among the nations like an undesirable vessel. 8:9 For they, they go up to Assyria, a wild donkey by himself. Ephraim, they hire lovers. 8:10 Also, because they hire among the nations, now I will gather them, and they will begin to be few because of [the] burden of [the] king of princes [mlt Mss: king and princes].[92] 8:11 For Ephraim multiplies altars in order to sin. They are to him altars for sinning. 8:12 Though I write for him the ten thousand things [qere: multitudes] of my instruction, it is like a stranger that they are reckoned. 8:13 As for the sacrifices of my gifts [i.e., my sacrificial gifts], they sacrifice [Rashi: let them sacrifice] meat and eat. The LORD, he does not accept them. Now he will remember their iniquity and visit their sins. As for them, it is to Egypt that they will return [LXX adds: and among Assyrians they will eat unclean things; cf., Hos 9:3]. 8:14 And Israel forgot his maker and built temples / palaces. (And Judah, he multiplied fortified cities.) And I will send fire into his cities, and it will consume the citadels of each one.

This chapter begins by sounding another warning (Hos. 8:1; cf., Hos. 5:8). The comparison of the coming enemy to an eagle (or vulture) is familiar from elsewhere (e.g., Hab. 1:8). It is not clear, however, what "the house of the LORD" is in this context. This is not so much a question of meaning as it is one of referent. The phrase most likely refers to a sanctuary or temple. The true temple of the LORD was in Jerusalem, but the present text seems to have the northern kingdom in view primarily (but see Hos. 8:14). The reference to Samaria in Hosea 8:6 might suggest the Baal temple there (1 Kgs. 16:32). Other candidates include but are not necessarily limited to Dan, Bethel, and Shiloh (1 Kgs. 12:29; Jer. 7:12–15). The coming of an enemy against the temple is in accordance with the curses for disobedience to the covenant (Deut. 28:49).

Israel cries out to the LORD (Hos. 8:2), but their cry is not genuine (Hos. 8:3; cf., Hos. 7:14). They install and remove kings apart from the LORD's approval (Hos. 8:4a; cf., Isa. 30:1). The verb השירו is an unusual form either way the interpreter parses it. If the root is שרר, then the verb means, "they install officials," but the spelling would ordinarily be השרו (see GKC §67v). If the root is שור, then the verb means, "they remove," but the spelling would ordinarily be הסירו. The latter option has in its favor another occurrence in Hos. 9:12b of the root סור spelled שור. The history of the monarchy in Israel was not off to a good start

---

92. LXX: "and they will cease a little from anointing king and rulers" (ויחדלו מעט ממשח מלך ושרים).

when they expressed the desire to have a king like all the other nations had (1 Sam. 8–12). The LORD gave them such a king (Saul), but it was more of a judgment than a concession (cf., Hos. 13:11). It is not the people's prerogative to manipulate the throne through conspiracy. The LORD is the one who installs and removes kings (Dan. 2:21).

The people take the LORD's blessings of silver and gold and make for themselves idols, resulting in perishable objects and perishable worshipers (Hos. 8:4b; cf., Hos. 2:10 [Eng., 2:8]; 13:2; Ps. 115:4–8). When used as a conjunction, למען ordinarily indicates purpose ("in order that"; BDB, 775), but in this context it appears to indicate result, unless the reader is to think of unintended purpose. Just as Israel has "rejected" (זנח) what is good (i.e., true worship; Hos. 8:3), so the LORD has "rejected" (זנח) Samaria's calf (i.e., false worship; Hos. 8:5a). It is not necessary to revocalize זנח as an imperative (as the LXX) or to change the form to first person. The reader only needs to keep in mind that the prophet is still the primary speaker. There has been no formal introduction of the LORD's discourse, so the prophet can be the voice of the LORD, or he can refer to the LORD in the third person. Samaria's calf is not necessarily a calf idol located in Samaria, although it could be. Jeroboam had established the calf idols in Dan and Bethel (1 Kgs. 12:29; Hos. 10:5), but Samaria later became the capital city of the north (1 Kgs. 16:29, 32) and so was guilty by association of reenacting the downfall at Sinai (Exod. 32).

The words of lament in Hosea 8:5b (cf., Isa. 6:11; Ps. 6:4 [Eng., 6:3]) speak volumes about Israel's binding sin problem and fundamental inability to please God under the terms of the old covenant (Hos. 5:4). They also serve as a sobering reminder to any new covenant believer who might attempt to live under law rather than under grace (Ezek. 20; Rom. 7; Gal. 3). The calf idol is from Israel of all places (Hos. 8:6; cf., Jer. 2:10–11). But it is not their maker (Jer. 10:11–12). Rather, it is something made by a craftsman (Isa. 44:9–20). What was intended to be a symbol of strength is nothing more than a grass-eating bull (Ps. 106:20). It is a non-god (cf., Deut. 32:21; Ps. 96:5 [Eng., 96:4]; see GKC §152a[1]). The calf of Samaria will ultimately meet the same fate as the original calf at Sinai (Exod. 32:20).

Israel will reap what they sow (Hos. 8:7; cf., Gal. 6:7–8). The idolatry that they thought would bring fertility will only result in futility (Hos. 2:14 [Eng., 2:12]; cf., Jer. 2:5b). Strangers will "swallow" (יבלעהו) their produce (Hos. 8:7b2; cf., Hos. 7:9). Thus, Israel itself is "swallowed" (נבלע; Hos. 8:8a). This is either a reference to foreign occupation of the land (Deut. 28:33) or a reference to land goods squandered on worship of strange gods (Deut. 32:16; Jer. 3:24). Israel's idolatry has made them like the nations, but the prophet also envisions Israel already scattered among the nations in exile like an undesirable vessel and like a divorced woman (Hos. 8:8b; cf., Isa. 62:4; Jer. 48:38b; Hos. 7:8; 9:3, 17). They go up to Assyria to hire lovers (Hos. 8:9)—perhaps an instance of double entendre, suggesting acts of spiritual infidelity (Hos. 2:14–15 [Eng., 2:12–13]) and attempts to secure foreign aid by means of an alliance rather than trusting in the LORD (Hos. 5:13; 7:11). Here Ephraim is compared to Ishmael ("a wild donkey"; Gen. 16:12)—not a very flattering image for the descendants of Isaac through whom the line of blessing was to come (Gen. 21:12; 25:11).

Because Ephraim hires among the nations, the LORD will "gather" them (Hos. 8:10a). The irony is that this is usually a term for gathering the people from the nations in a future time of restoration (BDB, 868), but here it speaks of judgment (cf., Hos. 9:6). They will begin to be "few" (מעט)—a reversal of their fortunes (Deut. 26:5)—because of the burden of the king of princes (Hos. 8:10b).[93] Keil suggests that this is a reference to the king of Assyria, but it could also be a reference to Israel's own corrupt leaders ("king and princes/officials"). Ephraim multiplies altars in order to sin, thus the altars are purely for the purpose of sinning (Hos. 8:11; cf., Jer. 11:13; Hos. 10:1). In spite of the fact that the LORD himself wrote the many things of his instruction for them (Exod. 31:18; Deut. 4:13), it is now as if they were a complete stranger to the people (Hos. 8:12; cf., Hos. 4:2).[94] The strange gods are more familiar to them than God's own instruction.

In Hosea 8:13a, the LORD is either saying that the people are consuming offerings that should have been wholly devoted to him (see Lev. 1–7) or he is essentially commanding them to break the law in doing so given the fact that the offerings are really for Baal and therefore do not require any adherence to the LORD's instruction (cf., Isa. 29:1; Jer. 7:21). Contrary to the people's expectations, the LORD will remember their sins and punish them (Hos. 5:3; 8:13b; cf., Jer. 14:10). This is not yet the new covenant (Jer. 31:34). In this context of judgment, a return

---

93. The MT's vocalization of ויחלו as a *wayyiqtol* should probably be changed to *waw* + *yiqtol*.

94. The *qere* (רבי) would be a unique instance of the plural of רב. The number "ten thousand" (רבו) is the highest number that can be expressed by a single word in Hebrew. It can thus have the sense "myriad" (BDB, 914). The traditional number of laws in the Pentateuch is either 611 (the numerical value of תורה) or 613 (the numerical value of בתורה), which would include Exodus 20:1 and the Shema (Deut. 6:4). See John H. Sailhamer, *The Pentateuch as Narrative* (Grand Rapids: Zondervan, 1992), 481–516.

to Egypt does not appear to be a literal appeal for foreign aid or political alliance as in Hosea 7:11. Rather, it is a metaphorical return to Egypt, the original place of captivity (cf., Hos. 9:3; 11:5; see also Deut. 28:68). Thus, any future Assyrian or Babylonian captivity will in this sense be a recapitulation of Israel's history, and any future deliverance from said captivity will be a new exodus (Hos. 2:16–17 [Eng., 2:14–15]; 11:11).

The use of *wayyiqtol* forms in Hosea 8:14a summarizes and tells the story of Israel's apostasy. They forgot their maker, as evidenced by their worship of "made" things (Hos. 8:6), and they built temples (perhaps also palaces) such as the one for Baal in Samaria (1 Kgs 16:32). Judah is added to this by way of comment (x + *qatal*). Their multiplication of fortified cities not only shows where they put their trust but also parallels their multiplication of altars for Baal (Jer. 11:13). The LORD's fire of judgment will consume the very citadels in which they place their faith (Hos. 8:14b). This last part of Hosea 8:14 is the standard judgment for the kingdoms surrounding Israel, according to Amos 1:7, 10, 14; 2:2, 5.

HOSEA 9

9:1 Do not be glad, O Israel, to the point of rejoicing like the peoples [LXX: and do not rejoice like the peoples; cf., Syr., Tg. Jon.]. For you fornicate from with your God. You prefer a harlot's pay upon every threshing floor of grain. 9:2 As for a threshing floor or a wine vat, that will not feed them [LXX: know them], and as for new wine, it will deceive [i.e., fail, disappoint] them [reading □□ w / mlt Mss]. 9:3 They will not live in the land of the LORD. And Ephraim will return to [LXX: live in] Egypt, and in Assyria unclean food is what they will eat. 9:4 They will not pour out to the LORD wine, and their sacrifices will not be pleasing to him [2 Mss: and they will not arrange to him sacrifices]. Like bread of troubles [food for idols?] will it be to them, all those who eat it will make themselves unclean. For their bread is for themselves, it will not enter the house of the LORD. 9:5 What will you do on a day of an appointed time and on the day of the LORD's festival? 9:6 For look, they go from destruction [or, if they go from destruction], Egypt will be the land to gather them, Memphis will be the city to bury them. As for the desirable things of their silver, thistles will be the ones to possess them, thorns will be in their tents.[95] *9:7 The days of visitation have come, the days of recompense have come. Let Israel know [LXX: And Israel will be treated badly; or, Let Israel*

---

95. LXX: "they go forth from the trouble of Egypt, and Memphis will receive them, and Machmas will bury them. Their silver, destruction will inherit it."

shout (יָרֵעוּ, hiphil jussive 3mp רוּעַ)]. "A fool is what the prophet is, a madman is what the man of the Spirit is." Because of the abundance of your iniquity, animosity is great. 9:8 The watchman of Ephraim is with my God—a prophet [MT: Ephraim watches with my God, a prophet; Stuart: Is Ephraim a watchman? Is God's people a prophet?]. A fowler's snare is on all his paths, animosity in the house of his God. 9:9 They act very corruptly [see GKC §120g] like the days of Gibeah. He will remember their iniquity, he will visit their sins.

This chapter begins with a warning to Israel not to celebrate the festival of the LORD to the point of doing it the way the Gentiles do (cf., Job 3:22), but the people already fornicate spiritually away from their God. This hearkens back to what was said in Hos. 2:12–15 (Eng., 2:10–13). The people prefer the "harlot's pay" that they wrongly think they receive from Baal on their threshing floors. That is, they prefer it to recognition of blessings from the LORD and fidelity to their covenant relationship with him. Therefore, the very threshing floor or wine vat from which the people expect to receive remuneration for their infidelity will in the end disappoint them and fail to feed them (Hos. 9:2). Their false religion will prove to be deceptive, and the LORD will remove the blessings that have gone unacknowledged.

Ephraim will no longer live in the LORD's land (i.e., the land of the covenant). They will return to Egypt in the sense that they will recapitulate their history by going back to a place of captivity and servitude (Hos. 9:3). Exile in Assyria will be their new Egypt in which they will stand in need of a new exodus. There they will eat unclean food (Lev. 11) in an unclean land (cf., Amos 7:17). Israel has lived and worshiped like a foreign people, and so the LORD will put them where they belong (cf., Hos. 3:4). Their libations in that context will not be for the LORD, and their sacrifices will be unacceptable to him (Hos. 9:4). Their food offerings to idols (see BDB, 20) in which they partake are what will make them unclean. In reality, this food is only for themselves and not for the LORD. It will not enter his temple, not only because it is unacceptable, but also because the people will no longer have any access to the true temple in Jerusalem.

The prospect of exile inevitably raises the question of how Israel could do anything pleasing to the LORD in that context, including celebration of festivals (Hos. 9:5; cf., Lev. 23). The exile will put the people in a position where divine initiative will be necessary in order to have any possibility of restoration. The "festival of the LORD" in Hosea 9:5 is likely the Feast of Tabernacles (Lev. 23:39). Jeroboam had already perverted this festival in the north by changing it from the seventh month to the eighth month and by changing the location from Jerusalem to Bethel in direct violation of the centralization of worship prescribed by Deuteronomy 16:15 (1 Kgs. 12:32–33). This celebration also involved worship of the calf idols and the service of the alternative priesthood established by Jeroboam.

Interpretation of Hosea 9:6a depends upon whether Egypt is literal or figurative. Assuming that it is literal, the text would mean that even if some of the people were to survive destruction at the hands of the Assyrians, the Egyptians would gather them (perhaps because the people would flee there to seek refuge), and Memphis specifically would be the place where they would die and be buried. That is, the alternative to Assyrian captivity is not all that appealing. On the other hand, if Egypt is figurative, then those who survive destruction would not be those who escape captivity but those who survive Assyrian invasion. The new Egypt (i.e., Assyria) would then gather them to the place of exile where they would eventually die and be buried, never to return to their land again. In their absence, the land will become a thorny overgrowth (Hos. 9:6b; cf., Isa. 7:23–25; see also 2 Kgs. 17), which will "possess" their dwellings and the precious things that they so notoriously misused (Hos. 8:4).

The days of visitation/punishment and recompense have come, which Israel now knows all too well primarily because of the ministry of the prophet (Hos. 9:7). But Hosea is no different from other true prophets in that his message is generally not well received (cf., Isa. 6:9–10; Jer. 1:18–19; Ezek. 2:5). The people prefer the false sense of security provided by the prophets of Baal (see 1 Kgs. 22). Thus, they call the prophet a fool (cf., Isa. 28:9–13). To them the man of God, the man of the Spirit, is nothing but a madman (cf., 2 Kgs. 9:11; Jer. 29:26). But the distinctive trait of the true prophet is that he possesses the Spirit of God (Num. 11:29; Ezek. 2:2; Joel 3:1–2 [Eng., 2:28–29]; Mic. 3:8) no matter how unusual or unappealing his words or actions might be (e.g., Ezek. 4:1–3). It is only because of the greatness of the people's iniquity that their animosity toward the prophet is so great. They have developed such a taste for deception that they have no appetite for the truth.

The above translation of Hosea 9:8 assumes a revocalization of צֹפֶה to the construct state. A prophet is the watchman of Ephraim (cf., Ezek. 3:17). This is true of Hosea or any other genuine prophet of the north, which is why Hosea can refer to the watchman in the third person as a category and then use the pronominal suffix "my" in reference to his God. Such a prophet bears an unpopular burden and is subject to the possibility of entrapment at any point along the way (e.g., Jer. 37:12–16). Even in the temple itself this animosity is felt (e.g., Jer. 26:1–11). The depth of the people's corruption has reached that of what happened at Gibeah in the tribe of Benjamin according to Judges 19–21 (Hos. 9:9; cf., Hos. 10:9). There Israel became the new Sodom and Gomorrah (cf., Gen. 19). But more importantly for the present context, the people in that story failed to heed the same kind of call to repentance that Hosea is issuing (Judg. 20:12–13). The LORD, however, will not forget their iniquity (Hos. 5:2–3). Their day of visitation is imminent.

9:10 It was like grapes in the wilderness that I found Israel, it was like an early fig on a fig tree at its beginning that I saw your forefathers. As for them, they came to Baal Peor and consecrated themselves [LXX: were estranged] to shame, and they became detested things according to their preference. 9:11 Ephraim is like a bird, their glory will fly away so that there will be no childbearing or belly or conception [see BDB, 583]. 9:12 For if they raise their children, I will bereave them so that there are no people. Indeed, woe to them when I depart [LXX: my flesh] from them. 9:13 Ephraim, as I have seen in Tyre, is planted in a pasture [LXX: to hunting they presented their children]; and Ephraim, is to bring forth to a slayer his children [see GKC §114k]. 9:14 Give to them, O LORD—what will you give?—give to them a bereaving womb and shriveling breasts. 9:15 All their evil is in Gilgal, for it was there that I rejected them. Because of the evil of their deeds, it is from my house that I will drive them. I will not love/choose them again. All their princes [or, officials] are rebels. 9:16 Ephraim is stricken [cf., LXX], their root is dry. As for fruit, they do not produce it. Also, when they give birth, I will kill the desired children of their belly. 9:17 My God [LXX: God] will reject them, for they have not listened to him, and they will be wanderers among the nations.

Many critical interpreters see in Hosea 9:10 a suppressed tradition about the discovery of Israel in the wilderness as opposed to the election of Israel in Egypt or in the patriarchal traditions (cf., Deut. 32:10; Jer. 2:2–3; Hos. 2:16–17 [Eng., 2:14–15]).[96] This is often understood as an ideal, romanticized stage of Israel's faithfulness to the LORD. But such a reading does little justice to the context. The phrase "in the wilderness" does not modify the verb "found" but the noun "grapes" (cf., Hos. 9:10a2). Furthermore, the second half of Hos. 9:10 indicates

---

96. E.g., Wolff, *Hosea*, 164.

that Israel was already idolatrous in the wilderness (cf., Deut. 9:24; Hos. 10:1; Amos 5:25–27). Hosea is well aware of the fact that Israel's story did not begin in the wilderness (Hos. 12:5 [Eng., 12:4]; 13:4–6). Other texts cited in favor of this supposed tradition also fail to pass the test. For example, Deuteronomy 32:8 already shows awareness of something prior to the "finding" of Israel in the wilderness in Deuteronomy 32:10. The use of the verb "find" is simply a poetic way of describing how the LORD met the people in real time and space to provide for them during an important period of their history (BDB, 593). This faithfulness is then contrasted with the people's record of infidelity beginning in Deuteronomy 32:15. The text of Jeremiah 2:2–3 does not refer to Israel's covenant loyalty during the wilderness journey but to the LORD's loyalty (see Calvin).

So, in what way was the discovery of Israel like finding grapes in the wilderness, or how was the sight of the forefathers like seeing an early fig on a fig tree at its beginning? The wilderness period was a time of great potential for Israel. They had departed Egypt, and they were on the cusp of entry into the land of the covenant. But they began to squander this privilege as early as the grumbling in Exodus 16–17 (cf., Num. 11–20), the golden calf incident (Exod. 32; Deut. 9), and the worship of goat idols (Lev. 17:1–7). Thus, the worship of the local manifestation of Baal at Peor in Numbers 25 is part of a well-established pattern of behavior (cf., Ps. 106:28–31). The term "shame" (בשׁת) in Hosea 9:10b stands for Baal himself (cf., Jer. 11:13). And so, Israel became like the detestable idols that they preferred to the LORD (cf., Ps. 115:8).

The metaphor shifts in Hosea 9:11 to that of a bird because Israel's glory will fly away. Earlier in Hosea, Israel's glory was the LORD himself (Hos. 4:7; cf., Isa. 17:3–4; Jer. 2:11). Here there is likely an allusion to the story of the loss of the ark of the covenant to the Philistines in 1 Samuel 4 (see Hos. 10:5). The departure of the ark, which was housed at Shiloh (1 Sam. 4:3), is said to be the departure of Israel's glory (1 Sam. 4:22), presumably because of the way it represented the LORD's presence and word among the people. This event is later symbolic of the exile of the northern kingdom (Jer. 7:12–15; Ps. 78:60–64). The reference to the loss of childbearing, belly, and conception (a reversal of the natural order: conception, belly, childbearing) in Hosea 9:11b is reminiscent of the bittersweet conception and birth of Ichabod in the wake of the deaths of his father (Phineas) and grandfather (Eli) in 1 Samuel 4:19–21. According to Hosea 9:12a, even if they manage to raise their children, they will be lost, suggesting strongly the significant loss of life coming in the Assyrian invasion, captivity, and exile.

Woe to them because of the LORD's departure (Hos. 9:12b; cf., Hos. 7:13), indicating that the departure of Israel's glory is in some sense the departure of the LORD's protective presence.

Many translators and commentators prefer to follow the LXX for Hosea 9:13, but the more difficult reading represented by the MT is by no means an impossible one. Like the wealthy seaport of the city of Tyre, Ephraim has been blessed with prosperity in a fertile land, yet the people have fallen because of their pride (cf., Ezek. 26–28). Ephraim is fully responsible for bringing its own children to the destruction described in Hosea 9:11–12 (see also Ezek. 20:31). Thus, the prophet prays that the LORD will give them what they deserve (Hos. 9:14)—an imprecatory prayer designed to put the matter in God's hands and honor his justice. It may very well be a prayer for a reversal of Israel's earlier fortunes (e.g., Gen. 11:30).

In what sense is all the evil of Israel at Gilgal (Hos. 9:15)? There is clearly a close relationship between Gilgal and the idolatrous activities at Bethel (Hos. 4:15; 12:12 [Eng., 12:11]; Amos 4:4). But there is also a strong connection between Gilgal and the establishment and rejection of Saul's kingship (1 Sam. 11:15; 15:12, 21). The anointing of Saul as king was essentially a judgment on the people's request to have a king like the other nations (1 Sam. 8). The LORD gave them what they wanted to see how they would like it, but his chosen king was ultimately David (1 Sam. 16). After the division of the united kingdom, it was the northern kingdom of Israel that continued the tradition of political and religious independence from the LORD, as attested by Hosea and (Hos. 8:4) other prophets to the north (e.g., Amos). Their leaders are rebels (Hos. 9:15b; cf., Hos. 7:3–7). The LORD will drive them out of his sanctuary because of the evil of their deeds (cf., Gen. 3:24). When he says that he hates them and no longer loves them, he means that he rejects them and no longer chooses them (cf., Hos. 9:17; 14:5 [Eng., 14:4]; Mal. 1:2). Because of the broken covenant relationship, God is no longer under any obligation to devote or to commit himself to them.

Verse 16 goes back to the thought of Hosea 9:11–13. Ephraim will dry up and fail to produce the fruit of the womb. Even if they manage to bear children, the LORD himself will kill them. In verse 17, the prophet's voice comes into the foreground as it did in Hosea 9:14 (but see the LXX). It has now become a regular occurrence for the prophet to move seamlessly from the LORD's voice to his own and then back again. The LORD will reject the people because they do not listen to him (cf., 2 Kgs. 17:14a). They will be wanderers among the nations (cf., Gen. 4:12; Hos. 8:8).

HOSEA 10

10:1 A luxuriant grapevine is what Israel is.[97] Fruit is what he produces for himself. According to the abundance of his fruit he increases altars. According to the good of his land they adorn pillars. 10:2 Their heart is deceptive [Syr., Tg. Jon., Vulg.: Their heart is divided; LXX: They divide their hearts]. Now they are guilty. As for him, he will break the neck of their altars, he will destroy their pillars. 10:3 Indeed, now they will say, "We have no king, for we have not feared the LORD. And as for the king, what will he do for us?" 10:4 They speak words, swearing falsely, making a covenant. And like poison justice sprouts upon furrows of a field. 10:5 The calves [LXX, Syr.: calf] of Beth Aven are what the inhabitants [cf., LXX, Syr.] of Samaria fear [Tg. Jon.: worship]. Indeed, its people mourn for it—and its priests rejoice over it, over its glory—for it goes into exile from it. 10:6 Also it to Assyria will be carried as a gift for king Yarev [see Hos. 5:13]. Shame is what Ephraim will receive, and Israel will be ashamed of his counsel. 10:7 Samaria, her king, is destroyed like a splinter [Tg. Jon.: anger] on top of water.[98] 10:8 And the high places of Aven [Ms: Beth Aven; or, the high places of iniquity] will be destroyed, the sin of Israel. Thorns and thistles are what will go up over their altars. And they will say to the mountains, "Cover us," and to the hills, "Fall on us."

The comparison of Israel to a grapevine and/or a vineyard is not unique to Hosea (cf., Isa. 5:1–7; 27:2–6; Ezek. 15; 17; 19:10–14; Hos. 9:10; Ps. 80:9–14 [Eng., 80:8–13]; Matt. 21:33–46; John 15:1–17).[99] Typically it is a negative image. According to Isaiah 5:1–7, the LORD did everything that could have been expected of him to prepare his vineyard (i.e., Israel) for production of good fruit, but the vineyard only produced bad grapes (i.e., injustice). Only in the eschaton will the LORD make his vineyard fruitful (Isa. 27:2–6; cf., Hos. 14:8 [Eng., 14:7]). In Ezekiel, Israel (i.e., Judah and Jerusalem) is the good-for-nothing grapevine (Ezek. 15) that will find itself in exile (Ezek. 17; cf., Ps. 80) and whose

---

97. Rashi takes בוקק from the root בקק ("empty"), yielding the sense that Israel is a vine devoid of fruit fitting for it. The tendency of modern English translations (e.g., NET) to render this verse in the past tense seems misguided. The context indicates that judgment is imminent but not currently present. The prophet's words are directed against the kind of behavior described in this verse, which has yet to cease.
98. Or, "Samaria is destroyed. Her king is like a splinter on top of water."
99. See Shepherd, *Text in the Middle*, 135–36.

fruit will dry up and be consumed by fire (Ezek. 19:10–14). Hosea's use of the metaphor is designed to juxtapose the great abundance of the grapevine's fruit—a sign of the LORD's blessing (Deut. 28:4)—with the increase of altars and pillars to Baal (cf., Deut. 32:15; Jer. 11:13; Hos. 2:4–15 [Eng., 2:2–13]; 8:11; 11:2).

The verb חלק at the beginning of Hosea 10:2 is either the *qal* stem of a root that means "to be smooth" (i.e., deceptive) as in the MT or the *pual* stem of a root that means "to divide" as in the Syriac, *Targum Jonathan*, and Latin Vulgate. This is a matter of vocalization, and both senses would fit the context well. It is not out of the question that the author employs double entendre here. Israel has acted deceptively in that the people have pledged allegiance to the LORD, but their actions indicate that their real loyalty belongs to Baal. But this also means that Israel is in some sense divided (cf., 1 Kgs. 18:21). The people are thus guilty of a crime against God, one that they themselves have yet to recognize (Hos. 5:15). As for the LORD's part, he will break the very altars that they have increased and destroy their pillars—a judgment already anticipated in Hosea 3:4.

Similarity to Hosea 3:4 continues in Hosea 10:3 with the reference to the people's future acknowledgment of the loss of their king due to their own lack of the fear of the LORD (cf., Hos. 7:7b; 10:7, 15). The king will obviously do them no good in exile. But such words are currently not part of Israel's vocabulary. Their words are marked by false swearing (Hos. 10:4; cf., Exod. 20:7, 16; Deut. 5:11, 20; Jer. 7:9; Hos. 4:2). When they made their covenant with God (Exod. 24:3, 8; see Calvin), they took an oath that they could not possibly keep (Hos. 6:7; 8:1), bearing false witness to themselves and swearing falsely in the LORD's name (cf., Jer. 4:2; 5:2). It is also possible that this is a reference to the making of a treaty with Assyria (Hos. 12:2 [Eng., 12:1]). Their brand of justice, which is really injustice, is like poison in a field (cf., Hos. 12:12 [Eng., 12:11]; Amos 5:7; 6:12).

The golden calves of Bethel, Dan, and Samaria are well known to the reader of Hosea by now (1 Kgs 12:28–29; Hos 4:15; 5:8; 8:4–5; 13:2). Here in Hosea 10:5, the focus is on the one at Beth Aven (i.e., Bethel), which is the object of worship for all Israel as represented by the capital city of Samaria. They mourn for it because it goes into exile just like the departure of the glory of Israel, the Ark of the Covenant, when it was taken by the Philistines (1 Sam. 4:22; Hos. 9:11 [cf., Jer. 2:11; Hos. 4:7]). The comment about the priests rejoicing over it is apparently parenthetical. The term for "priest" here is not כהן but כמר, a word reserved in the Hebrew Bible for idol-priests (2 Kgs. 23:5; Zeph. 1:4). This idol will be carried off along with the people of Israel as a gift for the king of Assyria (Hos. 10:6; cf., Hos. 5:13). Such a turn of events will be a source of great shame for Ephraim inasmuch as the object of their worship will be reduced to tribute for a foreign king (2 Kgs. 17:3; Mic. 1:7).[100] Furthermore, Samaria itself is doomed, and her king is left helpless like a splinter floating on the surface of the water (Hos. 10:7).

The high places of Aven ("iniquity")—likely a reference to Jeroboam's high places, which were so closely associated with the calves at Bethel (Beth Aven) and Dan (1 Kgs. 12:31) and together with them constituted the sin of Israel (i.e., alternative worship to Jerusalem) that characterized every subsequent king of the north (1 Kgs. 12:30)—will be destroyed. Not only will the altars that they once increased be broken (Hos. 10:1–2), but also they will be overrun by thorns and thistles—a sign of the curse (Gen. 3:18; Isa. 7:23–24; Hos. 9:6). The judgment will be so severe that the people will prefer death to life, calling for the mountains to cover them and for the hills to fall on them (cf., Isa. 2:10; Rev. 9:6). This last part of Hosea 10:8 has been understood in an eschatological sense by Luke 23:30; Rev. 6:15–16. The warrant for this comes from the use of language known from Hosea 3:4–5—the programmatic passage of the Twelve—to frame the chapter as a whole (Hos. 10:1–2, 8, 12, 15).

In Hosea chapter 10 Israel faces judgment for her idolatry (Hos 10:1–4). This judgment involves the removal of all external means of worship and the removal of Israel's king—a clear echo of the eschatological judgment that precedes ultimate restoration in the programmatic passage of Hosea 3:4–5 (see again the phrase "at the end of the days" in Hosea 3:5). Israel will go into exile to Assyria (Hos. 10:5–7). Their places of sin will be destroyed, and they will seek the release of death (Hos. 10:8). According to Hosea 10:9–10, Israel has in fact sinned, and the LORD will discipline them. The people were supposed to sow righteousness and seek the LORD (Hos. 10:11–12), but instead they have plowed wickedness and have not trusted in the LORD (Hos. 10:13). Devastation is inevitable, and the king of Israel will be destroyed (Hos. 10:14–15). According to Hosea 3:5, the people will only seek the LORD "at the end of the days." By presenting the threat of Assyrian exile through the lens of Hosea 3:4–5, the author has made the historical circumstances of eighth-century Israel into an occasion to speak of eschatological judgment and deliverance. This is, after all, the usual mode of operation in the prophetic texts. The historical situations of the prophets are the immediate contexts and springboards from which the

---

100. In place of Israel being ashamed of its "counsel," the NET Bible says that Israel will be ashamed of its "wooden idol" (cf., Jer. 6:6).

texts are able to speak prefiguratively about the future. In Hosea, Assyria represents the enemies of God's people.[101]

10:9 Since the days of Gibeah you have sinned, O Israel [LXX: Israel has sinned]. There they remain. Was it not in Gibeah that warfare overtook them in addition to sons of injustice [or, Will it not be in Gibeah that warfare will overtake them because of sons of injustice?]? 10:10 In my desire [LXX: I have come], and I will discipline them [see GKC §71], and against them peoples will be gathered when he binds them to their two iniquities [LXX: when they are disciplined for their two iniquities]. 10:11 And Ephraim was a trained heifer that loved to thresh, and I, I passed over the goodness of her neck. I would cause Ephraim to pull. Judah would plow. Jacob would harrow for him. 10:12 Sow for yourselves according to righteousness, reap according to covenant loyalty [LXX: according to fruit of life], break up for yourselves untilled ground [LXX: shine for yourselves light of knowledge]. And it is time to seek the LORD until he comes and sends showers of righteousness to you [or, teaches righteousness to you (cf., Syr., Tg. Jon., Vulg.); LXX: until products of righteousness come to you].[102] 10:13 You have plowed wickedness, injustice is what you have reaped, you have eaten deception's fruit. For you have trusted in your way [LXX: your chariots; cf., Ps. 20:8 (Eng., 20:7)], in the abundance of your warriors. 10:14 A crash will rise up against your people, and each one of your fortresses will be destroyed like Shalman's [LXX[764]: Shalmaneser] destruction of Beth-arbel in a day of warfare. Mother upon [or, in addition to] children was dashed to pieces. 10:15 Thus he does [LXX: I will do; Ms: will be done] to you, O Bethel [LXX: house of Israel], because of your great evil [see GKC §133i]. At dawn the king of Israel will be completely destroyed [or, silenced].

Verse 9 refers once again (cf., Hos. 9:9) to the story of Gibeah in Judges 19–21 where what took place in the territory of the tribe of Benjamin recapitulated the story of Sodom and Gomorrah, demonstrating how far Israel had fallen in its cycle of rebellion since the days of Joshua. It is in that state of sin that Israel currently remains in Hosea's context.

---

101. Shepherd, *The Twelve Prophets in the New Testament*, 16. This is a good example of the way in which the composer of the Twelve influences the way Hosea's prophecies are read.
102. *Tg. Jon.*: "House of Israel, do for yourselves good works, walk in the way of innocence, maintain for yourselves the teaching of the Torah. Look, at every time the prophets say to you, 'Return to the worship of the LORD.' Now he will be revealed and he will bring innocence to you."

Wolff understands the second half of verse 9 in the future tense, taking the "sons of injustice" to be the Israelites (cf., Hos. 10:13), so that what happened in Gibeah in the past will in some sense happen again (*Hosea*, 184). This leads him to understand the two iniquities in verse 10 to be the past and present iniquities of Gibeah. But the use of the phrase "sons of injustice" in 2 Samuel 7:10 to refer to the foreign enemies who ruled Israel throughout the book of Judges suggests that the second half of Hosea 10:9 is still talking about Gibeah past as an analogy for Israel present. Israel has not merely committed two iniquities. They have persisted in the same sin throughout their history.

The LORD's voice comes once again into the foreground through the prophet by means of the first-person verbs and pronouns in Hosea 10:10–11. The nations (presumably Assyria and then Babylon, but see also Ezek. 38–39) will be gathered against Israel for the purpose of discipline (as opposed to punishment). Commentators do not agree on the two iniquities at the end of Hosea 10:10, but in the context of the chapter (Hos. 10:5) and the book (Hos. 8:5; 13:2) it seems best to refer them to the two golden calves at Bethel and Dan (1 Kgs. 12:28–30). This would then be a fitting segue into Hosea 10:11, which compares Ephraim to a trained heifer or female calf. Verse 11 hearkens back to a time when Ephraim had great potential (cf., Hos. 9:10). It also mentions Judah and even appears to use "Jacob" in the sense of the united kingdom of Israel, Ephraim, and Judah together (cf., Hos. 3:5). This then becomes the basis for the present imperatives in Hos 10:12 to sow according to righteousness and to reap according to covenant loyalty (see Hos. 2:25 [Eng., 2:23]; 6:6; 12:7 [Eng., 12:6]) and to break up untilled ground (cf., Jer. 4:3), for it is time to seek the LORD until he comes (cf., Gen. 49:10b) and either showers (cf., Hos. 6:3) or teaches (Isa. 2:3) righteousness. But such is not the case currently for the land of Israel where they plow wickedness, reap injustice, and eat the fruit of deception (Hos. 7:3; 12:1 [Eng., 11:12]), trusting in themselves and in their own resources rather than in the LORD (Hos. 10:13; cf., Jer. 17:5–8; Ps. 20:8 [Eng., 20:7]). Only in the last days will the people seek the LORD (Hos. 3:5).

Verse 14 compares the coming destruction of Israel's fortifications (in which they trusted) to Shalman's destruction of Beth-arbel, using the image of mother and children to illustrate the heinousness of what is to come (cf., 2 Kgs. 8:12; Isa. 13:16; Hos. 14:1 [Eng., 13:16]; Nah. 3:10). The exact identity of this Shalman and the location of Beth-arbel are unknown to modern interpreters, but the use of the analogy implies that Shalman's destruction of Beth-arbel should be very well known to the readers of Hosea—an event so notorious that it would not be obscured by the mere passing of time. One possibility is that "Shalman" is a shortened form of "Shalmaneser" (LXX[764]), the Assyrian king who captured Hoshea, the last king of the northern kingdom of Israel, and took Israel into exile (2 Kgs. 17:1–6). The house of אַרְבֵּאל would then not be a particular location in Israel but a general designation for the place where "God" (אֵל) lay in wait to "ambush" (אָרַב) his own people (cf., Tg. Jon.; see also Hos. 5:14; Lam. 3:10). Of course, this would also mean that the scope of this chapter looks beyond Assyrian captivity to a future judgment for which Assyrian captivity serves as a fitting analogy. Thus God does to Bethel (i.e., Israel) because of their great evil (Hos. 10:15). At dawn (cf., Hos. 6:3; Ps. 110:3) the king of Israel will surely be destroyed (cf., Hos. 7:7; 10:3), setting up the hope of a messianic king who will rise out of the land of Egypt to lead a new exodus (Hos. 11:1, 5, 11; cf., Num. 23:22; 24:8; Matt. 2:15).

HOSEA 11

11:1 When Israel was a youth, I chose him, and it was out of Egypt that I summoned my son [LXX: his children]. 11:2 They summoned them [Tg. Jon.: I sent my prophets to teach them; LXX: As I called them], thus they went from before them [LXX: from before me]. It was to the Baals that they would sacrifice, and to the carved / sculpted idols they would make sacrifices smoke. 11:3 But I was the one who taught Ephraim to walk, (He took them on his arms) [LXX: I took him on my arms; cf., Syr., Tg. Jon., Vulg.], and they did not acknowledge that I healed them. 11:4 It was with humane cords [or, leather cords; see Arabic root] that I would draw them, with cords of love [or, cords of leather (cf., Song 3:10); see root in Arabic]. And I was to them like those who raise a yoke over their jaws [LXX: like one striking a man on his jaws; BHS: like one who raises a child to his cheeks], and I would incline to him, I would feed him [read לוֹ instead of אֵל].[103] 11:5 He will return to the land of Egypt

---

103. This translation assumes that לֹא (i.e., לוֹ) at the beginning of Hosea 11:5 belongs at the end of Hosea 11:4. See Michael B. Shepherd, "Is It 'To Him' or Is It 'Not'? Intentional Variation between לוֹ and לֹא," *JSOT* 39 (2014): 121–37. The LXX also makes this assumption, although it renders אוֹכִיל as if it were from the root יכל: "I would overcome him" (אוּכַל לוֹ). It is also possible to render the end of Hosea 11:4 in the MT as follows: "And gently (אַט) I would feed him," but fronting the object and marking it with the preposition אֶל would be highly unusual. This would also leave the negation לֹא at the beginning of Hosea 11:5, forcing the reader to interpret Hosea 11:5a as a rhetorical question expecting an answer of yes ("Will he

[LXX: Ephraim lived in Egypt], and Assyria, he will be his king, for they refuse to return. 11:6 And a sword will flash in his cities, and it will destroy its bars [or, its empty talkers], and it will consume because of their counsels. 11:7 And my people are hung on turning away from me. And upward [or, to Most High (cf., Hos. 7:16)] they call him, altogether he will not raise [them].[104] 11:8 How can I give you over [to an enemy], O Ephraim? [How] can I deliver you [to an enemy], O Israel? How can I make you like Admah? [How] can I make you like Zeboiim? My heart is turned upon me, altogether my compassion grows warm. 11:9 I will not perform the burning of my nostril [or, anger], I will not return to destroy Ephraim [i.e., I will not destroy Ephraim again]. For God is who I am and not man, in your midst holy, and I will not enter a city [or, excitement; see BDB, 735]. 11:10 After the LORD is where they will go, like a lion he will roar. Indeed [or, When], he will be the one who roars, and sons / children will tremble from [the] sea / west. 11:11 They will tremble like a bird from Egypt, and like a dove from the land of Assyria. And I will make them live in [LXX: return them to] their homes, the prophetic utterance of the LORD.

When the nation of Israel was in its early stages ("a youth"), the LORD "elected" (אהב) him (Hos. 11:1a; cf., Hos. 12:14 [Eng., 12:13]; 13:4). This sense of אהב (normally "love") corresponds to its antonym שנא (normally "hate"), which often has the meaning "reject" (e.g., Deut. 7:7–11; Mal. 1:2).[105] As opposed to the more common pair, בחר/מאס ("choose"/"reject"), אהב and שנא seem to include an element of devotional attachment/detachment that בחר and מאס lack. The LORD may have "discovered" Israel in the wilderness in some sense (Deut. 32:10; Hos. 9:10), but the present text shows an awareness of the election of Israel in Egypt. The following chapter will push that back even further to the patriarchs (Hos. 12:5 [Eng., 12:4]).

It was out of Egypt that the LORD called his son (Hos. 11:1b). Reference to Israel as God's son recalls Exodus 4:22 (see also Hos. 13:13). This text has attracted a great deal of attention due to its citation in Matthew 2:15, the context of which recounts the flight of Jesus's family to Egypt and their subsequent return to the land of Israel. Faced

---

not return to the land of Egypt? Yes, he will"). A statement that he will not return to Egypt would clearly be out of sorts with the context of the book (Hos. 8:13b; 9:3) and the chapter (Hos. 11:11).

104. *BHS:* "And to Baal he calls, but he altogether will not raise them."

105. See chapter 7 in Michael B. Shepherd, *Textuality and the Bible* (Eugene, Ore.: Wipf & Stock, 2016).

with a text in Hosea that seems on the surface only to speak of the historical exodus, and a text in Matthew that appears to speak of an entirely different situation, interpreters usually resort to *sensus plenior* and typology to account for Matthew's citation.[106] But such interpreters characteristically do not take the time to consider carefully the context of Hosea's source text, Matthew's source text, or the book of Matthew itself. Hosea has already demonstrated up to this point a tendency toward exegesis of the Pentateuch (e.g., Hos. 1:9 [Exod. 3:14]; 4:2 [Exod. 20]), a tendency that continues in the latter part of the book (e.g., the Jacob story from Gen. in Hos. 12). John Sailhamer has proposed that the cited text in Hosea 11:1b is Numbers 23:22; 24:8:[107]

God brings them (מוֹצִיאָם) out of Egypt (Num. 23:22).

God brings him (מוֹצִיאוֹ) out of Egypt (Num. 24:8).

Balaam's second oracle speaks of Israel coming out of Egypt like a lion (Num. 23:18–24). His third oracle, however, speaks of a lion king coming out of Egypt (Num. 24:3–9; cf., Gen. 49:8–12), a king that Israel does not yet have. According to the Hebrew text behind the LXX, this king is an eschatological one who will defeat Gog (Ezek. 38–39; Rev. 20:8) in the last days (Num. 24:7, 14; cf., Hos. 3:5).[108]

Thus, the figurative relationship between the original exodus and the new exodus is already established in the composition of the Pentateuch. Hosea's citation in Hosea 11:1b is only the beginning of a section that moves from the original exodus (Hos. 11:1b) to the metaphorical return to Egypt (Hos. 11:5) and finally to the new exodus out of Egypt (Hos. 11:11). And for the composer of the Twelve, this new

---

106. E.g., Craig L Blomberg, "Matthew," in *Commentary on the New Testament Use of the Old Testament*, eds. G. K. Beale and D. A. Carson (Grand Rapids: Baker, 2007), 7–8.

107. John H. Sailhamer, "Hosea 11:1 and Matthew 2:15," *WTJ* 63 (2001): 87–96.

108. See LXX and *Tg. Onk.* Num. 24:17. See also William Horbury, *Jewish Messianism and the Cult of Christ* (London: SCM, 1998), 5–35. The MT of Numbers 24:7 has historicized the text to make it refer to Agag (1 Sam. 15), a tendency common to the MT. For example, the Hebrew text behind LXX Jeremiah speaks of an unidentified enemy from the north who could be understood in an eschatological sense (Jer. 25:1–13; Ezek. 38:14–17; Dan. 9), but the MT historicizes this and says the enemy from the north is Babylon. See Shepherd, *Daniel*, 39, 95–96; idem, *Twelve Prophets*, 91–101; Tov, *Textual Criticism*, 286–94.

deliverance would not take place apart from the eschatological king of Hosea 3:5. The prophet's interest in a recapitulation of Egyptian bondage (Hos. 8:13; 9:3) and the hope of a new exodus (Hos. 2:16–17) has been well developed by the time the reader reaches this juncture, and the remainder of the Twelve will sustain this interest (e.g., Mic. 7:15; Zech. 10:10).[109] As for Matthew's context, the citation of the opening verse of Hosea 11 is similar to the citation of the opening verse of Psalm 22 in Matthew 27:46—it is a way to refer the reader to the entire passage, not merely to the cited verse.[110] Matthew shows an awareness of the context of Balaam's oracles when he refers to the star of Numbers 24:17 (Matt. 2:1–12). He also shows an awareness of the larger Book of the Twelve when he cites Micah 5:1 (Eng., 5:2; Matt. 2:6). And so, Jesus's flight to Egypt (Matt. 2:13–15) and subsequent return (Matt. 2:19–23) inaugurate and make possible the fulfillment of a new act of deliverance that will include his death, resurrection, and coming again (Luke 9:31). This new deliverance is already revealed by the Pentateuch and interpreted by the Prophets. It is not Matthew's task to reveal it. It is his task to identify the historical Jesus of Nazareth with the messianic king revealed in the Tanakh (Matt. 1:1; 5:17).

According to Hosea 11:2, Israel's subsequent history stands in stark contrast to their relationship with the LORD that he established by means of the exodus from Egypt. The LXX has altered the opening verb of this verse as well as one of the following pronominal suffixes to make them fit with the use of the first person in Hosea 11:1. The MT, however, requires the reader to understand the subject of a third person plural verb and the referent of a third-person plural pronominal suffix. *Targum Jonathan* takes this subject to be the prophets, and there is some exegetical warrant for it. The language is very similar to 2 Kings 17:13–17, which explains Israel's apostasy and downfall in terms of their rejection of the prophets. It also corresponds to the way Hosea describes the reception of the prophets elsewhere (Hos. 9:7–9). The situation was such that the ministry of the prophets only exposed

---

109. See Shepherd, *Twelve Prophets*, 17–24; idem, "The New Exodus in the Composition of the Twelve," in *Text and Canon: Essays in Honor of John H. Sailhamer*, ed. Robert L. Cole and Paul J. Kissling (Eugene, OR: Pickwick, 2017), 120–36.

110. This practice is well known from the rabbinic literature before the insertion of chapter and verse numbers, but there are other examples from the NT. For instance, the citation of Psalm 110:1 in Hebrews 1:13 likely assumes the entire psalm (Heb. 7:17, 21). See also Luke 4:18–19 (Isa. 61:1–2) and Mark 12:26.

and exacerbated the people's problems (cf., Isa. 6:9–10; Jer. 1:18–19; 11:13; Ezek. 2:5; Hos. 4:7; 10:1).[111] It was to the local manifestations of Baal that they sacrificed rather than to the LORD (cf., Hos. 2:15 [Eng., 2:13]). But it was not Baal who taught Ephraim how to walk (Hos. 11:3; cf., Deut. 1:31; Ezek. 16).[112] The LXX changes the second clause of Hosea 11:3 to first person in order to make it fit with the first and third clauses of the verse. It is likely an authorial comment inserted between the parallel clauses and should be left in the third person within parentheses (cf., Exod. 19:4; Deut. 32:11; 33:27).[113] The LORD was the one who taught them how to walk—indeed, he carried them—but the people did not acknowledge him for this or for the fact that he healed them (see Exod. 15:26; Hos. 6:1; BDB, 950). They credited Baal instead (Hos. 2:10 [Eng., 2:8]).

Interpretation of Hosea 11:4 depends in part on whether the reader understands אדם and אהבה in their usual Hebrew sense or according to Arabic parallels (see *HALOT*). If these are in fact terms for leather, it is a fair question to ask what would be the point of using rare words at this juncture to describe the material out of which the cords and bonds were made. After all, there is a perfectly good Hebrew word for leather (עור). On the other hand, given the fact that the cords and bonds are clearly metaphorical here, it would work well with the remainder of the verse to speak of the way in which the LORD "pulled" Israel by these means (i.e., humanely and with devoted love; cf., Jer. 31:3; Hos. 10:11; 11:1). The LORD was like one who lifts an animal's yoke so that he might bend down and feed it—a beautiful picture of his tender care for Israel. But Israel did not respond well to this (Deut. 32:15; Isa. 1:3).

The people of Israel will return to the land of Egypt from which the LORD once delivered them (Hos. 11:5). This is not a reference to an appeal to Egypt for aid or refuge as in Hosea 7:11 (cf., Hos. 5:13). It is also not about a literal return to servitude in Egypt as a nation (Exod. 14:13). Rather, it is a figure for future captivity in Assyria, as the second clause of Hosea 11:5 indicates (cf., Hos. 8:13; 9:3). This is due to the people's refusal to turn and indeed their inability to do so (Hos. 5:4). Lest the reader think that the idea of a new exodus would thus lose any eschatological sense that it might otherwise have, it is important to keep in mind that the prophets use both Assyria and Babylon to prefigure judgment in the last days and the context out of which

---

111. The syntax of Hosea 11:2 may be compared to Exodus 1:12.
112. This is a rare occurrence of the *tiphel* stem, which is essentially equivalent to the more frequent *hiphil* stem (see GKC §55h).
113. For the form קחם, see GKC §19i.

final deliverance comes (e.g., Isa. 13–14). Thus, even prophecies from a post-exilic perspective about the future work of God use the language of Babylonian exile to depict the situation from which restoration will occur (e.g., Isa. 61; Zech.; Luke 4:16–30) precisely because the kind of deliverance envisioned by the exilic prophecies (e.g., Isa. 40–55) did not find their fulfillment in the immediate return to the land (Ezra-Neh.).

Verse 6 describes the devastating effects of the enemy's sword (cf., Hos. 10:6). Nevertheless, it is as if the people are hung on their apostasy, unable to free themselves (Hos. 11:7). They may call upward for help, but it is too late (cf., Hos. 7:16). There will be no one to lift them from the consequences of their covenant infidelity. Yet the emotion expressed in Hosea 11:8 shows that the LORD is not finished with his people (cf., Amos 9:8b). This is not so much a change of mind as it is something consistent what the LORD had already revealed about what he would do in the wake of exile (Deut. 29–30; Jer. 3:11–18). The LORD will judge Israel, but how can he treat Israel like Admah and Zeboiim who were given to permanent destruction along with Sodom and Gomorrah (Gen. 10:19; 19)? His compassion for the true people of God will ultimately not cease (cf., 1 Kgs. 3:26; Lam. 3:22–23).[114] God's emotion has traditionally been explained in terms of a helpful metaphor rather than true emotion, since such emotion would imply change. But texts cited in support of this do not speak of God's inability to experience emotion (e.g., Mal. 3:6). They are in fact talking about his faithfulness and reliability. Thus, it is not necessary to speak of the LORD as a static God. It is possible for him to experience genuine emotion that remains consistent with his revealed character.

When Hosea 11:9 says that the LORD will not perform his anger, it does not mean that he will not judge Israel at all, but, as the second clause indicates, he will not destroy Ephraim again (i.e., a second time; cf., Gen. 8:21; GKC §114n[2]). The stated reason for this is that the LORD is God and not a man. Similar statements are made in Numbers 23:19 and 1 Samuel 15:29, where the idea is that the LORD is not prone to lie or does not change his mind the way humans are. He is completely set apart (קְדוֹשׁ) in this regard. He will not so much as threaten destruction by entering a city (see LXX; Syr.; *Tg. Jon.*; Vulg.; Luther). He will reliably and undeterredly stay the course of eventually establishing a new covenant people of God.

---

114. The use of הָפַךְ in the expression, "My heart is turned upon me," may be a deliberate play on the use of the same word in Genesis 19 to describe the overturn or overthrow of Sodom and Gomorrah (including Admah and Zeboiim). See, e.g., Gen. 19:25.

There is a touch of irony in the image of the people following after the LORD who roars like a lion (Hos. 11:10; cf., Jer. 25:30; Joel 4:16 [Eng., 3:16]; Amos 1:2). It recalls the picture of judgment painted in Hosea 5:14 where the LORD said he would tear them the way a lion tears its prey. But Hosea 6:1 also expressed the hope that the one who tore the people would also be the one to heal them. Likewise, the image of the people ("sons") trembling from the sea/west does not on the surface appear to be a positive one (cf., Exod. 19:16b; see BDB 353). But it is important to note the movement of this in Hosea 11:10–11. It is "out of the sea/west," "a bird out of Egypt," and "a dove out of the land of Assyria" (cf., Isa. 10:26; 11:16; 27:13). Furthermore, the direction is not away from the LORD but toward him and into the land (Hos. 11:11b), similar to the direction of the fear in Hosea 3:5 (in contrast to Micah 7:17). Verse 5 has already set up the notion of a new exodus out of a new Egypt, and the idea of Assyria/Babylon as the context from which future and final deliverance comes even after the return from exile has already been discussed above. But what can be said about a return from the west (i.e., the Mediterranean Sea; Hosea 11:10b)? This may very well contain a hint of things to come—ships from Kittim or Cyprus, perhaps a reference to Greece and/or Rome (see Num. 24:14, 24; Dan. 11:30).

HOSEA 12 (ENG., 11:12–12:14)

12:1 (Eng., 11:12) With lying Ephraim surrounds me, and with deceit the house of Israel. But as for Judah, still he wanders with God, with the Most Holy [GKC §124h] he is faithful.[115] *12:2 (Eng., 12:1) Ephraim feeds on wind [BDB, 945], and he pursues east wind all the day. (Lie and destruction he increases.) And a covenant with Assyria they make, and olive oil to Egypt is carried. 12:3 (Eng., 12:2) And the LORD has a point of contention with Judah. And he will punish Jacob according to his ways, according to his deeds will he repay him. 12:4 (Eng., 12:3) In the belly [i.e., in the womb] he grabbed his brother's heel, and in his vigor [i.e., in his adulthood; cf., LXX] he persisted with an angel [see Tg. Jon., Vulg.; cf., Gen. 48:15–16]. 12:5 (Eng., 12:4) And he persisted against an angel and prevailed. He wept and ingratiated himself to him. It was at Bethel that he would find him, and it was there that he would speak with us [Syr.: with him]. 12:6 (Eng., 12:5) And the LORD,*

---

115. LXX: "Ephraim surrounds me with deception, and with ungodliness the house of Israel and Judah. Now God knows them, and the holy people is called God's."

the God of hosts, the LORD [i.e., YHWH] is his memorial [see Tg. Jon.].
12:7 (Eng., 12:6) And as for you [sg.], with faith in your God you must
turn.[116] *Covenant loyalty and justice are what you are to maintain, and*
wait for your God continually. 12:8 (Eng., 12:7) A merchant in whose
hand are scales of deceit loves to oppress/extort. 12:9 (Eng., 12:8) And
Ephraim said, "Surely I am rich. I have found wealth for myself. In all
my labors they will not find in me iniquity,[117] *which is sin." 12:10 (Eng.,*
12:9) But as for me, I am [or, have been] the LORD your God from [or,
since] the land of Egypt [cf., LXX]. Again I will cause you to live in tents
like days of an appointed time. 12:11 (Eng., 12:12) And I spoke to the
prophets, and for my part, prophetic vision is what I increased. And
by the hand of the prophets I make comparisons. 12:12 (Eng., 12:11) If
in Gilead there is trouble/idolatry—surely nothing are they—in Gilgal
bulls/oxen [LXX: rulers] are what they sacrifice.[118] *Also their altars are*
like heaps upon furrows of a field. 12:13 (Eng., 12:12) And Jacob fled to
the country of Aram, and Israel worked for a wife, and it was for a wife
that he kept [Tg. Jon. adds: sheep]. 12:14 (Eng., 12:13) And it was by
a prophet that the LORD brought Israel out of Egypt, and it was by a
prophet that he was kept. 12:15 (Eng., 12:14) Ephraim provoked [him]
bitterly [GKC §118q]. And as for his bloodshed, on him will he leave it,
and as for his reproach, his Lord will cause it to return to him.

It is not immediately clear whose voice is heard in Hosea 12:1 (Eng.,
11:12)—the prophet's or the LORD's through the prophet. It may be that
the LORD's voice continues from Hosea 11:11, but that unit formally
concluded with נאֻם יהוה. The second half of Hosea 12:1 (Eng., 11:12)
through Hosea 12:9 (Eng., 12:8) appears to be the prophet's voice until
the sudden shift in Hosea 12:10–11 (Eng., 12:9–10). Israel's deceit is well
established by now (e.g., Hos. 4:2; 10:4), but the present chapter will
compare it to the story of the deceit of their patriarch Jacob/Israel whose

---

116. Wolff (*Hosea*, 207) says that this is a *constructio praegnans* in which a
    second verb of trust is implied.
117. Cf., 1 Sam. 29:3, 6, 8; 2 Kgs. 17:4; Jer. 2:5.
118. NIV renders Hosea 12:12a (Eng., 12:11a) as a two-part question, but
    אִם would ordinarily introduce the second part of a disjunctive question
    (GKC §150c; BDB, 50). RSV renders all of Hosea 12:12 (Eng., 12:11)
    with two protasis-apodosis (if-then) constructions, but גַם would be an
    odd choice to introduce the supposed apodosis in Hosea 12:12b (Eng.,
    12:11b). The present translation takes Hosea 12:12a (Eng., 12:11a) to be
    a protasis-apodosis construction with a parenthetical comment inserted
    between the two parts (see GKC §159v).

namesake they are (Hos. 12:8 [Eng., 12:7]). What appears to be a contrast with Judah in the MT of Hos. 12:1b (Eng., 11:12b; cf., LXX) raises several problems for the reader. First, Judah is included with Israel in the point of contention (ריב) that begins in Hosea 12:3 (Eng., 12:2). Nevertheless, this would not be the first time that such a favorable contrast for Judah has occurred (see Hos. 1:7). Another issue is the wording. What does it mean that Judah still "wanders" (רד) with God? This would not seem to be a particularly positive description (e.g., Jer. 2:31), yet it runs parallel to the word "faithful" (נאמן), and "wander" (רוד) simply does not occur frequently enough to establish that it bears a negative connotation (BDB, 923–24). Still another problem is the translation of קדשים. Should it be "holy ones" (cf., LXX) or "the Most Holy"? The parallelism ("with God and with קדשים") seems to suggest the latter option. At the time of Israel's downfall (722 BC), Judah would still have some good years left (e.g., the reigns of Hezekiah and Josiah), but they would eventually exceed Israel's sin and fall for many of the same reasons (2 Kgs. 17:13, 19; Jer. 3; 25:4; Ezek. 23). Meanwhile, Ephraim chases the wind (Hos. 12:2 [Eng., 12:1]), not only in their false religion but also in their attempts to make treaties with their foes, all the while refusing to put their trust in the LORD (Hos. 5:13; 7:11).

The following commentary is an extended quotation from my book, *The Text in the Middle* (151–54):

> Hosea 12 draws an analogy between the patriarch Jacob/Israel and the northern kingdom of Israel/Jacob, creating a mosaic of inner-biblical citations from Genesis.[119] Of course, it is possible to insist that Hosea 12 represents a different Jacob tradition from the one found in Genesis, but since there is no direct access to this alleged variant tradition against which to test the hypothesis, it is at least advisable to look for verbal correspondences between the two biblical texts. If verbal correspondences are present, and if a straightforward and plausible explanation of them on the basis of textual dependence is possible, then there is no reason to deny the presence of textual exegesis. At the very least, it can be said that readers of the biblical canon would be expected to make the association between Hosea 12 and Genesis.
>
> The passage begins by saying that YHWH has a point of "contention" (ריב) with Judah (Hos 12:3 [Eng., 12:2]; cf., Hos 12:1–2) to punish Jacob

---

119. Cf., Jer 9:3–5 (Eng., 9:4–6). Nahum 1 and Habakkuk 3 are two other examples in the Twelve of mosaics of primarily pentateuchal material used for figural purposes.

according to his ways. There is then a reference to the birth account of Jacob and Esau: "In the belly (בטן) he followed at the heel (עקב) of his brother (אחיו)" (Hos. 12:4a). This is the explanation for the name of "Jacob" (יעקב) in Genesis 25:24–26. When the twins were in their mother's "belly" (בטן), Esau came out first. Jacob, "his brother" (אחיו), was grasping Esau's "heel" (עקב).

The second half of Hosea 12:4 moves to a story in Jacob's adult life (באונו; cf., Gen 49:3): "He persevered with *elohim*" (שרה את אלהים). This is a reference to the story of Genesis 32:23–33. There the man with whom Jacob wrestled says, "Jacob will no longer be your name but Israel (ישראל: "God perseveres" or "He perseveres with God"), for you persevered (שרית) with God (אלהים) and with men and prevailed (ותוכל)" (Gen 32:29). Thus, Hosea 12:4 refers to the two accounts of the naming of Jacob/Israel (cf., Gen. 35:10). It is clear that Jacob understood his encounter with the "man" (Gen. 32:25; *Tg. Neof.*: Sariel) to be an encounter with God: "And Jacob called the name of the place Peniel (פניאל: "face of God"), for, 'I saw God (אלהים) face to face (פנים אל פנים), and my life was rescued'" (Gen. 32:21; cf., Exod. 33:11, 20). But was this actually the case? Elsewhere the appearance of mysterious men is the appearance of angels (e.g., Gen. 18:2; 19:1; Dan. 8:15–16). It is possible that Jacob makes the same mistake as Manoah in the account of the announcement of Samson's birth (Judg. 13). Manoah thought that he and his wife would die because they had seen God (Judg. 13:22), but they had in fact only seen an "angel" (מלאך) (Judg. 13:21). This is the same term that Hosea 12:5a1 uses to explain אלהים: "And he persevered with an angel and prevailed" (ויכל וישר אל מלאך). This meaning for אלהים is attested elsewhere (Ps. 97:7; cf., LXX). *Targum Jonathan* even translates אלהים in Hosea 12:4 with "angel." The latter part of Hosea 12:5a—"He wept and ingratiated himself to him" (בכה ויתחנן לו)—comes from Genesis 33:4, 8:

And Esau ran to meet him, and he embraced him and fell on his neck and kissed him. And they wept (ויבכו).

And he said, "Who to you is all this camp that I encountered?" And he said, "To find favor (חן) in the eyes of my lord."

Hosea 12:5b1 says, "At Bethel he found him" (בית אל ימצאנו). Elsewhere in Hosea "Bethel" ("house of God") is "Beth Aven" ("house of trouble") (Hos 4:15 [cf., *Tg. Jon.*]; 5:8). It was one of two places (along with Dan) where Jeroboam set up his golden calves (1 Kgs 12:25–30; 2 Kgs 17:21; Hos 10:5, 8; cf., Exod 32). But it was also the place where Jacob had his encounters with God in Genesis 28:10–22; 35:9–15. To whom do the pronouns "he" and "him" refer in Hosea 12:5b1? Some understand the verse to mean that Jacob found God at Bethel (e.g., NET), but elsewhere God is the one who does the finding (e.g., Deut. 32:10; Hos. 9:10). Hosea 12:5b2 says, "And there he spoke with us." That is, the words of the covenant that God spoke to Jacob at Bethel were also true for Jacob's seed. This kind of solidarity between generations past and present is attested elsewhere (e.g., Deut. 26:5–9; Josh. 24:1–15; cf., Rom. 4:23–24; 15:4; 1 Cor. 9:10; 10:11).

According to Hosea 12:6, YHWH the God of hosts is "his (i.e., Jacob's) memorial" (זכרו). This is a reference to Exodus 3:14–15 (cf., Hos. 1:9) where God says that his name (YHWH) is "my memorial" (זכרי) for generation upon generation. Verse 7a then addresses Israel: "And you, in your God you must return" (ואתה באלהיך תשוב) (cf., Hos. 6:1). This should perhaps read, "And you, in your tents (באהליך) you must return" (cf., Hos. 12:10b). It could then be an allusion to Genesis 25:27b: "And Jacob was a pious man, inhabiting tents (אהלים)" (cf., Luther; *Tg. Neof.*; Gen. 6:9; 17:1; Job 1:1). Israel was to maintain covenant loyalty and justice and wait on their God (Hos 12:7b), not perverting the law (Hos. 12:8; cf., Deut. 25:13). The term for "deceit" (מרמה) in the phrase "scales of deceit" (Hos. 12:8) is the same one found in Isaac's description of Jacob to Esau: "Your brother came in deceit (מרמה)" (Gen. 27:35). But Ephraim/Israel was confident that their sins would not be discovered: "Surely I am rich. I have found (מצאתי) vigor/wealth (און; cf., Gen. 35:18; 49:3) for myself. In all my labors they will not find (ימצאו) to me iniquity (עון), which is sin" (Hos. 12:9).

In Hosea 12:10a, YHWH turns from Israel to himself (ואנכי) in what is most likely a citation of Exodus 20:2: "And I (have been) YHWH your God from the land of Egypt" (cf., "I am YHWH your God who brought you out of the land of Egypt" [Exod. 20:2; cf., Gen. 15:7; Hos. 13:4]). He adds, "Again I will cause you to live in tents like days of an appointed time" (Hos. 12:10b; cf., Hos. 12:7a). This is a reference to the "appointed times" of Leviticus 23 and more specifically the Feast of Tabernacles (Lev. 23:42–43). YHWH then points out the fact that he has spoken by the prophets and increased prophetic visions (Hos. 12:11a). It is by the hand of the prophets that YHWH "makes comparisons" (אדמה) (Hos. 12:11b). The *piel* of דמה likely does not mean "destroy" (cf., Hos. 6:5). The root with that meaning occurs elsewhere in the *qal* and *niphal* stems (e.g., Hos. 4:5). Here the homonym דמה occurs as elsewhere in the *piel* to refer to the use of analogies, metaphors, and figures so common to the prophetic literature (BDB, 198; e.g., Hos. 11:1, 5, 11). It is this practice of the prophets that makes the comparison between Jacob and Israel possible.

Hosea 12:12 refers to the "trouble" (אָוֶן) in Gilead (גִּלְעָד) and the sacrifices of oxen in Gilgal (גִּלְגָּל) where their altars are like "heaps" (גַּלִּים)
(cf., Hos. 6:8; 9:15; 10:1, 4). There may be a subtle allusion here to
Jacob's "heap of witness" (גַּלְעֵד) (Gen. 31:47). Verses 13 and 14 of Hosea
12 make a comparison between Jacob's flight to Aram and Moses's departure from Egypt:

And Jacob fled (וַיִּבְרַח) to the country of Aram, and Israel worked (וַיַּעֲבֹד)
for a wife (בְּאִשָּׁה), and for a wife he kept (שָׁמָר).

And by a prophet YHWH brought up (הֶעֱלָה) Israel from Egypt, and by a
prophet he was kept (נִשְׁמָר).

Verse 13 uses two *wayyiqtol* forms to recount Jacob's flight (Gen. 27:43)
and his work (Gen. 29:20). The "x + *qatal*" clause at the end of the verse
explains how Jacob worked for his wife: he "kept" (שָׁמָר). That is, he kept
flocks (Gen. 30:31). Verse 14 uses two "x + *qatal*" clauses in its reference to
Israel's exodus from Egypt. Moses is the prophet by whom YHWH brought
Israel up from Egypt (Deut. 18:15, 18; 34:10), and by the shepherd Moses
Israel was "kept" (נִשְׁמָר) like a flock (cf., Ps. 77:21). What is the point of
this comparison? Israel had followed in the sins of their forefather Jacob
(Hos. 12:3–9, 12, 15), but there was also a positive analogy to be made between Jacob and Moses, the prophet *par excellence*. The true prophets are
still the ones by whom Israel is kept (Hos. 12:10–11).

The final verse of the chapter ends on a sour note (Hos. 12:15 [Eng.,
12:14). Ephraim's rebellious provocation of the LORD will not go unpunished (cf., Ps. 106:29). Their bloodshed and reproach will come back
to haunt them (Gen. 9:6; Hos. 4:2; 12:3 [Eng., 12:2]; Obad. 15).

HOSEA 13:1–14:1 (ENG., 13:1–16)

*13:1 As soon as Ephraim spoke there was trembling. He was exalted
[נָשָׂא] in Israel, and he was guilty by Baal and died. 13:2 And now they
sin again, and they make for themselves a molten image. From their
silver according to their understanding [LXX: according to image] they
make idols, each one the work of craftsmen. To them they say, "As for
those who sacrifice of mankind [either "people who sacrifice" or "those
who sacrifice people"], calves are what they kiss." 13:3 Therefore, they
will be like a morning cloud and like the dew that passes away early,
like chaff that is storm driven [יְסֹעֵר] from a threshing floor and like
smoke from a window. 13:4 But I am [or, have been] the LORD your*

God[120] *from [or, since] the land of Egypt, and a god apart from me you should not acknowledge, and there is no savior except me. 13:5 I knew you [LXX: tended you] in the wilderness, in a land of drought. 13:6 According to their pasture they were satisfied. They were satisfied, and their heart was exalted. Therefore, they forgot me. 13:7 And I was to them like a lion, and like a leopard upon a path do I watch [LXX: like a leopard along the path of Assyria]. 13:8 I will meet them like a bereaved bear and tear the enclosure of their heart. And I will devour them there like a lion [LXX: cubs of a thicket will devour them there], and a wild beast [or coll., wild beasts; lit., the creature(s) of the field] will be the one to split them open.*

The first three verses of this section take the form of a judgment oracle: introduction (Hos. 13:1), accusation (Hos. 13:2), and announcement of judgment (Hos. 13:3). Ephraim and its capital city of Samaria represent the corrupt leadership of the northern kingdom of Israel, which struck fear into the hearts of the people. Their pride and idolatry led to their downfall (Hos. 13:1, 6; 14:1 [Eng., 13:16]; cf., Isa. 2:6–22). Nevertheless, they persist in their idolatry (Exod. 32; Deut. 9; 1 Kgs. 12:28–30; Hos. 8:5; 10:5; 13:2). They kiss or pay homage to their molten calves, the mere works of craftsmen (cf., 1 Kgs. 19:18). The phrase זבחי אדם is unique in the Hebrew Bible. It is thus an unusual way to refer either to people who sacrifice or to those who sacrifice people (child sacrifice? see Rashi, NIV). The description of what the people will be as a result of their idolatry in Hosea 13:3a is identical to the description of their fickleness in Hosea 6:4b. In a remarkable instance of poetic justice, the people will reap what they sow (cf., Hos. 12:15b [Eng., 12:14b]), passing away from the scene every bit as quickly as their covenant loyalty did. The latter part of the verse extends the metaphor from morning fog and dew to chaff and smoke, all of which are gone in a moment (cf., Ps. 1:4–6).

John Day has made the case on the basis of the following parallels that Isaiah 26:13–27:11 depends upon Hosea 13:4–14:10 (Eng., 14:9):[121]

---

120. LXX adds: "who strengthens sky and creates land, whose hands created all the host of the sky, and I did not reveal these things to you to follow after them, and I brought you up" (cf., 4QXII^c; LXX Hos. 12:10 [Eng., 12:9]). See also Jer. 7:31b; 10:12; 19:5b; 51:15.

121. John Day, "A Case of Inner Scriptural Interpretation: The Dependence of Isaiah XXVI.13–XXVII.11 on Hosea XIII.4–XIV.10 (Eng., 9) and its Relevance to Some Theories of the Redaction of the "Isaiah Apocalypse," *JTS* NS 31 (1980): 309–319.

1. Israel knows no lords/gods but Yahweh (Hos. 13:4; cf., Isa. 26:13 [LXX])
2. Imagery of birthpangs but child refuses to be born (Hos. 13:13; cf., Isa. 26:17–18)
3. Deliverance from Sheol (Hos. 13:14 [LXX, etc.]; cf., Isa. 26:19)
4. Imagery of destructive east wind symbolic of exile (Hos. 13:15; cf., Isa. 27:8)
5. Imagery of life-giving dew (Hos. 14:6 [Eng., 14:5]; cf., Isa. 26:19)
6. Israel blossoming and like a vineyard (Hos. 14:6–8 [Eng., 14:5–7]; cf., Isa. 27:2–6)
7. Condemnation of idolatry, including the Asherim (Hos. 14:9 [Eng., 14:8]; cf., Isa. 27:9)
8. The importance of discernment; judgment for the wicked (Hos. 14:10 [Eng., 14:9]; cf., Isa. 27:11)

Granting the verbal similarities and the general agreement in sequence (but see #4), there are some remaining questions for this proposal. First, it is not immediately obvious what the direction of dependence is here (Isa. 1:1; Hos. 1:1). The problem of intentionality arises when the reader cannot establish what text should be read in the light of the other. On the other hand, the lack of any such clear indicators may reflect the perspective of those who gave the Prophets their final shape, suggesting to their readers that the two texts should be mutually influential.[122] A second issue involves Day's example from Hosea 14:10 (Eng., 14:9) and Isaiah 27:11. The verbal parallel is very weak here, and the final verse of Hosea is not an integral part of the passage that precedes it. The text of Hosea 14:10 (Eng., 14:9) is actually part of a compositional seam that connects the book of Hosea to the book of Joel (see Introduction, The Composition of the Twelve).

Richard Schultz has also raised several concerns about Day's proposal.[123] He wonders why the author of the Isaiah passage would have chosen the Hosea passage in particular for his prophecy of Israel's future beyond exile. This is not really an argument against Day. It would suffice to say that the Hosea passage offers a unique combination of imagery that other prophecies of restoration do not possess. Furthermore,

---

122. As opposed to something like the parallel passages in Isaiah 2:1–5 and Micah 4:1–5 where Isaiah is designated the primary prophet by means of the superscription in Isaiah 2:1. The Micah passage contains no such attribution to the prophet.
123. Richard L. Schultz, *Search for Quotation: Verbal Parallels in the Prophets*, JSOTSupp 180 (Sheffield: Sheffield Academic, 1999), 93–95.

it is not as though the author of the Isaiah passage necessarily had the whole Bible at his disposal. Schultz also asks whether there is any evidence that the Isaiah passage not only cites but also interprets the Hosea passage and whether the Hosea passage aids understanding of Isaiah. On the one hand, Isaiah makes Hosea's eschatology more explicit, much the same way the composer of the Twelve has made it so. On the other hand, a text like Isaiah 26:19 is informed not only by the cited text in Hosea 13:14 but also by the larger context of Hosea (e.g., Hos. 6:1–3). It is certainly worth noting that Paul's citation of Hosea 13:14 in his discussion of the resurrection includes reference to the Isaiah context (Isa. 25:8; 1 Cor. 15:54–55). Finally, Schultz offers some statistics. The Isaiah passage only borrows nine of the twenty-two verses from the Hosea passage. Only twelve of the twenty verses in the Isaiah passage contain borrowings from Hosea. Does Isaiah have to use all or most of the Hosea passage for it to be a legitimate citation? Who says so? Is it a requirement that all of the material in the Isaiah passage bear some direct relationship to Hosea? Again, who says so?

Verse 4a of Hosea 13 is identical to Hosea 12:10a (Eng., 12:9a; cf., Gen. 15:7; Exod. 20:2; Deut. 5:6). The second half of the verse either means that because of the exodus Israel should not acknowledge any other so-called god (Hos. 2:10 [Eng., 2:8]; 4:1, 6), or it means that Israel has in fact not really known any God other than the LORD precisely because he is the one true God (Isa. 45:5). All other "gods" (like Baal) are merely false gods and idols (Ps. 96:5). There is no other savior besides the LORD (Isa. 43:11). Verse 5 plays on the verb "know" (ידע) from verse 4b. Israel should not or does not know any god apart from the LORD, and the LORD knew Israel in the wilderness (cf., Jer. 2:2; Hos. 9:10). Verses 5 and 6 follow the sequence of Deuteronomy 32:10, 15 (cf., Ezek. 16). The LORD took care of Israel in the wilderness and guided them, but when he satisfied them they became prideful and rebellious (cf., Hos. 13:1; Neh. 9:25–26). They forgot the LORD and did not remember the exodus or his provision at all (Ps. 78:11). Verses 7 and 8 use imagery similar to that of Hosea 5:14 to describe vividly and graphically the LORD's judgment of his people in terms of a predator-prey relationship (cf., 2 Kgs. 2:24; Jer. 5:26; Joel 1:6).

13:9 The fact that you are against me, against your very help, has destroyed you, O Israel [cf., ASV]. 13:10 Where [LXX] is your king then that he may deliver you in all your cities [GKC §107q], and your judges to whom you said, "Give to me king and princes"? 13:11 And I gave [וָאֶתֶּן wyyqtl; cf., LXX, Syr.] to you a king in my anger, and I took [וָאֶקַּח wyyqtl; MT: and I will take] in my fury. 13:12 Bound is the punishment for Ephraim's iniquity, hidden/stored is the consequence for his sin. 13:13 Pains of a woman in labor are what will come to him, he is an unwise son. When it is time, he will not stand at the children's place of breach [i.e., the mouth of the womb]. 13:14 From the hand of Sheol [LXX: Hades] will I purchase them [or, From the hand of Sheol will I purchase them?], from death will I buy them back [or, from death will I buy them back?]. [124] *Where [LXX] are your plagues [LXX: your judgment], O death? Where [LXX] is your destruction [LXX: sting, goad], O Sheol? Will comfort be hidden from my eyes [or, Comfort will be hidden from my eyes]? 13:15 Though [BDB, 473] he, a son of brothers, shows fruitfulness [LXX: between brothers divides; or,* מפריא אחו בין*, among reeds shows fruitfulness], an east wind will come, the wind of the LORD. From a wilderness it goes up. And his source will be ashamed [4QXII*ᶜ ויבש*: will be dry; LXX: And it will dry up his veins], and his spring will be dried up [LXX: and it will devastate his springs]. It will plunder the storehouse of every desirable vessel [LXX: It will dry up his land and all his desirable vessels]. 14:1 (Eng., 13:16) Samaria is guilty [LXX: will be destroyed], for she has rebelled against her God. It is by the sword that they will fall. As for their infants, they will be dashed in pieces. And as for his pregnant women, they will be ripped open [GKC §145u].*

Israel has essentially self-destructed by standing against the very God who intends to help them (Hos. 13:9; cf., Ps. 118:7). Neither Baal nor their king (nor any foreign ruler) will be able to deliver them (Hos. 13:10a; see Hos. 5:13; 7:7, 16; 10:3, 6, 15; 11:7, 9). The word אהי at the beginning of Hos. 13:10 looks like a shortened first common singular *qal yiqtol* from היה ("to be"; cf., Hos. 13:7).[125] But the same word occurs twice in Hos. 13:14b apparently with the sense of איה "Where?" (see LXX; *Tg. Jon.*; BDB, 13). The latter part of Hosea 13:10b seems to allude to the people's request for a king to judge them "like all the nations" in 1 Samuel 8:5 (see also Hos. 8:4).[126] The LORD gave them what they wanted in the person of King Saul (Hos. 13:11; see 1 Sam. 9–11), and they paid the price for it (1 Sam. 8; 12; 13; 15). Thus, Saul was removed and replaced by David. But that crucial moment in Israel's early history was indicative of what their relationship with the LORD would continue to be. The

---

124. For the difference between פדה and גאל, see *TLOT* 1:291.
125. See Rashi. See also Exod. 3:14; Hos. 1:9; 12:6 (Eng., 12:5).
126. Passages like Judges 9 and 1 Samuel 8–12 are not against kingship in general (*contra* Rolf Rendtorff, *The Old Testament: An Introduction*, trans. John Bowden [Philadelphia: Fortress, 1986], 169, 171). They are against corrupt kingship and kings not appointed by God.

punishment for Ephraim's iniquity is bound like a document (cf., Isa. 8:16), stored for the proper time of judgment (Hos. 13:12; cf., Isa. 8:16; Job 15:22). It thus feels like the brink of childbirth without any release (i.e., forgiveness; Hos. 13:13; cf., Isa. 66:9). This is due to the fact that Israel is an unwise son (cf., Deut. 32:6, 28–29; Prov. 10:1).

Interpretation of Hosea 13:14 largely turns on whether the first two clauses are statements (cf., LXX) or questions (but see *Tg. Jon.*). Both options have their problems, and it would be brutish to insist that one or the other is immediately obvious from the context. Paul's quote of the second half of the verse in 1 Corinthians 15:55 appears to presuppose that the first half consists of positive statements rather than questions that require a negative response. He cites the verse with reference to the resurrection. Such an understanding is not without exegetical warrant, granted the verbal similarity between Hosea 13:14 and Psalm 49:16 (Eng., 49:15).[127] The initial difficulty with this view is the fact that the immediately preceding and following context of Hosea 13:14 is not about restoration but judgment. But then again sudden shifts from one to the other are the hallmark of the Prophets. For instance, Isaiah begins with judgment (Isa. 1:2–17) followed by restoration (Isa. 1:18–31). The oracle of deliverance in Isaiah 2:1–5 is followed by three judgment sections (Isa. 2:6–22; 3:1–15; 3:16–4:1), salvation (Isa. 4:2–6), and judgment (Isa. 5:1–7). Within the context of Hosea, this kind of shift has already occurred in places like Hosea 11:2–6 (words of judgment) and Hosea 11:7–11 (words of restoration). Thus, Hosea 13:14 can be read positively in anticipation of the restoration described in chapter 14.

On the other hand, it is possible that the first two clauses of Hosea 13:14 are rhetorical questions that presuppose a negative answer. Questions in Hebrew do not necessarily require a formal marker such as the prefix ה (GKC §150a). In favor of this interpretation are the immediate context of judgment and the fact that the second half of the verse contains two clearly marked questions (see אֱהִי in Hos. 13:10). Against this view are: (1) the fact that the two halves of the verse would have two different addressees; and (2) the problem of interpreting the second half of the verse in light of the first half. According to the above view that Hosea 13:14a contains positive statements, the second half of the verse is easily interpreted as an instance of a figure of speech known as apostrophe in which inanimate objects or abstract ideas are

---

127. See the above commentary on Hosea 6:2. See also Shepherd, *Twelve Prophets*, 24–25; von Rad, *Old Testament Theology*, vol. 1, 46.

addressed as if they were real individuals.[128] It would thus be a challenging (and a mocking) of death/Sheol.[129] But according to the latter view that the clauses in Hosea 13:14a are questions, the second half of the verse would have to be some sort of an unusual summons for death to bring its destructive power. The final clause of Hosea 13:14b can also be either a question or a statement, depending upon what decision the interpreter makes for the first part of the verse.

Looking at the textual options for Hosea 13:15 (see translation above), it would seem that the MT's "son of brothers" is the more difficult reading that gave rise to the existence of all others whether extant or conjectured. Perhaps the best way to explain the MT is to take it as an allusion to Jacob's words to Joseph in Genesis 49:22–26 where Joseph is depicted as a fruitful bough and a blessed son who is under attack from his own brothers but who nevertheless prevails to be the consecrated one among his brothers. Such an allusion would be pertinent to the context of Hosea 13 where the tribe of Joseph's son Ephraim represents the northern kingdom of Israel as its leadership (Hos. 13:1). But an east wind, the very wind of the LORD himself (cf., Exod. 14:21), will dry up the water sources that have made Israel so fruitful and abundant (cf., Hosea 2:11 [Eng., 2:9]). It will plunder the storehouse of every desirable thing—a fitting metaphor for the attack of an invading nation.

The final verse of this unit is marked off from what follows in the MT by the setting of Hosea 14:2 (Eng., 14:1) flush right. This is indicated in *BHS* by the the sign פ (פתוחה "open[ed]") after Hosea 14:1 (Eng., 13:16). The verse reiterates the guilt of Samaria for its rebellion against God and thus brackets the whole of chapter 13, which began with Samaria's guilt in Hosea 13:1 (see also Hos. 13:6; Neh. 9:26). It is by the sword that they will fall (cf., Hos. 11:6). The image of dashed infants and pregnant women ripped apart is not a pleasant one (Isa. 13:16; Hos. 10:14; Amos 1:13; Ps. 137:9). It is a testimony to Israel's hard heart that such a graphic and unsettling picture did not move them to repentance (cf., Rev. 9:20–21).

---

128. Bullinger, *Figures of Speech*, 901–905.
129. "Sheol" is simply a poetic term for the place of the dead (= pit, grave). The descriptions of Sheol as an "underworld" (e.g., Isa. 14:9–11) are nothing more than poetic depictions of death. They should not be interpreted literally as primitive views of the afterlife. *Contra* Philip S. Johnston, *Shades of Sheol: Death and Afterlife in the Old Testament* (Downers Grove, IL: InterVarsity, 2002), 85.

HOSEA 14:2–10 (ENG., 14:1–9)

14:2 (Eng., 14:1) Return, O Israel, to the LORD your God, for you have stumbled over your iniquity. 14:3 (Eng., 14:2) Take with you words and return to the LORD. Say to him, "May you completely forgive iniquity [GKC §128e] and receive what is acceptable [NET: prayer] that we might pay the fruit [LXX; MT: bulls] of our lips. 14:4 (Eng., 14:3) As for Assyria, he will not deliver us, upon a horse we will not ride. And we will not say again, 'Our god(s),' to the work of our hands, for it is in you that an orphan receives compassion." 14:5 (Eng., 14:4) I will heal their apostasy [LXX: dwellings], I will love them freely [GKC §118q], for my anger has turned away from him [LXX: them]. 14:6 (Eng., 14:5) I will be like the dew to Israel. He will sprout like the lily, and he will strike [4QXIIᶜ: כ] his roots like Lebanon. 14:7 (Eng., 14:6) His tender shoots will go, and let his splendor be like the olive tree and his scent like Lebanon. 14:8 (Eng., 14:7) Those who live in his shadow will return. They will revive grain. And they will sprout like the grapevine. His remembrance will be like the wine of Lebanon.[130] 14:9 (Eng., 14:8) Ephraim, what do I [LXX: what does he; cf., Syr., Tg. Jon.; see also BDB, 553] still have to do with shapes / idols? I am the one who answered, and I will watch [LXX: I humbled him, and I will strengthen him]. I am like a flourishing cypress tree. It is from me that your fruit is found.

The final section of the book begins with a call for Israel to return to the LORD from the iniquity over which the people had stumbled (Hos. 14:2 [Eng., 14:1]; cf., Hos. 12:7 [Eng., 12:6]; Joel 2:12). This call already strikes a new chord in the sense that such a return was simply not a possibility in the context of the old covenant made at Sinai (Hos. 5:4). Indeed, it had only been a hypothetical ideal (Hos. 6:1–3). But now the people are instructed to take words with them in their return to the LORD (Hos. 14:3 [Eng., 14:2])—words that pray for the new covenant realities of forgiven iniquity (Jer. 31:31–34) and spiritual sacrifices (Heb. 13:15).[131] Neither

---

130. *Tg. Jon.*: "They will be gathered from among their captivities, they will dwell in the shade of their Messiah, the dead will live, and the goodness will increase in the land. And the remembrance of their good things will continue without ceasing like the remembrance of trumpet sounds over old wine, which is poured out in the Temple." See Samuel Levy, *The Messiah: An Aramaic Interpretation, The Messianic Exegesis of the Targum* (Cincinnati: Hebrew Union College Press, 1974), 90–91.

131. See Shepherd, *Text in the Middle*, 120–22. See also Bullinger, *Figures of Speech*, 575.

Assyria nor any other military power ("horses") will be able to deliver Israel (Hos. 14:4 [Eng., 14:3]; cf., Hos. 5:13; Ps. 20:8 [Eng., 20:7]). Never again will the people refer to the work of their hands as their god(s) (cf., Hos. 8:4; 10:5; 13:2; 14:9 [Eng., 14:8]). It is only in the LORD that an orphan like Israel (see *Tg. Jon.*) will find compassion (Exod. 34:6–7; Deut. 10:18). This last part hearkens back to the prophecy of Israel's rejection in the name of Hosea's daughter Lo Ruhamah ("she has not received compassion"; Hos. 1:6–7). The first indication of the reversal of this was in Hosea 2:25 (Eng., 2:23): "I will have compassion on Lo Ruhamah."

When the LORD says through the prophet that he will heal Israel's apostasy/rebellion (Hos. 14:5 [Eng., 14:4]), he is saying that he will heal their "turning" from which they should now return (Deut. 30:3; Jer. 30:17; 31:18; Hos. 5:13; 6:1). This is precisely because his anger has "turned" from them. He will now love (i.e., choose and devote himself to) them freely and willingly (cf., Exod. 36:2–7; Deut. 7:7–11)—the exact opposite of the way the breaking of the old covenant relationship was described in Hosea 9:15. The new covenant relationship will be like the dew (cf., Hos. 6:3–4), causing the people to sprout and to send roots like the notorious cedars of Lebanon (BDB, 527) so that they might bear the fruit of righteousness (Isa. 27:6; 61:3b; Hos. 14:3b [Eng., 14:2b]). Israel's splendor will be like that of the olive tree, and his scent like that of the cedars of Lebanon (Hos. 14:7 [Eng., 14:6]; cf., Song 4:11).

When those who live in the LORD's shadow or shade return (Hos. 14:8 [Eng., 14:7]; cf., Isa. 4:6; 25:4; Pss. 17:8; 36:8 [Eng., 36:7]; 57:2 [Eng., 57:1]; 63:8 [Eng., 63:7]), they will revive the grain that was lost (Hos. 2:11 [Eng., 2:9]). They will sprout like the grapevine (cf., Hos. 10:1). According to Hosea 14:8b (Eng., 14:7b), "his remembrance" will be like the wine of Lebanon—a third reference to Lebanon. That is, his remembrance will only get better with age. But is this Israel's remembrance or the LORD's? A comparison with Exodus 3:14–15 and Hosea 12:6 (Eng., 12:5) suggests that it is the remembrance of God's name YHWH, but the immediate context would seem to indicate that this is the lasting fruitfulness of God's people. *Targum Jonathan* takes the LORD's shade in this verse to be the shade of the Messiah. It also takes the revival of the grain to be the resurrection from the dead. It would be easy to be dismissive of such a rendering, but it is important to bear in mind that only two other passages in the Targum of Hosea use the language of the Messiah (Hos. 3:5) and the resurrection (Hos. 6:2). In other words, the Targum does not throw this language around lightly, and it usually has some exegetical warrant for the interpretive decision. In the case of the Messiah, the shade metaphor for the LORD's protection also occurs in a passage from Hosea's contemporary, Isaiah

(Isa. 4:6). This text also happens to mention the messianic Branch (Isa. 4:2; cf., Isa. 11:1; Jer. 23:5–6; Zech. 6:12–13). As for the resurrection, the Targum has identified the *piel* of חיה with the occurrence of the same root and stem in Hosea 6:2. The language of Hosea 14:8 (Eng., 14:7) is figurative, and the Targum is simply making an attempt to understand the metaphors on the basis of analogous texts.

According to the Syriac and *Targum Jonathan* of Hosea 14:9 (Eng., 14:8), there is an implied introductory formula at the beginning of the verse that makes Ephraim the one who says, "What do I still have to do with idols?" This would make sense in light of Hosea 13:2. Unmarked shifts of voice between that of the prophet and that of the LORD are frequent in this chapter, but the only other example in context of the voice of the people (or, at least, what should be the voice of the people) is formally introduced in Hosea 14:3b (Eng., 14:2b). Another option would be to follow the LXX's change of pronoun so that the LORD is saying something about Ephraim: "What does he still have to do with idols?" But both renderings appear to reflect intentional efforts to avoid the initial awkwardness of what is said in the MT where the LORD seems to be saying that he no longer has anything to do with idols, as if he did have something to do with idols in the past. In favor of this reading is the remainder of the verse, which features the voice of the LORD in the first person, but what sense is to be made of the initial statement? It is perhaps an instance of metonymy. The people had become so closely associated with the idols they worshiped (cf., Ps. 115:8) that to say that one will no longer have anything to do with idols is to say that one will no longer have anything to do with those who worship them. The LORD had already cut off his relationship with the idol worshipers by fulfilling his obligations to the terms and consequences of the broken covenant, but now he will have nothing to do with them in the sense that there will be no idol worshipers in the new covenant community. He has answered the cry of the people (cf., Jer. 33:3) and will watch over them to ensure their fruitfulness (cf., Isa. 27:2–6).

14:10 (Eng., 14:9) Who is wise? [or, Whoever is wise,] Let him understand these things. [Who] has understanding? [or, (Whoever) has understanding,] Let him know them. Indeed, upright are the ways of the LORD, righteous people are the ones who walk in them. But as for transgressors, they stumble over them.

This last piece of text in Hosea does not belong to the main body of the book. It is part of a compositional seam that connects the book of Hosea to the book of Joel (see Introduction, Internal Evidence for the

Composition of the Twelve). The three criteria for identification of the activity of the composer of the Twelve are distinction from surrounding context at the junctures between books, development of the program in Hosea 3:4–5, and citation from Jeremiah. Wolff notes well the first and third criteria:

> Wisdom teachers often employ concluding questions like those in v 10a (cf. Eccl 8:1; Ps 107:43). We also find such questions added to the sayings of Jeremiah in 9:11. They belong to a period when the prophetic traditions had long since been preserved as literature and their interpretation had become problematic.

> The didactic proposition in the second sentence (v 10b) intercepts the provocative double question. The connection made by the deictic כִּי, which we have often found in the book, leaves open the possibility that v 10b did not originally belong with v 10a. Its vocabulary and antithetic structure are also typical of Wisdom (cf. Prv 10:29; 24:16b).[132]

The wisdom language ("wise," "understanding"; contrast of righteous and wicked) of the final verse of Hosea fits well with Joel 1:2–3, which adopts the wisdom tradition of passing instruction from the older generation to the younger (cf., Prov. 1–9). This text in Joel also stands apart from the material that follows it.

How does a seam based on wisdom themes develop the program of eschatological judgment and messianic restoration set forth in Hosea 3:4–5? According to the seams of the Tanakh (Deut. 34:5–Josh. 1:9 and Mal. 3:22 [Eng., 4:4]–Ps. 1), it is the wise person who studies the Torah (Deut. 34:9; Josh. 1:8; Ps. 1:2) in order to gain wisdom about the coming of the forerunner prophet like Elijah (Mal. 3:1, 23 [Eng., 4:5]) and the ultimate messianic prophet like Moses (Deut. 18:15, 18; 34:10). And so it is with the Book of the Twelve. This first compositional seam of the Twelve offers a wisdom reading strategy for the book as a whole. The wise reader will follow the clues and gain understanding not only about the past but also about the future work of God in Christ.

SOME THOUGHTS ON TEACHING
AND PREACHING THE BOOK OF HOSEA

Teaching and preaching from the book of Hosea should be done in the context of the Book of the Twelve. A weekly series on the Twelve covering roughly a chapter per week would finish in a little over a year.

---

132. Wolff, *Hosea*, 239.

One way to work through Hosea in particular would be to follow the divisions provided in the present commentary for weekly lessons. It is important not to succumb to the pressure of making the book into mere lists of life principles and things to do. It is not the author's intent to do this, so it would be completely arbitrary for the interpreter to do so. Remember, this is only the beginning of the Twelve. Give the composer time to develop his message. There is no need to interrupt him constantly with things that you are adding to the book. Your job is to provide a guided tour of the composition on its own terms and for its own sake in a way that will equip your hearers with tools to read the Twelve on their own. Trust that the application will come in the author's own sweet time, and keep in mind that the application is not always something to do but something to understand and believe. This is also true of the author's presentation of the Messiah. The textual portrait of Christ emerges over the course of the Twelve as whole as passages like Hosea 3:5 make their contribution. It does not appear all at once in a single passage, nor does every passage need to say the same thing. The composer of the Twelve has worked hard to make his book one that would be relevant to future generations by giving it an eschatological message. It is thus not the interpreter's necessary duty to update the book. The task is not to contextualize the book to the readers but to contextualize the readers to the book.

BOOK OF THE TWELVE

JOEL

JOEL 1:1–3

1:1 The word of the LORD that came to Joel the son of Pethuel.

1:2 Hear this, O elders, and give ear, all you inhabitants of the land. Did this happen in your days or in the days of your forefathers? 1:3 Concerning it, to your children recount, and your children to their children, and their children to another generation.

The form of the superscription in Joel 1:1 is identical to that of Hosea 1:1 minus any indication of the date of the prophet's ministry. It indicates the content of the book rather than the author of the book.[1] This is not to say that Joel cannot be the author of the book. It is only to say that the superscription is not intended to make such a claim. There are no narratives about Joel or Pethuel elsewhere in the Bible, so the reader primarily knows Joel from the words he speaks in the book that bears his name. Conjectures about the date of the prophet range from the ninth or eighth century BC (in part because of the placement of Joel between two eighth-century prophets, Hosea and Amos) to the post-exilic period (in part because of the reference to the Greeks in Joel 4:6 [Eng., 3:6]; cf., Zech. 9:13). For the purposes of the present commentary, however, the focus of interest lies in the role that the prophetic composer of the Twelve has designed for Joel. Within the composition

---

1. *Targum Jonathan*: "The word of prophecy from before the LORD that was with Joel the son of Pethuel."

of the Twelve, the function of the book of Joel is to introduce the Day of the LORD theme (Joel 1:15; 2:1, 11; 3:4; 4:14 [Eng., 2:31; 3:14]).[2]

The outline of the book of Joel follows the general pattern of judgment (Joel 1:4–2:17) and restoration (Joel 2:18–4:21 [Eng., 3:21]).[3] But prior to the main body of the book are two verses in Joel 1:2–3 that form a compositional seam with Hosea 14:10 (Eng., 14:9) in order to connect the books of Hosea and Joel and to develop the message of the composer of the Twelve (see above commentary on Hosea 14:10 [Eng., 14:9]). This piece of text stands apart first and foremost due to its dependence upon the language of the wisdom literature (cf., Prov. 1–9; see also Deut. 32:1, 7; Ps. 78:3–6). The call to understand and to pay attention in these verses points forward to the words of the prophets that must now be passed on to future generations along with the words of the Torah (see, e.g., Zech. 7:12). There is something unprecedented in them that demands retelling.[4]

JOEL 1:4–20

1:4 What remains from the cutting locusts is what the abundant locusts devour, and what remains from the abundant locusts is what the licking locusts devour, and what remains from the licking locusts is what the consuming locusts devour. 1:5 Wake up [LXX: Sober up], you drunkards, and weep, and wail, all you drinkers of wine, over sweet wine, for it is cut off from your mouth [LXX: for removed from your mouth is merriment and joy]. 1:6 For it is a nation that comes up against my land, mighty [or, numerous] and without number. Its teeth are lion's teeth, and it has a lion's incisors. 1:7 It makes my grapevine into a desolation, and my fig tree into a splintering. It completely strips it bare and throws it down, its twigs show white. 1:8 Wail [Tg. Jon.: Congregation of Israel, make lamentation] like a virgin girded with sackcloth over the husband of her youth. 1:9 Grain offering and drink offering are cut off from the house of the LORD. The priests, the servants of the LORD, mourn [Syr.: The kings sit in mourning, and the priests, the servants of the LORD]. 1:10 A field is destroyed, ground

---

2. See Rolf Rendtorff, *The Canonical Hebrew Bible: A Theology of the Old Testament*, trans. David E. Orton (Leiden: Deo, 2005), 276, 278.

3. Cf., the program of the Twelve in Hosea 3:4–5.

4. The questions in Joel 1:2b are essentially rhetorical ones that assume a negative response (see E. W. Bullinger, *Figures of Speech Used in the Bible* [London: Eyre and Spottiswoode, 1898; reprint, Grand Rapids: Baker, 1968], 950).

mourns. For grain is destroyed, new wine dries up, fresh olive oil lan-guishes. 1:11 Be ashamed, O farmers, and wail, O vinedressers, over wheat and over barley, for a field's harvest perishes. 1:12 The grape-vine dries up, and the fig tree languishes. Pomegranate, also palm tree and apple tree, all the trees of the field, they are dry. Indeed, rejoicing dries up from humanity. 1:13 Gird and mourn, O priests, wail, O altar servants. Come, spend the night in [or, on; see BDB, 974] sackcloth, O servants of my God [LXX: ministering to God]. For from the house of your God grain offering and drink offering are withheld. 1:14 Set apart a fast, call an assembly, gather elders, all the inhabitants of the land to the house of the LORD [> LXX] your God, and cry out to the LORD. 1:15 Ahah [LXX, Vulg.: Alas Alas Alas; Syr.: Oh Oh] for the day! For near is the day of the LORD, and like destruction [LXX: misery; Syr., Tg. Jon.: plunder] from Shaddai [LXX: misery; Vulg., Luther: the Almighty] will it come. 1:16 Is it not before our eyes that food is cut off, from the house of our God joy and gladness? 1:17 Grains shrivel under their shovels.[5] Storehouses are desolate, granaries are torn down, for grain dries up. 1:18 How the large livestock groan [LXX: What will they put away for themselves?], [how] the herds of cattle are confused! For they have no pasture. Also the flocks of sheep / goats are desolate [נֶאְשָׁמוּ; MT: guilty]. 1:19 To you, O LORD, I call [Tg. Jon.: pray], for fire consumes wild pastures, and a flame engulfs all the trees of the field. 1:20 Also [or, Even] wild beasts collectively long for you, for channels of water are dry, and fire consumes the wild pastures.

Translations and commentaries differ on the terminology of Joel 1:4. Some understand the Hebrew words to refer to different types of in-sects. Others see the same insect at different stages. Still others treat the terms synonymously. The above translation reflects the under-standing that these words describe different characteristics of the same insect (cf., Lev. 11:22; Joel 2:25; Amos 4:9; 7:1–3; Nah. 3:15–17). The destruction wrought by the locusts cannot be good news for the drunkards who depend upon the production of vineyards for their way of life (Joel 1:5; cf., Joel 4:18 [Eng., 3:18]; Amos 9:13b). It is quite possible that the "drunkards" here are the leaders of the nation (cf., Isa. 28:1).

Interpreters also disagree about whether the "nation" (גוֹי) in Joel 1:6 is a figure for the locust plague or a literal invading army for which

---

5. LXX: "Heifers leap in their stalls"; 4QXII^c: "Heifers decay under . . .";
Syr.: "The heifers roast in their stalls"; *Tg. Jon.:* "Jugs of wine decay under their seals."

the locusts are a figure.[6] Neither figure would be a common one in the Hebrew Bible (see Amos 6:14–7:3; Zeph. 2:14 [but LXX]; Prov. 30:25). In favor of the former interpretation is the description of the destruction in chapter 1 and the comparison of the locusts to an army in chapter 2. How can the locusts be a metaphor for an army when an army is being used as a metaphor or as a simile for the locusts? In favor of the latter interpretation is the scope of the book's prophecy, which looks well beyond any historical locust plague to the Day of the LORD, especially in the latter half of the book. It is certainly not the intent of the composer of the Twelve to include Joel solely for the purpose of recounting a locust plague from the past. Keil's understanding of this hermeneutical issue may very well be the most balanced.[7] The prophet does use the nation and its invading army as a figure for the locust plague, but in this he sees the destruction of judgment in the Day of the LORD. In other words, it is precisely because a real, historical locust plague reminds the prophet of an invading army that he goes to such great lengths to describe it in those terms. The locust plague is "like" an invading army in the sense that it is a fitting picture of things to come. Within the final form of the book of Joel, and certainly within the composition of the Twelve, there is no need to limit the referent of this army to Assyria or Babylon. It is now a final enemy to be defeated in the Day of the LORD prior to the restoration of his people (see Joel 2:20; cf., Jer. 25:1–13 [LXX]; Ezek. 38:14–17; 39:25–29; Dan. 9).

After describing the "nation" as innumerable in Joel 1:6a, the word of the LORD through the prophet mixes metaphors in Joel 1:6b and compares the "teeth" of the locusts to those of a lion. This so-called nation of locusts makes God's grapevine ("my grapevine") and his fig tree ("my fig tree") into a desolation and a splintering respectively (Joel 1:7). Some translations will render these terms as collectives (i.e., "grapevines" and "fig trees") and understand the first common singular possessive pronominal suffix "my" to refer to the prophet. But it

---

6. For the former view, see James L. Crenshaw, *Joel*, The Anchor Bible 24c (New York: Doubleday, 1995), 91–95; see also Rashi and Redak. For the latter view, see Alberto Ferreiro, ed., *The Twelve Prophets*, ACCS 14 (Downers Grove, IL: InterVarsity, 2003), 60; John Calvin, *Commentaries on the Twelve Minor Prophets*, vol. 2, *Joel, Amos, Obadiah* (reprint, Grand Rapids: Baker, 2005), 25–26; Douglas Stuart, *Hosea–Jonah*, WBC 31 (Nashville: Thomas Nelson, 1987), 241–42.

7. C. F. Keil, *The Minor Prophets*, trans. James Martin, Keil & Delitzsch Commentary on the Old Testament 10 (Edinburgh: T&T Clark, 1866–91; reprint, Peabody, MA: Hendrickson, 2001), 121–24.

is important to remember that this is still "the word of the LORD" (Joel 1:1) through the prophet until the reader is notified of a clear shift in voice (e.g., Joel 1:19). It is also important to keep in mind that the singular forms ("my grapevine" and "my fig tree") create the opportunity for double entendre. That is, this is not only about the actual destruction of grapevines and fig trees (cf., Hos. 2:14 [Eng., 2:12]) by locusts. It is also an image of a nation's destruction of Israel who up until this point in the Book of the Twelve has been known as God's grapevine (Hos. 10:1; 14:8 [Eng., 14:7]; cf., Jer. 24 for the fig tree).

The above reading of Joel 1:7 proves to be helpful at the beginning of Joel 1:8, which uses a feminine singular imperative ("Wail"). This imperative is generally understood to be directed toward Israel (see, e.g., *Tg. Jon.*), but "Israel" normally agrees with masculine verbs in Hebrew. This is different from other lands and cities in Hebrew because the terms "land" (ארץ) and "city" (עיר) are grammatically feminine. But the nation of Israel is so tied to the patriarch Israel (see Hos. 12) that the masculine gender sticks. The interpreter might suppose that the feminine imperative is directed to a city like Jerusalem or to the land in general as metonymy for the people, but there is no such indication in the text. It is also unlikely that the comparison to a virgin has influenced the gender of the imperative, especially because the feminine imperative is relatively rare and because feminine forms are often not used even when required for agreement (GKC §145p, t, u). It seems more likely that the imperative is directed to the "grapevine" (גפן) of Joel 1:7 (תאנה "fig tree" is also feminine), a feminine noun used as a figure for Israel in the Prophets (Ezek. 15:2, 6; 17:6–8; 19:10; Jer. 2:21; 6:9; Hos. 10:1; Ps. 80:9, 15 [Eng., 80:8, 14]). The image in Joel 1:8 of a virgin girded in sackcloth to mourn the loss of the husband she married in her youth is reminiscent of the language used in Hosea to describe the broken covenant relationship (Hos. 1–3; cf., Jer. 3). The Hebrew word בתולה ("virgin") normally describes a young woman who has not yet conceived (e.g., Gen. 24). The use here of a woman who had a husband is probably not enough to warrant the overthrow of the general definition. It is perhaps a picture of a newly married woman who has lost her husband prior to conception, or virginity is possibly a way to describe her new status without a husband (as opposed to אלמנה "widow").

The priests and the temple are deeply affected by the ravages of the locust plague precisely because the destruction of the fields means that there is nothing to give for grain offerings and drink offerings (Joel 1:9–10, 13; see Lev. 2; cf., Hos. 2:10 [Eng., 2:8]; see also Hos. 4:9). These things will have to be restored on the other side of judgment (Joel 2:19, 21–22). Of course, it is difficult not to see in these verses an allusion to the destruction of the temple itself (2 Kgs. 25; Jer. 39; 52; 2 Chr. 26). Farmers are put to shame, and vinedressers howl, over the loss of their harvest (Joel 1:11). Verse 12 picks up the language of Joel 1:7 and speaks of a situation that forces the remnant of the people of God to trust in the LORD despite their circumstances (cf., Hab. 3:17–19). The latter part of verse 12 talks of joy drying up from "humanity" (cf., Joel 1:16; 2:21). The use of the Hebrew phrase for "humanity" (בְּנֵי אָדָם) may be intended to distinguish the people of the land from what is said about animals in Joel 1:18, 20, but it may also be intended to broaden the scope to a worldwide judgment of mankind (see Joel 4 [Eng., 3]; cf., Nah. 1:1–9; Zeph. 1:1–3:8). The calling of a fast in Joel 1:14 is yet another way for the priests, the elders and the general populace to express their mourning and to entreat their God in the temple (cf., Joel 2:15–17).

Joel introduces the Day of the LORD theme to the Book of the Twelve in Joel 1:15 by declaring its imminence (cf., Joel 2:1; 4:14 [Eng., 3:14]; Obad. 15). Other prophets speak of this Day (e.g., Isa. 13:6, 9), but it is particularly prominent in the composition of the Twelve. Most commentators interpret the references to the Day of the LORD to indicate that there are many such days in the past, present, and future that lead up to the final Day.[8] Another possibility is that there is only one true Day of the LORD reserved for the eschaton, but the prophets see illustrations of certain features of that Day in historical events. So, for example, the locust plague serves to illustrate something about judgment in that Day. But the Day of the LORD is not just about judgment. It is also a day of restoration for the true people of God (Joel 3:1–5 [Eng., 2:28–32]). This is what makes the Day of the LORD theme so fitting for the composer of the Twelve whose program and message are all about final judgment and messianic restoration in the last days (Hos. 3:4–5). The text of Joel 1:15 encourages the reader to live with a sense of immediacy about the Day of the LORD so that what is said about the future actually shapes faith and life today (cf., 2 Pet. 3). The latter part of the verse employs a wordplay in the Hebrew text: "and like destruction (שֹׁד) from Shaddai (שַׁדַּי) it will come."[9] This text

---

8. E.g., Terence E. Fretheim, *Reading Hosea–Malachi: A Literary and Theological Commentary* (Macon, GA: Smyth & Helwys, 2013), 90–92.

9. This is probably not intended to be an etymological explanation of "Shaddai." Most translations both ancient and modern generally render the term as "Almighty" (cf., the rabbinic explanation: "the one who is sufficient"). Modern scholars often opt for "the one of the mountain" on the basis of comparative evidence, even though the contexts in which "Shaddai" occurs typically have nothing to do with a mountain. See *TLOT* 3:1304–1310.

is virtually identical to Isaiah 13:6, although it is not immediately evident what the direction of dependence is. Those who gave the prophetic corpus its present shape would have read the two in light of one another, and it is informative to see that Isaiah uses the judgment of Babylon to depict final judgment in the Day of the LORD. That is, the judgment of the Day of the LORD is not only for the unfaithful of Israel but also for the enemies of God's people, resulting in the vindication of the true remnant.

Verse 16 reiterates the thought of Joel 1:9–14, now with the conception of the Day of the LORD in full view (cf., Joel 2:21). There is no more produce for the offerings and festivals of the temple. Verse 17 laments the lack of grain in particular, although the early textual witnesses (see translation above) attest to a different reading of Joel 1:17a1 wherein the main verb is from עפש ("decay") instead of עבש ("shrivel"). The subject is פרות ("heifers") instead of פרדות ("grains"), and the object of the prepositional phrase is רפתיהם ("their stalls"; cf., Hab. 3:17) instead of מגרפתיהם ("their shovels"). Lack of pasture and water causes the livestock to groan just as the prophet calls to the LORD on behalf of the people (Joel 1:18–20; cf., Joel 2:22). The image of fire in these verses is possibly another metaphor for the destruction of the locust plague, but it could also be an allusion to the destruction of foreign invasion (see 2 Kgs. 25:9; Joel 2:3).

JOEL 2:1–17

2:1 Blast a shofar in Zion and sound an alarm in my holy mountain. Let all the inhabitants of the land be upset, for the Day of the LORD is coming. Indeed, it is near [Syr. puts this last part at the beginning of v. 2]. 2:2 A day of darkness and gloom, a day of cloud and heavy cloud, like blackness [כְּשָׁחֹר instead of MT כְּשַׁחַר (like dawn)] spread over the mountains, a people great and mighty. Like it there has not ever been, and after it there will not be again for generations to come. 2:3 Before it a fire consumes, and after it a flame engulfs. Like the Garden of Eden is the land before it, and after it a desolate wilderness. (And also an escape [or, escaped survivor] it does not have.) 2:4 Like an appearance of horses is its appearance, and like steeds so they run. 2:5 Like a sound of chariots, upon the tops of the mountains they leap. Like a sound of a fiery flame consuming stubble. Like a mighty people arranged for battle. 2:6 From before it peoples writhe; all faces, they gather beauty [i.e., grow pale; LXX: every face is like burn marks of a clay pot; cf., Syr., Tg. Jon.]. 2:7 Like mighty men they run, like warriors they ascend a city wall. And each in his ways they go, and

*they do not twist [יְעַבְּתוּן; MT יְעַבְּטוּן: lend on pledge] their paths. 2:8
And each his brother [i.e., one another] they do not crowd, each strong
man in his highway they go. And through the weapon they fall, they
do not break their course. 2:9 Against the city they rush, upon the city
wall they run; on the houses they go up, through the windows they
enter like the thief. 2:10 Before it land rages, sky quakes. Sun and
moon, they are dark; and stars, they gather their brightness. 2:11 And
the LORD, he gives his voice before his army. Indeed, very great is his
encampment. Surely mighty he makes his word. Certainly great is the
Day of the LORD and very terrifying, and who can endure it [4QXII^c:
who can support it]?*

*2:12 "And also now," the prophetic utterance of the LORD, "return to
me with all your heart and with fasting and with crying and with
mourning. 2:13 And tear your heart and not your garments and return
to the LORD your God, for gracious and compassionate is he, slow to
anger [lit., long of nostrils] and abundant in covenant loyalty and relenting with regard to calamity." 2:14 Who knows? Perhaps he will turn
and relent and leave after him a blessing—grain offering and drink
offering for the LORD your God. 2:15 Blast a shofar in Zion, set apart
a fast, call an assembly. 2:16 Gather people, set apart a congregation,
gather elders, gather children and infants [lit., suckers of breasts].
Let a groom go forth from his chamber and a bride from her canopy.
2:17 Between the porch and the altar let the priests, the servants of the
LORD, weep and say, "Have pity, O LORD, upon your people and do
not allow your people to be an object of reproach by nations ruling over
them [NET: to become a proverb (לִמְשָׁל) among the nations]. Why should
they say among the peoples, 'Where is their God?'"*

The imperative to blast a shofar and to sound an alarm issues a warning
from Jerusalem to the inhabitants of the land with regard to the imminent Day of the LORD (Joel 2:1; cf., Num. 10:1–10; Jer. 4:5; 6:1; Hos.
5:8; Joel 1:15; 2:10, 11, 15). The fact that this day is imminent and
not yet present helps the reader understand the relationship between
what Joel sees in his own day and what is still to come. According to
Joel 2:2, it is a day of deep darkness and heavy clouds, an image likely
drawn from the way the locust plague obscures the luminaries (Exod.
10:15; cf., Exod. 10:22; Deut. 4:11; Ezek. 30:3; 32:7; 34:12; Joel 2:10,
28–32 [Eng., 3:1–5]; Zeph. 1:15; Ps. 97:2). This is exactly the opposite
of what many expect the Day of the LORD to be (Amos 5:18–20). It
will not be a day of deliverance for those to whom judgment is due.
The blackness of the locusts spreads over the mountains like a great

and mighty people (cf., Joel 1:6).[10] It is clear from what follows in this chapter that locusts are being compared to such a people and not vice versa, yet the Day of the LORD is ultimately about people in the future and not merely about a locust plague from the past (Joel 2:28–32 [Eng., 3:1–5]).[11] This can be reconciled by thinking about the fact that the choice of metaphor here is not arbitrary. Why does Joel compare the locust plague to a human army? Is it not because the historical event is a fitting way to call to mind what is not yet a reality? The prophet could have started with something not yet experienced (i.e., the Day of the LORD) and compared it with the locust plague, but it makes more sense to move from the familiar to the less familiar, thus achieving the same goal by a more effective means. The basic correctness of this interpretation is confirmed immediately by the latter part of Joel 2:2, which says that the event is completely unprecedented and never to be repeated for the indefinite and foreseeable future.[12] Such a description has already been applied to the locust plague in Egypt (Exod. 10:14)—a subtle clue from the prophet to the careful reader that what is said in Joel 2:2 ultimately applies not simply to another plague but to the eschatological Day of the LORD.

Before the "people" of Joel 2:2 a fire consumes, and in their wake a flame engulfs (Joel 2:3a), recalling the imagery of destruction caused by the locusts in Joel 1:19–20 but also anticipating future and final judgment by fire (e.g., Isa. 66:15–17; 2 Pet. 3).[13] The before-and-after picture of Joel 2:3b is that of the Garden of Eden turned into a desolate wilderness. This is reminiscent of the original state of Sodom and Gomorrah prior to their destruction by fire (Gen. 13:10; 19:24)—not a very flattering comparison for Israel (cf., Gen. 19 and Judg. 19).[14]

---

10. Keil follows the MT vocalization and separates this part of the verse from what precedes: "like morning dawn is it spread over the mountains" (*Minor Prophets*, 127).

11. Ferreiro, ed., *The Twelve Prophets*, 64; Calvin, *Twelve Minor Prophets*, vol. 2, 46–47.

12. It is important for the reader not to read this Hebrew idiom in an overly literal fashion, as if the text were leaving open the possibility of repetition (see BDB, 189).

13. Note the *qatal-yiqtol* sequence of the verbs in the parallel clauses of Joel 2:3a. See James L. Kugel, *The Idea of Biblical Poetry: Parallelism and Its History* (New Haven, CT: Yale University Press, 1981; reprint, Baltimore: Johns Hopkins University Press, 1998), 17.

14. The flood of fire takes the place of the flood of water (Gen. 6–7). See Michael B. Shepherd, *The Text in the Middle* (New York: Peter Lang, 2013), 19–20. See also Deut. 29:22 (Eng., 29:23); 32:32; Isa. 1:9–10.

But both Isaiah and Ezekiel look forward to a new Garden of Eden (Isa. 51:3; Ezek. 36:35). The latter part of Joel 2:3 is an authorial, parenthetical comment that stands apart from the poetic parallelism. It is similar to the description of the locust plague in Egypt (Exod. 10:5). Nothing (and no one) will escape the destruction of the "people," yet in the Day of the LORD anyone who calls on the name of the LORD will in fact escape (Joel 3:5 [Eng., 2:32]).

Verse 4 of chapter 2 begins a series of similes that runs through verse 7. The comparison of the "people" (i.e., the locusts) to horses in Joel 2:4 has long prompted commentators to point out the similarity in appearance of the head of a locust to that of a horse. But this can hardly be the point of the imagery in the present context. Rather, the text looks at the locusts en masse as a stampede of horses or as an army of horses arrayed for battle (cf., Jer. 51:27; Rev. 9:7). This continues in verse 5 with comparison to the sound of chariots, the sound of fire consuming stubble, and to a mighty army arranged for battle. It is important to stay with the biblical imagery here. The passage is not an invitation for the reader to delve into historical research on locust plagues in an effort to find features of such plagues that match the metaphors, nor is there any guarantee that ancient readers in Joel's context would have all automatically known and/or experienced the discovered phenomena. Rather, it is the task of the reader to allow the text to transport him or her from the locust plague to the image of an invading army. From before this "people" other peoples writhe and grow pale (Joel 2:6; cf., Nah. 2:11 [Eng., 2:10]).[15] They are like mighty warriors scaling a city wall (Joel 2:7a; cf., 2 Sam. 22:30). They march in order (and do not break formation) in an effort to stay the course (Joel 2:7b–8a). The second half of Joel 2:8 is difficult, but the general sense seems to be that they are able to withstand any armed defense and to continue their advance unabated.

Verse 9 marks a progression from the advance against the city limits to the city wall to the houses within the city and finally into the houses themselves through the windows as a thief would enter (cf., Jer. 9:20 [Eng., 9:21]). Before this advancing army, the land and the sky rage/quake just as the inhabitants do (Joel 2:10a; cf., Joel 2:1; 4:16 [Eng., 3:16]). The luminaries gather their brightness just as the people's faces gather their glow (Joel 2:10b; cf., Joel 2:2, 6; 3:4; 4:15 [Eng., 2:31; 3:15]; see also Isa. 13:10, 13; Ezek. 32:7). Such a setting makes

---

15. *Tg. Jon.*: "all faces are covered with a black covering like a pot." This rendering is based on understanding the Hebrew פָארוּר ("beauty, glow") as if it were פָרוּר ("pot").

way for the image of a morning sunrise as a picture of future salvation
(e.g., Mic. 7:8). Verse 11 then provides important theological insight
into these events. It is the LORD himself who commands this army (cf.,
Joel 4:16 [Eng., 3:16]). The military encampment is his instrument of
judgment, which moves at his strong word. In what sense then is the
Day of the LORD "great" (Joel 2:11b; cf., Mal. 3:23 [Eng., 4:5])? The immediate context seems to suggest that it has to do with its magnitude
and its overwhelming terror.

The opening words of Joel 2:12 (וגם עתה "And also now") and the
formula נאם יהוה ("the prophetic utterance of the LORD") set apart a new
subsection that runs through verse 14 (see BDB, 610).[16] Having primed
the pump with words of judgment thus far in the book, the prophet now
quotes the LORD himself with a call to repentance (cf., Deut. 30:2; Hos.
14:2 [Eng., 14:1]), knowing that the reader is now ripe for such a response. It is somewhat ironic that verse 12 calls for outward signs of
repentance such as fasting, weeping, and mourning (cf., Isa. 58; Zech.
7), yet verse 13 seems to call for inward change rather than external
expression (i.e., tearing garments) (see 4Q266 11:4–5).[17] This latter emphasis has already been encountered within the Twelve (Hos. 6:6; cf.,
Amos 5:21–24; Mic. 6:6–8). Psalm 51 finds the balance of this when it expresses in its final verses the idea that God first desires a contrite heart
and then (and only then) accepts the outward worship of the believer.

Verse 13 also adds that the rationale for repentance is the character
of God revealed to Moses at Mount Sinai: "gracious and compassionate,
slow to anger and abundant in covenant loyalty, and relenting with
regard to calamity" (see Exod. 34:6–7).[18] It is worth noting that there
is no reference here to the other half of God's character: "he will by no
means leave the guilty unpunished, visiting the iniquity of the fathers
upon the sons and grandsons to the third and fourth generations."
Divine justice has already been established in the preceding context,
and there would be no reason to include it here as part of a rationale
for turning to God. The last part of Joel 2:13 ("relenting with regard
to calamity") does not appear in the Exodus 34:6–7 text. It does, however, surface in the citation of Exodus 34:6–7 found in Jonah 4:2. There

---

16. See Christo van der Merwe, Jackie Naudé, and Jan Kroeze, *A Biblical
    Hebrew Reference Grammar* (Sheffield: Sheffield Academic, 1999), 333.
17. There is some question about whether the quote ends with verse 12 or
    verse 13. Because of the *waw* at the beginning of verse 13, it seems best to
    include it within the quote. The prophet then speaks in verse 14.
18. See Michael Fishbane, *Biblical Interpretation in Ancient Israel* (Oxford:
    Clarendon, 1985), 335–50.

Jonah confesses that he knew God's revealed character and thus fled precisely because he anticipated the possibility that the LORD would relent with regard to the calamity announced for Nineveh if they would only repent. Even verse 14 of Joel 2 finds a parallel in the Jonah story where the Assyrian king says, "Who knows? Perhaps God will turn and relent and turn from the burning of his anger, and we will not perish" (Jon. 3:9; cf., Jon. 1:6). This kind of language indicates that the LORD is under no obligation to relent. The prophet in Joel 2:14 conjectures that the LORD may leave "after him" (אחריו) a blessing. This recalls what was said about the destruction left in the wake of the invasion in Joel 2:3, but also with the citation of Exodus 34:6–7 it is difficult not to hear an echo here of Exodus. 33:23: "And I will remove my palm, and you will see my back (אחרי), but my face will not be seen." In context, the "blessing" of Joel 2:14 is the restoration of the land's produce— enough to bring offerings of grain and drink to the LORD (cf., Joel 1:9, 13). This is in line with the realism of depictions of the messianic kingdom found elsewhere (e.g., Amos 9:11–15). The kingdom will be a full and everlasting restoration of what was lost in the Garden of Eden.

The end of Joel's judgment section concludes with a small unit that echoes the language from the beginning of chapter 2 (Joel 2:15; cf., Joel 2:1, 12; see also Joel 1:14). People of all ages are to gather for a fast and a solemn assembly (Joel 2:15–16; see BDB, 783–84). This even includes those who might otherwise be dismissed for special reasons (Joel 2:16b; cf., Deut. 20:7; 24:5). "Between the porch and the altar" is where the priests mourn (Joel 2:17a; cf., Joel 1:9, 13). This is evidently a merism for the entire temple structure. Their prayer is that God would have pity on his people lest his inheritance become the object of reproach (Joel 2:17b; cf., Isa. 19:25; Jon. 4:11; Neh. 1:3). There is an implicit admission of guilt in this insofar as there is no appeal to their own merit (cf., Lam. 5:19–22). The phrase למשל בם גוים either indicates that they would be the object of reproach by being ruled by foreign nations, or it parallels the thought of being an object of reproach by saying that they would become a proverb or saying among the nations, depending on the vocalization of למשל. The motive for God to respond to this prayer is in the rhetorical question at the end: "Why should they say among the nations, 'Where is their God?'" Such an appeal to God's concern for his reputation and glory is consistent with the pattern of laments and with biblical prayers in general (e.g., Exod. 32:11–14; Deut. 9:25–29; Ps. 42:11 [Eng., 42:10]; Dan. 9:3–19; Ezra 9:6–15; Neh. 1:5–11).[19] This is God's primary

---

19. See Hermann Gunkel, *Introduction to Psalms: The Genres of the Religious Lyric of Israel*, completed by Joachim Begrich, trans. James D. Nogalski

motive for action, and any reproach against his people and on his city is also a reproach against his name (see Deut. 12:5; Ezek. 48:35).

JOEL 2:18–27

2:18 And the LORD was zealous for his land, and he spared his people. 2:19 And the LORD answered and said to his people, "Look, I am about to send to you the grain and the new wine and the fresh olive oil, and you will be satisfied with it [4QXII^c has "and you will eat" written above the line]. And I will never again make you an object of reproach among the nations. 2:20 And as for the northerner, I will remove him far away from upon them, and I will drive him to a land of dryness and desolation, his face to the eastern sea and his end to the latter sea. And his stench will go up, and his foul smell will go up. (For he [i.e., the LORD] does great things.)[20] 2:21 Do not fear, O land. Rejoice and be glad. (For the LORD does great things [Tg. Jon.: For the LORD multiplies to do with you goodness for his people].) 2:22 Do not fear, O beasts of the field, for wild pastures grow green, because trees bear their fruit; fig trees and grapevines, they give their strength. 2:23 And O sons of Zion, rejoice and be glad in the LORD your God, for he has given to you the early [i.e., fall] rain [LXX, Syr.: food] for prosperity,[21] and he brought down to you rain—early rain

---

(Macon, GA: Mercer University Press, 1998), 91, 155–57. "The people are not the center of God's world. God is the center of God's world, and the people reap the benefits of that reality (Michael B. Shepherd, *Daniel in the Context of the Hebrew Bible* [New York: Peter Lang, 2009], 96).

20. *Tg. Jon.* takes the subject of the last clause to be the "northerner": "For he has multiplied to do harm."

21. The interpretation of מורה as "early rain," while seemingly appropriate to the context, is not without its problems. The term מורה normally means "teacher," in which case the phrase המורה לצדקה would mean "the teacher of righteousness" (see James VanderKam and Peter Flint, *The Meaning of the Dead Sea Scrolls: Their Significance for Understanding the Bible, Judaism, Jesus, and Christianity* [New York: HarperCollins, 2002], 282–85; see also *Tg. Jon.*, Vulg, and Luther). While it is difficult to see what this would mean in context, it at least has in its favor the most common meanings for מורה and צדקה. The common spelling for "early rain" is יורה, which is attested in the textual witnesses as a variant reading for the second occurrence of מורה in Joel 2:23b where it is coordinated with the word for "latter rain." The only other place where מורה apparently has the sense "early rain" is Psalm 84:7. Furthermore, the interpretation "early rain" for Joel 2:23a requires the reader to understand צדקה in the unusual sense of "prosperity" (cf., Prov. 8:18).

and latter [i.e., spring] rain as before [read כראשון *or* כראשונה *(see BDB, 911; see also Ms, LXX, Syr., Vulg.)].*[22] *2:24 And the threshing floors are full of grain, and the vats overflow with new wine and fresh olive oil. 2:25 And I will repay to you the years that the abundant locusts devoured— the licking locusts and the consuming locusts and the cutting locusts, my great army that I sent against you.*[23] *2:26 And you will eat to the point of satisfaction [GKC §113s], and you will praise the name of the LORD your God who has dealt with you wonderfully, and my people will never be ashamed. 2:27 And you will know [or, acknowledge] that in the midst of Israel am I and that I am the LORD your God, and there is none besides. And my people will never be ashamed."*

The restoration section begins with an answer to the prayer in Joel 2:17. This is why the first three verbs of Joel 2:18–19 are *wayyiqtol* forms.[24] The priests had asked that the people not be an object of reproach, lest the wrong message about the LORD be sent to the nations (cf., Deut. 32:27), and the LORD responded in the prophet's day with words of hope for the future. This was precisely because of the LORD's own zeal for his name (Exod. 20:5; 34:14; Nah. 1:2). The expression, "Look, I am about to send" (הנני שלח), using הנה plus pronominal suffix and participle, indicates the imminence of the LORD's action (GKC §116p). Here the text speaks of replenishing what was lost in Joel 1:10 (cf., Hos. 2:24 [Eng., 2:22]) so that the people will never again be an object of reproach, thereby vindicating the LORD's own name.[25]

Commentators typically identify "the northerner" in Joel 2:20 with the locust plague or with a historical nation such as Assyria or Babylon (see Rashi, Calvin, and Keil). Such identifications are usually accompanied by explanation of how a locust plague could have come from the north even though they would normally come from the south, or how a nation from the east would have invaded from

---

22. ב and כ are two of the most commonly confused letters in textual transmission of the Hebrew Bible in the square script (see Emanuel Tov, *Textual Criticism of the Hebrew Bible*, 3d ed. [Minneapolis: Fortress, 2012], 231).

23. *Tg. Jon.*: "And I will pay back to you the good years in place of the years that the peoples and tongues, the rulers and the kingdoms, plundered you—the vengeance of my great army that I sent against you."

24. See Keil, *Minor Prophets*, 133.

25. The importance of this theologically and practically can hardly be overstated. God does not act because the people are so loveable or valuable. He acts because he is worthy of their worship.

the north (but see Gen. 14). Few, however, discuss the possibility that this is the "biblical" northerner rather than a historically reconstructed one. The enemy from the north in the LXX of Jeremiah (Jer. 1:13–15; 25:8–13) is never identified as the historical nation of Babylon the way it is in the MT, leaving open the possibility that it is an eschatological enemy. This is the manner in which Ezekiel 38–39 reads Jeremiah's prophecy. The text says that the enemy from the north is the unidentified Gog who will appear in the last days and be defeated before the establishment of the messianic kingdom (Ezek. 38:14–17; cf., Num. 24:7, 23 [LXX]; Rev. 20:8).[26]

The LORD says that he will remove the northerner and drive him to a dry and desolate place. The northerner's face will be toward "the eastern sea" (i.e., the Dead Sea), and "his end" will be toward "the latter sea" (i.e., the Mediterranean Sea). This is usually taken to mean that one half of the locusts (or the human army) falls into one sea and the other half into the other sea. But this does not fit very well with the picture of being driven into a wilderness, nor does it work nicely with the following line about the rising stench. The reference to the two seas is not a way to speak of the division of the northerner. It is a way to show the direction in which the northerner will depart the land.[27] Movement eastward is an indication of judgment in Genesis (Gen. 3:24; 4:16; 11:2; 13:11; 25:6). Here the image is that of a decaying body whose smell rises in the heat of wilderness outside of the land of the covenant (cf., Isa. 34:3; Amos 4:10). On the basis of the parallel in Joel 2:21, the above translation understands the LORD to be the subject of the last clause of Joel 2:20 (cf., Ps. 126:2–3).

Verses 21 and 22 of Joel 2 repeat, "Do not fear," first to the land and then to the animals—a figure of speech known as apostrophe (cf., Ps. 96:11–12).[28] The land is likely not metonymy for the people here because verse 23 addresses the inhabitants of Zion directly and calls on them to rejoice and be glad likewise. What was lost in Joel 1:12,

---

26. "'The northerner' thus functions as a play on a prophetic symbol for the ultimate adversary; in so doing, it provides a powerful image to describe YHWH's sinister harbingers of a final day of judgment. The imagery continues that of 2:11 ('his army'), reiterated in 2:25 ('my formidable army')" (Crenshaw, *Joel*, 151).

27. According to Ezekiel 39:4 and Daniel 11:45, the final enemy will die in the land of Israel. If Joel 2:20 is about the same enemy, then it would be a reference to his expulsion from the land after his death—a rotting corpse in the wilderness.

28. Bullinger, *Figures of Speech*, 904–905.

16, 19 will be restored. This includes the outpouring of fall and spring rains resulting in full threshing floors and overflowing vats (Joel 2:23–24; cf., Amos 4:7–8). Keil understands the phrase המורה לצדקה in Joel 2:23 to mean "the teacher of righteousness," but he does not refer it to anyone in particular (see note to translation above).[29] For him it is an all-inclusive phrase for the gift of teachers generally from Moses to the priests and prophets and finally to the Messiah.

Verse 25 returns to the list of terms for locusts from Joel 1:4 and speaks of paying back the years that were lost to the plague (cf., Deut. 28:38). But *Targum Jonathan* sees the "great army" here as a human army (cf., Joel 2:11), perhaps taking its cue from the comparison of the locust plague to real horses, chariots, and warriors in Joel 2:4–7. Within the context of the Day of the LORD the historical locust plague is now the metaphor for the enemy to be defeated in the last days once it has served its purpose as God's instrument of judgment. Just as the locusts once "devoured" (אכל) the land, so the restored people will "eat" (אכל) the land's produce to the point of satisfaction (Joel 2:26). It is not necessary to spiritualize this. Such is the realism of the messianic kingdom and the new creation—a combination of the physical and the spiritual (Gen. 1–2; Isa. 11:1–10; 65:18–25; Rev. 21–22). But this time the people's satisfaction will not lead to the forgetting of their God (cf., Deut. 32:15). This is what makes the new covenant "new" in the sense of "better." They will instead praise the name of their God—the direct result of the LORD pursuing the vindication of his name by removing the reproach against his people (Joel 2:17–19)—their God who has dealt wonderfully with them (see BDB, 810–11). The final clause of Joel 2:26 repeats at the end of Joel 2:27, highlighting the fact that God's people will never again be ashamed. Sandwiched in between is the assurance that the people will acknowledge that the LORD is present and active among them and that he alone is their God (Gen. 15:7; Exod. 7:5; 9:16; 20:2; 29:46; Isa. 45:5–6, 14, 18, 21, 22; 46:9; Ezek. 34:27; Hos. 6:3; 12:10 [Eng., 12:9]; 13:4; see Joel 4:17 [Eng., 3:17]).[30]

---

29. Keil, *Minor Prophets*, 136–38.
30. This is apparently the meaning of the divine name YHWH as given in Exodus 3:12, 14–15 (Rendtorff, *The Canonical Hebrew Bible*, 40). The text of Exodus 6:3 is not intended to say that God was previously unknown by this name (cf., Gen). Rather, it indicates that he appeared by this name to the patriarchs primarily in visions, whereas now he will appear or show himself in the signs and wonders performed in Egypt (John H. Sailhamer, *The Pentateuch as Narrative* [Grand Rapids: Zondervan, 1992], 250–51).

JOEL 3:1–5 (ENG., 2:28–32)

3:1 (Eng., 2:28) "And it will be after thus, I will pour out my Spirit [LXX: from my Spirit; Tg. Jon.: my Holy Spirit] upon all flesh, and your sons and your daughters will prophesy; your elders will have dreams, your choice, young men will see prophetic visions. 3:2 (Eng., 2:29) And also upon the male servants and upon the female servants in those days will I pour out my Spirit [LXX: from my Spirit; Tg. Jon.: my Holy Spirit]. 3:3 (Eng., 2:30) And I will put wonders in the sky and in the land—blood and fire and pillars of smoke. 3:4 (Eng., 2:31) As for the sun, it will be turned into darkness, and the moon to blood, before the coming of the great and terrible [LXX: manifest] Day of the LORD. 3:5 (Eng., 2:32) And it will be, every person who calls on the name of the LORD will escape. For on Mount Zion and in Jerusalem there will be an escaped remnant, just as the LORD said, and among the survivors [LXX: and those who hear / announce good news (from בשׂר)] whom the LORD calls."

The phrase "after thus" (אחרי כן) at the beginning of Joel 3:1 (Eng., 2:28) is either a general indication that what follows will occur after the judgment described in Joel 1:4–2:17, or it is showing that the events prophesied here take place in sequence after the restoration of the land described in Joel 2:18–27. Either way the phrase signals that what the reader finds in this passage belongs to the future (see Rashi, Ibn Ezra). The image of the outpouring (שׁפך) of God's Spirit that brackets Joel 3:1–2 (Eng., 2:28–29) also occurs elsewhere in the Prophets (Ezek. 39:29; Zech. 12:10; cf., Isa. 32:15; 44:3). What makes Joel's depiction unique is the fact that the outpouring is upon all "flesh" (בשׂר) rather than upon the house of Israel (Ezek. 39:29) or the house of David (Zech. 12:10) in particular.[31] All "flesh" does not necessarily mean every living being as in Genesis 6:17, 19; 7:21; 9:11, 15, 16, 17. It more likely has the sense here of humanity as opposed to a specific ethnic group (Gen. 6:12, 13; Num. 16:22; 27:16; Deut. 5:23; Pss. 65:3 [Eng., 65:2]; 145:21; Isa. 40:5, 6; 49:26; 66:16, 23, 24; Jer. 12:12; 25:31; 32:27; 45:5; Ezek. 21:4, 9, 10; Zech. 2:17).[32] The second person plural pronominal suffixes in the remainder of Joel 3:1 (Eng., 2:28) would thus refer to the believing remnant of the people of God from all the nations—something very close to the heart of the composer of the Twelve (e.g., Amos 9:11–15; cf., Hos. 3:4–5).

---

31. *Contra* Crenshaw, *Joel*, 165.
32. See Bullinger, *Figures of Speech*, 616. This is also the way the passage is interpreted in Acts 2.

There is no *a priori* reason to believe that the "Spirit" (רוח) of Joel 3:1 (Eng., 2:28) is merely an impersonal force.[33] Such a concept would certainly be lost on someone like Luke or Peter (Acts 2). If the modern reader's assumption is that the Hebrew Bible is essentially equivalent to the religious practices of ancient Israel or to the post-exilic religion of Judaism, then it is understandable that he or she would have a difficult time seeing a personal Holy Spirit of God in these texts. But the Hebrew Bible is the product of the prophets— i.e., those who were contrary to the mainstream—and is thus cited in favor of Christianity over against Judaism (e.g., Hebrews). The NT authors use the very language of the Hebrew Bible to describe a personal Spirit (e.g., Isa. 63:10; Eph. 4:30). It is true that the Spirit in the Hebrew Bible sometimes comes upon an individual only for a particular task (e.g., Judges), but it is also true that the Hebrew Bible provides some of the most outstanding examples of Spirit-filled lives in all of Scripture (Joseph [Gen. 41:38]; Daniel [Dan. 4:5, 15 (Eng., 4:8, 18)]; cf., Eph. 5:18).[34] This is not to deny the uniqueness of the Pentecost event in history. It is only to affirm that the Hebrew Bible has a full revelation of the Spirit in its own right.

The future outpouring of God's Spirit according to Joel 3:1–2 (Eng., 2:28–29) is indiscriminate—male and female, old and young, servant and free.[35] It is difficult not to hear an echo of this in Paul's description of the gift of salvation in Galatians 3:28. Why does the text depict the recipients of God's Spirit as prophets—those who will prophesy and have prophetic dreams and visions (Num. 12:6)? This is because of the close association in the Hebrew Bible between the gift of the Spirit and true prophecy (e.g., Mic. 3:8). In the story of Numbers 11, the LORD takes "from" the Spirit that is on the prophet Moses and puts it on the seventy elders so that they can prophesy and help Moses in his leadership role (Num. 11:25; cf., LXX Joel 3:1–2 [Eng., 2:28–29]). When the Spirit then rests on Eldad and Medad, and they prophesy in the camp, Joshua urges Moses to restrain them (Num. 11:26–28). But Moses responds with the hope of the new covenant ideal that all the people would be prophets with the Spirit upon them. Thus, to call everyone a prophet in a poetic passage like Joel 3:1–2 (Eng., 2:28–29) is a way to say that they all will have the Spirit.[36]

---

33. *Contra* Crenshaw, *Joel*, 164.
34. See Shepherd, *Daniel*, 78.
35. See James B. Pritchard, ed., *Ancient Near Eastern Texts Relating to the Old Testament*, 3d ed. (Princeton, NJ: Princeton University Press, 1969), 627.
36. See Keil, *Minor Prophets*, 140.

The LORD says in Joel 3:3 (Eng., 2:30) that he will put "wonders" (מוֹפְתִים) in the sky and in the land. This term is usually coordinated with אוֹתוֹת ("signs") (BDB, 68–69). Signs and wonders in the Bible are designed to be indicators of something and/or someone and to engender faith in that something or someone. Thus, the signs and wonders in the exodus narrative (Exod. 7:3) indicate that God is actively present with his people (Exod. 7:5) and that he is superior to the Egyptian gods (Exod. 12:12; Num. 33:4), encouraging faith in him (Exod. 14:31).[37] In Joel 3:3–4 (Eng., 2:30–31), the wonders are the blood and fire and pillars of smoke, the sun turning to darkness and the moon to blood (cf., Joel 2:2, 10, 11; Matt. 24:29; Rev. 6:12). These are indicators of the Day of the LORD insofar as they are prior to its coming, much like the role of the prophet like Elijah who will prepare the way (Mal. 3:1, 22–24 [Eng., 3:1; 4:4–6]). According to Joel 3:5 (Eng., 2:32), such signs demand faith expressed in the form of calling upon the name of the LORD. The imagery of Joel 3:3–4 (Eng., 2:30–31) is likely intentionally reminiscent of the Egyptian plagues (cf., Exod. 7:17; 10:21), but it is important to keep in mind the genre differences between a poetic text like Joel and a narrative text like Exodus. When Exodus 7:20 says that the water of the Nile turned to blood, there is no simile or metaphor involved. It is a literal and realistic depiction of actual events. But when Joel 3:4 (Eng., 2:31) says the moon will turn to blood, the expectation is that this is figurative language for darkness.

To call upon the name of the LORD is either to invoke his name (e.g., 2 Kgs. 5:11) or to proclaim his name (e.g., Exod. 34:5) (see Isa. 43:7; Zeph. 3:9; Zech. 13:9; Ps. 80:19 [Eng., 80:18]; BDB, 895). In the present context, this is the expression of faith that makes the Day of the LORD a day of deliverance rather than a day of judgment for the escaped remnant (Obad. 17). It is a false dichotomy to say that Paul's citation of this in Romans 10:13 is about spiritual salvation by faith in Christ, while Joel 3:5 (Eng., 2:32) is about physical deliverance by faith in the LORD. Both are concerned with physical and spiritual deliverance that will involve a real, bodily resurrection, an earthly messianic kingdom, and a new creation (Dan. 12:1–2; 1 Cor. 15). The composer of the Twelve is every bit as interested in faith in Christ as Paul is (Hos. 3:5). The centrality of Mount Zion and Jerusalem in this deliverance in no way excludes the nations (Isa. 2:1–5; Mic. 4:1–5). They too will be among the survivors whom the LORD calls. Thus, those who call on the name of the LORD will be those called by the LORD.

---

37. See Hans-Christoph Schmitt, "Redaktion des Pentateuch im Geiste der Prophetie," *VT* 32 (1982): 170–89. See also John 20:30–31.

The form of citation of Joel 3:1–5 (Eng., 2:28–32) in Acts 2:17–21 initially favors the LXX where it differs from the MT for Joel 3:1a, 2b, 4b (Eng., 2:28a, 29b, 31b), but the citation does not include Joel 3:5b (Eng., 2:32b), so it is impossible to determine if the text at hand included the distinctive LXX reading there. It would be incorrect to conclude that the citation is in its entirety the LXX reading. It is certainly like the LXX in many ways, but the transmission of Acts in Greek (regardless of a possible Semitic original)[38] lends itself to this without indicating a text-critical preference.[39] Furthermore, the citation includes additions and changes that come from Peter, Luke, or another source (or some combination thereof). The text of Acts 2:17 interprets the phrase "after thus" in Joel 3:1 (Eng., 2:28) to mean "in the last days." It also switches the order of the clauses about the elders and the young men, perhaps in an attempt to link the young men with the preceding reference to sons and daughters. The text of Acts 2:18 adds "and they will prophesy" to the end of Joel 3:2 (Eng., 2:29). The textual apparatus of the Göttingen Septuagint indicates other textual witnesses to this reading, perhaps under the influence of Acts 2:18 (see also Acts 2:19). The text of Acts 2:19 adds "signs" to Joel 3:3 (Eng., 2:30) as might be expected from the above discussion. It also adds "above" and "below" to the text. While it is clear that Peter's citation of this passage indicates belief that the Pentecost event in some way was part of the inauguration of the last days, it is also clear from Luke's juxtaposition of Peter's speech in Acts 3:11–26 that this was not considered an exhaustive fulfillment of Joel's prophecy. "Times of refreshing" were still to come (Acts 3:20).[40]

---

38. See Matthew Black, *An Aramaic Approach to the Gospels and Acts*, 3d ed. (Oxford: Oxford University Press, 1967; reprint, Peabody, MA: Hendrickson, 1998).

39. The NT authors quote from a wide variety of textual witnesses to the Hebrew Bible. Sometimes the source text aligns with what can be established as the original text. Sometimes a reading is cited because it offers an accurate interpretation of the original (e.g., LXX Amos 9:12; Acts 15:17). Sometimes the reading simply fits the particular argument that the author wants to make (e.g., LXX Hab. 2:4; Heb. 10:38). Sometimes a specfic source is cited and then ignored in the exposition. For example, Hebrews 12:5–6 cites the LXX form of Proverbs 3:11–12, but the exposition actually depends upon the word "father" in the MT form (Heb. 12:7–11). This is like a modern preacher who shares a common English translation with his congregation but occasionally departs from it in his exposition on the basis of conviction about the original text. See Shepherd, *Text in the Middle*, 162.

40. See Michael B. Shepherd, *The Twelve Prophets in the New Testament* (New York: Peter Lang, 2011), 31–38. See also James C. VanderKam, "The

JOEL 4 (ENG., 3)

4:1 (Eng., 3:1) "For look, in those days [MurXII: in that day] and at that time when I restore the fortunes [qere: when I restore the captivity] of Judah and Jerusalem, 4:2 (Eng., 3:2) I will gather all the nations and bring them down to the valley of Jehoshaphat [Tg. Jon.: to the valley of the decision of judgment]. And I will enter into judgment with them there concerning my people and my inheritance, Israel, whom they scattered among the nations. And my land they distributed, 4:3 (Eng., 3:3) and for my people they each cast a lot. And they gave the boy for the prostitute, and the girl they sold for the wine, and they drank.

4:4 (Eng., 3:4) And also, what are you to me, Tyre and Sidon and all you regions [4QXII^g: נלילת] of Philistia? Is it recompense that you are paying to me, or are you paying back to me? Very quickly I will return your recompense on your head, 4:5 (Eng., 3:5) since it was my silver and my gold that you took, and my good desirable things were what you brought to your temples [or, palaces; MurXII: sg.], 4:6 (Eng., 3:6) and the Judeans and the Jerusalemites were the ones whom you sold to the Greeks in order to remove them from their border. 4:7 (Eng., 3:7) Look, I am about to arouse them from the place to which you sold them, and I will return your recompense on your head. 4:8 (Eng., 3:8) And I will sell your sons and your daughters into the hand of the Judeans, and they will sell them to the Sabeans [LXX: to captivity (= לשבי)], to a nation far away." Indeed [or, For], it is the LORD who has spoken.

This section continues the LORD's discourse from the previous chapters. The opening verse begins with several words and phrases that direct the reader back to the temporal context set by Joel 3:1 (Eng., 2:28). The conjunction כי ("For") introduces an explanation of the message of judgment and restoration in the Day of the LORD. The deictic particle הנה ("look") points to what will happen "in those days" and "at that time," creating the effect of unfolding the events in textual form before the reader's eyes. In other words, the description of judgment of the nations in this chapter is an eschatological one.[41] It is the final

---

Festival of Weeks and the Story of Pentecost in Acts 2," in *From Prophecy to Testament: The Function of the Old Testament in the New*, ed. C. A. Evans (Peabody, MA: Hendrickson, 2004), 185–205.

41. "[T]he reference here is to the judgment which would come upon all nations after the outpouring of the Spirit of God upon all flesh, and that it is not till vv. 4–8 that Joel proceeds to speak of the calamities which

vindication of the people of God over against their enemies.[42] Redak in particular interprets the opening verses of this chapter to be a reference to the war of Gog and Magog (cf., Ezek. 38–39; Zech. 12; 14).[43]

The *qere* ("what is read") of Joel 4:1b (Eng., 3:1b) is the *hiphil* stem of the verb שׁוּב ("return") and thus requires: "when I restore the captivity of Judah and Jerusalem," taking the noun שְׁבוּת as if it were from the root שׁבה ("take captive"; cf., LXX). While this sense fits the present context and many others, it cannot be sustained consistently (e.g., Job 42:10; see *TLOT* 3:1314–1315). Usage of the combination of שׁוּב and שְׁבוּת elsewhere suggests that the verb should be in the *qal* stem according to the *kethiv* ("what is written"). It also suggests that it is a cognate construction wherein the noun שְׁבוּת is from the root שׁוּב, resulting in the rendering: "when I restore the fortunes of Judah and Jerusalem." This restoration is the new covenant relationship anticipated in Deuteronomy 28:69; 29:3 (Eng., 29:1, 4); 30:3, 6.[44]

The LORD will gather all the nations and bring them down to the valley of Jehoshaphat and enter into judgment with them there concerning his people whom they scattered among the nations (Joel 4:2 [Eng., 3:2]; cf., Ezek. 20:34–36; Zech. 14:2). This is not merely a reference to judgment of nations like Assyria and Babylon whom the

---

neighbouring nations had inflicted upon the kingdom of Judah. The words presuppose as facts that have already occurred, both the dispersion of the whole nation of Israel in exile among the heathen, and the conquest and capture of the whole land by heathen nations, and that in the extent to which they took place under the Chaldeans and Romans alone" (Keil, *Minor Prophets*, 146).

42. "For what else was the Jewish restoration, but a prelude of that true and real redemption, afterwards effected by Christ? The Prophet then does not speak only of the coming of Christ, or of the return of the Jews, but includes the whole of redemption, which was only begun when the Lord restored his people from the Babylonian exile; it will then go on from the first coming of Christ to the last day; as though he said, 'When God will redeem his people, it will not be a short or momentary benefit, but he will continue his favour until he shall visit with punishment all the enemies of his Church." In a word, the Prophet here shows, that God will not be a half Redeemer, but will continue to work until he completes everything necessary for the happy state of his Church, and makes it in every respect perfect. This is the import of the whole" (Calvin, *Joel*, 114).

43. See *Mikraoth Gedoloth: The Twelve Prophets*, vol. 1, trans. A. J. Rosenberg (New York: Judaica, 1986), 107.

44. See Shepherd, *Text in the Middle*, 96–99. See also Jer. 29:10–14; 30:2–3, 18; 31:23; 32:44; 33:7, 11; Hos. 6:11; Amos 9:14; Zeph. 2:7; 3:20.

LORD used as his instruments of judgment against Israel and Judah but who also overstepped their bounds (e.g., Isa. 10:5–7; 47:6; Zech. 1:15). It is the future and final judgment of all worldly opposition to the true people of God.[45] According to some commentators, the valley of Jehoshaphat (Joel 4:2, 12 [Eng., 3:2, 12]) is none other than the Valley of Berakhah or the Valley of Blessing (2 Chr. 20:26) where the people blessed the LORD for their victory over their enemies (Moab, Ammon, and Edom) after king Jehoshaphat encouraged them to trust in the LORD (2 Chr. 20:20; cf., Isa. 7:9).[46] That is, according to this view, what happened in Jehoshaphat's day in some way prefigures what will take place in the future. Others prefer not to take the valley of Jehoshaphat as a reference to a specific place but as a general reference to a place of judgment that plays on the meaning of Jehoshaphat's name ("the LORD judges"). *Targum Jonathan's* rendering provides a third option: "the valley of the decision of judgment." This rendering has in its favor the phrase "the valley of decision" in Joel 4:14 (Eng., 3:14). Stuart wonders whether an original phrase like "valleys of judgment" (עמקי משפט) could have given rise to the phrase "the valley of Jehoshaphat" (עמק יהושפט).[47] The last clause of Joel 4:2 (Eng., 3:2) is parallel to the first clause of Joel 4:3 (Eng., 3:3). It was the LORD's land that the nations distributed, and it was his people for whom they cast lots (cf., Obad. 11; Nah. 3:10). Therefore, the LORD will act to vindicate his own name that his land and his people bear (cf., Joel 2:17–19). The nations paid for prostitutes with captive boys and bought wine to drink with captive girls (cf., Amos 2:6; 8:6). Such disregard for human life will not go unnoticed.

---

45. "The people and inheritance of Jehovah are not merely the Old Testament Israel as such, but the church of the Lord of both the old and new covenants, upon which the Spirit of God is poured out; and the judgment which Jehovah will hold upon the nations, on account of the injuries inflicted upon His people, is the last general judgment upon the nations, which will embrace not merely the heathen Romans and other heathen nations by whom the Jews have been oppressed, but all the enemies of the people of God, both within and without the earthly limits of the church of the Lord" (Keil, *Minor Prophets*, 147).
46. There is some question about whether Joel would have known the written form of this story since it appears in Chronicles but not in Kings. It is possible that he only knew an oral form of it, but the Chronicler does cite an older written source for his account (2 Chr. 20:34). Of course, depending upon the date of Joel's prophetic ministry, Chronicles may have been available to him.
47. Stuart, *Hosea–Jonah*, 264. See 4QXII[c] Joel 4:12 (Eng., 3:12): יושפט.

"And also" (וגם) at the beginning of Joel 4:4 (Eng., 3:4) marks the material in Joel 4:4–8 (Eng., 3:4–8) as something that is in addition to what the reader finds in Joel 4:1–3 (Eng., 3:1–3). One possibility is that this is recognition that the passage comes from a later time than that of the prophet Joel. Others see in this text evidence of a late date for Joel's ministry in general. But for the purposes of exegesis, these verses seem to serve to illustrate what is said about the nations in Joel 4:1–3 (Eng., 3:1–3) with regard to the people of God. The attachment begins with a question about what Phoenicia and Philistia have to do with the LORD. These nations border Israel on the west, the same ones cited in Zech. 9:1–8 (cf., Judg. 3:3) prior to the depiction of the coming of the Messiah in Zech. 9:9–10. Using rhetorical questions (see GKC §150h), the LORD accuses them of acting as though they were dealing him some sort of recompense that he deserved. But it will be the LORD who quickly returns their recompense on their head (cf., Obad. 15).

This retributive justice from the LORD (cf., Exod. 21:23–25) is due to the fact that they were actually his silver and gold and desirable things that the nations took for their own temples and/or palaces (Joel 4:5 [Eng., 3:5]; cf., 2 Kgs. 12:19; 16:18; 25:13–17; Dan. 1:2; 5:2).[48] His people were the ones whom they sold to the Greeks to move them far away from their border (Joel 4:6 [Eng., 3:6]; see Num. 24:14, 24; Zech. 9:13; Dan. 8:21–26; 2 Chr. 21:16–17). Again, because the LORD's people bear his name, he acts for the sake of his glory and his reputation among the nations (Joel 2:17–19; 4:1–3 [Eng., 3:1–3]). The LORD will rouse his people from the place to which they were sold and do unto the nations (represented by Phoenicia and Philistia) as they once did to Judah and Jerusalem (Joel 4:7 [Eng., 3:7]; see Deut. 30:7). Now their sons and daughters will be sold to the Judeans who will in turn sell them to the Sabeans in the Arabian desert (Joel 4:8 [Eng., 3:8]; cf., 2 Kgs. 18:8; 2 Chr. 26:6–7; see also Isa. 43:3; 45:14; Ps. 72:10; Job 1:15).[49] The above translation understands the final clause of Joel 4:8

---

48. "It may refer to cooperative involvement in looting the Jerusalem temple (2 Kgs 24:13–14) in the first great Babylonian exile (598 B.C.) with deals having been struck with the Babylonians for purchase of some furnishings, but more likely it refers to the plunder from the border wars of various occasions" (Stuart, *Hosea–Jonah*, 268).

49. It is generally recognized that there is no historical record of a sale of Phoenicians and Philistines to the Sabeans by the Judeans. "When God says, 'I will sell,' it is not meant that he is to descend from heaven for the purpose of selling, but that he will execute judgment on them; and then the second clause,—that they shall be sold by the Jews, derives its

(Eng., 3:8) to be the prophet's conclusion to the LORD's discourse (cf., Isa. 1:20; 40:5; 58:14; Mic. 4:4). To say that the LORD is the one who has spoken is to lend a clear sense of authority and certainty to the words of the prophecy.

4:9 (Eng., 3:9) "Proclaim this among the nations: 'Consecrate war. Arouse the mighty men, let the warriors draw near, let them go up [LXX has imperatives]. 4:10 (Eng., 3:10) Beat your plowing tools into swords and your pruning tools into spears. Let the weak man be the one to say, "A mighty man is who I am." 4:11 (Eng., 3:11) Lend aid [LXX, Syr., Tg. Jon.: Gather] and come all you nations from around, and gather [GKC §51o] to there.'" (Cause to descend, O LORD, your mighty men.) [LXX: Let the gentle man be a warrior; Syr.: And there the LORD is about to break your might (cf., Tg. Jon.)] 4:12 (Eng., 3:12) "Let the nations be aroused and let them go up to the valley of Jehoshaphat [Tg. Jon.: to the valley of the decision of judgment], for it is there that I will sit to judge all the nations from around. 4:13 (Eng., 3:13) Send a sickle, for harvest is ripe. Come, go down [or, rule; LXX, Syr.: trample], for winepress is full. The wine vats overflow. Indeed, great is their evil.[50] *4:14 (Eng., 3:14) Crowds, crowds [i.e., countless multitudes] in the valley of decision [see GKC §147c], for near is the Day of the LORD in the valley of decision. 4:15 (Eng., 3:15) Sun and moon, they are dark; and stars, they gather their brightness."*

4:16 (Eng., 3:16) And as for the LORD, it is from Zion that he roars, and it is from Jerusalem that he gives his voice. (And sky and land quake.) But the LORD is a refuge for his people, and a stronghold for the children of Israel [LXX, Syr.: But the Lord will spare his people, and the Lord will strengthen the children of Israel].

---

meaning from the first; and this cannot be a common sale, as if the Jews were to receive a price and make a merchandise of them. But God declares that the Jews would be the sellers, because in this manner he signifies his vengeance for the wrong done to them" (Calvin, *Joel*, 126). Calvin's explanation here is in accord with the common understanding of the *lex talionis*. The literal "eye for an eye" is not so much the concern as it is that the punishment fit the crime. See Brevard S. Childs, *The Book of Exodus: A Critical, Theological Commentary* (Louisville: Westminster John Knox, 1974), 472–73.

50. *Tg. Jon.*: "Stretch out against them the sword, for the time of their end [קיצהון] has arrived. Descend, thresh the slain of their mighty men like stamping that is done in the winepress. Pour out their blood, for their evil is great."

4:17 (Eng., 3:17) "And you will acknowledge that I, the LORD, am your God [or, that I am the LORD your God], dwelling [4QXII^c: השׁכן who dwells] in Zion my holy mountain.[51] And Jerusalem will be holy [lit., holiness]; and strangers, they will never again pass through it."[52]

Contrary to earlier Christian commentary,[53] this passage is not addressed to the people of God or even to the people of God scattered among the nations.[54] It is a summons for heralds to proclaim something among the very nations referenced in Joel 4:2 (Eng., 3:2). This proclamation is an imperative for the nations to participate fully in a war that will be the means of their ultimate judgment and defeat (cf., Ezek. 38:7–8; Rev. 16; 20). It is not against the nations per se but against the nations insofar as they represent enmity toward God and his people. To "consecrate" war means to open a campaign by sacrifice (BDB, 873; cf., 1 Sam. 7:9; Jer. 6:4; 22:7; 51:27, 28; Mic. 3:5). The nations are to arouse their mighty men so that all their warriors might draw near and go up (Joel 4:9b [Eng., 3:9b]; cf., Dan. 11:2).

Joel 4:10a (Eng., 3:10b) is a reversal of the image of peace found in Isaiah 2:4 and Micah 4:3.[55] Whereas Isaiah and Micah speak of the nations turning their weapons of war into agricultural tools, Joel envisions the exact opposite. Of course, the nations' participation in this war means defeat for the enemies of the people of God, which leads to the picture of peace painted by Isaiah and Micah. That no one is excluded from this war is indicated by Joel 4:10b (Eng., 3:10b): "Let the weak say, 'A mighty man is who I am'" (see Exod. 17:13; 32:18; cf., Deut. 20:5–9). Verse 11a is yet another call for the nations to lend help to one another in this effort as they come and gather for war. The

---

51. See Cynthia L. Miller-Naudé, "Mismatches of Definiteness within Appositional Expressions Used as Vocatives in Biblical Hebrew," *JNSL* 40/2 (2014): 97–111.
52. A slight change from the verb יעברו ("pass") to יעבדו ("serve") would yield the following translation: "and strangers, they will never again serve by it [i.e., by the people of the city of Jerusalem]." This would be virtually identical to the text of Jeremiah 30:8b, the idea being that the people would no longer be subjected to servitude at the hands of foreigners. Printed editions of the Hebrew Bible read יעברו ("pass"), but the writing of the supposed letter ר in the Leningrad Codex is ambiguous, leaving open the possibility that it is the ד of יעבדו ("serve").
53. E.g., Ferreiro, ed., *The Twelve Prophets*, 81; Calvin, *Joel*, 127–30.
54. See Keil, *Minor Prophets*, 149.
55. See Shepherd, *Text in the Middle*, 130–34.

parenthetical comment added to this in Joel 4:11b (Eng., 3:11b) is a prayer for the LORD to "bring down" his warriors (i.e., "mighty men") even as the enemy army from the nations is commanded to "go up" (cf., Joel 2:11). These could be human warriors (cf., Jer. 21:13), but Ibn Ezra and Redak suggest that they are angels.[56] The term "mighty men" (גבורים) is used of angels in Psalm 103:20. This reading has been echoed more recently by Crenshaw, following W. Rudolph.[57]

Verse 12a reuses the language of verse 9b and then revisits the reference to the valley of Jehoshaphat from verse 2. But this time the LORD says that he will "sit" to judge the nations, casting the image of a court in session (cf., Dan. 7:9–10). Verse 13 uses the imagery of sending a sickle to a ripe harvest (cf., Jer. 50:16; LXX Zech. 5:1; Rev. 14:15, 18), a full winepress (cf., Isa. 63:1–6; Rev. 14:20; 19:13), and overflowing wine vats to depict the judgment of the nations' great evil (cf., Gen. 6:5). The time is ripe for their judgment (cf., Gen. 15:16; 1 Thess. 2:16). This stands in stark contrast to the hope of threshing floors full of grain and vats overflowing with new wine and fresh olive oil for the people of God (Joel 2:24). The gathering of the nations for war and judgment results in a mass of noisy crowds in "the valley of decision" (cf., Isa. 10:23; 28:22; Dan. 9:26, 27; 11:36), which is apparently the internal interpretation of the valley of Jehoshaphat (Joel 4:14a [Eng., 3:14a]). Since חרוץ ("decision") has a homonym that means "sharp," Crenshaw suggests that the term has a dual sense here, possibly referring to the use of iron threshing instruments mentioned in Amos 1:3.[58]

The Day of the LORD in Joel 4:14b (Eng., 3:14b) not only supports the eschatological interpretation of the chapter but also adds yet another facet to the reader's overall conception of the Day. Earlier in the book the Day of the LORD was something mentioned in warnings issued to those in the land of the covenant who thought they could live however they wanted and yet still expect deliverance in the Day (Joel 1:15; 2:1, 2, 11; cf., Amos 5:18–20). Then it was depicted as a day of restoration for "all flesh" on whom the LORD would pour out his Spirit indiscriminately and for all who would call on the name of LORD (Joel 3:1–5 [Eng., 2:28–32]). Those who do not participate in the Day in this fashion will face the judgment side of it. Now the present passage clarifies that judgment in the Day of the LORD is not just for unbelieving Israel or Judah. It is also for all those among the nations who oppose God's Spirit and do not call on his name. Thus, just as restoration is

---

56. *Mikraoth Gedoloth: The Twelve Prophets*, vol. 1, 110.
57. Crenshaw, *Joel*, 190.
58. Ibid., 192.

for "all flesh" (those who believe from Israel/Judah and the nations), so judgment is for all flesh (those who do not believe from Israel/Judah and the nations). Once the descendants of Abraham fulfill their role as God's instrument of restoration of the lost blessing of life and dominion in the land (primarily through the coming of the Messiah), the essential distinguishing factor for the true people of God is not ethnicity but faith (Gen. 12:1–3; 15:6, 18; 17:5, 16; 22:18; 26:4; 35:11; 27:29; 49:8–12; Num. 24:7–9, 17; Rom. 4:11). The darkness of the Day of the LORD in Joel 4:15 (Eng., 3:15) is already familiar to the reader of the book (Joel 2:11; 3:4 [Eng., 2:31]). Judgment of the enemies of God in the Day of the LORD means deliverance for the people of God (Isa. 61:2).

Verse 16 is an insertion that interrupts the LORD's discourse, which continues in verse 17. It is a third person reference to the LORD and likely comes from the composer of the Twelve for several reasons. First, verse 16a is a citation from Jeremiah 25:30, which is in a context that also deals with judgment of the nations. It was established in the introduction to this commentary that one of the marks of the composer's work is dependence upon the book of Jeremiah. Second, this text is also cited and inserted at the beginning of Amos (Amos 1:2a) between the superscription (Amos 1:1) and the section on the nations (Amos 1:3–2:16), creating a compositional seam that connects the book of Joel to the book of Amos. Third, the context of the citation in Joel 4:16a (Eng., 3:16a) is the message of the Day of the LORD, a message that is near and dear to the composer's program of eschatological judgment and messianic salvation (Hos. 3:4–5).

The Hebrew verb used for the LORD's roar in Joel 4:16a (Eng., 3:16a) can be the roar of a lion (e.g., Jer. 2:15; Hos. 11:10; Amos 3:4, 8) or the roar of thunder (e.g., Job 37:4). This roar signals the defeat of the enemy and the vindication of the true people of God, but it is also the roar of revelation (see LXX Jer. 32:16 = MT 25:30). At Mount Sinai, the "voice" (קוֹל) of the LORD was also heard like thunder (Exod. 19:16a, 19b; 20:18a; Deut. 5:23a; cf., Gen. 3:8). It resulted in the people trembling with fear (Exod. 19:16b, 18b; 20:18b). Likewise, Joel 4:16a (Eng., 3:16a) adds the comment that the sky and the land "quake" at the roaring of the LORD (cf., Joel 2:10)—something that the beginning of Amos echoes with its reference to the "quake" (Amos 1:1b). The Amos 1:2a text also calls to mind the Sinai account. It sets up the words of judgment directed toward the nations, but such words are almost a foil for the words of judgment to Judah and to Israel in particular for their failure to keep the terms of the Sinai covenant. But Joel 4:16a (Eng., 3:16a) and Amos 1:2a also speak of something new, because now the revelation is not from Sinai but from Zion (Hag. 2:6, 7, 21; Heb.

12:18–29; cf., Isa. 65:18; Gal. 4:25–26). Joel 4:16b (Eng., 3:16b) adds that the LORD will be a refuge and a stronghold for his people no matter how bad things may be in those days for the nations who oppose God (cf., Isa. 4:6; Nah. 1:7).

When the LORD's discourse resumes in Joel 4:17 (Eng., 3:17), it is in the form of a recognition formula that it does so (cf., Ezek. 36:11; Joel 2:27). It is difficult to decide precisely how to word the translation of this formula in English: (1) "And you will acknowledge that I, the LORD, am your God"; or (2) "And you will acknowledge that I am the LORD your God." According to the first option, the idea would be that the people will acknowledge that the LORD and not some other so-called god like Baal is their God. This was more of an issue in Hosea than it has been in Joel. According to option two, the people will acknowledge that God is the LORD (i.e., Yahweh)—the one who is present with his people (Exod. 3:12, 14). This would be fitting in the Joel context where judgment in the past, present, or future might give the impression that the LORD is absent (cf., Isa. 40:27). It also fits with the description of the LORD as the one who dwells in Mount Zion (Exod. 29:45–46; Lev. 26:11–12; Ezek. 37:27). It is worth noting that the recognition formula in Joel 2:27 seems to accommodate both options. The LORD is in the midst of Israel, and he alone is their God (cf., Joel's name: "The LORD is God"). Jerusalem will be set apart in that day not merely because of the temple (1 Kgs. 8:13, 27; Jer. 7; Isa. 66:1–2) but because of the LORD's presence (Isa. 2:1–5; Ezek. 48:35 [cf., Deut. 12:5]; Mic. 4:1–5) and because of the absence of any who are not part of the people of God. The "strangers" who will never pass through the new Jerusalem are not simply the Gentiles. Even the old covenant accommodated resident aliens (e.g., Lev. 19:33–34). No, the strangers in this context are those who are foreign to the new covenant relationship whether they are of Israelite/Judean ethnicity or any other.

*4:18 (Eng., 3:18) "And it will be in that day [see GKC §112y], the mountains will drip [4QXII*c*: יטיפו] sweet wine, and the hills will flow with milk, and all the ravines of Judah will flow with water. And a spring, from the house of the LORD will it go forth, and it will water the wadi of Shittim [acacia trees].[59] 4:19 (Eng., 3:19) As for Egypt, a desolation is what it will become; and as for Edom, a desolate wilderness is what it will become, because of the violence done to the sons of Judah in whose land they poured out innocent blood. 4:20 (Eng.,*

---

59. 4QXII*c* adds כול ("all") above the line before the phrase "the wadi of Shittim."

3:20) But as for Judah, forever it will live, and Jerusalem for genera-
tion upon generation. 4:21 (Eng., 3:21) And I will leave their blood
unpunished [LXX, Syr.: And I will avenge their blood]. I do not leave
unpunished [LXX, Syr.: And I will not leave unpunished]." And the
LORD dwells in Zion.

The phrase "in that day" at the beginning of Joel 4:18 (Eng., 3:18) locates this final sub-unit firmly within the eschatological context set by Joel 3:1; 4:1 (Eng., 2:28; 3:1). Verse 18 is a poetic image of mountains covered with productive vineyards, hills filled with cattle (and thus their abundant milk), dry ravines running with water, and a water source from the temple that will replenish even the driest places. There is no need to spiritualize this (*contra* Calvin). The realism of the prophets embraces both the physical and the spiritual realities of the messianic kingdom and the new creation. The hope of sweet wine is a reversal of the manner in which the book of Joel began (Joel 1:5). It is also something that is reiterated in the seam that connects the following book of Amos to Obadiah (Amos 9:13b). The picture of a great water source from the temple is perhaps the most obviously eschatological feature of this image, since it bears no relationship to the historical Jerusalem. Nevertheless, it is a picture familiar from other passages of Scripture (Ezek. 47:8–12; Zech. 14:8; Rev. 22:1). The wadi of Shittim could simply be a place with acacia trees, but it could also be a reference to the place name Shittim where Joshua and the Israelites departed the land east of the Jordan to enter the land of the covenant (Josh. 2:1; Mic. 6:5). It is also mentioned at the beginning of the account of Baal of Peor, which led Rashi to see here atonement for the iniquity of Peor according to the midrashic meaning of Joel 4:18 (Eng., 3:18).[60]

Egypt and Edom represent the enemy nations in Joel 4:19 (Eng., 3:19) as did Phoenicia and Philistia in Joel 4:4 (Eng., 3:4). They are fitting representatives due to their notorious historical and biblical relationship to Israel (Exod. 1–15; Num. 24:18; 2 Sam. 8:14; 2 Kgs.

---

60. "*Rashi's* intention is to the sins committed by the Israelites when they abode in Shittim (Num. 25:1–3), when they worshiped Baal-peor and committed harlotry with the Moabite women. According to the Midrash (*Tanchuma, Balak* 17; *Num. Rabbah* 20:22), this tendency toward harlotry was due to their drinking the water of Shittim. The Rabbis state, therefore, that, in the future, God will dry up and renew the waters of Shittim, or, according to other readings, will cure the waters of Shittim" (*Mikraoth Gedoloth: The Twelve Prophets*, vol. 1, 112).

8:20–22; Isa. 19; 34; Jer. 46; 49:7–22; Ezek. 25:12–14; 29–32).[61] Egypt has already played a role in setting up the hope of a new exodus in the book of Hosea (Hos. 2:17 [Eng., 2:15]; 8:13; 9:3; 11:1, 5, 11) and will continue to do so throughout the Twelve. Mention of Edom (Esau!) at the end of Joel anticipates the central role that Edom will play in the connection between Amos (Amos 1:6, 9, 11; 2:1; 9:12) and Obadiah. Both Egypt and Edom will be turned into desolate places because of acts of violence committed against the Judeans "in whose land they poured out innocent blood" (cf., Obad. 10). Syntax would seem to favor understanding this to mean that Egypt and Edom attacked the land of Judah and poured out innocent blood there (1 Kgs. 14:25–26; 2 Kgs. 23:29–34; 2 Chr. 12:2–12; 14:9–15; 16:8; 20:1, 22). Furthermore, while the servitude in Egypt is well known, no such corresponding experience in Edom is on record. It is, however, possible that the expression is intentionally ambiguous in order to allow for all acts of violence against Judah committed by the nations whether domestic or abroad.

In contrast to the enemy nations, Judah and Jerusalem will live forever (Joel 4:20 [Eng., 3:20]) in accordance with the terms of the covenant with David (2 Sam. 7:13). This is the everlasting kingdom that will consist of all the true remnant of the faithful from all the nations to whom the lost blessing of life and dominion in the land will be restored through the Judean and Davidic Messiah (Gen. 1:26–28; 12:1–3; Isa. 66:18–25; Dan. 7). There is a direct correlation between this everlasting life and the presence of the LORD there as indicated at the end of Joel 4:21 (Eng., 3:21; cf., Hab. 1:12a; 2:4b). That last clause of the book is an authorial comment added after the conclusion of the LORD's discourse. It is a reiteration of Joel 4:17a (Eng., 3:17a), and, according to Redak, it runs parallel to the end of Ezekiel's prophecy (Ezek. 48:35; cf., Rev. 21:22), achieving the ultimate goal of the LORD's presence with his people (Exod. 29:45–46).

The two short clauses at the beginning of Joel 4:21 (Eng., 3:21) are perhaps the most difficult of the passage.[62] A straightforward rendering of the MT—"And I will leave their blood unpunished. I do not leave unpunished"—is easily the most challenging of the options. The phrase "their blood" presumably refers to the innocent blood of the Judeans

---

61. "*Ibn Ezra* states that both Egypt and Edom were laid waste during the reign of Nebuchadnezzar, and that the present-day Egypt is not ancient Egypt. *Redak* identifies Egypt with the Ishmaelites, or the Arabs, and Edom with Rome. These two nations are long powerful and will remain so until the redemption" (ibid., 113).

62. See Crenshaw, *Joel*, 202–203.

poured out by Egypt and Edom (Joel 4:19b [Eng., 3:19b]). The MT of Joel 4:21a (Eng., 3:21a) then looks like an incorrect reading ("And I will leave their blood unpunished") followed by a correction ("I do not leave unpunished"). On the other hand, the reading usually suggested on the basis of the LXX and Syriac is by far the easiest to explain: "And I will avenge [= וְנִקַּמְתִּי] their blood, and I will not leave unpunished [= וְלֹא אֲנַקֶּה]." But there are other possibilities for the rendering of the MT. One is that verse 21a is a rather unusual way of expressing Exodus 34:7: "And I will by no means leave their blood unpunished." In favor of this option is the citation of Exodus 34:6 in Joel 2:13. Another possibility is the one promoted by Calvin and Keil: "And I will cleanse their blood that I have not cleansed." This view takes the *piel* of נקה, which normally means "acquit, leave unpunished" (BDB, 667), to mean "cleanse" (cf., *niphal*). Calvin understands this to be the final cleansing of God's own people, while Keil seems to understand it to be the cleansing of the nations' guilt,[63] in which case the reader might expect the plural of דם ("bloodshed") rather than "their blood" (BDB, 196–97). This view also assumes that the second clause is an unintroduced relative clause, which is nothing unusual in poetic texts. Yet another possibility is that the first clause is a question: "And will I leave their blood unpunished?"[64] The second clause then gives a negative response. In favor of this option is the similar wording of Jeremiah 25:29, especially since Jeremiah 25:30 has already been cited in Joel 4:16 (Eng., 3:16). The only problem is that Jeremiah 25:29 uses the *niphal* for the main verb rather than the *piel* of Joel 4:21a (Eng., 3:21a). One last option is that the *piel* in Joel 4:21a (Eng., 3:21a) is declarative (GKC §52g): "And I will declare their blood innocent, which I have not declared innocent." This would then be something of an explanation for the wording of verse 19b. Judah was certainly not innocent in its previous relationship with the LORD, but now in its final vindication it is declared to be so insofar as it now represents the true people of God.

FINAL THOUGHTS ON JOEL

It would be a shame to lose the intended contemporary relevance of the book of Joel by treating it in isolation from the Twelve or by becoming bogged down in the assumed reconstruction of the prophet's historical context. There is a reason why such context is so obscured by the book itself. It would be a disservice to the author to take what he intends to keep in the background and to move it into

---

63. Calvin, *Joel*, 142; Keil, *Minor Prophets*, 153.
64. See Stuart, *Hosea–Jonah*, 264–65.

the foreground. Elaborate explanations of historical locust plagues tend to take the place of the biblical depiction and thus become the platform for all kinds of unbiblical messages. The loss of the book's eschatological message is only one version of what such an approach can produce. The success of the incorporation of the book of Joel into the overall program of the Twelve (Hos. 3:4–5) is attested by the citation of the book to explain the Pentecost event and to look forward to times of refreshing when Christ returns in the Day of the LORD (Acts 2–3). Here is the ongoing significance of the book as Christian Scripture for the church. It is indispensable for our understanding of the eschatological Day of the LORD in the Twelve, the Hebrew Bible, and in Christian theology. Without such hope, it is difficult for the individual believer to make sense of his or her daily life and struggles.

BOOK OF THE TWELVE

AMOS

The book of Amos begins with a superscription (Amos 1:1) and seam work (Amos 1:2a) that links the book to the end of Joel (Joel 4:16a [Eng., 3:16a]). It then divides into three main sections: Nations (Amos 1:3–2:16), Words and Woes (Amos 3–6), and Visions (Amos 7:1–9:10). The section on the nations crisscrosses the land of the covenant with very formulaic and stylized addresses to six surrounding foreign nations (Amos 1:3–2:3) before addressing Judah briefly (Amos 2:4–5) and reaching the ultimate goal, Israel (Amos 2:6–16). The words (Amos 3:1; 4:1; 5:1) and woes (Amos 5:18; 6:1) are each marked clearly at the beginning of their respective sub-units. Likewise, the five visions in the last section of the book are clearly delineated for the reader (Amos 7:1, 4, 7; 8:1; 9:1). This section also includes a brief narrative about Amos' encounter with Amaziah (Amos 7:10–17). The last five verses of the book (Amos 9:11–15) do not belong to the main body of the book and are part of a compositional seam that connects the book of Amos to the following work of Obadiah. Their message stands in stark contrast to that of the prophet Amos, but they make an important contribution to the overall composition of the Twelve.

AMOS 1:1–2

1:1 The words of Amos who was among the herdsmen [or, sheep/goat raiser/dealer/tender/breeder] from Tekoa, which he saw concerning Israel in the days of Uzziah the king of Judah and in the days of Jeroboam, the son of Joash, the king of Israel two years before the quake.

149

1:2 And he said, "The LORD, from Zion he roars, and from Jerusalem he gives his voice. And the pastures of the shepherds languish, and the top of Carmel withers."

The phrasing, "The words of Amos," (Amos 1:1a) is unique among super-scriptions within the Twelve, but it is found both in prophetic literature (Jer. 1:1; cf., LXX) and in non-prophetic literature (Prov. 30:1; 31:1; Eccl. 1:1; Neh. 1:1). It indicates that the book as a whole features the collected words of the prophet now organized in textual form. That is, the reader does not encounter the historical prophet delivering his oracles orally in flesh and blood. The prophet has been textualized in the literature of the book, and so the reader must interpret what is before him or her in literary categories. Amos is said to have been among the "herdsmen" (נקדים) from Tekoa about five or six miles south of Bethlehem (see Jer. 6:1), which is remarkable given the fact that he is primarily a prophet to the northern kingdom. Amos later indicates that he is not a profes-sional prophet for hire (Amos 7:14). Rather, he is a "herdsman" (בוקר) and "someone who tends sycamore trees" (בולס שקמים). Despite compar-ison to Mesha the Moabite king (2 Kgs. 3:4), these terms do not precisely define Amos' socioeconomic status, nor do they reveal the exact nature of Amos' occupation. What they do suggest is that it was only the call of God that compelled Amos to be a prophet (Amos 3:7–8).

The words of Amos are not the prophet's own. They are the words that the prophet "saw" (cf., Isa. 1:1; 2:1; 13:1; Hab. 1:1). That is, they were revealed to the prophet by means of prophetic vision. Furthermore, they are the words that Amos saw "concerning Israel." Apart from the brief address to Judah in Amos 2:4–5 (see also Amos 6:1), the prophet only has words of judgment for the northern kingdom of Israel. The reference to the fallen booth of David in Amos 9:11 belongs to the work of the composer of the Twelve (Amos 9:11–15) and likely envisions a united kingdom. Amos' prophetic ministry is set during the mid-eighth century BC in the days of Uzziah and Jeroboam II (cf., Isa. 1:1; Hos. 1:1; Mic. 1:1) for which 2 Kings 14–15 provides the narrative context. The reference to the Judean king Uzziah parallels the practice in the book of Kings of correlating the reigns of the kings in the north and the south. The designation "Jeroboam, the son of Joash" is to distinguish Jeroboam II from the original king of the north, Jeroboam I (1 Kgs. 12:25–33). It will be evident from the content of Amos that this period of time was one of great prosperity for the north that led to equally great complacency with regard to the covenant relationship (Amos 6:1). Amos shares a negative assessment of Israel with the author of Kings and with the prophet Hosea.

The superscription further indicates that Amos saw his words "two years before the quake," perhaps the same quake referenced in Zech. 14:5. This quake was apparently so well known that one could refer to it simply as "the quake" without any further designation. Thus, someone with this later historical perspective was able to look back at the prophet's words and give such a point of reference. Why? One very real possibility is the link between Joel 4:16a (Eng., 3:16a) and Amos 1:2a. In Joel 4:16a (Eng., 3:16a), the result of the LORD roaring from Zion is the quaking of sky and land. The book of Amos begins with the LORD roaring from Zion (Amos 1:2a), and the superscription informs the reader of a quake two years after the words of judgment in Amos' book.

As noted in the Introduction and in the commentary on Joel 4:16a (Eng., 3:16a), Amos 1:2a forms part of a compositional seam that connects Joel to Amos. It meets the criterion of distinctiveness in that it is neither part of the superscription nor part of the first section of the book in Amos 1:3–2:16.[1] It features citation from the book of Jeremiah (Jer. 25:30), which is the calling card of the composer of the Twelve. And it ties into the Twelve's message of eschatological judgment and messianic salvation (Hos. 3:4–5) by means of the context of Joel 4:16a (Eng., 3:16a), which mentions the Day of the LORD (Joel 4:14 [Eng., 3:14]; see also Joel 2:2; Amos 5:18). The image of the LORD roaring like a lion anticipates the comparison between the LORD and a lion in Amos 3:4, 8. The giving of his voice from Jerusalem raises the expectation of words of judgment directed to the nations as in Joel 4:16a (Eng., 3:16a), only now the words will include Israel as the LORD's words once did when he gave his voice from Sinai (Exod. 19:16, 19; see commentary on Joel 4:16a [Eng., 3:16a]).

The line about the languishing of the shepherds' pastures and the withering of the top of Carmel is fitting for several reasons (Amos 1:2b). First, it speaks to the effect of the LORD's roaring and the giving of his voice. Second, the pastoral context matches the description of Amos' occupation in the superscription. Third, the image of the desolation of once fertile places is reminiscent of what the reader has just encountered in the book of Joel with the locust plague (see Amos 7:1–3). It also contrasts with the picture of the transformation of dry places into well-watered places in Joel 4:18 (Eng., 3:18). Shepherds' pastures obviously had to be fertile in order to be functional, and Carmel was a notoriously fertile location on the Mediterranean coast (see BDB, 502). In fact, the phrase "the top of Carmel" could also be translated "the

---

1. In fact, the verb וַיֹּאמַר ("And he said") at the beginning of Amos 1:2 could easily be the introduction to Amos 1:3 (cf., Josh. 24:2).

best of the plantation." It would do no good to illustrate the effects of judgment by speaking of the decline of an average location. That would be like showing the force of hurricane winds by pointing the camera at a bank rather than a palm tree.

AMOS 1:3–2:3

1:3 "Thus says the LORD, 'For the three transgressions of Damascus and for four I will not turn it back [Tg. Jon.: I will not forgive them; GKC §134l, s], for their threshing with the iron sledges Gilead [Tg. Jon.: the inhabitants of the land of Gilead; LXX: because they cut with iron saws the pregnant women who were in Gilead; GKC §158c]. 1:4 And I will send fire against the house of Hazael, and it will consume the fortresses of Ben Hadad. 1:5 And I will break the bar of Damascus, and I will cut off inhabitant [or, the one who sits on the throne] from the valley of Aven [or, valley of trouble] and one grasping a ruler's scepter from Beth Eden [or, house of luxury; LXX: I will cut off a tribe from the men of Haran], and the people of Aram will go into exile to Kir,' says the LORD."

1:6 "Thus says the LORD, 'For the three transgressions of Gaza and for four I will not turn it back, for their taking into exile a complete group of exiles [LXX: the captives of Solomon] to deliver to Edom. 1:7 And I will send fire against the city wall of Gaza, and it will consume its fortresses. 1:8 And I will cut off inhabitant [or, the one who sits on the throne] from Ashdod and one grasping a ruler's scepter from Ashkelon; and I will turn my hand against Ekron, and the remainder of Philistines will perish,' says the LORD."[2]

1:9 "Thus says the LORD, 'For the three transgressions of Tyre and for

---

2. The MT has אָמַר אֲדֹנָי יְהוִה ("says the Lord GOD"), following the practice of vocalizing the divine name with the vowels of *Elohim* whenever it stands next to *Adonai*, whose vowels the divine name would normally take according to the *qere perpetuum*. The LXX, however, simply reads κύριος as if the original text were what the reader finds in Amos 1:5, 15; 2:3. This discrepancy between the MT and the LXX occurs throughout the book of Ezekiel in particular, suggesting that early insertion of אֲדֹנָי into the consonantal text was a way to guide the reader as to the appropriate substitute for the divine name, which was not to be pronounced, when reading the text aloud. It was only much later that the *kethiv/qere* tradition could be expressed through vowel pointing.

four I will not turn it back, for their delivering a complete group of exiles to Edom, and they did not remember an agreement of brothers [GKC §114r]. 1:10 And I will send fire against the city wall of Tyre, and it will consume its fortresses.'"

1:11 "Thus says the LORD, 'For the three transgressions of Edom and for four I will not turn it back, for his pursuing with his sword his brother, and he destroyed his compassion [or, allies; LXX: womb], and he tore them like prey continually [LXX: as a witness] in his anger [Syr.: he kept his anger continually], and as for his fury, he kept it [GKC §58g, 91e] perpetually. 1:12 And I will send fire against Teman, and it will consume the fortresses of Bozrah [LXX: the foundations of its walls].'"

1:13 "Thus says the LORD, 'For the three transgressions of the sons of Ammon [or, the Ammonites] and for four I will not turn it back, for their splitting apart the pregnant women of Gilead in order to expand their border. 1:14 And I will kindle a fire against the city wall of Rabbah, and it will consume its fortresses, with a shout in a day of battle, with a tempest in a day of storm wind [LXX: it will be shaken in the day of its completion]. 1:15 And their king [Syr.: Milcom] will go into exile [or, with the exiles], he and his princes/officials [Syr.: his priests and his nobles] together,' says the LORD."

2:1 "Thus says the LORD, 'For the three transgressions of Moab and for four I will not turn it back, for his burning the bones of the king of Edom into lime. 2:2 And I will send fire against Moab, and it will consume the fortresses of Kerioth [Tg. Jon.: the city]. And Moab will die with a crash [LXX: with impotence], with a shout, with a sound of a shofar. 2:3 And I will cut off judge from its midst, and all its officials will I slaughter with him,' says the LORD."

Oracles directed to the nations are familiar to the reader of the Prophets (e.g., Isa. 13–23; Jer. 46–51; Ezek. 25–32). Such oracles are not always words of judgment (e.g., Isa. 19:16–25), nor are they always strictly historical; that is, they can be eschatological (e.g., Jer. 48:47; 49:39). The oracles in Amos 1:3–2:3 do follow the pattern of a judgment oracle: introduction (Amos 1:3a, 6a, 9a, 11a, 13a; 2:1a), accusation (Amos 1:3b, 6b, 9b, 11b, 13b; 2:1b), and announcement of judgment (Amos 1:4–5, 7–8, 10, 12, 14–15; 2:2–3). These addresses to six different nations are designed to prime the pump for the words of judgment directed to Judah (Amos 2:4–5) and Israel (Amos 2:5–16). They begin with Damascus in the northeast (Amos 1:3–5) and move to Gaza in the southwest (Amos 1:6–8), then to Tyre in the northwest (Amos 1:9–10) and finally to Edom (Amos 1:11–12), Ammon (Amos 1:13–15), and Moab (Amos 2:1–3) in the east and southeast before hitting squarely on the land of the covenant.

Each introduction features a prophetic formula ("Thus says the LORD") and a numerical formula ("For the three transgressions of . . . and for four I will not turn it back"). Unlike the use of the numerical formula in Proverbs 30, the examples in Amos 1:3–2:3 do not actually enumerate three or four items. It appears to be a stylistic device designed to express the completeness of the crimes committed, as the numbers three, seven, and ten are known to do throughout biblical literature. The use of the number four is a feature of the Hebrew parallelism. That is, there is no synonym for a number like three, so the next number above three is given in order to advance the thought in the parallel. What is it exactly that the LORD will not turn back? Since there is no obvious antecedent for the pronoun, it is likely a proleptic use that points forward to the announcement of judgment. In other words, the LORD will not relent with regard to the judgment that he plans to bring against the nations. In addition to similarity of introduction, the oracles also share a common element in their announcements of judgment: fire (Amos 1:4, 7, 10, 12, 14; 2:2). Stories and images of divine judgment by fire (e.g., Gen. 19; Isa. 66:15–17) are well known to readers of the Bible, but the present context likely has in view the practice of burning conquered cities (e.g., 2 Kgs. 25:9).

What really sets apart the different oracles in this section are the specific accusations leveled against the individual nations. These all have to do with international war crimes. From a biblical standpoint, such crimes are in direct violation of the terms of the covenant with Noah (Gen. 9:5–7), which God established with all the nations (Gen. 10). Thus, regardless of the religious allegiances of these different nations, the one true God holds them accountable for their breach. It is not as though the nations listed here were unaware of the God of Israel. On the other hand, the actions committed by these nations would have been recognized as war crimes without any special revelation, as they have been throughout history. It is worth noting that the time of judgment for the nations is not always given in the oracles. The use of the phrase "in that day" in Amos 2:16 is perhaps designed to lend an eschatological sense to Amos 1–2 (cf., Joel 4:18 [Eng., 3:18; Amos 9:11; Mic. 4:1, 6), indicating that a final day of judgment may very well be in view. If this was not the case for Amos, it certainly would have been for the composer of the Twelve.

The accusation against Damascus has to do with their egregious and violent threshing of nearby Gilead with sharp instruments of iron

(Amos 1:3b). The LXX interprets this to be the same as what is said about Ammon in Amos 1:13b, the splitting apart of pregnant women, although the expression in Amos 1:3b is not necessarily limited to such action (but see 2 Kgs. 8:12). The announcement of judgment in Amos 1:4 is directed specifically against the house or dynasty of Hazael and the fortresses of Hazael's son Ben Hadad (2 Kgs. 8:12; 13:3; cf., Jer. 49:27). The *BHS* apparatus suggests rearranging the clauses of Amos 1:5 according to what the reader finds in Amos 1:8a so that the parallelism is tighter, but there is no textual evidence to make this decision. As it stands, the verse is arranged in chiastic fashion. The breaking of the bar of Damascus indicates the destruction of the city's defenses. The next two clauses are likely references to the ruler (cf., Isa. 10:13), following the mention of Hazael and Ben Hadad. These references use pejorative names for Damascus ("valley of trouble" and "house of luxury"). The final clause forecasts a reversal of Aram's history. According to Amos 9:7, the Arameans originally came from Kir. The LORD will essentially send them back to where they belong. The text of 2 Kings 16:9 narrates the fulfillment of this prophecy.

The accusation against Gaza deals with their taking into exile "a complete group of exiles" for the purpose of delivering them to Edom (Amos 1:6b). The text does not provide the details of the identity of the exiles, the nature of the transaction, or what Edom did with the exiles once they were delivered. Keil suggests that this is a reference to what the reader finds in Joel 4:4–8 (Eng., 3:3–8) and 2 Chronicles 21:16. A complete group of exiles is presumably a collection of captives without discrimination against age, gender, or civilian status (see Calvin). The announcement of judgment in Amos 1:7–8 mentions three other Philistine cities in addition to Gaza: Ashdod, Ashkelon, and Ekron (cf., Amos 3:9; Zeph. 2:4–7; Zech. 9:5–6). There were five major Philistine cities in all (1 Sam. 6:17). Perhaps the reference to "the remainder of the Philistines" is a reference to the fifth city, Gath. The accusation against Tyre in Amos 1:9b is initially similar to the one against Gaza, but then it mentions their failure to remember "a covenant of brothers." This is usually taken to mean that they forgot the healthy relationship that Hiram the king of Tyre once had with David and Solomon, as it is described in 1 Kings 5:15, 26 (Eng., 5:1, 12).

The accusation against Edom in Amos 1:11b comes in the midst of several references to Edom in the immediate context (Amos 1:6b, 9b; 2:1b; see also Joel 4:19 [Eng., 3:19]). Edom will play a major role in the connection between the end of Amos (Amos 9:12) and the following book of Obadiah as the representative Gentile nation, both positively and negatively (cf., Isa. 34; Ezek. 34–36). Here Edom/Esau is accused of pursuing his own brother, Israel/Jacob, with the sword (cf., Gen. 27:40). Of course, Jacob and Esau had their problems as brothers (Gen. 27:41), but this also played itself out in the subsequent history of the relationship between the two nations that came from them (Gen. 25:23; Num. 20:14–21; 2 Sam. 8:14; 2 Kgs. 8:20–22; Mal. 1:2–5; 2 Chr. 28:17). Verse 12 mentions two Edomite cities in the announcement of judgment by fire: Teman and Bozrah.

The origin of Ammon and Moab is well known from the story of Lot and his daughters in Genesis 19:29–38 (see also Deut. 2; Judg. 11; Zeph. 2:8–11). Ammon's heinous crime was the ripping apart of pregnant women for the sole purpose of expanding its territory (Amos 1:13b; cf., 2 Kgs. 8:12; Isa. 13:16; Hos. 10:14; 14:1 [Eng., 13:16]; Nah. 3:10; Ps. 137:9). It was not enough to defeat their enemies. They humiliated the peoples they conquered and put the fear of such atrocities in any who would oppose them. The announcement of judgment in Amos 1:14–15 includes not only the judgment by fire but also the accompanying battle cry (cf., Jer. 49:2), storm wind (cf., Nah. 1:3b), and the exile of the Ammonite king and his officials (cf., Jer. 49:3). The Syriac version vocalizes the word translated "their king" (מלכם) as "Milcom," the name of the Ammonite god (1 Kgs. 11:5, 33; Jer. 49:1, 3 [LXX, Syr., Vulg.]). The stated offense of Moab is his burning of the bones of the king of Edom into lime (Amos 2:1b; cf., 2 Kgs. 3:26–27; Isa 33:12; see also 1 Kgs. 13:2; 2 Kgs. 23:16, 20; 2 Chr. 34:5). This is sometimes described as desecration of the dead for the mere purpose of making plaster (see Deut. 27:2). The fire against Moab will consume the fortresses of Kerioth (Amos 2:2a; see Jer. 48:24, 41). Moab will perish amidst the sounds of battle (Amos 2:2b). Amos 2:3 is roughly parallel to Amos 1:15 with the term "judge" carrying the sense of "ruler" or "king" (BDB, 1047).

AMOS 2:4–16

2:4 "Thus says the LORD, 'For the three transgressions of Judah and for four I will not turn it back, for their rejecting the instruction of the LORD, and his statutes they did not keep, and their lies after which their forefathers went led them astray. 2:5 And I will send fire against Judah, and it will consume the fortresses of Jerusalem.'"

2:6 "Thus says the LORD, 'For the three transgressions of Israel and for four I will not turn it back, for their selling for silver a righteous person, and a needy person for a pair of sandals, 2:7 those who trample on the dust of the ground the head of the poor [cf., LXX] and turn aside the way of the afflicted. Both a man and his father go to the young woman in order to profane my holy name. 2:8 And on clothes taken in pledge [LXX: binding with ropes] they stretch out next to every altar, and wine from those fined they drink in the house of their God [or, their god(s); Tg. Jon.: their idols]. 2:9 But as for me, I destroyed the Amorite from before them whose height was like the height of cedar trees, and strong was he like the oaks, and I destroyed his fruit from above and his roots from below. 2:10 And I am the one who brought you up out of the land of Egypt, and I walked you through the wilderness for forty years to possess the land of the Amorite. 2:11 And I raised up some of your sons for prophets and some of your choice, young men for nazirites [LXX: holiness; Tg. Jon.: teachers]. Is this not indeed the case, O sons of Israel?' the prophetic utterance of the LORD. 2:12 'And you gave the nazirites wine to drink, and to the prophets you commanded saying, "Do not prophesy." 2:13 Look, I am about to press [LXX: roll; Syr.: loathe, be weary; grieve][3] you in your place just as the full cart that has a sheaf presses.[4] 2:14 And flight will perish from a swift person, and a strong person, he will not make firm his strength; and a mighty man, he will not deliver himself, 2:15 and the holder of the bow [i.e., the archer], he will not remain; and a person swift in his feet, he will not deliver himself [see BDB, 572; LXX: escape (= niphal)], and the rider of the horse, he will not deliver himself; 2:16 and a person strong in his heart [GKC §128y; 4QXII[c]: ומוצא] among the mighty men [LXX: and he will find his heart in powers], naked will he flee in that day,' the prophetic utterance of the LORD."

The *BHS* textual apparatus marks Amos 2:4–5 as an addition. This is because these verses address the southern kingdom of Judah in a book otherwise largely devoted to words of judgment directed to the northern kingdom of Israel. It is true that the address to Israel in Amos 2:6–16 is the ultimate goal of the first two chapters, as its placement and length suggest, but it is important to keep in mind that Amos 1:3–2:3 featured all the kingdoms that surrounded Israel with the exception of Judah, so it would actually be somewhat unusual not to see any reference to the south. Furthermore, there is no textual support for the omission of Amos 2:4–5. In contrast to the nations in Amos 1:3–2:3, the accusation against Judah has nothing to do with war crimes. The LORD accuses them of rejecting his *torah* ("instruction") (cf., Isa. 5:24b). The coordination of this

---

3. Several suggestions from Arabic have been made for this verb (see *HALOT* 1:802). The present translation understands עוק to be the Aramaic form of צוק (BDB, 734).

4. *Tg. Jon.*: "Look, I am about to bring upon you distress and oppress you in your place just as the cart to which is loaded the sheaf totters."

term with "his statutes," which they did not keep, suggests that it is not a specific reference to the Book of the Torah (i.e., the Pentateuch) but a reference to the kinds of laws found therein that formed the basis of the old covenant relationship. In particular, "their lies" (i.e., their idols) led them astray (cf., Ps. 40:5 [Eng., 40:4]; see BDB, 469). Idolatry was at the heart of covenant failure (Exod. 20:2–6; 32), and it was something that passed from one generation to the next (Jer. 2:5, 9). (For the announcement of judgment in Amos 2:5, see Jer. 17:27b; Hos. 8:14.)

The address to Israel divides into three sub-units: introduction and accusation (Amos 2:6–8), narrative context (Amos 2:9–12), and announcement of judgment (Amos 2:13–16). Naturally the tendency of critical scholarship has been to regard Amos 2:9–12 as a secondary interruption of the typical pattern of a judgment oracle.[5] Once again, there is no textual evidence for this decision, but more importantly, it is not out of character for the prophets to set their oracles within the context of the larger biblical narrative (e.g., Isa. 63:7–14; Jer. 2:1–13; Ezek. 20; Hos. 12; Mic. 6:1–8).[6] The accusation against Israel in Amos 2:6b–8 is the only one in Amos 1–2 that actually enumerates the four transgressions of the accused: (1) selling the righteous, (2) trampling the poor, (3) profanation of the LORD's name, and (4) misuse of items taken in pledge or by fine. Like Judah, these offenses are not general, international crimes. They are breaches of the terms of the covenant relationship established with Israel at Sinai.

The first accusation in Amos 2:6b refers to seizure of the property of the innocent on the basis of false accusation and corrupt judgment (cf., Exod. 21:2–11; Lev. 25:35–55; Deut. 15:12–18; 25:9–10; 1 Kgs. 21; Amos 8:6).[7] This suggests that the accusation here primarily deals with

---

5. Jörg Jeremias, *The Book of Amos: A Commentary*, trans. Douglas W. Stott, OTL (Louisville: Westminster John Knox, 1998), 38–39. Jeremias believes that these verses derive from Deuteronomistic theology and belong to an exilic edition of the book of Amos. He cites W. H. Schmidt, "Die deuteronomistische Redaktion des Amosbuches," *ZAW* 77 (1965): 168–93.

6. See Michael B. Shepherd, *The Textual World of the Bible* (New York: Peter Lang, 2013), 34–42.

7. See William R. Harper, *A Critical and Exegetical Commentary on Amos and Hosea*, ICC (New York: Charles Scribner's Sons, 1905), 49; C. F. Keil, *The Minor Prophets*, trans. James Martin, Keil & Delitzsch Commentary on the Old Testament 10 (Edinburgh: T. & T. Clark, 1866–91; reprint, Peabody, MA: Hendrickson, 2001), 170. Tertullian believed that this was a prophecy about Judas' betrayal of Jesus for silver as in Zechariah 11:12–13; Matthew 27:9–10 (Alberto Ferreiro, ed., *The Twelve Prophets*, ACCS XIV [Downers Grove, IL: InterVarsity, 2003], 88).

those in positions of privilege, power, and authority who have abused their position (cf., Mic. 3). The oppression of the lowly in Amos 2:7a continues along this line of thought. Those who were entrusted with the responsibility of fair judgment have turned aside the way to justice for the afflicted and the marginalized (cf., Isa. 10:12; Amos 4:1; 5:12; 8:4; Job 24:4; Prov. 18:5; Lam. 3:35).

The nature of the third accusation in Amos 2:7b is debated, although it is clear to all that the purpose or result of the offense of the accused is the profanation of the LORD's name (cf., Lev. 22:32). Some think that the offense is a father and son having sex with the same woman (see Lev. 18), but there are several problems with this interpretation. For instance, the expression "Both a man and his father" does not necessarily mean that the two did something "together" (יחד). It may simply be an indication that the sons follow in the sins of the fathers (cf., Amos 2:4b). Furthermore, the expression "go to" (הלך אל) a woman is not the normal Hebrew idiom for sexual relations (cf., בוא אל). The word for the woman is נערה, a "girl" or "young woman," which has led to the suggestion that this is an abused servant girl, but this reading has little support from the context. The use of the definite article with this term does not require the sense "the same young woman." The article here may only indicate class (GKC §126m). Perhaps the most plausible interpretation given the cultic references in verse 8 is that the father and the son, whether separately or together, go to the cultic site to have sexual relations with prostitutes (cf., Deut. 23:18; Hos. 4:14).

The fourth accusation deals first with the misuse of garments taken in pledge (Amos 2:8). Such necessities were not to be withheld from their owners (Exod. 22:25–26), and they certainly were not to be used for spreading out next to altars at alternative worship sites. Given that this address is to the northern kingdom of Israel, the reader can be quite confident that the altar and the temple mentioned in this verse have nothing to do with the temple in Jerusalem (1 Kgs. 12:25–33).[8] These people also bought wine for their inappropriate religious practices (cf., Amos 6:6) with the money seized from the fined (whether justly or unjustly). In their minds, this was all done in the house of their God, but the true God obviously considered their so-called temple to be the house of their god(s).

The fronted pronoun (ואנכי) at the beginning of Amos 2:9a marks the shift to the recounting of the LORD's faithfulness (see also Amos

---

8. See John Calvin, *Commentaries on the Twelve Minor Prophets*, vol. 2, *Joel, Amos, Obadiah*, trans. John Owen, Calvin's Commentaries XIV (reprint, Grand Rapids: Baker, 2005), 186.

2:10a). It is always the mode of operation for the prophets to see the biblical story as their story and to orient their own prophecies to the framework of the biblical narrative. The text of Amos 2:9–12 does not represent a variant oral tradition independent of the Pentateuch, which in any case would not be demonstrable given the lack of access to such a tradition. Rather, the text is aligned with what the reader finds in the book of Moses. Thus, on the basis of this evidence it should be interpreted as the prophet's exegesis of the biblical text.

At first glance the presentation appears to be out of chronological order, starting with the conquest and then moving back to the exodus (Amos 2:9–10). But the wording of Amos 2:9a, which uses the term "Amorite" for all the peoples of the land of Canaan, derives from the forecast of the conquest in the story of the making of the covenant with Abram (Gen. 15:16; cf., Gen. 48:22) prior to the account of the exodus in the sequence of the Pentateuch (Exod. 14). Again, this indicates awareness of the actual text of the book of Moses. Such a detail would be difficult to explain from oral tradition. Verse 9b describes the inhabitants of the land as being as tall as trees (Num. 13:33; Deut. 1–3; CD-A 2:19) and then extends the simile by describing their destruction as the cutting down of trees from top (fruit) to bottom (root). These were the kind of people whom the LORD (and no other) destroyed on Israel's behalf (Josh. 10:42).

The book of Amos references the exodus several times as the central act of divine deliverance and the foundation for the making of the covenant (Amos 2:10a; 3:1; 9:7; cf., Exod. 20:2). The LORD, the very one whose covenant Israel has broken, is the one who brought them out of Egypt, not the so-called gods/idols of the surrounding peoples. He also led them through the wilderness and provided for their every need for forty years not only because of their rebellion but also in spite of their rebellion (Amos 2:10b; see Num. 11–20; cf., Deut. 29:4 [Eng., 29:5]; Jer. 2:6). This was all with the purpose of granting possession of the land of the covenant in accordance with what was spoken to the patriarchs, yet the conquest remained incomplete (Josh. 13:1; Judg. 1:27–36; Heb. 4:9), in large part because the people quickly forgot what the LORD had done and thus persisted in their rebellion due to their unbelief (Ps. 78; 106; Neh. 9).

One particularly important expression of God's grace that the people failed to appreciate, although the rhetorical question in Amos 2:11b suggests that they knew about it enough to be held accountable for it, was the extension of the role of Moses through the establishment of the office of the true prophet (Amos 2:11–12; see Deut. 18). The prophet was to be God's means of communicating to the people through the explication of the book of Moses, the Torah. The people were not to seek revelation by any other means (Isa. 8:16–20). But they rejected the prophets (2 Kgs. 17:13–14) in favor of false prophets who told them what they wanted to hear (Jer. 6:14; 23; 27–28; Ezek. 13–14)—messages of restoration rather than messages of judgment. They so much desired this false sense of security that they commanded the true prophets not to prophesy (Isa. 30:10; Jer. 11:21; Amos 7:13; Mic. 2:6), something that simply was not an option for someone genuinely called by God (Jer. 20:9; Amos 3:8; 7:14–17).

Given the importance of the prophets, it is worth asking why they are coordinated with nazirites in this passage (Num. 6; Judg. 13; Jer. 35).[9] This is not to downplay the nazirite vow, but it is difficult to see how the typical nazirite compares to the role of the prophet. *Targum Jonathan* renders "nazirites" as "teachers," that is, those consecrated to the study of the Torah (see Rashi). According to this reading, "nazirites" (i.e., consecrated ones) are not specifically those who have taken the nazirite vow. Rather, the term is parallel to "prophets." The prophets were the ones set apart for the study and teaching of the Torah (see 2 Kgs. 17:13; Dan. 9:10; Ezra 9:10–11; see also Prov. 29:18 LXX). But does not Amos 9:12a argue against this when it says that the people gave the nazirites wine to drink (supposedly in violation of their vow), either by force or by a general culture of influence that discouraged or failed to encourage strict adherence to the terms of the vow? Actually, this refers to dilution of the prophets by encouraging them to tell the people what they wanted to hear in exchange for wine and strong drink (cf., Mic. 2:11).

The announcement of judgment in Amos 2:13–16 begins with a verse whose translation is disputed, although it is usually understood to indicate that the LORD is about to put pressure on Israel in some way. There will be no escape from this judgment (cf., Amos 9:1–4), even for the fastest and the strongest among them (cf., 1QM 14:11). Warriors will not be able to save themselves, and archers will not remain. Neither on foot nor on horse will the swift deliver themselves. Not even the most stouthearted of the mighty men will be able to avoid running away naked and ashamed. As noted above, the phrase "in that day" leaves the prophecy somewhat open ended and undefined

---

9. Note the chiastic structure of Amos 2:11–12: prophets, nazirites, nazirites, and prophets. Douglas Stuart suggests that the expected term here would be the priests (cf., Jer. 2:8), but the illegitimacy of the northern priesthood (1 Kgs. 12:31–32) led to the choice of another term (*Hosea–Jonah*, WBC 31 [Nashville: Thomas Nelson, 1987], 318), but this does not explain the selection of nazirites in particular.

temporally (cf., Amos 4:2; 5:13; 6:3; 8:3, 9, 11, 13; 9:11, 13). The *BHS* apparatus raises the question of whether this is an addition, but it is probably best seen as an authorial attempt to give an eschatological sense to the oracles, a sense that would ensure the ongoing relevance of their message for future generations of readers.

AMOS 3

3:1 "Hear this word that the LORD has spoken against you, O sons of Israel [LXX, Syr.: house of Israel], against all the family that I brought up out of the land of Egypt, saying, 3:2 'Only you have I known from all the families of the earth. Therefore, I will visit upon you all your iniquities [i.e., the punishments for your iniquities].'"

3:3 "Do two walk together unless they have met by appointment? 3:4 Does a lion roar in the forest, and it has no prey? Does a young lion give its voice from its den unless it has captured something? 3:5 Does a bird fall upon the trap [> LXX] of the ground, and there is no bait for it [or, it (i.e., the ground) has no bait]? Does a trap spring up from the ground, and it does not indeed capture anything? 3:6 If a shofar is blasted in a city, do people not tremble? If calamity occurs in a city, is the LORD not the one who has done it? 3:7 Certainly [BDB, 472; LXX, Syr., Tg. Jon., Vulg., Luther: For] the LORD [or, Lord GOD]¹⁰ does not do a thing unless he reveals his counsel to his servants the prophets. 3:8 It is a lion that has roared, who does not fear? It is the LORD [or, Lord GOD] who has spoken, who does not prophesy?"

Amos 3:1 ("Hear this word") marks the first of three messages of judgment from the prophet to Israel (Amos 4:1; 5:1; cf., Deut. 4:1; 5:1; 6:4; Hos. 4:1; 5:1). It is the message that the LORD has spoken against the Israelites in particular (cf., Amos 2:6). This raises a question about the identity of "all the family that I brought up out of the land of Egypt," since this would presumably have included the ancestors of those now in the land of Judah as well.¹¹ In response, it must be noted that the

---

10. The combination אֲדֹנָי יהוה is likely an early attempt to indicate in the consonantal text what should be read (אֱלֹהִים) for the divine name (יהוה). See LXX Ezekiel, which often has κύριος where the MT has אֲדֹנָי יהוה. See also Amos 3:8.

11. See Calvin, *Amos*, 200. The switch to first person here is admittedly odd at first sight (see Jeremias, *Amos*, 49), but there is no textual evidence that omits it. The reader of the Twelve, however, is now accustomed to

earlier reference to the exodus in Amos 2:10 was given in the context of the address to Israel (Amos 2:6–16; see also Amos 9:7). Psalm 78 provides a helpful model for the resolution of this apparent discrepancy. After the introduction (Ps. 78:1–8), the psalm walks through the biblical narrative beginning with the exodus account (Ps. 78:12–13), specifically highlighting the unbelief of the people in spite of the LORD's faithful provision (Ps. 78:22, 32). On the surface this would appear to be the story of all Israel/Judah. But closer examination reveals that Psalm 78:9 alerts the reader to the fact that the failures documented in the psalm are actually the failures of Ephraim (i.e., the northern kingdom of Israel), setting up the contrast with the chosen tribe of Judah in Psalm 78:67–72.

The LORD says, "Only you have I known from all the families of the earth" (Amos 3:2a). This special recognition of Israel is a reference to the unmerited election of Abraham and his descendants to be the instrument of the restoration of the lost blessing of life and dominion in the land to all the nations (Gen. 12:3; 28:14; Exod. 19:5; Deut. 7:7–11; Neh. 9:7). The choice of the term מִשְׁפָּחָה ("family") as opposed to גּוֹי ("nation"), עַם ("people"), or even שֵׁבֶט/אֵלֶף ("tribe") likely stems from its use in Genesis 12:3; 28:14, which is broader in its application than a mere subset of a tribe within a larger people or nation (BDB, 1047). Because of Israel's elected status, the people bear a greater responsibility than the other nations, and with that responsibility comes stricter judgment (Amos 3:2b; cf., Luke 12:48; Jas. 3:1).[12] This was already anticipated in Amos 2:4–16 where the special revelation from the LORD and the special history with the LORD meant that words of judgment for both Judah and Israel would look different than those directed to the other nations for war crimes.[13]

---

unmarked shifts from the voice of the prophet to the voice of the LORD and back (cf., Hosea, Joel). It is difficult to label this piece of text as part of a systematic redaction of the book.

12. *"Ibn Ezra* and *Redak* explain that, since Israel is closer to God than the other nations, being His nation and witnessing His wonders and miracles, God is stricter with them than with the other nations. They give the example of the king, who is stricter with his servants who stand before him to serve him, who are familiar with the procedure of his court, than he is with the villagers, who are totally unfamiliar with it" (*Mikraoth Gedoloth: The Twelve Prophets*, vol. 1, trans. A. J. Rosenberg (Brooklyn: Judaica, 1986), 126.

13. Jeremias notes well the importance of this verse for the book as a whole: "With v. 2, the tradents positioned a summary of the commissioned divine oracle before Amos' own reproofs against individual circumstances of sin in vv. 9ff. Its position between the superscription and the pericope of

The series of rhetorical questions in Amos 3:3–6 is designed to set up the main point in Amos 3:7–8. Earlier commentators sought to find in these questions veiled references to the relationship between Israel and the LORD,[14] but more recently the tendency has been to regard them as references to common features of everyday life that would be recognizable to all with the hope that what is then said in Amos 3:7–8 would be accepted as equally obvious and self-evident.[15] Two people do not walk together randomly or arbitrarily (Amos 3:3). A lion does not roar without reason (Amos 3:4; cf., Isa. 5:29; 31:4). A bird does not normally descend upon a trap unless there is bait to attract it, and a trap does not usually spring unless there is something in it to trigger the mechanism for the capture (Amos 3:5). A warning alarm does not sound in a city without striking some measure of fear within the people (Amos 3:6a; cf., Jer. 4:5; 6:1; Hos. 5:8). And no "calamity" (רעה) occurs in a city apart from divine providence (Amos 3:6b; cf., Gen. 50:20; Job 2:10; Eccl. 7:14; Lam. 3:37–38).[16]

Jeremias considers Amos 3:7 to be part of a later deuteronomistic redaction that attempts to make Amos 3:8 into "a timelessly valid doctrinal statement."[17] It is true that Amos 3:7 interrupts the poetic parallelism in Amos 3:3–8, but there are several problems with Jeremias' formulation. First, such a conversion of Amos 3:8 would be expected after the verse, not before it. Second, there is no textual evidence to suggest that Amos 3:7 was ever absent.[18] And finally, the language of Amos 3:7 is not uniquely deuteronomistic. For instance, the term סוד

---

legitimation show two things: First, it attests the great import of this divine oracle, which stands representatively for all of Amos' divine oracles—'this also could have served as a motto for the entire book' (Wellhausen); second, it indicates that in the eyes of the readers this oracle will be an extremely unusual, indeed offensive statement in need of special justification. Whoever wishes to understand the book of Amos must above all understand Amos 3:2 in the sense of its first edition" (*Amos*, 49). Jeremias also believes that the terminology of this verse is unique within the book of Amos and intentionally creates associations with Hosea (e.g., Hos. 13:5).

14. E.g., Calvin, *Amos*, 204–210; Keil, *Minor Prophets*, 175–76.
15. Stuart, *Hosea–Jonah*, 324; Jeremias, *Amos*, 51.
16. See John Chrysostom's distinction between two kinds of evils (Ferreiro, ed., *Twelve Prophets*, 92).
17. Jeremias, *Amos*, 54.
18. The lack of textual evidence is not by itself an argument against the claim. It is certainly possible that there was revision of the book that resulted in discontinued transmission of previous versions. But variant literary editions of sections and books are often supported by textual witnesses (see

("counsel") does not appear anywhere in Deuteronomy–Kings. Amos 3:7 is the author's own preemptive effort to make his point in the form of a propositional statement, thus making it impossible for the reader to miss the meaning of the line of questioning in Amos 3:8.

The asseverative כִּי at the beginning of Amos 3:7 lends the same certitude to the statement that the preceding rhetorical questions are intended to provide. The LORD does not do a thing unless he reveals his counsel (cf., Prov. 3:32) to his servants the prophets (cf., Gen. 18:17; 20:7; 2 Kgs. 4:27; 17:13, 23; Dan. 9:10; Ezra 9:10–11). That is, the LORD established the role of the prophet to communicate his will to his people (Deut. 18; Amos 2:11). Amos clearly sees himself as one of the truly called prophets of the LORD with a message to deliver and he wants his audience to know the legitimacy of what he has to say however unpleasant and unpopular it may be (cf., Mic. 3:8).[19] Amos 3:8 is the poetic version of this. If a lion roars, who does not fear or respect that roar (cf., Joel 4:16 [Eng., 3:16]; Amos 1:2)? If the LORD speaks, who does not prophesy? Amos 3:8b is the interpretation of Amos 3:8a.[20] The true prophet is compelled to speak not by the pay of a professional prophet or prophet for hire (Amos 7:14; Mic. 2:11; 3:5, 11) but by the genuine call of God (Amos 7:15; cf., Jer. 20:9).

3:9 "Make proclamation to fortresses in Ashdod [LXX: among Assyrians], and to fortresses in the land [> LXX] of Egypt, and say, 'Gather on the mountains [LXX: mountain] of Samaria and see great confusion [GKC §124e] in its midst and oppression [or, oppressed] within it [> Syr.].' 3:10 'And they do not know to do right [Tg. Jon.: Torah; LXX: And it does not know what things will be before it],' the prophetic utterance of the LORD, 'those who store violence and destruction in their fortresses.' 3:11 Therefore, thus says the LORD [MT: Lord GOD; אֲדֹנָי > Syr.], 'A foe [LXX: Tyre], and he is around the land [Syr., Tg. Jon.: Trouble surrounds the land], and he will bring down from you your strength [pc Mss: and

---

chapter 7 of Emanuel Tov, *Textual Criticism of the Hebrew Bible*, 3d ed. [Minneapolis: Fortress, 2012]).

19. "The Rabbis (*San.* 89b) understand this verse to mean that, whenever a prophecy is transmitted to one prophet to proclaim to the people, it is revealed to all other prophets. Although these prophets are not enjoined to proclaim it—indeed, they are forbidden to proclaim it, since it is not their prophecy—they are, nevertheless, informed of it" (*Mikraoth Gedoloth: The Twelve Prophets*, vol. 1, 127).

20. E. W. Bullinger, *Figures of Speech Used in the Bible* (London: Eyre and Spottiswoode, 1898; reprint, Grand Rapids: Baker, 1968), 402.

your strength will be brought down from you], and your fortresses will be plundered.' 3:12 Thus says the LORD, 'Just as the shepherd rescues from the mouth of a lion two legs or a piece of an ear, so will the sons of Israel be rescued, those who sit in Samaria on a corner of a bed [LXX, Syr., Tg. Jon.: מִטָּה] and on damask [i.e., silk; LXX, Syr., Tg. Jon., Vulg.: Damascus] of a couch.' 3:13 'Hear and warn [or, testify against] the house of Jacob,' the prophetic utterance of the LORD, the God of hosts [cf., LXX; MT: the Lord GOD, the God of hosts]. 3:14 'For in the day of my visiting the transgressions of Israel upon him, I will visit upon the altars of Bethel, and the horns of the altar will be cut off, and they will fall to the ground. 3:15 And I will strike the house of winter [LXX: And I will mingle together and strike the house encircled with columns] in addition to the house of summer, and the houses of ivory will perish, and many [or, great] houses will come to an end [or, be swept away; LXX: and many other houses will be added],' the prophetic utterance of the LORD."

The use of plural imperatives in Amos 3:9 is likely not intended to address any group in particular, unless a plurality of prophets is in view (Amos 3:7). It is probably a rhetorical device designed for an imaginary summons to two perennial enemies of Israel—Philistia and Egypt (cf., Joel 4:19 [Eng., 3:19]; Amos 1:6–8)—to bear witness to the evil deeds of Israel and their judgment (cf., Mic. 1:2; Lam. 2:17). The fortresses of these lands represent the peoples, and they were to come see the confusion and oppression from the vantage point of the stadium seating provided by the mountains of Samaria (1 Kgs. 16:24). This was to add insult to injury given the fact that both Philistia and Egypt were guilty before the LORD as well. The people of Israel would be humiliated in front of their own nemeses. Ironically, the words of accusation in Amos 3:10 could apply equally to Israel or its enemies. It is only the announcement of judgment in Amos 3:11 that speaks to Israel directly. When Amos 3:10 says that they did not know to do right, it apparently does not mean that the ignorance was such that the people could not be held responsible for their actions. Rather, Israel is accountable for hoarding in its fortresses plunder taken by acts of violence and destruction (cf., Hab. 1:3). The judgment announced in Amos 3:11 indicates that an unidentified foe (Assyria?) will surround the land. That foe will bring down Israel's strength, and Israel's fortresses will be plundered. In other words, the crime that the people of Israel committed will be done to them (*lex talionis*).

The image in Amos 3:12a of a shepherd salvaging two legs or a piece of an ear of one of his sheep from a lion's mouth is not intended to engender hope beyond judgment as in Amos 9:8b (cf., Amos 4:11). The sheep is dead. The remains simply show this to be the case and thereby vindicate the shepherd against any charge of theft (Exod. 22:12–13). It is in this way that Israel will be "rescued" (Amos 3:12b). The description of Israel in Amos 3:12b probably tells of the way the wealthy inhabitants of Samaria currently are—self-satisfied in their prosperity and indifferent to the LORD and his will (cf., Amos 3:15; 4:1; 6:4).

Once again, the plural imperatives in Amos 3:13 are perhaps not directed to any group in particular (cf., Amos 3:9). The punishment for Israel's transgressions (Amos 3:14; cf., Amos 2:6; 3:2) will be a punishment against the altars of Bethel where Jeroboam set up one of his golden calves (1 Kgs. 12:29). The horns of the altar (1 Kgs. 1:50; 2:28) will be cut off. This will be in fulfillment of the Josiah prophecy (1 Kgs. 13:2; 2 Kgs. 23:15–16). The LORD will strike the wealthy and the prosperous mentioned in Amos 3:12b—those like the royalty who could afford winter homes (Jer. 36:22), summer homes, houses of ivory (1 Kgs. 22:39), and great (or, many) houses (Amos 3:15).

AMOS 4

4:1 "Hear this word, O heifers of Bashan [Tg. Jon.: rich with possessions] who are in Mount Samaria [Tg. Jon.: the fortress of Samaria], who oppress poor [or, lowly] people, who crush needy people, who say to their lords [i.e., husbands; Tg. Jon.: nobles; see GKC §144a], 'Bring [4QXIIᶜ: הביאו; GKC §135o] so that we may drink [GKC §108d; Tg. Jon.: Give us authority to plunder].' 4:2 The LORD [LXX: κύριος; MT: Lord GOD] swears by his holiness [LXX: against his holy ones], 'Look, days are coming upon you, and he will take you away with hooks [LXX, Syr.: weapons; Tg. Jon.: the peoples will lift you up on their shields], and your end will be in fishing pots [or, your posterity with fishing hooks; 4QXIIᶜ: בסופות with fish beaters; LXX: and burning pestilences will throw those with you into heated cauldrons; Tg. Jon.: and your daughters in skiffs of hunters; cf., Syr.]. 4:3 And through breaches each woman will go forth straightforward [LXX: And naked you will be brought out before one another], and you will be cast [cf., LXX] toward Harmon [ארמון? Hermon? LXX: Mount Remmon; Syr.: the mountain of Armenia],²¹ the prophetic utterance of the LORD."

4:4 "'Enter Bethel and transgress, in Gilgal transgress greatly, and

---

21. *Tg. Jon.*: "And they will tear down upon you the wall, and they will surround you like women each before him, and they will take you into exile beyond the mountains of Armenia."

bring in the morning your sacrifices, for three days [or, every three days;
LXX: on the third day] your tithes.[22] *4:5 And burn from leaven a thank*
offering [LXX: And they read the law outside; Tg. Jon.: And they levy
payment of a thank offering by force], and proclaim freewill offerings,
announce [LXX: and they called for confessions. Announce that . . .;
Syr.: and make vows and pay; Tg. Jon.: and they bring it with song and
say, This is for acceptance], for you like it that way, O sons of Israel,' the
prophetic utterance of the LORD [MT: Lord GOD]."

4:6 "'And also I, I gave to you cleanness of teeth [LXX: I will give to you
grinding of teeth] in all your cities and lack of bread in all your places,
but you have not returned to me [Tg. Jon.: to the worship of me],' the
prophetic utterance of the LORD."

4:7 "'And also I, I withheld from you the rain. In yet three months to
the harvest, I would cause rain to fall on one city [GKC §112h], and on
another city I would not cause rain to fall. One portion of land would
receive rain, and another portion, which would not show rainfall on it
[LXX: on which I would not cause rain to fall], it would dry up. 4:8 And
two, three cities would stagger [LXX, Syr.: gather / assemble] to one city
to drink water and not be satisfied, but you have not returned to me,' the
prophetic utterance of the LORD."

4:9 "'I struck you with blight and mildew. The increase [cf., LXX, Syr.,
Tg. Jon., Vulg.] of your gardens and your vineyards and your fig trees
and your olive trees is what the cutting locust devours, but you have not
returned to me,' the prophetic utterance of the LORD."

4:10 "'I sent against you a plague in the manner of Egypt. I slaughtered
by the sword your choice, young men with the captivity of your horses,
and I brought up the stench of your camps, that is, in your nostril [LXX:
and I offered up in fire your camps in my wrath], but you have not re-
turned to me,' the prophetic utterance of the LORD."

4:11 "'I overturned you [or, I turned against you; Tg. Jon.: I rejected you]
like the divine overthrow of Sodom and Gomorrah, and you were like a
firebrand rescued from burning, but you have not returned to me,' the
prophetic utterance of the LORD."

---

22. The LXX renders all the imperatives in this verse as second plural aorist
active indicatives.

4:12 "'Therefore, thus will I do to you, O Israel. On account of the fact that [Tg. Jon.: Because you did not return to the Torah] this is what I will do to you, prepare to meet your God [Tg. Jon.: prepare to accept the instruction of the Torah of your God], O Israel.' 4:13 For look, he is [LXX: I am] the one who fashions mountains [LXX: thunder] and creates wind [Syr.: creates wind and creates mountains] and declares to mankind what his thought is [LXX: his anointed one; Syr.: his praise; Tg. Jon.: his work]. He makes dawn into darkness [LXX: dawn and mist/fog][23] and treads upon land's high places. The LORD God of hosts is his name."

The judgment oracle in Amos 4:1–3 does double duty for the composition of the book. On the one hand, it concludes the material that began in Amos 3:9. On the other hand, it begins with one of the major structural devices in Amos—"Hear this word" (Amos 3:1; 4:1; 5:1). The unit is thus a kind of a hinge between two sections. The address is to the wealthy women of the capital city of Samaria. They are characterized here as heifers fattened by the fertile land of Bashan (BDB, 143). This is not because the wealthy women are the only ones to be judged. Rather, it is because the outward depiction of the loss of their prosperity in exile is a particularly striking illustration of what will happen to the northern kingdom of Israel in general (cf., Isa. 3:16–4:1; Hos. 10:11; Amos 3:9, 12; 6:1–7). The accusation against them is that they oppress those with a low societal status (cf., Amos 2:7; 5:11; 8:4) and disrespect their husbands (cf., Gen. 18:12; 1 Pet. 3:6; see also Amos 6:6), treating them as if they were servants. The announcement of their judgment begins with a divine oath in which the LORD swears by his own holiness that the days of reckoning are coming upon them (Amos 4:2a). This is because there is none greater by which the LORD can swear (Amos 6:8; 8:7; Heb. 6:16). Despite the difficulties of translating Amos 4:2b–3 (see above), it is clear that it is an unflattering picture of the removal of the wealthy women through the war-torn wall of Samaria and away to a place of exile.

The command to go to Bethel and Gilgal for the purpose of transgression is both ironic and sarcastic (Amos 4:4a; cf., Isa. 29:1; Jer. 7:21–22; Hos. 8:13). These sites had great tradition (Gen. 12:8; 28; 35; Josh. 5:9; 1 Sam. 11:14–15; Hos. 12:12 [Eng., 12:11]), but they had also become alternatives to the centralization of worship in Jerusalem (Deut. 12:5; 1 Kgs. 12:25–33; Hos. 4:15; 9:15; 10:5; Amos 5:5). Thus,

---

23. *Targum Jonathan* makes this into a contrast between the light of the righteous and the darkness of the wicked.

any kind of worship that took place at these locations was automatically contrary to the LORD's design. The people could bring their sacrifices early in the morning to show their zeal. They could even bring their tithes every three days instead of every three years to demonstrate their eagerness (Amos 4:4b; cf., Deut. 14:28; Rom. 10:2), but they still lacked the justice and righteousness that the LORD required of them (Amos 5:21–27). They might as well break the law by burning thank offerings made from leaven (Amos 4:5a; cf., Lev. 2:11; 7:13) or by commanding offerings that should be voluntary rather than mandatory (Exod. 35:4–36:7). This is unfortunately the way the people liked their worship, because it required so little of them apart from empty ritual (Amos 4:5b). The message is clear, "Since you refuse to listen, you may as well do what you like, thus proving that your judgment is just."

The next section in Amos 4:6–11 contains a series of references to covenant curses for disobedience that have already occurred (Lev. 26; Deut. 28). These are all punctuated with the same conclusion: "'And you have not returned to me,' the prophetic utterance of the LORD" (Amos 4:6b, 8b, 9b, 10b, 11b). Thus, in spite of the initial prodding of judgment, the people have refused to turn (cf., Rev. 9:20–21). They have not responded to famine or lack of rain (Amos 4:6–8; see 1 Kgs. 8:35–40; 17:1; 2 Kgs. 6:24–31),[24] nor have they responded to blight, mildew, or locust plagues (Amos 4:9; cf., Joel 1:4; Amos 5:11; 7:1–2; Hag. 2:17). Verses 10 and 11 of Amos 4 form two analogies with iconic moments in biblical narrative: the Egyptian plagues (Exod. 7–14) and the overthrow of Sodom and Gomorrah (Gen. 19). The return-to-Egypt metaphor has already surfaced in the Twelve (Hos. 8:13; 9:3; 11:5). Here the specific term "plague" (דבר) comes from Exod. 9:3 (cf., Hab. 3:5). In what sense, however, was the judgment against Israel "in the manner of Egypt" (cf., Exod. 15:26)? This phrase occurs in Isa. 10:24, 26 with reference to the oppression of Israel in Egypt and with reference to the dividing of the sea. But Amos 4:10 speaks of a slaughter of young men by the sword with the captivity of their horses (which either means that they took their horses captive or they slaughtered horses that had been taken captive), resulting in the rising stench of their corpses (cf., Isa. 34:3; Joel 2:20). Thus, the analogy is invoked primarily because of the parallel death and destruction, not because of any corresponding slaughter of young men by the sword in Egypt. Sodom and

---

24. The repetition of וגם אני ("And also I") in Amos 4:6, 7 highlights the relationship between what the people have done (Amos 3:9–4:3) and what the LORD has done (Amos 4:6–11).

Gomorrah, on the other hand, are the biblical model for wickedness (Deut. 32:32), and their overthrow is the model of divine judgment (Deut. 29:22 [Eng., 29:23]; Isa. 13:19; Jer. 49:18; 50:40). Israel had essentially become the new Sodom and Gomorrah (Judg. 19; Isa. 1:10; Jer. 23:15) and thus faced a similar judgment,[25] only as a firebrand rescued from burning (cf., Amos 3:12; 9:8b; Zech. 3:2).

According to the conclusion in Amos 4:12, the LORD will do to Israel what he has already done. That is, the past judgments have been a foretaste of things to come. Therefore, the people of Israel must prepare to meet their God (cf., Exod. 19:17). The rationale for this is given in the form of a brief hymn dominated by participial descriptions of the LORD (Amos 4:13; cf., Isa. 42:5; Amos 5:8; 9:5–6; Zech. 12:1).[26] He is the maker who fashions mountains and creates wind/breath/spirit and declares to mankind what his thought is (Prov. 20:27; Heb. 4:12).[27] Therefore, all must give an account to him. He makes the light of the morning dawn into darkness, just as he is able to do the opposite and turn deep darkness into morning light (Amos 5:8). He treads upon the land victoriously (BDB, 119; cf., Deut. 33:29; Mic. 1:3).[28] Yahweh, the God of angelic hosts, is his name (Exod. 3:12, 14–15).

---

25. See Michael B. Shepherd, *The Text in the Middle* (New York: Peter Lang, 2014), 19–20.
26. See Hermann Gunkel, *Introduction to Psalms: The Genres of the Religious Lyric of Israel*, completed by Joachim Begrich, translated by James D. Nogalski (Macon, GA: Mercer University Press, 1998), 30–31.
27. This is not intended to say that God reveals his own thoughts to mankind but that mankind's thoughts are known to God and not hidden. The LXX translator read מְשִׁיחוֹ ("his anointed one") rather than מַה שֵּׂחוֹ ("what his thought"). It would be easy to dismiss this as either a misreading of the Hebrew or a deliberate creation of a messianic reading (see Aaron Schart, "The Jewish and the Christian Greek Versions of Amos," in *Septuagint Research: Issues and Challenges in the Study of the Greek Jewish Scriptures*, eds. Wolfgang Kraus and R. Glenn Wooden [Atlanta: SBL, 2005], 168–69). But the MT is not without its problems. The spelling and vocalization of שֵׂחוֹ are highly unusual (cf., 2 Kgs 9:11; Ps 102:1). According to Cyril of Jerusalem, "The prophet was not ignorant of him [Christ] when he said, 'And declaring his Christ to men.' Moses also knew him, and Isaiah and Jeremiah as well. None of the prophets was ignorant of him. Even the devils acknowledged him, for he rebuked them, and Scripture adds, 'Because they knew that he was the Christ'" (Ferreiro, ed., *The Twelve Prophets*, 96).
28. See Humphrey Hill Hardy II and Benjamin D. Thomas, "Another Look at Biblical Hebrew *bama* 'High Place,'" *VT* 62 (2012): 175–88.

AMOS 5

5:1 "Hear this word that I am lifting up against you, a lament, O house of Israel. 5:2 The virgin Israel [GKC §128k] has fallen, she will not rise up again. She is forsaken upon her land, there is no one raising her up. 5:3 For thus says the LORD [MT: Lord GOD; cf., LXX], 'The city that goes out to fight [BDB, 424] with a thousand will have one hundred left, and the one that goes out to fight with one hundred will have ten left for the house of Israel.'"

5:4 "For thus says the LORD to the house of Israel, 'Seek me and live [or, so that you may live; GKC §110f; Luther]. 5:5 And do not seek Bethel, and into Gilgal you shall not enter [BDB, 518], and to Beersheba you shall not cross over. For as for Gilgal, it will surely go into exile,[29] and as for Bethel, it will become trouble [Tg. Jon.: those who worship idols in Bethel will become nothing].' 5:6 Seek the LORD and live [or, so that you may live], lest he rush like fire upon the house of Joseph [or, O house of Joseph], and it [i.e., fire] consume, and there be no one to extinguish it for Bethel [LXX: for the house of Israel]."

5:7 "They are those who turn justice into wormwood. And as for righteousness, it is to the ground that they put it."[30]

5:8 "He is the one who makes Pleiades and Orion and turns deep darkness [LXX: shadow of death][31] into the morning light and darkens day into night. He is the one who summons the waters of the sea and pours them on the surface of the earth. Yahweh [pc Mss add: of hosts; LXX adds: God Almighty] is his name. 5:9 He is the one who flashes destruction upon a strong one [LXX: divides ruin upon strength; Syr., Tg. Jon.: empowers the weak against the strong], and destruction comes upon [LXX: he brings upon] a fortification."

5:10 "They hate in the city gate someone who reproves [i.e., someone who administers reproof; or, arbitrates; Tg. Jon.: someone who reproves

---

29. The Hebrew text here features a wordplay on the place name Gilgal: הגלגל גלה יגלה (*haggilgal galoh yigleh*). Cf., Josh. 5:9.
30. The LXX makes this about the LORD: "The Lord is the one who makes judgment on high and puts righteousness on earth."
31. See James Barr, *Comparative Philology and the Text of the Old Testament*, with additions and corrections (Winona Lake, IN: Eisenbrauns, 1987), 375–80.

them in court with the words of the law],[32] *and as for one who speaks with integrity, they abhor him. 5:11 Therefore, because you trample on a poor / lowly person [NET: because you make the poor pay taxes on their crops], and because an exacted portion of grain is what you take from him, houses of cut stone are what you have built, but you will not live in them; desirable vineyards are what you have planted, but you will not drink their wine. 5:12 For I know how abundant are your transgressions and how many are your sins, those who are hostile to a righteous person, those who take a bribe, and needy people in the city gate they turn aside. 5:13 Therefore, the one who is wise [or, the one who has success], at that time, he will be silent [or, he will wail], for an evil time is what it will be."*

*5:14 "Seek good and not evil in order that you may live, and thus the LORD God of hosts will be with you just as you said [or, and thus may the LORD God of hosts be with you just as you said; see GKC §109k]. 5:15 Reject [4QXII*ᵍ*: שנאו] evil and choose good and set up in the city gate justice. Perhaps the LORD God of hosts will be gracious [4QXII*ᵍ*: יחננו] to the remnant of Joseph."*

5:16 "Therefore, thus says the LORD God of hosts [MT adds: Lord], 'In every square there will be wailing, and in every street they will say, "Ho, ho." And they will call a farmer to mourning, and wailing to those who know lamentation [i.e., professional mourners]. 5:17 And in every vineyard there will be mourning, for I will pass through your midst,' says the LORD."

The third and final "message" of judgment begins in Amos 5:1—"Hear this word" (cf., Amos 3:1; 4:1). The prophet sounds the death knell for the house of Israel by lifting up a "lament" (קינה) against them (cf., 2 Sam. 1:17; Amos 8:10; see BDB, 884). This has a powerful rhetorical effect, indicating the inevitability of Israel's demise. The only hope at this point is that of restoration for a faithful remnant (Amos 5:15b). Virgin Israel (i.e., the unconquered nation in the prime of life; see BDB, 144) has in essence fallen on the battle field and will not rise up again (Amos 5:2; cf., 2 Sam. 1:19, 25, 27; Isa. 24:20; Jer. 8:4; Amos 8:14). This prophecy is grounded in what the LORD himself says about the decimation of

---

32. English versions typically understand the phrase "in the city gate" to modify the participle "someone who reproves," but the word order and the Masoretic accentuation suggest that it modifies the main verb.

Israel's armies (Amos 5:3). Only a tenth of the soldiers who go out to engage in warfare will return (cf., Isa. 6:13).

In light of the funeral dirge/elegy in Amos 5:2, the divine exhortation to seek the LORD and live cannot simply mean to seek the avoidance or survival of disaster (Amos 5:4, 6a; cf., Deut. 4:29; 30:20; Isa. 55:6; Zeph. 2:3). It must have something to do with future and final restoration of the true people of God (see Hos. 3:5; Amos 9:12; Hab. 1:12a; 2:4b; cf., *Tg. Onk.* Lev. 18:5). To seek the LORD according to Amos 5:5 means not to seek the idols of Bethel (Gen. 28), Gilgal (Josh. 5:9; 1 Sam. 11:14), or Beersheba (Gen. 21:31; 26:33).[33] These important sites in the history of Israel had become places of alternative worship (Deut. 12:5; 1 Kgs. 12:25–33; Hos. 4:15; 9:15; 10:5; Amos 4:4; 8:14). In the case of Beersheba, this even involved crossing the border into the southern kingdom of Judah. These locations will not experience life. Rather, they will face exile and the consequences of *aven* ("trouble/idolatry"; see BDB, 19–20). Bethel even became known as Beth Aven ("house of trouble/idolatry"; Hos. 4:15; 5:8; 10:5, 8). Failure to seek the LORD would result in judgment by fire for the house of Joseph as represented by Bethel (Amos 5:6b; cf., Amos 1:4, 7, 10, 12, 14; 2:2, 5; see also Isa. 66:24).[34]

Verses 7–9 of Amos 5 shift from the problem of Israel's idolatry to the problem of Israel's lack of justice and righteousness, which will remain the focus in one way or another for the remainder of the chapter. These are not, however, unrelated issues, as the conclusion of the chapter in Amos 5:21–27 will make clear. Even the contrast between Israel (Amos 5:7) and the LORD (Amos 5:8–9) is a contrast between an unjust people and a God who alone is worthy to be worshiped. The call for justice and righteousness in this chapter is coupled with a call to seek the LORD and forsake idols. Thus, justice and righteousness are ultimately theological issues. The people of Israel are described as those who pervert justice and abandon righteousness (Amos 5:7; cf., Deut. 29:17; 32:32; Hos. 10:4; Amos 6:12b). Use of the participle to describe Israel in this way works nicely with the hymnic material in Amos 5:8–9 (cf., Amos 4:13; 9:5–6; see also Job 9:5–10). His name is Yahweh who makes the constellations of the sky (cf., Job 9:9; 38:31).

---

33. Such a practice was in direct violation of Exodus 20:2–6 (cf., Exod. 32).
34. The house of Joseph stands here for the ten tribes of the northern kingdom of Israel. Two of the tribes were named for Joseph's sons, Ephraim and Manasseh, the latter of which was divided between the east of the Jordan and the west. Ephraim's prominence in the north led to the use of "Ephraim" to represent the northern kingdom in general as opposed to Judah in the south.

He is the one who providentially oversees the changes from night to day and from day to night (Gen. 1:3–5). He alone is able to summon the water of the sea for such catastrophic events as the flood (Gen. 6–7). Only he can bring destruction against a strong fortification in an instant. The distribution of this hymnic material throughout Amos forces the reader to reflect on whom to worship and whom to follow.[35]

The people of Israel hate to have judges making legal decisions in the city gate with integrity because that would mean reproof for their oppression of the poor for their own personal gain (Amos 5:10–12; cf., Isa 29:21; Amos 2:7; 4:1; 8:4). They much prefer to have someone in that position who is susceptible to bribes (cf., Mic. 3:11), someone who is willing to wrong the righteous and turn aside the needy from their path to justice. But both the prophet and the LORD are well aware of the extent of their sin (cf., Isa. 29:15; Hos. 5:3). Their judgment will be that they will not be able to enjoy the wealth that they have so wrongly amassed (cf., Deut. 28:30; Mic. 6:9–16; Zeph. 1:13). In fact, there appear to be two announcements of judgment here marked by לְכֵן ("Therefore"; Amos 5:11, 13). If that is the case, then Amos 5:13 should probably be rendered, "Therefore, the one who has success, at that time, he will wail, for an evil time is what it will be." On the other hand, since there is already an announcement of judgment in Amos 5:11, verse 13 may very well be a word of advice for the wise: "Therefore, the one who is wise, at that time, he will be silent, for an evil time is what it will be" (cf., Prov. 9:8; 10:19; Lam. 3:26).

The call to seek good and not evil in order to live (Amos 5:14a) runs parallel to the one to seek the LORD and live (Amos 5:4, 6a; cf., Exod. 33:19; Deut. 30:15–20). There may also be an echo here of the gift of the tree of life and the prohibition of the tree of knowing good and evil (Gen. 2:9, 16–17). It is only by this means that the people will truly experience the LORD's presence in their midst as they have so presumptuously claimed in the past (Amos 5:14b; cf., Jer. 7:4; Mic. 3:11). The corollary to Amos 5:14a then is to reject evil and choose good (Amos 5:15a; cf., Isa. 1:17), which will manifest itself in the establishment of true justice in the city gate contrary to what is said of the

---

35. The question of whether Amos 4:13; 5:8–9; 9:5–6 originally constituted one poem is somewhat beside the point (see James L. Crenshaw, *Hymnic Affirmation of Divine Justice: The Doxologies of Amos and Related Texts in the Old Testament*, SBLDS 24 [Missoula, MT: Scholars, 1975]; Jeremias, *Amos*, 76–79). What matters now is the function of this material in its present position and in relationship to the surrounding context and to the compositional strategy of the book as a whole.

people in Amos 5:10 (see Amos 5:24). This will create the possibility of the LORD's graciousness toward the faithful remnant of Joseph (Amos 5:15b). That is, the judgment presupposed by Amos 5:1–3 will still come, but those who seek the LORD can look forward to restoration (Isa. 8:19–20; Hos. 3:5; Amos 9:12; Nah. 1:7).

The last two verses of this unit (Amos 5:16–17) attach one last announcement of judgment marked by לכן ("Therefore"). This one is a forecast of widespread mourning. Not only will this involve every square and street in the cities, but also the farmers will be summoned from their work in the fields. They will join in with the professional mourners (cf., Jer. 9:16–20 [Eng., 9:17–21]). The LORD will pass through to destroy what Israel has so unjustly built for itself (Amos 5:11b, 17a) just as he once passed through the land of Egypt to judge Israel's enemies and redeem his people (Exod. 12:12). Only in the messianic kingdom will what is lost here be fully restored (Amos 9:14).

5:18 "Woe [BDB, 222], those who long for the Day of the LORD. To what purpose is the Day of the LORD to you? It will be darkness and not light, 5:19 just as a man flees from before the lion, and the bear meets him, and he enters the house and leans his hand upon the wall, and the serpent bites him. 5:20 Is it not darkness that the Day of the LORD will be, and not light, and gloomy, and without brightness to it?"

5:21 "'I hate, I reject your festivals, and I do not delight in your solemn assemblies. 5:22 Even if you offer up to me burnt offerings and your grain offerings, I will not accept them. And as for the peace offering of your fatlings, I will not regard it. 5:23 Take away from me the noise of your songs, and the music of your harps I will not hear. 5:24 But let justice roll [i.e., flow down] like water, and righteousness like a perennial stream.'"

5:25 "'Sacrifices and offering, did you draw them near to me in the wilderness [LXXᵂ] for forty years, O house of Israel [see GKC §100l]? 5:26 And you will lift up the tent of your king [LXX: Moloch] and the pedestal [or, shrine] of your images, the star of your god(s) [LXX adds: Raifan] that you made for yourselves. 5:27 And I will cause you to go into exile beyond Damascus [Acts 7:43: Babylon], says the LORD.' The LORD God of hosts is his name [cf., Amos 4:13b; MT: God of hosts is his name (haplography)].

This section opens with a woe oracle (Amos 5:18–20; cf., Amos 6:1). The wealthy oppressors condemned in Amos 5:1–17 had claimed that the LORD was present with them (Amos 5:14b; cf., Jer. 7:4; Mic. 3:11). They thought that the Day of the LORD would be a day of deliverance for them regardless of their religion and behavior. But according to Joel 3:1–5 (Eng., 2:28–32), the Day of the LORD would only be a day of deliverance for those who genuinely call on the name of the LORD. For everyone else it will be a day of darkness and judgment, contrary to expectation (cf., Joel 2:2; Amos 8:9; Mic. 7:4b; Lam. 3:2). Salvation, on the other hand, will be like the light of a morning sunrise to those who trust in the LORD (Isa. 9:1 [Eng., 9:2]; 60:1–3; Mic. 7:8–10; Mal. 3:20). What then is the point of the comparison of the darkness to the sequence of unfortunate events in Amos 5:19 (cf., Isa. 24:18; Jer. 48:43–44; Ps. 7:16 [Eng., 7:15]; Lam. 3:47; Eccl. 10:8–9)? It would seem to be not only a picture of stumbling in darkness from one unknown encounter to the next but also a way of illustrating the inescapability of the darkness.

Earlier in Amos 4:4–5, the LORD sarcastically urged the people to engage in their unlawful religious practices with enthusiasm. Now he speaks frankly about his rejection of the festivals, offerings, and songs of the cult (Amos 5:21–24; cf., Isa. 66:3; Jer. 14:12; Ezek. 26:13; Amos 6:5). The prophets generally set this up for rhetorical effect as an either-or proposition rather than a both-and one (e.g., 1 Sam. 15:22; Isa. 1:10–17; Jer. 7:21–23; Hos. 6:6; Mic. 6:6–8).[36] The conclusion to Psalm 51, which accepts the sacrifices as the legitimate expression of worship from a contrite heart, is a rare exception. Of course, the cult was established according to Leviticus 1–7, but this was not an original or essential part of the covenant relationship (Jer. 7:21–23). It was added secondarily because of transgression (Gal. 3:19). Thus, without justice and righteousness the practice of the cult was completely worthless, not to mention offensive. Keil understood the call for justice and righteousness in Amos 5:24 to be the desire for God's punitive judgment and righteousness to come on the basis of similar flood imagery in Isa. 10:22 (cf., Isa. 48:18).[37] But this does not take into account the use of the same terminology in the preceding context. According to Amos 5:15, "justice" (מִשְׁפָּט) is something that the LORD wants the people to set up in the city gate (cf., Isa. 56:1; Amos 5:7).

In Amos 5:25–27 the LORD addresses the people of Amos' day as if they were the wilderness generation.[38] Most interpreters understand

---

36. See Shepherd, *Text in the Middle*, 120–22.
37. Keil, *The Minor Prophets*, 194.
38. "He addresses them as though *they* had perverted God's worship in the desert, and yet they were born many ages after; what does he mean? Even this—the Prophet includes the whole body of the people from their first

Amos 5:25 to be a question that expects a negative answer (cf., LXX), although it is possible to read it as a simple statement.[39] Many take this to mean that sacrifices were initially not part of the people's relationship with the LORD (Jer. 7:21–23).[40] According to this reading, Amos 5:26 would either be a second part to the question in Amos 5:25 or part of the announcement of judgment in Amos 5:27. Another, perhaps more likely possibility, is that the connection between Amos 5:25 and 5:26 is intended to suggest that Israel did in fact offer sacrifices in the wilderness, but they offered them to idols rather than to the LORD (see Lev. 17:7; Num. 25:1–3; Deut. 4:19; 32:17). This has been Israel's problem from its inception to the present day (Deut. 9:24; 2 Kgs. 17:16; Jer. 32:30; Mal. 3:7; Acts 7:39–43). Therefore, they will take their idols and go into exile (Amos 5:26–27; cf., Amos 6:7, 14; 7:11).

The Masoretes have vocalized סכות and כיון after the pattern of שִׁקּוּץ ("detested thing").[41] Modern interpreters often prefer to see references to the Mesopotamian gods Sakkuth and Kayamanu here. The LXX, however, reads the text differently and presents it in a slightly different word order: "And you took up the tent of Moloch [cf., 1 Kgs. 11:7b] and the star of your god Raifan, their images that you made for yourselves" (cf., Acts 7:43). In this translation, the word מלך is read as the name of the Ammonite god מֹלֶךְ ("Molech") rather than מֶלֶךְ ("king"). According to the Damascus Document (CD 7:14–21), the tent of the king (i.e., the assembly) represents the books of the Torah (citing Amos 9:11), and the foundation of the images stands for the books of the Prophets. The star is the interpreter of the Torah who will come to Damascus (citing Num. 24:17). This is said to be the escape of the faithful to the north—a decidedly more positive understanding of Amos 5:26 than the Hebrew text would seem to yield.

Stephen's quote in Acts 7:42–43 comes toward the end of a lengthy rehearsal of the biblical narrative in response to the accusation that

---

beginning, as though he said, 'It is right to inclose [sic] you in the same bundle with your fathers; for you are the same with your fathers in your ways and dispositions'" (Calvin, *Amos*, 293).

39. The Babylonian Talmud (*b. Hag.* 6b) understands the question to mean that regular public offerings were not brought, but that the tribe of Levi brought offerings.

40. E.g., Stuart, *Hosea–Jonah*, 355.

41. Shalom M. Paul, *Amos*, Hermeneia (Philadelphia: Fortress, 1991), 195–96. This is similar to the practice of vocalizing the place name תֹּפֶת ("Topheth") after the word בֹּשֶׁת ("shame"). But see 2 Kgs. 17:30.

he has spoken against Moses, God, and the temple (Acts 6:8–15).[42] His use of "tent" (σκηνή) from Amos 5:26 works well with the reference to "the tent of the testimony" in Acts 7:44 and the reference to the "dwelling place" (σκήνωμα) that David requested to find (Acts 7:46). Stephen identified in his own day what had plagued Israel throughout its history: idolatry (Acts 7:39–43), rebellion, and rejection of the Holy Spirit and the prophets (Acts 7:51–53; cf., Neh. 9:29–31). Misguided trust in cherished institutions had blinded Stephen's accusers to the work of God in their midst.

AMOS 6

6:1 "Woe, those who are at ease in Zion [LXX, Syr.: those who despise Zion] and those who trust in Mount Samaria, the distinguished of the best of the nations [LXX: they have picked the first of the nations], and it is to them that the house of Israel comes [Syr.: they exile].[43] 6:2 Cross over to Calneh [Calneh > LXX] and see, and go from there to Great Hamath, and go down to Gath in the land of the Philistines. Are they better than these kingdoms [i.e., Judah and Israel]? Is their border greater than your border,[44] 6:3 you who put away an evil day [or, for an evil day] and draw near a seat of violence [LXX: you who are coming to

---

42. See Shepherd, *Textual World*, 84; idem, *Twelve Prophets*, 38–40. Cf., Acts 7:42a and Rom. 1:24–32. A major part of Luke's compositional strategy is to employ speeches from major characters (e.g., Peter and Paul) to punctuate and interpret the narrative.

43. The LXX reads "house of Israel" with the beginning of Amos 6:2 as the group to which the plural imperatives are addressed there.

44. The NET understands this to be a quote from the leaders who considered themselves to be from the best of the nations (i.e., Judah and Israel). It is what they would tell the people to assure them that they would not fall to the Assyrians like other nations (cf., 2 Kgs. 18:33–35). The *BHS* apparatus, however, suggests emendation of the second half of the verse so that it reads like an address from the prophet to the leaders: "Are you better than these kingdoms? Is your border better than their border?" Cf., Nah. 3:8. Stuart renders, "Are you better than these kingdoms?" taking "these kingdoms" to refer to those listed in the first half of Amos 6:2 (*Hosea–Jonah*, 357–59). But this hardly fits with the second part of the question. Another possibility is that the prophet is in fact highlighting the superiority of Israel in order to condemn the leaders for their squandering of God's blessings (see Amos 3:2; Keil, *Minor Prophets*, 199–200). This option is also consistent with the Hebrew syntax, which extends the description of those addressed here through Amos 6:3 (cf., RSV)

an evil day, who are approaching and reaching a Sabbath of lies]? 6:4 [Woe,] those who lie upon beds of ivory and are unrestrained on their couches and eat lambs from a flock and calves from within a stall, 6:5 those who sing [LXX: applaud] according to the sound of the harp, like David[45] *they invent for themselves instruments of song [LXX: as permanent they reckoned and not as fleeting], 6:6 those who drink from [lit., in] sacred ritual bowls filled with wine [LXX, Syr.: strained wine], and with the best of oils anoint themselves. (And they are not sickened over the breaking of Joseph.) 6:7 Therefore, now they will go into exile at the head of the exiles, and the feast of the unrestrained [LXX: neighing of horses from Ephraim; Syr.: gladness from their rulers] will turn aside."*[46]

6:8 *"The LORD [L: Lord GOD; > Ms, LXX] swears by himself [L adds: the prophetic utterance of the LORD God of hosts; > Ms, LXX], 'I loathe the pride of Jacob [Tg. Jon.: the sanctuary, the greatness of Jacob], and his fortresses [LXX: places] I hate, and I will deliver the city [i.e., Samaria] and its fullness [LXX: inhabitants] to the enemy.' 6:9 And so it will be, if ten men are left in one house, they will die [LXX adds: and the remaining ones will be left]. 6:10 And his uncle (that is, the one who burns him) will lift him up [LXX: and their family members will take and persuade] to bring forth bones from the house, and he will say to the one who is in the innermost parts of the house [LXX: the managers of the house], 'Is there anyone still with you?' And he will say, 'There is not.' And he will say, 'Hush, for not to mention the name of the LORD [or, for there is no one (GKC §114l) to mention the name of the LORD (or, in the name of the LORD)].' 6:11 For look, the LORD commands, and he will strike the large house into fragments and the small house into pieces.*[47] *6:12 Do horses run on the cliff? Does one plow the sea with oxen [*בבקר ים*; MT: Does one plow with oxen? LXX: Will they be silent*

---

45. The spelling of David's name here (דויד) is not what one would expect from an eighth-century prophet. Early biblical Hebrew (e.g., Samuel and Kings) spells the name without the *yodh* (דוד). It is in late biblical Hebrew (e.g., Chronicles) that the spelling in Amos 6:5 primarily occurs.

46. For the term מרזח ("feast"), see Jer. 16:5; *KTU* 1.114; 3.9; *HALOT* 1.634. See also J. McLaughlin, *The marzēaḥ in the Prophetic Literature: References and Allusions in Light of Extra-biblical Evidence*, VTSup 86 (Leiden: Brill, 2001).

47. Syr.: "Because of which look, the Lord is going out, and he will strike the high house and cause it to tremble, and the small house and lay it waste." *Tg. Jon.*: "For look, the Lord commands, and he will strike a great kingdom with a strong blow, and he will strike a small kingdom with a weak blow."

among mares?]? For you have turned justice into poison and the fruit of righteousness into wormwood, 6:13 you who rejoice about Lo-Debar [or, nothing] and you who say, 'Was it not by our strength that we took for ourselves Karnaim [or, two horns]?' 6:14 'For look, I am about to raise up against you, O house of Israel [MT adds: the prophetic utterance of the LORD the God of hosts; > LXX], a nation, and they will oppress you from the entrance to Hamath to the wadi of the Arabah.'"

Amos 6:1 begins the second of two woe oracles in the book (cf., Amos 5:18; see also Isa. 5:8–24; Hab. 2:5–20). The accusation consists of the descriptions in Amos 6:3–6. Amos 6:7 is the formal announcement of judgment, but this is now extended somewhat by the words of judgment in Amos 6:8–14. The woe is against those who are at ease in Zion (cf., Isa. 32:9, 11; Amos 4:1) and those who trust in Mount Samaria (1 Kgs. 16:24, 29, 32), the distinguished or the elite of the best of the nations to whom the house of Israel comes (Amos 6:1). The reference to Zion here is somewhat unusual in Amos (but see Amos 2:4–5). The LXX and Syriac attempt to avoid this problem by rendering, "those who despise Zion," but this neither reflects a different Hebrew text nor translates accurately the text found in the MT. There is a not-so-subtle reminder here that what was true for Israel was also true for Judah (see 2 Kgs. 17:18–19; Jer. 3; Ezek. 23). This address then is for the wealthy leaders who had developed a false sense of security in their political and religious institutions. They had forgotten the LORD, and they had shown little concern for the people entrusted to them. They did belong to the "best" of the nations (e.g., Exod. 19:5–6; Deut. 4:7–8; 2 Sam. 7:23; Jer. 1:3), but this should have been cause for humility and gratitude rather than pride and abuse of privileges. With their special status came great responsibility (Amos 3:2) and subsequently greater judgment for failure to maintain that responsibility (cf., Amos 1:3–2:3 and 2:4–16).

Interpretations of Amos 6:2 vary from commentary to commentary (see note to the translation above), but the one that requires no emendation and also fits syntactically and conceptually with the surrounding context reads this as part of the prophet's address to the leadership as a call to go and see if there is any other nation (such as those where Calneh, Hamath, and Gath were found [Gen 10:10, 14, 18]) as blessed as Israel and Judah (cf., Jer. 2:9–13). That is, no other nation was the specially chosen instrument of God to redeem the nations (Amos 2:8–11), and yet the response of the leaders particularly in Israel at this point was to behave in the manner outlined in Amos 6:3–6. There is no indication in the text that this is talking about how Israel would fall to the Assyrians in the same way that the nations represented in Amos 6:2 had fallen or would fall, however true that would be (cf., Isa. 10:9–11; 14:31; Jer. 7:12; Nah. 3:8).

These leaders were those who put off the impending day of calamity and judgment, thinking wrongly that it would not be for them (Amos 6:3; cf., Joel 2:2; Amos 5:18). They promoted violence rather than peace and justice from their position ("seat"; cf., 1 Kgs. 10:19) of authority. They indulged in luxuries at an inappropriate time and at the expense of others (Amos 6:4–6; cf., 2 Kgs. 5:26; Isa. 5:12; Amos 2:7; 3:12; 4:1; 5:23; see also Gen. 9:21; Est. 1; Dan. 5). Calvin suggested that there may have been an appeal to prominent figures such as Abraham (Gen. 12:16), David (1 Sam. 16:23; 1 Chr. 23:5; 2 Chr. 29:26–27; 34:12), and Solomon (1 Kgs. 5:3 [Eng., 4:23]; 10:18) who enjoyed items such as those listed here.[48] The difference between these men and the leaders of Amos' day is stated in the parenthetical authorial comment added at the end of Amos 6:6. Amos' contemporaries were not sickened or upset by the plight of their own people (cf., Gen. 37:25; Est. 3:15; see also Amos 5:15). Therefore, they will lead the people one last time—into exile (Amos 6:7). And there will be no more unrestrained feasting.

The oath language of Amos 6:8 is similar to that of Amos 4:2; 8:7. Here the LORD swears by himself (cf., Heb. 6:16). In Amos 4:2 he swears by his holiness, and in Amos 8:7 he ironically swears by the pride of Jacob, which is the perpetual attribute of Israel that the LORD abhors according to Amos 6:8 (cf., Amos 5:10). *Targum Jonathan* understands "the pride of Jacob" in Amos 6:8 to be the sanctuary, although it is not clear what sanctuary is in view. This is an intriguing interpretation, given the fact that "his holiness" in Amos 4:2 could also be "his sanctuary" (cf., Matt. 5:33–37). The sanctuary would also make a nice structural parallel to the fortresses that the LORD hates in Amos 6:8. The problem is that the attestation of the phrase "the pride of Jacob" for a sanctuary is neither clear nor consistent (but see Ps. 47:5 [Eng., 47:4]). It seems rather to be the case that the pride of Jacob is manifested in the people's (and particularly the leadership's) misplaced trust in their fortifications. Thus, the LORD will deliver the city of Samaria and its inhabitants to the enemy in order to expose their failure to trust in him (cf., Amos 2:4, 6b, 7, 9b, 10, 12, 14a; 2:2a, 5).

The oath taken in Amos 6:8 is illustrated by the death of ten people remaining in a single house in the wake of deliverance to the enemy (Amos 6:9; cf., Amos 5:3; 8:3). The difficulties of interpreting Amos 6:10 are evident in the varied attempts of commentators. An uncle comes to take each body and burn it in order to bring out the bones from the

---

48. Calvin, *Amos*, 310.

house (for ossuaries?). Some take this to mean that spices are burned for the dead (see 1 Sam. 31:12; Jer. 34:5; 2 Chr. 16:14). This relative then asks someone in the house whether there is anyone left. It is not clear who this person in the house might be. The LXX suggests that there were people managing the house between the time of the deaths and the time of the arrival of the uncle. A voice replies that there is in fact no one left. The reintroduction of discourse indicates that the uncle speaks again at the end of the verse, "Hush, for not to mention the name of the LORD." This is unquestionably the most unusual feature of the verse, and the difficulty of it is compounded by the fact that it apparently does not form an independent clause (but see translation options above). The reference to mentioning the name of the LORD has led to several suggestions since such an expression can occur in a wide variety of contexts (see BDB, 270–71). But the clearest guide seems to be the word "Hush." This word occurs four other times in the Book of the Twelve (Amos 8:3; Hab. 2:20; Zeph. 1:7; Zech. 2:17 [Eng., 2:13]). Each time it calls for silence in the presence of the LORD in light of the imminent Day of the LORD. Amos 6:11 adds that what the reader finds in Amos 6:9–10 is but a mere microcosm of what the LORD decrees for the entire land, for houses both large and small.

Amos 6:12 turns the reader back to the reason for such severe judgment. It begins with an analogy: "Do horses run on the cliff? Does one plow the sea with oxen?" It is possible to make sense of the second question according to the MT by adding the word "there": "Does one plow with oxen there [i.e., on the cliff]?" The absurdity of these scenarios is intended to illustrate Israel's perversion of justice and righteousness (Hos. 10:4; Amos 5:7). They had taken what should have been healthy and sweet and made it into something poisonous and bitter. Amos 6:13 describes them as those who rejoiced in "nothing" (Lo-Debar) and who boasted that they had acquired symbols of strength ("two horns" [BDB, 901–902]; or, Karnaim) on their own. It is not obvious that these are references to the place names Lo-Debar and Karnaim, but even so, it is the play on the meanings of these names that is primarily in view. The beginning of Amos 6:14 then follows the wording and pattern of the first part of Amos 6:11 for the final announcement of judgment. An unnamed nation will oppress the house of Israel from the entrance to Hamath in the north to the wadi of the Arabah in the south.[49] These

---

49. The lack of clear identification of this nation here and elsewhere in Amos should be considered deliberate. It is not the place of the commentator to override the decision of the author by suggesting Assyria. Even if the historical identity was evident to Amos and his early readers, it was still

were considered the boundaries of the northern kingdom of Israel to its fullest extent (2 Kgs. 14:25).

A REMINDER ABOUT TEACHING AMOS 1–6

Working through the details of the judgment oracles, messages of judgment, and woe oracles of the first six chapters of Amos might seem laborious to an audience listening to this material in a typical sermon setting during a weekly worship service. The temptation might be to skip these chapters or to make them say something that they are really not intended to say. But a better decision would be to move the teaching of these texts to a setting more appropriate for their content— perhaps a smaller setting with more interaction led by someone with expertise in the Prophets. Even in a more ideal environment, however, it will be important to remind the audience that these texts are just as much part of Scripture as other texts that they might find more accessible on the surface. One way to relieve some of the pressure that may build during this stretch would be to give the listeners a sense of how the sub-units contribute to Amos as a whole and to the overall compositional strategy of the Twelve.

AMOS 7

7:1 "Thus the LORD [L: Lord GOD] showed me, and look, he was fashioning a swarm of locusts at the first stage of the sprouting of the spring crop. (And look, the spring crop was after the royal mowing [or, shearing; LXX: And look, one locust, Gog the king]). 7:2 And so [GKC §112uu], when [BDB, 50] it [i.e., the swarm of locusts] finished devouring the herbage of the land, I said, 'Lord GOD, forgive [Tg. Jon. adds: the sins of the remnant of the house of Jacob]. How [HALOT 1.575] will Jacob rise up? For he is small.' 7:3 The LORD relented concerning this [LXX: 'Repent, O Lord, concerning this']. 'It will not happen,' said the LORD."

7:4 "Thus the LORD [MT: Lord GOD] showed me, and look, the LORD [MT: Lord GOD] was calling to contend by fire, and it [i.e., the fire]

---

a choice not to mention the nation by name. A parallel example of this phenomenon is Isaiah 33. Commentators normally assume Assyria to be the referent, yet Assyria is never mentioned by name in the chapter. This leaves the text open to other possibilities, especially within the now larger context of the composition of Isaiah, the prophetic corpus, and the Tanakh. See the treatment of this example in Brevard S. Childs, *Isaiah: A Commentary*, OTL (Louisville: Westminster John Knox, 2000), 246–49.

consumed the great deep, and it consumed the portion of land.[50] 7:5 And I said, 'Lord GOD, stop [Syr.: have pity; Tg. Jon.: forgive]. How will Jacob rise up? For he is small.' 7:6 The LORD relented concerning this [LXX: 'Repent, O Lord, concerning this']. 'Also it, it will not happen,' said the LORD [L: Lord GOD]."

7:7 "Thus he showed me, and look, the LORD [L: Lord] was standing beside [or, on] a city wall built with a plumb line [or, a city wall made with tin / lead; LXX, Syr.: an adamantine wall; Tg. Jon.: a wall of judgment], and in his hand was a plumb line [or, tin / lead]. 7:8 And the LORD said to me, 'What do you see, Amos?' And I said, 'A plumb line [or, tin / lead].' And he [see 2 Mss, LXX; L: the Lord] said, 'Look, I am about to put a plumb line [or, tin / lead] in the midst of my people Israel. I will never cross over to him again [Tg. Jon.: I will never forgive him again; see BDB, 717]. 7:9 And the high places of Isaac [LXX, Syr.: laughter] will be desolate, and the sanctuaries of Israel will be waste, and I will rise up against the house of Jeroboam with the sword.'"

The first nine verses of chapter 7 feature three of the five visions of judgment that appear in Amos 7:1–9:10. The third and fourth (Amos 8:1–3) visions are now separated by the narrative in Amos 7:10–17, and the fourth and fifth (Amos 9:1–4) are separated by the intervening material in Amos 8:4–14. Furthermore, there is text in chapter 9 beyond the fifth and final vision. Thus, the reader of these last chapters must reckon with more than the visions, and it is the interpreter's task to contemplate the strategy behind the decision to intersperse the visionary material in this way, given the fact that the five visions could conceivably have appeared in simple succession much like the first three. Jeremias has noted five ways in which Amos' visions differ from those of other prophets: (1) the lack of an interpretive angel as in Zechariah 1–6 and Daniel (but see Jer. 1:11–14; 24; Ezek. 37), (2) the

---

50. GKC §112tt considers the "wayyiqtol . . . waw + qatal" sequence in Amos 7:4b to be an error, presumably because of the expectation of two wayyiqtol forms. But this is likely not a simple narrative sequence. It is the simultaneous presentation of two actions performed by the same grammatical subject with two different objects. This is similar to chiastic structuring of clauses ("wayyiqtol . . . waw + x + qatal") with the same, similar, or opposite verbal roots (e.g., Gen. 1:5a). See Francis I. Andersen, The Sentence in Biblical Hebrew (The Hague: Mouton, 1974), 119–40. The other option would be to treat the second verb as weqatal ("and it will consume the portion of land").

lack of commission for proclamation (cf., Isa. 6), (3) the structuring of the first four visions in pairs, (4) indication of a change from messenger of divine patience to one of divine judgment, and (5) placement of the visions at the end of the book rather than the beginning (cf., Jer. 1:11–14; Zech. 1–6; but see Ezek. 1; 8–11; 37; 40–48).[51] The lack of an angelic guide to the visions is not entirely unique to Amos. The lack of commission for proclamation applies specifically to the content of the visions and does not imply that Amos was not called as a prophet (Amos 3:7–8; 7:10–17). These visions were not part of Amos' public preaching, but as part of his book such encounters with God provide the reader with special insight into the nature of Amos' prophetic ministry and thus work well with the narrative in Amos 7:10–17. The visions are then effectively located after the messages of judgment and the woes in Amos 1–6 to answer a question that naturally arises in the reading of those chapters: Why does Amos only preach a message of judgment? Or, why is there no message of restoration in Amos' preaching? The seam work from the composer of the Twelve now alleviates this problem in a different way at the end of the book (Amos 9:11–15),[52] but at this particular juncture in the reading of the book the answer provided in the present section is still very helpful.

The visions are not only about what is seen but also about what is heard. The first four visions begin, "Thus the LORD showed me, and look . . ." (Amos 7:1, 4, 7; 8:1). The fifth begins, "I saw" (Amos 9:1). But then in each case the LORD speaks (Amos 7:3b, 6b, 8; 8:2–3; 9:1–4). The first two visions share the pattern of the prophet's response to what he saw ("forgive," "stop") followed by an indication that the LORD relented (Amos 7:1–6). The third and fourth visions feature a question-and-answer format initiated by the LORD (Amos 7:8; 8:2). The fifth vision stands apart from the others and includes the longest discourse from the LORD (Amos 9:1–4).

The first vision features the LORD's fashioning of a swarm of locusts during the first stage of the sprouting of the spring crop (Amos 7:1a; cf., Joel 1:4–2:27). The parenthetical note in Amos 7:1b indicates that this spring crop was after the royal mowing (or sheep shearing). Several suggestions have been offered for what this royal mowing might have been, none of which is conclusive: (1) the king's mowing of his own land first, (2) a royal tax on the crops of the land (NET), (2) a royal decree

---

51. Jeremias, *Amos*, 124–26.
52. See Ronald E. Clements, "Patterns in the Prophetic Canon," in *Canon and Authority: Essays in Old Testament Religion and Theology*, eds. George W. Coats and Burke O. Long (Philadelphia: Fortress, 1977), 42–55.

to start the mowing of the land (Calvin), and (4) the LORD's mowing (Keil).[53] What is important for the vision, however, is the devastation caused by the swarm of locusts (Amos 7:2). This devastation was such that it prompted the prophet to seek forgiveness for small Jacob who could not possibly recover from such a fall unless the LORD were to relent (Amos 5:2; Mic. 7:8; Ps. 130:3–4; see also "Jacob" in 2 Kgs. 17:34; Hos. 12). The reader has not seen this side of Amos thus far in the book, and the LORD's response indicates that there may in fact be hope for Israel (Amos 7:3 [see also LXX]; cf., Amos 9:8b). Some prefer to translate נחם ("relent") here as "repent" or "change the mind." Such translations are potentially misleading for readers who might take this to mean that God repents or changes his mind the way a human does (Num. 23:19; 1 Sam. 15:29). God always relents in such a way that is consistent with his revealed character and purposes (e.g., Gen. 6:6; 1 Sam. 15:35; Jon. 3:10). Judgment for the broken covenant relationship is inevitable in order for God's faithfulness to the terms of the covenant to stay intact, but the judgment as stated here does not exclude the possibility of restoration. The reader of Amos 1–6 alone might conclude differently. In the second vision, the prophet was shown judgment by fire, which is nothing new to the book of Amos (Amos 7:4; cf., Amos 1:3–2:5). This time the prophet asked the LORD to stop or cease, and the LORD relented (Amos 7:5). It is not immediately clear whether the locusts and the fire were depictions of simultaneous judgments or sequential ones, but they were apparently not intended to be different depictions of the same judgment. This is clear from the wording of Amos 7:6b: "Also [or, In addition (גם)] it, it will not happen" (cf., Isa. 7:7).

In both visions three (Amos 7:7) and five (Amos 9:1), the LORD is standing by or on an object. The difficulty with the third vision is the phrase "city wall of tin/lead." Does this refer to a city wall built according to the standard of a lead plumb?[54] If so, does Amos 7:8 then mean that the LORD is putting a standard of measure among his people in order to show why he will not cross over to them again (cf., *Tg. Jon.*)?[55] Or, does it mean that the city is being measured for destruction (2 Kgs. 21:13; Isa. 34:11)? On the other hand, the phrase "city wall of tin/lead" could mean that the wall is made out of tin/lead, symbolizing either weakness or strength (cf., LXX). It would not be clear,

---

53. The LXX rendering ("And look, one locust, Gog the king") gives the vision a decidedly eschatological bent (Ezek. 38–39). Cf., LXX Num. 24:7, 23.
54. See Harper, *Amos and Hosea*, 166.
55. This crossing over is represented by Amos' journey from Tekoa in the south to deliver his message to the northern kingdom of Israel.

however, why then the LORD has in his hand some of this tin/lead or why it is put among the people. Another option is to consider אֲנָךְ ("tin/ lead") to be a play on the root אנק/אנח ("groan").[56] This would be similar to the visions in Jeremiah 1:11–14 and Amos 8:1–3 where the objects in the visions are not as significant to the message as the words with which they form a sound play in the Hebrew text. The difference in the case of Amos 7:7–9, however, is that the word play does not actually occur in the text. That is, the root אנק/אנח does not appear. These unresolved issues in the interpretation of the vision make the role of Amos 7:9 that much more important. It clarifies that this too is a vision of judgment. The high places of Isaac were the alternative places of worship (1 Kgs. 12:31).[57] The illegitimate sanctuaries of Israel are the parallel. They will all be laid waste, and the LORD himself will rise up against the dynasty of Jeroboam II (Amos 7:10) with the sword. This speaks not only of the household of Jeroboam II (2 Kgs. 15:10) but also of everything that was started by Jeroboam I (1 Kgs. 12:25–33), which will ultimately end in exile (Amos 7:17).

7:10 And Amaziah the priest [Tg. Jon.: leader] of Bethel sent to Jeroboam the king of Israel saying, "Amos has conspired [Syr., Tg. Jon.: rebelled] against you in the midst of the house of Israel. The land is not able to endure all his words. 7:11 For thus says Amos, 'By the sword Jeroboam will die, and as for Israel, he will surely go into exile from upon his land.'" 7:12 And Amaziah said to Amos, "Seer, go, flee for yourself [GKC §119s] to the land of Judah and eat there bread/food [LXX: spend your life there], and it is there that you should prophesy. 7:13 But in Bethel you must never again prophesy, for a royal sanctuary is what it is, and a kingdom temple [or, palace; lit., house] is what it is." 7:14 And Amos answered and said, "Not a prophet am I [LXX: was I], and not a member of a prophetic guild [GKC §128v] am I [or, was I]. For a herdsman is what I am [LXX: was], and someone who tends sycamore trees [Tg. Jon. adds: because of the sins of the house of my people am I afflicting

---

56. Stuart, *Hosea–Jonah*, 373. Stuart also points out that the usual terms for "plummet" and "line" would be מִשְׁקֹלֶת and קָו (2 Kgs. 21:13).

57. The use of Isaac's name here is somewhat unusual (see also Amos 7:16). It would seem that "Jacob" would make a better parallel and stylistic variant to "Israel." The spelling of Isaac's name is also unusual (יִשְׂחָק [4x] instead of יִצְחָק [108x]). The LXX thus does not understand this to be the name of the patriarch. It translates the meaning of the root as "laughter," perhaps intending to indicate that Israel's religious practices would become a laughingstock.

myself]. 7:15 And the LORD took me from after the flock, and the LORD said to me, 'Go, prophesy to my people Israel.' 7:16 And now, hear the word of the LORD. You say, 'Do not prophesy against Israel, and do not drip against the house of Isaac [LXX: Jacob].' 7:17 Therefore, thus says the LORD, 'Your wife, in the city she will be a prostitute; and your sons and your daughters, by the sword will they fall. And your land, by the cord it will be divided; and you, upon an unclean land you will die. And Israel, he will surely go into exile from upon his land.'"

Critical scholars generally understand Amos 7:10–17 to be an excerpt from a larger narrative whose later insertion into the middle of Amos' visions was prompted by the content of Amos 7:9.[58] It is obvious to anyone that this piece of text is of a different genre than the rest of the book, but it is the task of the interpreter to explain the present role of the unit within the final form of the composition. The text not only confirms the call of Amos in the prophet's own terms (cf., Isa. 6; Jer. 1; Ezek. 1–3) but also explains why the prophetic plea for forgiveness and the divine willingness to relent so evident in the first two visions (Amos 7:1–6) must ultimately give way to the announcement of the end of Israel (Amos 8:1–3). It will remain for the conclusion of the book to give indication of what, if any, hope of restoration lies ahead in the future.

Amaziah, who is otherwise unknown to the reader, is identified in the narrative as "the priest of Bethel" (not "a priest of Bethel"). This immediately flags him as a key member of the false priesthood established by Jeroboam I (1 Kgs. 12:31; see Rashi). Amaziah sent (perhaps by letter) to Jeroboam II a charge of conspiracy (קשר), indicating that the land would not be able to endure the prophet's words (Amos 7:10). Such an accusation would have suggested to the king that there were political ambitions behind Amos' announcement of judgment in Amos 7:9 (e.g., 2 Kgs. 10:9; 11:14; 12:21; 14:19; 15:10, 15, 25, 30; 21:23, 24; cf., Isa. 8:12). Ironically, Amaziah's concerns about the land's ability to bear the prophet's words would be alleviated all too well, for there would be a famine of the word of the LORD in the coming judgment (Amos 8:11–12). Amaziah's charge against Amos also included a misrepresentation of his prophecy (Amos 7:11). The prophecy in Amos 7:9 was against "the house of Jeroboam" and all that it represented—namely, the northern kingdom of Israel with all of its idolatrous practices

---

58. See Peter R. Ackroyd, "A Judgment Narrative between Kings and Chronicles? An Approach to Amos 7:9–17," in *Canon and Authority: Essays in Old Testament Religion and Theology*, eds. George W. Coats and Burke O. Long (Philadelphia: Fortress, 1977), 71–87.

and social injustices. This certainly would have included Jeroboam, but Amaziah made the prophecy personal and exclusive to Jeroboam, making the charge of conspiracy that much more pointed. Only the second half of Amaziah's "quote" of Amos is reiterated in Amos 7:17, forming a literary *inclusio*. But despite Amaziah's efforts to incite Jeroboam against Amos, there is no indication in the narrative of a response from the king. All signs suggest that Amaziah was working alone to stop the prophetic ministry of Amos in Israel.

Amaziah then took matters into his own hands and spoke directly to Amos (Amos 7:12–13). In the discourse, he refers to Amos as "prophetic visionary" (חֹזֶה), although the reader might expect "seer" (רֹאֶה) from the wording of Amos 7:1, 4, 7; 8:1; 9:1 (cf., 1 Sam. 9:9; 2 Kgs. 17:13; but see Amos 1:1).[59] He then instructs Amos to "flee" (as if threatened) back to Judah from which he came (Amos 1:1) in order to make his living as a prophet there in a place where a message against the north would be more palatable and perhaps more profitable (cf., Mic. 2:11; 3:5, 11). Amaziah adds that Amos is never again to prophesy in Bethel precisely because of its status as a "royal sanctuary" (cf., the capital Samaria). This is not merely a reference to a particular structure in Bethel. It is a description of Bethel as a whole and all that it represented as a place of idolatry sanctioned by the king (1 Kgs. 12:28–30). It is a far cry from the initial designation of Bethel as a place where God was surely present in a special way (Gen. 28:17, 19; 31:13; 35:7, 15).

The LXX rendering of Amos' response to Amaziah ("I was not a prophet") understands the prophet's words to be an account of how he was once not a prophet and then became one (Amos 7:14–15). While this translation works well syntactically with the *wayyiqtol* at the beginning of Amos 7:15,[60] it hardly seems necessary for Amos to point out that he was not born a prophet, since that would have been true of anyone. In context, it seems rather to be the case that he needed to clarify precisely what kind of a prophet he was.[61] The declaration, "I

---

59. This acknowledgement from Amaziah raises the underlying question of whether he actually believed Amos' prophecy. He certainly never explicitly denies the truth of it in the story. He only misrepresents Amos' intentions and insists that Amos prophesy elsewhere. If he did in fact believe him, the situation would have been that he chose to live in denial at the risk of very grave consequences, or it would have been that he had a very false sense of security in the Bethel establishment (cf., Jer. 7:1–15).

60. Jeremias, *Amos*, 139.

61. See Harper, *Amos and Hosea*, 171. Stuart thinks that the most contextually appropriate rendering is "No, I am a prophet though I am not a

am not a prophet," is clarified by the following clause, "and I am not a member of a prophetic guild (lit., son of a prophet)." That is, Amos does not deny here that he was in fact a true prophet (cf., Zech. 13:5), rather he denies that he was the kind of prophet that Amaziah took him to be. He was not simply a professional prophet for hire who could be dismissed so easily. Rather, his actual profession was of a different nature ("herdsman and someone who tends sycamore trees"), while his prophetic ministry was under the compulsion of a divine calling (Amos 3:7–8). He had no choice but to fulfill his mission. When Amos recounts in Amos 7:15 that the LORD took him "from after the flock," the language is reminiscent of the election of David (2 Sam. 7:8; Ps. 78:70), but it need not imply that Amos was required to abandon his profession completely (cf., Amos 1:1).

So, Amos continued unabated with his proclamation of the word of the LORD to the very man who forbade him to prophesy/drip (Amos 7:16; cf., Mic. 2:6). Contrary to Amaziah's characterization of Amos' prophecy as a personal attack on Jeroboam II, the words of the prophecy in Amos 7:17 are designed specifically for Amaziah himself. (Notice the fronting of the subject in each of the clauses of the Hebrew text.) It is Amaziah's wife who will shamefully become a prostitute in the city. His children will be the ones to die by the sword (cf., Amos 7:9, 11). It is Amaziah's land that will be divided and redistributed. Amaziah himself as a priest (albeit a false one) will die in an unclean/ defiled (i.e., foreign) land. This will all be part of the larger judgment against the people of Israel who will go into exile (cf., Amos 5:27; 6:7; 7:11).[62]

AMOS 8

8:1 "Thus the LORD [L: Lord GOD] showed me, and look, a basket of summer fruit [LXX: a fowler's basket; Syr.: the sign of the end]. 8:2 And he said, 'What do you see, Amos?' And I said, 'A basket of summer fruit

---

professional prophet" (*Hosea–Jonah*, 376). But this option has by no means been an obvious one to the majority of interpreters historically, in part because it requires two different treatments of the same negation. Furthermore, the initial objection makes it sound like Amaziah had claimed that Amos was not a prophet, which was not the case.

62. There is a certain rhetorical effect to the fact that Amos has the last word in this conversation (cf., Gen. 34:31; Jon. 4:11). See Meir Sternberg, *The Poetics of Biblical Narrative: Ideological Literature and the Drama of Reading* (Bloomington: Indiana University Press, 1985), 472–75.

[Heb., qayits].' And the LORD said to me, 'The end [Heb., qets] has come to my people Israel. I will never cross over to him again [see Amos 7:8b]. 8:3 And songs [LXX: rafters; NET: women singing (= שָׁרוֹת)] of temple / palace will wail in that day,' the prophetic utterance of the LORD [MT: Lord GOD; cf., LXX]. Great is the number of corpses. In every place he casts them. Hush!"

8:4 "Hear this, you who trample the needy [LXX: destroy the poor in the morning; Tg. Jon.: despise like the dust of the ground the poor] and cause the afflicted [Tg. Jon.: the words of the poor] of the land to cease [GKC §53q],[63] 8:5 saying, 'When will the new moon festival pass so that we may sell grain [Heb., shever]; and the Sabbath [or, mid-month][64] so that we may open grain [Heb., bar; LXX, Syr., Tg. Jon.: storehouses] to make small an ephah and to make great a shekel and to pervert scales of deceit, 8:6 to acquire lowly people for silver and needy people for a pair of sandals, and droppings [i.e., chaff] of grain is what we will sell.' 8:7 The LORD swears by the pride of Jacob, 'I will never forget any of their works' [GKC §149]."

8:8 "On account of this will not the land quake, and will not every inhabitant therein mourn, and will not all of it [i.e., the land] go up like the Nile [כִיאֹר; cf., Amos 9:5; L: like the light / dawn], and will it not be driven and sink [BDB, 1054] like the Nile of Egypt?"[65]

8:9 "'And so, in that day,' the prophetic utterance of the LORD [MT: Lord GOD; cf., LXX], 'I will bring in the sun at noon, and I will cause the land to be dark at a time when it should be light; 8:10 and I will turn your festivals into mourning and all your songs into lament; and I will bring upon all loins sackcloth and upon every head baldness; and I will make it [GKC §135p] like mourning for an only child and its end like a bitter day.'"

8:11 "'Look, days are coming,' the prophetic utterance of the LORD [MT: Lord GOD; cf., LXX], and I will send a famine in the land, not a famine for bread / food (and not thirst for water) but for hearing the word [L:

---

63. For other examples of the infinitive construct used as an indicative verb, see 2 Kgs. 3:24; Ezek. 22:3; Neh. 8:13; 1 Chr. 9:25; 2 Chr. 7:3; 11:22.
64. See Michael Fishbane, *Biblical Interpretation in Ancient Israel* (Oxford: Clarendon, 1985), 145–51.
65. *Tg. Jon.*: "and a king will go up with his armies, who is great like the water of a river, and he will cover all of it and drive out its inhabitants."

*words; pc Mss, LXX, Syr., Vulg.: word] of the LORD. 8:12 And they will
totter from sea to sea, and from north to east will they go to and fro to
seek the word of the LORD, but they will not find it. 8:13 In that day,
the beautiful virgins (and the choice, young men) will faint because of
thirst.*[66] *8:14 Those who swear by the guilt [Syr.: idol] of Samaria and
say, "As your god lives [GKC §93aa], O Dan," and, "As the way [LXX: god;
Tg. Jon.: laws] of Beersheba lives," they will fall and never rise again.'"*

The fourth vision (Amos 8:1–2) follows the pattern of the third (Amos
7:7–8; cf., Jer. 1:11–14). The prophet is shown a basket of "summer
fruit" (קָיִץ) (see Gezer Calendar). Some commentators have seen something in the nature of this type of fruit that illustrates the condition of
Israel, but it seems rather to be the case that what is seen in the vision
is only there for the wordplay that the Hebrew term creates with the
key word of the LORD's message, which is presumably why the LORD
has the prophet say out loud what it is that he has seen. The "end" (קֵץ)
has come to Israel (cf., Gen. 6:13).[67] The prophet Ezekiel later reap-
plies this language to the southern kingdom of Judah (Ezek. 7:2, 6) in
a prophecy whose words are confirmed in the text of Lam. 4:18b. Amos
8:2 then concludes in the manner of the end of Amos 7:8 ("I will never
again cross over to him"; but see BDB, 717). Verse 3 of Amos 8 has attached itself to the vision much in the same way as Amos 7:9 in relation to Amos 7:7–8. It illustrates what is meant by the end of Israel by
means of a devastating picture of wailing for widespread death. This is
punctuated by הָס ("Hush!"), which gives the reader a hint of the Day of
the LORD (Amos 6:10; Hab. 2:20; Zeph. 1:7; Zech. 2:17 [Eng., 2:13]).[68]

The summons to hear at the beginning of the unit in Amos 8:4–7
recalls language employed in the first half of the book (Amos 3:1;
4:1; 5:1), and indeed much of the wording found here revisits earlier

---

66. *Tg. Jon.*: "At that time, the congregations of Israel, who are like beautiful
virgins who go astray in their beauty with sinful young boys, will be weary
and stricken, cast down with thirst."

67. The MT vocalization of "summer fruit" (קָיִץ) reflects the two-syllable
pronunciation of Judean Hebrew. The Proto-Semitic vocalization used a
diphthong (קַיְץ), which would have been monophthongized in Northern
Hebrew (קֵיץ)—a pronunciation virtually identical to the word for "end"
(קֵץ). See Joshua Blau, *Phonology and Morphology of Biblical Hebrew*,
LSAWS 2 (Winona Lake, IN: Eisenbrauns, 2010), 96–97.

68. Malbim suggested gematria for הָס (65) in order to link it with the
prophecy of sixty-five years in Isaiah 7:8 (*Mikraoth Gedoloth: The Twelve
Prophets*, vol. 1, 158).

material. The unit is addressed to those who trample the needy and destroy the afflicted (Amos 8:4; cf., Amos 2:7; 5:11). They are quoted as asking when the new moon festival (Num. 10:10; 28:11; 1 Sam. 20:24–25; 2 Kgs. 4:23; Isa. 1:13; Hos. 2:13 [Eng., 2:11]) and the Sabbath (Exod. 20:8; Jer 17:19–27; Neh. 13:15–22; or, mid-month [Lev. 23:11]) will be over so that they can resume their corrupt commerce (Amos 8:5; cf., Lev. 19:35–36; Deut. 25:13–15; Hos. 12:8 [Eng., 12:7]; Mic. 6:11; Prov. 11:1; 20:10, 23). This corruption facilitated the "purchase" of the poor by means of the resulting indebtedness to the sellers who sold a bad product at a high price (Amos 8:6; cf., Amos 2:6). The LORD swears (sarcastically by the unwavering pride of Jacob [cf., Amos 4:2; 6:8]) that he will never forget their works. What they do will not go unnoticed, and they will face judgment for their actions.

The rhetorical question in Amos 8:8 indicates what will happen as a consequence of the accusation in Amos 8:4–7 and serves as a bridge to the units that follow where the details of what will occur in the Day of Judgment unfold. The imagery of the land rising and falling like the water level of the Nile hearkens back to the reference to the quake in Amos 1:1 (also Joel 4:16 [Eng., 3:16]; cf., Isa. 57:20; Jer. 46:7–8; Ezek. 27:28) and anticipates the use of similar imagery in the little hymn of Amos 9:5–6, which is connected to the fifth and final vision (Amos 9:1–4). Such a cosmic and eschatological depiction of mourning and loss in the judgment of Israel is consistent with what the reader finds in Amos 8:9–14 where the Day of the LORD comes into the foreground. Israel's historical judgment has become an occasion to speak of broader implications.

The phrase "in that day" in Amos 8:9 (cf., Amos 2:16; 8:3) recurs in Amos 8:13 (see also "days are coming" in Amos 8:11; 9:13) and serves to set the material in this section within the same eschatological context as what the reader finds in the work of the composer of the Twelve, which begins in Amos 9:11. The transformation of light into darkness (Amos 8:9) is familiar not only from the earlier hymns (Amos 4:13; 5:8) but also from the descriptions of the Day of the LORD in both Joel and Amos (Joel 2:2; 3:4 [Eng., 2:31]; Amos 5:18). The LORD says that he will turn the festivals that he rejects (Amos 5:21) into mourning and the songs to which he will not listen (Amos 5:23) into lament (Amos 8:10; cf., Amos 5:1; 8:3, 8; Tob. 2:6). This mourning will be expressed outwardly in the wearing of sackcloth and in the shaving of heads (Isa. 3:24; 15:2; Jer. 47:5; 48:37; Mic. 1:16; Ezek. 7:18; 27:31). It will be like mourning the loss of an only child (cf., Zech. 12:10). Its outcome will be very bitter indeed.

Earlier in Amos it was indicated that one of the initial signs of judgment to which the people did not respond was the lack of food—a literal famine (Amos 4:6). Now the LORD says that days are coming when there will be a different kind of famine: lack of the word of the LORD (Amos 8:11; cf., Deut. 8:3; 1 Sam. 3:1; Isa 29:9–12; Lam. 2:9; 4Q387 2:8–9). The phrase "the word of the LORD" is a key component of several prophetic superscriptions (Jer. 1:1 LXX; Ezek. 1:3; Hos. 1:1; Joel 1:1; Jon. 1:1; Mic. 1:1; Zeph. 1:1; Hag. 1:1; 2:1, 10, 20; Zech. 1:1, 7; 7:1; 8:1; 9:1; 12:1; Mal. 1:1), and the anticipated lack thereof in this passage likely refers to the removal of oral prophecy from the northern kingdom of Israel (cf., 1 Sam. 28:6–7).[69] Something similar would eventually happen to Judah as well (Ezek. 7:26; Mic. 3:6). Of course, prophets continued to appear in the postexilic period (e.g., Haggai and Zechariah), but they increasingly adopted the role of exegete of the written texts of earlier prophets (e.g., Zech. 1:4–6; Prov. 29:18 LXX). Oral prophecy virtually ceased with the last of the biblical prophets (but see John the Baptist and Agabus [Acts 11:27–30; 21:10]) and was replaced by the written corpus of prophetic literature. The existence of this literature has been threatened in the history of the persecution of the people of God (cf., 1 Macc. 1:56–57), but the absence of it in the last days might take a different form—willful neglect. John Chrysostom commented, "This very thing that the Lord threatened to inflict on them by way of punishment we now of our own volition secure for ourselves despite God's show of care for us and his provision for us, through the advice of mentors, as well as the reading of Scriptures."[70] That is, the wandering described in Amos 8:12 may very well be self-induced not for the lack of Scripture but for the lack of teaching it (cf., Jer. 5:1; Amos 4:6; Dan. 12:4; 2 Tim. 3:10–4:5).[71] What was once rejected (Amos 7:10–13) will become sought out of spiritual hunger, but the people will not even know where to look at that point to find satisfaction. They will have brought the judgment on themselves.

In that day, the beautiful virgins and the choice, young men will faint due to thirst (Amos 8:13; cf, Deut. 32:25; Zech. 9:17; Ps. 78:63).

---

69. This is likely not a reference to the Second Temple period (contra *Mikraoth Gedoloth: The Twelve Prophets*, vol. 1, 162) if for no other reason than the fact that prophecy had become a literary phenomenon by then and could be accessed at any time by those who could read or hear the reading of the texts.
70. Ferreiro, ed., *The Twelve Prophets*, 113.
71. The expression "from sea to sea" in this verse is normally understood to indicate east (Dead Sea) to west (Mediterranean Sea) (cf., Zech. 9:10; Ps. 72:8), but the corresponding "from north to east" is somewhat odd. The reader might expect "north to south" or something like "from the river (i.e., the Euphrates) to the ends of the earth (or, to the wadi or river of Egypt [e.g., Gen. 15:18])." These boundaries designate the land of the covenant.

That is, not only the old and weak but also the young and strong will faint. Following Amos 8:11–12, this is likely a reference to spiritual thirst for the word of the LORD rather than physical thirst for water (cf., Amos 4:7–8). Those who swear by the "guilt" of Samaria will fall and never rise again (Amos 8:14; cf., Isa. 24:20; Amos 5:2). The guilt of Samaria is indicated in the words of their oath (see 1 Kgs. 12:29; 2 Kgs. 17:30). They swear by the golden calf at Dan and by the "way" (דֶּרֶךְ) of Beersheba (Gen. 21:31; 26:33; Amos 5:5; Hos. 8:5). This "way" of Beersheba is either a reference to pilgrimage or a reference to the manner of false worship at that location.

AMOS 9:1–10

9:1 "I saw the Lord standing on / by the altar, and he said, 'Strike the capital [LXX: the place of propitiation (i.e., the lid of the ark; see Exod. 25:22)] so that the thresholds shake, and cut them off on the head / top of all of them; and as for their end, it is by the sword that will I slay them. A fleeing person of theirs will not flee, and an escapee of theirs will not escape.[72] *9:2 If they dig into Sheol, from there my hand will take them. And if they ascend the sky, from there I will bring them down [cf., Tg. Jon.]. 9:3 And if they hide at the top of Carmel, from there I will search and take them. And if they hide from before my eyes on the floor of the sea, from there I will command the serpent, and it will bite them [cf., Tg. Jon.]. 9:4 And if they go into captivity before their enemies, from there I will command the sword and slay them. And I will put my eye on them for harm and not for good.'"*

9:5 "And the Lord GOD of hosts is the one who strikes the land, and it melts, and all the inhabitants therein mourn [MurXII: every inhabitant therein mourns], and all of it [i.e., the land] goes up like the Nile and sinks like the Nile of Egypt [see Tg. Jon.; Amos 8:8]. 9:6 He is the one who builds in(to) the sky his steps; and his vault [LXX, Syr.: promise;

---

72. *"The prophet said, 'I saw the glory of the Lord; it ascended by the cherub and rested on the altar, and he said, "If my people Israel will not return to the law, extinguish the lamp; king Josiah shall be slain, the temple shall be laid waste, and the temple courts shall be destroyed; and the vessels of the Sanctuary shall be taken into captivity."'"* (*The Targum of the Minor Prophets; Translated, with a Critical Introduction, Apparatus, and Notes,* trans. Kevin J. Cathcart and Robert P. Gordon, The Aramaic Bible 14 [Collegeville, MN: Liturgical, 1989], 94). *Targum Jonathan* reads the text as a reference to the Jerusalem temple and the downfall of Judah.

Tg. Jon.: congregation], on land he establishes it. He is the one who summons the waters of the sea and pours them on the surface of the land. The LORD [Yahweh; LXX adds: God Almighty (cf., Amos 4:13)] is his name."

9:7 "'Are you not like Cushites [Tg. Jon.: beloved children] to me, O children of Israel?' the prophetic utterance of the LORD. 'Was it not Israel that I brought up out of the land of Egypt, and Philistines from Caphtor [LXX, Syr., Tg. Jon., Vulg.: Cappadocia], and Aram from Kir? 9:8 Look, the eyes of the Lord GOD are on the sinful kingdom, and I will destroy it from upon the surface of the earth. But not completely [GKC §113v] will I destroy the house of Jacob,' the prophetic utterance of the LORD. 9:9 'For look, I am commanding, and I will shake [LXX: winnow] with / among all the nations the house of Israel, just as grain is shaken [LXX: winnowed] in the sieve [LXX: with a winnowing fork], and a pebble [LXX: fragment] does not fall to the ground. 9:10 It is by the sword that all the sinners of my people will die—those who say, "The calamity will not approach or meet us from every side."'"

The fifth and final vision (Amos 9:1–4) begins differently from the other four. The prophet does not state that he was shown something. Rather, he simply says what it was that he saw (cf., 1 Kgs. 22:19; Isa. 6:1). Furthermore, there is no verbal exchange between the prophet and the LORD. The fifth vision does, however, have a point of contact with the third vision (Amos 7:7–8) in that the prophet sees in both the LORD standing on or by an object (cf., Isa. 3:13).[73] Here that object is the altar. The context suggests that this was most likely the altar at Bethel (Amos 5:5; 7:10; 8:14; see 1 Kgs. 13:1–3). The command to strike the capital of each of the pillars of the sanctuary is given to no one in particular in the vision. This strike would result in the shaking of the thresholds (cf., Isa. 6:4). The second command is to cut down the pillars on top of the false priests and the idol worshipers therein (cf., Judg. 16:29–30). Anyone left would be slaughtered by the sword (cf., Amos 7:9, 11, 17; 9:4, 10). No one would be able to flee or escape the judgment (cf., Amos 2:14–16).

The remainder of the vision is devoted to an expansion of the concept of the inescapability of divine judgment by means of a series of hypothetical (אם) scenarios outlined in the LORD's discourse (Amos 9:2–4). Even if the guilty were to flee to Sheol or go up into the sky,

---

73. Amos did not actually see the LORD (Exod. 33:20). He only saw him in a vision.

they would not be out of the LORD's reach (Amos 9:2; cf., Obad. 4; Ps. 139:7–10). These are not references to hell (i.e., place of eternal punishment) and heaven (i.e., the dwelling place of God). Rather, Sheol is the burial place of the dead, and the sky is the place where the birds fly and the clouds float. Thus, there is no place either high or low where the guilty can flee in this earthly realm. This is reiterated in Amos 9:3 using different imagery. Even at the top of Mount Carmel or at the bottom of the sea it is not possible to hide from the LORD (cf., Isa. 27:1; Amos 5:19; Job 38:16). It is not even enough for the people to be taken captive by their enemies (Amos 9:4; cf., Amos 7:17). From there the LORD will decree their slaughter by the sword (cf., Amos 7:9, 11, 17; 9:1, 10). The LORD will put his eye on them for bad and not for good (cf., Jer. 21:10; 39:12; Amos 9:8).

The hymn in Amos 9:5–6 is similar to Amos 8:8, but each text performs a different function in its given setting. The image in Amos 8:8 contributes to the depiction of the Day of the LORD (Amos 8:9–10). In Amos 9:5–6, the idea is to illustrate how the destruction of the sanctuary at Bethel (Amos 9:1–4) is but a microcosm of God's judgment of the world, which is his sanctuary (Isa. 66:1). This is the reason for the structural terminology in Amos 9:6. The LORD is the one who oversees the earthquakes and floods therein (cf., Isa. 24:4; Nah. 1:8). They are his instruments of judgment (Gen. 6–7).

The worldwide perspective of Amos 9:5–6 forms a nice segue to the comparison of Israel to the nations in Amos 9:7. Israel's uniqueness among the nations was not due to its ethnic superiority but to the unmerited election of God who chose Israel to be the means by which he would restore the lost blessing to all humanity (Gen. 12:1–3; Deut. 7:7–11). The revelation of this made Israel accountable in a way that other nations were not (Amos 3:1–2). Thus, Israel was and is in fact very special, but not in such a way that they were immune to the consequences of their failures. They had in many ways become like the nations that surrounded them (cf., Ezek. 16:3). In what way then were they like the Cushites? Jeremiah's analogy appears to bring out the point of comparison (Jer. 13:23). Israel and Judah were as likely to change their ways on their own as the Cushites were to change the distinctive color of their skin. It was Israel whom the LORD brought out of Egypt (Amos 2:10),[74] but it was not as if the LORD was inactive

---

74. In the present context, "Israel" is the northern kingdom of Israel, even though the exodus obviously included ancestors of the people of Judah as well. It is simply the case that the story is told with reference to one particular group, even though others were involved (cf., Ps. 78:9–17).

among the other nations (Gen. 10; Amos 1:3–2:3). He also brought the Philistines from "Caphtor" or Crete (cf., Jer. 47:4; Zeph. 2:5) and the Syrians from Kir (cf., Amos 1:5).[75] This is not to say that the biblical exodus was not unique. It is only to say that the LORD is the God of all nations precisely because he is the only true God (Isa. 37:16), whether they acknowledge him or not. He providentially orchestrates all the events of history. Therefore, the exodus from Egypt ultimately has significance for all.

The fact that the LORD is putting his eye on Israel for bad and not for good (Amos 9:4b) means that he is watching the sinful kingdom for the time when he will destroy it from the surface of the earth (Amos 9:8a; cf., Gen. 6:7; Zeph. 1:3b). This is consistent with the message of Amos in general (e.g., Amos 5:1–3). But Amos 9:8b mitigates this message of judgment, indicating that the destruction of the house of Israel will not be complete (cf., Lev. 26:44; Jer. 4:27; 5:10, 18; 30:11; Amos 3:12; 4:11; Neh. 9:31). The Hebrew syntax suggests that the translation should be "not completely will I destroy" rather than "I will not destroy completely" (GKC §113v). That is, the negation is for the manner in which the destruction is conducted, not for the destruction itself.

Verse 9 of Amos 9 brings the nations back into view (cf., Amos 9:7), which now anticipates the message about the nations in Amos 9:12. The LORD decrees that he will shake Israel with all the nations as in a sieve through which a pebble does not fall. It matters very little what decision the interpreter makes about what the pebble or the grain represents in this analogy. The idea is that there will be a separation of the wicked from the righteous remnant. The fact that Israel and the nations are in the sieve together means that members from both groups will come from both Israel and the nations. That is, it would hardly make sense in the context of Amos 9:7–8 to say that the metaphorical sieve is designed to separate righteous Israel from the wicked nations. No, the wicked from Israel and the nations will be judged, and the righteous from Israel and the nations will be delivered.[76] It is by the sword that all the sinners of God's people will die (Amos 9:10a; cf., Amos 7:9, 11, 17; 9:1, 4)—all those of Israel who dismiss the prophetic warning about the coming calamity (Amos 9:10b; cf., Amos 5:18; Mic. 3:11).

---

75. The word "Caphtor" is the same word translated "pillar" in Amos 9:1.
76. This will be treated more fully in the discussion of the seam in Amos 9:11–15 and its connection to Obadiah and Jonah.

AMOS 9:11–15

9:11 "In that day, I will raise up the fallen [or, falling; cf., LXX, Syr.; see GKC §116d] booth [f. sg.] of David, and I will wall up their [f. pl.; LXX: f. sg.; Syr.: m. pl.] breaches, and his [LXX: f. sg.; Syr.: m. pl.] torn down places will I raise up, and I will build it [f. sg.; Syr.: m. sg.] like days of old [Syr. adds: and as the years of generations past],[77] 9:12 in order that they may possess [יירשו] the remnant of Edom [אדום][78] and all the nations upon whom my name is called," the prophetic utterance of the LORD who does this. 9:13 "Look, days are coming," the prophetic utterance of the LORD, "and one who plows will draw near with the one who harvests, and one treading grapes with the one who draws the seed. And the mountains will drip sweet wine, and all the hills will melt. 9:14 And I will restore the fortunes [LXX, Syr., Tg. Jon.: return the captives][79] of my people Israel. And they will build desolate cities and live in them. And they will plant vineyards and drink their wine. And they will make gardens and eat their fruit. 9:15 And I will plant them on their land, and they will never again be uprooted from upon their land that I have given to them," says the LORD your God [LXX: the Lord God Almighty].

Amos 9:11–15 forms the first part of a compositional seam that also includes the material in Obadiah 1–5 (see Introduction). This material is distinctive in that it does not belong to the nations corpus (Amos 1–2), the messages of judgment and the woes (Amos 3–6), or the visions of judgment (Amos 7:1–9:10). It is rather a prophecy of restoration unparalleled anywhere in the book of Amos. Furthermore, it reflects the perspective of the falling or fallen Davidic kingdom (i.e., Judah), which was not the perspective of the eighth-century prophet. It is true that

---

77. *Tg. Jon.*: "At that time, I will raise up the kingdom [f. sg.] of the house of David that has fallen, and I will build their [m. pl.] fortresses, and their [m. pl.] congregations will I prepare, and it [f. sg.] will rule over all the kingdoms, and it will destroy and finish many armies, and it will be built and completed like the days of old."

78. LXX (Alexandrinus): "in order that the remnant of mankind [= אדם] may seek [ידרשו] the Lord [את]." The direct object marker (את) features the first and last letters of the Hebrew alphabet (*aleph* and *taw*). The LXX (Alexandrinus) translates it with "the Lord," understanding the letters to represent the fact that God is the beginning and the end (Isa. 41:4; 44:6; Rev. 1:8; 22:13; cf., Acts 15:17). See also Schart, "Versions of Amos," 169–77.

79. For discussion of this idiom, see the translation note and commentary for Hosea 6:11b.

Amos 2:4–5 and Amos 6:1 anticipate judgment for Judah, but Amos 9:11 is not a prediction of Judah's fall. It is a prophecy about the future that presupposes the fall of Judah as a present reality. Amos 9:11–15 also meets the second criterion of a compositional seam, which is the development of the program set forth in Hosea 3:4–5.[80] There it was said that Israel would seek the LORD and David their king in the last days. Now it is added that Gentiles will also be part of the people of God in the messianic kingdom (Amos 9:12; Acts 15:17).[81] Lastly, this compositional seam cites from the book of Jeremiah, which is a feature common to the other seams of the Twelve. The primary citation occurs in the Obadiah portion of the seam (Jer. 49:9, 14–16; Obad. 1–5), but the expression "restore the fortunes" in Amos 9:14, while not unique to Jeremiah (e.g., Deut. 30:3), is more frequent in Jeremiah than in any other biblical book (e.g., Jer. 29:14; 30:3; 31:23; 32:44; 33:7).

The phrase "In that day" (Amos 9:11a; cf., Amos 2:16; 8:3, 9, 13) must be defined by the immediate context. It is clear from what follows that the prophecy envisions an eschatological time that has not come to fruition at any point in previous world history. At that time, the LORD says that he will raise up "the fallen booth of David" (see LXX, Syr.). *Targum Jonathan* rightly understands this to be a reference to the fallen kingdom of David, which from the present perspective has been left like a hut in a field (cf., Isa. 1:8; 4:6; Zech. 12:7).[82] 4Q*Florilegium* (4Q174) cites this text with reference to the covenant with David (2 Sam. 7:12–14) and the branch of David (Jer. 23:5–6; Zech. 6:12–13) will who rise up in the last days. The Masoretic Text of Amos 9:11b contains three

---

80. Augustine explicitly linked Amos 9:11 with Hos. 3:5 (Ferreiro, ed., *The Twelve Prophets*, 116).

81. "Verse 12 picks up the theme of the small book of Obadiah and constructs a bridge to it; v. 13 provides a link back to Joel 4:18 and thereby simultaneously a closure with the beginning of the present book in Amos 1:2, which in its own turn alludes to Joel 4:16. We do not need to address the difficult problem of the priority of these connections in order to see clearly that these relationships are to prevent the reader of the book of Amos from reading it in isolation. This device assumes that the reader has the perseverance to consider the book of Amos together with the other prophetic books comprising the Twelve Prophets" (Jeremias, *Amos*, 169–70).

82. The Babylonian Talmud (*b. Sanh.* 96b, 97a) derives from this a title for the Messiah: "the son of the fallen one." Stuart thinks that the Hebrew word translated "booth" should be revocalized so that it is the place name Succoth, which he says was the location from which David dominated Israel's neighbors to the east and south (*Hosea–Jonah*, 398). Its restoration would signal the return of that former dominance.

different pronominal suffixes that have given rise to various attempts to resolve the situation in the textual witnesses. The first occurs where the LORD says, "And I will wall up their (f. pl.) breaches." One possibility is that the preceding feminine singular "fallen booth of David" should be revocalized in the Hebrew text so that it reads "fallen booths of David," making it the antecedent of the third feminine plural suffix. Another possibility is that it refers to the broken "city walls" (חומות) of the Davidic kingdom (cf., 2 Kgs. 14:13; Neh. 6:1). The second pronominal suffix occurs in the next clause, "And his (m. sg.) torn down places will I raise up." This one seems most likely to be a reference back to David in Amos 9:11a. The last pronoun is then a reference to the booth/kingdom: "And I will build it (f. sg.) like days of old" (cf., Isa. 44:26; 49:17 [1QIsaᵃ]; 58:12). What does it mean for the kingdom to be rebuilt like olden days? It will be a return to the golden age of the united kingdom of Israel under David and Solomon without any of their problems—much the same way that kingdom is depicted in Chronicles. This is a common way among the prophets to describe what the messianic kingdom will be like (e.g., 1 Kgs. 5:5 [Eng., 4:25]; Mic. 4:4; Zech. 3:10).

Amos 9:12 indicates that the purpose for the restoration of the Davidic kingdom is the possession of the remnant of Edom. There is some question here about the subject of the third masculine plural verb ("in order that they may possess"). Does this refer to the members of the kingdom? It is quite possible that the subject is indefinite, in which case the verb could be translated as a passive ("in order that the remnant of Edom may be possessed"). What is the sense of the verb "possess" here? Does it have a positive connotation such as inclusion within the kingdom, or does it have a negative one as in the sense of dispossession? It is clear from the use of this verb in Obadiah 19 that Israel will conquer the land of Edom and defeat any enemies therein, but Amos 9:12 seems to allow for a believing remnant of Edomites who are representative of all Gentiles who bear the name of the LORD (cf., Zech. 2:15 [Eng., 2:11]).[83] This is the way the LXX (Alexandrinus) understands the text (see note to translation above). It takes "in order that they may possess

---

83. "יִירְשׁוּ, to take possession of, is chosen with reference to the prophecy of Balaam (Num. 24:18), that Edom should be the possession of Israel (see the comm. on this passage). Consequently the taking possession referred to here will be of a very different character from the subjugation of Edom and other nations to David. It will make the nations into citizens of the kingdom of God, to whom the Lord manifests Himself as their God, pouring upon them all the blessings of His covenant of grace (see Isa. 56:6–8)" (Keil, *Minor Prophets*, 222).

(*yiyreshu*) the remnant of Edom" and renders, "in order that the remnant of mankind (*adam*) may seek (*yidreshu*) the Lord."[84] This is, of course, adopted in Acts 15:17 where Luke presents James at the Jerusalem council making the definitive argument for the inclusion of the Gentiles in God's kingdom from this very text.[85] Such a reading seems warranted by the latter part of Amos 9:12, which reads, "and all the nations upon whom my name is called." This expression is so strongly associated with Israel as the people of God (e.g., Deut. 28:10; Isa. 63:19; Jer. 14:9; 2 Chr. 7:14) that Redak (Rabbi David Kimhi) thought that the relative clause ("upon whom my name is called") must apply to Israel rather than the nations, although the syntax does not really allow for this as the most likely option.[86] Such language is employed here to show that a remnant of believing Gentiles will become part of the people of God.

It is fair to ask why Edom is the representative Gentile nation. One reason is the graphic similarity between "Edom" and *adam* ("mankind") highlighted by the LXX here and by other texts elsewhere (e.g., Ezek. 34:31; 35; 36:37–38). Thus, for instance, Isaiah can use Edom's judgment (Isa. 34:5–17) to represent worldwide judgment (Isa. 34:1–4). Edom also has a long history with Israel in the biblical narrative going back to the relationship between the brothers Jacob and Esau. Edom was, of course, a perennial enemy of Israel (Jer. 49:7–22), but there were also benefits that Edom enjoyed as the result of its familial relationship to Israel (Deut. 2:2–8). The story of David's conquest of Edom (2 Sam. 8:14; but see 2 Kgs. 8:20–22) along with other surrounding nations (2 Sam. 8) is in many ways a prefiguration of what will take place in the messianic kingdom (Amos 9:12; Obad. 15–21). Following the book of Amos, the book of Obadiah highlights the judgment of Edom (Obad. 1–14). Its conclusion, however, looks forward to what will take place in the eschatological Day of the LORD (Obad. 15). Obadiah 16–21 uses the root ירשׁ ("possess") from Amos 9:12 five times to describe both the conquest and the possession of the territory to be incorporated into the kingdom of God (Obad. 21), including the mountain of Esau/Edom (Obad. 19). For the enemies of the people of God, this will mean defeat and dispossession. For the believing Gentile remnant, this will mean

---

84. It is possible that the LXX translator had a slightly different Hebrew text here, but given the correspondence with the meaning of the consonantal text now represented by the MT, it seems more likely that the translator brought out the sense of the proto-MT on the basis of similarities known to him (Edom/*adam* and *yiyreshu*/*yidreshu*).
85. Shepherd, *The Twelve Prophets*, 12.
86. *Mikraoth Gedoloth: The Twelve Prophets*, vol. 1, 169.

participation in the kingdom of God and membership among God's people. And the assurance is that the LORD is the one who will accomplish this (Amos 9:12b; cf., Isa. 9:6b [Eng., 9:7b]).

The expression "Look, days are coming" at the beginning of Amos 9:13 invites the reader to picture the eschaton (cf., Amos 8:11). It will be a time when the land of the covenant will be so productive and bountiful that the seasons of planting and harvesting will overlap (cf., Lev. 26:5). This is the ideal of the new and improved Garden of Eden (Isa. 51:3; Ezek. 36:35). The grape harvest will be so abundant that it will be as if the mountains were dripping with sweet wine, and all the hills flowing therewith (cf., Joel 4:18 [Eng., 3:18]). The LORD will restore the fortunes of his people (Amos 9:14; see comment at Hos. 6:11b). That is, they will rebuild desolate cities and live in them. They will plant vineyards and drink their wine. They will make gardens and eat their fruit. This is the language Isaiah uses to describe the new creation and the new Jerusalem (Isa. 65:17–18, 21–22; cf., Deut. 6:10–15; Jer. 31:5; Ezek. 28:26). Never again will the enemy come to take what belongs to them (Deut. 28:30–31). And just as they will plant vineyards, so will the LORD plant them in such a way that they will never again be uprooted (Amos 9:15; cf., Isa. 60:21; 61:3; Jer. 31:40; 32:41; Ezek. 34:29). It is important to note that these physical realities are just as much a part of the eschaton as the spiritual ones are. There is no exegetical warrant for spiritualizing a passage like this into a series of metaphors. God created a real world (Gen. 1–2), and he intends to restore it in the last days.[87] The composer personalizes this for the reader when he adds to the end of Amos 9:15, "says the LORD your (m. sg.) God."[88]

THE BOOK OF AMOS AS CHRISTIAN SCRIPTURE
The book of Amos is cited as Christian Scripture (Acts 15:17) precisely at the point where it intersects with the work of the composer of the Twelve. This is a good lesson for a modern Christian teacher or preacher to learn. Contemporary application of the book of Amos in the church should not come in the form of artificial appropriation

---

87. "When applied to biblical prophecy, biblical realism believes that future events are also described in the Bible just as they will happen. That is, both future events and past events are recounted realistically—though one must remain sensitive to the various types of literature used by the biblical authors to depict future events" (John H. Sailhamer, *Biblical Prophecy* [Grand Rapids: Zondervan, 1998], 18).
88. Redak read this as part of God's address to the prophet (*Mikraoth Gedoloth: The Twelve Prophets*, vol. 1, 170).

of the prophet's words of judgment to a new audience. That ship has already sailed. Amos' message of judgment was delivered and received by an audience that saw the fulfillment of his words historically in the Assyrian captivity. Those words are now at best a reminder of God's faithfulness to the terms of the old covenant and a glimpse of what the final judgment might be. They are preserved for the reader in order to set up the eschatological and messianic hope in Amos 9:11–15. This is what makes the book relevant for the new covenant believer.[89] That is, what did not take place historically was the redemption from Assyrian captivity or the inclusion of the Gentiles. Not even the later Judean return from Babylon fulfilled the prophecy in Amos 9:11–15. It is the future hope of every believer in Christ dead or alive today. Therefore, any exposition of Amos' message of judgment must always have Amos 9:11–15 and its role in the development of the Twelve in view. The judgment is only the context out of which the hope of the gospel emerges.

---

89. "Actualization has already been built into the canonical text. Thus, the book of Amos is not a dead relic of the past which needs to be made relevant" (Brevard S. Childs, *Introduction to the Old Testament as Scripture* [Philadelphia: Fortress, 1979], 408). "They [the scribal elite] redefined prophecy in terms of the records of past revelations rather than oracles currently being spoken, and they reshaped the prophetic tradition by delimiting the prophets and oracles that make up the prophetic canon. In the way that they integrated interpretive commentary with the oracle collections that provided the raw material for the prophetic books, they also modeled and thus defined the right way of interpreting this canon. Only if just these books were read in just this way would the authentic 'word of YHWH' be revealed for the present time" (Michael H. Floyd, "New Form Criticism and Beyond: The Historicity of Prophetic Literature Revisited," in *The Book of the Twelve and the New Form* Criticism, eds. Mark J. Boda, Michael H. Floyd, and Colin M. Toffelmire [Atlanta: SBL, 2015], 30). "[T]he Bible, despite its textual heterogeneity, can be read as a self-glossing book. One learns to study it by following the ways in which one portion of the text illumines another. The generation of scribes who shaped and reshaped the Scriptures appear to have designed them to be studied in just this way" (Gerald Bruns, "Midrash and Allegory," in *The Literary Guide to the Bible*, eds. Frank Kermode and Robert Alter [Cambridge, MA: Belknap, 1987], 626–27).

BOOK OF THE TWELVE

OBADIAH

OBADIAH 1–14

1 The prophetic vision of Obadiah. Thus says the Lord GOD to Edom: A report have we heard [LXX: I heard (cf., Jer. 49:14)] from the LORD, and a messenger among the nations has been sent [cf., Jer. 49:14 שלוח*; see also Jer. 49:14 LXX: send]. "Arise so that we may rise up against her for battle [Jer. 49:14 Gather together and come against her and rise up for battle]." 2 "Look, small is how I have given you among the nations,[1] despised are you very much so [Jer. 49:15 among mankind]. 3 The presumption of your heart is what has deceived you [Jer. 49:16 Your horror, the presumption of your heart has deceived you]—living in clefts of rock, the high place of his dwelling [Jer. 49:16 grasping high place of hill],[2] saying in his heart, 'Who will bring me down to ground?' 4 If [Jer. 49:16* כי*] you were to make high like the eagle, and if among stars were set [> Jer. 49:16] your nest, from there I would bring you down," the prophetic utterance of the LORD. 5 "If robbers were to come to you, if nighttime despoilers (O how you are ruined! [LXX: where would you be cast aside? Tg. Jon.: how would you sleep until . . .; cf., Syr.]), would they not steal only what is enough for them [Jer. 49:9b If robbers were to come to you, they would damage only what is enough for them]? If grape gatherers were to come to you, would they not [Jer.*

---

1. The *qatal* forms in Obadiah need not be translated as future tenses. They serve to back reference or establish what it is that the LORD has decreed for Edom.
2. *Targum Jonathan* makes a comparison to an eagle here, anticipating the imagery of Obadiah 4.

49:9a אֹל] leave gleanings? 6 How Esau is searched, his hidden treasures are searched out! 7 To the border all the men of your agreement send you. The men of your peace deceive you, they overcome you. As for your bread [Tg. Jon.: those who eat at your table], they will put an ambush [LXX, Syr.] in your place. (There is no understanding in him.) 8 Will it not be in that day," the prophetic utterance of the LORD, "and I will destroy wise men from Edom and understanding from the mountain of Esau? 9 And your mighty men, O Teman, will be shattered in order that each one might be cut off from the mountain of Esau. Because of killing [cf., LXX, Syr., Vulg.], 10 because of violence done to your brother Jacob shame will cover you, and you will be cut off forever. 11 In the day of your standing from before, in a day of strangers taking his army captive—and foreigners, they entered his gate [qere: gates], and for Jerusalem they cast a lot [or, cast lots]—also you were like one of them. 12 And do not look upon the day of your brother in the day of his misfortune [LXX, Syr.: foreigners], and do not rejoice about the sons of Judah in the day of their perishing, and do not cause your mouth to say great things in a day of distress. 13 Do not enter the gate of my people in the day of their calamity [LXX: toil]. Do not look also you upon his evil [LXX: congregation] in the day of his calamity [LXX: destruction]. And do not send against his army [cf., LXX; or, in his wealth; see Tg. Jon., GKC §47k] in the day of his calamity [LXX: perishing]. 14 And do not stand upon the parting of ways [NET: fork in the road] to cut off the life of his people who escape, and do not deliver his survivors to the enemy in a day of distress."[3]

There are two parts to the heading of Obadiah. The first part designates the content of the book as the "prophetic vision" (חֲזוֹן) of Obadiah ("servant of the LORD") (cf., Isa. 1:1; Mic. 1:1; Nah. 1:1). There is no date formula attached to this (cf., Joel 1:1; Jon. 1:1; Nah. 1:1; Mal. 1:1), and no further information appears in the book with regard to the prophet's life or background (cf., Joel, Nah., Mal.)—presumably because such information is irrelevant to the purpose and message of the book. Any attempt to "rectify" this situation runs the risk of obscuring what it is that the author wants the reader to see. The second part of the heading is the messenger formula: "Thus says the Lord GOD to Edom" (cf., Jer. 49:7). But the direct address to Edom does not begin until verse 2 and ends after verse 15, so some prefer to say that this

---

3. The use of prohibitions in Obadiah 12–14 for actions already committed (see Obad. 10–11) creates a powerful rhetorical effect.

is "about/concerning/with regard to Edom" rather than "to Edom."[4] For other oracles about Edom, see Numbers 24:18; Isaiah 63:1–6; Jeremiah 9:24–25 (Eng., 9:25–26); 25:21; 27; 49:7–22; Ezekiel 25:12–14; 32:29; 35–36; Amos 1; 9:12; Joel 4:19 (Eng., 3:19); Malachi 1:2–5 (see also 2 Sam. 8:14; 2 Kgs. 8:20–22; 2 Chr. 21:8–10).

The first five verses of Obadiah connect the book to the end of Amos (see commentary on Amos 9:11–15). This is where the composer of the Twelve characteristically cites from the book of Jeremiah (Jer. 49:9, 14–16). Historically the debate about the direction of dependence here has focused on whether Obadiah was prior to Jeremiah or later than Jeremiah. But when this material is assigned to the composer of the Twelve it becomes clear that it is part of a larger pattern of dependence upon Jeremiah within the seam work of the Book of the Twelve. The Obadiah text is consistently longer than the Jeremiah text, which is a sign of dependence and expansion, and it seems more likely in general that the Obadiah text is the result of careful selection from the larger Jeremiah section devoted to Edom (Jer. 49:7–22). It is less likely that the Jeremiah section began as a disintegration and rearrangement of the smaller Obadiah unit and then grew into the present state in which the reader finds it.[5]

Obadiah 1 says, "A report have we heard," rather than, "A report have I heard" (LXX; Jer. 49:14). Given the fact that the "report" here is specifically a prophetic report (cf., Isa. 28:9, 19; 53:1), it is likely that the prophetic composer speaks here on behalf of the prophets (cf., Amos 3:7), although it is not out of the question that he speaks on behalf of the people in general. The other option is that of the editorial "we." The report is from the LORD himself, and a messenger/envoy has been sent among the nations to deliver it. It is not clear whether this is a heavenly messenger or an earthly one, although contextually it seems probable that this is the prophet's depiction of his own role and the

---

4. Paul Raabe provides several examples from Jeremiah (Jer. 27:19–22; 30:5–7; 31:35–36; 45:2–5) of gaps between a messenger formula and the beginning of divine speech (*Obadiah: A New Translation with Introduction and Commentary*, AB 24D [New York: Doubleday, 1996], 108–112).

5. For arguments in favor of the priority of Jeremiah's text, see Julius A. Bewer, *A Critical and Exegetical Commentary on Obadiah and Joel*, ICC (New York: Charles Scribner's Sons, 1911), 33–37; Raabe, *Obadiah*, 22–31. Keil, on the other hand, argued for the priority of Obadiah (*Minor Prophets*, 229). Still others argue for a third, common source, which is difficult to prove given the lack of evidence (e.g., Hans Walter Wolff, *Obadja und Jona*, BKAT 13/4 [Neukirchen: Neukirchener, 1977], 12, 20).

role of his book. The call to rise up against the land of Edom for battle is not the full extent of the report in the present form of the text. The LORD's direct address to Edom in the following verses now provides an explanation for the summons that belongs to the overall message that the prophetic book delivers.

The LORD begins his speech by pointing out that he has already made the decision to make Edom small/insignificant and despised among the nations (Obad. 2).[6] It is the presumption of Edom's heart, which Jeremiah 49:16 calls Edom's "horror," that has deceived the nation into thinking that it is somehow safe from the LORD's judgment (Obad. 3). Living in clefts of "rock" (*sela*, cf., Judg. 1:36; 2 Kgs. 14:7; Isa. 16:1), the high place of his dwelling, he says in his heart, "Who will bring me down to the ground?" In the Jeremiah 49:16 text, the LORD says that even if Edom were to put its nest (i.e., dwelling place) in a high place like an eagle would, he would still be able to bring the nation down from there (cf., Num. 24:21; Amos 9:2). The Obadiah text expands on this and adds, "and if among stars it were set," making it even more impossible for Edom to flee from the LORD (Obad. 4).

The hypothetical scenarios in Obadiah 5 suggest that there will be no mercy for Edom. Even thieves steal only what suffices for them, but the thought of how nothing at all will be left behind for Edom leads to the interjection of a lament: "O how you are ruined!" This interjection is part of what has been added to the text from Jeremiah 49:9b. The second example then is like the first. Grape gatherers leave some gleanings behind in accordance with the law (Lev. 19:9–10), but there will be nothing left in the wake of Edom's destruction. Obadiah 6 echoes the thought of the interjection in Obadiah 5. Esau's (i.e., Edom's) hidden treasures will be thoroughly ransacked. Verse 7 indicates that the people of Edom will be sent to their own border by those whom they consider allies (cf., Ezek. 11:10–11). They will deceive and overcome them (cf., Jer. 38:22). Those who eat their bread will set an ambush for them (cf., Dan. 11:26). Parenthetically, Edom has no understanding in the sense that what will happen will be completely unexpected.

The rhetorical question in Obadiah 8 indicates that in the day of judgment (cf., Obad. 15) the LORD will destroy the wise men from Edom and understanding from the mountain of Esau (cf., Jer. 49:7). The "wise men" here are perhaps not a random reference to sages but a reference to Edom's political officials (cf., Isa. 19:11). Teman's (i.e., Edom's) warriors will be shattered or dismayed, resulting in the loss of each one (Obad.

---

6. The use of the phrase "among mankind" in Jeremiah 49:15 allows for the play on *adam* ("mankind") and "Edom."

9). The phrase "because of killing" at the end of verse 9 can be construed with what precedes it, but it likely belongs with verse 10 (LXX, Syr., Vulg.). It is because of Esau's/Edom's violence done to his own brother Jacob/Israel that the nation will be covered with shame and cut off forever (Obad. 10; see Gen. 25:19–34; 27; 33; Ezek. 35:5; Joel 4:19 [Eng., 3:19]). What was the day of Edom's standing opposite Judah (Obad. 11)? The text describes this as the day when strangers took Judah's army captive. Foreigners entered Judah's gates and cast lots for Jerusalem. The most immediately recognizable event in the biblical narrative that the reader would associate with this is the Babylonian invasion of Judah and Jerusalem in 587/586 BC (2 Kgs. 25; cf., Ps. 137:7; Lam. 4:21).[7] In what way then was Edom like one of Judah's Babylonian enemies? At first glance it looks like Edom was simply standing by, passively approving the actions of the Babylonians. It is true that this alone would have made Edom a kind of participant, but verse 10 has already suggested that Edom was somehow actively involved in the violence done to Judah. Such action is addressed in Obadiah 12–14.

Verses 12–14 consist of a series of eight prohibitions. In light of verses 10 and 11, it seems best to understand these as prohibitions against what Edom has already committed in the wake of the Babylonian invasion rather than as prohibitions against what Edom might potentially do. Verse 12a deals with what verse 11 describes— standing opposite Judah, looking upon their calamity, and rejoicing (cf., Lam. 4:21; see also Prov. 24:17–18). Judah's downfall should not be a reason for Edom to boast (Obad. 12b). Verses 13 and 14 deal more with Edom's active violence against Judah as referenced in Obadiah 10. Edom should not enter the gate of Judah as the Babylonians had done (Obad. 11, 13a). The verb "send" (שלח) in Obadiah 13b is usually understood in terms of the expression "to stretch out the hand," in which case the phrase בחילו could be either "in his wealth" or "against his army" (see BDB, 1018), indicating either looting or attack. Verse 14 then forbids picking off Judeans who are fleeing the Babylonian invasion in an attempt to escape. It also forbids capturing any survivors and delivering them to the enemy.

OBADIAH 15–21

15 "For near is the Day of the LORD upon all the nations. Just as you have done, it will be done to you. Your dealing, it will return on your head. 16 For just as you [pl.] drank on my holy mountain, all

---

7. See Bewer, *Obadiah*, 26; Raabe, *Obadiah*, 51.

the nations will drink continually [mlt Mss: around; LXX: wine].[8] *And they will drink and swallow and be as they were not. 17 But on Mount Zion will be an escaped remnant, and it will be a place set apart. And the house of Jacob will possess their possessions [MurXII, LXX, Syr., Tg. Jon., Vulg.: their possessors]. 18 And the house of Jacob will be a fire, and the house of Joseph will be a flame, and the house of Esau will become chaff. And they will burn against them and consume them. And there will not be a survivor of the house of Esau, for it is the LORD who has spoken. 19 And the south will possess the mountain of Esau, and the lowland [will possess] the Philistines. And they will possess the field / land [LXX: mountain] of Ephraim and the field / land of Samaria, and Benjamin [will possess] Gilead [LXX: and Benjamin and Gilead]. 20 And the exiles of this army / fortress of the sons of Israel [will possess] that of Canaanites up to Zarephath [cf., LXX]. And the exiles of Jerusalem who are in Sepharad, they will possess the cities of the south. 21 And deliverers [LXX: delivered men; cf., Syr.] will go up in / on [LXX: from] Mount Zion to judge the mountain of Esau, and to the LORD will the kingdom belong [Tg. Jon.: and the kingdom of the LORD will be revealed to all the inhabitants of the earth]."*

Obadiah 15 is a hinge that makes the transition from Obadiah 1–14 to Obadiah 16–21. On the one hand, it completes the direct discourse to Edom from Obadiah 2–14. On the other hand, it moves from the message of a historical day of judgment against Edom (Obad. 8–14) to the message of eschatological judgment and deliverance in the Day of the LORD (Obad. 16–21).[9] The book of Obadiah thus continues the development of the theme of this Day in the Book of the Twelve (Joel 1:15; 2:1, 11; 3:4 [Eng., 2:31]; 4:14 [Eng., 3:14]; Amos 5:18). The historical judgment against Edom now prefigures the eschatological judgment

---

8. *Tg. Jon.*: "For just as you rejoiced over the wound of my holy mountain, all the peoples will drink the cup of their repayment continually."

9. "The primary meaning is not the day of judgment, but the day on which Jehovah reveals His majesty and omnipotence in a glorious manner, to overthrow all ungodly powers, and to complete His kingdom. It was this which gave rise to the idea of the day of judgment and retribution which predominates in the prophetic announcements, but which simply forms one side of the revelation of the glory of God, as our passage at once shows; inasmuch as it describes Jehovah as not only judging all nations and regarding them according to their deeds (cf. vv. 15b, and 16), but as providing deliverance upon Zion (v. 17), and setting up His kingdom (v. 21)" (Keil, *Minor Prophets*, 244).

against the nations in the always imminent Day of the LORD. Just as Edom represented the nations in a positive way in Amos 9:12, so Edom represents the nations in a more negative way in Obadiah (cf., the positive role of Nineveh as the representative in Jonah and its negative role as such in Nahum). The justice that will be dealt to Edom and all the nations in that final Day will be according to the law of retaliation or *lex talionis* (Exod. 21:23–25; cf., Judg. 1:6–7; Jer. 50:15; Joel 4:4 [Eng., 3:4]; Ps. 7:17 [Eng., 7:16]). They must consider their present actions (e.g., Obad. 10–14) in light of that Day.

The first part of Obadiah 16 ("For just as you drank on my holy mountain") uses a second masculine plural verb ("you drank") in the Hebrew text. The subject of this verb is likely not Edom (contra *Targum Jonathan*'s attempt to interpret this as Edom's reveling in victory on Mount Zion), given the fact that Edom is addressed using the second masculine singular throughout Obadiah 2–15. The nations cannot be the subject. They are the subject of the next part of the verse. The only suitable solution seems to be that the Judeans are the subject.[10] If it is objected that they have not been addressed this way thus far, the reply is that no one has been addressed this way thus far, and the Judeans have not been addressed at all. The comparison would then be that just as Judah drank the LORD's cup of judgment at the hands of the Babylonians, so will all the nations drink that same cup in the Day of the LORD (Jer. 25:15–26; 49:12; Lam. 4:21). They will drink it in such a way that they will return to their state of being prior to their existence as nations. That is, they will cease to exist.

But as for Mount Zion, there will be a remnant of God's people (Obad. 17; cf., Joel 3:5 [Eng., 2:32]). The place will be a sanctuary (cf., Isa. 2:1–5; Mic. 4:1–5), and the house of Jacob will possess its land. The early versions, however, followed a slightly different reading, which said that the house of Jacob would possess those who had possessed them (cf., Jer. 49:2b). The combination of the house of Jacob and the house of Joseph in Obadiah 18 suggests a reunited kingdom of Judah and Israel as in the days of David and Solomon (cf., Jer. 3:17–18). This will be confirmed in Obadiah 19. They will be a fire/flame (i.e., instrument of divine judgment) to the stubble of the house of Esau and all the nations represented by them (cf., Amos 1:12; Zech. 12:6). There will be no remnant of wicked and unbelieving Gentiles. The message is certain, for it is the LORD (and not merely the prophet) who says this.

---

10. Raabe, *Obadiah*, 203.

Verses 19 and 20 outline the territory to be possessed or repossessed in the kingdom of God (Obad. 21), essentially forecasting the restoration of the lost blessing of life and dominion in the land of the covenant (Gen. 1:26–28; 2:11–14; 15:18). Those living in the southern portion of Judah (the Negev) will possess the mountain of Esau (i.e., Edom). It is likely that Edom represents here the nations or Gentiles to be possessed or dispossessed in God's kingdom. According to Amos 9:12, there will be some from Edom/humanity (i.e., the nations or Gentiles) who will believe and become part of the people of God in his kingdom. Others will simply be conquered, displaced, and judged. The same can be said for Israel. Only those who believe will take part in this kingdom (see Isa. 65:8–16). Those living in the lowland or foothills (Shephelah) will possess the Philistine territory to the southwest. They will also possess Ephraim and Samaria (i.e., the northern kingdom of Israel). Benjamin will possess Gilead on the other side of the Jordan, indicating that even the land of Reuben, Gad, and the half tribe of Manasseh will be restored (Num. 32; Josh. 22; 2 Kgs. 10:32–33). The exiles of the "army" (cf., Obad. 11, 13) of Israel will possess the land of Canaan all the way up to Zarephath of Sidon in the northwest (Obad. 20; see 1 Kgs. 17:9). This is perhaps not so much an end point as it is an indication of direction (i.e., northward). The exiles of the city of Jerusalem who are in Sepharad will be the ones to possess the cities of the south (i.e., those mentioned at the beginning of Obadiah 19). The location of Sepharad (traditionally Spain) is uncertain, but it is clear from the context that it is a distant place of exile from which the people will return.

According to the MT of Obadiah 21a, "deliverers" (מוֹשִׁעִים) will go up "in/on Mount Zion" (בהר ציון) "to judge" (לשפט) the mountain of Esau. According to the LXX, "delivered men" (= מוּשָׁעִים) will go up "from Mount Zion" (= מהר ציון) "to take vengeance" on the mountain of Esau. The language of the MT is familiar to readers of the book of Judges (e.g., Judg. 2:16; 3:9–10; Neh. 9:27) where the "judges" are not those who decide legal cases (but see Judg. 4:4–5). Rather, they are instruments of military deliverance. The MT sees this happening in/on Mount Zion (cf., Isa. 2:2–4; Mic. 4:1–3). It is highly unlikely, however, that it envisions a return to the period of the judges as the eschatological ideal, for "in those days there was no king in Israel, everyone would do what was right in his own eyes" (Judg. 17:6; 18:1; 19:1; 21:25).[11] Redak identified the deliverers here as the Messiah and his

---

11. "Consequently the fulfilment of vv. 17–21 can only belong to the Messianic times, and that in such a way that it commenced with the founding of the

colleagues, as in Mic. 5:4 (Eng., 5:3; cf., Jer. 3:15; 23:4). Malbim, on the other hand, explained that the two messiahs—the son of Joseph and the son of David—and the seven shepherds from Micah 5:4 (Eng., 5:3) will be revealed at the commencement of the war of Gog and Magog (Ezek. 38–39; see *Tg. Ps.-J.* Exod. 40:9–11; *Tg. Song.* 4:5; *b. Sukkah* 52a; *b. Sanh.* 98a; cf., *b. Pesah* 118a; *4 Ezra* 7:28–29; see also 4QD[a] 10 I, 12; 1QS 9:11; 1QSa 2:11–22).[12] The LXX text, which requires almost no change to the consonantal text of the MT, sees men delivered by the LORD not going up "in/on" Zion but going up "from" Zion to take vengeance on the mountain of Esau as in Obadiah 18 (cf., Isa. 59:20 LXX [Rom. 11:26]; Ps. 14:7). This reading, which leaves little room for messianic interpretation (but see Hab. 3:13; Zech. 9:9), was probably motivated by the difficulty of explaining how the judgment of the mountain of Esau could take place in/on Zion. The MT, however, understands Zion to be the seat of judgment.

This hope of the united kingdom of God (Obad. 21b; cf., Ps. 22:29 [Eng., 22:28]) that includes believing Jews and Gentiles is in fact the new covenant ideal. The book of Obadiah thus serves to balance the role of Edom as the representative nation in Amos 9:12 and also forms a bridge to the following book of Jonah where Nineveh will take up the mantle as the representative of the Gentiles. The Amos-Obadiah-Jonah sequence is perhaps the most important of all for the efforts of the composer of the Twelve to demonstrate that the message of Hosea 3:4–5 is also for the nations. The modern preacher likely has little use

---

kingdom of Christ on earth, advances with its extension among all nations, and will terminate in a complete fulfilment at the second coming of our Lord" (Keil, *Minor Prophets*, 252).

12. *Mikraoth Gedoloth: The Twelve Prophets*, vol. 1, 180. See the marginal Palestinian reading to the Targum of Zech. 12:10 in Codex Reuchlinianus (A.D. 1105): "And I will let rest upon the house of David and upon the inhabitants of Jerusalem the Spirit of prophecy and true prayer. Afterwards Messiah son of Ephraim will go out to wage war with Gog, and Gog will kill him before the gate of Jerusalem. And they will look at me and ask why the peoples pierced Messiah son of Ephraim, and they will mourn over him." This theory of a Messiah son of Joseph/Ephraim was designed for passages that spoke of a suffering Messiah, allowing the Davidic Messiah to reign without suffering. The Qumran community developed the idea of a Messiah of Aaron to explain how there could be a Messiah who occupied the office of a priest, since David's lineage did not allow the Davidic Messiah to be one (Zech. 6:12–13). The NT authors, however, understood that the Davidic Messiah would both suffer and reign (e.g., Ps. 22) and that he would occupy the offices of king and priest (e.g., Ps. 110; Heb. 7).

for a message about the historical judgment of Edom (Obad. 1–14), but that message has already been made relevant to contemporary audiences as a picture of eschatological judgment on the wicked and messianic deliverance of the righteous from all the nations (Obad. 15–21). This, along with Obadiah's relationship to Amos and Jonah, is what enables the book to function as Christian Scripture.

BOOK OF THE TWELVE

JONAH

JONAH 1

1:1 And the word of the LORD came to Jonah [Tg. Jon.: And a word of prophecy from before the LORD was with Jonah] the son of Amittai saying, 1:2 "Arise, go to Nineveh the great city and call against it [LXX: preach in it; Tg. Jon.: prophesy against it], for their evil has come up before me." 1:3 And Jonah arose to flee to Tarshish [Tg. Jon.: to the sea] from before the LORD [Tg. Jon.: from before that he would prophesy in the name of the LORD]. And he went down to Joppa and found a ship going to Tarshish [Tg. Jon.: in the sea]. And he paid its fare and went down in it to go [LXX: to sail] with them to Tarshish [Tg. Jon.: in the sea] from before the LORD [Tg. Jon.: from before that he would prophesy in the name of the LORD].

The Hebrew text of the "superscription" in Jonah 1:1 differs from other similarly worded headings (cf., Hos. 1:1; Joel 1:1; Mic. 1:1; Zeph. 1:1) in that it begins with the verbal form of narration (ויהי) rather than the phrase "the word of the LORD" (see GKC §111f; cf., Ezek. 6:1; 7:1; Hag. 1:3; 2:20; etc.). Jonah is identified as the son of Amittai. That is, he is the same prophet from the historical narrative about the reign of Jeroboam II (c. 793–753 BC) recorded in 2 Kings 14:23–29, making him a contemporary of Hosea (Hos. 1:1) and Amos (Amos 1:1). According to that account, Jeroboam II restored the border of Israel from the entrance to Hamath in the north to the sea of the Arabah in the south (2 Kgs. 14:25; cf., Amos 6:14). This was "according to the word of the LORD the God of Israel who spoke by the hand of his servant Jonah the son of Amittai, the prophet who was from Gath Hepher" (as opposed to Gath of the Philistines).[1]

Such an intertextual link between Jonah 1:1 and 2 Kings 14:25 provides several pieces of valuable information to the reader of the book of Jonah. The first item to take into consideration is the genre clue. Unless otherwise noted, the reader should take it for granted from this point that the author intends the book to be read as historical narrative. The historical critic might deny the historicity of the story, but that is a matter for biblical apologetics to address. Such a denial does not grant the reader the right to ignore the way in which the author intends his book to be read. Of course, many commentators choose to have it both ways. They concede that Jonah was a historical prophet, but they believe that the book is a work of fiction based on Jonah. The burden of proof is on these commentators to demonstrate that the book contains sufficient genre indicators of fiction to override the initial signal sent to the reader by the very first verse of the book. At the very least, critics should be willing to concede that the book of Jonah is much closer in genre to the historical narratives of the prophets Elijah and Elisha in the book of Kings than it is to something like Jotham's fable in Judges 9:8–15.

Another way in which 2 Kings 14:25 is helpful to the reader of Jonah is the information that it provides about Jonah's status as a true prophet. The text describes Jonah as the LORD's "servant" and indicates that Jonah's prophecy actually came to pass (see Deut. 18:22). Thus, the reader encounters in the book of Jonah not merely a true prophet or a false prophet but a disobedient true prophet. This is totally unprecedented. There is the example of Balaam who was a false teacher (Num. 31:16) and yet was an instrument of true prophecy (Num. 23–24), but the idea of a disobedient true prophet is completely unexpected and creates a sense of suspense and adventure for the reader. Much like a Steve McQueen or Clint Eastwood character in the

---

1. Gath Hepher was in the Galilee region. Most textual witnesses to John 7:52 have the Pharisees telling Nicodemus to search and see that from Galilee "a prophet" (or, "a prophet" from Galilee) is not raised up. This makes it seem like the Bible experts of the day were ignorant of a fact as basic as Jonah's place of origin, which is highly unlikely. The original reading of P[66], however, is "the prophet." In other words, the Pharisees were saying that the messianic prophet like Moses (Deut. 18:15, 18; 34:10) is not raised up from Galilee. They believed he would come from Bethlehem according to Micah 5:1 (Eng., 5:2; see Matt. 2:5–6).

movies, it is difficult to tell whether Jonah is a good guy or a bad guy, although readers typically do not sympathize with Jonah.

The fact that the book of Jonah is story rather than a collection of oracles sets it apart from the other books of the Twelve. Verses 2 and 3 of chapter 1 provide the initial setting and problem of the story, but the story's problem looks different depending upon whose perspective is taken. For Jonah, the problem is his response to his calling. He does eventually go to Nineveh (Jon. 3), but the problematic motive behind his initial flight is never completely resolved (Jon. 4). For Nineveh, the problem is the threat of judgment. This is resolved in chapter 3. But the heart of the book's message comes in the LORD's rhetorical question to Jonah in the final verse of the book, suggesting that the real intent is to address a potential problem in the reader.

The LORD commands Jonah in verse 2 to arise and go to Nineveh "the great city." Nineveh the capital of Assyria, was a large (Jon. 3:3) and densely populated (Jon. 4:11) city, but the designation "the great city" probably has more to do with importance than size in this context. Nineveh was a strategic center in the Gentile world (see Gen. 10:11–12), making it an ideal candidate to represent the nations in general. Just as Edom represented the nations—both the good and the bad—in Amos and Obadiah partly because of the play on *adam* ("mankind"), so Nineveh represents the nations in books like Jonah and Nahum, demonstrating God's right to have compassion on Gentiles who believe and his obligation to judge Gentiles who do not believe. Here the LORD instructs Jonah to call against the city (i.e., to proclaim a message of judgment) because the report of their evil has come to his attention, not unlike the outcry against Sodom and Gomorrah that led to an investigation of their actions (Gen. 18:20–21).[2]

Jonah does arise (Jon. 1:3), but instead of going to Nineveh he "flees" to Tarshish from before the LORD. This is where the story gets interesting. The reader cannot imagine someone like Isaiah, Jeremiah, or any other biblical prophet acting with such blatant disregard for God's command. Furthermore, there is no explanation at this point as to why Jonah is fleeing. The reader will have to wait until chapter 4 for that. The place name "Tarshish" (Spain?) is probably not intended to designate a specific location or destination in this context. Rather, it indicates a direction from the perspective of Israel, as in the rendering of *Targum Jonathan*, "to the sea." Thus, "the ships of Tarshish" (1 Kgs.

---

2. This language is not intended to call God's omniscience into question. It only indicates that he interacts with humanity in real time and space. He communicates his action in such a way that it is understandable.

219

10:22; 2 Chr. 9:21) are seagoing ships. The following phrase, "from before the LORD," clarifies that this is the opposite direction from which God intends Jonah to go in the story. Of course, it is not actually possible to flee from before the LORD (Ps. 139:7), but the idea here is that he attempts to flee from his responsibility as a prophet (*Tg. Jon.*: "from before that he would prophesy in the name of the LORD"), which is difficult to do to say the least (see Jer. 20:7–9; Amos 3:8). The LORD pursues Jonah not only because he has a mission to accomplish but also because there is an important lesson to teach the reader about the role of the Gentiles in his plan. Jonah "goes down" (from Gath Hepher?) to Joppa on the Mediterranean coast of Israel and finds a ship going toward Tarshish. He pays the ship's fare and "goes down" into it to go with them (i.e., the sailors, see GKC §135p) toward Tarshish and away from the LORD's commission. Jonah's descent will continue down into the innermost parts of the ship below the deck (Jon. 1:5b) and finally down to the extremities of the mountains below the surface of the sea (Jon. 2:7 [Eng., 2:6]).

1:4 Now as for the LORD,[3] he hurled a great wind to the sea, and a great storm was in the sea. And as for the ship, it was about to be broken [lit., it considered to be broken]. 1:5 And the sailors[4] were afraid, and they cried out each to his god(s) [Tg. Jon.: and they sought each man from his object of fear/worship and saw that there was no use in them] and hurled the vessels that were in the ship into the sea to lighten from upon them. But Jonah, he had gone down into the innermost parts below the ship's deck [LXX: the belly of the ship] and had lain down and fallen into a deep sleep. 1:6 And the captain [lit., the chief of the ropepullers] drew near to him and said to him, "Why are you sleeping [lit., What to you sleeping? see GKC §120b; cf., RSV: What do you mean, you sleeper?]? Arise, call to your god. Perhaps that god will have consideration for us [LXX: so that that god might rescue us; Tg. Jon.: Perhaps there will be compassion from before the LORD upon us], and we will not perish." 1:7 And they said each to his neighbor, "Come and let us cast lots so that we may know on whose[5] account this calamity is to us."

---

3. See Wolfgang Schneider, *Grammar of Biblical Hebrew*, trans. Randall L. McKinion (New York: Peter Lang, 2016), 162–63.
4. See James Barr, *Comparative Philology and the Text of the Old Testament* (Oxford: Oxford University Press, 1968; reprint, with additions and corrections, Winona Lake, IN: Eisenbrauns, 1987), 109–110.
5. See John Huehnergard, "On the Etymology of the Hebrew Relative šɛ-," in *Biblical Hebrew in Its Northwest Semitic Setting: Typological and*

*And they cast lots, and the lot fell to [or, on] Jonah. 1:8 And they said
to him, "Tell us, on whose account is this evil to us? What is your occupation? And from where do you come? What is your land? And from
what people are you [lit., And where from this people you]? 1:9 And he
said to them, "A Hebrew [GKC §2b; LXX: servant of the Lord[6]; Tg. Jon.:
Judean] is who I am. And the LORD the God of heaven is the one whom
I fear [cf., 4QXII[a]], the one who made the sea and the dry land." 1:10
And the men were greatly afraid [lit., feared a great fear] and said to
him, "What have you done?" For the men knew that it was from before
the LORD that he was fleeing, for he had told them.[7] 1:11 And they
said to him, "What should we do to you so that the sea might be quiet/
calm from upon us?" For the sea was storming continually [lit., going
and storming; see GKC §113u]. 1:12 And he said to them, "Lift me up
and hurl me into the sea so that the sea might be quiet/calm from upon
you, for I know that it is on my account that this great storm is upon
you." 1:13 And the men rowed [lit., dug; LXX, Syr.: tried hard] to show
an effort to return [or, to cause the ship to return] to the dry land, but
they were not able, for the sea was continually storming [lit., going and
storming] upon them. 1:14 And they called to the LORD and said, "Ah
LORD, do not let us perish because of this man's life and do not put on
us innocent blood, for you, O LORD, just as you please, you do." 1:15
And they lifted up Jonah and hurled him into the sea, and the sea stood
still from its raging. 1:16 And the men greatly feared [lit., feared a great
fear] the LORD, and they sacrificed to the LORD [Tg. Jon.: they said to
sacrifice before the LORD] and made vows.*

The "*waw* + x + *qatal*" clause at the beginning of Jonah 1:4a resets the
stage for the new scene—the storm at sea. The verb "hurl" becomes
a kind of keyword that runs throughout the passage in various ways
(Jon. 1:4, 5, 12, 15). The background information in Jonah 1:4b is either a personification of the ship or an instance of metonymy where
the ship stands for the people on it (cf., 1 Kgs. 22:48; Ps. 48:8 [Eng.,

---

Historical Perspectives, eds. Steven E. Fassberg and Avi Hurvitz (Winona
Lake, IN: Eisenbrauns, 2006), 103–125. See also Robert D. Holmstedt, *The
Relative Clause in Biblical Hebrew*, LSAWS 10 (Winona Lake, IN: Eisenbrauns, 2016), 85–101, 244–47.
6. The LXX translator apparently read עבדי (as an abbreviation for עבד
יהוה) instead of עברי. See Emanuel Tov, *Textual Criticism of the Hebrew
Bible*, 3d ed. (Minneapolis: Fortress, 2012), 238–39. Cf., 2 Kgs. 14:25.
7. See Michael B. Shepherd, "So-called Emphasis and the Lack Thereof in
Biblical Hebrew," *Maarav* 19.1–2 (2012), 183–86, 188–90.

48:7]). This section of Jonah's story in Jonah 1:4–16 and the poem in chapter 2 has had a great influence on Psalm 107, particularly the material bracketed by inverted *nun* letters in Ps. 107:21–26 (see also Matt. 8:23–27; Mark 4:35–41; Luke 8:22–25; Acts 27:13–44).[8]

The "sailors" (Jon. 1:5a; cf., Ezek. 27:29) are understandably afraid at this point in the story and subsequently cry out to their individual god or gods (*elohim*). They hurl the ship's vessels overboard in an attempt to lighten the load, hoping that this might make the ship more buoyant in the midst of the turbulent sea. Where is Jonah in all of this? The background information provided in Jonah 1:5b indicates that he went down below the ship's deck prior to the storm and fell asleep. This is a sign of Jonah's false sense of security that he has successfully fled from the LORD's commission. The captain approaches Jonah and questions his sleeping in such dire circumstances (Jon. 1:6a; cf., Matt. 8:24–25). His words to Jonah—"Arise, call to your god" (the captain does not know at this point that Jonah is a servant of the LORD, the one true God)—echo the language of the LORD's commission in Jonah 1:2 to "arise" and "call" against Nineveh—a stark reminder that Jonah has not escaped at all. The captain thinks that perhaps Jonah's god will be the one to give them consideration so that they do not perish in the storm (cf., Jon. 3:9). This obviously reflects a belief system in which certain gods are assigned to certain people and to certain domains (cf., 1 Kgs. 20:23). The assumption is that they must discover which god has been offended and find a way to appease that god before it is too late.

The sailors decide to cast lots in an effort to learn who is responsible for their calamity, believing that the casting of lots is divinely controlled (Jon. 1:7a; cf., Prov. 16:33). Of course, the lot falls to Jonah (Jon. 1:7b), but the sailors do not assume that Jonah is the guilty one. They think that Jonah is the one selected to reveal the person responsible for the storm (Jon. 1:8a), so they question him about his occupation, his place of origin, his land, and his people (Jon. 1:8b). This information is somewhat tangential to their primary question, but their line of questioning does show that Jonah is unknown to the other men on board and that he has become a person of interest to them as a consequence of his identification by lot. It also gives Jonah the opportunity to say some things that the sailors do not think to ask. Jonah first identifies himself as a "Hebrew" (Jon. 1:9a; cf., LXX), a term immediately recognizable to foreigners (Gen. 39:14, 17; 41:12; 1 Sam. 14:11). This suffices to answer all the questions in Jonah 1:8b except the one about

---

8. See Michael B. Shepherd, *The Text in the Middle* (New York: Peter Lang, 2014), 154–55.

Jonah's occupation. Jonah never tells the sailors that he is a prophet.[9] He then moves on from their questions to inform them that the LORD (Yahweh) the God of heaven (Gen. 24:7; Dan. 2; Ezra 1:2; Neh. 1:4, 5; 2:4, 20; 2 Chr. 36:23) is the one whom he worships (even though his actions do not show it!) (Jon. 1:9b). Jonah does not worship some personal or local god. He worships the very maker of the sea and the dry land (see Gen. 1:9–10; Ps. 95:5).[10] Why does Jonah decide to make such a confession at this point? It seems that Jonah is fully aware of what is happening. He realizes that he will not be able to flee from the LORD, but he does not yet surrender to the LORD's commission. He would rather be thrown overboard! Thus, Jonah's suggestion in verse 12 is not an act of self-sacrifice. It is suicide. And as with many failed suicide attempts, Jonah's deliverance enables him to value life again (at least temporarily [see Jon. 2:2, 10 (Eng., 2:1, 9); 4:3, 8, 9]) and to reassess his response to God's calling on his life.

Now the men are greatly afraid (Jon. 1:10a), presumably because, given the circumstances, they take Jonah at his word without disputing the nature of the God he claims to worship. It is one thing to be in a storm in the hands of a so-called god (Jon. 1:5). It is quite another to be at the mercy of the creator. They ask Jonah, "What have you done?" This requires the narrator to explain to the reader that Jonah has already told the men about the fact that it is from before the LORD that he is fleeing (Jon. 1:10b), revealing that Jonah is not merely the one who will unveil the person responsible for their calamity. He is the man himself. The sailors wonder how Jonah could be so careless as to put others in harm's way by boarding the ship in the first place.

And so, the sailors ask what should be done to Jonah to make the sea calm down (Jon. 1:11a). The narrator explains that this request is due to the continuous storming of the sea (Jon. 1:11b). Jonah, however, does not suggest obedience to the will of God on his part. Rather, he instructs the men to throw him overboard (Jon. 1:12). This will do the trick, he says, because he is the responsible one. But the men do not see this as an attractive option for them. They seek in vain to row the ship ashore (Jon. 1:13a), perhaps in an attempt to show Jonah's God that they would rather not take Jonah's life. As the narrator explains,

---

9. Jonah may have been a prophet like Elisha who enjoyed the support of others (2 Kgs. 4:8–10) or he may have had an occupation of his own like Amos (Amos 1:1; 7:14). There is no indication that he was ever a mere professional prophet for hire.
10. Incidentally, the reader's adoption of this theology allows him or her to see the realism of chapter 2.

however, their efforts to make it to dry land do not succeed on account of the continuously storming sea (Jon. 1:13b). Thus, they decide to cover their bases by appealing directly to the LORD himself (Jon. 1:14a). As they see no other way than to follow Jonah's instructions, they plead with the LORD that they not perish on account of Jonah's life. They fear that they will be held accountable for innocent blood. That is, they do not feel that the death penalty is warranted for Jonah's actions. The men make their appeal on the basis of good biblical theology (Jon. 1:14b; cf., Pss. 115:3; 135:6; Eccl. 8:3; Dan. 4:32 [Eng., 4:29]), which can be deduced from the revelation of Jonah's God as the creator. The LORD does as he pleases. Therefore, they acknowledge that they are at his mercy and are not in a position to demand anything from him. His bidding will be done.

With that said, the men lift up Jonah and throw him into the sea (Jon. 1:15a). And as predicted by Jonah himself (Jon. 1:12a), the sea stands still from its raging (Jon. 1:15b; cf., Matt. 8:26). Now the object of the men's "great fear" is the LORD himself (Jon. 1:16a). Given the parallel with Jonah 3:5, it is likely that this use of the word "fear" (ירא) falls within the semantic field of "faith" (see *TLOT* 1:143; cf., Exod. 14:31). This strikes at the heart of the book's message. The Gentile sailors are the ones who believe in the LORD, while the Hebrew prophet who claims to fear/worship the LORD flees in disobedience (cf., Matt. 8:10; 15:28). If it is objected that the men are simply assimilating the LORD into their polytheistic religion, it should be noted that there is no indication of this. Furthermore, it would not serve the author's purpose very well for their faith to be anything but genuine. The men express their faith in Jonah 1:16b the same way Jonah does in Jonah 2:10 (Eng., 2:9). They offer a sacrifice and make vows. It has been suggested that there may be a significant difference between the narration time and the time narrated here.[11] That is, there is some question about whether the sacrificed is offered on the ship or at some later time. On the other hand, the making of vows does not require this distinction.

JONAH 2 (ENG., 1:17–2:10)

2:1 (Eng., 1:17) And the LORD appointed a great fish [LXX: large sea creature (cf., Gen. 1:21)] to swallow Jonah, and Jonah was in the inward parts of the fish for three days and three nights. 2:2 (Eng., 2:1) And Jonah prayed to the LORD his God from the inward parts of the fish [see GKC §122s, t]. 2:3 (Eng., 2:2) And he said, "I called from my

---

11. See Shimon Bar-Efrat, *Narrative Art in the Bible* (London: T&T Clark, 2004), 141–96.

distress to the LORD, and he answered me [Tg. Jon.: he received my prayer]. From the belly of Sheol [Tg. Jon.: From the bottom of the ocean] I cried out. You heard my voice [Tg. Jon.: You did what I requested]. 2:4 (Eng., 2:3) And you cast me into the deep, in the heart of the seas. (And a current, it would surround me.) All your breakers and your rollers [i.e., waves; Tg. Jon.: All the storms of the sea and its waves], over me they passed. 2:5 (Eng., 2:4) And I, I thought, 'I am driven out from before your eyes. Surely / Yet [Theodotion: How?] will I look again to your holy temple.' 2:6 (Eng., 2:5) Water encompassed me up to life [i.e., to the point that I almost drowned; Tg. Jon.: to the point of death] (The ocean, it would surround me.), reeds [LXX: last; Tg. Jon.: the Sea of Reeds] were bound to my head.¹² 2:7 (Eng., 2:6) To the extremities of the mountains I went down [BHS: I descended the earth]; the earth, its bars were about me indefinitely. And you brought up from the pit [LXX, Syr., Tg. Jon., Vulg., Luther: from corruption (cf., Ps. 16:10)] my life [4QXII^g: the life of my soul], O LORD my God. 2:8 (Eng., 2:7) When my life fainted on me, the LORD [Tg. Jon.: the worship of the LORD] was the one whom I remembered. And my prayer came to you, to your holy temple. 2:9 (Eng., 2:8) As for those who keep idols [lit., empty things of nothingness], their covenant loyalty is what they abandon [cf., Tg. Jon.]. 2:10 (Eng., 2:9) But as for me, it is with a voice of thanksgiving [LXX: praise] that I resolve to sacrifice to you. That which I have vowed I am determined to pay. Salvation [Syr.: Recompense; see GKC §90g] belongs to the LORD [Tg. Jon.: The deliverance of my life is through prayer before the LORD]." 2:11 (Eng., 2:10) And the LORD said to the fish, ". . . ." And it vomited Jonah to the dry land.

When the text says that the LORD appointed a great fish to swallow Jonah and that Jonah was inside the fish for three days and three nights (Jon. 2:1 [Eng., 1:17]), it presupposes the world of the Bible (i.e., the real world) in which Jonah's God is the creator (Gen. 1:1; Jon. 1:9) and can do with his creation as he pleases (Jon. 1:14b; cf., Num. 22:28). It is by no means suggested that an event such as the one narrated here is "normal," but if the reader can accept the theology of the very first verse of the Bible, there should be no problem with what he or she finds

---

12. Rashi, from *Pirke d'Rabbi Eliezer* ch. 10: "For the Holy One, blessed be He, showed him the Red [lit. Reed] Sea and how Israel crossed in its midst, for the fish's two eyes were like two windows, and he would look and see everything in the sea" (*Mikraoth Gedoloth: The Twelve Prophets*, vol. 1, 188). See also *Tg. Neof.* Deut. 30:13. *BHS* arranges the text so that Jonah 2:6b (Eng., 2:5b) is read with the first part of Jon. 2:7a (Eng., 2:6a).

in this text. The specific kind of sea creature that the LORD appoints is not known. The Hebrew text uses the very broad, all-inclusive term דָּג, which is usually translated "fish" throughout the Hebrew Bible. But the reader must not assume modern scientific taxonomical distinctions of species. The Hebrew word does not mean "fish" as opposed to mammals, reptiles, et cetera. Rather, it stands opposite words like אָדָם ("mankind"), עוּף הַשָּׁמַיִם ("the flying creatures of the sky"), בְּהֵמָה ("large land animals"), and רֶמֶשׂ ("creeping things" [on land]) (Gen. 1:26).

The time designation "three days and three nights" can refer to all or part of three separate twenty-four hour periods (cf., Est. 4:16; 5:1) and likely represents a complete period of time (cf., use of the numbers seven and ten elsewhere [e.g., Gen. 2:2–3; Dan. 1:12]).[13] This time period is analogous to the stretch from the evening of Good Friday to the morning of Resurrection Sunday, but it is likely not what is meant by "the sign of Jonah" in the NT:

> When the scribes and Pharisees ask Jesus for a sign in Matthew 12:38, he responds that none will be given except that of Jonah the prophet (Matt. 12:39). Many have understood the sign of Jonah to be the following analogy between Jonah's stay in the belly of the fish for three days and nights and that of the Son of Man in the heart of the earth for the same period of time (Matt. 12:40). But the parallel pericope in Luke 11:29–32 also speaks of the sign of Jonah yet makes no reference to the three days and nights in the fish. What both texts share are the references to the Ninevites' repentance at the preaching of Jonah and the response of the Queen of Sheba to the reports about Solomon's wisdom (Matt. 12:41–42; Luke 11:31–32). The Jews of Jesus's day failed to do as well as the Gentiles in the days of Solomon and Jonah. Jesus was a greater wise man than Solomon and a greater preacher with a greater message than Jonah and yet his own people for the most part did not receive him. The sign of Jonah is thus identical to the message of the text of Jonah, an indictment against Israelite (and later Jewish) rejection of God's plan in the midst of Gentile faith and inclusion.[14]

Jonah's prayer of thanksgiving comes from the belly of the fish (Jon. 2:2 [Eng., 2:1]), which means he understands the appointment of the fish to be his deliverance. The prayer follows the pattern of a typical thanksgiving psalm (cf., Ps. 30): opening declaration of deliverance from distress (Jon. 2:3 [Eng., 2:2]), poetic narrative of deliverance from

---

13. Bullinger, *Figures of Speech*, 845.
14. Michael B. Shepherd, *The Twelve Prophets in the New Testament* (New York: Peter Lang, 2011), 13.

distress (Jon. 2:4–9 [Eng., 2:3–8]), and vow (Jon. 2:10 [Eng., 2:9]).[15] In fact, this prayer of thanksgiving is essentially a mosaic of texts from the book of Psalms, which will be noted in the following commentary. Thus, the prayer captures the authentic voice of the historical prophet Jonah, but it does so in a highly stylized fashion appropriate to its literary context. Biblical authors of largely narrative works often employ poetic units to punctuate or to frame their texts and to provide theological interpretation of the stories (e.g., Gen. 3:14–19; 49; Exod. 15:1–18; Num. 23–24; Deut. 32–33; Judg. 5; 1 Sam. 2:1–10; 2 Sam 22:1–23:7).[16]

In his opening declaration, Jonah says that he called to the LORD from his distress, and the LORD answered him (Jon. 2:3 [Eng., 2:2]; cf., Pss. 18:7; 22:25; 81:8 [Eng., 18:6; 22:24; 81:7]; 107:28; 116:1–4; 120:1; 130:1–2; 138:3; Lam. 3:55–56). He describes the place of distress from which he cried as "the belly of Sheol." This is a figurative description of the ocean depths. Sheol being a poetic term for the burial place of the dead, Jonah sees his descent into the waters of the sea as bringing him to the brink of death. At the end of Jonah 2:3 (Eng., 2:2), Jonah switches from third person reference to the LORD to second person: "You heard my voice." This sets up the prayer-like quality of the psalm in which Jonah addresses his account of what happened directly to the LORD himself. Unlike other thanksgiving psalms (e.g., 2 Sam. 22) in which the psalmist recounts to an audience what the LORD has done, the context of the story of Jonah requires that this one must stay between the prophet and the LORD. The reader is thus privy to a very personal moment.

Verse 4 (Eng., v. 3) offers a theological interpretation of what happened in the story of chapter 1 (cf., Pss 42:8; 68:23; 69:3; 88:8 [Eng., 42:7; 68:22; 69:2; 88:7]; 107:24). According to Jonah 1:15, the sailors hurled Jonah into the sea, but now Jonah says to the LORD, "And you cast me into the deep" (cf., Exod. 14:23; 15:1). The word "deep" (מצולה) is explained by the prepositional phrase "in the heart of the seas" placed in apposition to it. The following clause ("And a current, it would surround me"), however, is an added parenthetical comment that stands apart from the parallelism as indicated by its syntax and choice of verb (*waw* + x + *yiqtol*) (cf., Jon. 2:6a [Eng., 2:5a]). The waves that Jonah encountered in the stormy sea were not merely a natural phenomenon according to Jonah 2:4b (Eng., 2:3b). They were "your" (i.e., the LORD's) waves.

---

15. See Hermann Gunkel, *Introduction to Psalms: The Genres of the Religious Lyric of Israel*, completed by Joachim Begrich, trans. James D. Nogalski (Macon, GA: Mercer University Press, 1998), 199–221.

16. See John H. Sailhamer, *The Meaning of the Pentateuch: Revelation, Composition, and Interpretation* (Downers Grove, IL: InterVarsity, 2009), 323–44.

Jonah thought at that time that he had been driven out from the LORD's watching care, according to his quote of himself in Jonah 2:5a (Eng., 2:4a; cf., Lam. 3:54). The MT then has, "Surely/Yet (אַךְ) I will look again to your holy temple." This seems like a premature expression of confidence at this point in the structure of the thanksgiving psalm. There is a close parallel in Psalm 31:23 (Eng., 31:22), but it comes toward the end of a lengthy petition psalm where the reader would normally expect it (following the outline of outcry, petition, and trust). Theodotion reads אַךְ as a defectively written אֵיךְ (אֵיךְ ="How?"). This would make for an expression of lament and despair (cf., 2 Sam. 1:19): "How will I look again to your holy temple?" It is not uncommon for a psalmist to cite a former lament while recounting past distress in the structure of a thanksgiving psalm (e.g., Ps. 30:7–10 [Eng., 30:6–9]). To be able to look toward the temple is to have the hope that the God whose special presence it marks will hear and answer prayer (1 Kgs. 8:22–53; Dan. 6:11 [Eng., 6:10]).

Jonah recounts in Jonah 2:6 (Eng., 2:5) how he almost drowned (Pss. 18:5–6; 69:2 [Eng., 18:4–5; 69:1]; 116:3; 124:4–5), not only because the water was so overwhelming but also because his head was wrapped in reeds or reed-like growth (e.g., seaweed). Jonah's descent into the ocean felt like it reached the very base of the mountains far below the surface of the sea (Jon. 2:7a [Eng., 2:6a]). It was as if the earth itself had the bars of a city gate keeping in Jonah indefinitely (cf., Ps. 107:16; see BDB, 138). Yet it is precisely at this point that Jonah's story takes a turn for the better (Jon. 2:7b [Eng., 2:6b]). The poetic narrative advances with a *wayyiqtol* form for the first time since the beginning of Jonah 2:4 (Eng., 2:3).[17] In the early versions, Jonah says that the LORD ("you") brought up his life from "corruption" (from the root שׁחת). Modern English versions, however, prefer the translation "pit" (from the root שׁוח) (cf., Ps. 16:10b), which parallels the expression "from the belly of Sheol" in Jonah 2:2b (Eng., 2:1b; cf., Ps. 30:4 [Eng., 30:3]).

Jonah then says that when his life fainted on him it was the LORD whom he remembered (Jon. 2:8a [Eng., 2:7a]; cf., Jon. 4:8; Pss. 42:7; 77:4 [Eng., 42:6; 77:3]; 107:5). Against all hope (Jon. 2:5b [Eng., 2:4b]) his prayer came to the LORD, that is, to his holy temple (Jon. 2:8b [Eng., 2:7b]; Pss. 5:8 [Eng., 5:7]; 11:4; 138:2). Jonah's reference to idolaters in Jonah 2:9 (Eng., 2:8; cf., Ps. 31:7 [Eng., 31:6]) is ironic given the fact that idolaters were the ones who made Jonah look bad in chapter 1 when

---

17. See Diethelm Michel, *Tempora und Satzstellung in den Psalmen* (Bonn: H. Bouvier u. Co., 1960). Thus far the psalm has made primarily independent statements using *qatal* forms.

they came to faith in the LORD while the prophet persisted in his disobedience. The clause, "their covenant loyalty is what they abandon," can either refer to the abandonment of faithfulness to the LORD or to the abandonment of the benefits of the LORD's faithfulness. Jonah contrasts himself with idolaters by expressing his resolve to sacrifice to the LORD with thanksgiving, his determination to pay what he has vowed (Jon. 2:10 [Eng., 2:9]; cf, Jon. 1:16; Pss. 22:26 [Eng., 22:25]; 50:14–15; 56:13 [Eng., 56:12]; 116:14, 17, 18). His final confession is that salvation (or deliverance) belongs to the LORD (cf., Ps. 3:3, 9 [Eng., 3:2, 8]).

When the narrative resumes in Jonah 2:11 (Eng., 2:10), there appears to be an ellipsis: "And the LORD said (ויאמר) to the fish, '. . . .'" English versions translate the verb here as if it were וידבר: "And the LORD spoke to the fish" (cf., Jon. 2:1 [Eng., 1:17). But direct discourse almost always follows the verb ויאמר ("And he said, '. . . .'"). In fact, this is so consistent that when it does not happen in Gen. 4:8, the LXX (and some English versions) is compelled to supply the discourse in its translation. Whatever was said to the fish, the next part of the narration is that the fish vomited Jonah to the dry land. Even the fish follows the LORD's instructions better than Jonah (cf., Jon. 1:1–3)!

JONAH 3

3:1 And the word of the LORD came to Jonah a second time saying, 3:2 "Arise, go to Nineveh the great city and call against[18] it the proclamation that I am speaking to you." 3:3 And Jonah arose and went to Nineveh according to the word of the LORD. And as for Nineveh, it was a very great city [lit., a great city to God],[19] a walk of three days.

---

18. The change of preposition from על in Jonah 1:2 to אל in Jonah 3:2 probably does not indicate a change in the original commission from a negative proclamation ("call against it") to a more positive one ("call to it"). There is no reason for such a change. There is no indication that the report about Nineveh's evil is any different at this point (see the content of the message in Jonah 3:4). Furthermore, the prepositions על and אל are often used interchangeably (see BDB, 40–41) to the point that they not infrequently appear in separate textual witnesses to the same passage (e.g., Jer. 11:11). The decision to use אל in Jonah 3:2 is most likely a choice based on stylistic variation.

19. The expression "a great city to God" probably does not mean that God was somehow impressed with the city or that the city was known to belong to God in some way. Still less likely is the idea that it means "a great city of gods," since that would have nothing to do with the following phrase, "a

3:4 And Jonah began to go through the city [or, enter the city] a walk of one day. And he called and said, "Yet forty days [LXX: three days], and Nineveh is overturned." 3:5 And the men [i.e., the people] of Nineveh put their faith in God [Tg. Jon.: in the word of the LORD], and they called a fast and put on sackcloth from the greatest to the least of them [GKC §133g]. 3:6 And the word reached the king of Nineveh, and he arose from his throne and removed his royal robe from upon him [Syr.: and he took up his crown from him] and covered himself with sackcloth and sat on ashes. 3:7 And he summoned [or, made a proclamation] and said, "In Nineveh from the judgment [i.e., decree] of the king and his nobles saying:²⁰ The people and the animals, the cattle and the flocks, let them not taste anything. Let them not graze, and water let them not drink. 3:8 And let the people and the animals cover themselves with sackcloth and call to God loudly [lit., with strength; LXX: earnestly]. And let them turn each from his evil way and from the violence that is in the palms of their hands.²¹ 3:9 Who knows if this God will turn back and relent and turn from the burning of his anger so that we might not perish?"²² 3:10 And the one true God [BDB, 43] saw their works, that [or, for] they turned from their evil way, and the one true God relented concerning the calamity [lit., evil] that he spoke to do to them, and he did not do it.

The beginning of chapter 3 deliberately follows the pattern of the opening verses of chapter 1 in order to create the sense that the story is in effect starting over (Jon. 3:1–2; cf., Jon. 1:1–2). The main difference this time is that Jonah does not flee to Tarshish (Jon. 3:3; cf., Jon. 1:3). Jonah has learned that he cannot escape the LORD's commission, but it remains to be seen whether the motive behind his initial flight stays with him. He goes to Nineveh "according to the word of the LORD" (i.e., to proclaim the message that the LORD speaks), but chapter 4 will expose the fact that the traumatic events of the first two chapters have done little to change Jonah's attitude. The background information provided in Jonah 3:3b informs the reader that the great city of Nineveh was a walk of three days. In context, this probably indicates not the city's circumference or how

---

walk of three days." The phrase "to God" most likely gives "a great city" a superlative or elative sense (cf., Gen. 30:8; Exod. 9:28; 1 Sam. 14:25; Pss. 36:7; 80:11 [Eng., 36:6; 80:10]).

20. Or, And he summoned and said in Nineveh from the judgment of the king and his nobles saying, ". . . ." Cf., Ezra 1:1–4.
21. The LXX uses aorist verbs for this verse.
22. Or, "Who knows? Perhaps this God will turn back and relent and turn from the burning of his anger, and we will not perish."

long it would take to walk from one side of the city to the other or how long it would take to see the whole city. Rather, this is how long it would take the prophet to deliver his message in every part of the city so that it would be sufficiently distributed in order to hold the entire city accountable for its response. Verse 4 only narrates the first day of this preaching tour. The brevity of Jonah's message—"Yet forty days and Nineveh is overturned" (cf., Gen. 19:25)—could be a summary of Jonah's words or an indication that Jonah did not have long to preach at each location. It could also be an indication of Jonah's lack of enthusiasm for the task at hand. The LXX has "three days" instead of "forty days." This was likely a translator's decision to depart from the Hebrew source on the basis of context. The thinking was perhaps that the judgment should come immediately at the conclusion of the three-day preaching tour. But the period of forty days as found in Jonah's message according to the MT allows time for the Ninevites to respond and perhaps to repent, thus avoiding the potential judgment. This will be important to keep in mind when the reader comes to Jonah 3:10 and Jonah 4:2. The fact that God ultimately relents is not at odds with the message of judgment, precisely because the opportunity for repentance on the part of the Ninevites is built into the message. Likewise, Jonah's revelation of his reason for running in the first place is not to be understood in terms of a concern about being labeled a false prophet for preaching a judgment that never came.[23] He could only be labeled as such if there were no opportunity for repentance.

Much like the Gentile sailors in chapter 1, the Ninevites take Jonah at his word and put their faith in Jonah's God (Jon. 3:5a). Lest the reader think that this is faith in any god of their choice, the parallel with Jonah 1:16 strongly suggests that it is faith specifically in the LORD (Yahweh). The author does not feel compelled to explain how such faith could have occurred. It is not clear what the temporal relationship of this response is to the king's decree in the following verses. It is only clear that it precedes the decree in the narrative sequence. The people express their repentance with the calling of a fast and the wearing of sackcloth (Jon. 3:5b; cf., Neh. 9:1–3). The expression "from the greatest to the least of them" does not necessarily mean "every single individual" but "the general populace" (cf., 2 Kgs. 23:2; 25:26; Jer. 42:1, 8; Est. 1:5; 2 Chr. 34:30). Critics have a difficult time reconciling this account of the mass conversion of the Ninevites with the lack of any independent historical verification of such an event. Furthermore, how does the reader

---

23. See Rolf Rendtorff, *The Canonical Hebrew Bible: A Theology of the Old Testament*, trans. David E. Orton (Leiden: Deo, 2005), 292. See also *Lives of the Prophets* 10:1–3 and Rashi's comment on Jonah 4:1.

reconcile what he/she finds here with the later history of the Assyrian captivity (2 Kgs. 17) and the negative portrayal of Nineveh in the book of Nahum? Of course, the book of Jonah is part of the historical record. If it is objected that its account must be dismissed on the basis that it is ideological literature, it is important to remember that no historical account is completely objective. Moreover, the embrace of a particular ideology does not necessarily mean the account is false. As for the depiction of Nineveh elsewhere, there is nothing about the Jonah narrative that requires the conclusion that every successive generation of Ninevites would sustain the faith of the awakening in Jonah's day. Every nation, including Israel, will ultimately have those who believe and those who do not. There is no indication in the story that the Ninevites made a record of what took place. Moreover, such a record of credence to a foreign God would likely not have survived through future generations. Nations tended to maintain records that portrayed them and their own in a very positive light and not in submission to other nations or their gods (e.g., the Mesha Stele; cf., 2 Kgs. 3:4).[24]

When the word reaches the "king of Nineveh" (cf., Gen. 14:1–2, 18; Josh. 2:2; 8:1b; 10:1; 1 Kgs. 21:1b; Isa. 37:13), he rises from his place of authority (i.e., his throne) and removes his symbol of authority (i.e., his royal robe) and expresses his repentance by covering himself with sackcloth and sitting on ashes (Jon. 3:6; cf., Job 42:6; m. Taan. 2:1). The royal proclamation in Jonah 3:7–8 features a play on the noun טַעַם ("judgment" = Aramaic "decree" [BDB, 1094]) and the verb טָעַם ("to taste"). Inclusion of animals in the decree naturally raises a question for the reader, but announcements of judgment often include both humans and animals (e.g., Gen. 6:7; Exod. 12:12; 13:15; Jer. 7:20; 36:29; Ezek. 14:13, 17, 19, 21; 25:13; 29:8; Zeph. 1:3; Hag. 1:11). Therefore, the wording of the king's decree is designed to call for ways for the people to show their repentance outwardly by their own actions and by what they do with their livestock. They are not to allow their animals to "graze" (רָעָה), thus having them participate in the fast. Both humans and animals are to be covered with sackcloth. But then the calling to God (cf., Jon. 1:5) and the turning from evil and violence applies specifically to the people (cf., Isa. 59:6; Ps. 58:3 [Eng., 58:2]; Job 16:17; 1 Chr. 12:18).

The king expresses the hope that God might relent and that they might not perish (Jon. 3:9; cf., Joel 2:13–14), much like the captain of the ship in Jon. 1:6. As noted above, this possibility was worked into the wording of Jonah's message in Jon. 3:4b (cf., Jer. 18:7–8; 26:3). God

---

24. Thus, for example, one would not expect to find an account like Exodus 1–15 among the Egyptian records.

sees their works (Jon. 3:10), the demonstration of their faith (Jon. 3:5; cf., Gen. 15:6; 22; Jas. 2:14–26), and relents concerning the "calamity" (רעה) that he spoke to do to them (cf., Exod. 32:14; Num. 23:19; 1 Sam. 15:29, 35; see comment at Amos 7:3, 6). He turns from the burning of his anger because they turn from their "evil" (רעה) way.

JONAH 4

4:1 And it was very bad to Jonah [LXX: And Jonah was very grieved], and he burned with anger [LXX: and he was confused]. 4:2 And he prayed to the LORD and said, "Ah, LORD, was this not my word when I was still on my land? Therefore, I fled beforehand [GKC §114n²] to Tarshish, for I knew that you are a gracious and compassionate God, slow to anger [lit., long of nostrils] and abundant in covenant loyalty and relenting concerning the calamity. 4:3 And now, O LORD, take my life from me, for my death is better than my life." 4:4 And the LORD said, "Is it for good reason that you burn with anger [LXX: Are you very grieved]?" 4:5 And Jonah went out from the city and sat east of the city [LXX: opposite the city]. And he made for himself there a booth and sat under it in the shade until he would see what would happen in the city. 4:6 And the LORD God [4QXIIᵍ: Lord GOD; cf., Gen. 2–3] appointed a little plant [LXX: gourd] and caused it to go up [or, and it went up] over Jonah to be shade over his head to rescue him [LXX: to give him shade] from his bad situation. And Jonah rejoiced greatly over the little plant. 4:7 And the same God appointed a worm when the dawn went up on the next day. And it struck the little plant, and it withered. 4:8 And so, as soon as the sun arose, God appointed a plowing [or, autumnal; LXX: burning] east wind. And the sun struck upon Jonah's head, and he fainted [or, covered himself (cf., Gen. 38:14)]. And he asked his life to die and said, "My death is better than my life [Syr.: It has come into your hand, O Lord, to take my life from me because I am not better than my fathers (cf., 1 Kgs 19:4b)]." 4:9 And God said to Jonah, "Is it for good reason that you burn with anger concerning the little plant?" And he said, "It is for good reason that I burn with anger to the point of death." 4:10 And the LORD said, "As for you, you had pity on the little plant for which you did not toil and that you did not grow, which came overnight and perished overnight [GKC §128v]. 4:11 And as for me, should not I have pity upon Nineveh the great city in which there are more than 120,000 people who do not know their right hand from their left and many animals?"

The Ninevites turned from their "evil" (רעה) way, and the LORD turned from the "burning" (חרון) of his anger and relented concerning the "calamity" (רעה) that he spoke (Jon. 3:9–10), but now the situation is a great "evil" (רעה) to Jonah, and he "burns" (חרה) with anger (Jon. 4:1; cf., Gen. 4:5b).[25] It is safe to say that Jonah and the LORD are still not on the same page even though Jonah has fulfilled his mission. It is at this point that Jonah reveals why it was that he fled at the beginning of the story. He prays to the LORD (Jon. 4:2) as in Jonah 2:2 (Eng., 2:1), but this time it is not a psalm of thanksgiving but a complaint. Jonah unveils the fact that he thought from the outset that something like this would happen (cf., Exod. 14:12). He did not want to see a wicked city like Nineveh have the opportunity to repent and to receive God's compassion (cf., Ps. 59:6 [Eng., 59:5]). He knew how the LORD had revealed himself to Moses as "gracious and compassionate, slow to anger and abundant in covenant loyalty" (Exod. 34:6).[26] Of course, the LORD had also revealed himself to Moses as a God who does not leave the guilty unpunished (Exod. 34:7), but that part of his character was of little concern to Jonah. Now Jonah asks the LORD to take his life from him, concluding that his death is better than his life (Jon. 4:3; cf., Num. 11:15; 1 Kgs. 19:4; Jon. 1:12). He cannot bear the thought that he has become the instrument of compassion to the wicked. The LORD questions whether Jonah is rightfully angry (Jon. 4:4; cf., Gen. 4:6). Jonah does not respond at this point, but the dialogue will be revisited later in Jonah 4:9.

Verse 5 of Jonah 4 appears at first glance to be out of temporal sequence. Jonah goes outside the city and sits east of it (cf., Gen. 3:24; 4:16; 11:2; 13:11; 25:6). He makes a shelter to shield himself from the sun while he waits to see what will happen in the city. It seems that he is still hoping to see the destruction of Nineveh at the end of the forty-day period. Thus, the *BHS* apparatus suggests relocating this verse between verses 4 and 5 of chapter 3, but there is no textual evidence to support this move. Stuart argues that Jonah 4:5 is a flashback, but this requires

---

25. For a comparison of Jonah with both Cain and Elijah, see Michael B. Shepherd, *The Text in the Middle* (New York: Peter Lang, 2014), 18.
26. Jonah adds, "and relenting concerning the calamity," in accordance with the context (Jon. 3:9–10). See comment at Joel 2:13–14. The citation of Exodus 34:6 in Jonah 4:2 anticipates the seam work that connects the following book of Micah to the book of Nahum (Mic. 7:18–20; Nah. 1:2b–3a; cf., Exod. 34:6–7). This is not unlike the way material at the end of the book of Joel (Joel 4:18 [Eng., 3:18]) anticipates material in the seam work that connects the following book of Amos to the book of Obadiah (Amos 9:13). See also Num. 14:18; Pss. 111:4; 112:4; 145:8; Neh. 9:17.

him to render the *wayyiqtol* forms as pluperfects.[27] Whether or not Jonah 4:5 is in temporal sequence, the writer has chosen to maintain the narrative sequence by means of these forms. But it is also possible that Jonah 4:5 is in temporal sequence. The above suggestions are based on the assumption that neither the Ninevites nor Jonah would have known that God relented prior to the transpiring of the forty-day period, but the granting of such a period was an opportunity for repentance that would avert the disaster. Widespread repentance on the part of the Ninevites was in itself a sign that God would relent. The king's question in Jonah 3:9 was not so much an indication of doubt about what God would do as it was an expression of hope in what he would do if in fact the people were to respond to the terms of the decree. Jonah knows this all too well (Jon. 4:1–3), but in lieu of God taking his life (Jon. 4:4) he decides to wait on the inevitable conclusion to the forty-day period to confirm that his desire for the destruction of the city will not come to fruition, thinking perhaps that there is still some small chance that it will.

Back in Jonah 2:1 (Eng., 1:17), the LORD "appointed" a great fish to do his bidding. Now in Jonah 4:6–8 he appoints a little plant, a worm, and then an east wind. There is nothing unrealistic about this at all. God is in control of his own creation. The appointment of the plant sets up an object lesson for Jonah and ultimately for the reader. The plant becomes a welcome replacement for the insufficient shade of Jonah's shelter, thus delivering Jonah from his "bad situation" (רעה). Jonah is naturally very pleased about this, but it exposes the fact that Jonah has a double standard. When God relented concerning the "calamity" (רעה) that he spoke to do to the Ninevites, Jonah was very displeased (Jon. 3:10–4:1). He did not rejoice for them then as he does for himself now. God then appoints a worm early the next morning to kill the plant, thus removing Jonah's shade. With the rising of the sun and the appointment of an east wind (a symbol of judgment [Exod. 10:13; 14:21; Ezek. 19:12; Hos. 13:15]), the hot sun becomes unbearable for Jonah, and he faints (cf., Amos 8:13; Jon. 2:8 [Eng., 2:7]). Jonah asks a second time to die, asserting once again that his death is better than his life. And so, while Jonah would like nothing more than to see "calamity" (רעה) come upon the Ninevites, his own "misfortune" (רעה) makes him despair of life itself. Jonah's attitude reflects an unbalanced view of himself and the Ninevites, and it amounts to a denial of God's right to have compassion on the Gentiles on his own terms.

God asks whether Jonah is rightfully angry about the plant (Jon. 4:9), echoing his earlier question about whether Jonah was rightfully

---

27. Stuart, *Hosea–Jonah*, 504.

angry about the fact that he relented concerning the judgment of the Ninevites (Jon. 4:4). But this time Jonah defiantly responds that he is rightfully angry to the point of death. This is not simply an idiom that means Jonah is extremely angry (*contra* NET). It is clear from Jonah 4:8 that Jonah literally wants to die. The LORD then drives home the point of his object lesson by means of the contrast between Jonah's action (Jon. 4:10) and his own action (Jon. 4:11). Jonah had pity on the little plant, which really represented his own personal comfort, even though he had made no real investment in it. The plant was gone as quickly as it came. On the other hand, does not God have the right to have compassion on a great city like Nineveh consisting of more than 120,000 people, especially when they repent (cf., Matt. 6:30; Luke 12:18)? The designation "who do not know their right hand from their left" is likely not a way to describe the children of the Ninevite population (cf., Isa. 7:16), in part because the introduction of such a consideration at this point in the narrative would be extraordinarily odd. God relented because the general populace repented, not because there were too many children. Rather, those who do not know their right hand from their left are those who are in need of special revelation such as what Jonah delivered to the Ninevites. They are simply not in a position to know how to respond to God unless he reveals himself to them. The addition of "many animals" at the end can be explained by the inclusion of the animals in the decree of Jonah 3:7–8. The lack of response from Jonah at the end of the book is significant because it gives God the last word (cf., Gen. 34:31).[28] It also invites the reader to consider how he or she might respond. As far as the author is concerned, the point of the object lesson has been conceded. God does in fact have the right to show compassion to the Gentiles. Only one other book of the Twelve concludes with a rhetorical question—Nahum (Nah. 3:19). There the question has a similar effect, but Nineveh represents the unbelieving Gentiles in that context. According to Hosea 3:5; Amos 9:12; Mic. 4:1–5; Zech. 8:20–23, the inclusion of the Gentiles will ultimately take place in the last days.[29] The following book of Micah likewise sees Assyria as a type of the Gentile domain to be possessed in the messianic kingdom (Mic. 5:1–5 [Eng., 5:2–6]).

---

28. See Meir Sternberg, *The Poetics of Biblical Narrative: Ideological Literature and the Drama of Reading* (Bloomington: Indiana University Press, 1985), 474–75.
29. See Gregory Goswell, "Jonah among the Twelve Prophets," *JBL* 135 (2016): 283–99.

BOOK OF THE TWELVE

MICAH

MICAH 1

1:1 The word of the LORD that came [LXX: And the word of the Lord came; cf., Jon. 1:1] to Micah the Morashtite [Tg. Jon.: The word of prophecy from before the LORD that was with Micah who was from Mareshah] in the days Jotham, Ahaz, Hezekiah, the kings of Judah, which he saw concerning Samaria and Jerusalem.

1:2 Hear, O peoples, all of them [GKC §135r; LXX: words], pay attention, O earth and its fullness, so that the LORD [L: Lord GOD; cf., LXX] may be [but see 8ḤevXII gr; GKC §109k] against you as a witness, the Lord from his holy temple. 1:3 For look, the LORD is going forth from his place [Tg. Jon.: is revealed from the place of the house of his Shekhinah], and he will come down and tread on earth's high places. 1:4 And the mountains will melt under him, and as for the valleys, they will be split apart [LXX: melt], like wax from before the fire, like water poured on a slope. 1:5 It is because of the transgression of Jacob that all this occurs, and it is because of the sins [LXX: sin] of the house of Israel. Who [Syr.: What; Tg. Jon.: Where; see GKC §37a, 137a] is the transgression of Jacob? Is it not Samaria? And who are the high places of Judah [LXX, Tg. Jon.: the sin of the house of Judah; cf., Syr.]? Is it not Jerusalem? 1:6 "And I will make Samaria into the ruin [LXX: lodge; Syr.: country house; cf., Isa. 1:8] of the field, into places for planting a vineyard, and I will pour into the valley its stones, and its foundations will I uncover. 1:7 And as for all her carved / sculpted images, they will be crushed; and as for all her harlot's wages, they will be burned in the fire; and as for her shaped / fashioned idols, I will make a desolation. For it was from a harlot's wage that she

237

gathered [Syr., Tg. Jon., Vulg.: they were gathered], and it will be unto a harlot's wage that they will return."

The wording of the superscription in Micah 1:1 most closely corresponds to Isaiah 1:1 and Hosea 1:1. The link to Isaiah in particular will prove to be helpful to the reader of the book.[1] According to this superscription, Micah is "the Morashtite," usually understood to mean that Micah's home was Moresheth Gath (Mic. 1:14; see also Mareshah in Mic. 1:15). The list of kings (Jotham, Ahaz, Hezekiah) indicates that the narrative context for Micah's prophecies is 2 Kings 15–20, which includes the downfall of the northern kingdom of Israel (2 Kgs. 17). This explains in part why the word of the LORD to Micah concerns both Samaria and Jerusalem, even though Micah was primarily a prophet to the south. Another reason for this is the comparison between Samaria and Jerusalem at the outset of the book (Mic. 1:5–7).[2]

Micah is the namesake of the prophet Micaiah from 1 Kings 22. Thus, his book begins with a quote from that prophet: "Hear, O peoples, all of them" (Mic. 1:2; cf., 1 Kgs. 22:28b [> LXX]; 2 Chr. 18:27b). It is worth noting then that Micah's contemporary, Isaiah, also quotes from Micaiah (Isa. 6:1–2; cf., 1 Kgs. 22:19). Micah 1:2 is the first of three major headings that address three different groups in the book (see also Mic. 3:1; 6:1). This raises a question about why a section devoted to Samaria and Jerusalem is addressed rhetorically to the "peoples." There is a sense in which the nations were to bear witness to the judgment of God's people for their covenant infidelity (cf., Jer. 6:18–19; Mic. 6:2). This judgment would be played out on an international stage.[3] But it is also true that God's dealings with Israel would have and still have implications for his dealings with the nations (e.g., Mic. 4:1–5; 7:8–13).

Micah 1:3 envisions the LORD going forth from his place (cf., Isa. 26:21). The end of Micah 1:2 suggests that this place is his holy temple, but Micah 1:3 likely does not refer to a departure from the earthly

---

1. See Brevard S. Childs, *Introduction to the Old Testament as Scripture* (Philadelphia: Fortress, 1979), 434–38.
2. See Michael H. Floyd, "New Form Criticism and Beyond: The Historicity of Prophetic Literature Revisited," in *The Book of the Twelve and the New Form Criticism*, eds. Mark J. Boda, Michael H. Floyd, and Colin M. Toffelmire (Atlanta: SBL, 2015), 31–36.
3. There is continuity here with the cited text in 1 Kings 22:28b. There the context is the coalition between the northern kingdom of Israel (Ahab) and the southern kingdom of Judah (Jehoshaphat) against Syria. The judgment of Ahab unfolded on the world stage.

temple. It speaks of a descent from a heavenly temple (cf., Isa. 66:1; Ps. 11:4). The LORD will tread upon earth's high places in victory (cf., Amos 4:13). The imagery of Micah 1:4 could be a depiction of a volcano or an earthquake and a landslide (cf., Isa. 34:4 [1QIsa^a]; Nah. 1:5; Jdt 16:15; 4Q201). It is also possible that this could be a way to describe how the inhabitants of the earth will feel (cf., Josh. 2:9–11; 1QH^a 12:33–34). Psalm 97:5 cites from Micah 1:4 (and Mic. 4:13b) and provides valuable insight into the early history of interpretation of Micah's opening passage. The psalm presents the LORD as a king (Ps. 97:1; cf., Mic. 2:13) surrounded by dark clouds whose throne is righteousness and justice and before whom fire goes (Ps. 97:2 – 3; cf., Dan. 7:9–10). His lightning lights up the world (Ps. 97:4). The heavens declare his righteousness (Ps. 97:6a; cf., Ps. 19:2 [Eng., 19:1]), and all "the peoples" see his glory (Ps. 97:6b; cf., Mic. 1:2). All idolaters will thus be ashamed (Ps. 97:7; cf., Mic. 1:5–7), and the true people of God will rejoice in the light of his deliverance (Ps. 97:8–12; cf., Mic. 7:8–13).

All of what Micah 1:2–4 describes is due to the transgression of Jacob and the sin(s) of the house of Israel (Mic. 1:5a). It is the stated purpose of the prophet Micah to declare this to Jacob and to Israel (Mic. 3:8).[4] The questions in Micah 1:5b are not about what or where the transgression of Jacob is or about what or where the high places (i.e., the sin[s]) of Jerusalem are,[5] although this is the way versions both ancient and modern have often rendered them (cf., 1Q14). The questions are literally about "who" (מִי) the transgression of Jacob is and about "who" the high places of Jerusalem are. They are asking who is responsible for the religious practices of idolatry and the worship of other gods (Mic. 1:7). It will be evident from the content of Micah's book that the abandonment of true worship of the LORD led in particular to the corruption of the nation's leadership (e.g., Mic. 3). The northern kingdom of Israel had become like its Canaanite neighbors, and the southern kingdom of Judah was becoming like Israel, only much worse (Jer. 3; Ezek. 23). Therefore, Judah and Jerusalem would have to face the same judgment as Israel—exile (Isa. 10:10–11; see Deut. 28–29). Just as the LORD says that he will make Samaria into a "ruin" (Mic. 1:6), so he will make Jerusalem into "ruins" (Mic. 3:12). Samaria will no longer be a place for a city but a place for a vineyard. The stones

---

4. See the comparison between the patriarch Jacob/Israel and the nation of Jacob/Israel in Hosea 12.
5. The high places here are not the same as the ones in Micah 1:3 (see BDB, 119). These high places were alternative places of worship that still had to be removed in the time of Hezekiah (2 Kgs. 18:4).

of its buildings will be poured into a valley, laying bare its foundations. Likewise, Jerusalem will become a field to be plowed. The temple
mount will be a forest. Micah 1:7 describes a reversal of the process of
idol manufacturing. The gold used to make idols is compared to a harlot's wage because of the people's spiritual infidelity (cf., Jer. 3; Ezek.
16; Hos. 1–3). The idols will be reduced to the material from which they
came (see Exod. 32; 1 Kgs. 12:28; Hos. 2:10 [Eng., 2:8]; 4:12; 8:4).[6]

*1:8 Concerning this I resolve to wail and howl [LXX: she will mourn
and lament]. I will go stripped / barefoot and naked [LXX: she will go
barefoot and naked; Tg. Jon.: in chains; Vulg.: plundered]. I [LXX:
she] will make wailing like the jackals and mourning like ostriches.
1:9 For her wound [MT: wounds; see LXX, Syr., Tg. Jon.] is incurable,
indeed, it has come to Judah. It has extended to the gate of my people,
to Jerusalem. 1:10 In Gath do not declare, certainly do not cry [LXX:
you in Akim do not rebuild from a house according to laughter]. In Beth
Leaphrah [house of dust] roll in the dust [LXX: sprinkle dust on your
laughter].[7] 1:11 Cross over for yourselves, O inhabitant [yoshebheth] of*

---

6. A word of caution is in order here to preachers and teachers of this text in
the church. The pressure to "apply" every single subunit of the Scripture
regardless of authorial intent might lead to a message about modern forms
of so-called idolatry such as money, success, et cetera. There are two main
problems with this approach. The first is that this is only the introduction
to the book. It is simply laying the groundwork for what is to come. If the
reader will allow the author to do his job, then the relevance of the book's
message and its relationship to the Twelve will emerge in good time. It may
help to compare this to one of Paul's epistles. In Romans 1–11, Paul is not
trying to give application to his readers. He wants them to listen and to
understand certain things. Then, when the time is right, he transitions to
application in Romans 12–15 on the basis of the theology in the first eleven
chapters. If the reader spends all of his/her time attempting to apply Romans 1–11, then the force of Romans 12–15 is easily missed. The second
problem with contemporary messages about idolatry from texts like Mic.
1:2–7 is the misuse of the term. It is true that Paul uses "idolatry" in two
cognate texts to describe greed (Eph. 5:5; Col. 3:5), but this is a very isolated
and unusual use in the Bible. Idolatry is normally the conscious worship of
an object as God (e.g., Exod. 32) or as other so-called gods. Of course, it is
wrong to spend too much time and energy on things like money and success,
but such action would only be idolatry in a metaphorical sense. People do
not consciously worship those things as a religious act.
7. The Hebrew verb translated "roll in the dust" sounds like "Philistia" where
Gath was located.

Shaphir [pleasant], in nakedness, that is, shame [bosheth]. The inhab-
itant of Tsaanan [sheep] does not go out [yatseah]. The wailing of Beth
Etsel [the house of nearness], he will take from you his support [LXX:
she will receive a blow of pain from you]. [8] *1:12 Indeed, it is for good that*
the inhabitant of Maroth [bitter; LXX: pains; Tg. Jon.: rebellious to turn
to the Torah] waits [qal qatal 3fs חִיל*; LXX =* מִי יחל *(hiphil yiqtol 3ms*
חלל*); BHS: piel qatal 3fs* יחל*], although evil [ra] has come down from*
[meeth] the LORD to the gate [LXX, Syr., Tg. Jon.: gates] of Jerusalem.
1:13 Bind the chariot to the steeds [larekhesh], O inhabitant of Lachish
[or, Lakhish]. The beginning of sin is she to the daughter of Zion, for
in you were found the transgressions of Israel. 1:14 Therefore, you will
give parting gifts to Moresheth [LXX, Syr.: inheritance] Gath, the houses
of Achzib [or, Akhzibh] will become deceptive [akhzabh] to the kings of
Israel. 1:15 "Again [LXX: until] the (dis)possessor [hayyoresh] will I
bring to you, O inhabitant of Mareshah. To Adullam the glory of Israel
will come [NIV: He who is the glory of Israel will come to Adullam]."
1:16 Make bald and shave for the children of your delight. Make wide
your baldness as the eagle, for they go into exile from you.

The MT of Micah 1:8 features the prophet speaking in the first
person. The LXX has third person verbs for which Samaria continues
as the subject from Micah 1:6–7. According to the MT, the prophet
determines to mourn over the coming judgment by going barefoot and
naked. This is a sign act that Micah borrows from Isaiah (Isa. 20:2).
Isaiah's action symbolized how the king of Assyria would drive the
captives of Egypt and the exiles of Cush both young and old naked
and barefoot (Isa. 20:3). Likewise, Micah's action symbolizes how the
inhabitants of "Shaphir" will experience the shame of nakedness at
the hands of a foreign enemy (Mic. 1:11). He says that his wailing
will be like the howling of jackals. The sound of his mourning will be
like that which ostriches make. This is because Samaria's wound is
incurable, and it has now reached Judah and Jerusalem (Mic. 1:9; cf.,
Isa. 1:6; Jer. 30:12–17; Mic. 1:12). According to Isaiah 8:5–8, Assyria's
invasion of the northern kingdom would have some negative consequences for the south.

Some commentators think that Micah 1:10–16 portrays a historical invasion of Judah and Jerusalem such as Sennacherib's invasion
in 701 BC (2 Kgs. 18:13).[9] In favor of this view are the references to

---

8. The LXX does not render "Shaphir" and "Beth Etsel" as place names.
9. E.g., Terence E. Fretheim, *Reading Hosea–Micah: A Literary and Theo-*
   logical Commentary (Macon, GA: Smyth & Helwys, 2013), 195–96.

several well-known locations like Gath, Jerusalem, and Lachish (Mic. 1:10, 12, 13). Others say that the passage is more of a generalization of Judah's entire history of judgment.[10] In favor of this are the unknown place names like Beth Leaphrah, Shaphir, Tsaanan, Beth Etsel, and Maroth whose presence in the text seems to be entirely for the sake of wordplay (Mic. 1:10–12). The passage is in many ways comparable to Isaiah 10:27–34, and Brevard Childs' commentary on that text is applicable here:

> In my opinion, this historical debate is of limited value in interpreting the passage. It aids to the extent in which the deviant path of attack described increases the effect of an unstoppable, invincible, and utterly terrifying enemy. Yet it is fully clear that the passage in its present form is a prophetic oracle, not a historical report. It is very possible that the geographical details derive from a memory of a past event, but recovering this particular invasion, even if possible, leaves the interpreter still a great distance from the meaning of the text. The exegetical task remains crucial to determining how the prophet construed his material and to what end.[11]

It is worth noting in addition to this that the Isaiah context is both eschatological (Isa. 10:22–23; cf., Dan. 9:27) and messianic (Isa. 11:1–10). Thus, whatever historical connection Isaiah 10:27–34 may have to an event like what occurred in 701 BC, the text now serves to illustrate something bigger than that particular moment. The same can be said for Micah 1:10–16. What happened historically to Judah and Jerusalem now functions within the context of the book of Micah and the Twelve to depict future realities of judgment (Mic. 1:10–14) and restoration (Mic. 1:15; see Hos. 3:4–5; Mic. 4:1–5, 10).

Verse 10 of Micah 1 begins with a quote from David's lament for Saul and Jonathan when they died at the hands of the Philistines (2 Sam. 1:20): "In Gath do not declare." The idea is not to spread the news among the enemies of Judah and Jerusalem that Samaria's incurable wound has arrived. Rather, their "rolling in the dust" (cf., Ezek. 27:30) should be done in the so-called "house of dust" (Beth Leaphrah). The inhabitants of Shaphir are to cross over into exile (Mic. 1:11). On the other hand, the inhabitants of Tsaanan cannot go out because they are under siege. As for Beth Etsel, the conqueror will take its place. The inhabitants of Maroth wait for something good

---

10. E.g., Keil, *Minor Prophets*, 297.
11. Brevard S. Childs, *Isaiah*, OTL (Louisville: Westminster John Knox, 2001), 96–97.

to happen, but evil/calamity is what comes down from the LORD to the gate of Jerusalem (Mic. 1:12).

The inhabitants of Lachish (Josh. 10:34–35) are commanded to bind their chariots to their horses in a vain attempt to flee (Mic. 1:13). The prophet calls Lachish the "beginning of the sin of Daughter Zion." He explains that the transgressions of Israel were found in her, suggesting a special connection to the practices referenced in Micah 1:5–7. It is also possible that the term "sin" here means "punishment for sin" (BDB, 309; Zech. 14:19). The invasion of Lachish was prior to or simultaneous with the invasion of Jerusalem (or the threat of its invasion) in both the Assyrian (2 Kgs. 18:14) and the Babylonian campaigns (Jer. 34:7). Micah 1:14a is worded as an announcement of judgment for Lachish, although the image of a father (Lachish) giving parting gifts to a newly married daughter (Moresheth Gath) might give the impression that Moresheth Gath, Micah's hometown, is the city going into captivity. But the only other use of the term in 1 Kings 9:16 features Pharaoh giving Gezer as a parting gift to his daughter (recently married to Solomon) before his return to Egypt, allowing for the possibility that Mic. 1:14a is describing the departure of Lachish. The houses of Achzib (or, Akhzibh; "deception"; Josh. 15:44) will become "deceptive" (*akhzabh*) to the kings of Israel like a disappointing stream (Mic. 1:14b; see Isa. 58:11; Jer. 15:18). That is, the people will prove to be unreliable to the authorities in the midst of the judgment.

The first-person voice of the LORD emerges in Micah 1:15 with what appears to be a glimmer of hope beyond judgment (cf., Mic. 2:12–13; 4:1–8; 5:1–8 [Eng., 5:2–9]; 7:8–20). He speaks of "the possessor" (cf., Amos 9:12; Obad. 15–21) whom he will bring "again" (עֹד) to Judah (cf., Deut. 33:7) as represented by Mareshah (2 Chr. 20:37). He also mentions the glory of Israel who will come to Adullam, a location traditionally associated with David (1 Sam. 22:1; 2 Sam. 23:13; cf., Mic. 7:12). The use of the same verb (בוֹא) in both clauses suggests that the glory of Israel here is not an object (1 Sam. 4:21–22) or a status ("glorious") but a title for the possessor (cf., Isa. 11:10). According to the MT, the possessor will come "again," perhaps a reference to a new David. The LXX, however, reads עֹד as עַד ("until"), possibly alluding to the messianic prophecy in Genesis 49:10b: "until (עַד) the one to whom it belongs comes, and to him will belong obedience of peoples."[12] In the meantime

---

12. For the different ways to interpret the wording of Genesis 49:10b and its context see Richard C. Steiner, "Four Inner-Biblical Interpretations of Genesis 49:10: On the Lexical and Syntactic Ambiguities of עַד as Reflected in the Prophecies of Nathan, Ahijah, Ezekiel, and Zechariah," *JBL*

the inhabitants of the land are commanded to shave their heads as an outward expression of their mourning over the loss of their children in exile (Mic. 1:16; cf., Jer. 31:15; Mic. 2:9; Job 1:20).

MICAH 2

2:1 Woe, planners of trouble and doers of evil on their beds. In the light of the morning they do it, for it belongs to the power of their hand [LXX: therefore, they do not lift up to God their hands; Syr., Vulg.: their hand is against God]. 2:2 And they desire fields and rob them [LXX: plunder orphans], and houses, and they take them. And they extort a man and his house, and a man and his inheritance. 2:3 Therefore, thus says the LORD, "Look, I am planning against this family calamity [lit., evil] from which they will not move their necks. And they will not walk haughtily [LXX adds: suddenly], for a time of calamity [lit., evil] will it be." 2:4 In that day he [but see GKC §144d] will lift up against you a saying and wail a wailing and say, "We are completely destroyed. As for the portion of my people, he will exchange it [LXX: it will be measured with a rope/cord]. O how he will move it for me! To an apostate our fields will he divide." 2:5 Therefore, you will not have someone casting a cord by lot in the assembly of the LORD.

2:6 "Do not drip [Tg. Jon.: prophesy]," they drip, "they should not drip of these things." Reproaches will not depart [BHS: "Shame will not over-take us"].[13] 2:7 Is it said, O house of Jacob, "Is the patience of the LORD short, are these things his deeds?" Do not my words cause good with the upright walking [GKC §118n; LXX: Are not his words good with him, and have they not gone upright]? 2:8 And yesterday [LXX: before; Syr.: were filled] my people as an enemy [Syr.: thief] arose. From before a garment [LXX, Syr.: his peace] a robe you strip [BHS: you strip a robe from upon a friend; LXX: they flayed his skin; cf., Syr.] from passers-by in security, those returned from war [LXX: to take away hope in the crushing of war]. 2:9 As for the women of my people, you drive them out each from her house of delights, from upon her children you take my glory forever [LXX: Therefore, the leaders of my people will be thrown out from their luxurious homes, because of their evil practices they are

---

132 (2013): 33–60; Michael B. Shepherd, *The Text in the Middle* (New York: Peter Lang, 2014), 46–49.

13. LXX: "Do not weep tears, and do not let them weep over these things, for disgrace will not be set aside" (cf., Syr.).

driven out. Draw near to the eternal mountains].[14] *2:10 Arise and go, for not this is the resting place on account of uncleanness [טָמְאָה; MT: it is unclean]. It will destroy, and destruction will be severe. 2:11 If a man walking in a spirit of deception [lit., spirit and deception] were to lie [LXX: You have fled, no one pursuing . . .], "I will drip to you for wine and for strong drink [or, of wine and of strong drink]," he would be a dripper for this people.*

2:12 "I will surely gather, O Jacob, all of you [LXX: Jacob will surely be gathered with all], I will surely gather the remnant of Israel [Tg. Jon.: your exiles, O remnant of Israel]. Together I will make him like the sheep of Bozrah [Tg. Jon.: in the fold], like a flock in the midst of the pasture, and they will make noise [read הדבר ותהימנה] on account of mankind [BDB, 580]." 2:13 The one who breaks through goes up before them [cf., LXX]. They break through and pass through a gate and go out through it. And their king passes through before them, and the LORD is at their head.

The first five verses of Micah 2 follow the pattern of a woe oracle: introduction (Mic. 2:1), accusation (Mic. 2:2), and announcement of judgment (Mic. 2:3–5). The words are directed against "planners of trouble" and "doers of evil" (Mic. 2:1), which in context refer to those who commit the injustices of Mic. 2:2. When the text says, "doers of evil on their beds," it does not refer to actions performed in bedrooms. Rather, it is a reference to the nighttime thoughts that precede what is actually done in the light of the morning (cf., Ps. 36:5 [Eng., 36:4]). These people are early to the task and unashamed to oppress others in broad daylight. The end of Micah 2:1 provides a clue to the identity of the evildoers. They are the ones in whose hand is the power to do these things (cf., Gen. 31:29; Mic. 7:3; Neh. 5:5). That is, they are the leaders who are in positions of authority and who have abused their privileges by taking advantage of those in their care. They desire the fields and homes of others who are defenseless against seizure and extortion, and they take them simply because they can (Mic. 2:2; see Exod. 20:17; Isa. 3:14–15). The story of Naboth's vineyard is an excellent illustration of this (1 Kgs. 21). King Ahab wanted Naboth's vineyard because it was adjacent to his palace, but Naboth refused because the vineyard was his family's inheritance. Queen Jezebel then made arrangements for

---

14. The differences between the MT and the LXX of Micah 2:8–9 seem drastic in English translation. In actual fact, the differences in translation reflect only very slight differences in the spelling and vocalization of the Hebrew text.

false accusations to be brought against Naboth so that he would be put to death, paving the way for Ahab to take the vineyard for himself.

The announcement of judgment in Micah 2:3 comes from the LORD himself and plays on the wording of the introduction, creating a sense of poetic justice (cf., Amos 3:1–2). The LORD has "plans" of his own for those who "plan" trouble and do "evil," but the "evil" that the LORD "plans" is better rendered as the "calamity" of judgment. They will not be able to move their necks from this calamity, and they will no longer walk in pride because the time of their judgment will come (cf., Isa. 3:16). The announcement continues in Micah 2:4 with the phrase, "In that day." This phrase occurs several other times in the book (Mic. 4:6; 5:9; 7:11–12 [MurXII]) with an eschatological sense (Mic. 4:1), suggesting that whatever historical judgment may be in view here, there is also an image of things to come. This is a feature that plays directly into the program of the Twelve (Hos. 3:4–5). A saying will be lifted up (cf., Hab. 2:6) against the guilty, and a wailing will be made. The quote of this is from the voice of the very ones who will face destruction and loss of land to a foreign enemy ("apostate"). Ironically, those who unjustly seized the fields of others (Mic. 2:2) will have their own fields divided. In the end, they will have no one "casting a cord by lot in the assembly of the LORD" (Mic. 2:5). In other words, they will have no portion in the land of the covenant (Ps. 16:6).[15]

The next section (Mic. 2:6–11) highlights the unfortunate response to true prophecy (cf., Isa. 6:9–10; 30:10; Jer. 1:18–19; Ezek. 2:5; Hos. 9:7; Amos 2:12; CD-A 4:20). They say to the prophet, "Do not drip," which is apparently a derogatory way of saying, "Do not prophesy" (cf., *Tg. Jon.*; Amos 7:16; Mic. 2:11). Of course, the prophet returns the favor ("they drip"). He laments the fact that reproach for the true prophet never ceases (cf., Jer. 20:7–12). The house of Jacob is quoted as insinuating that Micah's words of judgment make the LORD seem impatient (Mic. 2:7a). They believe that the LORD tolerates their injustice (cf., Mic. 3:11). They cannot accept that the acts of judgment described by Micah can be attributed to the LORD. But the prophet responds that the words he speaks on behalf of the LORD only cause good for those who live uprightly (Mic. 2:7b). Evildoers can and should expect judgment (cf., Amos 5:18).

Given the context, "my people" in Micah 2:8 likely refers to the leaders of the prophet's people. They are the ones who formerly arose as an enemy both to God and to their own people. This is illustrated by the practice of stripping the robes of men returning from battle who

---

15. Bullinger, *Figures of Speech*, 548.

expect to find security in their own land for which they have fought. Instead they are plundered and treated like foreigners by their own leaders (cf., Obad. 14). These same leaders drive out the women—the women they should be protecting—from their homes (Mic. 2:9; cf., Mic. 2:2; see also Deut. 10:12–22), forever taking away the inheritance that ought to belong to their children (cf., Mic. 1:16; Lam. 1:6). Therefore, they must go into exile (Mic. 2:10; see Deut. 28–29). The land of the covenant cannot be the place where they rest (cf., Isa. 11:10). This is because of their uncleanness that destroys it (cf., Lev. 18:27–29; Jer 2:7; 4Q177). Micah sarcastically concludes that the "dripper" (i.e., prophet) for this people would be the false prophet (cf., Jer. 5:31; 6:13–15; 23:9–40; 27–28; Ezek. 13), someone who would tell them what they want to hear for a price (Mic. 2:11; cf., Isa. 56:9–12; Amos 7:14; Mic. 3:5–8, 11; 2 Tim. 4:3).

According to Calvin, the gathering in Micah 2:12 is for judgment rather than restoration (cf., Zeph. 1:2).[16] This suggestion is primarily due to the preceding context of judgment, but it is difficult to reconcile with the language of Micah 2:12–13 (see also Mic. 4:6; Zeph. 3:18–20). Furthermore, it is not unusual in the prophetic literature to move suddenly back and forth between judgment and restoration (e.g., Mic 3:1–12; 4:1–5). The LORD says that he will certainly gather "the remnant of Israel" (cf., Ezek. 11:17; 20:34; 36:24). This is not merely a reference to those who survive the judgment (i.e., Isa. 56–59; Zech. 1–6; Ezra-Neh.). It is the faithful remnant, the flock that God himself will shepherd (cf., Ezek. 34; Mic. 4:7; 5:3, 6–7 [Eng., 5:4, 7–8]; 7:14, 18). The LORD will make this remnant collectively like the sheep of Bozrah (see Amos 1:12). Some translators and commentators prefer to revocalize "Bozrah" so that it reads, "in the fold" (see *Tg. Jon.*), but this misses the possible connection to Edom. The end of Micah 2:12 says that the remnant will be "like a flock in the midst of the pasture, and they will make noise on account of mankind (*adam*)." The reader of the Twelve is already familiar with the use of "Edom" to represent *adam* ("mankind") from Amos 9:12. It also occurs in Ezek. 34:31; 36:37–38 (*adam*) where the shepherd-and-flock imagery is prominent (see "Edom" in Ezek. 35:15; see also Gen. 1:26–28; Ezek. 36:10–12). But the point is not simply to say that the remnant of Israel is a large "flock" of people. Rather, the idea is that the faithful remnant of Israel will include believers from the nations (Mic. 4:1–5).

---

16. John Calvin, *Commentaries on the Twelve Minor Prophets*, vol. 3, *Jonah, Micah, Nahum*, trans. John Owen, Calvin's Commentaries XIV (reprint, Grand Rapids: Baker, 2005), 212.

The one who leads the remnant is the one who "breaks through" the enclosure (Mic. 2:13a; cf., John 10:9). Thus, the remnant is able to pass through the gate and go out—a metaphor for deliverance and perhaps an allusion to the new exodus (Isa. 52:12; Mic. 7:15). There is some question about whether Micah 2:13b speaks of two leaders ("their king" and "the LORD") or, because of the parallelism and/or the potential explicative use of the *waw* conjunction (GKC §154a), one leader ("their king," that is, "the LORD"). John Smith comments that double headship with a messianic ruler finds no parallel in the Old Testament, yet he cites Zephaniah 3:15 (cf., Zeph. 3:14; Zech. 2:14 [Eng., 2:10]; 9:9–10).[17] Actually, double kingship is quite prominent in the Pentateuch (e.g., Gen. 49:8–12; Exod. 15:18; Num. 24:7–9), Prophets (e.g., Isa. 9:5–6 [Eng., 9:6–7]; 10:21; Mic. 5:3 [Eng., 5:4]; 7:14), and Psalms (e.g., Pss. 2; 72; 93; 97; 99).[18] The two are held in balance without any feeling of tension from the biblical authors.

MICAH 3

3:1 And I said [LXX: And he will say; Syr.: And he said], "Hear, O heads of Jacob and leaders [LXX: remnant] of the house of Israel. Is it not for you to know what true justice is, 3:2 you who reject good and choose evil, you who tear away their skin from upon them and their flesh from upon their bones, 3:3 and those who devour the flesh of my people [Tg. Jon.: plunder the possessions of my people], and their skin from upon them they strip, and their bones they break, and they spread them just as [LXX: like flesh (כשאר)] in the pot and like meat within a cauldron? 3:4 Then they will cry out to the LORD, but he will not answer them, and he will hide [or, may he hide (GKC §109k)] his face from them at that time because [BDB, 455] they have acted wickedly in their deeds."

3:5 Thus says the LORD, "Concerning the prophets who lead my people astray [or, Thus says the LORD concerning the prophets who lead my people astray; or, Thus says the LORD concerning the prophets, "They are leading (הם מתעים) my people astray"], who bite with their teeth and proclaim peace, and whoever does not give upon their mouth [or, according to their command (BDB, 805)], they sanction against him

17. John Merlin Powis Smith, *A Critical and Exegetical Commentary on the Books of Micah, Nahum and Zephaniah*, ICC (New York: Charles Scribner's Sons, 1911), 69.

18. See William Horbury, *Jewish Messianism and the Cult of Christ* (London: SCM, 1998), 37–46.

war.[19] 3:6 Therefore, it will be night for you without a prophetic vision [GKC §119w; or, too night-like for you for a prophetic vision (BDB, 582)], and it will grow dark for you without divination by casting lots [or, too dark for you for divination by casting lots]. And the sun will set on the prophets [Tg. Jon.: false prophets], and the day will be dark on them. 3:7 And those who see prophetic visions [LXX: dreams] will be ashamed, and those who divine by casting lots will feel humiliation [LXX: be laughed at]. And they will cover over moustache, all of them [LXX: And all will speak against them], for there will be no answer from God [LXX: no one who listens to them]." 3:8 But as for me, I am full of strength (namely, the Spirit of the LORD [LXX: with / in the Spirit; Luther: and the Spirit]) and justice and might to declare to Jacob his transgression and to Israel his sin.

3:9 Hear this, O heads of the house of Jacob and leaders of the house of Israel who consider justice an abomination [or, make justice an abomination; Snaith, Ms. Or. 2626-2628: הַמְתַעֲבִים], and all of what is upright they twist, 3:10 who each build Zion with bloodshed and Jerusalem with injustice. 3:11 As for her heads, it is for a bribe that they judge. And as for her priests, it is for a price that they teach. And as for her prophets, it is for money that they divine by casting lots. And it is on the LORD that they lean saying, "Is not the LORD in our midst? Calamity will not come upon us." 3:12 Therefore, because of you, Zion will be plowed like a field, and Jerusalem will be ruins [GKC §87e], and the mountain of the house [i.e., the temple mount] will become high places of a forest.

Micah 3:1 begins the second of the three major divisions in the book (cf., Mic. 1:2; 6:1). It is addressed to "the heads of Jacob and the leaders of the house of Israel." Thus, it picks up the criticism of the leadership in chapter 2 and contrasts the headship of the LORD and the messianic king in the pastoral image of Micah 2:12–13 with that of those who are like wolves among the flock. The critique of the current state of affairs in chapter 3 also sets up a contrast with the messianic kingdom in Micah 4:1–5 and the ideal leadership of the messianic king in Micah 5:1–5 (Eng., 5:2–6; cf., Isa. 28). Chapter 3 divides into three judgment oracles: (1) introduction (Mic. 3:1), accusation (Mic. 3:2–3),

---

19. *Tg. Jon.*: "Thus says the LORD about the false prophets who lead my people astray, who, whenever someone feeds them a meal of meat, they prophesy to him peace, and whoever does not feed them, they prepare against him battle."

and announcement of judgment (Mic. 3:4); (2) introduction (Mic. 3:5a), accusation (Mic. 3:5b), and announcement of judgment (Mic. 3:6–7); and (3) introduction (Mic. 3:9a), accusation (Mic. 3:9b–11), and announcement of judgment (Mic. 3:12).

The rhetorical question in Micah 3:1b clearly implies that the leadership has the responsibility to know what true justice is and to do it (see Deut. 16:18–20; Mic. 6:8), but these leaders reject what is good and choose what is evil (Mic. 3:2a; cf., Gen. 2:17; Isa. 5:20; Mal. 2:17). Those who should be like shepherds feeding and watching over their flock are behaving like ravenous wolves. Note the structure of their description: (A) who tear away their skin from upon them, (B) and their flesh from upon their bones, (B¹) and those who devour the flesh of my people, (A¹) and their skin from upon them they strip (Mic. 3:2b–3a). They break their bones and spread them out as in a pot and like meat in a cauldron (Mic. 3:3; cf., Ezek. 11:2–13). Of course, they do not literally do these things, so what does the metaphor describe? It describes their oppression of the people to their own advantage as in Mic. 2:2, 8–9; 3:9b–11. It also includes the actions of the false prophets (Mic. 3:5–7, 11) who put themselves in a leadership role. In this way, the leaders "devour" those entrusted to their care. Therefore, the LORD will not answer them when they cry to him for help (Mic. 3:4a; cf., Deut. 32:37–38; Judg. 10:14; Jer. 11:12). He will hide his face from them at that time because of their wicked deeds (Mic. 3:4b; cf., Num. 6:24–26; Deut. 32:20; Jer. 25:5; Hos. 9:15).

The second judgment oracle in Micah 3 is addressed to the false prophets who lead the people astray by telling them what they want to hear and by giving them a false sense of security for a price (Mic. 3:5–7; cf., Mic. 2:11; 3:11). *Targum Jonathan* interprets Mic. 3:5b to mean that the false prophets proclaim peace to those who feed them for their services (cf., Ezek. 13:19), but they declare war against anyone who does not (cf., Joel 4:9 [Eng., 3:9]). But it is also possible that the expression "who bite with their teeth" is a figure for oppression (BDB, 675) rather than a description of the false prophets eating food. Furthermore, the expression "give upon their mouth" is not necessarily a reference to feeding the false prophets. It could be a more general reference to giving according to what they say. Either way, they proclaim peace for those who pay and war for those who do not.

Therefore, it will be nighttime for the false prophets without a prophetic vision, and it will grow dark for them without divination by casting lots (Mic. 3:6a; cf., Isa. 8:20; Ezek. 12:24; 21:26–27; Lam. 2:9b). The proverbial sun will set on them, and the day will be dark (Mic. 3:6b). The darkness is a metaphor for the lack of true revelation from the LORD (cf., Ezek. 7:26; Amos 8:11–12). Ironically, prophetic visions sometimes appear at night (e.g., Zech. 1–6), but the false nature of the "prophecy" of these self-proclaimed prophets is evident in their practice of divination (Deut. 18:10). It has been suggested that the darkness here is that of judgment in the Day of the LORD (Joel 2:2; Amos 5:18), although that association is not made explicit in the text of Micah itself.[20] Those who falsely claim to see prophetic visions and to foretell the future will be ashamed in the exposure of their hoax (Mic. 3:7; see Deut. 18:22; Zech. 13:4). They will cover their mouths (cf., Lev. 13:45; Ezek. 24:17, 22), for there will be no answer from God (cf., 1 Sam. 28:6; Amos 8:11–12; Mic. 3:4), and everyone will know it.

Micah takes this opportunity to contrast himself with the false prophets (Mic. 3:8). What is it that sets a true prophet apart from a false one other than the fact that his prophecy actually comes to pass? Micah says that he is full of three things—"strength and justice and might"—for the purpose of declaring to Jacob his transgression and to Israel his sin (Mic. 1:5). The syntax of this triad is interrupted between its first and second parts by את רוח יהוה. Some versions (e.g., LXX) render את as the preposition "with": "with the Spirit of the LORD." But this would be a highly unusual use of that preposition (see BDB, 86). Others (e.g., Luther) simply add the Spirit of the LORD to the list by putting the conjunction "and" in front of it, but this clearly has no warrant from the Hebrew text. The definite direct object marker את is sometimes used to indicate parenthetical scribal or authorial comments/interpolations or glosses (e.g., 1 Sam. 2:23; Isa. 29:10; Hag. 2:5a; Zech. 12:10).[21] A secondary scribal or editorial insertion will be flagged by textual variation (e.g., 1 Sam. 2:23; Hag. 2:5a). A genuine authorial comment will not be (e.g., Isa. 29:10; Mic. 3:8; Zech. 12:10). The parenthetical nature of the phrase is thus brought out in the above translation: "But as for me, I am full of strength [namely, the Spirit of the LORD] and justice and might to declare to Jacob his transgression and to Israel his sin." What this means is that Micah is not claiming physical strength but spiritual strength and fortitude to fulfill his task (cf., Zech. 4:6). True prophets have the Spirit of the LORD (Num. 11:29; Hos. 9:7; Neh. 9:30; see commentary on Joel 3:1 [Eng., 2:28]). This is not merely the spirit of prophecy. Paul uses this language to describe the Spirit filling the believer (Eph. 5:18; cf., Gen. 41:38; Exod. 31:3; Dan. 4:5, 15 [Eng., 4:8, 18]; 5:11) much the same way that he uses the language of Isaiah 63:10 to describe the Spirit in personal terms (Eph. 4:30).

---

20. See J. Smith, *Micah, Nahum and Zephaniah*, 75.
21. See Michael Fishbane, *Biblical Interpretation in Ancient Israel* (Oxford: Clarendon, 1985), 48–51.

Thus, in the current climate the proclamation of true justice does not come through those in leadership positions (Mic. 3:1, 9). It comes through the rejected yet true prophets (Mic. 2:6) by the work of the Spirit of the LORD (Mic. 3:8). But it would be a reduction of Micah's message to say that he only declares the sins of idolatry and social injustice and announces judgment. Furthermore, it would be blatantly inaccurate to say that he is merely attempting to call the leadership back to the terms of the Sinai covenant. Yes, he is exposing the breaking of that covenant and the consequences thereof, but this is not for the purpose of a return or a renewal. It is ultimately to look beyond the now inevitable judgment to the hope of a new exodus and a new covenant relationship in the messianic kingdom (Mic. 4:1–5; 5:1–5 [Eng., 5:2–6]; 7:14–17, 18–20).

The third and final judgment oracle in chapter 3 (Mic. 3:9–12) begins the same way the first did (Mic. 3:1a, 9a), but this time the prophet leaves aside the rhetorical question (Mic. 3:1b) and launches directly into his accusation against the leaders who consider (or make) justice an abomination and twist all that is upright (Mic. 3:9b). They build the royal city for their own benefit at the expense of the lives and the justice of others (Mic. 3:10; cf., Hab. 2:12). The clauses in Micah 3:11a front three different groups: (1) heads/leaders judge for a bribe (see Exod. 18; Deut. 10:17; Mic. 4:3; 7:3); (2) priests teach for a price (see Deut. 17:11; 33:10; 2 Chr. 17:7–9); and (3) prophets divine for money (cf., Mic. 2:11; 3:3). Yet their mindset is that the presence of the LORD will protect them from any calamity announced by a prophet like Micah regardless of their behavior (cf., Jer. 7:4; Amos 9:10; Mic. 2:7).

The marginal note in the MT indicates that the announcement of judgment in Micah 3:12 is the middle verse of the Book of the Twelve (cf., 4Q371, 372). Jeremiah 26:18 is usually understood to be a citation of Mic. 3:12, but the spelling of "ruins" (עִיִּין) in Micah 3:12 suggests that the textual form of the prophecy in the book of Micah is actually later than the one in Jer. 26:18 (see GKC §87e; see also Mic. 1:6), even though the prophecy itself is attributed to Micah. Thus, what Jeremiah 26:18 cites is the oral prophecy of Micah. The composer of the Twelve, who consistently cites the book of Jeremiah in his work, quotes Jeremiah 26:18 in a deliberately later form to mark the middle of his composition. The connection to the Jeremiah context suggests a more positive reception of Micah than what he received according to Mic. 2:6. Was Micah's prophecy not fulfilled simply because the Assyrians did not capture Jerusalem in the time of Hezekiah (Jer. 26:19)?[22] This

---

22. See Fretheim, *Reading Hosea–Micah*, 204.

is apparently not the inner-biblical understanding of the prophecy. Hezekiah was able to avoid disaster (2 Kgs. 18–19), but the prophecy was ultimately about what would happen to Jerusalem in the hands of the Babylonians (2 Kgs. 20; Mic. 4:10; Ps. 79:1) in fulfillment of words once spoken to Solomon (1 Kgs. 9:8; 2 Chr. 7:21).

APPLICATION OF MICAH 3

It is important to recognize that the charge of injustice in Micah 3 is directed against those in leadership positions and not against those in the general populace. The people in the general populace were the victims of oppression and were not in a position to inflict the same harm on others.[23] Therefore, it would be a misapplication of the text to use it to condemn a church congregation for social injustices over which they have little control and for which they have little responsibility. In an effort to stress that believers continue to struggle with sin and must fight against it, preachers too often speak to their congregations from texts like these as if the people were unredeemed sinners, failing to make a distinction between unbelievers and those who have the power of the Spirit. It would be more accurate to compare the wolves among the flock in Micah 3 to false teachers in the church (Acts 20:29) or to corrupt civil leaders (cf., Ezek. 22:27; Zeph. 3:3). But the real message for the Christian is that injustice is part of living in a fallen world. Efforts to combat injustice are noble, but true justice will only come in the messianic kingdom (Mic. 4:1–5). Thus, the Christian should not put his or her hope in the leaders or the courts but in the coming of Christ.

MICAH 4–5

4:1 And it will be at the end of the days, the mountain of the house of the LORD [LXX: the mountain of the Lord] will be [LXX: will be visible] established at the top of the mountains, and it will be lifted up above hills. And peoples [Isa. 2:2: all the nations] will flow [or, shine; LXX: hasten] to it [Tg. Jon.: And all the kingdoms will turn to worship on it], 4:2 and many nations [Isa. 2:3: peoples] will go and say, "Come, and let us go up to the mountain of the LORD [to the mountain of the LORD > 1QIsaᵃ] and [and > Isa. 2:3] to the house of the God of Jacob, and he will [or, so that he may] teach us from his ways [or, some of his ways; LXX:

---

23. This is not to say that the people were innocent of all wrongdoing. It is only to say that the particular charges brought by the prophet in Micah 3 are specific to the leadership.

they (the priests?) will show us his way], and we will walk [or, and so that we may walk] in his paths." For it is from Zion that Torah will go forth, and the word of the LORD from Jerusalem. 4:3 And he will judge between many peoples [Isa. 2:4: nations], and he will decide for mighty / many nations [Isa. 2:4: many peoples] even to afar [> Isa. 2:4]. And they will crush their swords into plowing tools and their spears into pruning tools. They will not lift up nation to nation a sword [Isa. 2:4: Nation will not lift up to nation a sword], and they will never again learn war. 4:4 And each will dwell under his grapevine and under his fig tree, and there will be no one causing trembling, for it is the mouth of the LORD of hosts that has spoken. 4:5 Though [Vss.: For] all the peoples walk each in the name of his god [LXX: his way], we, on the other hand, will walk in the name of the LORD our God forever and ever.[24]

Micah 3 ended with a very dismal picture of what would happen to Jerusalem (Mic. 3:12). Now, at the beginning of Micah 4, the text turns to one of the most magnificent depictions of what the holy city will be in the last days as part of the messianic kingdom. The passage in Micah 4:1–5 is a careful reading and interpretation of Isaiah 2:1–5, which is the programmatic passage of the book of Isaiah (cf., the corresponding bookend in Isaiah 66:18–25).[25] There is no substantial reason or extant evidence to suggest that the two texts were independently following a common written source or oral tradition. The similarity of wording and the signs of exegesis between the two point to direct dependence. Micah has already given notice of following Isaiah's work, particularly in chapter 1. According to Isaiah 2:1, the text in view is the word that Isaiah saw. Since there is no such superscription with Micah's name, it stands to reason that readers of the prophetic corpus have given priority to Isaiah's passage as the one that is read and interpreted by Micah rather than vice versa.

Other clues to the direction of dependence increase as the reader progresses through the Hebrew text of the Micah passage. Micah 4:1 changes the position of נכון ("established") and inserts the pronoun הוא ("it"). It also uses the preposition על ("to") for אל ("to"), and עמים ("peoples") for כל הגוים ("all the nations"). Conversely, the beginning of Micah 4:2 has גוים ("nations") for עמים ("peoples"). Micah 4:2 also adds

---

24. Isaiah 2:5: "O house of Jacob, come and let us walk [or, that we may walk] in the light of the LORD."
25. See Richard L. Schultz, *The Search for Quotation: Verbal Parallels in the Prophets*, JSOTSup 180 (Sheffield: Sheffield Academic, 1999), 290–307; Shepherd, *Text in the Middle*, 130–34.

the conjunction *waw* ("and") before "to the house of the God of Jacob" and has the fuller spelling of וְיֹרֵנוּ ("and he will teach us") for וִירֵנוּ. Longer text and fuller spellings, both of which continue to appear in the Micah passage, are typical features of dependent texts rather than source texts. Micah 4:3 uses עַמִּים רַבִּים ("many peoples") for הַגּוֹיִם ("the nations"), and לְגוֹיִם עֲצֻמִים עַד רָחוֹק ("for mighty/many nations even to afar") for לְעַמִּים רַבִּים ("for many peoples"). Note also the orthographic variants in this verse: חַרְבֹתֵיהֶם for חַרְבוֹתָם ("their swords"), וַחֲנִיתֹתֵיהֶם for וַחֲנִיתוֹתֵיהֶם ("and their spears"), and יִלְמְדוּן for יִלְמְדוּ ("learn"). The verb יִשְׂאוּ ("lift up") is plural for the singular יִשָּׂא. Micah 4:4a comes from 1 Kings 5:5 (Eng., 1 Kgs. 4:25), but Micah 4:4b appears to depend on an expression that serves to mark the three major divisions of the book of Isaiah (Isa. 1:20; 40:5; 58:14). Finally, Micah 4:5 is an interpretation of what is meant by "walking" (הָלַךְ) in the light of the LORD in Isaiah 2:5, which is an explication of what Isaiah 2:3 (Mic. 4:2) means by "going" or "walking" to the mountain of the LORD to learn the Torah and the word of the LORD in order to "walk" in his ways.

The phrase "at the end of the days" (Mic. 4:1) is the same one that occurs in the programmatic passage of the Twelve (see commentary for Hosea 3:5). Micah envisions the eschaton as a time when the temple mount (Mount Zion) will be established at the top of the mountains (cf., Ezek. 38:12; Dan. 2:34–35, 44–45). Given the parallelism and the poetic nature of this passage, this does not necessarily mean that Zion will become geographically higher than all other mountains in the world. It is more likely a way to show that Zion will be the most important and honored of all the mountains in the last days.[26] This is consistent with the sustained biblical interest in the land of the covenant, and specifically the city of David, as the location central to God's plan of redemption for humanity (e.g., Gen. 2:11–14; 15:18; 22:2 [2 Chr. 3:1]; 2 Sam. 6–7; Isa. 65:18; Ps. 46; Rev. 21–22).

But the exiles of Judah and Jerusalem are not exclusively the ones that the prophecy sees returning or going to Zion (Mic. 4:1b–2). It anticipates that "peoples" and "many nations" will flow to it like a river (see Mic. 1:2)—those who are the children of Abraham by faith (Gen. 17:5, 6, 16; 35:11; Rom. 4:11; see also Gen. 12:3; 27:29; 49:8, 10). This continues the development within the Twelve of the inclusion of the nations in God's kingdom as established by the Amos-Obadiah-Jonah sequence.

---

26. Redak: "The prophet mentions this because the nations were wont to worship the gods on the mountains and the lofty hills" (*Mikraoth Gedoloth: The Twelve Prophets*, vol. 2, trans. A. J. Rosenberg [New York: Judaica, 1996], 213–14).

Some early church fathers believed that this prophecy was fulfilled in the worldwide apostolic preaching of the gospel (Col. 1:23),[27] but that would be the opposite of the movement in the text. It is not the spread of a message from Jerusalem as in Acts 1:8. It is the coming of the nations to Jerusalem in the last days (Isa. 66:18; Dan. 7:14). Furthermore, the reader must resist the temptation to spiritualize this kingdom (*contra* Calvin). Regardless of the reader's ability or lack thereof to imagine the logistics of such a mass of people flowing to Zion, it is imperative to maintain the Bible's realism when it comes to the hope of a new and better Garden of Eden and that of a literal reign of Christ on earth.

The discourse of the nations is quoted in Micah 4:2a as expressing the desire to go up to the mountain of the LORD and to the house of the God of Jacob that the LORD might teach them his ways and that they might walk in his paths (cf., Exod. 19:12–13; Ezek. 11:19–20; Zech. 8:20–23; Rom. 8:4). That is, they want to receive the LORD's instruction in order to live a life of faith in his kingdom. This stands in stark contrast to the situation described in Micah 3:10–11 where the corrupt leadership in Zion, particularly the priesthood, disseminated teaching for their own personal gain. There will be no such mediation in the New Jerusalem. The fronting of "from Zion" in the Hebrew syntax of Mic. 4:2b makes it clear that the going forth of the Torah here is not the same as the giving of the Torah on Mount Sinai (Exod. 19–Lev. 27). The giving of the Torah at Sinai was ineffective because it was on tablets of stone but not on the hearts of the people (Deut. 29:3 [Eng., 29:4]; 2 Cor. 3:3). In the new covenant, the Torah will be written on the hearts of the people (Jer. 31:31–34). But Micah 4:2b does not merely speak of the LORD's instruction and word in a general sense or even his law and oral prophecy in a limited sense. The combination "Torah and the word of the LORD" shows an early, inner-biblical awareness of the canonical designation "Moses and the Prophets" (i.e., the Pentateuch and the books of the Prophets as an abbreviated reference to the Tanakh [cf., Luke 24:27, 44]; see also Isa. 1:10; 8:16; Zech. 7:12), the phrase "the word of the LORD" being a familiar introduction to prophetic speech in the literature.[28] Thus, the hope of Micah 4:2 is that of the Torah piety and devotion to Scripture

---

27. Alberto Ferreiro, *The Twelve Prophets*, ACCS XIV (Downers Grove, IL: InterVarsity, 2003), 160–61.
28. See Michael B. Shepherd, *Textuality and the Bible* (Eugene, Ore.: Wipf & Stock, 2016), 28–32. Lest the reader find this anachronistic, it is to be noted that this is the vantage point of those who gave the Bible its final shape in its entirety (Ezra 7:6, 10). See Karel van der Toorn, *Scribal*

known to the reader of texts like Psalms 1, 19, and 119, or Nehemiah
8–9.[29] Such devotion is considered the highest act of faith, obedience,
and worship now and in the last days.

The LORD himself will bring justice and peace to the nations,
turning weapons of warfare into agricultural tools, according to Micah
4:3 and in contrast to the kind of leadership seen in Micah 3:1–3, 9–11
(see commentary on Joel 4:10 [Eng., 3:10]; see also Hos. 2:20 [Eng.,
2:18]). Redak (Rabbi David Kimchi) commented that the judge here is
King Messiah.[30] This interpretation is not without reason. Justice and
peace are consistently the hallmarks of the Messiah and his kingdom
in the Prophets (e.g., Isa. 9:5–6 [Eng., 9:6–7]; 11:1–10; Jer. 23:5–6; see
also Ps. 72). Furthermore, Micah himself seems to make this connection
with the citation of 1 Kings 5:5 (Eng., 4:25; cf., 2 Kgs. 18:31) in Micah
4:4. The image of each dwelling under his grapevine and under his fig
tree without anyone causing trembling was originally used to describe
the peace and prosperity of the golden age of the kingship and kingdom
of Solomon whose wise judgment (1 Kgs. 3) had established justice and
righteousness in the land. Now the prophet envisions a new and better
Solomon (cf., Matt. 12:42) in a new and better kingdom that will last
forever (2 Sam. 7:12–16). The certitude of this is confirmed by Micah
4:4b. Zechariah will later pick up this citation and tie it to the messianic
"Branch" (Zech. 3:8, 10; cf., Isa. 4:2; 11:1; 53:2; Jer. 23:5–6; Zech. 6:12–13).

Micah 4:5a can hardly be a description of the way in which the
peoples are to go to Mount Zion in the last days. Their worship sounds
more like what is described in 2 Kings 17:29–41. The syntax of Micah
4:5b (*waw* + x + *yiqtol*) sets the prophet and the true people of God who
walk in the name of Yahweh in clear contrast to those in Micah 4:5a.
It appears then that Micah 4:5a describes the current state of affairs.
The peoples presently do not walk in the name of Yahweh, but the
true people of God will do so until the future hope of Micah 4:1–4 is
realized. To walk in the name of Yahweh is to live a life of faith in him
and to bear his name (see Gen. 5:24; 6:9; 17:1; Mic. 5:3 [Eng., 5:4]; 6:8;
Zech. 10:12; Prov. 18:10). This is Micah's interpretation of what Isaiah
means by walking in the "light" (אוֹר) of the LORD. Both prophets are
expounding what it means to "walk" or go to Zion to learn the "Torah"
(Aramaic: אוֹרָיה). The Torah provides the light of wisdom and salvation

---

Culture and the Making of the Hebrew Bible (Cambridge, MA: Harvard
University Press, 2009).

29. See Shepherd, *The Textual World of the Bible* (New York: Peter Lang,
2014), 97–107.
30. *Mikraoth Gedoloth: The Twelve Prophets*, vol. 2, 214.

that the Messiah will bring (Deut. 4:6; Isa. 9:1–6 [Eng., 9:2–7]; 42:6; 49:6; Mic. 7:8–9; Ps. 19:8–10 [Eng., 19:7–9]; 119:105; Prov. 6:23; John 1:4; 5:39, 46; 2 Tim. 3:15).

4:6 "In that day," the prophetic utterance of the LORD, "I will gather the limping [see GKC §122s], and the driven out will I gather, and those whom I treated badly [Tg. Jon. adds: because of the sins of my people].[31] *4:7 And I will make the limping into a remnant, and the removed far off [BDB, 229; cf., LXX, Syr. Tg. Jon.] into a mighty nation." And the LORD will be king over them in/on Mount Zion [Syr. adds: and in Jerusalem] from now and to forevermore.*

4:8 And as for you, Migdal-eder [Tower of Flock], fortified hill [BDB, 779] of Daughter Zion, to you the former dominion will come and enter, a kingdom [LXX adds: out of Babylon] for Daughter Jerusalem.[32]

4:9 Now [pc Mss, LXX: And now (cf., Mic. 4:11, 14 [Eng., 4:11; 5:1])], why do you shout a shout [LXX: know evil]? Is there no king over you? Has your counselor [LXX: counsel] perished so that writhing has gripped you like a woman in labor? 4:10 Writhe and burst forth [LXX: Writhe and be a man and draw near], Daughter Zion, like a woman in labor. For now you will go forth from a city and live in the country. And you will come to Babylon. There you will be rescued. There the LORD will buy you back from the palm of your enemies.

4:11 And now many nations are gathered against you, those who say, "Let it be profaned [LXX: We will rejoice] so that our eye [L, LXX: our eyes; 4 Mss, Syr., Tg. Jon., Vulg.: our eye] may look upon Zion." 4:12 But as for them, they do not know the thoughts of the LORD, and they do not discern his counsel, for he gathers them like the sheaf to the threshing floor. 4:13 "Arise and thresh, Daughter Zion, for it is your horn that I will make iron, and your hooves are what I will make bronze, and you

---

31. For stylistic variation, this verse uses two different verbs for "gather" somewhat synonymously: אסף and קבץ. The verb קבץ normally has people for its object, while אסף can have a broader range of objects. The verb כנס ("gather") is a synonym that occurs in later texts (*TLOT* 3: 1100–01).

32. *Tg. Jon.*: "And you, Messiah of Israel, who is hidden from before [or, because of] the sins of the assembly of Zion, to you the kingdom is about to come, and the former dominion will come to the kingdom of the assembly of Jerusalem."

*will crush many peoples." And you will devote [GKC §44h] to the LORD
their unjust gain, and their wealth to the Lord of all the earth.*

*4:14 (Eng., 5:1) Now gather in troops [or, cut yourself], daughter of a
troop [NET: daughter surrounded by soldiers; BDB: warlike city; LXX:
daughter Ephraim will be stopped up in a wall]. A siege [LXX: distress]
is what he has set against us. With the scepter they will strike upon the
cheek the judge [LXX: tribes] of Israel. 5:1 (Eng., 5:2) "And as for you,
Bethlehem Ephrathah, too little/insignificant to be among the tribes
[or, families] of Judah, from you for me he will go forth [Tg. Jon.: before me the Messiah will go forth] to be a ruler over Israel, and his origins [or, activities] are from long ago, from days of old." 5:2 (Eng., 5:3)
Therefore, he will give them until time when she who is in labor gives
birth. And as for the rest of his brothers, they will return to [or, in addition to] the sons of Israel. 5:3 (Eng., 5:4) And he will stand [LXX adds:
and see] and shepherd in the strength of the LORD, in the majesty of the
name of the LORD his God. And they will live [Syr., Vulg.: return; Tg.
Jon.: gather], for now [or, at that time] he will be great to land's ends.
5:4 (Eng., 5:5) And this one will be peace. As for Assyria, when he comes
into our land, and when he treads on our fortresses [LXX: ground], we
will establish against him seven shepherds and eight installed kings
of mankind. 5:5 (Eng., 5:6) And they will shepherd [or, break] the land
[> LXX] of Assyria by the sword, and the land of Nimrod in her gates
[BHS: with a drawn sword]. And he will rescue from Assyria when he
comes into our land and when he treads on our border.*

The phrase "In that day," at the beginning of Micah 4:6, refers the
reader back to the phrase, "at the end of the days," at the beginning
of Micah 4:1, putting what follows in an eschatological context. The
LORD says he will gather the limping and the driven-out (cf., Deut.
30:4; Jer. 31:8; Zeph. 3:19; Neh. 1:9). The use of feminine singular par-
ticiples in the Hebrew text suggests the feminine singular noun צאן
("flock"), in which case the imagery of Micah 4:6–7 is very similar to
that of Micah 2:12–13. The LORD will make those who limp into a remnant (Mic. 4:7a; cf., Mic. 2:12; 5:6 [Eng., 5:7]). Fretheim misreads this
to say that those who limp *are* the remnant.[33] That is, they are merely
the injured survivors of the judgment. According to Fretheim, they are
not the faithful remnant. But the text says that the LORD makes them
into a remnant, which Zephaniah 3:19 interprets to be the true people
of God. Furthermore, Micah 4:7a says that he will make the exiles into

---

33. Fretheim, *Reading Hosea–Micah*, 208.

a mighty nation (cf., Exod 32:10; Deut. 9:14; 26:5). The LORD will be their king on Mount Zion forever (Mic. 4:7b; cf., Exod. 15:18; Mic. 2:13; 4:1–5; Zeph. 3:14–15; Zech. 2:14 [Eng., 2:10]). According to Calvin, the LORD himself is in the place of David's posterity here (2 Sam. 7:12–16; Mic. 2:13; 4:8; 5:3 [Eng., 5:4]; Zech. 9:9–10).[34] The Davidic king is God in the flesh (Isa. 9:5–6 [Eng., 9:6–7]; 10:21; Zech. 12:10).

The first part of Micah 4:8 ("And as for you, Migdal-eder") is conspicuously similar to the beginning of the messianic prophecy in Micah 5:1 (Eng., 5:2) ("And as for you, Bethlehem Ephrathah"). The proximity of Migdal-eder to Bethlehem Ephrathah and Jerusalem is evident from Genesis 35:19, 21 (see also Luke 2:4, 8) and *m. Sheqal.* 7:4. The name "Migdal-eder" ("Tower of Flock") also continues the shepherd imagery from Micah 2:12–13; 4:6–7 (see also Mic. 5:3, 7 [Eng., 5:4, 8]; 7:14). The prophet calls Migdal-eder "the fortified hill of Daughter Zion." The terms "Daughter Zion" and "Daughter Jerusalem" are terms of affection for the inhabitants of the city (Mic. 1:13; 4:8, 10, 13; Zeph. 3:14; Zech. 2:14 [Eng., 2:10]; 9:9; BDB, 123). This once destroyed city (Mic. 3:12) will become the center for the whole world in the last days (Mic. 4:1; cf., Isa. 65:18). It is to Zion that the former dominion will come, a kingdom for Daughter Zion (Mic. 4:8; cf., Deut. 33:7).[35] Rashi says that the former dominion is the united kingdom under David and Solomon. The basic correctness of this view is confirmed by Mic. 4:4, which uses the imagery of Solomon's kingdom (1 Kgs. 5:5 [Eng., 4:25]) to describe what will be a new and better version in the messianic kingdom. Thus, several key exegetical factors have contributed to the messianic rendering of Micah 4:8 in *Targum Jonathan* (see above) wherein Migdal-eder is associated by metonymy with the Messiah himself. According to this rendering, the Messiah is currently hidden because of the sins of the assembly of Zion and needs to be revealed (see *Tg. Jon.* Zech. 4:7; 6:12).[36] It is to him that the kingdom will come (cf., Dan. 7:13–14, 27).

---

34. Calvin, *Micah*, 276–77.

35. The verb אתה only occurs in poetry in Hebrew (BDB, 87) and is the primary verb for "come" in Aramaic (BDB, 1083). It is possible that the presence of the usual Hebrew verb for "come" (בוא) is for explanatory purposes, but it is also possible that it creates a link to Deut. 33:7 understood in a messianic sense, which uses the *hiphil* of בוא: "Hear, O LORD, the voice of Judah, and to his people bring him" (cf., Gen. 49:10b).

36. Cathcart says that the term "hidden" is based on reading עפל ("fortified hill") as אפל ("dark") (Kevin J. Cathcart and Robert P. Gordon, *The Targum of the Minor Prophets: Translated, with a Critical Introduction, Apparatus, and Notes*, The Aramaic Bible 14 [Collegeville, MN: Liturgical, 1990], 120).

The next three subunits each begin with עתה ("Now") or ועתה ("And now"): Micah 4:9–10; Micah 4:11–13; and Micah 4:14–5:5 (Eng., 5:1–6).[37] There is some debate about whether such an introduction has a logical ("Therefore") or temporal ("Now") force in this context. It is possible to understand the questions at the beginning of Micah 4:9 as a logical inference from Micah 4:8, but taken on the whole it becomes apparent that each of the three subunits begins with a description of the current state of affairs and then moves to what God will do in the future, thus favoring a temporal interpretation.

The shout that the prophet questions in Micah 4:9a is likely a cry of distress from Daughter Jerusalem (cf., Isa. 15:4; but see BDB, 929).[38] It is as if there were no king or counselor (Mic. 4:9b; cf., Isa. 9:5 [Eng., 9:6]; Hos. 10:3; Mic. 4:14 [Eng., 5:1]). It is admittedly difficult to tell how the reader is supposed to understand the questions about the absence of the king. Does the prophet mean to suggest that the reason for the cry of distress is the actual or virtual absence of a king (see Calvin)? Does he mean to say that their cry for help from foreign kings implies that they have no king of their own (see Rashi)? Is he suggesting that they are acting as if God is not their king (see Ibn Ezra; cf., Mic. 2:13; 4:7)? According to Micah 4:14 (Eng., 5:1), they do have a king ("the judge of Israel" [see BDB, 1047]), but the king is in trouble, and the people are ultimately in need of the ideal ruler described in Micah 5:1–3 (Eng., 5:2–4). Thus, writhing has gripped Daughter Jerusalem like a woman in labor (cf., Isa. 26:17–18). The prophet encourages Daughter Zion to go ahead and writhe and burst forth like a woman in labor (Mic. 4:10a). That is, she must face the consequences of the broken covenant relationship by leaving the city of Jerusalem to go to the country and finally into exile in Babylon (Mic. 4:10b; see Deut. 28–29; 2 Kgs. 24–25).[39] It is from there that Daughter Zion will

---

37. Commentators often separate Micah 5:4–5 (Eng., 5:5–6) from Mic. 4:14–5:3 (Eng., 5:1–4), but the understanding here is that the antecedent of the masculine singular demonstrative pronoun in Micah 5:4a (Eng., 5:5a) and the subject of the third masculine singular verb ("And he will rescue") in Micah 5:5b (Eng., 5:6b) is the ruler described in Micah 5:1–3 (Eng., 5:2–4), making the two verses an integral part of the unit.

38. The verb ("shout") is second feminine singular.

39. The *BHS* apparatus questions whether the reference to Babylon here is a later addition to the text. This is because of the critical consensus that the eighth-century prophet Micah would have had no knowledge of what would transpire in the sixth century (e.g., J. Smith, *Micah*, 92). But Micah's contemporary, Isaiah, fully anticipated what would happen at the

be rescued. It is from there that the LORD will redeem her from her enemies (cf., Isa. 40–66).[40]

The sub-unit that begins with Micah 4:11 features a different view of the nations than the one in Micah 4:1–3 (cf., Mic. 5:6–8 [Eng., 5:7–9]). It describes the relationship of the people of God to the nations prior to the establishment of the messianic kingdom. In fact, the picture of many nations gathered against the city of Jerusalem and seeking to profane and to destroy it is not unlike the descriptions of a final battle with Gog and his horde of nations elsewhere (Ezek. 38–39; Joel 4:2 [Eng., 3:2]; Zech. 12; Rev. 20).[41] But the thoughts of the nations are not those of the LORD (Mic. 4:12; cf., Isa. 55:8–9; Jer. 29:11). They may be "gathered" (אסף) against his people (Mic. 4:11), but he will "gather" (קבץ) them like the sheaf to the threshing floor (Mic. 4:12). The privilege of threshing is then granted to Daughter Zion herself with an iron horn and bronze hooves (Mic. 4:13; cf., 1Q28b 5:26). She will crush many peoples (cf., Dan. 2:44–45) and "devote" their unjust gain to the LORD (see Lev. 27:28), and their wealth to "the Lord of all the earth" (cf., Ps. 97:5b).

The imperative at the beginning of the third subunit (Mic. 4:14 [Eng., 5:1]) can be either "gather in troops" or "cut yourself" (BDB, 151). The rendering "gather in troops" fits well with the addressee "daughter of a troop," which apparently describes the city of Jerusalem as surrounded by an army. But the context of the verse suggests that to gather in troops would be in vain in the present situation. Thus,

---

hands of the Babylonians (Isa. 39:6), and it appears that this is exactly what the prophecy in Jeremiah 26:18 and Micah 3:12 envisions.

40. "We must therefore not restrict his threats in ch. 3:12 and 4:10 even to the Chaldean catastrophe, nor the promise of Israel's deliverance in Babel out of the hands of its foes to the liberation of the Jews from Babylon, which was effected by Cyrus, and their return to Palestine under Zerubbabel and Ezra; but must also extend the threat of punishment to the destruction of Jerusalem by the Romans and the attendant dispersion of the Jews over all the world, and the redemption out of Babel promised in ch. 4:10 to that deliverance of Israel which, in the main, is in the future still. These two judgments and these two deliverances are comprehended in an undivided unity in the words of the prophet, Babel being regarded not only in its historical character, but also in its typical significance, as the beginning and the hearth of the kingdom of the world. Babel has this double significance in the Scriptures from the very commencement" (Keil, *Minor Prophets*, 318).

41. See Keil, *Minor Prophets*, 319–21. The expression "to look upon" (חזה ב) is the poetic equivalent of ראה ב (see BDB, 302).

"cut yourself" as a command to mourn might seem preferable, unless "daughter of a troop" describes Jerusalem as a city characterized by its own soldiers. In any case, the city is clearly under attack, and things are not going very well. The enemy humiliates the king by striking him on the cheek or jaw with his own royal scepter (cf., 2 Kgs. 24:6–7; Isa. 50:6). According to Ralph Smith, this ruler stands in contrast to the Messiah revealed in Micah 5:1–3 (Eng., 5:2–4; cf., Mic. 4:8–9).[42]

Both Jewish and Christian interpreters have long understood the prophecy in Micah 5:1–3 (Eng., 5:2–4) to be eschatological and messianic according to the context set by Micah 4:1, 6 (*Tg. Jon.*; Matt. 2:6; John 7:42; *b. Yoma* 10a; *b. Sanh.* 98b; Rashi).[43] Micah 5:1 (Eng., 5:2) is addressed from the LORD to Bethlehem Ephrathah (see GKC §90g), the home of David (see Gen. 35:19, 21; 1 Sam. 16:1; 17:12; Mic. 4:8; Ps. 132:6; Ruth 4:11), which is said to be too small or too insignificant to be among the families of Judah (cf., Deut. 7:7). The word אֶלֶף normally means "tribe," but a town or a city would not be considered to form a tribe regardless of its size or importance, unless it is a tribe in a representative sense. It seems rather that Bethlehem is too small to qualify as one of the larger tribal subdivisions of a certain size, roughly a thousand (see BDB, 49). That is, it is not the kind of place from which a ruler like David would be expected to come (2 Sam. 17:33, 42; Ps. 118:22). Of course, this is precisely the point. God humbles the proud and exalts the lowly (1 Sam. 2:1–10). Matthew's citation of this text understands "tribe" to be "ruler of a tribe" (see Exod. 18:21, 25), which fits with "ruler" later in the verse, and it renders the description of Bethlehem almost as if it were a question expecting the answer "no": "by no means least among the rulers of Judah" (Matt. 2:6). The Messiah will come from a seemingly insignificant place to be the greatest ruler of all. According to Matthew's text, this very fact makes Bethlehem significant.[44] Thus,

---

42. Ralph L. Smith, *Micah–Malachi*, WBC 32 (Nashville: Thomas Nelson, 1984), 43–44.

43. See Ferreiro, *The Twelve Prophets*, 163–68. The citation of Micah 5:1 (Eng., 5:2) in Matthew 2:6 comes in the context of Herod's inquiry about the birthplace of the Messiah (Matt. 2:4). The chief priests and scribes indicate that the birthplace of the Messiah will be Bethlehem of Judea (Matt. 2:5). It is not clear whether the citation of the Micah text in Matthew 2:6 is from the chief priests and scribes or from Matthew himself. Normally Matthew uses a formal "fulfillment" introduction (Matt. 1:22–23; 2:15, 17–18, 23; 4:14–16; but see Matt. 3:3).

44. The last part of Matthew's text, which says, "who will shepherd my people Israel," draws from 2 Samuel 5:2; Micah 5:3 (Eng., 5:4); and 1 Chronicles 11:2. "It is possible that Matthew's text is an ad hoc rendering, but it is

it is from Bethlehem of all places that one will go forth for the LORD himself to be a ruler not merely over Judah but over the whole of Israel just as David was (see 2 Sam. 5:1–3; 7:12–16; Isa. 40:10–11; Jer. 30:21; Mic. 2:13; Ps. 22:28–29 [Eng., 22:27–28]. This ruler will be "from long ago, from days of old." Rashi explains that this means the name of the Messiah is from before creation (see *Pirqe R. El.* ch. 3; *b. Ned.* 39b; *b. Pesah.* 54a; *b. Sanh.* 98b). Cyril of Jerusalem, Calvin, and Keil all interpret it to mean that the Messiah is eternal (cf., Hab. 1:12; Prov. 8:22). In context, it is possible that this is a reference to his lineage, which goes back to David and his former dominion (Amos 9:11; Mic. 4:8). It is also possible that these are the "days of old" mentioned in Micah 7:14, 20 (see Isho'dad of Merv). In other words, the Messiah is of old in the sense that he will lead a new version of the old exodus and fulfill the words spoken long ago to the patriarchs.

The inference drawn in Micah 5:2 (Eng., 5:3) is that the present time of judgment (NET: "the LORD will hand the people of Israel over to their enemies") is only temporary until the coming of the prophesied ruler. The use of the woman in labor to mark the time can be understood in at least two ways. One possibility is that it is an allusion to the prophecy in Isaiah 7:14b: "Look, the maiden is pregnant and about to give birth to a son, and she will call his name Immanuel" (see Matt. 1:23).[45] But it is equally plausible in context to say that giving birth is a metaphor for fulfillment (cf., Mic. 4:9–10). At that time, the remainder of the Davidic king's brothers (i.e., the exiled Judeans) will return to or in addition to the sons of Israel (i.e., the northern kingdom). This envisions a return to the united kingdom under David and Solomon (see Jer. 3:18; Ezek. 37:15–28; Hos. 3:5; Mic. 4:4, 8). The Davidic Messiah

---

also possible that Matthew preserves the text of an ancient Greek version. The evidence suggests that different Greek versions of the Hebrew Scriptures may have existed in Matthew's time, versions no longer extant. The *Letter of Aristeas* 30, 314 (c. 100 BC) shows awareness of earlier Greek translations in addition to the one for which the letter gives an account. Early, pre-Christian fragments of the Greek Bible include Papyrus Greek 458 of the John Rylands Library, Papyrus Fouad 266, and the Greek Minor Prophets Scroll from Naḥal Ḥever (also fragments from Qumran caves 4 and 7). Whether different Greek versions represent different Hebrew texts is another matter" (Michael B. Shepherd, *The Twelve Prophets in the New Testament* [New York: Peter Lang, 2011], 41–42). See Paul E. Kahle, *The Cairo Geniza*, 2d ed. (New York: Praeger, 1960), 209–264. Citations from the Bible in the New Testament, Josephus, and Philo often differ from extant witnesses.

45. See J. Smith, *Micah*, 104.

is the shepherd-king who will stand/remain and tend his flock (i.e., the people) in the strength of the LORD, that is, in the majesty of the name of the LORD his God (Mic. 5:3a; cf., Exod. 15:7; Isa. 9:5–6 [Eng., 9:6–7]; 40:11; 61:5; Ezek. 34:23; Mic. 2:13; 4:5; 7:14; Prov. 18:10; Php. 2:9–11). And the people will live in security (cf., Ezek. 34:25b) because at that time their Messiah will be great to the ends of the land of the covenant (Mic. 5:3b; cf., Gen. 2:11–14; 15:18; Zech. 9:9–10; Ps. 72:8).[46]

Some commentators separate Micah 5:4–5 (Eng., 5:5–6) from Micah 4:14–5:3 (Eng., 5:1–4).[47] According to this view, the masculine singular demonstrative pronoun ("this one") in Mic. 5:4a (Eng., 5:5a) does not refer to the messianic king in Micah 5:1–3 (Eng., 5:2–4) but to the general situation or period of peace. Also, according to this view, the subject of the third masculine singular verb ("And he will rescue") at the beginning of Mic. 5:5b (Eng., 5:6b) is either God or the shepherds mentioned in Mic. 5:4b (Eng., 5:5b). Some translations (e.g., NRSV) even translate the verb as if it were plural ("they will rescue"). But there are several problems with this exegetical work. To refer to a general situation or period of peace in Micah 5:4a (Eng., 5:5a) the reader would expect to see the feminine singular demonstrative זאת rather than the masculine singular זה (see BDB, 260; see also GKC §135p). The masculine singular demonstrative refers back to the messianic ruler revealed in Micah 5:1–3 (Eng., 5:2–4) as the one who will bring peace. This is consistent with other prophetic descriptions of the Messiah and his kingdom (e.g., Isa. 9:5–6 [Eng., 9:6–7]; 11:6–8; Mic. 4:3; Nah. 2:1 [Eng., 1:15]; Zech. 6:13b; 9:9–10; Ps. 72:3, 7; Eph. 2:14). The subject of the third masculine singular verb in Mic. 5:5b (Eng., 5:6b) is most likely not God or the LORD because God has not been the subject of a main verb in the present context since at least Mic. 5:2a (Eng., 5:3a), and even there he is not the explicit subject. There is no clear indication that God is the new subject in Micah 5:5b (Eng., 5:6b). The subject is also not likely to be the shepherds (plural) from Mic. 5:4b (Eng., 5:5b) because Mic. 5:5a (Eng., 5:6a) uses a plural verb for them. Rather, the subject is the ideal individual shepherd of Micah 5:3 (Eng., 5:4; cf., Jer. 23:4–5; see also Redak).

Assyria, the world power in Micah's day, is typologically the Gentile domain to be conquered and possessed in the messianic kingdom according to Micah 5:4–5 (Eng., 5:5–6; see Gen. 10:8–12; cf., Isa. 19:24–25). Foreign enemies will be defeated, but the nations will also be included

---

46. The Syriac and the Latin Vulgate read the verb וישבו as if it were from the root שוב ("return") rather than the root ישב ("live"). This may be due to the presence of the verb "return" in Micah 5:2 (Eng., 5:1).
47. E.g., R. Smith, *Micah–Malachi*, 45.

in the kingdom (Mic. 4:1–3). This is much like the role of Edom in Amos 9:12 and Obadiah, a representative of those who believe and of those who do not believe from among the nations. It is also the role of the Assyrian capital Nineveh to represent believing (the book of Jonah) and unbelieving (the book of Nahum) Gentiles. The prophet, speaking on behalf of the people of God, says that "we" will establish against "Assyria" seven shepherds and eight installed kings of mankind (Mic. 5:4b [Eng., 5:5b]). This is similar to the numerical device employed in Amos 1:3–2:6 and Proverbs 30 (see GKC §134s). The number seven stands for completeness and/or perfection (BDB, 988). Since there is no such thing as a synonym for a number, the writer simply uses the next number above seven for the parallelism. The phrase "installed kings of mankind" (אָדָם נְסִיכֵי) is difficult for two reasons. First, נָסִיךְ is normally used of foreign rulers elsewhere (see Josh. 13:21; Ezek. 32:20; Ps. 83:12 [Eng., 83:11]). The object of the verbal form of the same root in Psalm 2:6, however, is the messianic king (see BDB, 651; see also Prov. 8:23). Second, what does it mean to say the installed kings are "of mankind"? One very good possibility is that this is a way to say "royal men" (GKC §128l). Another option is that it is a clarification of what is meant by "shepherds." That is, they are not leaders of flocks but leaders of men. Yet another possibility is that the qualifier "of mankind" here indicates that the kings are not merely rulers of one nation (Israel). They are the rulers of all humanity.[48]

What then is to be made of the shift from plural verb ("And they will shepherd the land of Assyria by the sword") to singular verb ("And he will rescue from Assyria") in Micah 5:5 (Eng., 5:6)? One way to understand this is to say that there will be a plurality of shepherd-kings and one messianic shepherd. This seems to be the idea expressed in texts like Jeremiah 3:15 and Jeremiah 23:4–5 (see also Isa. 32:1). That is, Christ will rule, and the saints will reign with him (Dan. 7:13–14, 27; Rev. 5:10; 20:6; 22:5). It is also possible to say that the number seven in Mic. 5:4b (Eng., 5:5b) is not intended to indicate a plurality of shepherds. Rather, it signifies the perfection of the Messiah's reign.

5:6 (Eng., 5:7) And the remnant of Jacob will be [LXX adds: among the nations] in the midst of many peoples like dew from the LORD, like copious showers [LXX: lambs] upon herbage, which does not wait for a

---

48. The Babylonian Talmud actually names seven shepherds and eight kings: "Who are the seven shepherds? David in the middle, Adam, Seth, and Methuselah on his right, Abraham, Jacob, and Moses, on his left. And who are the eight kings among men? Jesse, Saul, Samuel, Amos, Zephaniah, Zedekiah, the Messiah, and Elijah" (b. Sukk. 52b).

man and does not hope for humanity [LXX: so that no one be gathered
or stand among sons of men]. 5:7 (Eng., 5:8) And the remnant of Jacob
will be among the nations, in the midst of many peoples like a lion
among forest animals, like a young lion among flocks of sheep, which,
if he crosses over and tramples and tears prey, there is no one rescuing.
5:8 (Eng., 5:9) May your hand be exalted [mlt Mss, Vrs: Your hand will
be exalted] against your foes; and as for all your enemies, may they be
cut off [or, they will be cut off].

5:9 (Eng., 5:10) "And it will be in that day," the prophetic utterance of
the LORD, "I will cut off your horses from your midst and destroy your
chariots. 5:10 (Eng., 5:11) And I will cut off the cities of your land and
throw down all your fortifications. 5:11 (Eng., 5:12) And I will cut off
sorcerers from your hand; and as for soothsayers, they will not belong
to you. 5:12 (Eng., 5:13) And I will cut off your carved/sculpted images and your standing objects [Syr.: altars; RSV: pillars] from your
midst, and you will never again bow down to the work of your hands.
5:13 (Eng., 5:14) And I will pluck up your Asherah poles [LXX: woods,
sacred groves] from your midst and destroy your cities [Tg. Jon.: foes].
5:14 (Eng., 5:15) And I will perform in anger and in wrath vengeance
with the nations who [LXX: because they] did not listen [Tg. Jon.: did
not receive the instruction of the Torah]."

Following Micah 5:4–5 (Eng., 5:5–6), where Assyria represents the enemies of the people of God, the text of Micah 5:6–8 (Eng., 5:7–9) returns
to the scene of Micah 4:11–13 where the nations are not yet part of
God's people as in Micah 4:1–3. They are gathered against God's people
and must be defeated by them (cf., Ezek. 38–39; Joel 4:2 [Eng., 3:2];
Obad. 15–21; Redak: Gog). The remnant of Jacob is said to be "in the
midst of many peoples like dew from the LORD, like copious showers
upon herbage" (Mic. 5:6a; see Deut. 32:2; Mic. 2:12; 4:7). This could be
a messianic image (see Ezek. 34:26; Hos. 6:3–4; Ps. 72:6), but the context seems to favor a comparison between the multitudes of God's army
and the many drops of morning dew or those of a heavy rain shower
(see 2 Sam. 17:12). Such widespread moisture does not depend upon
mankind but upon God himself (Mic. 5:6b [Eng., 5:7b]; cf., Isa. 25:9).
The remnant among the nations will be "like a lion among forest animals, like a young lion among flocks of sheep" (Mic. 5:7a [Eng., 5:8a];
cf., Gen. 49:8–12; Num. 23:24; 24:9; Ezek. 19:1–9). There will be no one
to rescue the nations from the remnant (Mic. 5:7b [Eng., 5:8b]). Thus,
the prophet prays for the remnant, "May your hand be exalted against

your foes; and as for all your enemies, may they be cut off" (Mic. 5:8 [Eng., 5:9]; cf., Exod. 14:8b; Num. 33:3b).

The phrase "in that day" in Micah 5:9 (Eng., 5:10) serves to maintain the eschatological context set by Micah 4:1, 6. The LORD is speaking in Micah 5:9–14 (Eng., 5:10–15), but commentators are divided on who is being addressed. Fretheim suggests that the unit is addressed to the nations and to the unfaithful of Israel.[49] In favor of this is the end of Micah 5:8 (Eng., 5:9), which expresses the hope that all the remnant's enemies would be "cut off." This verb ("cut off") is repeated at the beginning of Micah 5:9a2, 10a, 11a, 12a (Eng., 5:10a2, 11a, 12a, 13a).[50] The problem with this interpretation is that the three second masculine singular pronominal suffixes in Micah 5:8 (Eng., 5:9) all refer to the remnant. Thus, when the reader comes to the twelve second masculine singular pronominal suffixes in Micah 5:9–13 (Eng., 5:10–14), it is only natural to assume that they too refer to the remnant. Furthermore, Micah 5:14 (Eng., 5:15) refers to the nations in the third person. This is why commentators like Rashi, Redak, Calvin, and Keil all say that the remnant is addressed in this section.[51] But the passage is not primarily about the removal of things like horses and chariots in which the people might be tempted to trust (Mic. 5:9 [Eng., 5:10]; cf., Ps. 20:8 [Eng., 20:7]). It is about the eradication of things needed for warfare such as horses, chariots, and fortified cities (Mic. 5:9–10 [Eng., 5:10–11]; cf., Ezek. 36:35) in the peacetime of the messianic age (Mic. 4:3; 5:4a [Eng., 5:5a]; Zech. 9:10). It is also about the removal of foreign religious influence (Mic. 5:11–13; see Deut. 13; 18:9–13; 31:29; Judg. 2:11–13; Jer. 25:6; Hos. 3:4; Mic. 1:7). Finally, the LORD says that he will exact vengeance on the nations "who did not listen" (Mic. 5:14 [Eng., 5:15]; cf., Mic. 4:11–13; 5:6–8 [Eng., 5:7–9]). This implies that there will be nations who did listen and who will be included in the kingdom of God (Mic. 4:1–3; cf., Amos 9:12).

MICAH 6

6:1 Hear what the LORD says [LXX: Hear the word of the Lord. The Lord says]: "Arise, contend with the mountains, and let the hills hear your voice." 6:2 Hear, O mountains, the contention of the LORD, and O perennial ones, earth's foundations. For the LORD has a point of

---

49. Fretheim, *Reading Hosea–Micah*, 213.
50. This technique is known as anaphora (Bullinger, *Figures of Speech*, 201).
51. *Mikraoth Gedoloth: The Twelve Prophets*, vol. 2, 223; Calvin, *Micah*, 318–26; Keil, *Minor Prophets*, 331.

contention with his people, and it is with Israel that he will argue his case. 6:3 "My people, what have I done to you [LXX adds: or how have I grieved you; Tg. Jon.: My people, what good did I say I would do for you that I did not do] and how have I wearied you? Answer me [or, Testify against me]. 6:4 When I brought you up out of the land of Egypt and from a house of servitude I redeemed [or, purchased] you, I sent before you Moses, Aaron, and Miriam [Tg. Jon.: I sent before you my three prophets: Moses to teach tradition and judgments, Aaron to atone for the people, and Miriam to teach the women]. 6:5 My people, remember what Balak the king of Moab planned and how Balaam the son of Beor answered him. [Remember] from Shittim [LXX: the reeds] to Gilgal [Tg. Jon.: Were mighty deeds not done for you from the valley of Shittim to the house of Gilgal] in order to know the righteous acts of the LORD."

6:6 "With what should I come before the LORD? How should I bow to the high God [Tg. Jon.: the God whose dwelling is in the high places]? Should I come before him with burnt offerings, with year-old calves? 6:7 Will the LORD be pleased with [or, accept] thousands of rams, with myriads of streams of olive oil? Should I give my firstborn for my transgression, the fruit of my womb for the sin of my soul?" 6:8 He has told you [LXX: Has it been told to you], O man, what is good [or, acceptable]. And what does the LORD seek from you but to do justice and to choose covenant loyalty and without presumption to live a life of faith with your God [LXX: to be ready to walk with the Lord your God; Tg. Jon.: to be set aside to walk in the fear of your God]?

Micah 6:1 begins the third and final major division of the book (see Mic. 1:2; 3:1). In contrast to Micah 1:2 and 3:1, which are addressed to the peoples and to the leaders respectively, the opening address in Mic. 6:1a is not directed to anyone in particular. This is further complicated by the fact that the initial imperative ("Hear") in the prophet's address is plural, but the following imperatives at the beginning of the LORD's discourse in Micah 6:1b ("Arise, contend") are singular. Verse 2 clarifies that the prophet is addressing the mountains (plural) as the perennial witnesses to the LORD's history with his people (cf., Deut. 4:26; 30:19; 31:28; 32:1; Isa. 1:2, 18; Hos. 4:1; 12:3 [Eng., 12:2]). On the other hand, the LORD is addressing his people (singular) and asking them rhetorically what charge they would bring against him that would explain their covenant infidelity (Mic. 6:3; cf., Isa. 7:13; Jer. 2:5).

The LORD then makes the case for his faithfulness from the biblical narrative itself (Mic. 6:4–5; cf., Deut. 6:20–25; 26:5–9; 32; Josh. 24:1–15; Judg. 2:1–5; 6:7–10; 10:11–15; 1 Sam. 12:6–17; Isa. 63:7–14; Jer. 2:1–13;

Ezek. 20; Hos. 12; Amos 2:9–12; Hab. 3:3–15; Pss. 78; 105; 106; 135; 136; Neh. 9; Acts 7; 13; 13–41; Heb. 11).[52] He refers to the time of the exodus when he sent Moses, Aaron, and Miriam before the people (Mic. 6:4; cf., Exod. 1–17; Num. 12; Jer. 2:6; Hos. 2:16–17 [Eng., 2:14–15]; Mic. 7:15).[53] That is, the LORD not only delivered them but also provided prophetic and priestly leadership for them. He also calls on the people to remember the story of Balak the king of Moab and Balaam the son of Beor (Mic. 6:5a; see Num. 22–24; Josh. 24:9–10).[54] Balak, feeling threatened by the people of Israel passing along the east side of the Jordan, summoned Balaam to curse them (Num. 22), but the LORD only allowed Balaam to speak words of blessing (Gen. 12:3; Num. 23:7–10) and prophecies of eschatological and messianic salvation (Num. 24:7–9, 14, 17). From Shittim, which was the last place where Israel camped before crossing the Jordan and thus signified everything up to that point (Num. 25:1; Josh. 3:1), to Gilgal, which was the first place where Israel camped after crossing the Jordan and thus signified everything after that point (Josh. 4:19), the LORD was faithful, demonstrating his righteous acts of loyalty to the terms of the covenant by bringing his people out of Egypt and into the land of the covenant (Mic. 6:5b; cf., 1 Sam. 12:7).

What then is the appropriate response to the biblical history of the LORD's faithfulness? This is the question posed by the hypothetical worshiper in Micah 6:6a. It is certainly not correct to respond with the idolatry, social injustice, and corruption condemned by Micah 1–3. The hypothetical worshiper assumes that he should come before the LORD with burnt offerings and streams of olive oil (Mic. 6:6b–7a; see Exod. 12:5; Lev. 1–2; 9:3). But the reader of the Tanakh knows that this cannot possibly be the right answer (see 1 Sam. 15:22; Isa. 1:10–17; 40:16; Jer. 7:21–23; Hos. 6:6; Amos 5:21–24; Mal. 1:10; Pss. 40:7; 51:18–21 [Eng., 40:6; 51:16–19]; Prov. 21:3).[55] The worshiper then asks if he should give his firstborn for his transgression (Mic. 6:7b). The parallel to this ("the fruit of my womb for the sin of my soul") indicates that he is not talking about firstborn animals. It is a question about child sacrifice. The Pentateuch (Lev. 18:21; Deut. 12:31; 18:10; cf., Gen. 22), the books of Kings and Chronicles (2 Kgs. 16:3; 17:17, 31; 21:6 [2 Chr. 33:6]; 23:10), and the book of Ezekiel (Ezek. 16:21; 20:26, 31;

---

52. See Shepherd, *Textual World*.
53. Note how the people in Micah's day are addressed as if they were the ones whom the LORD brought out of Egypt (cf., Josh. 24:6–8; Hos. 12:5b [Eng., 12:4b]; Rom. 4:23–24; 15:4; 1 Cor. 9:10; 10:11; 1 Pet. 1:12).
54. See how Israel forgot in Psalm 78:11; 106:21; and Nehemiah 9:17.
55. See Shepherd, *Text in the Middle*, 120–22.

23:37) all forbid and/or condemn the practice. So why does the worshiper even raise the question? The references to child sacrifice in the book of Jeremiah all include a clause ("which I did not command") that suggests the Israelites thought their practice was in obedience to the law (Jer. 7:31; 19:5; 32:35). The LORD's insistence that he did not command child sacrifice seems to presuppose a claim or assumption on the part of the people that he did.

> It is possible that the current placement of the law in Exodus 13:2 provides a clue to the ancient misunderstanding. As it stands, the law in Exodus 13:2 instructs the people to set apart the firstborn of humans and animals to YHWH without qualification (cf., Neh. 10:37). It is only much later in the chapter and in the Pentateuch that the reader learns of the redemption of the firstborn (Exod. 13:13; Num. 18:15–16). It is also later in the Pentateuch that the reader learns how the tribe of Levi will take the place of the firstborn (Num. 3:12–13, 41; 8:16–17). It seems likely then that the people understood the law in Exodus 13:2 in isolation and apart from its present context and thus found warrant for the practice of child sacrifice.[56]

The prophet responds to this line of questioning, "He has told you, O man, what is good/acceptable" (Mic. 6:8a; cf., Rom. 12:1). Where has the LORD told what is good or acceptable? Micah's text (Mic. 6:8b) is based on a passage that begins in Deuteronomy 10:12: "And now, O Israel, what does the LORD your God ask from you but to fear the LORD your God, to walk in all his ways and to love/choose him and to serve/worship the LORD your God with all your heart and with all your soul." This intertextual link is a tremendous help in understanding what Micah means by doing justice, loving/choosing covenant loyalty, and living without presumption a life of faith with God (see Zech. 7:9; 1QS 5; *b. Sukk.* 49b). To begin, doing "justice" (משפט) involves things like not showing favoritism, not taking a bribe, giving justice to orphans and widows, and loving resident aliens by giving them food and clothing (Deut. 10:17–19; cf., Mic. 3:9–11). To love or choose "covenant loyalty" (חסד) is often mistranslated as to love (as in "to have strong feelings for") "mercy." But "love" (אהב) here is not so much an emotion as it is an act of devotion or commitment.[57] Furthermore, there is a long tradition of translating חסד as "mercy" and the like, but this goes back to the use of *eleos* ("mercy") to translate the word in the LXX and the NT where it does not mean "mercy" but is a mere symbol for חסד

---

56. Ibid., 59.
57. See Shepherd, *Textuality and the Bible*, 94–102.

and its meaning, which is often parallel to terms like אֱמוּנָה ("faithfulness"; see *HALOT* 1:336–37; see also comment on Hosea 6:6). In the Deuteronomy passage, to choose covenant loyalty is an act of faithfulness to the covenant relationship wherein the believer fears and worships the LORD with all of the heart/mind and soul/life (i.e., all of one's being) by obeying him, given the fact that he is the God of creation who has elected a people for himself and demonstrated his faithfulness to them in the exodus (Deut. 10:12–15, 20–21; cf., Deut. 6:4–9). This is ultimately something that happens only in the new covenant relationship characterized not merely by the physical circumcision of the flesh (Gen. 17) but by the spiritual circumcision of the heart (Deut. 10:16; see Deut. 28:69; 29:3 [Eng., 29:1, 4]; 30:6; Jer. 4:4; 31–34; Ezek. 11:19–20; Rom. 2:28–29). The third and final requirement is to "walk" or live a life of faith with God (Deut. 10:12: "walk in all his ways"; cf., Gen. 5:24; 6:8; 17:1) in a manner that is void of presumption (see Prov. 11:2). These are the weightier matters of the Torah (Matt. 23:23).

6:9 The voice of the LORD [Tg. Jon.: The voice of the prophets of the LORD], to the city it calls. (And it is wisdom to fear [יִרְאָה] your name [LXX: And he will deliver those who fear his name].) "Hear, O tribe, and who appointed it [LXX: and who will adorn a city]? 6:10 Again [BDB, 209–10], is there [see Tg. Jon., GKC §47b¹; cf., LXX, Syr., Vulg.: fire] in the house of the wicked treasures of wickedness and a denounced ephah of leanness [Tg. Jon.: deceptive measures bringing a curse]? 6:11 Am I pure [Vulg.: Will I justify] with scales of wickedness and with a bag of stones of deceit? 6:12 which [or, because; LXX: from which; Vulg.: in which; Luther: through which?], her rich people, they are full of violence; and her inhabitants, they speak deception, and their tongue is deceit [LXX: exalted] in their mouth. 6:13 And also I, I make sick / sore your striking [or, make you sick / sore by striking you; LXX: begin to strike you], destroying because of your sin. 6:14 As for you, you will eat and not be satisfied, and your emptiness / hunger [see BDB; cf., HALOT: filth] will be in your inner parts [LXX: and it will become dark in you; see BHS apparatus]. And you will remove [BDB, 691; LXX: he / it will leave; NET overtake], but you will not carry off [LXX: be delivered]. And whatever you take / secure, to the sword will I give it [see BDB, 812]. 6:15 As for you, you will sow but not reap; as for you, you will tread / press olives but not anoint yourself with olive oil, and fresh juice will you squeeze but not drink wine. 6:16 And each one keeps for himself [Syr., Vulg.: you kept] the statutes [i.e., customs / practices (BDB, 350)] of Omri [LXX: Zimri] and all the work of the house of Ahab. And you [pl.] went in their counsels in order that [or, so that] I might give each one of you [sg.] to destruction [or, make you into an object of horror] and her inhabitants into an object of whistling / hissing. And the reproach of my people is what you [pl.] will bear."

Because of the many difficulties in the Hebrew text of this section, critical scholars will usually rearrange it (see, e.g., the *BHS* apparatus). Some of the suggestions make good sense. For instance, the placement of Micah 6:12 directly after Micah 6:9 provides an antecedent for the relative pronoun at the beginning of Micah 6:12. Also, the first part of Micah 6:14 seems to go with Micah 6:15. The problem, however, is that there is no textual evidence (i.e., no extant textual witnesses) for these adjustments. Therefore, the reader must be content to work out an understanding of the text as it is.

The prophet introduces the discourse as the voice of the LORD calling to the city, which is presumably the city of Jerusalem (Mic. 6:9a). This is followed by a parenthetical comment directed to the LORD himself: "And it is wisdom to fear your name."[58] This is a familiar concept from the wisdom literature (e.g., Job 28:28; Prov. 9:10).[59] Rashi suggests that it is the wisdom of the Torah from Micah 6:8 (see Deut. 4:6; 10:12). The point of adding this comment seems to be to suggest that it would be wise to heed the voice of the LORD in the present context.

The LORD's discourse begins in Micah 6:9b with a call to the "tribe" (מטה; cf., שבט) of Judah to hear (cf., Mic. 1:2; 3:1, 9; 6:1). This is followed by a rhetorical question: "and who appointed it?" The feminine singular pronominal suffix "it" refers to the feminine singular noun "city" (i.e., the city of Jerusalem), and the assumed answer to the question is that LORD appointed it (2 Sam. 5:9–10). That is, the city belongs to him. Therefore, its leaders must pay attention to his voice (cf., Mic. 3:1, 9–11). The specific accusation against them is that they are the wicked who have amassed treasures by means of dishonesty, charging high prices for lean measures (Mic. 6:10). The question in Micah 6:11 ("Am I pure?") seems strange coming from the LORD or even from the prophet. Keil suggests that it is the voice of the conscience.[60] It is perhaps prefer-

---

58. The MT has the verb "he sees" ("And wisdom he sees your name" or "And wisdom your name sees"), but a slight revocalization of the Hebrew text yields "to fear" (see translation above; cf., LXX).

59. The Hebrew word for "wisdom" here, תושיה, seems to run somewhat parallel to the more common חכמה ("wisdom") in the wisdom literature (e.g., Prov. 3:21), sometimes indicating its effect (e.g., Prov. 2:7). See *HALOT* 2:1713–15.

60. Keil, *Minor Prophets*, 337.

able to follow the lead of the Latin Vulgate and revocalize the verb so that it is in the *piel* stem: "Will I justify (or, make/declare pure)?" The answer, of course, is no. The use of uneven scales and disproportionate bags of stones to deceive buyers is consistently prohibited elsewhere (Deut. 25:13; Ezek. 45:10; Hos. 12:8 [Eng., 12:7]; Amos 8:5; Prov. 11:1; 20:10, 23). The occurrence of אֲשֶׁר ("which") at the beginning of Micah 6:12 is problematic not because it is an impossible reading but because there are too many legitimate possibilities from which to choose (see translation above; see also versions and commentaries). Nevertheless, the verse is a continuation of Micah 6:11. The city's wealthy are full of violence in that they have gained their riches by deceit and at the expense of the livelihood of others (cf., Ps. 5:10 [Eng., 5:9]).

Thus, the announcement of judgment is that the LORD will strike them (Mic. 6:13). He will destroy them because of their sin. The idea that they each would eat and not be satisfied (Mic. 6:14a) recalls the covenant curses of Deuteronomy 28:30–44 (cf., Amos 5:11; Zeph. 1:13; 1Q14). Whatever or whomever they attempt to take with them (into exile?), they will not successfully carry them off (Mic. 6:14b; cf., Isa. 5:29). They will be lost to the sword. Along the same line of thought as Micah 6:14a, they each will sow but not reap (Mic. 6:15a). They will do the hard work of treading or pressing the olives, but they will not enjoy anointing themselves with the olive oil they produce (Mic. 6:15b; see Ps. 133). They will do the hard work of squeezing the fresh juice from the grapes, but they will not enjoy the wine made from that juice.

Micah 6:16 compares the leaders of Judah and Jerusalem in Micah's day to those of Samaria and the northern kingdom of Israel in the days of the Omride dynasty, of which the most notorious member was Ahab (1 Kgs. 16:23–2 Kgs. 10; see 2 Kgs. 8:18, 27; 21:3). This, of course, recalls the comparison to Samaria in Micah 1:5–7 and the fact that Micah is the namesake of Micaiah (see comment for Micah 1:2) who prophesied during the reign of Ahab (1 Kgs. 22). The verb at the beginning of Micah 6:16 in the MT is masculine singular, which means that the feminine plural "statutes" is not the subject (contra ASV). Some English versions (e.g., ESV, NET) prefer to follow the Syriac and the Latin Vulgate by translating the verb as second person. The above translation of Micah 6:16 is an attempt to distinguish the use of a third masculine singular verb, second masculine plural verbs, and a second masculine singular pronominal suffix in the verse—all presumably with the same referent. The customs and practices of Omri and Ahab referenced here include Baal worship (1 Kgs. 16:30–33; cf., Mic. 1:5–7), corruption, and social injustice (e.g., 1 Kgs. 21; cf., Mic. 3). The adoption of such behavior would result in the destruction of Judah and Jerusalem (Jer. 3; Ezek. 16; 23;

Mic. 3:12), making them the object of horror and hissing (cf., Jer. 25:9). The conclusion to Micah 6:16—"And the reproach of my people is what you (pl.) will bear"—appears on the surface to make a distinction between two groups: "my people" and "you" (pl.). But the most probable interpretation is that this is a way of saying, "You, my people, will bear the responsibility that comes with being my people" (cf., Amos 3:2).

MICAH 7

7:1 [Tg. Jon.: The prophet said] Woe to me! For I am like gatherings of summer fruit [LXX: like one gathering straw in harvest; cf., NIV, NET], like gleanings of vintage. There is no cluster to eat, no first ripe fig that my soul desires [GKC §152z; BDB, 660]. 7:2 A loyal person perishes from the land, and an upright person among mankind does not exist [GKC §152k]. As for all of them, it is for bloodshed [Tg. Jon.: innocent blood] that they lie in ambush. Each his brother they hunt with a perforated net [BDB, 357]. 7:3 Concerning the evil, palms to do well [LXX: their hands prepare]. The official asks, and the judge, for a bribe [BDB, 1024; LXX: the judge speaks peaceful words], and the noble speaks the evil desire of his soul [GKC §135f], and they weave it. 7:4 The best of them [GKC §133g] is like a brier, their most upright is a hedge of thorns [see BHS apparatus]. The day of your watchmen, your visitation, it has come. Now their confusion will be.[61] *7:5 Do not put your faith in a friend / neighbor, and [see MurXII, mlt Mss] do not trust in an intimate friend [LXX: leaders]. From the woman who lies in your bosom [Syr., Tg. Jon.: wife] keep the openings of your mouth. 7:6 For [Tg. Jon.: Look, at that time] a son treats a father like a fool [LXX: dishonors a father], a daughter rises up against her mother, a daughter-in-law against her mother-in-law. A man's enemies are the people of his house [NET: servants (Gen. 14:14)]. 7:7 But as for me, it is for the LORD that I will watch [Tg. Jon.: rejoice loudly], and I will wait [Tg. Jon.: dance] for the God of my salvation [Syr., Vulg.: savior]. My God will hear me.*

This unit takes the form of a lament (cf., Ps. 13; Job 10:15): introductory cry (Mic. 7:1), lament (Mic. 7:2–6), and trust (Mic. 7:7). According to the MT of Micah 7:1a, the prophet says that he is like gatherings of summer fruit. The NIV, following the LXX, says that he is "like one

---

61. LXX: "And I will take away their good things like a moth devouring and walking on a rail [or, going by a rule] in a day of watchtower. Woe, woe, the acts of vengeance against you have come. Now their weeping [or, lamentations] will be."

275

who gathers summer fruit," but this does not fit very well with the parallel "like gleanings of vintage." The NET suggests that the prophet does not really mean what he says, positing an ellipsis of some sort so that the gatherings and gleanings are merely temporal indicators. But Redak, Calvin, and Keil have all understood that the prophet, by comparing himself to scarce clusters of grapes and desirable first ripe figs, is illustrating the fact that the righteous are lacking from the land.[62] This reading is confirmed by Micah 7:2a: "A loyal person perishes from the land, and an upright person among mankind does not exist" (cf., Isa. 57:1). The righteous are the victims of all those who lie in wait for bloodshed, each man hunting his brother with a net as if he were an animal (cf., Prov. 1:11).

When it comes to evil, the leaders of the people have the hands to do it well, and it is in their power to do it (Mic. 7:3; cf., Mic. 2:1). Both the official and the judge request a reward (i.e., a bribe) for their services (cf., Mic. 3:11). That is, they are more concerned with money than with justice (Mic. 3:1, 9). The nobles speak out loud the evil desires of their thoughts, and they weave them. In other words, they brazenly do what is necessary to put their plans together and bring them to fruition (cf., Mic. 2:1–2). According to Micah 7:4a, even the best of them is like a brier, their most upright a hedge of thorns (cf., Mic. 7:2a; Prov. 15:19). The prophet then adds, "The day of your watchmen, your visitation, it has come. Now their confusion will be." It is not immediately clear to whom the second masculine singular pronominal suffixes ("your") refer, but it seems most likely given the use of the phrase "your visitation" that they refer to the leaders either individually or collectively. "Their confusion" apparently refers to the confusion of the evil plans of the leaders (cf., Isa. 22:5). But what is "the day of your watchmen" or "your visitation"? The watchmen could be the prophets like Micah who have warned of the coming day (see Ezek. 3:17; 33:7; Hos. 9:8), or they could be the false prophets who will also be subject to judgment in that day (see Isa. 56:10; Jer. 6:17; Mic. 3:5–7). The watchmen could also be those who literally watch on the city wall for the day of attack (see Isa. 21:6; 62:6–7; Hab. 2:1; Pss. 127:1; 130:6). The day of visitation is most likely the day of judgment (see Isa. 10:3; Jer. 6:15; 8:12; 23:12; Hos. 9:7). The only question is whether this is a historical day (e.g., Mic. 4:10) or an eschatological day (Mic. 4:1, 6; 1Q14). It appears from early readings of Micah 7:5–6 that it was understood eschatologically (e.g., *Tg. Jon.* Mic. 7:6a; Matt. 34–39).

---

62. *Mikraoth Gedoloth: The Twelve Prophets*, vol. 2, 230; Calvin, *Micah*, 361; Keil, *Minor Prophets*, 340.

Micah 7:5–7 encourages readers not to put their faith in friends or family members, even the closest ones, but to trust in the LORD in the last days, following the example of Micah himself (cf., Deut. 13:7–12; Jer. 9:3–4 [Eng., 9:4–5]; 12:6; Zech. 8:10; 2 Tim. 3:2). Only with the coming of the prophet like Elijah will the hearts of the fathers return in addition to the sons and the hearts of the sons in addition to the fathers (Mal. 3:23–24 [Eng., 4:5–6]; Luke 1:17). The rabbinic literature understands Micah 7:6 to be a description of relationships in the days of the Messiah (*b. Sanh.* 97a; *m. Soṭah* 9:15; *b. Soṭah* 49b; *Midr. Song* 2:13). This is very similar to the reading of the text in Matthew's gospel (cf., Mark 13:12; Luke 12:53; 14:26):

> Matthew 10 is Jesus's second major discourse in the Gospel of Matthew. He commissions the twelve to proclaim the kingdom of heaven (Matt. 10:1–15) and then warns them of coming postresurrection persecution (Matt. 10:16–25). They are not to fear men during this time of tribulation, but they are to confess Christ (Matt. 10:26–33). The gospel will be divisive—even within the family—due to the fact that not all will embrace the peace Christ brings (Matt. 10:34–39; cf., 12:46–50). It is within this context that Jesus quotes Micah 7:6, accommodating the wording to the flow of his discourse. Christ's followers must love him more than family (see Exod. 32:26–29; Deut. 33:9).[63]

The prophet expresses his resolve, in contrast to others, to "watch" for the LORD and to wait for the God of his salvation (Mic. 7:7; cf., Isa. 8:17; Mic. 3:8; 7:4b; Hab. 2:1; 3:18; Dan. 12:12–13). He knows that his God will hear him. This sets up the following section in Micah 7:8–13 where the prophet speaks of "light" (salvation) coming out of "darkness" (judgment) in the last days.

7:8 Do not rejoice [Tg. Jon. adds: O Rome], my enemy [GKC §122s] at me. Though I have fallen, I will rise up. Though I dwell in the darkness, the LORD will be my light. 7:9 The indignation [or, raging] of the LORD is what I must bear [Tg. Jon. adds: says Jerusalem], for I have sinned against him, until he pleads my case [lit., contends my contention] and accomplishes my justice. He will bring me forth into the light. I will look upon his righteousness [NET: deliverance]. 7:10 And my enemy [f.] will see [or, let my enemy see; or, so that my enemy may see], and shame will cover her who says to me, "Where is he, the LORD your God?" My

---

63. Shepherd, *Twelve Prophets*, 43. See Keil, *Minor Prophets*, 342; R. Smith, *Micah–Malachi*, 55.

eyes, they will look upon her. Now [or, At that time] she will become a trampling place like street mud.

7:11 A day to build your walls, in that day [ההוא ביום][64] *boundary [lit., statute; cf., LXX, Tg. Jon.] will be far away. 7:12 In that day [see MurXII; GKC §126aa], and to you he [Tg. Jon.: the exiles from Assyria] will come from Assyria and the cities of Egypt [BHS: and to Egypt; LXX: your cities (= עריך) will come to a leveling and division of Assyrians and your fortified cities to a division from Tyre (cf., Syr.)] and from Egypt and to River [Tg. Jon.: Euphrates; LXX: river of Syria]*[65] *and sea from sea and the mountain of the mountain [Vulg.: and to mountain from mountain; LXX: a day of water and confusion; BHS: from sea to sea and from mountain to mountain]. 7:13 And the land will become a desolation because of its inhabitants, because of the fruit of their deeds.*

The small unit in Micah 7:8–10 picks up the thread of confidence expressed in Micah 7:7. The prophet, speaking on behalf of the faithful remnant, addresses the unidentified enemy rhetorically, prohibiting the enemy to rejoice at his fall (cf., Prov. 24:17–18). The prophet is confident that he will rise from his fall. He will emerge from his present darkness (Mic. 7:8). In context, these are figures both for the consequences of the broken covenant relationship endured even by the faithful (e.g., Daniel; see Mic. 4:10) and for the trials and tribulations of the last days (see the temporal indicators in Micah 4:1, 6; 5:9 [Eng., 5:10]; 7:11–12). The use of light or a morning sunrise to depict the LORD's salvation is not unique to Micah (e.g., Isa. 9:1 [Eng., 9:2]; 42:6; 49:6; 60:1–3, 19–20; Mal. 3:20 [Eng., 4:2]; Ps. 27:1; John 8:12). It likely stems from Genesis 1:3: "And God said, 'Let there be light.' And there was light." This completes the cycle in the book of Micah wherein there is literal light (Mic. 2:1), the light of prophetic revelation (Mic. 3:6), the light of the wisdom of the Torah (Isa. 2:5; via Mic. 4:5), and now the light of salvation (Mic. 7:8).

---

64. The MT's גדריך יום ההוא ("your walls, day the that") is the result of haplography. Prior to the consistent introduction of final forms, which did not take place until after the Dead Sea Scrolls, the original would have been written גדריכ ביום ההוא. The non-final letter כ on the end of גדריכ was confused with the letter ב at the beginning of the following ביום, resulting in the loss of ב.

65. Some witnesses to LXX Mic. 7:12 do not have "of Syria," which is the reading favored by the Göttingen Septuagint volume edited by J. Ziegler. But here the shorter reading is considered a secondary attempt to align with the text now represented by the MT.

At first glance, Micah 7:9a hardly sounds like the voice of the faithful, but other exemplary believers have expressed this kind of solidarity with their people who, on the whole, have not been faithful to their God. Daniel, Ezra, and Nehemiah, for instance, all show a willingness to confess the sin of their people for which they are not personally responsible (Dan. 9:5; Ezra 9:6–7; Neh. 1:6–7). It is a way to affirm that God's judgment is just (cf., Lam. 1:18; 3:42). The prophet says that he must bear the LORD's indignation, indeed the LORD's contention (Mic. 6:2), until the LORD contends for him and accomplishes his justice (Mic. 7:9b; cf., Ps. 35:23). According to Isaiah 40:27, the Babylonian exiles would question whether the LORD had any concern for their justice, even contemplating the worship of the Babylonian gods (Isa. 40:12–26). But the faithfulness of the LORD and his word is above reproach and in stark contrast to the fickleness of the people (Isa. 40:6–8; 55:10–11). He is not created. He is the one true creator God who is able to declare things before they happen, and those who wait on him for final deliverance will find their strength renewed (Isa. 40:28–31). Thus, the prophet affirms that the LORD will in fact bring him forth into the light (i.e., salvation). He will look upon the LORD's righteousness, which, in context, refers to the LORD acting in right relationship to his people by staying faithful to his message of deliverance (cf., Isa. 56:1).

Just as the prophet looks upon the righteousness of the LORD, so the enemy will see and be covered with shame (Mic. 7:10a; cf., Mic. 7:16), no longer having any reason to rejoice at the remnant's fall. This is the same enemy who says, "Where is he, the LORD your God" (cf., Isa. 36:19; Joel 2:17; Pss. 42:4, 11 [Eng., 42:3, 10]; 79:10; 115:2)? And so, not only will the prophet "look upon" the LORD's righteousness, and not only will the enemy "see" and be ashamed, but also the prophet's eyes will "look upon" the enemy in defeat (Mic. 7:10b; cf., Isa. 66:24; Pss. 112:8; 118:7). The enemy will be a mere trampling place like street mud (cf., Zech. 10:5).

The next unit in Micah 7:11–13 focuses on the eschatological day of restoration for the people of God (cf., Mic. 4:1, 6; 5:9 [Eng., 5:10]). It will be a day to rebuild the city's walls (Mic. 7:11; cf., Ezra 9:9; Neh 1–7; CD-A 4:12). The distant boundaries indicate the great length and breadth of the city and perhaps also the land of covenant (cf., Gen. 15:18; Isa. 49:20; Zech. 2:8b [Eng., 2:4b]). In that day "he" will come to "you" (Mic. 7:12a), but it is not immediately clear who will come to whom. It is possible that "he" stands for the returning exiles or perhaps the nations themselves coming to the LORD (cf., Mic. 4:1–3). But the reader would expect "they" for this, and why would the prophet suddenly address the LORD as "you" in a section where he does not otherwise do this at all (Mic. 7:8–13)? If the second feminine singular pronominal suffix in Micah 7:11 refers to the city of Jerusalem, then it is possible that the second masculine singular pronominal suffix in Micah 7:12 refers to the people (עַם) of the city. In this case, the text is speaking of an individual who will come to the people. This now sounds a great deal like Micah 1:15 and the use of language from Genesis 49:10 and Deuteronomy 33:7 (see commentary above). The Messiah to whom the kingship belongs will come, and the obedience of peoples will be his (Gen. 49:10). It is to his people (i.e., Judah) that the LORD will bring him (Deut. 33:7). According to this reading, the latter part of Micah 7:12 (lit., "from Assyria and the cities of Egypt and from Egypt and to River and sea from sea and the mountain of the mountain") would not be a description of the places from which the exiles or the nations would come to Mount Zion. It would actually be a description of the extent of the boundaries of the land of the covenant in the messianic kingdom (Gen. 2:11–14; 15:18; Isa. 19:25; Mic. 7:11; Zech. 9:10; Ps. 72:8). The present problems with the state of the Hebrew text here seem to be the mixed result of attempts to read the text in these two very different ways.

The final verse of this section speaks of the land becoming a desolation "because of its inhabitants, because of the fruit of their deeds" (Mic. 7:13). Commentators are divided on whether this is the land of the covenant (Calvin) or the land outside of it (Keil). The prophets certainly speak of the land of the covenant becoming a desolation because of the deeds of its inhabitants (e.g., Jer. 25:5–7, 11; Mic. 3:12), but such a thought hardly seems appropriate as a conclusion to a section that highlights the defeat of the enemy (Mic. 7:8–10) and the restoration of the city and the land of the covenant (Mic. 7:11–12). Rather, it appears that the land here is the land of the enemy defeated for its evil deeds against the people of God (see Isa. 10:5–7; 47:6; Jer. 25:12; Zech. 1:15).

7:14 Shepherd your people with your staff, the flock of your inheritance, you who dwell alone in a thicket [or, he/they who dwell(s) alone in a thicket (cf., LXX, Syr., Tg. Jon., Vulg.)], in the midst of Carmel [or, rich/ fertile pastureland; see Isa. 29:17; 32:15]. Let them graze in Bashan and Gilead like days of old. 7:15 "As the days of your going forth from the land of Egypt, I will show him [LXX: you will see] wonders." 7:16 Nations will see and be ashamed of all their military might. They will put hand over mouth, their ears will be deaf. 7:17 They will lick dust like the serpent, like land crawlers. They will quake from their strongholds to the LORD our God. They will dread and be afraid of you.[66]

---

66. The MT accentuation suggests a different arrangement of the latter part of this verse: "They will quake from their strongholds. To the LORD our God

The final prayer of the book revisits the earlier metaphor of the shepherd with his flock (Mic. 7:14; cf., Mic. 2:12–13; 5:3 [Eng., 5:4]; see also Isa. 40:11; Ezek. 34:11–31; Zeph. 2:7; 3:13; Pss. 23; 28:9; 74:1; 79:13; 95:7). The participle שֹׁכְנִי ("dwelling") either describes the people/flock or the LORD himself (see GKC §90m), although most translators and commentators choose the former option. The image of the people of Israel dwelling alone and apart from the other nations is well known from Numbers 23:9b. There may also be a hint here of Israel scattered and thus in need of a shepherd (cf., Num. 27:17; 1 Kgs. 22:17; Ezek. 34:5; Mic. 3:12; Zech. 10:2b). On the other hand, if the participle describes the LORD, the text is very likely to be a link to Deuteronomy. 33:16: שֹׁכְנִי סְנֶה ("one who dwelt in a bush"). This refers to the LORD as the one who spoke to the shepherd Moses by means of an angel in the burning bush and called him to lead the Israelites out of Egypt (Exod. 3:1–2, 10; cf., Ps. 77:21 [Eng., 77:20]). Such a reading is an attractive option for Micah 7:14 given the reference to the exodus in Micah 7:15. The prayer then is that the LORD would shepherd his people again in this way and lead them to the rich pastures and fertile hills of Bashan and Gilead as in the glory days of David and Solomon (Mic. 7:14b; cf., Mic. 4:4, 8; 5:1 [Eng., 5:2]; Nah. 1:4; see BDB, 143). Bashan and Gilead were east of the Jordan in the territory once occupied by Reuben, Gad, and the half tribe of Manasseh (Num. 32) but subsequently lost (2 Kgs. 10:32–33). Thus, the prophet prays for full restoration and enjoyment of the land of the covenant (cf., Mic. 7:11–12).

Micah 7:15 interjects the voice of the LORD (but see LXX), apparently in response to the prayer of Micah 7:14. The LORD says that he will show the people wonders as in the days of the original exodus from Egypt, anticipating a new exodus to come in the future (cf., Num. 24:8; Isa. 11:16; 43:19; Hos. 2:16–17 [Eng., 2:14–15]; 8:13b; 9:3b; 11:1, 5, 11). The Hebrew term נִפְלָאוֹת ("wonders") often refers to the great acts of God as narrated in the Pentateuch and elsewhere (e.g., Ps. 78:3, 11), but in Micah 7:15 it likely refers specifically to the extraordinary display of signs and wonders in the ten plagues and the exodus by which the LORD made himself known as the God who was present with his people (Exod. 3:20; 7:3). As for the prophet's choice of words in saying "your" going forth from the land of Egypt,

---

they will fear, and they will be afraid of you." The difficulty with this arrangement is that it sends conflicting signals. Trembling and being afraid indicate an unhealthy fear or fright, but the expression "fear to" (פָּחַד אֶל) indicates a healthy fear (see Hos. 3:5). On the other hand, "to fear from or away from" (פָּחַד מִן) is to dread (see Ps. 27:1).

Redak comments, "Since their forefathers left Egypt, it is as though they themselves left Egypt."[67]

Micah 7:16 picks up the picture of the defeated enemy from Micah 7:10 who sees the LORD's deliverance of his people and is ashamed of his acts of aggression against them. These are not the nations of Micah 4:1–3 to be included in God's kingdom. These are the nations who oppose God and his people. The act of putting their hand to mouth signifies that they have no answer for what God has said and done (cf., Judg. 18:19; Job 21:5; 29:9; 40:4; see also Isa. 52:15).[68] According to the NET, "Their inability to respond will make them appear to be deaf mutes." They will lick dust like the serpent (Mic. 7:17). That is, they will suffer the same fate as the ultimate enemy to be defeated (Gen. 3:1, 14–15; Isa. 11:6–8; 27:1; 65:25; Ps. 72:9; Rom. 16:20; Rev. 12; see also Mal. 3:21 [Eng., 4:3]).[69] They will come trembling from their strongholds to feign allegiance to the LORD with dread and fear (cf., Deut. 33:29b; 2 Sam. 22:45–46; Ps. 18:45–46 [Eng., 18:44–45]). Given the prayer language of Mic. 7:14, the second masculine singular pronominal suffix ("you") at the end of the verse likely has the LORD as its antecedent rather than the people.

7:18 Who is God like you, forgiving iniquity and passing over transgression for the remnant of his inheritance? (He does not hold on forever to his anger, but / for delighting in covenant loyalty is he. 7:19 He will have compassion on us again [BDB, 998]. He will subdue our iniquities.) And you will cast [LXX, Syr., Tg. Jon., Vulg.: he will cast] into sea's depths all their sins [LXX, Syr., Vulg.: our sins]. 7:20 You will give faithfulness to Jacob, covenant loyalty to Abraham, which you swore to our fathers long ago.[70]

This final hymn with its initial participial descriptions of God (Mic. 7:18a; cf., Exod. 15:11; Amos 4:13; 5:8; 9:5–6; Pss. 89:7–9 [Eng., 89:6–8]) stands apart from the preceding prayer in Micah 7:14–17 and forms the first part of a compositional seam that connects the book of Micah to the following book of Nahum (see Introduction). The composer of the

---

67. *Mikraoth Gedoloth: The Twelve Prophets*, vol. 2, 235; cf., Josh. 24:6–8; Hos. 12:5b [Eng., 12:4b]; Mic. 6:4; Rom. 4:23–24; 15:4; 1 Cor. 9:10; 10:11; 1 Pet. 1:12.
68. See Bullinger, *Figures of Speech*, 607.
69. See Shepherd, *Text in the Middle*, 14–16.
70. The rendering of Micah 7:20 in *Targum Jonathan* references Jacob's dream at Bethel (Gen. 28), the covenant with Abram (Gen. 15), and the binding of Isaac (Gen. 22). Cf., *Tg. Neof.* Exod. 12:42.

Twelve has already cited from Jeremiah 26:18 to mark the midpoint of his composition at Micah 3:12, allowing the cited material in this seam to be the language of the LORD's revelation of himself to Moses at Sinai according to Exodus 34:6–7 (cf., Joel 2:13–14; Jon. 4:2): "And the LORD passed by (ויעבר) before him and proclaimed, 'The LORD, the LORD, a compassionate and gracious God (אל רחום וחנון), slow to anger (ארך אפים) and abundant in covenant loyalty (חסד) and faithfulness (אמת), keeping covenant loyalty (חסד), forgiving iniquity and transgression and sin (נשא עון ופשע וחטאה), but by no means will he leave the guilty unpunished (ונקה לא ינקה), visiting the iniquity of the fathers (עון אבות) upon the sons and upon the grandsons to the third and to the fourth generations.'" This is a revelation of a God who not only forgives but also punishes iniquity, fitting nicely with the themes of judgment and restoration set forth in the program of the Twelve (Hos. 3:4–5) and in the unfolding picture of the Day of the LORD in the Twelve (Joel 2:2; 3:4 [Eng., 2:31]; Amos 5:18; Obad 15; Zeph. 1:7, 15; Zech. 14:1; Mal. 3:23 [Eng., 4:5]).

Thus, Micah 7:18–20 focuses on the first part of this description of the LORD: "Who is a God (אל) like you, forgiving iniquity (נשא עון) and passing over transgression (ועבר על פשע) for the remnant of his inheritance? (He does not hold on forever to his anger [אפו], but delighting in covenant loyalty [חסד] is he. He will have compassion on us [ירחמנו] again. He will subdue our iniquities [עונתינו].) And you will cast into sea's depths all their sins (חטאותם). You will give faithfulness (אמת) to Jacob, covenant loyalty (חסד) to Abraham, which you swore to our fathers (לאבתינו) long ago." The text of Nahum 1:2b–3a then completes the compositional seam by means of its insertion between the *aleph* and *beth* lines of the partial acrostic poem in Nahum 1:2–8 (see the arrangement of the lines in *BHS*) and by its citation from both parts of the LORD's self-description in Exodus 34:6–7. The LORD takes vengeance on his foes and keeps wrath for his enemies (Nah. 1:2b; cf., Exod. 20:5). He is "slow to anger" (ארך אפים) and great of strength, "but he will by no means leave the guilty unpunished" (ונקה לא ינקה) (Nah. 1:3a).

The rhetorical question at the beginning of Micah 7:18 ("Who is a God like you [מי אל כמוך]?") expects a negative answer. It also appears to be a play on the name "Micah" (מיכה ["Who is like Yah(weh)?"]; cf., "Michael" [מיכאל ("Who is like God?"); Dan. 10:13, 21; 12:1]). Forgiveness of iniquity and sin will take place in the new covenant relationship (Jer. 31:31–34) for the remnant of his inheritance (see Isa. 19:25; Mic. 2:12; 4:7; 5:6; 7:14; Zeph. 2:7; see also BDB, 635). The shift from second person address to God in Mic. 7:18a to third person reference in Micah 7:18b–19a is due to the fact that Micah 7:18b–19a is a parenthetical comment on what it means for God to forgive his people. The second person address resumes in Micah 7:19b–20. God does not hold on to his anger forever (Mic. 7:18b; cf., Isa. 57:16; 64:8; Nah. 1:2b–3a; Lam. 3:31–32; 5:22), for he delights in his own covenant loyalty (cf., Ezek. 18:23, 32). He certainly delights in the covenant loyalty of his people (e.g., Hos. 6:6; Mic. 6:8), but here his own faithfulness is in view. God will have compassion on his people again. He will "subdue" (יִכְבֹּשׁ) all their sins (Mic. 7:19a).[71]

God will cast all the sins of the people into the depths of the sea (Mic. 7:19b; cf., Ps. 103:12). He will give faithfulness and covenant loyalty to the patriarchs Jacob and Abraham, which he swore (or, bound himself by oath to) long ago (Mic. 7:20). The LORD made a covenant with the patriarchs to restore the lost blessing of life and dominion in the land (Gen. 1–3) through them and their seed (see Gen. 12; 15; 17; 26; 28). It would be to the true children of Abraham by faith (Rom. 4) that the LORD would give the land of the covenant (Gen. 12:7; 15:18). Thus, faithfulness to the "seed" (Gal. 3:16, 29) is faithfulness to Abraham and Jacob (see Deut. 7:8, 12; Neh. 9:8).

---

71. This is an unusual use of the verb "subdue." It is possible that it should be the verb "wash" (יְכַבֵּס = יְכַבֵּשׁ). See Jer. 2:22; 4:14; Ps. 51:4, 9 (Eng., 51:2, 7). But see also *Tg. Jon.* Zeph. 3:17.

BOOK OF THE TWELVE

NAHUM

NAHUM 1:1-8

1:1 The oracle against Nineveh. The document of the prophetic vision of Nahum the Elkoshite.[1]
1:2 [א] A jealous and avenging God is the LORD, the LORD is avenging and a lord of wrath.[2]
The LORD takes vengeance against his foes, and he keeps wrath for his enemies.
1:3 The LORD is slow to anger and great of strength [Tg. Jon. adds: and he forgives those who turn to his Torah], but the LORD will by no means leave the guilty unpunished.
[ב] In a storm-wind [LXX: completion] and in a tempest is his way, and a cloud is the dust of his feet.
1:4 [ג] He rebukes the sea and makes it dry, and all the rivers he dries up. [ד] Bashan and Carmel languish,[3] and the sprout of Lebanon, it languishes.

---

1. Syr.: "The wound/blow of Nineveh, which is in the document of the prophetic vision of Nahum the Elkoshite." *Tg. Jon.*: "A burden/oracle of a cup of curse to make Nineveh drink. In former times Jonah the son of Amittai, the prophet who was from Gath Hepher, prophesied against her, and she turned from her sins. But now she has sinned again. Nahum, from the house of Koshi [or, Beth Koshi], prophesied against her again as it is written in this document."
2. See GKC §128u. Cf., LXX, Syr., *Tg. Jon.*.
3. The *BHS* apparatus proposes דללו ("they hang/are low/languish") instead of אמלל ("languish") for the first verb of this line. This would provide a

285

1:5 [ה] Mountains,[4] they quake because of him, and the hills, they melt [LXX: are shaken].

[ו] And the earth is ruined [וַתִּשָּׂא][5] from before him, and the world and all inhabitants therein.

1:6 [ז] Before his indignation[6] who can stand? And who can rise up against the burning of his anger?

[ח] His wrath, it is poured out like fire, and the rocks, they are broken down[7] because of him.

1:7 [ט] The LORD is good, a place of safety [see BDB, 514, 732] in a day of distress.[8]

[י] And he acknowledges[9] those who seek refuge in him [LXX: reverence him].

1:8 [כ] Like a flood[10] crossing over, a complete destruction is what he will make its place, and his enemies will he pursue into darkness [LXX: darkness will pursue those who rise against him and his enemies].

The opening phrase of the superscription, "The oracle against Nineveh," indicates the content of the present book of Nahum as a whole (see the references to Nineveh in Nahum 2:9 [Eng., 2:8]; 3:7), even though the

---

word that begins with the letter *daleth*, although such a move is not necessary to maintain the acrostic. Other acrostic poems omit letters of the alphabet (e.g., Ps. 9–10; 25; 34; 145). The proposed plural verb would also fit better with the compound subject. Finally, it is somewhat unusual for a poet to repeat the same verb (as in the MT here) in reiterative parallelism.

4. MurXII, LXX, Syr., and *Tg. Jon.* have "The mountains." But see 4Q169 and GKC §126k.

5. Cf., *Tg. Jon.* The MT's וַתִּשָּׂא ("And it lifts up") does not work here because it is neither intransitive nor passive.

6. The word that represents the letter *zayin* is second in the Hebrew text. *Targum Jonathan* prefaces the verse with a reference to Sinai: "If, when he revealed himself in love to give the Torah to his people, thus the world trembled from before him, then when he reveals himself in rage to take vengeance on the enemies of his people."

7. One manuscript reads נִצְּתוּ ("they are burned"). Cf., Jer. 4:26.

8. LXX: "The Lord is kind to those who wait upon him in a day of trouble."

9. The *yodh*-initial word comes after the *waw* conjunction (cf., Ps. 37:39).

10. Read כְּשֶׁטֶף. Cf., Vulg. Dan. 9:26b. The MT is the result of dittography (*waw*) and confusion of *beth* and *kaph*. *BHS* puts the first two words of Nahum 1:8 with Nahum 1:7b: "And he acknowledges those who seek refuge in him and in a flood crossing over." This makes כְלָה the first word of the *kaph* line.

partial acrostic poem in Nahum 1:2–8 does not mention Nineveh at all. The placement of the superscription forces the reader to reckon with the relationship between the eschatological and worldwide judgment depicted in Nahum 1:2–8 and the rather specific and historical judgment of Nineveh in Nahum 1:9–3:19.[11] The "oracle" (מַשָּׂא) is not the load or burden that the prophet or someone else bears but the uplifted prophetic discourse itself (cf., Isa. 13:1; Hab. 1:1; Zech. 9:1; 12:1; Mal. 1:1). Duane Christensen translates, "The exposition of Nineveh," suggesting that מַשָּׂא does not refer to revelation but to explanation of revelation.[12] But this interpretation of the term works better in places like Zechariah 9:1; 12:1; and Malachi 1:1, where the translator could render, "The exposition of the word of the LORD." In Nahum 1:1, the term would be neither revelation nor explanation of revelation but exposition of a place, which makes very little sense. The appositional phrase, "The document (סֵפֶר) of the prophetic vision (חֲזוֹן) of Nahum the Elkoshite," clarifies that the "oracle" in this case is the written "prophetic vision" itself (cf., Isa. 1:1; Obad. 1:1). A מַשָּׂא is in fact something that can be "seen" (חָזָה) in a prophetic vision (Isa. 13:1; Hab. 1:1). This is the only prophetic superscription to refer to what follows as a written document (cf., Jer. 25:13; 30:2; 36; 45:1; 51:60; Mal. 3:16), showing a unique awareness that the content is not merely a recorded collection of oral prophecies but a work of literature. This is not to say that other prophetic books are simply collections of oral prophecies. It is to point out that Nahum in particular makes the textual phenomenon explicit from the outset. Thus, the task is to interpret the text according to literary categories. It is not to reconstruct what may or may not be behind the text. Nahum 1:1 is the only verse in the Bible that mentions the prophet Nahum ("comfort[ing]"; cf., "Nehemiah"). The only information provided about him is that he is "the Elkoshite," usually

---

11. "The psalm offers a theological interpretation of how to understand the oracles of judgment which constitute the main portion of the book" (Brevard S. Childs, *Introduction to the Old Testament as Scripture* [Philadelphia: Fortress, 1979], 443). "The canonical use of the psalm has relativized the historical particularity of Nineveh's destruction by viewing it as a type of a larger and recurring phenomenon in history against which God exercises his eternal power and judgment. . . . [T]he psalm in ch. 1 functions to transform the visions of Nahum which foretold the historical destruction of Nineveh into an eschatological prophecy of the end time" (ibid., 444).
12. Duane L. Christensen, *Nahum: A New Translation with Introduction and Commentary*, The Anchor Yale Bible 24f (New Haven, CT: Yale University Press, 2009), 152.

understood to indicate his place of origin or hometown rather than his family lineage. But nothing is known for certain about the location of Elkosh.[13] It appears that biographical details about the prophet are to play virtually no role in the interpretation of the book's message, which is by no means unusual (cf., Joel 1:1; Obad. 1; Mal. 1:1). The written prophetic vision itself is what is important.

The book of Nahum shares with the preceding books of Jonah (Jon. 1:2) and Micah (Mic. 5:4–5 [Eng., 5:5–6]) an interest in Assyria and its capital city Nineveh. Of course, in the book of Jonah Nineveh represents Gentiles who come to believe in the LORD (Jon. 1:16; 3:5; 4:11). In the book of Nahum, on the other hand, Nineveh represents Gentiles who do not believe. They are the enemies of the people of God (Nah. 3:19; cf., Mic. 5:4–5 [Eng., 5:5–6]). The arrangement of the Twelve in the LXX makes this relationship apparent by placing the book of Nahum directly after the book of Jonah. But this placement disrupts the compositional seam between Micah and Nahum noted in the Introduction and in the commentary on Micah 7:18–20. Furthermore, such an arrangement is not necessary to see the relationship between Jonah and Nahum in the composition of the Twelve. *Targum Jonathan*, which follows the arrangement of the Twelve according to the MT, notes the relationship well in its rendering of the superscription. According to the Targum, the Ninevites repented because of Jonah's prophecy, but now they have sinned again, requiring Nahum to prophesy against them. The Targum sees no contradiction between the two books. They show two sides of the same coin.

The Assyrians were God's instrument of judgment against the northern kingdom of Israel (2 Kgs. 17). They were also a threat to the southern kingdom of Judah (2 Kgs. 18). So, how can God judge his own instrument? This problem is addressed in the woe oracle pronounced against Assyria in Isaiah 10:5–19. Assyria was indeed God's instrument to plunder (Isa. 10:5–6), but Assyria went beyond this in order to destroy (Isa. 10:7–11). Therefore, when God is finished judging his own people by means of the Assyrians, he will judge the Assyrians themselves for this and for their claims to do what they have done by their own power (Isa. 10:12–19). The Assyrians, like the Babylonians who followed them, were an evil instrument of judgment (cf., Isa. 47:6; Hab. 1:12–13; Zech. 1:15). Nahum's message, however, is not like Jonah's (i.e., Jon. 3:4b). It is not designed to be proclaimed to the Ninevites directly, nor is there opportunity for repentance. Rather, it is a message

---

13. "Capernaum" ("village of Nahum") bears no traceable relationship to the biblical prophet.

of hope for the true people of God that their enemies will be defeated and that they themselves will be delivered (Nah. 1:7; 2:1 [Eng., 1:15]).

The fronting of the partial alphabetic acrostic in Nahum 1:2–8 has the effect of making the historical judgment of Nineveh in Nahum 1:9–3:19 into a lasting illustration of what future and final judgment of the enemies of the people of God will be.[14] That is, by starting with a picture of eschatological and worldwide judgment, the composer makes the book into something more than a mere documentary of a past event. It is now relevant Scripture for the people of God until the coming of the last days (Hos. 3:5). The poem in Nahum 1:2–8 has apparently been lifted from a larger, complete alphabetic acrostic for precisely this purpose. Juxtaposition of Nahum 1:2–8 and Nahum 1:9–3:19 has created new and ongoing meaning for future generations. The poem also forms

---

14. Early interpreters generally did not recognize the acrostic either because ancient Hebrew manuscripts did not arrange the lines accordingly to make the acrostic obvious (but see Ps. 119 in 11QPs[a]) or because the interpreters were working primarily with a translation (e.g., LXX). Medieval Masoretic manuscripts such as the Leningrad Codex feature verse divisions that enable the reader to see acrostics where the words representing the letters appear at the beginning of each verse (e.g., Ps. 25; 34; 145; Prov. 31:10–31). The *setuma* divisions help the reader to see the acrostics in Lamentations 1–4 (see Ernst Würthwein, *The Text of the Old Testament*, 2d ed., trans. Erroll F. Rhodes [Grand Rapids: Eerdmans, 1994], 20). The acrostic that can be seen most clearly in the Leningrad Codex is Psalm 119. Widespread acceptance of some form of acrostic in Nahum 1 came in the nineteenth and twentieth centuries, although attempts to reconstruct a full acrostic have not been sustained (see Hermann Gunkel, "Nahum 1," *ZAW* 11 [1893]: 223–44; John M. P. Smith, *A Critical and Exegetical Commentary on Nahum*, ICC [Edinburgh: T. & T. Clark, 1911]; Duane L. Christensen, "The Acrostic Poem of Nahum Reconsidered," *ZAW* 87 [1975]: 17–30; idem, "The Acrostic of Nahum Once Again: A Prosodic Analysis of Nahum 1:1–10," *ZAW* 99 [1987]: 409–415; Michael B. Shepherd, "Hebrew Acrostic Poems and Their Vocabulary Stock," *JNSL* 36/2 [2010]: 95–98). Those who now deny that there is any kind of acrostic in Nahum 1 are few and far between (e.g., Michael H. Floyd, "The Chimerical Acrostic of Nahum 1:2–10," *JBL* 113 [1994]: 421–37). The present commentary agrees with K. Seybold ("Vormasoretische Randnotizen in Nahum 1," *ZAW* 101 [1989]: 71–85) that Nahum 1:9 begins a separate unit. Thus, the partial acrostic goes halfway through the alphabet and stops after Nahum 1:8. Cf., the Masoretic division of the acrostic in Psalms 9 and 10, which form one psalm in the LXX (see H. Eshel and J. Strugnell, "Alphabetical Acrostics in Pre-Tannaitic Hebrew," *CBQ* 62 [2000]: 453–58). Psalm 9 only goes halfway through the alphabet.

bookends with the poem in Habakkuk 3:3–15 for the books of Nahum and Habakkuk. Both poems (Nahum 1:2–8 and Habakkuk 3:3–15) depict future appearances of God (theophanies) coming to judge the wicked and to deliver the righteous in terms drawn from the narratives in Genesis–Kings (e.g., the flood, the exodus, the conquest, etc.). Thus, the historical prophecies of Nahum and Habakkuk are recast as images of things to come.

The opening line of the acrostic declares that the LORD is a jealous and an avenging God (Nah. 1:2a). He avenges and is a lord of wrath. The LORD is jealous for his people (Isa. 42:13; 63:15; see also Isa. 9:6 [Eng., 9:7]; 37:32), his name (Ezek. 39:25), his city (Zech. 1:14; 8:2), and his land (Joel 2:18). He jealously demands exclusive worship of himself (Exod. 20:5; 34:14; Deut 4:24; 5:9; 6:15; Josh. 24:19). He avenges the blood of his servants (Deut. 32:43; cf., Ps. 94:1). Inserted between the *aleph* line (Nah. 1:2a) and the *beth* line (Nah. 1:3b) are two lines (Nah. 1:2b–3a) that draw from the language of Exodus 34:6–7 and form a compositional seam with Micah 7:18–20 (see commentary on the Micah passage). Thus, composition occurs here on two different levels. On the one hand, the acrostic poem is interrupted for the purpose of linking the beginning of the book of Nahum to the end of the book of Micah. On the other hand, the acrostic poem itself is an introductory piece of text designed to give the judgment of Nineveh a broader application. The poem is also intended to join the book of Nahum with the following book of Habakkuk for which the corresponding poem in Habakkuk 3:3–15 serves as a conclusion.

The first line of the compositional insertion reiterates that the LORD takes vengeance on his foes, then it takes the language of Exodus 34:7a—"keeping (נֹצֵר) covenant loyalty"—and transforms it into "and he keeps (נוֹטֵר) wrath for his enemies" (Nah. 1:2b; cf., Lev. 19:18; Jer. 3:5, 12; Ps. 103:9; see also CD 9:5). This is in accordance with Exodus 20:5, which says that the LORD punishes the iniquity of those who reject him. The second line of the insertion draws from Exodus 34:6b to say that the LORD is "slow to anger" (אֶרֶךְ אַפַּיִם; lit., "long of nostrils"; see Exod. 15:8; Ps. 18:16 [Eng., 18:15]) and "great of strength" (see BDB, 470–71) rather than "abundant in covenant loyalty" (Nah. 1:3a; cf., Pss. 145:8; 147:5). But he will by no means leave the guilty unpunished, as it says in Exodus 34:7b.

When the acrostic resumes in Nahum 1:3b, it is an image of the coming of God whose path is in the wind of a storm (cf., 2 Sam. 22:8–16; Isa. 29:6; 66:15; Ps. 18:8–16 [Eng., 18:7–15]). The dust of his feet (an anthropomorphism) is a cloud (cf., Isa. 19:1). He rebukes the sea and makes it dry (Nah. 1:4a; cf., Hab. 3:8). This is an image drawn from the story of the exodus (Exod. 14:21–22; 15:8; Ps. 106:9). He dries up all the rivers (cf., Josh. 3:13–17; 2 Kgs. 2:8, 14). Bashan (east of the Jordan) and Carmel (on the Mediterranean coast), places known for their fertile land (see Mic. 7:14), languish as a result of God's appearing (Nah. 1:4b; cf., Isa. 33:9). Lebanon (in the north), a place known for its cedars (BDB, 527), languishes as well. This creates a stark contrast between fertility (as opposed to a wilderness) and the desolation brought by divine judgment. *Pesher Nahum* from Qumran (4QpNah [4Q169]) interprets Nahum 1:4 to be the judgment of the Kittim, that is, the island of Cyprus to the west of the Mediterranean coast.[15] In biblical prophecy this island represents all enemies from the west, including the Greeks and the Romans, in the last days (Num. 24:14, 24; Dan. 11:30).

Mountains quake because of God (Nah. 1:5a; cf., Joel 4:16 [Eng., 3:16]; Hab. 3:6). Furthermore, the hills melt (cf., Mic. 1:4; Ps. 97:5). The earth is devastated before him, the world and all its inhabitants (Nah. 1:5b). Here it is clear that the scope of the judgment depicted in this passage goes well beyond any particular locale and well beyond any event that has occurred in history. It is a worldwide judgment that is still to come. The rhetorical questions in Nahum 1:6a expect the answer, "No one." Who can endure his indignation (cf., 1 Sam. 6:20; Mal. 3:2; Ps. 76:8 [Eng., 76:7]; 147:17)? Who can rise up against the burning of his anger (cf., Amos 7:2, 5)? His wrath is poured out like fire (Nah. 1:6b; cf., Isa. 66:15), and even the rocks are broken down because of him.

Given the questions in Nahum 1:6a, it is naturally a concern whether there is any hope for the righteous in the Day of Judgment (Ps. 1:6; Eccl. 12:14). Verse 7 addresses this concern: "The LORD is good (טוב)" (cf., Ps. 100:5). טוב ("good") is the most commonly occurring initial word for the *teth* line in biblical acrostic poems (see Ps. 25:8; 37:16; 112:5; 119:65, 66, 68, 71, 72; 145:9; Lam. 3:25, 26, 27; 4:9). The text explains that the LORD is good in the sense that he is a "place of safety" (i.e., a place in which to take refuge from the storm) for the faithful in a day of distress (cf., Isa. 25:4; Joel 4:16 [Eng., 3:16]; Ps. 27:1; 31:5 [Eng., 31:4]; 37:39; 52:9 [Eng., 52:8]). The "day of distress" becomes identified with the Day of the LORD in the composition of the Twelve (see Hab. 3:16b; Zeph. 1:15; see also Isa. 33:2; Ps. 59:17 [Eng., 59:16]; Dan. 12:1). The LORD acknowledges those who seek refuge in him (cf., Ps. 2:12). In his rage against the wicked, he remembers to have compassion on his own (Hab. 3:2).

---

15. *Pesher* ("interpretation") is a specific form of verse-by-verse biblical commentary.

The final verse of the acrostic (Nah. 1:8) says that the LORD is like a flood crossing over the land. This is perhaps an allusion to the flood narrative in Genesis 6–7 as an illustration of the final judgment of the wicked and the ultimate deliverance of the righteous (see Isa. 26:20; Dan. 9:26; see also Gen. 19; 2 Pet. 3).[16] The LORD will make a "complete destruction" (see Isa. 10:23; Zeph. 1:18; Dan. 9:27) of "its" (f.) place (i.e., the earth's [f.] place [Nah. 1:5b]). His enemies (cf., Nah. 1:2b) are the ones he will pursue into darkness (or, with darkness [cf., Jer 29:18; Ps. 83:16 (Eng., 83:15); Lam. 3:43, 66]). This is the darkness of divine judgment in the Day of the LORD (Joel 2:2; 3:4 [Eng., 2:31]; Amos 5:18, 20; Zeph. 1:15).

NAHUM 1:9–2:3 (ENG., 2:2)

1:9 What are you planning against the LORD?[17] A complete destruction is what he is making. Distress will not rise up two times [LXX: He will not take vengeance twice upon the same by affliction]. 1:10 For to the degree of [BDB, 724] entangled thorns [LXX: Because to their foundation he will be dried; Syr.: Because even their rulers are rebellious (cf., Tg. Jon.)] and like the strong drink of drunkards [lit., and like their strong drink, drunkards; LXX: and like entangled yew he will be consumed] they are consumed like fully dry chaff [cf., LXX, Tg. Jon.]. 1:11 It is from you [Tg. Jon. adds: Nineveh] that one planning against the LORD evil goes forth [LXX: a thought against the Lord goes forth; Tg. Jon.: the king who plans against the people of the LORD evil goes forth], a worthless advisor.

1:12 Thus says the LORD, "Though at full strength and thus many [LXX: ruler of many waters; Syr.: To the rulers of many waters], so are they sheared [LXX: they will be commanded; Syr.: who dragged away], and it crosses over [Syr.: and crossed over (pl.)]. And I afflicted you [NIV adds: O Judah]. I will not afflict you again [LXX: and the report of you will not be heard again].[18] 1:13 And now, I will break his yoke [LXX:

---

16. Use of flood imagery for the final judgment comes by way of flood imagery in the Sodom and Gomorrah account (a flood of fire). See Michael B. Shepherd, *The Text in the Middle* (New York: Peter Lang, 2014), 19–20.
17. *Targum Jonathan* addresses this to the peoples who plundered Israel.
18. *Tg. Jon.*: "Thus says the LORD, 'Though they are full in counsel and numerous in numbering, the peoples who gather together to oppress you, Jerusalem, though they cross over the Tigris and pass over the Euphrates and come to afflict you, and which I subdued you, I will not subdue you again.'"

scepter] from upon you, and your bonds will I tear off. 1:14 And the LORD has commanded against you [Tg. Jon. adds: O king of Assyria]: There will never be sown from your name again [Tg. Jon.: There will never be remembrance of your name again]. From the house of your god(s) I will cut off carved / sculpted image and molten image. I will make your grave [Tg. Jon.: There I will make your grave], for you are despised [Tg. Jon.: for this is light / easy before me]."

2:1 (Eng., 1:15) Look, upon the mountains are the feet of one proclaiming good news, one causing peace to be heard: "Celebrate, O Judah, your festivals. Pay your vows. For a worthless one [or, destroyer] will never again pass through you [LXX: For they will by no means pass through you again to decay]. All of him is cut off [LXX: He / It is finished. He / It is removed]." 2:2 (Eng., 2:1) One who scatters [Syr.: A ruler] has come up against your face. Guard the rampart [LXX: One who breathes in your face has come up delivered from trouble]. Watch the road.[19] Make firm your loins [Tg. Jon.: neck]. Make very strong your strength.[20] 2:3 (Eng., 2:2) For the LORD restores the majesty of Jacob as the majesty of Israel [LXX: For the Lord has turned away the pride of Jacob just as the pride of Israel]. Though those who empty have emptied them [LXX: For those who shake have shaken them], and their branches have they destroyed.

The partial acrostic poem ended with the *kaph* line in Nahum. 1:8. There is no reason to think that the poem continues in Nahum 1:9 with the *mem* line, having skipped the *lamedh* line. The direct question in Nahum 1:9 is out of character with the acrostic, but, as might be expected, there are some interesting verbal correspondences between Nahum 1:9 and the end of the partial acrostic. The author has not simply spliced the acrostic onto the front of the book arbitrarily. Commentators do not agree on the identity of the addressee in Nahum 1:9. Calvin argues that the enemies are addressed rhetorically (cf., *Tg. Jon.*),[21] which is the interpretation reflected in the above translation

---

19. *Tg. Jon.*: "For they were coming up and scattering themselves upon your land, besieging you in siege, setting watchmen on your roads."
20. The NET says that this is the voice of the watchmen of Nineveh. The verses that come before and after suggest that it is the voice of the prophet. The rhetorical warning of an attack directed to the enemy contributes to the words of encouragement for Judah in Nahum 2:1, 3 (Eng., 1:15; 2:2).
21. John Calvin, *Commentaries on the Twelve Minor Prophets*, vol. 3, *Jonah, Micah, Nahum*, trans. John Owen (reprint, Grand Rapids: Baker, 2005), 434–36.

(cf., Nah. 1:11). Keil thinks that the Judeans (and not the Assyrians or Ninevites) are addressed and renders, "What do you think with regard to Jehovah?"[22] It would thus be a question about whether the Judeans really think the LORD will fulfill his threat against Nineveh. The statement, "A complete destruction (כלה) is what he is making (עשה)," picks up the language of Nahum 1:8: "a complete destruction (כלה) is what he will make (יעשה) its place." Likewise, the statement about "distress" (צרה) not rising up two times now has a connection to the day of "distress" (צרה) in Nahum 1:7. Although it is true that God's historical judgment of Nineveh would be so effective that it would not require repetition, it is also true that Judah would soon thereafter fall into the hands of the Babylonians. The prefixing of the acrostic poem is thus already adding life to the historical prophecy. The day of distress (i.e., the eschatological Day of the LORD) will be a final judgment for all the enemies of the people of God.

Nahum 1:10 compares the destruction of the enemy to the consumption of three things: (1) entangled thorns consumed by fire (cf., Isa. 34:13), (2) strong drink consumed by drunkards, and (3) and very dry chaff consumed by fire (cf., Exod. 15:7). In this way, the enemy will be consumed by the LORD's judgment. According to the rendering of Nah. 1:11 in *Targum Jonathan*, it is from the city of Nineveh that a king goes forth who plans evil against the people of the LORD. This corresponds to the question in Nahum 1:9, "What are you planning against the LORD?" The one who plans this evil is called a "worthless advisor" (cf., 2 Sam. 15:12; Isa. 19:11; Nah. 2:1b [Eng., 1:15b]; 2 Chr. 22:4) or "one who advises worthlessness/ruin" (cf., 2 Sam. 22:5; Ps. 18:5 [Eng., 18:4]).

Nahum 1:12 begins with a common introductory formula for a prophetic oracle, "Thus says the LORD." It is most frequent in the book of Jeremiah. The oracle concedes that the members of the enemy army are at full strength and numerous, but they will nevertheless be sheared like a large flock of sheep (a metaphor for their humiliating defeat and subjugation). The singular verb, "and he/it crosses over," either has the individual enemy king or nation for its subject (cf., Nah. 2:1b [Eng., 1:15b]), or it has for its subject the shearing instrument that passes over the body (cf., Num. 8:7; Ezek. 5:1). Commentators are split on who it is in Nahum 1:12b that the LORD has afflicted but will never afflict again.[23] Some (e.g., Calvin, Keil) understand this to mean that though the LORD has afflicted Judah by means of the Assyrians he will never do so again by that particular nation. That is, it does not exclude

---

22. Keil, *Minor Prophets*, 360.
23. See Christensen, *Nahum*, 241.

the possibility that Judah would be afflicted by another nation like Babylon. Others (e.g., Rashi) take Nahum 1:12b to be another way of expressing what was said in Nahum 1:9b, "Distress will not rise up two times."[24] In other words, once the LORD afflicts the enemy (i.e., the city of Nineveh), he will not have to do it again. The judgment will be complete, and the enemy will never recover to full strength. This reading also works well with the wording of the decree against the enemy in Nahum 1:14: "There will never be sown from your name again."

So now the LORD will break the enemy's yoke from upon the land of Judah and the city of Jerusalem (Nah. 1:13; cf., Jer. 27:2). He will tear off the bonds. The people of Judah will no longer be subject to the enemy. The LORD's command for the enemy king/nation is that there will never be sown from his name again (Nah. 1:14a), which *Targum Jonathan* understands to mean that there will never be remembrance of his name again. It could also be a way to refer to offspring (see Jer. 22:30; Hos. 2:25 [Eng., 2:23]; Mal. 2:3; Ps. 21:11–12 [Eng., 21:10–11]). According to Nahum 1:14b, the LORD will cut off the idols from the house (or, temple) of the so-called god(s) of the enemy king/nation. He says that he will make the grave of the enemy king/nation because he is despised. This sounds very similar to the description of Sennacherib's death in 2 Kings 19:36–37: "And Sennacherib the king of Assyria traveled and went and returned and lived in Nineveh. And so, he was prostrating himself in the house of Nisroch his god, and Adrammelech and Sarezer his sons, they struck him with the sword." This is perhaps why *Targum Jonathan* renders in Nahum 1:14b, "There [i.e., in the house of your god] I will make your grave."

In Nahum 2:1a (Eng., 1:15a) the prophet points to the mountains, perhaps the hill country of Judah, and envisions on them the feet of "one proclaiming good news" (מבשר) to the people of God (cf., Isa. 40:9), someone causing peace to be heard (cf., Isa. 9:5 [Eng., 9:6]; Mic. 5:4a [Eng., 5:5a]; Zech. 9:9–10; Ps. 72:3). This is usually understood to be a reference to an unidentified herald with connections to Isaiah 52:7 and Romans 10:15. According to Keil, "The first clause is applied in Isaiah 52:7 to the description of the Messianic salvation."[25] But the links to the book of Isaiah run much deeper than this, making the identity of the one proclaiming good news even clearer. In Isaiah 41:25–26 there is a reference to the arousal of one from the north and the east, generally understood to be Cyrus (cf., Isa. 41:2; 44:28; 45:1), but then the LORD says in Isaiah 41:27 that he will give to Jerusalem "one

---

24. See J. Smith, *Nahum*, 304.
25. Keil, *Minor Prophets*, 363.

proclaiming good news" (מבשר). The problem is that there is no one, no "counselor" (cf., Isa. 9:5 [Eng., 9:6]), who responds (Isa. 41:28–29; cf., Isa. 59:16; 63:3), and so the LORD presents his "servant" on whom his Spirit rests and who will bring forth justice to the nations (Isa. 42:1–7; cf., Isa. 49:1–9; 50:4–11; 52:13–53:12; 61:1–9; see also Isa. 9:5–6 [Eng., 9:6–7]; 11:1–10). *Targum Jonathan* and Matt. 12:18–21 identify this individual as the Messiah. Furthermore, *11QMelchizedek* identifies the one proclaiming good news in Isaiah 52:7 as the Messiah in Daniel 9:25–26. According to Isaiah 61:1, it is the role of the one on whom the LORD's Spirit rests "to proclaim good news" (לבשר). This is the individual with whom Jesus identifies himself in Luke 4:16–30. Paul's use of the plural ("the feet of those who proclaim good news") in his citation of Isaiah 52:7; Nahum 2:1 (Eng., 1:15) is an extension of the ministry of the Christ to the ministry of the Christian church. It is similar to what Paul does with the role of the servant of the LORD as a light to the nations (Isa. 42:6; 49:6), extending it to the role of the apostles (Acts 13:47). The good news is that Judah can celebrate its festivals (Lev. 23; Zeph. 3:18) and pay its vows (cf., Jon. 2:10 [Eng., 2:9]) to express its worship and thanksgiving in response to the saving work of God (Nah. 2:1a [Eng., 1:15a]; cf., Ezra 3; Neh. 8). The worthless one from Nah. 1:11 will never again pass through the land of Judah. He will be completely cut off (Nah. 2:1b [Eng., 1:15b]).

There is some question about the identity of the "one who scatters" in Nahum 2:2 (Eng., 2:1).[26] Some consider him to be someone like Sennacherib who threatens Judah. Others think that this is Nebuchadnezzar coming against Assyria. A decision here depends partly on how the reader interprets the placement of the verse and partly on how Nahum 2:3a (Eng., 2:2a) is interpreted. Some scholars move Nahum 2:2 (Eng., 2:1) after Nahum 2:3 (Eng., 2:2) so that it is part of the beginning of the account of the siege of Nineveh (Nah. 2:4 [Eng., 2:3]).[27] According to this reading, Nahum 2:3a (Eng., 2:2a) is a positive reference to the restoration of Israel and should be read with Nahum 2:1 (Eng., 1:15). On the other hand, if Nahum 2:2 (Eng., 2:1) is understood to describe one coming against Judah, then Nah. 2:3a (Eng., 2:2a) will likely be read as a negative reference to the removal of the pride of Israel (cf., LXX). It is perhaps best to stay with the present order of the text due to the fact that there is no textual evidence for its rearrangement. But it is still possible to say that the one who scatters

---

26. See Christensen, *Nahum*, 262–63.
27. See *BHS* apparatus and Ralph L. Smith, *Micah–Malachi*, WBC 32 (Nashville: Thomas Nelson, 1984), 81.

in Nahum 2:2 (Eng., 2:1) is coming against Judah's enemy. According to this reading, the warning to prepare for an attack is directed to the enemy rhetorically (cf., Joel 4:9–12 [Eng., 3:9–12]), but it is ironic, and it serves as an encouragement to Judah that the LORD will use this instrument to remove their enemy. This then feeds directly into Nahum 2:3a (Eng., 2:2a) as a positive reference to the restoration of Israel (see 4Q198).[28] Nahum 2:3b (Eng., 2:2b) is thus read as a concession (cf., Isa. 5:6; 17:10; Ezek. 8:17; Nah. 2:11 [Eng., 2:10]).

NAHUM 2:4–14 (ENG., 2:3–13)

2:4 (Eng., 2:3) The shield [LXX, Syr., Tg. Jon.: shields] of his mighty men is reddened [LXX: from men], army men are clothed in crimson [LXX: playing with fire]. With fire of steel [Syr.: With lamps of fire] are the chariots [LXX: The reins of their chariots] in the day of his making ready; and as for the cypresses [LXX, Syr.: horsemen], they are made to quiver [ESV: the cypress spears are brandished; Tg. Jon.: the leaders of their armies are wrapped in dyed stuff; see Zech. 11:2].[29] 2:5 (Eng., 2:4) In the streets the chariots go madly [cf., Syr.], they rush to and fro in the squares. Their appearance is like that of torches, like lightning flashes they run about. 2:6 (Eng., 2:5) He remembers [NET: orders; DCH: boasts] his nobles [LXX: And their nobles will remember], they stumble in their going [cf., Nah. 3:3; LXX: flee for days and grow weak in their journey]. They hasten to the city wall [see BHS apparatus], the protecting structure [or, mantelet] is prepared. 2:7 (Eng., 2:6) As for the gates of the rivers [Syr.: the gates of Judah], they are opened [Tg. Jon.: The bridges of the rivers are cut off]; and as for the palace, it melts [Tg. Jon.: and the king in his palace trembles]. 2:8 (Eng., 2:7) And it is fixed/determined [Tg. Jon.: And the queen sits in a litter], and she is uncovered [or, taken into exile; LXX: And the foundation is revealed], she is taken up. And her maids moan [LXX: are led away; Tg. Jon.: led away, going after her moaning] like a sound of doves, beating on their hearts [LXX: uttering in their hearts]. 2:9 (Eng., 2:8) And Nineveh has been like a pool of water [cf., 8HevXII gr] throughout her days [cf., 4QXII^g, LXX], but they are

---

28. "Jacob" and "Israel" are used synonymously here for stylistic purposes. This use of "Israel" is not to be thought of in distinction from "Judah." It is simply a way to refer to the people of God (cf., Ps. 14:7).
29. The normal word for "brandish" or "wield" would be גוף. See Gregory Cook, "Nahum's Shaking Cypresses," *BBR* 26 (2016): 1–6.

fleeing.[30] *"Stand still, stand still" [LXX: they did not stand], but there is no one turning back [LXX: no one paying attention]. 2:10 (Eng., 2:9) Plunder silver, plunder gold,*[31] *and there is no end to what is in store [LXX: her adornment], wealth from every vessel of desire [LXX: he has been made heavy beyond all her desirable vessels]. 2:11 (Eng., 2:10) Emptiness and desolation and devastation*[32] *and a melting heart [LXX: Shaking and violent shaking and trembling and breaking of heart (cf., Syr.)] and tottering of knees and writhing in all loins; and the faces of all of them, they gather beauty [Evv.: grow pale; LXX: like burn marks of a clay pot (cf., Syr., Tg. Jon.)].*

2:12 (Eng., 2:11) Where is the habitation of the lions [Tg. Jon.: kings] and the feeding place of the young lions [Tg. Jon.: rulers] where the lion went to bring food [LXX, Syr.: to enter; or, lion(ness)] to the cub, and there was no one causing them to tremble with fear? 2:13 (Eng., 2:12) The lion tore prey for what sufficed for its cubs and strangled for its lionesses and filled its holes with prey and its habitats with torn flesh [Tg. Jon.: their fortresses with plunder]. 2:14 (Eng., 2:13) "Look, I am against you," the prophetic utterance of the LORD of hosts, "and I will cause her chariots [LXX, 4QpNah: your abundance] to burn with smoke [Tg. Jon.: fire], and your young lions a sword will devour, and I will cut off from the land your prey [Tg. Jon.: merchandise], and never again will the voice of your messengers [LXX, Syr.: works] be heard."

From this point forward the prophet envisions the siege of the city of Nineveh and its subsequent fall in 612 BC.[33] It is possible to understand Nahum 2:4–5 (Eng., 2:3–4) to be a description of the Assyrian army, but most interpreters agree that it is much more likely to be a depiction of the advancing Babylonians (cf., Ezek. 23:14). There is some question about whether the shields of the mighty men are reddened from the blood stains of conquered peoples (cf., Gen. 49:11b; Isa. 63:1–6) or from red dye (or from the glow of copper or brass in

---

30. Some English versions understand "they" to be the waters (e.g., ESV). Others interpret "they" to be the people of Nineveh (e.g., NET).
31. The NET understands Nahum 2:10a (Eng., 2:9a) to be the voice of the conquerors.
32. *Targum Jonathan* describes the city of Nineveh here as plundered and opened to the enemy.
33. See James B. Pritchard, ed., *Ancient Near Eastern Texts Relating to the Old Testament*, 3d ed. (Princeton, NJ: Princeton University Press, 1969), 304–305.

the sun). Some commentators consider blood stains to be premature prior to the battle itself and prefer to see the reddened shields as an intentional feature of the armor parallel to "clothed in crimson" (cf., Isa. 1:18), the idea being to strike fear in the heart of the enemy. But this is by no means a necessary reading. Blood stains could be on the shields from previously conquered peoples, and the parallelism with "clothed in crimson" need not be synonymous parallelism.

The Babylonian chariots are said to be "with fire of steel" when the army prepares for battle. The difficulty of this phrase is due to the uncertainty surrounding the Hebrew word פְּלָדוֹת (see Arabic cognate). Nevertheless, it is fairly clear that the phrase describes the fiery appearance of the chariots and bears some relationship to Nahum 2:5b (Eng., 2:4b), which says that their appearance is "like that of torches" (כַּלַּפִּידִם). The cypress trees made to quiver in Nahum 2:4b (Eng., 2:3b) are usually understood to be cypress spear shafts in motion, although it is not out of the realm of possibility that the cypresses are figurative for enemy leaders who quiver or reel because of the Babylonians (see, e.g., Zech. 11:1–3; 12:2). Some consider the presence of Babylonian chariots in the streets and squares of Nineveh in Nahum 2:5 (Eng., 2:4) to be too early in the sequence, assuming that the Babylonians have yet to breach the city wall at this point.[34] Therefore, they interpret the language of this verse to be a portrayal of what happens outside of the city. But there is no reason to think that the text provides a precise sequence of events. It seems to be of much greater importance to the prophet to give a sense of immediacy, as if to say, "The Babylonians are already among you, flashing like lightning!"

Yet another decision must be made about the subject of the verb ("he remembers") at the beginning of Nahum 2:6 (Eng., 2:5). Is this person (presumably the king) who remembers his nobles from the Assyrians or from the Babylonians? The LXX seems to prefer the former option, referring to the flight of the nobles. According to this reading, the Assyrians stumble to hasten to the city wall to establish a protective structure for themselves against the Babylonian invasion. On the other hand, the reader might expect here a continuation of the Babylonian advancement from Nahum 2:4–5 (Eng., 2:3–4), in which case their nobles stumble over the bodies of the slain (cf., Nah. 3:3b) to overtake the city wall of Nineveh, setting up a protective structure against the city's defenses.[35]

---

34. E.g., J. Smith, *Nahum*, 330.
35. See C. E. Armerding, *Nahum*, EBC 7 (Grand Rapids: Zondervan, 1985), 475.

Nahum 2:7 (Eng., 2:6) envisions the opening of the gates of the rivers (cf., Nah. 3:13). The text does not say who does the opening, nor does it go into the logistics of what this would involve. What it does indicate is the effect of the opening: the melting of the palace. There are at least two possibilities for the meaning of this expression. One possibility is that the palace melts in the sense that the structure of the palace erodes due to the flood waters. The other possibility is the one taken by *Targum Jonathan*. The palace stands by metonymy for the king, and his melting is figurative for his helplessness against the terror of the Babylonians and the destruction of the city (cf., Exod. 15:15; Josh. 2:9, 24; Nah. 2:11 [Eng., 2:10]). Nineveh's location along the Tigris River was both an advantage and a potential weakness due to its vulnerability to this kind of disaster.

According to *Targum Jonathan*, Nahum 2:8 (Eng., 2:7) is about the exile of the Assyrian queen and her maids, but given the lack of any clear reference to the queen, it is perhaps best to understand the subject of the third feminine singular verbs (and the referent of the third feminine singular pronominal suffix) to be the city (a feminine noun) of Nineveh. It is the city of Nineveh that will be uncovered and taken away. Her maids have been variously understood to be associated cities or the inhabitants of Nineveh, but associated cities are usually called "daughters" (e.g., Judg. 1:27), and Hebrew writers typically do not call inhabitants maids. Therefore, it seems more likely that the maids here are the women of Nineveh who mourn the defeat of their city (cf., Jer. 9:16–21 [Eng., 9:17–22]), making a sound like that of doves and beating their breasts (cf., Isa. 32:12). This is the opposite of the way the women would respond to victory over their enemies, in which case they would sing (rather than moan), beat tambourines (rather than their hearts) and dance (see Exod. 15:20–21; Judg. 11:34; 1 Sam. 18:6–7; Jer. 31:4).

The comparison of Nineveh to a pool of water in Nahum 2:9 (Eng., 2:8) is appropriate not only because of the city's location along the Tigris River but also because the name "Nineveh" means "fish-city."[36] Nineveh has always been this way, but now things are changing. According to Nahum 2:7 (Eng., 2:6), the gates of the rivers have been opened, and so the waters flee. But the flood waters are also symbolic of the flight of the people. Thus, the repeated command to stand still goes unheeded. It is not clear who is giving the command (the prophet, the Assyrian officials, the Babylonians), but such information is apparently not important for interpretation. It is often suggested, however, that the prophet is the one rhetorically giving the command to the Babylonians

---

36. See Christensen, *Nahum*, 293.

in Nahum 2:10 (Eng., 2:9) to plunder the silver and the gold of the city of Nineveh. This could also be the voice of the Babylonian officials. There was no end to the treasure found there, wealth made up of every kind of desirable object.

The text of Nahum 2:11 (Eng., 2:10) opens with a play on similar sounding words for rhetorical effect: בוקה ומבוקה ומבלקה ("Emptiness and desolation and devastation") (cf., Isa. 24:1; Nah. 2:3b [Eng., 2:2b]). This is the fate of the city of Nineveh. The reference to melting hearts uses different terminology in the Hebrew text but is similar to the idea expressed in Nahum 2:7 (Eng., 2:6). Tottering knees and writhing loins are well illustrated by Belshazzar's response to the writing on the wall in Daniel 5:6. Versions are divided on how to render the last clause of Nahum 2:11 (Eng., 2:10) (cf., Joel 2:6). Ancient versions generally understand פָּארוּר to be פָּרוּר ("pot"). That is, their faces gather (and thus display) the blackness of a pot. Modern versions tend to favor the sense "beauty" for this same word. Their faces gather (and thus remove) beauty. In other words, they grow pale. 4Q177 quotes Nahum 2:11 (Eng., 2:10) in an eschatological context, apparently under the influence of the effect of Nahum 1:2–8 on the final form of the text and perhaps also due to the larger context of the Twelve (Hos. 3:4–5).

The final sub-unit of chapter 2 features an analogy between the Assyrian kings and lions (Nah. 2:12–14 [Eng., 2:11–13]). This is not an invitation to conduct a separate study of lions either to embellish or to evaluate what the author does here. The task of the interpreter is to discern the specific way in which the writer draws the comparison. The initial question ("Where is the habitation of the lions?") can be read, "Where is the city (i.e., Nineveh) of the Assyrian kings?" This is the way *Targum Jonathan* interprets the text. The lion is a common metaphor for kings in biblical usage due to its stature in the animal kingdom (e.g., Gen. 49:9; Num. 24:9; Isa. 5:29; Ezek. 19:1–9). It is less clear what the young lions, the cubs, and the female lions represent in this passage. *Targum Jonathan* understands them to be the rulers, the sons, and the wives, although it is possible to use the Hebrew terms somewhat interchangeably in this figurative sense. The assumed answer to the rhetorical question in Nahum 2:12 (Eng., 2:11) is that the habitation is nowhere to be found according to what the prophet envisions in Nahum 2:4–11 (Eng., 2:3–10). The once powerful empire that did as it pleased without consequence and without fear is now no more. Nahum 2:13 (Eng., 2:14) depicts the violent manner in which the Assyrians plundered those they conquered in order to satisfy their appetites (see *Tg. Jon.*; Nah. 3:1; cf. 4QpNah). The LORD speaks in Nahum 2:14 (Eng., 2:13) in order to point out that he is against Nineveh (cf., Nah.

3:5). His discourse is a mix of the literal and the metaphorical. Thus, he speaks of burning actual chariots, but then he says the literal sword will devour the figurative young lions (cf., Nah. 3:15). He will cut off "prey" (i.e., plunder; cf., *Tg. Jon.*) from the land of Assyria, and the voice of Assyria's messengers (e.g., 2 Kgs. 18:17; see GKC §91e, 1) will never again be heard.

NAHUM 3

3:1 Woe, city of bloodshed. All of it is lying. It is full of plunder snatched away [LXX, Syr.: unrighteousness]. Prey does not depart [LXX, Syr.: will not be touched; Tg. Jon.: Killing does not cease]. 3:2 A sound of a whip and a sound of a wheel's shaking and a horse dashing [Syr.: snorting; Tg. Jon.: galloping] and a chariot skipping. 3:3 A horseman brings up, and a sword's flame and a spear's lightning and an abundance of slain and heaviness of corpses, and there is no end to the bodies [LXX: her nations], they stumble over their bodies [cf., 4QpNah].

3:4 "Because of an abundance of harlotries of a harlot [cf., LXX], good of grace, a lady of sorceries who sells [cf., 4QpNah: הממכרת*] nations by her harlotries and families by her sorceries, 3:5 look, I am against you," the prophetic utterance of the LORD of hosts, "and I will remove your skirts [LXX: the things after you; Tg. Jon.: the shame of your sin] over your face, and I will show nations your bareness [LXX, Tg. Jon.: shame] and kingdoms your disgrace. 3:6 And I will throw upon you detestable things [LXX: abomination according to your uncleannesses], and I will treat you as a fool and make you as a spectacle [4QpNah:* כאורה *(repulsive)]. 3:7 And so, everyone who sees you will flee [4QpNah:* ידודו*] from you and say [4QpNah:* ואמרו*], 'Nineveh has been devastated [LXX: Wretched Nineveh]. Who will mourn for her?' From where will I seek comforters for you [LXX: for her]."*

3:8 Are you better than [LXX: Prepare a portion, adapt a string, prepare a portion] No-Amon [or, Thebes; LXX: Amon; Syr.: Javan of Amon; Tg. Jon.: the great Alexandria (cf., Vulg.)] who lived by the banks of the Nile with water around her, whose rampart [LXX: power] was the sea [cf., MurXII], whose city wall was from the sea [Vulg.: water; cf., LXX, Syr.]? 3:9 Cush [or, Ethiopia / Sudan], her might [or, she was mighty; cf., LXX; 4QpNah: עוצמה*; Tg. Jon.: her troops], and Egypt, and there was no end. Put and Lybians, they were your help [LXX: her helpers (cf., Syr.); see GKC §119i]. 3:10 Yet she as an exile [4QpNah:* בגולה*] went into captivity. Even her infants would be dashed to pieces at the head of every street.*

And for [LXX adds: all] her honored ones they cast [4QpNah: יורו] a lot
[LXX: lots], and all her nobles would be bound with fetters.

3:11 Also you, you will be drunk, you will hide [cf., Syr.; see also GKC
§145p]. Also you, you will seek refuge from an enemy. 3:12 All your fortifications are fig trees [Syr.: like fig trees; LXX adds: having sentries]
with first-ripe fruit. If they are shaken [Syr.: boil], they will fall upon
an eater's mouth [Tg. Jon.: and raisins that are fit to eat will be left in
them]. 3:13 Look, your people are women [LXX, Syr.: like women; Tg.
Jon.: weak like women] in your midst. To your enemies the gates of your
land are opened wide. Fire devours your bars. 3:14 Water for a siege
draw for yourself. Strengthen your fortifications. Go into the mud and
trample the mortar. Take hold of a brick mold [LXX: Make stronger than
brick; Syr.: Cause your counsel to prevail]. 3:15 There fire will consume
you. A sword will cut you off. It will devour you like the licking locusts.
Make yourself [GKC §110k] dense like the licking locusts, make yourself
dense like the abundant locusts [cf., LXX].³⁷ 3:16 You have increased
your merchants more than the stars of the sky [8HevXII gr: as the stars
of the sky]. Licking locusts strip off and fly [LXX: rushed and spread].
3:17 Your courtiers [or, guards; see HALOT; cf., BDB: consecrated ones
(see Syr.); see also LXX: commingled one; Tg. Jon.: plates] are like the
abundant locusts, and your official scribes [cf., שטר] are like a swarm of
locusts that camp in the walls on a cold day. The sun rises and it flees,
and its place is not known. Where are they [or, and its place where they
are is not known; LXX: Woe to them]?

3:18 Your shepherds slumber [Tg. Jon.: Your mighty men (i.e., warriors) are defeated], O king of Assyria [Syr.: The friends of the king of
Assyria slumber]. What's more, your nobles [Syr.: those near you (2fs)]
settle down [LXX: The king of Assyria has put your mighty men to sleep;
Tg. Jon.: The people of your armies have gone into exile]. Your people
are scattered [Syr.: They are scattered with you] upon the mountains,
and there is no one gathering them. 3:19 There is no lessening [LXX:
healing] to your breaking [Syr.: There is no one who suffers over your
(2fs) breaking; cf., Tg. Jon.], your wound is sick [or, severe]. All those
who hear the report about you clap their hands over you [Tg. Jon. adds:
they rejoice]. For over whom has not your evil [Tg. Jon.: the striking of
your evil] passed continually?

---

37. *Targum Jonathan* says the armies of the peoples that are as numerous as
the locusts will assemble against the city.

Chapter 3 begins with a woe oracle complete with introduction, accusation, and announcement of judgment that now extends through verse 7 (cf., Isa. 10:5–11). Nineveh is the violent city of bloodshed in its dealings with other nations (Nah. 3:1; cf., Ezek. 22:2; 24:6; Hab. 2:12).[38] The city is completely deceptive in its international relationships, full of plunder seized therefrom. The kind of "prey" described so vividly in Nahum 2:13–14 (Eng., 2:12–13) does not depart from Nineveh in the sense that the city always has its fill of it. Verses 2 and 3 of chapter 3 likely do not describe the Ninevites in a state of frenzy. Rather, they envision the invading Babylonian army (cf., Nah. 2:5 [Eng., 2:4])—the sound of whips and shaking wheels, dashing horses, and skipping chariots (cf., Judg. 5:22; Jer. 47:3). The beginning of verse 3 indicates that the horsemen bring up something. A comparison with Jeremiah 51:27 suggests that they bring up horses. It is not immediately clear, however, what the syntactical relationship of this is to what follows: "and a sword's flame and a spear's lightning and an abundance of slain and heaviness of corpses" (cf., Hab. 3:11). These are likely separate flashes of images rather than additional items brought up by the horsemen, although this is not to exclude the possibility or the reality that horsemen were in fact armed with swords and responsible for many slain. It is only to say that they apparently do not form part of the preceding clause unless the presence of the supplied object for the participle is so felt that it is possible to coordinate other objects. There is no end to the corpses according to Nah. 3:3b, resulting in the Babylonians stumbling over the slain Assyrians as they advance (cf., Nahum 2:6 [Eng., 2:5]).

Nahum 3:4 depicts Nineveh's violence and deception (Nah. 3:1) in terms of prostitution and sorcery.[39] Again, the author must be allowed to use this metaphor as he sees fit. If the reader presses the analogy too far, then the details will become confusing. Nineveh is a harlot and a sorceress first of all in the sense that the city is very enticing ("good of grace") to other nations. Secondly, she "sells" those very nations by means of her acts of harlotry and sorcery. Prostitutes and sorcerers in the Bible deceive their customers with promises of good things, but those who follow them find that their path only leads to destruction (e.g., Jer. 27:9–10; Prov. 7). Commentators have historically struggled with the root "sell" (מכר) because they picture a prostitute selling herself rather

---

38. Note the eschatological interpretation of Nahum 3:1 in 4QpNah. Again, this may in part be due to the influence of Nahum 1:2–8 on the final form of the book.

39. Prostitution or sexual promiscuity is a familiar biblical metaphor for religious infidelity, but that does not seem to be directly in view here.

than selling others. This has led to a wide variety of textual and philological explanations for why "sells" should not be the translation in this context.[40] But this is a fundamentally backwards way of explaining the meaning of words. Words are not defined by the interpreter's ability to imagine or to reconstruct events and viewpoints. Words are defined by usage, and the reality is that מכר is a very well-attested root in biblical Hebrew that means "sell" (BDB, 569). Thus, the reader is left to ponder in what sense a prostitute sells her clients by means of her actions. The answer lies in the violent destruction that results from the deception (cf., Est. 7:4). Nations who are drawn by the seductive city of Nineveh find that they are metaphorically "sold" to their doom (cf., Rev. 18:23).[41]

The LORD of heavenly and earthly armies announces in Nahum 3:5 that he is against Nineveh (cf., Nah. 2:14 [Eng., 2:13]). The removal of the skirts over the face and the exposure of bareness might seem at first glance to be a strange judgment for a prostitute whose very livelihood depends upon sexual indiscretion (cf., Jer. 13:22; Ezek. 16:37; 23:10, 29; Hab. 2:15–16). But the judgment here is not a shameful act committed in private. It is a public disgrace.[42] The justice is thus poetic, and the punishment for the "detestable" (unclean and perhaps idolatrous) acts of the harlot city will be cast upon it (Nah. 3:6). The LORD will treat Nineveh as the senseless and disgraceful city that it is, and it will be a "spectacle" (Rashi: "dung"; cf., 4QpNah) to all. Therefore, all who see Nineveh will "flee" (from נדד) in horror at the sight of its demise (cf., Pss. 31:12; 64:9 [Eng., 31:11; 64:8]) and ask who will "mourn" (from נוד) for the devastated city (Nah. 3:7). Nahum 3:19 anticipates that everyone will celebrate this occasion (cf., Hab. 2:6). In addition, for rhetorical effect the LORD asks from where he will seek comforters for Nineveh (cf., Lam. 1:2), assuming that such comforters are nowhere to be found.

Christensen has noted well that the sense of the question in Nahum 3:8 is, "Will it go better with you? Shall you have a better fate?"[43] The downfall of Thebes took place at the hands of the Assyrians in circa 664 BC even though the city had the advantages of location along the Nile (cf., Nah. 2:7, 9 [Eng., 2:6, 8]). The Nile is called a "sea" in translation because this is a standard gloss for ים, but the Hebrew word does not always correspond strictly to the bodies of water designated by the

---

40. See Christensen, *Nahum*, 339–43.
41. Some think that the metaphor is that of selling into slavery, but the consequence appears to be even more severe than that.
42. 4QpNah interprets this to be the exposure of evil deeds in the last days.
43. Christensen, *Nahum*, 354. See also Ezek. 30:14–15; 4Q385c.

English words "sea" or "ocean" (e.g., Isa. 19:5). For instance, the Sea of Galilee and the Dead Sea are really lakes in English terminology, while the Mediterranean Sea is in fact a sea. Cush and Egypt were once strong just like Nineveh and Assyria. There was no end to their might (Nah. 3:9). Thebes even had Put and the Libyans in North Africa as allies to help them. Nevertheless, the city went into captivity as an exile (Nah. 3:10; see Isa. 18; 19:4; 20). The treatment of Thebes by the Assyrians was merciless. Even the infants were dashed to pieces at the head of every street (cf., 2 Kgs. 8:12; Isa. 13:16; Hos. 10:14; 14:1 [Eng., 13:16]; Ps. 137:9). As the Assyrians have done, so will it be done to them (cf., Obad. 15). They cast lots for the honored ones of Thebes and put their nobles in fetters (cf., Isa. 45:14; Joel 4:3 [Eng., 3:3]; Obad. 11; Ps. 149:8), treating their prominent ones as slaves. 4QpNah wrongly applies this to Manasseh but rightly reads the text under the influence of Nahum 1:2–8 as an illustration of things to come in the last days.

The repetition of "Also you" (אַתְּ גַּם) in Nahum 3:11 highlights the fact that the city of Nineveh will face a fate similar to that of Thebes. Nineveh will be drunk in the sense that the city will drink from the cup of God's judgment (cf., Jer. 25:15–26; Hab. 2:16).[44] Interpreters normally relate the *niphal* of עלם ("be concealed") to the drunkenness in the sense of being obscured, overcome by intoxication, or becoming unconscious (see *HALOT* 1:834–35; *DCH* VI: 427). It is also possible that the verb is simply intransitive ("hide") and is to be related to what follows (cf., the *niphal* of חבא and סתר). That is, when the cup of judgment comes, Nineveh will attempt to hide and to seek refuge from the enemy, but there will be no such refuge (cf., Nah. 1:7). All the city's fortifications are ripe for the picking so to speak (Nah. 3:12). They are like fig trees that only need to be shaken to cause their fruit to fall to the eater.[45] The prophet points out that the people of Nineveh are women (Nah. 3:13). *Targum Jonathan* takes this to mean that they are "weak

---

44. See Calvin, *Nahum*, 494.
45. Commentators are quick to point out that Sennacherib planted fig trees along the main streets in order to beautify the city, suggesting that the prophet might be implying some irony in the city's fate (e.g., Christensen, *Nahum*, 364). But there is no way to verify the certainty of this intention. Perhaps such irony would have been expressed differently as in the description of actual fig trees withering. As it stands, an allusion to literal fig trees would seem to detract from the purpose of the metaphor, which is to highlight the weakness of the city's fortifications. It is not out of the question, however, that what was intended to be a symbol of strength has now become a way to describe such weakness.

like women."[46] The gates of the land are opened (cf., Nah. 2:7 [Eng., 2:6]), and fire consumes the bars of the city's gates.

The imperatives in Nahum 3:14 are commands to do things in vain.[47] A city would normally need to draw water for a variety of reasons in preparation for a siege, but in this case the preparation will ultimately do the city little good. A city would normally want to strengthen its fortifications by making bricks for repairs, but when such fortifications are like fig trees (Nah. 3:12), it seems not to be worth the effort. It is there that fire will consume Nineveh (Nah. 3:15a; cf., Nah. 3:13b). The sword will cut off the city the way that locusts consume land (cf., Joel 1:4; Nah. 2:14 [Eng., 2:13]). *Targum Jonathan* interprets the command to be dense like locusts in Nahum 3:15b to be a description of the invading armies (cf., Num. 20:20), which is understandable given the end of Nahum 3:15a. But it is also possible to read Nahum 3:15b with Nahum 3:16–17. That is, Nineveh is commanded to make itself dense by the increase of its merchants, courtiers, and official scribes. All of this will also prove to be in vain. Even though Nineveh increases its merchants more than the stars of the sky, those very merchants will strip/raid and fly away like locusts.[48] This is either a reference to the shedding of the outer skin of locusts before flight, or it is a reference to the way locusts plunder the land before they fly away. It is not immediately clear what the point of including the shedding of the skin in the metaphor would be if the former option were intended. Nahum 3:17 appropriately uses two Assyrian loanwords for Nineveh's "courtiers" and "official scribes" who are as abundant as locusts camping in the walls on a cold day. But when the sun rises (i.e., when it gets hot), they flee and are nowhere to be found.

Nahum 3:18a addresses the king of Assyria and indicates that his shepherds slumber and that his nobles settle down (cf., Isa. 5:27). In other words, they will sleep the sleep of death and remain inactive (cf., Jer. 51:39, 57; Pss. 13:4; 76:6 [Eng., 13:3; 76:5]). It is a familiar metaphor in the Prophets to call kings shepherds (e.g., Jer. 23:1–4; Ezek. 34), but it is somewhat problematic when a single king is said to have a plurality of shepherds. Perhaps in this case the shepherds are officials below the king and parallel to the nobles. *Targum Jonathan* calls

---

46. Nogalski understands this literally to mean that actual women are open to rape by the enemy soldiers (*Literary Precursors to the Book of the Twelve*, BZAW 217 [Berlin: de Gruyter, 1993], 119–20).

47. See Bullinger, *Figures of Speech*, 515.

48. See Rashi and Redak (*Mikraoth Gedoloth: The Twelve Prophets*, vol. 2, 255). See also Keil, *Minor Prophets*, 377.

them mighty men or warriors. But these suggestions assume that the address is to a particular king of Assyria. It is possible that the address is to the office of the king (i.e., the kingship). As a result of the demise of the leadership, the people will be scattered on the mountains as in the story of Ahab (Nah. 3:18b; cf., Num. 27:17; 1 Kgs. 22:17; Isa. 13:14; Ezek. 34:5; Zech. 10:2).

According to the Masoretic vocalization, the address to the king of Assyria continues in Nahum 3:19 due to the use of second masculine singular pronominal suffixes. Second feminine singular pronominal suffixes would be required to address the city of Nineveh (see Syr.). Of course, the king represents the nation of Assyria in general and the capital city of Nineveh in particular. There is no relief for the fracture of the kingship and all that it symbolizes. The wound is too severe. Not only is there no one to comfort or to mourn Nineveh (Nah. 3:7), but also everyone who hears about the downfall of the city will rejoice (cf., Hab. 3:2; Zeph. 2:15; Ps. 47:2 [Eng., 47:1]). This is because there is no one who has not been a constant victim of Nineveh's evil (cf., Hab. 1:17). As mentioned in the commentary on Jonah 4:11, both the book of Jonah and the book of Nahum end with rhetorical questions about Nineveh, but the view of Nineveh at the end of Jonah is decidedly more positive than the one at the end of Nahum. This is the dual role of Nineveh in the Book of the Twelve. In the book of Jonah, Nineveh is "the great city" of the Gentiles that represents those from among the nations who believe (Jon. 1:16; 3:5; cf., Amos 9:12). In the book of Nahum, Nineveh represents the wicked from among the nations who will face judgment in the last day (Nah. 1:2–8). The two books thus employ Nineveh to illustrate the two parts of the program of the Twelve (Hos. 3:4–5).

A REMINDER ABOUT TEACHING/PREACHING NAHUM

It is important to remember that the book of Nahum is not just a vision of the historical siege of Nineveh.[49] Failure to keep this in mind will result in futile efforts to "update" the book in order to make it relevant as Christian Scripture today. Such efforts typically look like an

---

49. "But if Nahum's prophecy was thus fulfilled in the destruction of Nineveh, even to the disappearance of every trace of its existence, we must not restrict it to this one historical event, but must bear in mind that, as the prophet simply saw in Nineveh the representative for the time of the power of the world in its hostility to God, so the destruction predicted to Nineveh applied to all the kingdoms of the world which have risen up against God since the destruction of Asshur, and which will still continue to do so to the end of the world" (Keil, *Minor Prophets*, 383).

abstraction of the book into a set of widely applicable principles. But this approach not only misses the specifics of the book's own presentation, but also it fails to reckon with the influence of Nahum 1:2–8 and the wider context of the Book of the Twelve. The composition of the book of Nahum itself and the work of the composer of the Twelve have already done the job of giving Nahum's prophecy its ongoing significance by tying it into the unifying program of the Twelve as a whole. All the reader needs to do is interpret this well. Thus, the way in which the siege of Nineveh now illustrates God's future and final judgment (Nah. 1:2–8) is immediately relevant for today's reader. The same is true for the way in which the Micah-Nahum seam shows the manifestation of God's character (Exod. 34:6–7) in his eschatological judgment of the wicked and his ultimate deliverance of the righteous. Likewise, both Nahum 1:2–8 and Habakkuk 3:3–15 have rendered the historical prophecies between them as lasting images of things that God still has in store both for his own people and for those who reject him.

HABAKKUK 1

1:1 The oracle [Syr.: vision; Tg. Jon.: prophecy] that Habakkuk the prophet saw [Tg. Jon.: prophesied].

1:2 How long, O LORD, must I cry for help [Tg. Jon.: pray] without you hearing [see GKC §106h; Tg. Jon.: Is it not revealed before you]? I cry out to you, "Violence!" But you do not deliver [Tg. Jon.: Is there no ability before you to redeem?]. 1:3 Why do you cause me to see trouble? And why upon mischief do you [Syr., Tg. Jon.: I] look? Both destruction and violence are before me, (and there is contention), and strife is what one must bear [Syr.: and the judge receives a bribe].[1] 1:4 Therefore, instruction grows numb [LXX: law is scattered], and justice does not ever go forth [LXX: and judgment is not brought to an end]. For wicked people surround [LXX: oppress] the righteous. Therefore, justice [1QpHab: המשפט] goes forth perverted [Tg. Jon.: reliable judgment does not go forth].

The superscription in Habakkuk 1:1 designates the content of the entire book as the oracle that the prophet Habakkuk saw (cf., Isa. 13:1; Nah. 1:1; Hab. 2:2). There is very little information about this prophet outside of the book that bears his name. Neither the Hebrew root of his name ("embrace") nor the Akkadian meaning of his name (a garden plant) seems to play any role in the book. The pseudepigraphal work

---

1. LXX: "Why do you show me troubles and pains to look upon misery and ungodliness? And before me there is judgment, and the judge receives."

Lives of the Prophets chapter 12 says that Habakkuk was from the tribe of Simeon, from the countryside of Beth-Zechariah (cf., 1 Macc. 6:32) and alludes to a story in the apocryphal addition to the Greek translation tradition of the book of Daniel known as *Bel and the Dragon*. According to this story, Habakkuk brought food to Daniel in the den of lions at the prompting of an angel (cf., Dan. 6). The superscription to the Old Greek of this story says that Habakkuk was from the tribe of Levi.

The book itself, however, features a personal and somewhat autobiographical component not unlike what the reader finds in the so-called confessions of Jeremiah.[2] It opens with the prophet's complaint and the LORD's response. It concludes with the prophet's prayer. The prophecy of the book comes within the context of this exchange. The book begins like a lament or petition psalm with an opening cry from the prophet that questions how long and why the present problem must persist without any apparent response from the LORD (Hab. 1:2–4; cf., Hab. 1:13; 2:6b; Pss. 6:4; 13:2–4; 22:2; 62:4 [Eng., 6:3; 13:1–3; 22:1; 62:3]). But these introductory verses do not feature a request or motivation for the LORD to act, nor do they conclude with any expression of trust or confidence as petition psalms typically do. It is possible, however, that the petition is implied in the complaint. It is also possible that the expression of trust at the end of the book (Hab. 3:17–19) now functions to complete the sequence. Commentators generally agree that Habakkuk prophesied in the seventh century BC, but a more precise date depends upon how the reader identifies the foreign enemy in the book (see comments on Habakkuk 1:6).

The prophet feels like his cry for help is in vain (Hab. 1:2). It is as if the LORD does not hear. When he cries out, "Violence," there is no deliverance from the LORD (cf., Isa. 46:7; Ps. 55:10 [Eng., 55:9]; Job 19:7). The prophet wonders why he is forced to see the present situation without being able to do anything about it (Hab. 1:3). He also wonders why the LORD stands by and watches without taking action (cf., Hab. 1:13). There are three word pairs in Habakkuk 1:3 that describe the problem: "trouble" and "mischief" (cf., Num. 23:21; Isa. 10:1; 59:4; Hab. 1:13; 3:7; Pss. 7:15 [Eng., 7:14]; 10:7; 55:11; 90:10 [Eng., 55:10; 90:9]; Job 4:8; 5:6; 15:35), "destruction and violence" (cf., Gen. 6:11; Isa. 60:18; Jer. 6:7; 20:8; Ezek. 45:9; Amos 3:10; Hab. 1:9; 2:8, 17), and "contention" and "strife" (see Jer. 15:10; Ps. 55:10 [Eng., 55:9]). With regard to the last of these three, the more common word רִיב

---

2. Gerhard von Rad, *Old Testament Theology*, vol. 1, *The Theology of Israel's Historical Traditions*, trans. D. M. G. Stalker (Louisville: Westminster John Knox, 1962), 392.

("contention") seems to be added parenthetically to clarify the sense of the less common word מָדוֹן ("strife"), which is largely limited to occurrences in the book of Proverbs (see *BHS* apparatus). The inference is then drawn in Habakkuk 1:4 that "instruction" grows numb or ineffective (see Gen. 45:26; Ps. 77:3 [Eng., 77:2]). "Justice" never goes forth (cf., Hab. 1:12). This is because wicked people surround the righteous (cf., Hab. 1:13; 2:4; Ps. 22:13 [Eng., 22:12]), so that the only way that "justice" goes forth is in a perverted manner (cf., Hab. 1:7). The earliest commentary on this text in *Pesher Habakkuk* from Qumran (1QpHab) identifies the wicked as the Wicked Priest and the righteous as the Teacher of Righteousness.[3] More recent interpreters, however, are divided as to whether the problematic situation that the prophet describes arises from within Judah or from outside.[4] Those who contend for a foreign enemy here are further divided on whether that enemy is Assyria or Babylon (see Hab. 1:6). There is good evidence for both views.

On the one hand, the terminology in Habakkuk 1:3 is elsewhere descriptive of people living in the land of the covenant, as can be seen in the texts referenced above. Furthermore, the reader might expect terms like "instruction" (*torah*) and "justice" (*mishpat*) to be references to the Mosaic law for which Israel was responsible (Hab. 1:4a; cf., Deut. 4:44–45). According to this reading, the raising up of a foreign enemy (Hab. 1:6) is discipline in response to the failure of Judah as outlined in Habakkuk 1:2–4. On the other hand, the same words in Habakkuk 1:4a could refer to civil law and custom. Most of the terminology that describes the wicked and their activity in Habakkuk 1:2–4 is applied

---

3. See James C. VanderKam and Peter W. Flint, *The Meaning of the Dead Sea Scrolls: Their Significance for Understanding the Bible, Judaism, Jesus, and Christianity* (New York: HarperCollins, 2002), 282–86.
4. For the former see John Calvin, *Commentaries on the Minor Prophets*, vol. 4, *Habakkuk, Zephaniah, Haggai*, trans. John Owen, Calvin's Commentaries XV (reprint, Grand Rapids: Baker, 2005), 15–16; C. F. Keil, *The Minor Prophets*, trans. James Martin, Keil & Delitzsch Commentary on the Old Testament 10 (Edinburgh: T. & T. Clark, 1866–91; reprint, Peabody, MA: Hendrickson, 2001), 391; Ralph L. Smith, *Micah–Malachi*, WBC 32 (Nashville: Thomas Nelson, 1984), 99; J. J. M. Roberts, *Nahum, Habakkuk, and Zephaniah*, OTL (Louisville: Westminster John Knox, 1991), 81. For the latter see *Mikraoth Gedoloth: Twelve Prophets*, vol. 2, trans. A. J. Rosenberg (New York: Judaica, 1996), 257–58; Georg H. A. von Ewald, *Commentary on the Prophets of the Old Testament*, vol. 3, *Nahum, Zephaniah, Habakkuk, Zechariah 12–14, Jeremiah*, trans. John Frederick Smith (London: Williams and Norgate, 1878), 33.

to the foreign enemy elsewhere in the book (Hab. 1:7, 9, 13; 2:8, 17). According to this reading, the raising up of a foreign enemy is still discipline for Habakkuk's people (Hab. 1:12), but the description of that enemy already begins in Habakkuk 1:2–4. Of course, it is also possible that the idea is to say that both Judah and the foreign enemy exhibit the kind of behavior found in Habakkuk 1:2–4. As Judah has done, so it is done to Judah. In the end, a firm decision on this matter makes very little difference in how the reader understands the book as a whole. The remainder of the book focuses on how the historical enemy prefigures the way in which God will judge the wicked and deliver the righteous in the last days (cf., Nahum).[5] Childs has rightly noted, "The historical perspective from which the prophet now views world events is thoroughly eschatological."[6]

1:5 See among the nations [LXX: See, you despisers (= בֹּגְדִים, treacherous or unfaithful ones); cf., Syr., Acts 13:41] and look. And astonish yourselves, be astounded [cf., Isa. 29:9; LXX: And marvel at amazing things and be destroyed]. For a work is working in your days [Tg. Jon., Vulg.: For a work has been worked in your days; LXX: For I am working a work in your days; cf., Syr.; see GKC §116s; cf., 1 Sam. 3:11; Ps. 44:2 (Eng., 44:1)]. You will not believe when it is recounted [LXX: that you would not believe if someone were to tell it; cf., Syr.]. "Indeed, look, I am about to raise up the Chaldeans [LXX adds: the fighters; see GKC §116p], the bitter and hasty nation that goes to earth's broad places to possess dwellings [Tg. Jon.: cities] that do not belong to it. 1:7 Terrible and feared [LXX: manifest] it is. From it is its brand of justice. And

---

5. "The whole of the prophecy has an ideal and universal stamp. Not even Judah and Jerusalem are mentioned, and the Chaldeans who are mentioned by name are simply introduced as the existing possessors of the imperial power of the world, which was bent upon the destruction of the kingdom of God, or as the sinners who swallow up the righteous man" (Keil, *Minor Prophets*, 390). "Although the fact that the Chaldeans are mentioned by name leaves no doubt whatever that the judgment will burst upon Judah through this wild conquering people, the prophecy rises immediately from this particular judgment to a view of the universal judgment upon all nations, yea, upon the whole of the ungodly world, to proclaim their destruction and the dawning of salvation for the people of the Lord and the Lord's anointed" (ibid.).

6. Brevard S. Childs, *Introduction to the Old Testament as Scripture* (Philadelphia: Fortress, 1979), 453. "In the autobiographical style of the confession the prophet himself serves as an example of a faithful response of one person living between the promise of the end and its arrival" (ibid., 455).

as for its dignity [lit., lifting up; Syr., vision; Tg. Jon.: decree], it goes forth [LXX: And its profit will go forth from him].[7] *1:8 And its horses are swifter [1QpHab:* וקול*] than leopards [Syr.: eagles] and keener than wolves of evening [LXX: Arabia]. And its horsemen [or, horses] spring about [cf., 1QpHab]. And its horsemen [or, horses], from far away they come [> 1QpHab]. They fly like an eagle [or, vulture] hastening [Syr., that is hungry] to devour. 1:9 All of it [Syr., Tg. Jon.: All of them], it is for violence that it comes [Syr., Tg. Jon.: they come]. The totality of their faces is eastward [1QpHab:* קדים*; Syr.: The appearance of their faces is strong; Tg. Jon.: In front of their faces they resemble something like an east wind], and it gathers [Syr.: they gather] captives like the sand.*[8] *1:10 And as for it, kings are the ones whom it mocks [1QpHab:* יקלס*], and rulers are a laughingstock to it. It [1QpHab, pc Mss:* והוא *(cf., LXX)], at every fortification it laughs, and it heaps up dust [LXX: will throw a mound; NET: build siege ramps] and captures it [1QpHab:* וילכדהו *(cf., LXX)]. 1:11 Then it passes through like wind and crosses over. And this one [1QpHab:* זה*] whose strength is ascribed to his god is guilty [1QpHab:* וישם*]."*[9]

There is a difference of opinion on who is speaking and who is being addressed in Habakkuk 1:5. Some understand the LORD to be the speaker and Habakkuk and the Judeans to be the addressees. The

---

7. The MT accentuation suggests reading "its justice and its dignity" as the compound subject of the following verb "goes forth" (cf., ESV). The problem with this is that the Hebrew verb is singular (see Michael B. Shepherd, "The Compound Subject in Biblical Hebrew," *HS* 52 [2011]: 107–120). The LXX divides Habakkuk 1:7b into two clauses.
8. LXX: "Consummation will come to the ungodly who resist with their faces in opposition, and it will gather captivity like sand."
9. The MT accentuation arranges וְאָשֵׁם with what precedes it, requiring the following זוּ to be read as a demonstrative pronoun: "Then it passes through like wind and crosses over, and it is guilty. This is its strength to its god." But זוּ normally has a relative function (e.g., Exod. 15:13; see BDB, 262). The above translation follows the arrangement of the text in *BHS*. The LXX uses future tense verbs for this verse. Note the difference between Brenton's translation of the LXX and the more recent translation in the NETS. Brenton: "Then shall he change his spirit, and he shall pass through, and make an atonement, *saying*, This strength *belongs* to my god." NETS: "Then he will have a change of spirit and pass through and will appease. [line space] This strength belongs to my God." See also *Tg. Jon.*: "Then because its spirit is exalted upon it, it passes along from its kingdom and commits sin in that it increases honor to its idol."

addition of the pronoun "I" in the LXX and in many English versions of Habakkuk 1:5b presupposes that the LORD is the speaker. This pronoun, however, is not present in the Hebrew text. It is not until Habakkuk 1:6 that the LORD is clearly the speaker. It is possible then that the speaker is the prophet (i.e., the author). The Hebrew imperatives are plural, but the identity of those addressed depends in part upon the textual decision made between the MT's בגוים ("among the nations") and the LXX's "despisers" (= בגדים, "treacherous ones" or "unfaithful ones"). The graphic similarity between the two options would seem to suggest accidental change from one to the other, but it is also plausible that the MT reading is an intentional attempt to soften the harshness of the reading reflected by the LXX. 1QpHab is fragmentary at this juncture in the text, but the commentary uses הבוגדים three times to explain Habakkuk 1:5a. If that is the correct reading, then it is worth noting that the wicked foreign enemies in Habakkuk 1:13b are also called בוגדים. That is, the prophet addresses the treacherous, unfaithful enemies of the true remnant of the people of God. They are the ones to be astounded and astonished at what is happening. But this need not be limited to the foreign nation (see Isa. 5:12; Jer. 5:11; 9:1 [Eng., 9:2]; Mal. 2:10–11). It is inclusive of any who would fall prey to the temptation to lack faith in light of what the book reveals about both the historical and the future work of God. Thus, Habakkuk 1:5 serves to issue an initial warning to the readership (cf., Acts 13:41).

The text of Habakkuk 1:5 is the first of three verses that stand at the beginning of the three major divisions of the book (see also Hab. 2:4; 3:2). They share similar terminology and develop the theme of faith in the work of God. The historical work of God in the days of those addressed in Habakkuk 1:5 prefigures the eschatological work of God anticipated in Habakkuk 2:4 and Habakkuk 3:2 (see Hab. 2:2–3; 3:3–15). This is why 1QpHab is able to interpret Habakkuk 1:5 in terms of the new covenant and the last days. Some of the details of the interpretation are certainly problematic, and it would be easy to be dismissive of the way the Qumran community understood the text, but there is exegetical warrant for a future-oriented reading. This is also the reason why Paul is able to address his own generation directly from the text of Habakkuk 1:5 (Acts 13:41). Furthermore, when Habakkuk 1:5b says, "You will not believe when it is recounted," it is not simply another way of saying that the people will be astonished. There is also very little evidence to suggest that it means the people would have trouble standing firm (*TLOT* 1:142). 1QpHab understands it to be lack of faith in the covenant and statutes of God. The citation in Acts 13:41 interprets it to be lack of faith in the Messiah (see Hab. 3:13).

When the LORD begins to speak in Habakkuk 1:6, there is an affirmation that he is the one raising up the foreign enemy (cf., Jer. 27:6; Amos 6:14). The Hebrew construction here normally conveys a sense of imminence. That is, the LORD is not currently doing this, but he is about to do it. This might suggest to the reader that Habakkuk 1:6 is in response to the wickedness of Habakkuk's own people in Habakkuk 1:2–4. But it is not out of the realm of possibility that the action is presently underway in some fashion (see Hab. 1:5b: "a work is working in your days") yet still to come to fruition in the near future. Thus, if the prophet's complaint in Habakkuk 1:2–4 is already about the foreign enemy, then the LORD could very well be saying in Habakkuk 1:6 that he is the one orchestrating that situation. This is the test to the reader's faith. How can God use a wicked instrument to accomplish his purposes (see Hab. 1:12–13)? But that very instrument will also be the object of divine judgment (Hab. 2:5–20) not unlike the way that the final enemy of the people of God will face judgment in the day that the LORD delivers the righteous by faith (Hab. 2:2–4; 3:13–14; cf., Ezek. 38–39).

The MT of Habakkuk 1:6 says that the LORD is about to raise up "the Chaldeans" (i.e., the Babylonians). This is a very curious reading given the fact that the historical enemy is nowhere else mentioned by name in the book. Indeed, such a lack of historical particularity appears to be intentional, allowing the events of Habakkuk's day to foreshadow the events of the last days more effectively. It is well known that the MT tends to add or to clarify historical information (cf., MT and LXX Jer.). Thus, the reading found in the LXX ("the Chaldeans, the fighters") appears to preserve the original text in what is now a conflation of the original and a scribal clarification. The original text read, "Indeed, look, I am about to raise up the fighters." This was historicized in the tradition behind the MT to read, "Indeed, look, I am about to raise up the Chaldeans." The tradition behind the LXX was aware of both readings, and, instead of choosing one or the other, decided to preserve them both. While this does allow for the possibility that the historical enemy was a nation other than Babylon—perhaps Assyria (cf., Jonah, Micah, and Nahum)—such identification seems to be contrary to the author's intention. All the reader needs to know in Habakkuk. 1:6 is that the fighters are "the bitter and hasty nation that goes to earth's broad places to possess dwellings that do not belong to it" (cf., Hab. 2:6b). 1QpHab identifies the fighters as the Kittim (i.e., Cyprus; cf., 4QpNah). The Qumran community believed that they were actually living in the last days and that the Kittim were the Romans. But what is significant for the present commentary is that there was something in the larger context of the book of Habakkuk that prompted an eschatological reading (see Num. 24:24; Dan. 11:30).

The third masculine singular pronouns and pronominal suffixes in Habakkuk 1:7–11 all refer back to "the nation" (הגוי) in Habakkuk 1:6a as their antecedent. English versions often handle this by using "they" and "them" instead of "he" and "him" or "it." The problem with this approach is that it can obscure any attempt on the writer's part to make an association between the individual nation and an individual person (e.g., Hab. 1:11b and Dan. 11:38–39). The description of the "terrible and feared" nation in this passage is quite similar to that of the foreign enemy in Isaiah 5:26–30 (presumably the Assyrians, although they are not named in the text itself). This nation generates its own brand of justice and authority (Hab. 1:7), which, according to Habakkuk 1:4, is no justice at all. It is a very twisted kind of justice. But the speed with which the nation comes to conquer its enemies is very impressive, being compared to several different predators (Hab. 1:8). Its horses are swifter than leopards and keener than wolves of evening (cf., Jer. 4:13; 5:6; Zeph. 3:3). Some prefer to emend the text so that it says "desert wolves" (see *BHS* apparatus). Its horsemen (or, horses) leap about and come from far away (cf., Nah. 3:3). They seem to fly like an eagle or a vulture hastening to devour (cf., Deut 28:49; Job 9:26; Lam. 4:19).

All of the nation comes for violence (Hab. 1:9; cf., Hab. 1:2–3). The difficult phrase מגמת פניהם ("the totality of their faces") is apparently equivalent to כלה ("all of it"). To say that the totality of their faces is "eastward" is to view the coming of the enemy (whether Assyria or Babylon) from the perspective of someone living in Israel. That is, a witness to the coming of the enemy into the land of the covenant would see a nation whose place of origin was in the east. Thus, that nation is eastward and coming from the east. The nation gathers captives as easily and as abundantly as sand (cf., 2 Kgs. 17:6; 25:21; Hab. 2:5). (Note: the use of *wayyiqtol* forms in Hab. 1:9b, 10b, 11a is strictly for the purpose of sequencing and need not be rendered as past tense.) This same nation makes a mockery of other kings and rulers (Hab. 1:10). Its power is such that it need not take seriously the fortifications that it intends to conquer. According to the NET Bible, the piling up of dust in this verse is the building of siege ramps. The final verb ("captures it") in the MT of Habakkuk 1:10 features a third feminine singular pronominal suffix ("it") that likely refers to an implied feminine singular noun עיר ("city") as its antecedent. 1QpHab, which has a third masculine singular pronominal suffix on this verb, is probably a secondary reading designed to remove any potential ambiguity by allowing the preceding masculine singular noun "fortification" to serve as the antecedent.

It is possible that רוח in Habakkuk 1:11 means "spirit" and is the subject of the masculine verbs (cf., 1 Kgs. 22:24; Job 4:15).[10] רוח, however, normally agrees with feminine verbs and pronouns, so it seems best to maintain the foreign nation as the subject of the verbs and to understand רוח as an adverbial description of the manner in which the nation passes through and crosses over ("like wind"; cf., Isa. 8:8; Dan. 11:40). It is not necessary to emend the text to כרוח as suggested in the *BHS* apparatus (see GKC §118m). The MT verb ואשם declares guilty this one whose strength is ascribed to his god. (See the note to the above translation on the syntax of this verse.) 1QpHab, however, reads וישם, which is a third masculine singular prefixed form either from שמם ("destroy") or from שׂים ("put, set, place, give, make").

1:12 Are you not from aforetime [or, ancient time; Tg. Jon.: Did you not, O LORD, create the world from the beginning]? O LORD my God, my Holy One [LXX: my holy God; cf., Tg. Jon.],[11] we will not die [Tiq soph pro: you will not die; cf., Tg. Jon.]. O LORD, it is for judgment that you have appointed it [i.e., the foreign nation]. And O Rock [Tg. Jon.: O Strong One], it is to rebuke / correct [1QpHab: למוכיחו] that you have established it [LXX: And he has formed me to reprove his discipline]. 1:13 [You are] too pure of eyes to see evil [1QpHab: ברע], and to look upon mischief you are not able. Why do you look upon [1QpHab: תביטו] treacherous / unfaithful ones? [Why] are you silent [1QpHab: ותחריש] when wicked people swallow those more righteous than they are [LXX, Syr.: when the ungodly swallow the righteous]? 1:14 And you make [1QpHab: ותעש] mankind like the fish of the sea, like creeping things without a ruler [GKC §152u; 1QpHab: למשל] over them. 1:15 All of him [i.e., mankind; Tg. Jon.: All of them resemble a hunter / fisherman] with a fishhook it [i.e., the foreign

---

10. See the discussion in Roberts, *Nahum, Habakkuk, and Zephaniah*, 97–99.
11. English versions normally arrange the vocative ("O LORD my God, my Holy One") in Habakkuk 1:12a at the end of the opening rhetorical question. *BHS* arranges the line so that there are two vocatives—one at the end of the question and one at the beginning of the following declaration. The vocatives in Habakkuk 1:12b, however, are both at the beginning of their respective clauses. Therefore, the above translation follows suit and puts the vocative in Habakkuk 1:12a at the beginning of its clause. The MT accentuation seems to favor this. It is also possible that "the LORD" is the predicate in the first clause of Habakkuk 1:12a: "Are you not from aforetime the LORD?" Cf., Ps. 90:2.

nation] brings up. Furthermore, it drags him [1QpHab: וינרהו*; cf., LXX, 8HevXII gr] in its perforated net [or, throw net]. And it gathers him in its fishing net [or, dragnet]. Therefore, it is glad and rejoices [LXX: its heart rejoices].*[12] *1:16 Therefore, it sacrifices to its perforated net [or, throw net; Tg. Jon.: its weapons] and makes sacrifices smoke [or, burns incense] to its fishing net [or, dragnet; Tg. Jon.: its standards]. For it is by means of them that its portion [8HevXII gr: bread / food] is rich / robust and its food fat / healthy. 1:17 Therefore, will it empty [LXX, Syr., Tg. Jon.: cast] its perforated net [or, throw net; 1QpHab, 8HevXII gr: its sword] and continue to slaughter nations without sparing [lit., and continually to slaughter nations will it not spare]?*[13]

Habakkuk's initial response to the revelation that the LORD is the one raising up the fighters is essentially an affirmation of his faith (Hab. 1:12). He does not fail to believe when faced with the problem of evil, thus serving as a model for the reader (Hab. 1:5). His rhetorical question emphatically assumes that the LORD, the God who is set apart from all other so-called gods is in fact from the indefinite past (cf., Deut. 33:27). Some interpreters (e.g., Calvin) understand this to be a reference to the long history of the covenant relationship that began with the patriarchs. *Targum Jonathan* takes it back to the beginning of creation. The text itself, however, is not so specific. The fact that the LORD is from aforetime then serves as the basis for the following declaration, "We will not die." This is considered one of the *Tiqqune sopherim* ("corrections of the scribes") in the tradition of the Masoretes.[14] According to this tradition, the original reading was, "You will not die." The scribes subsequently changed this reading in order to avoid any speculation about whether God could die. If this reading is correct, then the idea of Habakkuk 1:12a would be that the LORD has always been around, therefore, he will always be around. In other words, God is present even when he seems to be absent. But given the lack of actual textual evidence for this reading, the intended statement in this half verse seems to be that God's true people (i.e., those who believe) will

---

12. 1QpHab reverses the order of Habakkuk 1:15b and Habakkuk 1:16a1.

13. 1QpHab: על כן יריק חרבו תמיד להרוג גוים ולוא יחמל ("Therefore, it unsheathes its sword continually to slaughter nations and does not spare"). ASV: "Shall he therefore empty his net, and spare not to slay the nations continually?" ESV: "Is he then to keep on emptying his net and mercilessly killing nations forever?"

14. See Ernst Würthwein, *The Text of the Old Testament*, 2d ed., trans. Erroll F. Rhodes (Grand Rapids: Eerdmans, 1994), 17–18.

not die precisely because their God has always existed and remained faithful (cf., Lam. 5:19–22). The true remnant of the people of God who are righteous by faith will live indefinitely (Hab. 2:4b). Thus, there is a clear distinction of three groups in this passage: the true people of God, wicked Judeans, and the foreign nation. These three are identified in 1QpHab: "God will not destroy his people by the hand of the nations, but in the hand of his chosen ones he will give the judgment of all the nations, and by their reproof all the wicked of his people will be guilty, (by the reproof) of those who have kept his commands."

The prophet understands from Habakkuk 1:6–11 that the foreign nation is the LORD's appointed instrument of judgment/justice against Judah's covenant infidelity (Hab. 1:12b; cf., Jer. 46:28), even though justice is currently perverted by both groups (Hab. 1:4, 7). It is the Rock in whom he takes refuge who has established the enemy to rebuke those who had abandoned his ways. Unfortunately for Habakkuk and those like him, they must endure the hardship that comes as a consequence of living among a wicked people. But such hardship will ultimately only strengthen their faith (see Hab. 3:17–19). The prophet knows that the LORD's "eyes" are too pure to see evil and that he is unable to stand by and look at mischief without having any purpose or response (Hab. 1:13a; cf., Isa. 33:15; Hab. 1:3). But understandably he still struggles with an experience that gives him the feeling that God is simply looking on in silence while the treacherous ones have their way (Hab. 1:13b). Why is it that the LORD has chosen a nation even more wicked than the Judeans to judge them (cf., *4 Ezra* 3:31)? The response in Habakkuk 2:2–20 is that the LORD will bring justice to all the wicked and will vindicate the righteous. The phrase, "when wicked people swallow those more righteous than they are," is not the same as the clause, "wicked people surround the righteous," in Habakkuk 1:4b. The difference, at least in the MT of Habakkuk 1:13b, is the comparative "more righteous." The Judeans were not righteous, but they were more righteous than the foreign nation. The righteous in Habakkuk 1:4b, however, would seem to be those like Habakkuk who are righteous by faith (Hab. 2:4b). The LXX and Syriac of Habakkuk 1:13b appear to harmonize with Habakkuk 1:4b by removing the comparative: "when the ungodly swallow the righteous."

The *wayyiqtol* at the beginning of Habakkuk 1:14 likely does double duty. On the one hand, it serves as a continuation of Habakkuk 1:13b (cf., Hab. 1:9b, 10b). On the other hand, it is reminiscent of the narrative in Genesis 1:26: "And God said, 'Let us make mankind in our image according to our likeness so that they may rule over the fish of the sea . . . .'" By saying that the LORD makes mankind like the

fish of the sea, the prophet is suggesting that judgment at the hands
of such a wicked foreign nation is a perversion of the created order (cf.,
Amos 4:2; Zeph. 1:3). Rather than ruling over the animals, mankind is
like creeping things (collective) without a ruler (cf., Isa. 63:19). 1QpHab
misses the irony by harmonizing with Genesis 1:26: "And you make
mankind like the fish of the sea, like creeping things to rule over them."
The phrase, "All of him/it," (Hab. 1:15) could either be the subject or the
object depending upon whether the pronoun refers to the foreign nation
(Hab. 1:9) or to mankind (Hab. 1:14). The foreign nation brings up mankind with a fishhook and drags him with a net (cf., Ezek. 47:10). The
nation gathers humanity with another kind of net. The nation rejoices
over this just as a fisherman would rejoice over a catch. Therefore, the
foreign nation sacrifices to the former kind of net and makes sacrifices
smoke or burns incense to the latter precisely because it is by means of
them that its portion is rich or robust and its food fat or healthy (Hab.
1:16). This is probably a way of describing worship of false gods and/or
idols for the defeat and the plunder of enemies (cf., Hos. 11:2; Hab. 1:11).
The difference between the MT and 1QpHab of Habakkuk 1:17 is rather
significant. According to the MT, the verse is essentially a question from
the prophet to the LORD about whether the foreign nation will empty
its net and continue to slaughter nations without sparing. That is, will
the fisherman continue his catch of mankind unabated as described in
Habakkuk 1:14–16? But according to 1QpHab, the verse is a concluding
inference from Habakkuk 1:14–16 that translates the fishing metaphor
into something more literal (see note to translation above). The foreign
nation unsheathes its sword continually to slaughter nations and does
not spare. It is worth noting that the *hiphil* of ריק is used several times
in the Hebrew Bible for the unsheathing of a sword. Furthermore, the
potential for graphic confusion between חרמו ("its net") and חרבו ("its
sword") was noted well before the discovery of 1QpHab among the Dead
Sea Scrolls (see BDB, 938).

HABAKKUK 2

*2:1 Upon my watch I resolve to remain standing, and I will station
myself upon a siege-enclosure [or, watchtower; 1QpHab: my siege-enclosure; LXX, Syr.: rock =* צור*],[15] and I will watch to see what he will*

---

15. The proposal in the *BHS* apparatus (מַצּוֹרִי from נצר = "my watch") makes
a nice parallel with משמרתי ("my watch"), but while the root of the proposed word is very common, the proposed word itself does not occur elsewhere in biblical Hebrew.

speak with me [or, by means of me (BDB, 181)] and what I will reply
[Syr.: what he replies to me] concerning my rebuke / argument [Tg. Jon.:
request]. 2:2 And the LORD answered me and said, "Write a prophetic
vision and so explain [Vulg., GKC §110f] upon the tablets [LXX: and
clearly / plainly on a tablet] in order that he who reads it aloud publicly
[1QpHab: בו הקורא] may run [LXX: so that the reader might pursue
them (n. pl.)].[16] 2:3 For yet is a prophetic vision for the appointed time
and a witness [LXX: and it will rise; BDB: and it pants; see HALOT,
DCH; 1QpHab: יפיח] for the end [Tg. Jon.: the end is fixed], and it will
not fail [or, disappoint]. If it tarries, wait for it, for it will surely [Syr.:
quickly] come. It will not delay [1QpHab, mlt Mss: and it will not delay].
2:4 Look, it [i.e., his soul] is swollen, his soul is not upright [1QpHab:
יושרה] within him [LXX: If he draws back, my soul is not pleased with
him; Tg. Jon.: the wicked in their heart say all these things are not], but
he who is righteous by his faith [LXX: my faithfulness (or, faith in me)]
is the one who will live."

Here the prophet uses cohortatives to express his determination to remain as a watchman looking for the word of the LORD to come not
only to him but also by means of him to the people (Hab. 2:1; cf., Isa.
21:6–12; Ezek. 3:16b–21; 33:1–9; Hos. 9:8; Hab. 3:18; Ps. 5:4 [Eng.,
5:3]; 130:5–6). He also anticipates that he himself will have something
to reply either concerning what he thinks will be the LORD's rebuke
of him concerning Habakkuk 1:12–17 or concerning his argument
in Habakkuk 1:12–17 in response to whatever the LORD has to say.
Thus, Habakkuk 2:1 is programmatic for the remainder of the book.
The LORD answers in Habakkuk 2:2–20, then follows the prayer of
Habakkuk in chapter 3. 1QpHab does not include chapter 3 in its text
and commentary, but the reason for this is not entirely certain. It is
fragmentary at the point where the verb אשיב ("I will reply") would
occur in Habakkuk 2:1b, so it is not possible to say whether it read ישיב
("he will reply"; cf., Syr.). One possibility is that 1QpHab bears witness
to the pre-history of the composition of the book of Habakkuk prior to
the inclusion of chapter 3. Another is that the Qumran community may
have had theological reasons for not including the chapter. What is certain, however, is that all other textual witnesses bear testimony to the
integral role of chapter 3 in the final composition of the book.

When the LORD answers in Habakkuk 2:2, he does not rebuke the
prophet. Rather, he instructs the prophet to write a prophetic vision

---

16. *Tg. Jon.*: "The prophecy is written and specified [or, explained] upon the
book of the Torah in order that whoever reads it may hasten to be wise."

that will serve to bolster the faith of the true people of God. The relationship of באר ("make plain") to this initial imperative is disputed. Many take it in the sense of Deuteronomy 27:8 that the vision should be written clearly (see LXX) so that even someone on the run (perhaps even a herald) could read it. Of course, those who understand it this way do not think that people were actually running by the tablets. It is simply an exaggerated way of describing the clarity of the writing. The other possibility is that באר means "make plain" in the sense "explain" as in Deuteronomy 1:5. This seems to be the way in which *Targum Jonathan* interprets the verse: "The prophecy is written and specified [or, explained] upon the book of the Torah in order that whoever reads it may hasten to be wise" (see Deut. 4:6). This raises the issue of where the prophecy is written. The Targum might presuppose that the vision is marked by הנה ("Look") in Habakkuk 2:4 and that the wording of Habakkuk 2:4b derives from the Torah in Genesis 15:6. It is also possible that Habakkuk 3:3–15, which draws upon imagery from the Torah, is the vision. Still others contend that the explanation was to be upon the tablets but not in the book (see Redak). This latter option is somewhat unlikely given the content of the book and given the wording of a text like Isaiah 30:8, where the terms "tablet" and "book/document" are parallel. The understanding of the present commentary is that whoever reads the explanation of the vision in the book of Habakkuk will "run" in the sense that the strength of his or her faith will be renewed (cf., Isa. 40:31).[17] According to 1QpHab, God told Habakkuk to write the things that would come upon the last generation, but the completion of the end he did not make known to him.

Inner-biblical and early postbiblical interpretation understood the language of Habakkuk 2:3 to be eschatological (Dan. 11:27; 12:4, 6, 7, 9, 12, 13; 1QpHab; Heb. 10:37–38).[18] According to this reading, the

---

17. Roberts has suggested a different rendering based upon the syntax of Prov. 18:10: "so that the one who reads might run into it (for refuge)" (*Nahum, Habakkuk, and Zephaniah*, 109). Thus, the content of the vision itself is a refuge for the reader. Roberts points out that content such as a vision or Torah is normally not the object of ב קרא ("call in" or "read aloud publicly") (see Deut. 17:19; Jer. 36:8, 10, 13; Neh. 8:3, 18; 13:1; 2 Chr. 34:18; but see Neh. 8:8). Normally the book is the object. This is why he construes the prepositional phrase with the verb "run." The problem with this suggestion is that the prepositional phrase in Habakkuk 2:2b follows the participle "reads" rather than the verb "run."

18. See Michael Fishbane, *Biblical Interpretation in Ancient Israel* (Oxford: Clarendon, 1985), 492–93. See also Keil, *Minor Prophets*, 400. Augustine:

LORD's initial response to Habakkuk in Habakkuk 2:2–4 pertains to the last days (cf., Hab. 3:3–15). It is only in the woes (Hab. 2:5–20) that he addresses the historical situation directly. Thus, hope in the future work of God is to shape the way the believer deals with the present, and the present in many ways foreshadows the future. The prophetic vision that the prophet is to write is for the "appointed time" (מוֹעֵד). It bears witness to the "end" (קֵץ) and will not disappoint. If it seems to tarry, the prophet is to "wait" (חכה) for it. Indeed, it may not even come in the prophet's lifetime, but it will surely come without delay in accordance with the LORD's timing (cf., Isa. 60:22). Following the wording of this text, Daniel receives instructions in the conclusion to the final vision of the book (Dan. 10–12) to seal the document until the time of the "end" (קֵץ) (Dan. 12:4; cf., Dan. 8:17, 19, 26; Rev. 10:4; 22:10). This was not merely to keep a record of the prophecy so that it could be vindicated or explained after its fulfillment. It was to preserve words of assurance to maintain the hope of the faithful (cf., Isa. 8:16–18). When Daniel inquires how long it will be until the end (Dan. 12:6b), the angel responds that it is for an "appointed time" (מוֹעֵד), appointed times, and a half (Dan. 12:7). Blessed is "the one who waits" (הַמְחַכֶּה) (Dan. 12:12; cf., Isa. 30:18). "Daniel then becomes a model for the reader in Dan. 12:13 much like Isaiah (Isa. 8:16–18) and Habakkuk (Hab. 3:17–19) before him, waiting on the future work of God whether or not it appears in his lifetime."[19] Much like the book of Daniel, 1QpHab interprets Habakkuk 2:3 to be about the final age, which will extend into the future and go beyond all that the prophets say. Likewise, the reading of Habakkuk 2:3b in Hebrews 10:37 is eschatological: "For he who is coming will come and not delay" (see also Isa. 26:20). This version of the text adds an article ("he who") and a conjunction ("and") in the Greek, and it translates the Hebrew infinitive absolute as a participle ("is coming"). It understands the content of the vision to be the coming of the unidentified "anointed" (i.e., messianic) king in Habakkuk 3:13.

Habakkuk 2:4 is the second of the three related texts that stand near the beginning of the three major sections of the book (Hab. 1:5; 2:4; 3:2). The fact that these three texts share the similar terminology of faith in the work of God not only helps to maintain the unity of the book's message but also creates a situation in which consultation

---

"Of what else than the advent of Christ, who was to come, is Habakkuk understood to say." (Alberto Ferreiro, ed., *The Twelve Prophets*, ACCS XIV [Downers Grove, IL: InterVarsity, 2003], 191).

19. Michael B. Shepherd, *The Twelve Prophets in the New Testament* (New York: Peter Lang, 2011), 49.

with all three texts can guide the reader to resolve difficulties in any one of them individually. Isolation of these verses results in unnecessary problems and a breakdown of the book's development. Nowhere is this more the case than with Habakkuk 2:4. The verse begins with the deictic marker הִנֵּה ("Look") and proceeds to contrast the wicked who will die with the righteous who will live, but it does so in a somewhat unexpected fashion. Given the eschatological context of Habakkuk 2:2–4, it does not appear to be the case that this is a contrast between the foreign nation (and/or the wicked Judeans) and the faithful like Habakkuk who will survive the historical crisis. Rather, it is a more general contrast between those who lack faith and those who have faith in the future work of God.

The syntax of the MT of Habakkuk 2:4a is difficult but not impossible. The feminine singular noun "soul" with its third masculine singular pronominal suffix "his" is apparently the subject of two third feminine singular verbs of the suffixed conjugation ("swollen" and "not upright"). The initial difficulty with this reading is the following prepositional phrase "in him." Roberts considers the first verb ("swollen") to be corrupt, and, on the basis of constructions elsewhere involving the Hebrew noun translated "soul" followed by the preposition "in" (Gen. 49:6; Num. 21:4; Isa. 46:2; 66:3), he renders, "Now the fainthearted, his soul will not walk in it [i.e., in the vision]."[20] Roberts has chosen the meaning "to walk straight" for the verb "to be upright/straight" (see 1 Sam. 6:12). This is to avoid what would be an uncommon occurrence of "soul" followed by the preposition "in" with the meaning "his soul in him." The closest examples of parallels to this would be the instances of "soul" and the preposition "upon" in which the pronominal suffix on "soul" has the same antecedent as the pronominal object of the preposition "upon" (e.g., Jon. 2:8 [Eng., 2:7]; Ps. 42:7 [Eng., 42:6]; 107:5; 131:2b).

The more significant issue in Habakkuk 2:4a is the meaning of the verb עֻפְּלָה ("it is swollen"). If this meaning is correct, then it is the only occurrence of the verb in the Hebrew Bible. Some understand the verb to mean that the one who is not upright or pleasing in God's sight is puffed up or swollen with pride (e.g., NIV). But the contrast with the righteous person who lives in Habakkuk 2:4b suggests that the one who is not upright in Habakkuk 2:4a swells up and dies. But why the choice of such an unusual verb? This is where the links with Habakkuk 1:5 and 3:2 can be helpful. The root עפל ("swell") features transposition or metathesis (הפך) of the first two root letters of the key word פעל ("work") in Habakkuk 1:5 and 3:2. This is a common technique for

---

20. Roberts, *Nahum, Habakkuk, and Zephaniah*, 107.

associating passages with one another in biblical composition, inner-biblical exegesis, and in rabbinic exegesis.[21] By means of this technique the author is able to maintain a connection with the key word "work" in Habakkuk 1:5 and 3:2 while also using the faith terminology of those two verses in Habakkuk 2:4b.

The rendering of Habakkuk 2:4a in the LXX ("If he draws back, my soul is not pleased with him") understands עפלה to be from the homonymic root עפל ("to be heedless"), which also only occurs once in the Hebrew Bible (Num. 14:44). The rendering, "my soul [= נפשי] is not pleased with him," rather than, "his soul [נפשו] is not upright within him," is perhaps due to the similarity of the *yodh* and *waw* suffixes in the writing at the time (cf., DSS). This translation fits well the warning against turning back in Hebrews 10:19–39. In fact, the citation of Habakkuk 2:4 in Hebrews 10:38 reverses the order of the clauses so that the verb "draw back" is immediately followed by the nominal form "drawing back" in Hebrews 10:39.

There are at least two ways to understand the syntax of Habakkuk 2:4b. Largely because modern commentary tends to historicize the meaning of the text, it is now commonly understood that the phrase באמונתו means "by his faithfulness" and that this phrase modifies the verb "live," yielding the following translation: "And the righteous will live by his faithfulness." According to this reading, the text is little more than an unnecessary statement designed to point out the obvious, namely, that righteous people will live faithfully through the historical crisis. The alternative to this is to understand the phrase באמונתו to modify the word "righteous" with the meaning "by his faith":[22] "but he who is righteous by his faith is the one who will live." According to this reading, the righteous person is the one who will live, and it is by faith that someone can be said to be righteous.

There are several reasons why the second of the two options mentioned above is preferable. First, the wording of the text appears to be based on Genesis 15:6 (cf., Ps. 106:31; Neh. 9:8): "And he had placed

---

21. E.g., ערף and פרע in Exodus 32:9b, 25a; also בער and עבר in Numbers 11:1 and Psalm 78:21. See Wilhelm Bacher, *Die exegetische Terminologie der jüdischen Traditionsliteratur* (Hildesheim: Georg Olms, 1965), 44.

22. "[I]n this particular context steadfastness can only mean the religious attitude of unshakeable trust, that is, faith" (Walther Eichrodt, *Theology of the Old Testament*, vol. 2, trans. J. A. Baker [Philadelphia: Westminster, 1967], 285). "[W]ithin the general context its value is to all intents and purposes that of our 'faith'" (James Barr, *The Semantics of Biblical Language* [Oxford: Oxford University Press, 1961], 173, n. 1).

his faith (וְהֶאֱמִן) in the LORD, and he reckoned it to him righteousness (צְדָקָה).” Thus, the apostle Paul quotes both Genesis 15:6 and Habakkuk. 2:4 for his doctrine of justification by faith in his letters to the Romans and to the Galatians. Second, even though אֱמוּנָה normally means “faithfulness,” the link to Habakkuk 1:5 suggests that in Habakkuk 2:4b it is the nominal expression (“faith”) of the *hiphil* verbal stem of the same root (“to believe” or “to have faith”). Indeed, there is really no other option in the language for the nominal form of “faith.” Third, the placement of the phrase “by his faith” immediately after “righteous” in the Hebrew syntax suggests that the former modifies the latter. If the writer had wanted the phrase “by his faith” to modify the verb “live,” it would have been much clearer to place that phrase after the verb (cf., Lev. 18:5).

Given the eschatological context set by Habakkuk 2:2–3, the message of Habakkuk 2:4b is that a person who is declared to be in right standing with God by means of his or her faith in the future work of God (i.e., Hab. 3:3–15) in Christ (i.e., the unidentified anointed one in Hab. 3:13; cf., Heb. 10:37) will live (cf., Ezek. 33:13). This eschatological context also has implications for the way in which the verb “live” is interpreted. According to Habakkuk 1:12, it is the fact that the LORD is from the indefinite past that serves as the basis for the hope that the true people of God will live into the indefinite future. Indeed, it would make very little sense for God to encourage Habakkuk to look forward to something that would not transpire in his lifetime unless there were some sort of hope in a resurrection and eternal life. A mere promise to survive the historical crisis or even to live a blessed life and then die seems to fall short of what the context envisions.[23]

The LXX of Habakkuk 2:4b—“but the righteous by my faithfulness will live”—involves the same shift from “his” (*waw*) to “my” (*yodh*) that occurred in the LXX of Habakkuk 2:4a when compared to the MT. This would change the focus from the righteous person’s faith to the faithfulness of the LORD. It is possible, however, that the translation of *pisteōs mou* as “my faithfulness” is not the correct understanding of the Greek text. This may very well be an example of an objective genitive (“faith in me”), resulting in the following translation: “but the righteous by faith in me will live” (cf., Rev. 2:13). The rendering of Habakkuk 2:4b in

---

23. “Hence, when Habakkuk promises life in future to the faithful, he no doubt overleaps the boundaries of this world, and sets before the faithful a better life that that which they have here, which is accompanied with many sorrows, and proves itself by its shortness to be unworthy of being much desired” (Calvin, *Habakkuk*, 76).

the Alexandrian text of Hebrews 10:38 displaces the first-person pronoun and says, "But my righteous one by faith will live," anticipating the list in Hebrews 11 of those who had faith. The Western text realigns this with the LXX, and the Byzantine text removes the pronoun so that it matches Paul's citations of Habakkuk 2:4b.

Paul's citation of Habakkuk 2:4 in Romans 1:17 is programmatic for the entire epistle to the Romans. His is unique in that there is no pronoun "his" or "my" as in the MT and the LXX: "But the righteous by faith will live." James Dunn argues that this was an intentional omission of the pronoun designed to give the term "faith" a new Christian sense.[24] But this is by no means a necessary conclusion. It is quite likely that Paul was well aware of the proto-MT "by his faith" and the LXX "by faith in me" and understood that there was ultimately no real difference between the two. Both were about the believer's faith in the LORD and his future work in Christ. According to Paul, Habakkuk 2:4b is about the revelation of God's righteousness in the gospel "by faith to those who believe" (*ek pisteōs eis pistin*) (Rom. 1:17; 3:22; see Isa. 53:1, 11; 56:1; 60:21; 61:3).[25]

The citation of Habakkuk 2:4b in Galatians 3:11 is specifically intended to counter the wording of Leviticus 18:5 (cf., Rom. 10:5–8), which extends a hypothetical offer of eternal life to anyone who does the works of the law. The text of Leviticus 18:5 is often understood to mean that anyone who keeps the law will have a long life or a blessed life. But several ancient sources interpret Leviticus 18:5 to mean eternal life (*Tg. Onk.* Lev. 18:5; *Tg. Jon.* Ezek. 20:11, 13, 21; Matt.

---

24. James D. G. Dunn, *Romans 1–8*, WBC 38A (Dallas: Word, 1988), 46.
25. The phrase *ek pisteōs eis pistin* in Romans 1:17 is often rendered "from faith to/for faith" (cf., 2 Cor. 2:16), but the meaning of this is far from clear. Others understand it in the sense "from God's faithfulness to the believer's faith" (cf., Rom. 3:3). These suggestions overlook the fact that the phrase *ek pisteōs* in the cited text of Habakkuk 2:4b does not mean "from faith" but "by faith." Imputed righteousness comes by faith to the faith of the believer (i.e., to the one who believes). This is essentially the same idea expressed in Romans 3:21–22: "But now apart from law the righteousness of God is manifested, being witnessed by the Law and the Prophets, namely, the righteousness of God by faith in Jesus Christ to all those who believe." For Paul, the testimony to this in the Law and the Prophets is primarily in Genesis 15:6 and Habakkuk 2:4b. A correct understanding of these texts reveals that Paul does not mean "by the faithfulness of Jesus Christ" but "by faith in Jesus Christ." These are not mutually exclusive concepts, but they are also not the same. It is clear that the focus of the cited texts is the believer's faith.

19:17).[26] Of course, no one is actually able to the keep the law (Deut. 31:29; Josh. 24:19–20; Jas. 2:10), and the giving of the law is designed to illustrate this very point (Rom. 5:13, 20; Gal. 3:19). It is only by faith that someone can be said to have kept the law. That is, it is only by faith that the righteousness embodied by the law can be reckoned to a person (Gen. 15:6; 26:5). Therefore, it is also only by faith that a person can obtain eternal life.

2:5 *"And also the wine acts treacherously [1QpHab:* הון יבגוד *("wealth acts treacherously")], a proud man, and he does not stay at home [LXX: And the drunkard and despiser, a boastful man, will not complete anything; Syr.: And the brazen and greedy man is not full; Tg. Jon.: And also look, like those who go astray with wine is a proud man with wickedness, and he will not be established], he who enlarges like Sheol his soul, and he is like death and is not satisfied [1QpHab, LXX, Syr.: and he like death is not satisfied]. And he collects [1QpHab: they collect] to himself all the nations and gathers [1QpHab: they gather] to himself all the peoples.[27] 2:6 Will not these [these > 1QpHab], all of them, against him lift up a saying and a satire, riddles against him [1QpHab: and interpreters of riddles against him]? And he will say [1QpHab, LXX, Syr.: And they will say], 'Woe, the one who increases what does not belong to him [1QpHab: and it does not belong to him] (How long?) [> 8ḤevXII gr],[28] and makes himself heavy with riches made from debts paid [or, makes himself heavy with debts owed; LXX: chain or collar; Syr.: cloud of dirt (=* עב טיט*); cf., 8ḤevXII gr].[29] 2:7 Will not those who pay you interest [LXX, Syr.: those who bite him; NET: your creditors] suddenly rise up [cf., 1QpHab], and those who shake you [or, cause you to tremble] awake [1QpHab:* ויקיצו*]? And you will become plunder to them. 2:8 Because you yourself [cf., 8ḤevXII gr] plundered many nations, all the rest of the peoples will plunder you [1QpHab:* וישלוכה*; cf., 8ḤevXII gr], because of bloodshed of mankind and violence of land, town [Tg. Jon.: the land of Israel, the city of Jerusalem] and all inhabitants therein.*

---

26. See Simon J. Gathercole, "Torah, Life, and Salvation: Leviticus 18:5 in Early Judaism and the New Testament," in *From Prophecy to Testament: the Function of the Old Testament in the New*, ed. Craig A. Evans (Peabody, MA: Hendrickson, 2004), 126–45.
27. This verse continues the LORD's discourse from Habakkuk 2:2–4.
28. See GKC §147c.
29. English versions typically end the reported discourse here, but it is possible that it extends all the way through Habakkuk 2:20.

2:9 Woe, the one who makes [1QpHab: הבוצע] evil unjust gain by violence for his house to set in the high place his nest to be rescued from disaster's palm. 2:10 You have advised shame for your house, cutting off many peoples and sinning against yourself [LXX: your soul has sinned]. 2:11 For a stone from a wall cries out [Tg. Jon. adds: against the one who takes it by force], and a beam [or, rafter; LXX: beetle; Syr.: peg / nail] from woodwork answers it.

2:12 Woe, he who builds a city with bloodshed and establishes a town with injustice. 2:13 Is it not, look, from [1QpHab: מעם] the LORD of hosts [LXX: Are not these things from the Lord Almighty] that peoples grow weary [1QpHab: יגעו] for fire, and peoples for emptiness grow faint. 2:14 For the earth will be filled with the knowledge of the glory of the LORD like the waters cover over the sea [1QpHab: הים; LXX: them].

2:15 Woe, he who gives his neighbor a drink, joining [DCH: pouring] your wrath [or, your poison; or, your water skin; 1QpHab: his wrath; BHS: from the cup of his wrath] and also [1QpHab: also] making drunk in order to look upon their nakedness [1QpHab: מועדיהם (their festivals); LXX: their caves]. 2:16 You are satisfied with dishonor rather than honor. Drink also you and be regarded as uncircumcised [1QpHab: והרעל (reel); cf., LXX, Syr.; Tg. Jon.: become naked]. The cup of the right hand of the LORD [Tg. Jon.: A cup of curse from before the LORD] will come around to you, and disgrace [Vulg.: vomit of disgrace] to your honor. 2:17 For the violence against Lebanon [Tg. Jon.: the sanctuary; cf., 1 Kgs. 5:19–20 (Eng., 5:5–6)] will cover you, and destruction of beasts [Tg. Jon.: the plunder of his people] that terrifies them [1QpHab: יחתה; LXX, Syr.: will terrify you], because of bloodshed of mankind and violence of land, town [Tg. Jon.: the land of Israel, the city of Jerusalem] and all inhabitants therein.

2:18 How does a carved / sculpted image [1QpHab: פסל] benefit when [or, that] its fashioner carves / sculpts it, a molten image and one teaching [1QpHab: ומרי] deception [LXX, 8HevXII gr: a false appearance]? For he who fashions his image [1QpHab: יצריו] trusts in it by making dumb worthless idols. 2:19 Woe [cf., 1QpHab], he who says to the wood, 'Wake up' [LXX: 'Sober up, rise up'], 'Rouse yourself,' to silent stone. (It teaches.)[30] Look, it is grasped [i.e., overlaid] with gold and silver [silver > Syr.], and there is no breath / spirit within it at all. 2:20

---

30. English versions tend to render this parenthetical comment as a question. Cf., LXX: "and it is an appearance." Syr.: "they are empty."

*But the LORD is in his holy temple [Tg. Jon.: But the LORD is pleased
to make his Shekhinah dwell in his holy temple]. Hush [LXX: Act rever-
ently] from before him [1QpHab:* מלפניו*] all the earth [Syr.: All the earth
will be shaken from before him; Tg. Jon.: Every object of worship on the
earth will come to an end before him]."*

The MT of Habakkuk 2:5–20 appears on the surface to be an introduction (Hab. 2:5–6a) followed by five woe oracles (Hab. 2:6b–8a, 9–11, 12–
14, 15–17a, 18–20) and two refrains (Hab. 2:8b, 17b).[31] But beneath the
surface the evidence suggests that the outline of this section of woe oracles against the historical enemy is quite different. To begin, the opening
words of Habakkuk 2:5—וְאַף כִּי ("And also")—are not reflected in the LXX
or the Syriac. There is then textual variation between the MT (הַיַּיִן ["the
wine"]) and 1QpHab (הון ["wealth"]), leading the *BHS* apparatus to suggest that הוֹי ("woe") is the original reading. The other major issue with
this section is that Habakkuk 2:12–14 does not really follow the pattern
of a typical woe oracle (i.e., introduction, accusation, and announcement
of judgment). It is generally recognized that Habakkuk 2:13–14 consists
of citations from Jeremiah 51:58 and Isaiah 11:9.[32] These do not come
from the prophet Habakkuk but from the composer of the Twelve, who,
according to the present commentary, consistently cites from Jeremiah
elsewhere in his work. This results in Habakkuk 2:12 standing apart
and now functioning as the second of three refrains that mention bloodshed (Hab. 2:8b, 12, 17b). If these observations are followed, the outline
of Habakkuk 2:5–20 becomes five woe oracles (Hab. 2:5–6a, 6b–8a, 9–11,
15–17a, 18–20), three refrains (Hab. 2:8b, 12, 17b), and one authorial
insertion of citations (Hab. 2:13–14).

The present form of the Hebrew witnesses (MT and 1QpHab) to
Habakkuk 2:5 employs וְאַף כִּי at the beginning to link the verse to
Habakkuk 2:4a (see the construction in Prov. 11:31 and BDB, 65).[33]
These witnesses also have either "the wine" (MT) or "wealth" (1QpHab)

31. The translation of Habakkuk 2:5–20 in this commentary follows the ancient
    practice of rendering הוֹי as "woe" (cf., LXX). It is understood that the word
    is a simple interjection and that it is not always appropriate to translate it
    this way (e.g., Isa. 55:1). The primary difference between הוֹי and אוֹי is syn-
    tactical. The latter is typically followed by the preposition "to."
32. See William Hayes Ward, *A Critical and Exegetical Commentary on Ha-
    bakkuk*, ICC (New York: Charles Scribner's Sons, 1911), 16–17; Roberts,
    Nahum, Habakkuk, and Zephaniah, 122–24.
33. See Smith, *Micah–Malachi*, 107–108; Roberts, *Nahum, Habakkuk, and
    Zephaniah*, 116.

as the subject of the following participle (MT) or finite verb (1QpHab), unless they are understood in an adverbial relationship (cf., *Tg. Jon.*).[34] It is highly unlikely that "a proud man" is the object of "acts treacherously" in the present form of the Hebrew text since this participle/verb is ordinarily intransitive (e.g., Hab. 1:13b; see BDB, 93). As it currently stands, "a proud man" is appositional and either personifies the wine/wealth or explains that the wine/wealth is metonymy for the proud man who consumes or amasses such things. But it is entirely possible that the original text read: הוי יבגוד גבר יהיר ("Woe, a proud man acts treacherously").[35] This proud man (i.e., the foreign enemy) does not stay at home. He is restless.

The אשר clause in Habakkuk 2:5b further describes the proud man as death personified. He enlarges himself like Sheol, and like death he is not satisfied (cf., Isa. 5:14; Prov. 27:20; 30:16).[36] His appetite is insatiable. The MT then uses narrative verbs (*wayyiqtol*) to translate the simile. He gathers the nations to himself seemingly without end (cf., Hab. 1:9b, 17). 1QpHab has plural verbs here. If this reading is correct, then the nations would be the subject of the verbs, and the sense would either be that the nations gather against the proud man or that they gather their belongings to the proud man. The LORD then raises the rhetorical question in Habakkuk 2:6a, "Will not all of these very nations be the ones to take up a saying/satire/riddle against the proud man" (cf., Mic. 2:4; Nah. 3:7; see BDB, 605)? That is, the tables will be turned in the judgment of the foreign enemy, and it is precisely this poetic justice that becomes the basis for the woe oracle in Habakkuk 2:6b–8a. The LORD thus reports through the prophetic voice the imagined discourse of each nation in Habakkuk 2:6b.

According to the introduction and accusation in Habakkuk 2:6b, the proud man increases what does not belong to him (cf., Hab. 1:6b, 10b).

---

34. Rashi understood the wine and the proud man to be references to Belshazzar and his feast in Daniel 5 (*Mikraoth Gedoloth: The Twelve Prophets*, vol. 2, 266), but this kind of historical particularity is remarkably absent from Habakkuk 2:5–20, making the transition to the vision of the future in Habakkuk 3:3–15 very easy. See also Hab. 2:15; Prov. 20:1.

35. The outline of the woe oracle would then be introduction (Hab. 2:5a), accusation (Hab. 2:5b), and announcement of judgment (Hab. 2:6a).

36. "Sheol" is simply a poetic term for the place of the dead (i.e., the grave) and is commonly parallel to terms like "pit" and "death." It is unsound methodologically to reconstruct an elaborate view of an underworld and the afterlife based on a literalistic reading of poetic imagery in passages like Isaiah 14:9–11.

There is then a parenthetical expression of lament in the text: "How long" (cf., Hab. 1:2; Ps. 6:4b [Eng., 6:3b])? The following parallel to the first part of Habakkuk 2:6b indicates that the proud man makes himself heavy with either debts paid or debts owed (but see Syr.). There is a sense in which both are true, and this may very well be an example of intentional ambiguity. The foreign enemy certainly makes himself rich by demanding payment from the nations, but because this is done unjustly he becomes a kind of debtor to those nations. A similar problem occurs in the announcement of judgment (Hab. 2:7–8a). Those who will rise up suddenly at the beginning of Habakkuk 2:7 are either those who pay the proud man interest or those who are his creditors. The LXX and the Syriac both understand the subject to be those who "bite" the proud man. Again, the sense of this may be that those who have been forced to pay interest unjustly will take a bite out of the foreign enemy in a new role as creditors. The proud man now owes those whom he has wronged. Thus, they will wake up and cause him to tremble as creditors do when it is time to pay (cf., Ps. 109:11). He will become plunder to them. Precisely because the proud man has been the one to plunder so many nations, they in turn will plunder him (Hab. 2:8a; cf., Jer. 30:16; Obad. 15; Zech. 2:13 [Eng., 2:9]).[37] The phrase "all the rest of the peoples" does not refer to those who happened not to fall under the wrath of the foreign enemy but to the remnant of those who did.[38] The refrain that occurs in Habakkuk 2:8b (see also Hab. 2:12, 17b) highlights the bloodshed and violence of the proud man as the reason for his judgment. In context, this would seem to be acts committed against multiple peoples, lands, and cities, but *Targum Jonathan* interprets the singular forms of the Hebrew text to be specific references to the land of Israel and the city of Jerusalem.

The introduction to the next oracle in Habakkuk 2:9–11 describes the proud man as one who makes "evil" (רֹע) unjust gain by violence for his house (Hab. 2:9a; cf., Jer. 6:13; 8:10; Ezek. 22:27; Prov. 1:19; 15:27). The purpose for this is to put his "nest" in a high place (Hab. 2:9b; cf., Num. 24:21; Jer. 49:16; Obad. 4) in an effort to rescue himself from the palm of "disaster" (רָע). But this will prove to be in vain. The accusation in Habakkuk 2:10 is that the proud man has advised shame for his house. This is explained in terms of the unjust cutting off of many peoples as depicted in Habakkuk 2:5–8. The proud man's action is also said to be sin against himself (cf., Exod. 5:16b; Prov. 20:2b). That is, his destruction of many peoples for personal gain has unwittingly

---

37. See 1QpHab for an eschatological interpretation of this.
38. See Keil, *Minor Prophets*, 406–408.

become the cause of his own downfall. The announcement of judgment in Habakkuk 2:11 is then given somewhat indirectly as an explanation of the accusation. Two inanimate witnesses (the stone and the beam/rafter) give voice to the cry of the oppressed, who cannot speak for themselves (cf., Gen. 4:10). The stone from the wall cries out against the oppressor, and the beam/rafter confirms the testimony with its response (cf., Deut. 17:6). These are the very materials out of which the proud man has built his house by means of injustice. They are like the all-seeing eyes of the sky and the land who are sometimes summoned to give testimony in a court of law (e.g., Deut. 32:1; Isa. 1:2; Mic. 6:1–2). The following text of Habakkuk 2:12 initially appears to be the introduction to the next woe oracle, but the two subsequent verses do not follow suit with an accusation and an announcement of judgment. It is clear that Habakkuk 2:12 bears a relationship to the building themes in Habakkuk 2:9–11 and Habakkuk 2:13–14 (cf., Jer. 22:13; Mic. 3:10; Nah. 3:1; Dan. 4:27 [Eng., 4:30]). As it now stands, however, Habakkuk 2:12 functions as the second of three refrains in this passage that share the key words "bloodshed" and "town" (Hab. 2:8b, 12, 17b).

The citation of Jeremiah 51:58 in Habakkuk 2:13 begins with a rhetorical question: "Is it not, look, from the LORD of hosts" (cf., "Thus says the LORD of hosts" [Jer. 51:58])? In other words, not only is the LORD responsible for raising up the foreign nation to judge Habakkuk's people (Hab. 1:6, 12), but also he will oversee the judgment of this wicked instrument and vindicate the true people of God. He himself will lead an army to victory. The Jeremiah 51:58 text is part of the address against Babylon in Jeremiah 50–51. It speaks of the destruction of Babylon's city walls and the burning of its gates (Jer. 51:58a). It also has the phrases "for emptiness" and "for fire" in the reverse order of the clauses in Habakkuk 2:13b (Jer. 51:58b). The proud man will find that the product of the weariness and fainting of the peoples he plundered and exploited for the building of his house will all go up in smoke and amount to nothing. On the other hand, those who trust in the LORD will find their strength renewed. They will run and not grow weary, they will walk and not grow faint (Isa. 40:31; 65:23; Hab. 2–4).

The citation of Isaiah 11:9 in Habakkuk 2:14 comes from a messianic prophecy (Isa. 11:1–10; cf., Isa. 9:5–6 [Eng., 9:6–7]) that anticipates a new exodus (Isa. 11:16) and links to the vision of a new creation (Isa. 11:6–8; 65:17–18, 25). In the messianic kingdom, no one will act badly or corruptly in God's holy mountain (cf., Isa. 2:1–5) because the earth will be full of the knowledge/recognition of the LORD as the waters cover the sea (Isa. 11:9). According to Habakkuk 2:14, the worldly kingdoms of nations like Assyria and Babylon will ultimately fail because the earth will be filled with the knowledge of the glory of the LORD like the waters cover over the sea (cf., Num. 14:21; Jer. 23:24; Hab. 3:3; Ps. 72:19; see also Dan. 2; 7). The addition of the phrase "the glory of the LORD" in Habakkuk 2:14 creates an association between the filling of the sanctuary, whether the tabernacle or the temple, and the filling of the earth as God's sanctuary (see Exod. 40:34; 1 Kgs. 8:11; Isa. 6:3–4; 66:1–2; Ezek. 43:5; Rev. 21:22).

The woe oracle in Habakkuk 2:15–17a begins with a description of the proud man as one who gives his neighbor a drink (see Hab. 2:5).[39] But this is not to be friendly. It is an expression of the foreign enemy's wrath. He makes others drunk in order look upon their nakedness (cf., Gen. 9:20–25; Nah. 3:5, 11).[40] In this the foreign nation is more satisfied with dishonor than with honor (Hab. 2:16; see Hos. 4:7; Prov. 3:35).[41] Therefore, for judgment he is commanded to drink also and be regarded as uncircumcised. *Targum Jonathan* interprets this to mean that the foreign enemy is to be exposed in the way that he has exposed others.[42] Just as the proud man has made others drunk with his cup of wrath, so the cup of the right hand of the LORD will come around to him, disgrace to his honor (see Exod. 15:6; Jer. 25:15–29; Lam. 4:21).[43] This is explained in terms of the violence done to Lebanon and the destruction done to animals by the proud man, which will cover the proud man himself (Hab. 2:17a; cf., Hab. 1:3, 9). It is possible that this is merely talking about violence done to the famous cedars of Lebanon and destruction of animal life in the land, in which case there would be a corresponding judgment for the enemy. But *Targum*

---

39. The MT "joining [or, pouring] your wrath" seems to be the more difficult reading that best explains the origin of the other readings.
40. 1QpHab ("their festivals") and the Hebrew text reflected by the LXX ("their caves") are graphically very similar to the MT ("their nakedness").
41. The Hebrew word translated "honor" here is the same one translated "glory" in Habakkuk 2:14. Several English translations render the first clause in Habakkuk 2:16 as part of the announcement of judgment, but the above translation interprets it to be the accusation (see Keil, *Minor Prophets*, 411).
42. The text of Habakkuk 2:16a in 1QpHab has "reel" instead of "be regarded as uncircumcised." This Hebrew text features transposition of two consonants in the middle of the word. The interpretation (*pesher*), however, in 1QpHab seems to presuppose the verb "be regarded as uncircumcised."
43. The Hebrew words behind "dishonor" (קלון) and "disgrace" (קיקלון) in this verse are very similar. The extra syllable on the beginning of the second word was interpreted by the Latin Vulgate to be a separate word: "vomit of disgrace" (קיא קלון).

Jonathan understands this to be a reference to the destruction of the sanctuary and the plundering of the people. This is based on the fact that Solomon's temple was built using cedars from Lebanon (see 1 Kgs. 5:19–20 [Eng., 5:5–6]).[44] According to the same association, the reader might also see a reference to Solomon's palace, which is called "the house of the forest of Lebanon" due to the extensive use of Lebanon cedars in its construction (1 Kgs. 7:2). If either of these readings is correct, then the corresponding judgment of the enemy would be destruction of sanctuaries or palaces. The conclusion of this oracle is followed in Habakkuk 2:17b by repetition of the refrain from Habakkuk 2:8b (see also Hab. 2:12).

The final "woe" is prefaced by a question in Habakkuk 2:18 about what is the benefit of a carved/sculpted and molten image (see Exod. 32; Deut. 9; 1 Sam. 12:21; Isa. 44:9–20; 57:12; Jer. 2:8, 11; 16:19; Hab. 1:11, 16).[45] It is a teacher of deception (cf., Isa. 9:14 [Eng., 9:15]; Jer. 10:8). According to Keil, "The idol is a teacher of lying, inasmuch as it sustains the delusion, partly by itself and partly through its priests, that it is God, and can do what men expect from God; whereas it is nothing more than a dumb nonentity."[46] The one who fashions such an image demonstrates his trust in the lie of idolatry by the very act of making "dumb" (אלמים) "worthless idols" (אלילים) rather than trusting in the one true "God" (אלהים) (see Ps. 96:5; 115:2–12; 135:15–18). Thus, woe to the one who tries to tell a block of wood to wake up or who tries to rouse silent stone as if such objects were alive and active (Hab. 2:19; cf., Isa. 51:9; Ps. 35:23; 44:24; 59:5–6 [Eng., 44:23; 59:4–5]). English versions typically render the first clause of Habakkuk 2:19b as a question, "Will it teach?" But in light of the description of the idol as a teacher of deception in Habakkuk 2:18a this is not so much a question about whether it will teach as it is a statement about the fact that it does teach lies (see Calvin, *Habakkuk*, 123). The remainder of Habakkuk 2:19b simply points out the fact that the idol is merely an image encased in gold or silver without any breath of life in it at all. On the other hand, the one true living God, the LORD, is in his holy temple (Hab. 2:20; cf., Ps. 96:5–6). There is some question, however, about whether this is a reference to the earthly temple (see the discussion of Habakkuk 2:14) or the

---

44. The interpretation of the destruction of animals as the plundering of the people is based on the understanding that the destruction of animal life would be the removal of the people's livestock.
45. A פסל is "a divine image carved from wood or sculpted from stone, but later cast in metal" (*HALOT* 2:949).
46. Keil, *Minor Prophets*, 413.

heavenly temple (Ps. 11:4). The call to all the earth to hush or be silent (see *Tg. Jon.*) is picked up in Zephaniah 1:7a with reference to the Day of the LORD and again in Zechariah 2:17 (Eng., 2:13).[47] 1QpHab and *Targum Jonathan* see here the end of all idol worship in the final Day of Judgment. This marks the beginning of a transition back to the Day of the LORD theme from Joel-Amos-Obadiah, which will resurface in the following books of Zephaniah, Zechariah, and Malachi.

HABAKKUK 3

3:1 A prayer of Habakkuk, according to shigyonoth [LXX: with song; Syr.: upon which he wandered, cf., Vulg., Luther].[48]

3:2 O LORD, I have heard your report [or, the report about you; Syr.: your name], I have feared your work. In midst of years revive it, in midst of years make it known [LXX: you will be known]. (In rage remember to have compassion.)[49]

---

47. See Mark J. Boda, "A Deafening Call to Silence: The Rhetorical 'End' of Human Address to the Deity in the Book of the Twelve," in *The Book of the Twelve and the New Form Criticism*, eds. Mark J. Boda, Michael H. Floyd, and Colin M. Toffelmire (Atlanta: SBL, 2015), 183–204.

48. BDB: "a wild, passionate song, with rapid changes of rhythm" (993). Cf., Ps. 7. *Tg. Jon.*: "The prayer that Habakkuk the prophet prayed when it was revealed to him concerning the prolongation that he gave to the wicked, that if they would return to the Torah with a whole heart, it would be forgiven them, and all their sins that they committed before him, look, as the mistake/error." Cf., Num. 15:25, 30; Dan. 4:24 (Eng., 4:27). According to Jerome, this is Habakkuk's reproof of himself for his words spoken in Habakkuk 1:2–4 (Ferreiro, *The Twelve Prophets*, 198).

49. LXX: "O Lord, I have heard of your renown and paid reverence; O Lord, I considered your works and was astonished. You will be known in the midst of two living creatures; you will be recognized when the years draw near; you will be displayed when the right time comes; you will remember mercy when my soul is troubled with wrath" (NETS). Caesarius of Arles interpreted the two creatures to be the Old and New Testaments in the midst of which Christ is known spiritually (Ferreiro, *The Twelve Prophets*, 198–99). According to Origen, however, the two creatures are Christ and the Holy Spirit (ibid., 199–200). Roberts suggests that the LXX translator had the two cherubim of the ark (Exod. 25:22) in mind (Roberts, *Nahum, Habakkuk, and Zephaniah*, 131). *Tg. Jon.*: "Lord, I have heard the report *of your strength and* I was afraid! O Lord, your works *are great, for you grant an extension of time to the wicked to see if they will return to your law; but they have not returned and they provoke before you* in the midst

3:3 *God, it is from Teman that he comes, and Holy One from Mt. Paran [LXX: from a shady, densely-wooded mountain; cf., LXX^Barb]. Selah [LXX: διάψαλμα].*[50]

His splendor covers sky, and his praise fills the land [or, the land is full of his praise]. 3:4 *And brightness is like the light,*[51] *two horns from his hand belong to him [Syr.: in the city of his hands]. (And there is the hiding place of his strength.)*[52] 3:5 *Before him goes a plague [or, a word (דֶּבֶר); cf., LXX; see also Syr., Vulg.: death; Tg. Jon.: the angel of death; Luther: pestilence], and a fire-bolt [LXX^Barb: the greatest of winged creatures; Syr.: fowl; Vulg.: the devil; Luther: plague] goes out at his feet [LXX: and he goes forth, in sandals his feet].*[53] 3:6 *He stands and shakes [or, measures] land, he sees and starts up [or, loosens] nations.*[54] *And mountains of antiquity are shattered [or, scattered], hills of long ago bow down. (Goings of long ago belong to him.)* 3:7 *Under trouble I see the tents of Cushan [LXX: Ethiopians], the curtains of the land of Midian rage.*[55] 3:8 *Is it with the rivers that it burns, O LORD? Is your*

---

of the years *in which you have given them life. Therefore you* will display *your might* in the midst of the years, *for you have promised to renew the world, to take vengeance on the wicked who have disregarded your Memra*; *but* in *the midst of your* anger you will remember in mercy *the righteous who do your will*" (Kevin J. Cathcart and Robert P. Gordon, *The Targum of the Minor Prophets: Translated, with a Critical Introduction, Apparatus, and Notes*, The Aramaic Bible 14 [Collegeville, MN: Liturgical], 156).

50. *Tg. Jon.*: "When he gave the Torah to his people, God revealed himself from the south, and the Holy One from Mt. Paran with everlasting strength."

51. The verb is feminine, but it is not clear from form or usage whether "brightness" is masculine or feminine, so the subject could be either "praise" or "land" from Habakkuk 3:3b (both of which are feminine). The Syriac has a masculine verb. *Targum Jonathan* interprets the light to be that of בראשית, which is a reference to Genesis 1:1, 3.

52. LXX: "And he makes strong love of his strength." Syr.: "He puts his power in an area of jurisdiction around a city."

53. *Tg. Jon.*: "and he goes forth in the flame of fire from his word."

54. The LXX makes "land" the subject of the first two verbs, but this cannot be right because "land" is feminine and the verbs are masculine. It also makes "nations" the subject of the next two verbs, which is incorrect because the verbs are singular. *Targum Jonathan* sees here references to the Flood (Gen. 6–8) and the Tower of Babel (Gen. 11:1–9). See also the longer version of this verse in LXX^Barb.

55. According to *Targum Jonathan*, when Israel worshiped idols, the LORD gave them into the hand of Cushan, but when they kept the Torah, he did great things and delivered them from the Midianites by means of Gideon.

anger with the rivers?[56] *Is your fury with the sea when you ride upon your horses, your chariots of salvation [GKC §131r; cf., LXX^{Barb}]? 3:9 In nakedness your bow is laid bare [Syr.: Your bow is surely aroused; cf., 8HevXII gr], oaths about rods are a decree [BDB, 57; or, rods are sworn in with a word; Syr.: and the arrows are filled with your word].*[57] *Selah.*

With rivers you split apart land [LXX: A land of rivers is torn apart; Syr.: And the land is renewed with rivers; Tg. Jon.: For them you split strong rocks, rivers washing the land came out], 3:10 mountains [LXX: peoples] see you,[58] *they writhe. A flood of water, it crosses over [MurXII: Clouds pour out rain; cf., Ps. 77:18 (Eng., 77:17); LXX: scattering waters of his journey; 8HevXII gr: the tempest of waters passed by], [the] deep gives its voice. On high he lifts up his hands [LXX: height of its appearance], 3:11 sun, moon, each stands / remains in a lofty abode [LXX: the sun is lifted up, and the moon stands in its order].*[59] *At the light of your arrows they go, at the brightness of the lightning of your spear [LXX: Into light your spears go, into light of lightning your weapons]. 3:12 In indignation you march on land [LXX: With a threat you diminish (from* צעד*) land], in anger you trample on nations. 3:13 You go out for the salvation of your people, for the salvation of your anointed one [pc Mss, LXX^{-BS}: your anointed ones; LXX^{Barb}: your chosen ones; Vulg.: salvation with your anointed one].*[60] *You strike [the] head of [the] house of [the] wicked, laying bare from foundation to neck [LXX: You cast death to the heads of the lawless, you raise up bonds to the neck].*[61] *Selah.*[62]

3:14 You pierce with his rods [LXX: in ecstasy] the head [LXX^{Barb}: leaders] of his warriors [MurXII, MT kethiv: warrior; 8HevXII gr: unfortified ones]. They storm to scatter me [8HevXII gr: us; LXX: They tremble in it; Syr.: And they trust in their ferocity]. Their exultation is

56. According to *Targum Jonathan*, the rivers represent kings and their armies.
57. LXX: "Surely you stretch your bow tight at the scepters, says the Lord." Cf., LXX^{Barb}. *Tg. Jon.*: "You certainly revealed yourself in strength because of your covenant, which was with the tribes."
58. *Tg. Jon.* adds at the beginning of the verse: "When you revealed yourself on Mt. Sinai."
59. According to *Targum Jonathan*, this refers to the story in Joshua 10.
60. Bede and Cyril of Alexandria interpreted the plural "christs" to be parallel to "your people" and thus "Christians" (Ferreiro, *The Twelve Prophets*, 205–206).
61. *Tg. Jon.*: "the feet of your people were upon the necks of their enemies."
62. Both the Syriac and *Targum Jonathan* have "forever" for "Selah."

as to devour an afflicted one in the secret place [LXX: They open their bridles like a poor man eating in secret].⁶³ 3:15 You tread on the sea with your horses [GKC §144l, m], a heap [or, foaming] of many waters [LXX: stirring up much water].

3:16 I have heard [LXX: I keep = שמרתי]⁶⁴, and my belly rages, at a sound my lips quiver [LXX: from the sound of the prayer of my lips]. Rottenness enters my bones, and in my place I rage, so that [or, where; see Vulg., BDB, 83] I rest for a day of distress to come up to a people that attacks us [LXX: to a people of my sojourning].⁶⁵ 3:17 Even though a fig tree does not sprout [LXX: bear fruit], and there is no produce among the grapevines. Even though an olive tree's work fails, and fields do not produce food. Even though he cuts off sheep from a fold, and there are no cattle in the stalls,⁶⁶ 3:18 as for me, it is in the LORD that I will exult, I will rejoice in the God of my salvation [Vulg.: in God my Jesus].⁶⁷ 3:19 The LORD [MT: GOD, the Lord] is my strength, and he makes my feet like the does [Tg. Jon.: light like the does; LXX: for perfection], and upon my high places [LXX: the high places] he causes me to tread.

For the one who endures, in my afflictions [or, For the director, on my stringed instruments; LXX: to have victory in his song; cf., LXXᴮᵃʳᵇ].

Habakkuk 3 in its entirety is designated by its superscription "A prayer of Habakkuk the prophet" (Hab. 3:1a; cf., Pss. 17:1; 72:20; 86:1; 90:1; 102:1; 142:1).⁶⁸ Added to this is the musical notation "according

---

63. *Targum Jonathan* sees in this verse references to the splitting of the sea by means of Moses's rod and the drowning of the captains of Pharaoh's armies in the Sea of Reeds because they enslaved God's people.

64. *Targum Jonathan* prefaces this verse with "Babylon said." According to the Targum, Babylon trembled at the judgment of the Egyptians as recounted in the Targum's version of Habakkuk 3:14.

65. NASB: "for the people to arise who will invade us." This translation presupposes that the foreign nation's attack is not already underway. See commentary on Habakkuk 1:2–4. See also LXXᴮᵃʳᵇ.

66. Those who do not think that the foreign nation's attack is already underway will render this verse as contrary to fact (e.g., ASV). *Targum Jonathan* interprets the images in this verse to be metaphors for the downfalls of Babylon, Media, Greece, and Rome.

67. According to *Targum Jonathan*, this is a celebration for God's deliverance of his anointed one and his people (see Hab. 3:13).

68. According to Calvin, this was to give the prayer authority and to show the people how to pray (*Habakkuk*, 133). Similarly, Smith suggests that the

to *shigyonoth*," which has been variously interpreted according to שׁגה ("to go astray, err"). It is not clear whether this is a style or a tune (or something else). The only parallel is the singular form of the word in Psalm 7:1. There the *shiggayon* is something that David sang to the LORD. But the form and content of the psalm, which is a petition psalm, does not have the character of the theophany in Habakkuk 3. The prayer in Habakkuk 3 is divided into sub-units by means of the marker "Selah," which is also a feature of many of the psalms (e.g., Ps. 3). The chapter concludes with what was apparently the superscription to the following psalm of the collection from which Habakkuk's prayer was taken (Hab. 3:19b). Thus, much like the adoption of the partial acrostic at the beginning of Nahum (Nah. 1:2–8), which gave the book a broader, eschatological context, the integral inclusion of Habakkuk's prayer at the end of the book puts the prophet's historical situation into perspective by means of its vision of things to come in the last days.

The prophet opens his prayer in Habakkuk 3:2 by addressing the LORD and stating that he has heard the report about the LORD's work (cf., Isa. 66:19; Ps. 44:2 [Eng., 44:1]). This is somewhat of a loaded declaration. On the one hand, Habakkuk has heard within the context of the book about the work of God in his own day, which involves the raising up of a foreign nation as God's chosen instrument of judgment (Hab. 1:5–6). He has also heard about the eschatological work of God in which the wicked will be judged and the righteous delivered (Hab. 2:2–4). On the other hand, it is clear from Habakkuk 3:3–15 that the prophet has heard the reading of the Torah, for it is precisely the narrative of the Torah that provides the storehouse of prefigurative imagery for his vision of the coming of the LORD in the future.[69] Parallel to this is Habakkuk's statement that he has feared the LORD's work.[70] In the

---

psalm, which defies simple categorization, should be classified as a liturgy that was used in temple worship (*Micah–Malachi*, 115). The more pressing hermeneutical issue, however, is the role that the prayer now plays in the composition of the book.

69. According to Redak, "The prophet relates the miracles God performed for Israel since the Exodus, and he is praying and prophesying that God will do likewise in this exile; when Israel emerges from this exile, and during the war of Gog and Magog" (*Mikraoth Gedoloth: The Twelve Prophets*, vol. 2, 272–73).

70. The NASB arranges the syntax here differently: "O LORD, I have heard the report about You *and* I fear. O LORD, revive Your work in the midst of the years." Not only does this ignore the parallelism of the Hebrew text, but also it misses the connection to Habakkuk 1:5 and 2:4, where the work of God is the object of faith. Technically, this syntactical decision would require

present context this is not a declaration of amazement, reverence, or terror. This usage of יָרֵא falls within the semantic field of "faith" (cf., Exod. 14:31; Jon. 1:16; 3:5; see also *TLOT* 1:143). Thus, Habakkuk 3:2 is the third and final of the three leading texts in the book that speak of faith in the work of God. The text of Habakkuk 1:5 warned the reader about lacking faith because of the historical work of God. That of Habakkuk 2:4 revealed that those who put their faith in the future work of God would be justified. And now in Habakkuk 3:2, prior to the vision of the future work of God, the prophet declares his faith in that very work. He prays that the LORD would revive his work even in the midst of his years—that he would make it known. According to Keil, "there is an evident allusion to the divine answer in ch. 2:3, that the oracle is for an appointed time."[71] Thus, the prophet wants to see the LORD's eschatological work in his own day, but he also expresses at the end of his prayer his resolve to trust in the LORD even if he must wait until the resurrection (Hab. 3:17–19; cf., Dan. 12:13). The clause in Hab. 3:2b is an additional parenthetical prayer that stands outside the poetic parallelism and clarifies what is meant by the request to revive the work. Habakkuk asks that in the rage of judgment against the wicked the LORD would remember to have compassion on those who are righteous by faith (see *Tg. Jon.*; cf., Mic. 7:18–20; Hab. 3:7).

The so-called "theophany" in Habakkuk 3:3–15 is neither a recounting of past events (past tense) nor a mere prediction of things to come (future tense). It is a timeless mosaic of images drawn from the narratives of the Pentateuch and designed like pictures at an exhibition to provide a comprehensive portrait of an artist's work. Therefore, the present tense is most suitable in translation.[72] The prophet wants to depict the future work of God, but he does not go outside the textual world of the Bible to do so.[73] The first part of this features third-

---

a hanging construction: "O LORD, your work, in the midst of years revive it." The LXX does something similar (see above), but it adds a verb ("I considered your works"). On this basis, the *BHS* apparatus suggests reading וְרָאִיתִי ("and I have seen") rather than יָרֵאתִי ("I have feared"). The problem with this is that the LXX translator clearly had יָרֵאתִי in his *Vorlage*, which he translated, "and I paid reverence." He then felt the need to supply a verb to what would otherwise be the beginning of a hanging construction.

71. Keil, *Minor Prophets*, 415.
72. See Calvin, *Habakkuk*, 161; Keil, *Minor Prophets*, 417; Ward, *Habakkuk*, 19–22; Roberts, *Nahum, Habakkuk, and Zephaniah*, 151.
73. See Michael B. Shepherd, *The Textual World of the Bible* (New York: Peter Lang, 2013).

person reference to God (Hab. 3:3–7), but then the second-person reference in Hab. 3:8–15 maintains the sense that this is still part of the prayer. Habakkuk begins with an image of God coming from Sinai (Hab. 3:3a; cf., Deut. 33:2; Judg. 5:4–5; Zech. 9:14; 14:5; Ps. 68:8–9, 18 [Eng., 68:7–8, 17]) in order to describe God's future deliverance of his people in terms of a new exodus. Just as he defeated the Egyptians and provided for his people in the wilderness (including the giving of the Torah) and brought them into the land, so will he judge the wicked and deliver the righteous in days to come.[74] God's splendor covers the sky, and his praise fills the land (Hab. 3:3b; cf., Exod. 13:21–22; 19:16–19; 20:18–21; Isa. 11:9; Hab. 2:14).

This brightness of God's splendor at Sinai is like the light of creation (Gen. 1:3) according to *Targum Jonathan's* interpretation of Hab. 3:4a. Others interpret this to be the light of the lightning (Hab. 2:11; cf., 2 Sam. 22:13, 15; Ps. 18:13, 15 [Eng., 18:12, 14]). The use of קְרָנַיִם ("two horns") in Habakkuk 3:4a is likely an example of double entendre. In context, it means "two rays of light" in reference the story in Exodus 34:29–30, where the skin of Moses's face "shone" (קָרַן) at Sinai (see Rashi). But "horn" in biblical Hebrew is often a symbol of strength (BDB, 901–902). This is the way Habakkuk 3:4b interprets the horns: "And there is the hiding place of his strength" (cf., 2 Sam. 22:12; Ps. 18:12 [Eng., 18:11]). The adverb "there" points back to "his hand" (likely the strong right hand [Exod. 15:6; Deut. 33:2]).[75]

The MT of Habakkuk 3:5a interprets דבר to be דֶּבֶר ("plague"), a reference to the plagues in Egypt (Exod. 9:15) or possibly a reference to the death of the wilderness generation (Num. 14:12). *Targum Jonathan* interprets it to be the angel of death that goes before the LORD (Exod. 12:23; 2 Sam. 24:13, 16; Ps. 78:49). On the other hand, the LXX reads דבר as דָּבָר ("word"), a reference to the giving of the Torah. Parallel to this is the going out of a "fire-bolt" at the LORD's feet (Hab. 3:5b; cf., Deut. 33:2b; Isa. 66:15–16; Pss. 50:3; 97:3). According to Rashi, this means that "angels of fire came with him to Sinai" (cf., Dan. 7:9–10).[76] This is an intriguing interpretation in light of the reference to Deuteronomy 33:2 in Habakkuk 3:3a. According to Deuteronomy 33:2a, when the LORD came from Sinai, he came from holy myriads (see also "angels" in LXX Deut. 33:2b [cf., Acts 7:53; Gal. 3:19; Heb.

---

74. According to BDB (699–700), "Selah" (Hab. 3:3a, 9a, 13b) is an imperative from *sll* ("lift up") that signals an option in the liturgy to insert a doxology or benediction.

75. See also Ps. 132:8 (Redak). The LXX reads שָׁם instead of שָׂם.

76. *Mikraoth Gedoloth: The Twelve Prophets*, vol. 2, 275.

2:2]). Rashi understands the holy myriads in Deuteronomy 33:2a to be holy angels.[77]

Interpretation of Habakkuk 3:6 largely depends upon whether וימדד is a *poel* of מדד ("measure") or a *polel* of מוד (= מוט ["shake"]; cf., LXX). Both formations are unusual. The former option would result in a reference to something like the Table of Nations or the Tower of Babel (Gen. 10–11; Deut. 32:8; see *Tg. Jon.*; see also *b. B. Qam.* 38a). But it could also be similar to the use in 2 Samuel 8:2 or the one in Psalms 60:8 and 108:8 (Eng., 60:7; 108:7). The latter option ("shake") seems to fit better with the second half of the verse, which speaks of shattering or scattering mountains of antiquity and the bowing down of hills of long ago (cf., Judg. 5:5; Mic. 1:4; Nah. 1:5; Ps. 114:6). Such ancient and imposing geographical features cannot stand before the LORD who possesses "goings of long ago" (cf., Hab. 1:12; Ps. 68:25 [Eng., 68:24]). According to Habakkuk 3:7, this is also true of the peoples. "Cushan" is a place name parallel to "Midian" and does not refer to the king in Judges 3:8, 10 (*contra* Calvin). The prophet "sees" in his vision the tents of Cushan "under trouble." The parallel to this is that the curtains of the land of Midian "rage" (cf., Exod. 15:14). *Targum Jonathan* sees here a reference to the story of Gideon who defeated the Midianites (Judg. 6–8), but it could just as well be a reference to Numbers 25 and 31.

The rhetorical questions in Habakkuk 3:8 expect the answer, "No." When the LORD split the waters of the Sea of Reeds (Exod. 14:21–22) and those of the Jordan River (Josh. 3:13–17; 2 Kgs. 2:8, 14), it appeared that he was angry with the waters (Exod. 15:8; Nah. 1:4; Ps. 114:3, 5), but he was in fact angry with the enemies of his people (Exod. 15:6–7).[78] The text of Habakkuk 3:8–15 bears a close relationship to Ps. 77:17–21 (Eng., 77:15–20). Keil argues that Habakkuk depends upon the psalm: "Habakkuk depicts a coming redemption under figures borrowed from that of the past, to which the singer of this psalm looks back from his own mournful times, comforting himself with the picture of the miraculous deliverance of his people out of Egypt."[79] On the other hand, Ward considers the psalm to be later, referring to its

---

77. It is worth noting that Rashi does not take the opportunity in his commentary on Habakkuk 3:5 to bolster his interpretation of אשדת in Deuteronomy 33:2b as "fire" plus "law."

78. See *Mikraoth Gedoloth: The Twelve Prophets*, vol. 2, 277; Calvin, *Habakkuk*, 151; Keil, *Minor Prophets*, 421.

79. Keil, *Minor Prophets*, 417.

use of tricola.[80] It is a difficult decision to make since the direction of dependence has been obscured. The good news is that the matter need not be settled in order to enjoy the benefits of comparing the two texts. Thus, the psalm personifies the waters of the sea as terrified at the sight of God, and it depicts God making a path in the many waters (Ps. 77:17, 20 [Eng., 77:16, 19]). Likewise, Habakkuk's image of God's anger with the waters refers to when God rides upon his horses, his chariots of salvation, and makes a path in the many waters of the sea (Hab. 3:8, 15; cf., 2 Sam. 22:11; Isa. 66:15; Ps. 18:11 [Eng., 18:10). The text of Hab. 3:9a adds that God exposes his weaponry—his bow and his rods.[81] The "oaths" in this half verse are not about the "tribes" (*contra* *Tg. Jon.*) but about the rods (cf., Hab. 3:14). What God swears about his use of weaponry against the enemy constitutes an official decree (cf., Deut. 32:40–42).

With rivers God splits apart land (Hab. 3:9b; cf., Ps. 74:15). Parallel to this is the thought that mountains see God and writhe (Hab. 3:10; cf., Hab. 3:6; Ps. 77:17 [Eng., 77:16]). According to *Targum Jonathan*, this happened when God revealed himself on Mt. Sinai. The imagery of flood waters passing over and the deep giving its voice is reminiscent of both creation (Gen. 1:2, 9–10; Ps. 104:5–9) and the Flood (Gen. 7:11, 19; 8:1–5), but in context this is likely intended to recall the exodus tradition (Exod. 15:5; Ps. 77:18 [Eng., 77:17]). It is not immediately clear then who or what the subject of the last clause of Habakkuk 3:10 is ("On high he lifts up his hands"). If the clause is read with what precedes it, then the deep would presumably be the subject. If it is read with Habakkuk 3:11a, then the subject could be God taking an oath with a raised hand in the context of the exodus (cf., Ezek. 20:5). It could also be the people of God defiantly departing Egypt with hands lifted high (cf., Exod. 14:8). It could also be Moses or Joshua defeating the enemy with raised hands (Exod. 17:8–16; Josh. 8:18). The parallel to this in Habakkuk 3:11a is apparently a reference to the story in Joshua 10 (see *Tg. Jon.*).[82] According to that story, Joshua came to defend the Gibeonites with whom he had foolishly made a covenant (Josh. 9:15; see Deut. 7:2) against the southern coalition of kings. He traveled all

---

80. Ward, *Habakkuk*, 23–24.
81. "The bow is made bare, not by the shooting of the arrows, but by its covering being removed, in order to use it as a weapon" (Keil, *Minor Prophets*, 421).
82. See Rashi and Calvin. Keil (*Minor Prophets*, 424) and Roberts (*Nahum, Habakkuk, and Zephaniah*, 141, 156) disagree. Roberts thinks that this is the darkness of the Day of the LORD (see Joel 2:2, 10–11; 3:4 [Eng., 2:31]; Amos 5:18–20; Zeph. 1:15)

the night before to come up from Gilgal (Josh. 10:9) and did not finish the job until sunset of the following day (Josh. 10:27). Thus, it felt like the LORD had granted in response to Joshua's request a longer day than normal to defeat the enemy. This is characterized poetically in Joshua 10:12–13 in terms of the sun and the moon standing still. The source citation in Joshua 10:13 indicates that this came from a larger collection of poetry called the Book of Jashar (see also 2 Sam. 1:18).

The language and imagery of Habakkuk 3:11b are very close to that of 2 Sam. 22:15; Zech. 9:14; Pss. 18:15; 77:18–19 (Eng., 18:14; 77:17–18); 97:4; 144:6. Flashes of lightning are the LORD's arrows and spear in the battle against the enemy (cf., Hab. 3:9). Translations understand the subject of "they go" differently. The LXX takes the weaponry to be the subject. It would then be possible to interpret the whole of verse 11 to mean that while the sun and the moon are darkened by the storm clouds, the lightning flashes are the only source of light. On the other hand, it is also possible that the nations of Habakkuk 3:12 are the subject. That is, the LORD's arrows made the seven nations of Canaan flee (see Rashi and Calvin on Habakkuk 3:12; see also Joshua 24:12). Verse 11 has already introduced the conquest as the latter part of the sequence that began with the plagues and the exodus. It is in indignation and in anger that the LORD marches on the land of the covenant and tramples the nations to be dispossessed (Hab. 3:12; see Gen. 15:16).

Most translations interpret Habakkuk 3:13a to envision that God goes out for the salvation of his people and to deliver his anointed king as in the past (e.g., 2 Sam. 8:14b; Zech. 9:9). According to this reading, the first occurrence of the prepositional phrase לישע ("for salvation") is in a construct relationship to "your people." But the second occurrence of this phrase in the parallel functions like an infinitive construct with a following definite direct object marker before the object "your anointed." The Latin Vulgate, however, interprets את to be the preposition "with" rather than the definite direct object marker: "for salvation with your anointed" (see also Calvin and KJV). This anointed king is not any particular historical king.[83] Indeed, the eschatological context

---

83. See Keil, *Minor Prophets*, 425. Ward thinks that the anointed one is Israel (*Habakkuk*, 24), but there is no real precedent for this. An anointed one is normally a king or, less often, a high priest (see BDB, 603). There is one reference to the patriarchs as kings (Ps. 105:15), but this is probably because of the reference to Abraham in Genesis 23:6, using Ezekiel's term for a king (e.g., Ezek. 34:24; see LXX Gen. 23:6).

of the vision would seem to suggest a messianic figure.[84] It is important to keep in mind that the source for the imagery of this vision is the exodus story, so it would be out of place for this to be a reference to David or one of the Davidic kings of the past. It is more likely that the anointed one here is the messianic king prophesied in Numbers 24:7–8 whom God brings out of Egypt in a new exodus (cf., Num. 23:22; see also LXX Num. 24:7–8). Some witnesses to Habakkuk 3:13a read the plural "your anointed ones." This is most probably a secondary attempt to historicize the text so that it refers to a succession of multiple Davidic kings, unless it is to be read according to what is found in texts like Jeremiah 23:4, 5–6; and Micah 5:4–5 (Eng., 5:5–6), where the plurality of saints reign with the one ideal Davidic king (cf., Dan. 7:13–14, 27; Rev. 5:10).

Striking the head of the enemy is a prominent theme in ancient Hebrew poetry and in messianic psalms (Hab. 3:13b; see Gen. 3:15; Num. 24:17; Deut. 32:39, 42; Judg. 5:26; Pss. 68:22 [Eng., 68:21]; 110:5–6). Here it results in laying bare the very foundation of the house of the wicked by tearing down its walls and structure from top to bottom. It matters very little whether the head in either Habakkuk 3:13b or 3:14a is a literal head or a leader. Either way the poetic imagery depicts a fatal blow to the enemy. According to Habakkuk 3:14a, the LORD pierces the head of the enemy's warriors either by means of the anointed king's rods or by means of the enemy's own rods (see Hab. 3:9a; cf., Exod. 14:28; 15:4).[85] The prophet takes the threat of the enemy personally ("They storm to scatter me"). The joy of the enemy warriors is to devour an afflicted one like Habakkuk in a secret place (Hab. 3:14b; cf., Ps. 10:8). The theophany concludes in Habakkuk 3:15 very fittingly by returning to the image of the exodus from Habakkuk 3:8 and Psalm 77:20 (Eng., 77:19).

The conclusion to Habakkuk's prayer in Habakkuk 3:16–19 hearkens back to the beginning in Habakkuk 3:2 ("I have heard"). The thought of enduring the attack of God's wicked instrument of judgment causes the prophet's belly to rage and his lips to quiver. It feels as though rottenness or decay enters his bones, and he is agitated and

---

84. Rashi took this king to be Saul and David, but Redak says it is a reference to the Messiah (*Mikraoth Gedoloth: The Twelve Prophets*, vol. 2, 279). "Since the vision refers to a set time in the future, there is no reason why Habakkuk need have had a particular Davidide in mind. On could easily think of Jeremiah's ideal Davidide of the future (Jer. 23:5–6; cf. Rudolph, 245)" (Roberts, *Nahum, Habakkuk, and Zephaniah*, 156).

85. See *Tg. Jon.* for reference to the exodus tradition in Habakkuk 3:14.

unsettled in the very place where he stands. Nevertheless, the knowledge that this is all part of the work of God results in an ability to rest/wait for the day of distress to come upon the people that attacks (see note to translation above). The LORD is good to those who take refuge in him in the day of distress (Nah. 1:7). This day of distress is none other than the Day of the LORD according to the way the following book of Zephaniah picks up this language (Zeph. 1:15). Habakkuk expresses his confidence in Habakkuk 3:17–18 when he resolves using cohortative forms (cf., Hab. 2:1) to exult in the LORD and to rejoice in the God of his salvation (cf., Hab. 3:13) despite the loss of figs, grape produce, flocks, and cattle (cf., Judg. 6:1–6; 1 Kgs. 5:5 [Eng., 4:25]; Isa. 54:10; Hos. 2:14 [Eng., 2:12]; Joel 1:12; Hag. 2:19). In this he is much like other prophets who wait on the future work of God even though it may not come in their lifetime (Isa. 8:16–18; Mic. 7:7; Dan. 12:13). Here Habakkuk is a model for the reader to follow. The LORD is his strength (Hab. 3:19; cf., Ps. 73:25–26), and the LORD makes him swift and sure-footed like a doe, enabling him to tread on high places with ease (cf., Deut. 33:29b; 2 Sam. 22:34; Ps. 18:34 [Eng., 18:33]; Isa. 58:14). That is, he gives him confidence in the midst of distress to live victoriously and to rise up on wings like eagles, running without growing weary and walking without growing faint (Isa. 40:31; Hab. 2:2).

The text of Habakkuk 3:19b is not a concluding musical notation for Habakkuk's prayer. The phrase למנצח is normally in a psalm superscription (see BDB, 663–64). As noted above, this superscription apparently belonged to the following psalm in the collection from which Habakkuk's prayer was taken. But its inclusion at the end of the book of Habakkuk is no accident. The usual translation ("For the director, on my stringed instruments"), however, probably does not reflect the intent of the author. The translation "director" for מנצח comes from the interpretation that the word refers to one who is pre-eminent in the musical setting. But the same word can also mean "one who endures." This is apparently reflected in the way the LXX often translates the phrase in the book of Psalms: *eis to telos* ("for the end"). That is, it designates the psalm as being for one who endures to the end (i.e., the last days) when God will complete his future and final work (e.g., LXX Pss. 63–69 [MT, Eng.: Ps. 64–70]; cf., Matt. 24:13). The following phrase (בנגינותי) does not mean "on my stringed instruments" but "in my afflictions."[86] Thus, the prayer of Habakkuk is for the one who endures to the end in the midst of such afflictions

---

86. See A. E. Cowley, ed., *Aramaic Papyri of the Fifth Century B.C.* (Oxford: Clarendon, 1923; reprint, Eugene, OR: Wipf & Stock, 2005), 100.

as what the prophet suffers—a very fitting conclusion to a prayer and a book that find great comfort from distress in the vision of the eschatological work of God in Christ.

CONCLUSION

It should be evident from the above commentary that the book of Habakkuk is not in need of an update or additional application/principles for teaching or preaching in the local church. For the apostle Paul, it is Christian Scripture. The text of Habakkuk 2:4, understood in the context of the book (Hab. 1:5; 3:2) and according to its intertextual link to Genesis 15:6, is the Christian doctrine of justification by faith in Christ. The connection between Habakkuk 3:3–15 and Nahum 1:2–8 provides a broader eschatological context for the historical prophecies that remains immediately relevant for today's reader. The connection to Zephaniah 1:7, 15 (Hab. 2:20; 3:16) reinforces this by making the transition back to the Day of the LORD theme. The prophet himself serves as a model for the Christian reader (Hab. 3:16–19), demonstrating how to wait on the future work of God in the midst of a fallen world. This is the application provided in the book itself: to be justified by faith in Christ and to live faithfully each day in expectation of his coming (Matt. 24:45–51).

BOOK OF THE TWELVE
ZEPHANIAH

ZEPHANIAH 1

1:1 The word of the LORD that came to Zephaniah [Tg. Jon.: The word of prophecy from before the LORD that was with Zephaniah] the son of Cushi, the son of Gedaliah, the son of Amariah, the son of Hezekiah [pc Mss, Syr.: Hilkiah], in the days of Josiah the son of Amon, the king of Judah.

1:2 "Gathering and taking away, I will make an end of [LXX: Let him completely abandon; Syr.: I am completely removing; Tg. Jon.: I will completely destroy; Vulg.: I will surely gather] everything from upon the surface of the ground," the prophetic utterance of the LORD.[1]

1:3 "I will make an end of mankind and beast, I will make an end of the birds of the sky and the fish of the sea (and the stumbling-blocks, namely, the wicked)[2] [> LXX]. And I will cut off mankind from upon the surface of the ground," the prophetic utterance of the LORD. 1:4 "And I will stretch out my hand against Judah and against all the inhabitants of Jerusalem, and I will cut off from this place the remnant of Baal [LXX: the names of Baal], the name of the idol-priests[3] [MT adds: with

---

1. See GKC §113w[3] and BDB, 692–93.
2. Or, "and the stumbling-blocks [i.e., the idols] with the wicked." Syr.: "And the offense I will cause to come upon the sinners." *Tg. Jon.*: "because the snares of the wicked are many." The Latin Vulgate has "ruins" rather than "stumbling-blocks."
3. mlt Mss, LXX, Syr., Vulg.: "and the name of the idol-priests."

*the priests, > LXX], 1:5 and [> 8HevXII gr] those who prostrate them-
selves on the rooftops to the host of the sky, and those who prostrate
themselves [> LXX], those who swear to the LORD and those who swear
by their king [LXX^L, Syr., Vulg., Luther: Milcom; Tg. Jon.: in the name
of their idols], 1:6 and those who turn back from after the LORD and
who do not seek the LORD and do not seek him in prayer and worship
[or, inquire of him].*"

*1:7 Hush [LXX: Act reverently; Tg. Jon.: All the wicked have ended]
from before the LORD [MT: Lord GOD], for near is the Day of the LORD.
For the LORD has established a sacrifice, he has set apart his invited
guests. 1:8 And so will it be in the day of the LORD's sacrifice: "And I
will visit upon the princes [or, officials / leaders; LXX: rulers] and upon
the sons [LXX: house] of the king] and upon all those who wear foreign
clothing [Tg. Jon.: all who stir themselves up to worship idols]. 1:9 And
I will visit upon everyone who leaps over the threshold [Tg. Jon.: all
who walk in the laws of the Philistines] in that day,^{4} those who fill the
house of their lord / master with violence and deceit.*

*1:10 And there will be in that day," the prophetic utterance of the LORD,
"a sound of a cry from the Fish Gate and a howling from the second district [Tg. Jon.: Ophel; cf., 2 Chr. 33:14] and a great breaking from the
hills. 1:11 Howl, O inhabitants of the Mortar [LXX: what is cut down;
Tg. Jon.: Kidron Valley], for all the people of Canaan [or, merchants; see
BDB, 488] are destroyed [LXX: all the people are like Canaan; cf., Tg.
Jon.], all those laden with silver are cut off.*

*1:12 And it will be in that day, I will search Jerusalem with lamps
[LXX, Syr.: a lamp],^{5} and I will visit upon the men who thicken upon
their lees [or, wine dregs, sediment; LXX: who despise their commands;
cf., Syr.; Tg. Jon.: who lie at ease upon their possessions], who say in
their heart, 'The LORD will not cause good, nor will he cause evil.'^{6} 1:13
And their wealth will become plunder, and their houses will become a
desolation. And they will build houses and not inhabit them, and they
will plant vineyards and not drink their wine."*

*1:14 Near is the great Day of the LORD, near and very swift. The sound
of the Day of the LORD is a mighty man bitterly crying there [BHS: The*

---

4. Cf., LXX and Syr.
5. According to *Tg. Jon.*, the LORD will appoint searchers to do this.
6. BDB (405): "in prov. phr., cannot *do good or ill*, =cannot do anything at all."

sound of the Day of the LORD is bitter, a mighty man is crying / roaring there; LXX: The sound of the Day of the Lord is bitter and harsh, it is appointed strong; cf., Syr., Tg. Jon.]. 1:15 A day of wrath is that day, a day of distress and stress, a day of ruin and desolation, a day of darkness and gloominess, a day of cloud and heavy cloud,[7] 1:16 a day of shofar and shout of war against the fortified cities and against the high corners [Tg. Jon.: the exalted hills / heights; NET: high corner towers].

1:17 "And I will cause distress for mankind, and they will go like blind men." (For it is against the LORD that they have sinned.) "And their blood will be poured out like the dust, and their bowels [LXX, Syr.: flesh; Tg. Jon.: corpse] like dung. 1:18 Neither their silver nor their gold will be able to rescue them." In the day of the LORD's wrath[8] and in the fire of his jealousy all the earth will be consumed [Tg. Jon.: in the fire of his vengeance all the wicked of the earth will come to an end], for a complete destruction, surely terrible [LXX: and haste], will he make all the inhabitants of the earth.

The superscription to "Zephaniah" ("The LORD hides")[9] indicates that the book as a whole is "the word of the LORD" (Zeph. 1:1; cf., Hos. 1:1; Joel 1:1; Mic. 1:1). That is, the book is not primarily Zephaniah's book. It is God's book. The word of the LORD came to Zephaniah, but there is no explanation of how this happened (see 2 Pet. 1:19–21). There are four names given in Zephaniah's lineage, more than the reader customarily sees in a prophetic superscription. Some think that this was to trace the prophet's ancestry back to Hezekiah, the great king of Judah, but there is no clear indication of this. A few witnesses even read "Hilkiah" instead of "Hezekiah." It seems rather more likely that the lineage is given simply to distinguish Zephaniah the prophet from others who bear the same name. The narrative context for Zephaniah's prophecy is 2 Kings 22–23, "the days of Josiah" (640–609 BC). This makes Zephaniah a contemporary of Jeremiah the prophet (Jer. 1:1–3). Commentators debate whether Zephaniah prophesied before or after Josiah's reform. On the

---

7. According to GKC §133l, "Sometimes the completeness of an action or state is expressed by placing together two or even three substantives of the same stem and of similar sound." The Syriac repeats "is that day" with each word pair.
8. English translations typically put the phrase "in the day of the LORD's wrath" with what precedes it, but see the arrangement in *BHS*.
9. See J. J. M. Roberts, *Nahum, Habakkuk, and Zephaniah*, OTL (Louisville: Westminster/John Knox, 1991), 165.

one hand, Zephaniah's words of judgment appear to presuppose that there has been no reform. On the other hand, it is quite possible that Josiah's reform simply did not have the desired widespread effect, as evidenced by the rapid decline that led to Babylonian exile in the two decades following the king's death.[10] But perhaps it is best not to make the context of Zephaniah's prophecy so specific. After all, the superscription refers generally to "the days of Josiah."

The book opens with two prophetic utterances of the LORD that declare the end of all creation (Zeph. 1:2–3; cf., Amos. 9:8; Mic. 1:2–7; Zeph. 1:18; 3:8). This is the context for the judgment of Judah (Zeph. 1:4–6; 3:1–8)), the Day of the LORD (Zeph. 1:7–2:3), and the judgment of the nations (Zeph. 2:4–15) prior to the words of restoration in Zephaniah 3:9–20. The text of Zephaniah 1:2 begins with a citation of Jeremiah 8:13. These are the only two places in the Hebrew Bible that feature a play on the *qal* infinitive absolute of אָסֹף ("gather") and the *hiphil* prefixed conjugation first common singular of סוּף ("end"). As noted above, Zephaniah was a contemporary of Jeremiah, but the inclusion of Zephaniah 1:2 is likely the work of the composer of the Twelve for two reasons. First, citation of Jeremiah at the beginning of books has already been part of the composer's seam work (Amos 1:2a [Jer. 25:30]; Obadiah 1–5 [Jer. 49:9, 14–16]). Second, the text of Zephaniah 1:3 essentially makes the same point without the presence of Zephaniah 1:2. The context of the quoted text in Jeremiah 8:13 is also the judgment of Judah. Furthermore, it refers to the loss of grape produce and figs in much the same way as Habakkuk 3:17 just prior to the beginning of the book of Zephaniah.

The language of Zephaniah 1:3 gives the impression of the reversal of creation in Genesis 1:20–28 (cf., Jer. 7:20; 9:9 [Eng., 9:10]; 15:3; Ezek. 38:20; Hos. 4:3; Hab. 1:14; Hag. 1:11; 2:6, 21), similar to what happens in the flood story, with the exception of the fish (see Gen. 6:7). Un-creation is necessary in order to pave the way for the new creation (Isa. 65:17–18; 2 Pet. 3; Rev. 21–22). The parenthetical comment at the end of Zephaniah 1:3a—"and the stumbling blocks, namely, the wicked" (or, "and the stumbling blocks with the wicked")—is missing from the LXX and probably should not be considered part of the original text. Nevertheless, it is a witness to early interpretation of the text. It is usually translated, "and the stumbling-blocks with the wicked," in

---

10. It is a curious thing that the superscription mentions Josiah's ignominious father Amon, suggesting that the practices of Manasseh and Amon persisted in Josiah's day and then resurfaced in full force after his death (see 2 Kgs. 23:26; 24:3).

which case the humans and animals of Zephaniah 1:3 are the images of idols (i.e., stumbling-blocks) that will be destroyed along with the wicked who make and worship them (cf., Ps. 115:8). Another possibility is that אֵת is not the preposition "with" but the marker of a clarification (cf., 1 Sam. 2:23; Hag. 2:5; Zech. 12:10) explaining to the reader that the stumbling-blocks are the wicked. According to this translation, the point of the scribal comment would be to say that the judgment is for the wicked in particular and not the righteous (see Nah. 1:7; Hab. 2:4).

Verses 4–6 of chapter 1 focus on the sins of Judah and Jerusalem for which the LORD will stretch out his hand in judgment (see BDB, 640). He will cut off from that place "the remnant of Baal." Some take this to refer to what is left of Baal worship in the land in the wake of Josiah's reforms. Others understand it to mean that the LORD will destroy every last vestige of Baal from beginning to end. According to the Leningrad Codex, "the name of the idol-priests" (see 2 Kgs. 23:5; Hos. 10:5) is in apposition to "the remnant of Baal." In other words, Baal is the name of the idol that these priests represent. Other witnesses use a copula: "the remnant of Baal and the name of the idol-priests." According to this reading, the name of the idol-priests is the reputation or memory of the priests that will perish from the land. The addition of "with the priests" at the end of Zephaniah 1:4 in the MT does not appear in the LXX. This addition uses the ordinary Hebrew term for "priests" and is apparently intended to associate the special class of "idol-priests" with the corrupt priesthood generally (cf., Jer. 2:8). Verse 5 adds that the LORD will also cut off "those who prostrate themselves on the rooftops to the host of the sky" (i.e., the sun, moon, and stars as gods; cf., Deut. 4:19; 2 Kgs. 21:3). The repetition of "those who prostrate themselves" at the beginning of Zephaniah 1:5b is not in the LXX and is likely not part of the original text. Rather, Zephaniah 1:5b speaks of those who swear to the LORD and yet at the same time swear by or in the name of their king (i.e., Baal; see *Tg. Jon.*). This is illustrative of the syncretistic worship in Judah and Jerusalem (cf., Jer. 5:2). It is possible that the MT's "their king" should be revocalized to "Milcom" (1 Kgs. 11:5, 33) or "their Molech" (1 Kgs. 11:7; patterned after *bosheth* ["shame"; cf., Jer. 11:13]). Verse 6 then adds finally those who turn back from after the LORD (cf., Isa. 59:13) and those who neither make the LORD the object of their seeking nor seek him in their religious activity or inquiry (see BDB, 205; see also Hos. 3:5; Zeph. 2:3; 1QS 5:11).

The text of Zephaniah 1:7 reintroduces the theme of the imminent Day of the LORD. This theme was initially developed in the Joel-Amos-Obadiah sequence, and it now plays a prominent role in the conclusion of the Book of the Twelve (Zephaniah, Haggai-Zechariah, and Malachi).

Verse 7 accomplishes this reintroduction by employing the language of Habakkuk 2:20—language that also anticipates Zechariah 2:17 (Eng., 2:13). This Day of the LORD is not the day of Judah's historical judgment. Indeed, much like the book of Habakkuk (see commentary on Habakkuk 1:6), the book of Zephaniah keeps the identity of Judah's foreign enemy and means of judgment in the distant background. According to Zephaniah 1:2–3, the Day of the LORD is an eschatological day of worldwide judgment, which Judah's historical judgment merely prefigures. The chosen image for this day of judgment is that of a sacrifice prepared by the LORD himself for his invited guests (cf., 1 Sam. 9:13; Isa. 34:6; Jer. 46:10; Ezek. 39:17). It is not clear, however, whether the invited guests are also the sacrifice.

In the day of the LORD's sacrifice, he will judge the "princes" (or, leaders) and "the king's sons" (Zeph. 1:8). Commentators typically point out that Josiah's sons would be too young in Zephaniah's context to be the object of divine judgment. But given the rather broad reference to "the days of Josiah" in Zephaniah 1:1, it is difficult not to think of the sons of Josiah who all lacked their father's righteousness, especially the way they are described by Zephaniah's contemporary, Jeremiah (Jer. 21:1–23:4). The latter part of Zephaniah 1:8 adds "all those who wear foreign clothing." Some take this to be a reference to the clothing of the idol-priests who worship foreign gods (Zeph. 1:4–5), but the immediate context of Zephaniah 1:8a suggests that this is the clothing of the Judean royalty. It is yet another sign that Judah has assimilated to the peoples from whom they should be distinct (see Lev. 11:44–45).

The LORD will also judge in the day of his sacrifice "everyone who leaps over the threshold" (Zeph. 1:9). The text further describes these people as "those who fill the house of their lord/master with violence and deceit." The specific language of the Hebrew text in Zephaniah 1:9a strongly suggests a connection to 1 Samuel 5:5, which says that the priests of the Philistine god Dagon, and those who entered Dagon's house (i.e., temple) in Ashdod, would not tread on the threshold because of the fallen and dismembered image of Dagon at that spot (1 Sam. 5:4). If this connection is correct, then the sense of Zephaniah 1:9 would be that the LORD will judge anyone who respects and worships the image of an obviously false god like Dagon. Such false gods are the lords or masters of those who worship them (cf., Zeph. 1:4–5), and their worshipers fill their houses/temples with the violence (or, wrong) and deceit of their religion (cf., Jer. 7:11; see also Isa. 53:9).[11]

---

11. Some interpreters prefer to read this verse as a description of robbers who fill their master's house with things acquired by violence and deceit. The

In the great Day of the LORD (i.e., in the day of the LORD's sacrifice), there will be "a sound of a cry" (cf., Jer. 48:3) from the Fish Gate (see Neh. 3:3), a "howling" from the second district (see 2 Kgs. 22:14), and "a great breaking" (cf., Jer. 48:3) from the hills (Zeph. 1:10). The fact that this parallels the judgment of Moab in Jeremiah 48:3 confirms for the reader that this Day of the LORD is not limited to the historical judgment of Judah. "Howling" characterizes the judgment of the nations generally (see Isa. 13:6; 14:12, 31; 15:2; 16:7; 23:1, 6, 14). The reference to the second district in Zephaniah 1:10 is especially notable because it was the place where Huldah the prophetess lived in the days of Josiah when she was consulted by his men (2 Kgs. 22:14). The term מִשְׁנֶה ("second") is also used in Deuteronomy 17:18 to refer to the copy of the Torah that the king was to have written and read publicly (Deut. 17:19; cf., Deut. 31:9–13), the latter of which is exactly what Josiah did according to 2 Kings 23:2. The imperative to the inhabitants of the Mortar in Zephaniah 1:11 is to howl, because all the people of Canaan (i.e., the merchants) are destroyed. The Mortar is apparently a reference to a low-lying place that resembles a mortar. By itself, the description of the Judeans as the people of Canaan might imply that they have become like the Canaanites in their religious practices (cf., Ezek. 16:3), but the parallel with the cutting off of all those laden with silver (or, weighing out silver) suggests the familiar use of "Canaan" to refer to merchants (see BDB, 488–89; Ezek. 16:29; 17:4; Zech. 11:7, 11; 14:21; Prov. 31:24).

At that same time, the LORD will search Jerusalem with lamps (Zech. 1:12). That is, he will search the innermost parts of the inhabitants therein (cf., Jer. 17:10; Prov. 20:27). And on that basis, he will judge those who "thicken upon their lees," those who have settled and grown complacent in response to the word of the LORD (cf., Ezek. 12:21–28). They are the ones who say to themselves that the LORD will do nothing at all, whether good or bad (cf., Isa. 41:23; Jer. 10:5; see also 4QpZeph [4Q170]). Their wealth will become plunder, and their houses a desolation (Zeph. 1:13). The LORD will reverse the blessing of Deuteronomy 6:10–11 (cf., Josh. 24:13; Amos 9:14) according to which the land of the covenant would be ready-made with houses full of every good thing to enjoy and with vineyards and fig trees already planted and bearing fruit to be consumed for satisfaction. Now they will not

---

problem with this interpretation is that there is nothing about the Hebrew expression "leap over the threshold" that even implies robbery. Furthermore, such a reading requires the translator to supply "things acquired by" or some other equivalent expression not present in the Hebrew text.

even inhabit the homes that they themselves build, nor will they drink the wine of the vineyards of their own planting (cf., Deut. 28:30; Amos 5:11; Mic. 6:14–15; Hag. 1:6).

The great Day of the LORD is always the imminent Day of the LORD (Zeph. 1:14a; cf., Isa. 13:6; Joel 1:15; 3:14 [Eng., 4:14]; Obad. 15; Zeph. 1:7). It will be very swift even when it is expected, because no one knows for sure exactly when it is coming (see Mark 13:32). According to the accentuation of the text of Zephaniah 1:14b in the MT, the sound of the Day of the LORD is that of a defeated mighty man or warrior bitterly crying "there" ("pointing to a spot in which a scene is localized vividly in the imagination" [BDB, 1027]). On the other hand, the arrangement of the syntax in *BHS* allows for the possibility that the warrior (perhaps the LORD himself) is roaring into battle (cf., Isa. 42:13; Zeph. 3:17): "The sound of the Day of the LORD is bitter, a mighty man is roaring there." Verses 15 and 16 of Zephaniah 1 use word pairs to describe this day. It is first of all "a day of wrath" (cf., Ezek 7:19; Zeph. 1:18). It is then "a day of distress and stress," linking the description of the Day of the LORD to the visions of God's future coming in Nahum 1:2–8 and Habakkuk 3:3–15 (see "day of distress" in Nahum 1:7 and Habakkuk 3:16). According to Nahum 1:7, the LORD is good to those who take refuge in him in the day of distress. The Day of the LORD is also a day of great devastation ("ruin and desolation" [cf., Job 30:3; 38:27]) and darkness ("darkness and gloominess" [cf., Joel 2:2; Amos 5:18]), "a day of cloud and heavy cloud" (cf., Deut. 4:11; Joel 2:2; Ezek. 34:12; Ps. 97:2; see also Add Esth A 7). This is consistent with the way judgment in the Day of the LORD is depicted elsewhere (e.g., Joel 3:4 [Eng., 2:31]). It is "a day of shofar and shout of war" (cf., Jer. 4:5; 6:1; Hos. 5:8) against the fortified cities and against the high corners. The "high corners" are usually understood to be battlements or towers strategically located for defense at the corners of the city walls (see 2 Chr. 26:15).

When the LORD says in Zephaniah 1:17 that he will cause distress for mankind, it is clear from the context of worldwide judgment in Zephaniah 1:2–3 and from the context of the Day of the LORD in Zephaniah 1:7, 14–16 that this is not merely for Judah and Jerusalem (see also Zeph. 2:4–15). Whatever historical judgment may have once been in view, it now simply prefigures what will take place in the eschatological Day of the LORD. Mankind will walk like blind men in that day, for it is against the LORD that they have all sinned (see Deut. 28:29; Lam. 4:14). Their blood will be poured out like dust, and their bowels (or, flesh) like dung. According to Keil, "The point of the comparison is not the quantity, as in Gen. 13:16 and others, but the worthlessness of dust, as in 2 Kings 13:7 and Isa. 49:23."[12] Neither their silver nor their gold will be able to rescue them in that day (Zeph. 1:18; cf., *1 En.* 52:7). In the day of the LORD's wrath and in the fire of his jealousy (Exod. 20:5), the whole of the earth will be consumed (cf., Ezek. 36:5; Zeph. 1:2–3, 15; 3:8; Zech. 1:14; Ps. 79:5; see 1Q15 [1QpZeph]). For it is a complete destruction, indeed a terrible one, that the LORD will make not only of Judah and Jerusalem but also of all the inhabitants of the earth (cf., Isa. 10:23; Nah. 1:8; Dan. 9:27).

ZEPHANIAH 2

2:1 Gather yourselves together like stubble and gather together [LXX, Syr.: be bound; Tg. Jon.: come and draw near], O nation not longing [or, not ashamed; see GKC §152a[1]; LXX, Syr.: undisciplined nation; Tg. Jon.: O scattered people who do not desire to return to the Torah; Vulg.: unlovable nation], 2:2 before what is prescribed gives birth (Like chaff, a day passes away.) [LXX: like a flower passing away; cf., Syr., Tg. Jon.], before the burning of the LORD's anger comes upon you [GKC §152y], before the day of the LORD's anger comes upon you. 2:3 Seek the LORD, all you afflicted of the earth [MurXII, pc Mss: earth] who do his justice [LXX: Do justice and righteousness; cf., Syr.]. Seek [> LXX] righteousness, seek [> Syr.] humility LXX: Seek and answer them]. Perhaps you will be hidden in the day of the LORD's anger.

2:4 For Gaza, it will be forsaken [LXX: plundered]; and Ashkelon, it will become a desolation. As for Ashdod, at noon they will drive it out; and Ekron, it will be uprooted. 2:5 Woe [or, Hey; cf., LXX], inhabitants of the sea region, nation of Cherethites [i.e., people who came from the island of Crete]. The word of the LORD is against you, Canaan, the land of the Philistines, "and I will destroy you without inhabitant [or, so that there is no inhabitant]." 2:6 And the sea region will be pastures for shepherds' wells [LXX: And Crete will be pasture for shepherds; cf., Syr.] and walls for flocks.[13] 2:7 And the region will [read וְהָיָה הַחֶבֶל; the article was lost by haplography; cf., LXX, Syr.: the sea region; see also Tg. Jon.] belong to the remnant of the house of Judah. Upon them they will graze,

---

12. Keil, *Minor Prophets*, 445.
13. The Hebrew phrase translated "the sea region" does not agree with the third feminine singular verb of being. On the basis of the LXX, it should probably not be considered part of the original text. This results in the following translation: "And it [i.e., the land (f.) of the Philistines] will be pastures for shepherds' wells and walls for flocks."

in the houses of Ashkelon in the evening they will lie down [LXX adds: from before the sons of Judah]. For the LORD their God will visit them and restore their fortunes [LXX, Syr., Tg. Jon., Vulg.: their captivity].

2:8 "I have heard the reproach of Moab and the revilings [LXX: blows with the fist (or, cruel acts)] of the sons of Ammon with which they have reproached my people and exalted themselves against their border [LXX: my borders].[14] 2:9 Therefore, as I live," the prophetic utterance of the LORD of hosts [hosts > LXX], the God of Israel, "surely Moab will be like Sodom, and the sons of Ammon like Gomorrah, a possession [LXX: Damascus; Syr.: will be destroyed; Tg. Jon.: abandoned land; Vulg.: dryness] of weeds [LXX: abandoned] and a pit of salt and a desolation forever. The remnant of my people will be the ones who will plunder them, and the remainder of my nation will be the ones who will inherit them." 2:10 This will be theirs in place of their pride, for they have reproached and exalted themselves against the people [people > LXX] of the LORD of hosts [see v. 8]. 2:11 The LORD is awesome [LXX, Syr.: will appear] over them, for he makes lean [read רָזָה; the MT is the result of haplography] all the gods [Syr.: kings] of the earth [LXX: nations of the earth], and they will prostrate themselves to him, each from his place, all the coastlands of the nations.

2:12 "Also you Cushites are the slain of my sword."[15]

2:13 And he will stretch out his hand against north, and he will destroy Assyria, and he will make Nineveh into a desolation, dryness like the wilderness [or, desert]. 2:14 And flocks will lie down [LXX: graze] in its midst, every creature of a nation [LXX: of the land; Tg. Jon.: of the field]. Both pelican [or, owl; LXX: chameleon] and porcupine [or, hedgehog; or, a type of bird] on its capitals [LXX: rafters] will lodge. A sound [BHS prp: owl; LXX:, Syr.: wild animals; Tg. Jon.: there is the sound of the bird which is chirping in the window; Vulg.: voice] will sing through the window, desolation [LXX, Vulg.: a raven] in the threshold, for he has

---

14. The above translation takes the *hiphil* of גדל to be an internal hiphil (cf., Dan. 8:8). It is also possible that the object "mouth" is implied (cf., Ezek. 35:13), yielding the sense "boast" or "gloat."

15. Lit., "Also you Cushites, the slain of my sword are they." It is possible that the pronoun "they" functions here as a copula (grammaticalization) (cf., Ps. 44:5 [Eng., 44:4]). See Robert D. Holmstedt and Andrew R. Jones, "The Pronoun in Tripartite Verbless Clauses in Biblical Hebrew: Resumption for Left-dislocation or Pronominal Copula?" *JSS* 59 (2014): 53–89.

laid cedar-work bare [LXX: a cedar is its rising; Syr.: its root was uncovered; Tg. Jon.: its cover they destroyed; Vulg.: I will cause its strength to waste away]. 2:15 This is the exultant city that dwelt in security, that said in its heart, "I am, and there is none besides." How it has become a waste [or, occasion for appalment or horror], a place where wild animals lie down! Every person who passes by it will whistle, each one will wave his hand [Syr. adds: and say].

The unit in Zephaniah 2:1–3 serves as a transition between Zephaniah 1:2–18 and Zephaniah 2:4–15. The imperatives in Zephaniah 2:1 are apparently directed to the nation of Judah generally (see Zeph. 1:4–6, 12–13; 1Q15 [1QpZeph]). The Judeans are to gather themselves together like highly flammable stubble (cf., Exod. 5:7, 12) before the "giving birth" (i.e., the time of the coming to fruition [cf., Mic. 4:9–10; 5:2 (Eng., 5:3)]) of the judgment decreed by the LORD in chapter 1—before the day of the "burning" of the LORD's anger comes upon them (Zeph. 2:1–2; cf., Joel 2:12–17). This choice of the root קשש for "gather" (rather than קבץ, אסף, or קהל) is likely based on the image of all the earth being consumed by the fire of the LORD's jealously (see Zeph. 1:18). The nation is described in Zephaniah 2:1 as one that is "not longing." Despite the wide variety of renderings of this verse in translations both ancient and modern, the *niphal* of כסף elsewhere in the Hebrew Bible has an active meaning ("long") followed by the preposition "for" (see Gen. 31:30; Ps. 84:3 [Eng., 84:2]; cf., *qal* in Ps. 17:12; Job 14:15). Thus, *Targum Jonathan's* understanding that the people do not desire or long for the Torah is actually closest to the mark among the ancient versions. The parenthetical comment in Zephaniah 2:2—"Like chaff, a day passes" (cf., Isa. 29:5; Jer. 13:24)—highlights how quickly time flies (and how quickly chaff or stubble is blown away by the wind or consumed by fire [see Ps. 1:4–6; Dan. 2:35]), making the call to seek the LORD all the more urgent before the coming of the imminent Day of the LORD.

The command to seek the LORD in Zephaniah 2:3 (cf., Isa. 55:6; Hos. 3:5; Amos 5:4–6; 9:12; Zeph. 1:6) is not directed to Judah generally but to "all the afflicted of the earth who do his justice" (cf., Mic. 6:8). The afflicted of the earth are the marginalized remnant of faithful believers who constitute the true people of God (see Isa. 11:4; Zeph. 3:12). As the following context makes clear, this includes not only believers from Judah (Zeph. 2:7, 9b) but also believers from the nations (Zeph. 2:11). They are the ones who are to seek righteousness and humility (see BDB, 776). The final clause of Zephaniah 2:3—"Perhaps you will be hidden in the day of the LORD's anger"—is not intended to cast doubt on whether the remnant will be hidden (cf., Joel 2:14; Jon. 1:6;

3:9).[16] Rather, it makes refuge in the Day of the LORD contingent upon demonstration of genuine faith (see Nah. 1:7).

Zephaniah's section on the nations (Zeph. 2:4–15; cf., Isa. 13–23; Jer. 46–51; Ezek. 25–32; Amos 1:3–2:16) begins in Zeph. 2:4 with the conjunction כִּי. This serves to connect Zephaniah 2:4–15 with Zephaniah 2:1–3. That is, the call for believers from Judah and the nations to seek the LORD is given in light of the fact that there will be a worldwide judgment in the Day of the LORD (Zeph. 1:2–3, 7, 14–16). The address to Philistia (Zeph. 2:5–7; cf., Isa. 14:28–32; Jer. 47; Ezek. 25:15–17; Amos 1:6–8) is preceded by wordplays on four of the five major cities of Philistia (see 1 Sam. 6:17; Zech. 9:5–6). Each name in the list is fronted in the Hebrew word order. עַזָּה ("Gaza") will be עֲזוּבָה ("forsaken"). אַשְׁקְלוֹן ("Ashkelon") will לִשְׁמָמָה ("become a desolation"). "Ashdod" (אַשְׁדּוֹד), at noon (cf., Jer. 6:4; 15:8) "they will drive it out" (יְגָרְשׁוּהָ). "Ekron" (עֶקְרוֹן) "will be uprooted" (תֵּעָקֵר).

The address to Philistia in Zephaniah 2:5–7 begins like a "woe" oracle (cf., Hab. 2:5–20; Zeph. 3:1), yet there is no formal accusation, only an announcement of judgment.[17] But it is well known to the reader of the Bible that the Philistines were a perennial enemy of Israel (e.g., Judg. 13–16; 1 Sam. 4–6; 2 Sam. 17). They were the inhabitants of the region of the Mediterranean Sea to the southwest who had originally come from the island of Crete (Zeph. 2:5a; see Ezek. 25:16; Amos 9:7). The word of the LORD is now against them (Zeph. 2:5b). The oracle puts "Canaan" in apposition to "the land of the Philistines," a reminder that this region is part of the land of the covenant with Abraham (Gen. 2:11–14; 15:18), a region that Joshua failed to possess in his conquest of the land (Josh. 11:22–23). Thus, the full restoration of the lost blessing of life and dominion in the land awaits the Day of the LORD (Gen. 1:26–28; Ps. 8:4–9 [Eng., 8:3–8]; 110:1; Dan. 7:13–14, 27; Heb. 4:8–9; Rev. 5:9–10). The latter part of Zephaniah 2:5b interjects the LORD's

---

16. According to BDB (19), אוּלַי ("perhaps") is "usually expressing a hope."

17. "Despite the stylistic feature of the direct address to the Philistines that characterizes the oracle, it is unlikely that the Philistines ever heard it. Though the Philistines are addressed in the second person, and the Judeans are referred to later in the oracle in the third person (v. 7), the Philistines are only the fictive audience; the real audience for whom the oracle was intended was Judean. The oracle was probably spoken originally to Judeans; its written circulation certainly envisioned a Judean readership. The announcement of judgment on the Philistines contained a promise to Judah, and it is as a promise to Judah for a better future that the oracle actually functions" (Roberts, *Nahum, Habakkuk, and Zephaniah*, 197).

discourse. He will destroy Philistia in such a way that there will be no inhabitants left (cf., Zeph. 3:6). The land of the Philistines will be pastures for shepherds' wells (see Gen. 26:25) and walls for flocks (Zeph. 2:6). The sea region will belong to the believing remnant of the house of Judah (Zeph. 2:7; cf., Mic. 7:18). It is not immediately clear what the antecedent is when the text says they will graze "upon them." Perhaps it is a reference to the Philistines (i.e., the land of the Philistines) in Zephaniah 1:5b. The image of the people of God grazing and then lying down in the dispossessed houses of Ashkelon in the evening is similar to other prophetic restoration passages that speak of the people as the LORD's flock (e.g., Ezek. 34:13–15; Mic. 7:14; see also Ps. 23:2). The LORD their God will visit them in a positive way (beyond their judgment [Zeph. 1:8–9]) and restore their fortunes (Deut. 30:3; Jer. 30:3; Amos 9:14; Zeph. 3:20; Job 42:10; for this expression, see commentary on Hos. 6:11; Amos 9:14).

The LORD says that he has "heard" the reproach of Moab and the revilings of the sons of Ammon (Zeph. 2:8; cf., Num. 22–24; Judg. 11; Isa. 15–16; Jer 48:1–49:6; Ezek. 25:1–11; Amos 1:13–2:3; see also Num. 11:1b). A reproach against God's people is a reproach against the God whose name they bear (see the LXX of Zephaniah 2:10b; see also Isa. 51:7; Jer. 48:26, 42; Obad. 10–11; Dan. 9:16–19). Thus, the LORD swears by himself (Zeph. 3:9; cf., Heb. 6:12) that Moab will be like Sodom, and the sons of Ammon like Gomorrah. The irony of this is that Moab and Ammon were born out of the story of Sodom and Gomorrah (Gen. 19:29–38). Their land will become a possession of weeds and a pit of salt, just as Lot's wife became a pillar of salt (Gen. 19:26). It will forever be a desolation. Why then would the remnant of God's people want to plunder and inherit such a desolate place? This question is somewhat beside the point of the poetic imagery. The focus is really on the judgment of the guilty parties, not the land itself. Just as the land of Philistia is to be depopulated in order to repopulate it with the remnant of God's people (Zeph. 2:5–7; see Zeph. 3:13), so it will be for the land of Moab and Ammon (cf., Obad. 16–21). This will be their lot in place of their pride, precisely because they reproached and exalted themselves (or, boasted) against God's people (Zeph. 2:10).[18]

---

18. "[N]either Philistia on the one hand, nor Moabites and Ammonites on the other, were ever taken permanent possession of by the Jews; and still less were they every taken by Judah, as the nation of God, for His own property. Judah is not to enter into such possession as this till the Lord turns the captivity of Judah (v. 7); that is to say, not immediately after the return from the Babylonish captivity, but when the dispersion of Israel among the

According to Zephaniah 2:11, the LORD will be awesome over them (i.e., Philistia, Moab, and Ammon), for he will make all the so-called gods (see Ps. 96:5) of the earth dwindle or disappear, and those who worship such gods from all the coastlands of the nations will prostrate themselves to the LORD, each one from his own place or land (see Gen. 10:5; Isa. 42:4; see also 1 Sam. 5:4–5; Zeph. 1:9). Critical scholars consider this verse to be a secondary addition because it speaks of the conversion of the nations in a context largely devoted to their judgment (see *BHS* apparatus). But there is nothing unusual about this (e.g., Isa. 19:24–25; Jer. 48:47; 49:6, 39), and there is no textual evidence for the removal of the verse. Furthermore, the hope of the remnant of Judah (Zeph. 2:7, 9; 3:13) is given in the same context as the judgment of Judah (Zeph. 1:4–6, 12–13; 3:1–8). The role of Zephaniah 2:11 in chapter 2 has been well noted by D. C. Timmer:

> [I]t becomes clear that 2:11 has nearly the same relation to 2:5–10 as does 2:1–3 to 1:2–18. Much as YHWH will come in judgment to destroy especially Judahite sinners in 1:2–18 but may also "hide" those Judeans who seek righteousness and humility, so alongside his coming judgment against nations all around Judah, YHWH will intervene in such a way as to realize (not merely make possible) a radically new relationship between some non-Israelites and the God of Israel while destroying others.[19]

The text of Zephaniah 2:12 turns back to the judgment theme and adds the Cushites to the list (cf., Isa. 18; 34:6).

The final oracle against Assyria in Zephaniah 2:13–15 obviously anticipates the same historical fate that the reader finds in the book of Nahum (see also Isa. 10:5–19; 14:24–27; 33), but the reader must also remember the eschatological context set by Nahum 1:2–8; and Zephaniah 1:2–3, 7, 14–16. The LORD will stretch out his hand against the north (Zeph. 2:13). Relative to Judah, Assyria is to the east, but the general understanding is that an invading army from the east would normally enter from the north. The LORD will destroy Assyria. In particular, he will make the capital city of Nineveh into a desolate, dry

---

Gentiles, which lasts till this day, shall come to an end, and Israel, through its conversion to Christ, be reinstated in the privileges of the people of God" (Keil, *Minor Prophets*, 450).

19. D. C. Timmer, "The Non-Israelite Nations in Zephaniah: Conceptual Coherence and the Relationship of the Parts to the Whole," in *The Book of the Twelve and the New Form Criticism*, eds. Mark J. Boda, Michael H. Floyd, and Colin M. Toffelmire (Atlanta: SBL, 2015), 253.

place like a wilderness or a desert. This is depicted in Zephaniah 2:14 by the image of flocks or herds of every kind of creature found in a nation like Assyria lying down within the city. That is, the city is depopulated, overrun by animals, and uninhabitable for humans. It is worth noting that there is no subsequent indication that the remnant of Judah will repopulate the land as in Zephaniah 2:7, 9. The exact identity of all the creatures in Zephaniah 2:14 is uncertain, but what is important is the recognition that these same creatures are listed in other passages intended to portray the same kind of desolation (e.g., Isa. 14:23; 34:11; cf., Rev. 18:2). The capitals, the window, and the threshold will all be occupied because the LORD has laid bare the cedar-work. The text of Zephaniah 2:15a can be rendered either as a statement or as a question. It comes from a perspective that assumes the fall of the city of Nineveh, highlighting the magnitude of that fall by recounting the city's former glory, its security, and its prideful assertion about itself using words that should only be heard from the one true God himself (see Isa. 37:24; 47:8, 10; cf., Rev. 18:7). The text of Zephaniah 2:15b can be rendered either as an exclamation or as a question (BDB, 32; see also Rev. 18:18), although the answer to the question would be immediately obvious from the context. It is the LORD who has made Nineveh into a desolation, a place where creatures lie down. The whistling and hand waving of passers-by are signs of derision (see BDB, 631, 1056; see also Nah. 3:19).

ZEPHANIAH 3

3:1 Woe [or, Hey; cf., LXX, Syr., Vulg.], rebellious [see GKC §75rr] and defiled is the oppressive city.[20] 3:2 It does not obey a voice [Tg. Jon.: the voice of his servants, the prophets], it does not take discipline [Tg. Jon.: instruction]. In the LORD it does not trust, to its God [Tg. Jon.: to the worship of its God] it does not draw near. 3:3 Its officials in its midst are roaring lions [see GKC §87m]. Its judges are wolves of evening [LXX: of Arabia]. They do not leave anything for the morning. 3:4 Its prophets are reckless, men of treachery. As for its priests, they profane holiness, they treat Torah violently [Luther: interpret the law wantonly]. 3:5 The LORD is righteous in its midst. He does not do injustice. Morning by morning his justice he gives, at the light [i.e., dawn; Tg. Jon.: like the light; cf., ASV] not lacking [see GKC §152a¹; LXX: and it is not hidden; at the light not lacking > OG], but an unjust one does not know shame [LXX: and he knows not justice by extortion, nor injustice in strife].

---

20. LXX: "O, the manifest and redeemed, the city, the dove." Cf., Syr., Tg. Jon.

3:6 "*I cut off nations [LXX: I pull down the proud; cf., Syr.], their corners [perhaps corner towers or battlements (cf., Zeph. 1:16; 2 Chr. 26:15); see also Tg. Jon.] are destroyed. I devastated their streets without passer-through. Their cities are laid waste without man, without inhabitant. 3:7 I thought, 'Surely you [LXX, Syr., Tg. Jon.: 2 pl] will fear me, you will take discipline. And its dwelling [LXX, Syr.: from its eyes; 8ḤevXII gr: its spring] will not be cut off, all that I visit upon it [Tg. Jon.: all the good that I said to them I will bring to them].' But they rise early to corrupt their deeds [or, early / eagerly they corrupt their deeds (GKC §120g); LXX: Prepare, rise, all their gathering is destroyed; cf., Syr.]. 3:8 Therefore, wait [LXX, Vulg.: sg] for me," the prophetic utterance of the LORD, "for the day of my rising up forever [LXX; Syr.: as a witness; BDB, NET: plunder]. For my judgment [or, decision] is to collect nations, to gather [read with Cairo Geniza: לקבץ] kingdoms, to pour out upon them my indignation, all the burning of my anger. For in the fire of my jealousy all the earth will be consumed.*"

Chapter 3 opens with a "woe" oracle (cf., Zeph. 2:5–7): introduction (Zeph. 3:1), accusation (Zeph. 3:2–7), and announcement of judgment (Zeph. 3:8). It is not uncommon for commentators to divide this section into separate units (e.g., Zeph. 3:1–4, 5, 6–8), but the contrast with the LORD's righteousness in Zephaniah 3:5 and the divine discourse in Zephaniah 3:6–7 are part of the accusation. And despite the fact that the announcement of judgment in Zephaniah 3:8 contains an element of surprise ("wait for me"), it is still formally marked by לכן ("Therefore") as the conclusion to the oracle (cf., Mic. 2:3). This time the words of judgment are not for the nations (Zeph. 2:4–15) but for Judah and Jerusalem (cf., Zeph. 1:4–6, 12–13) as is made clear by the wording of Zephaniah 3:3–4, 6–7. The oracle concludes the judgment section of the book and makes way for the restoration section in Zephaniah 3:9–20.

Verse 1 calls Jerusalem "the oppressive city," which the LXX reads as "the city, the dove" (cf., Hos. 7:11). The city is "rebellious and de-filed." The LXX interprets מראה as a *hophal* participle from the root ראה ("manifest") rather than a *qal* participle from the root מרא or מרה ("rebellious"). Some interpreters (e.g., Rashi) analyze this word as a denominative *hophal* participle according to the postbiblical noun ריאי ("excrement" [cf., Nah. 3:6b]) in order to create a better parallel with "defiled" (i.e., "sullied and defiled").[21] The LXX interprets the later bib-lical Hebrew root גאל ("defile") according to the more common homonym

---

21. See Marcus Jastrow, *Dictionary of the Targumim, Talmud Babli, Yerush-almi and Midrashic Literature*, 2d ed. (New York: Judaica, 1903), 1436.

גאל ("redeem"). The people of the city of Jerusalem do not obey the LORD's voice or receive his instruction (Zeph. 3:2; cf., Gen. 26:5; Prov. 1:3). *Targum Jonathan* takes this to mean that they do not listen to his servants, the prophets (cf., 2 Kgs. 17:13; Jer. 25:4–7). They do not trust in the LORD (cf., Ps. 20:8 [Eng., 20:7]; 115:9–11), nor do they draw near to their God to worship him or to seek his will (see 1 Sam. 14:36; Isa. 48:16; Ezek. 44:15).

The accusations in Zephaniah 3:3–4 against various groups of community leaders within Judah and Jerusalem (i.e., officials, judges, prophets, and priests) can be compared to similar passages elsewhere in the prophetic literature (see Jer. 2:8; 4:9; 5:31; Ezek. 7:26; 22:23–31). The passage in Ezekiel 22:23–31 in particular appears to be based on Zephaniah 3:3–4 and offers a very helpful exposition of the text. Verse 3 compares the city's officials to roaring lions. The MT of Ezekiel 22:25 uses this same metaphor for the prophets, but since the prophets are described later in that same passage (Ezek. 22:28), it is perhaps best to read "leaders" with the LXX of Ezekiel 22:25 rather than the MT's "prophets" (see the back-translation in the *BHS* apparatus). Thus, according to Ezekiel 22:25, the leaders are like a roaring lion tearing prey. They devour life and take riches and valuables for themselves, making many widows along the way. The text of Zephaniah 3:3b says that the city's judges are like "wolves of evening" (cf., Hab. 1:8), not leaving anything for the morning. Again, Ezekiel picks this up and says that the officials are like wolves tearing prey, pouring out blood and destroying lives ("destroying lives" > LXX) in order to make dishonest gain (Ezek. 22:27). The city's prophets are "reckless" (cf., Gen. 49:4), men of treachery (Zeph. 3:4a). These are the false prophets who prophesy by Baal and give the people a false sense of security (Jer. 2:8; 6:14; 23:9–40; Ezek. 13; Mic. 3:5–8; Zech. 13:2–6). According to Ezek. 22:28, the false prophets whitewash their message. They see empty visions and divine a lie, claiming to speak the word of the LORD when in fact he has said nothing to them. Last but not least, the city's priests profane or make common what is holy or set apart, and they treat Torah violently (Zeph. 3:4b). The text of Ezekiel 22:26 takes this to mean that they fail to distinguish between the holy and the profane, between the ceremonially clean and unclean (see Lev. 10:10; 11:47; Deut. 17:8–13; 33:10). They hide their eyes from the LORD's Sabbaths, and the LORD himself is profaned. According to Ezekiel 7:26, Torah perishes from the priests.[22]

---

22. Violence done to the Torah could also include mishandling of the text (Jer. 2:8) and tampering with the text (Jer. 8:8). For example, Jeremiah 33:14–26 was apparently added by a special interest group to the second

The contrast with the LORD in Zephaniah 3:5 is striking (cf., Jer. 23:1–4 and Jer. 23:5–6). The LORD is righteous in the midst of the city. He acts in right relationship to the people according to the terms of the covenant. He does not do injustice. This description of the LORD apparently derives from Deuteronomy 32:4: "The Rock, blameless is his work, for all his ways are just, a God of faithfulness and without injustice, righteous and upright is he." The reliability of the LORD's justice is depicted in terms of his faithfulness to summon the sunrise each and every morning (see Gen. 1:3; cf., Lam. 3:23; see also Jer. 21:12). The last clause of Zephaniah 2:5 can be interpreted in at least two different ways. Most understand it to mean that an unjust man knows no shame. That is, he is not ashamed of what he should be ashamed of (cf., Jer. 6:15). The LXX, on the other hand, understands the LORD to be the subject of this clause. It is possible to translate, "and he does not acknowledge an unjust one, shame." In this translation, the word "shame" could stand for Baal (see Jer. 11:13).

The LORD's discourse in Zephaniah 3:6 recounts how he cut off nations so that their "corners" are now destroyed. He devastated their streets so that their cities are laid waste without people and without inhabitant. No one passes through. It is not immediately clear to what this makes reference. Is this about the biblical history of the LORD's victories on behalf of his people (i.e., the defeat of the Egyptians, the conquest of the seven nations of Canaan, military deliverance by means of the judges, various victories over foreign enemies during the time of the monarchy and the divided kingdom, etc.)?[23] It is possible, however, that this is a reference to the announcement of judgment against the nations in Zephaniah 2:4–15 (and perhaps also the worldwide judgment in Zephaniah 1:2–3, 7, 14–18) as something that is as good as done (see Zeph. 2:5). The LORD thought that the city of Jerusalem would fear him as a result of this judgment of the nations (Zeph. 3:7; cf., Jer. 3:19–21). He thought that the people would accept his discipline so that the city's "habitation" (i.e., the LORD himself [see Deut. 33:27; Pss. 71:3; 90:1; 91:9]) would not be cut off from the people. This

---

edition of the book, which is represented by the MT. The passage does not appear in the LXX. The added text seeks to leverage the covenant with David (Jer. 23:5–6) in an effort to make the case for a covenant with the Levites separate from the biblical covenant with the Aaronic priesthood (see Num. 16–18). See the discussion in Michael B. Shepherd, *The Twelve Prophets in the New Testament* (New York: Peter Lang, 2011), 98–99.

23. Roberts prefers to avoid this problem by revocalizing גּוֹיִם ("nations") to גּוֹיָם ("their nation") (*Nahum, Habakkuk, and Zephaniah*, 208–209).

cutting off is everything that the LORD visits upon them in punishment for the broken covenant relationship (Exod. 20:5).[24] But despite what the LORD thought would be the case, the people have been eager to corrupt their deeds. Of course, this accommodating language is not intended to address the issue of divine foreknowledge. It is intended to highlight the fact that the LORD did everything to create the expectation that the people would fear him, but they did not (cf., Isa. 5:1–7; Jer. 2:1–13; Mic. 6:1–8). The failure of the people could not be more evident.

Right at the point where the reader expects an announcement of judgment marked by לכן ("Therefore") there is instead an imperative: "wait for me" (Zeph. 3:8). This is the same verbal root discussed in the commentary on Habakkuk 2:3 (cf., Dan. 12:12) where the prophet is encouraged to wait for the vision of the future work of God to come to fruition at the appointed time. The text of Zephaniah 3:8 is thus addressed to the same group called to seek the LORD in Zephaniah 2:3. They are the afflicted remnant of the true people of God from all the nations who do the LORD's justice (Zeph. 2:7, 9b, 11). They are the ones who, having sought righteousness and humility, will find that they are hidden in the judgment of the Day of the LORD (Zeph. 1:2–3, 7, 14–18). The LORD calls this the day of his rising up for judgment "forever" (i.e., indefinitely in the last days). The same Hebrew phrase rendered "forever" can also be translated "for plunder" (cf., Gen. 49:27). Furthermore, the same consonantal text can be revocalized to mean "as a witness" as in the LXX. All three options fit the context quite well. For it is the LORD's judgment/justice or decision to collect the unbelieving from the nations (cf., Joel 4 [Eng., Joel 3]) and to gather the kingdoms (including Judah and Jerusalem) in order to pour out on them his indignation (cf., Nah. 1:6; Hab. 3:12; Dan. 8:19), all the burning of his anger. For it is in the fire of his jealousy that the whole of the earth will be consumed. The similarity of language between Zephaniah 3:8 and Zephaniah 1:18 is unmistakable, making clear the connection to the eschatological and worldwide judgment in the Day of the LORD as depicted in Zephaniah 1:2–3, 7, 14–18. Thus, the message of the prophet Zephaniah forever remains a contemporary message.

3:9 *"For at that time I will restore to peoples [MurXII:* על העמים*] purified speech [lit., lip; LXX: language in its generation; Syr.: chosen speech; Tg. Jon.: one chosen speech] so that all of them may call on*

---

24. This is perhaps a play on the familiar Hebrew idiom "to cut a covenant" and the reference to the cutting off of the nations in Zephaniah 3:6.

the name of the LORD to serve / worship him with one shoulder [BDB, 1014: as one man; LXX, Syr.: one yoke]. 3:10 From beyond the rivers of Cush [LXX, Vulg.: Ethiopia] my supplicants, the daughter of my scattered ones [my supplicants, the daughter of my scattered ones > LXX, Syr.] will carry my offering [LXX, Syr.: sacrifices to me].²⁵ 3:11 In that day you will not be ashamed of all your deeds by which you have transgressed against me. For at that time I will remove from your midst the exultant ones of your pride [or, your proud, exultant ones; LXX: the detestable acts of your insolence], and you will never be haughty again in my holy mountain. 3:12 And I will leave in your midst a people afflicted and low, and they will take refuge in the name of the LORD [BHS: the remnant of Israel will take refuge in the name of the LORD (cf., LXX)]. 3:13 As for the remnant of Israel, they will not do injustice and they will not speak a lie. A tongue of deceit will not be found in their mouth. For they will be the ones who graze and lie down, and there will be no one causing trembling."

3:14 Shout, Daughter Zion [Tg. Jon.: congregation of Zion]! Cry out, O Israel! Be glad and exult with all your heart [cf., LXX, Syr.], Daughter Jerusalem [Tg. Jon.: congregation of Jerusalem]! 3:15 The LORD has removed your judgments [Syr., Tg. Jon.: judges], he has turned away [LXX: redeemed you from the hand of] your enemy [mlt Mss, MurXII, LXX, Syr., Tg. Jon.: your enemies]. The king of Israel, the LORD, is in your midst [LXXᴸ ᴹˢˢ: The Lord will be king in your midst; Tg. Jon.: The king of Israel, the LORD, has said to cause his Shekhinah to dwell in your midst]. You will never be afraid [2 Mss, LXX, Syr.: see] again. 3:16 In that day it will be said to Jerusalem, "Do not be afraid, Zion. Let not your hands go slack [see GKC §145p]. 3:17 The LORD your God is in your midst [cf., Tg. Jon. v. 15b], a mighty man who delivers [Syr.: a mighty man and a deliverer]. He will exult over you with gladness [LXX: He will bring joy upon you]. He will be silent in his love [or, will cause to be silent (i.e., soothe) in his love (cf., Job 11:3); LXX, Syr.: He will renew you in his love; Tg. Jon.: He will subdue your sin in his love (cf., Mic. 7:19)]. He will rejoice over you with a shout [LXX adds: as in a day of festival (see v. 18)]."

3:18 "Those grieved from an appointed time²⁶ have I collected [LXX: And I will gather the crushed; Tg. Jon.: Those who were holding back among

---

25. *Tg. Jon.*: "From beyond the rivers of India in mercy the exiles of my people who were exiled will return, and they will bring them lo as offerings."
26. *BHS* follows the LXX and puts this phrase with the end of v. 17.

*you the times of your festivals I will distance from you; cf., Vulg.]. From
you [f. sg.] are they. A burden upon it [f. sg.] is reproach [LXX: Woe, who
has taken against her a reproach? Syr.: And I will remove from you
those who spoke reproach against you; Tg. Jon.: Woe to them, because
they were lifting up their weapons before you and mocking you]. 3:19
Look, I am about to make [Tg. Jon. adds: a complete destruction; cf.,
Isa. 10:23] all those who afflict you [LXX: among you for your sake; Syr.:
to all of them when humbled in your midst] at that time [LXX adds:
says the Lord]. And I will deliver the limping [GKC §122s], and the
driven out will I gather. And I will make them into an object of praise
and renown [Syr.: renown and praise; cf., v. 20] in all the land where
their shame once was [cf., Syr., Tg. Jon., Vulg., Luther].[27] 3:20 At that
time I will bring you in [LXX: And they will be ashamed at that time
when I do well with you; Tg. Jon.: I will draw near your exiles], and at
the time of my gathering you [> Tg. Jon.]. For [or, Indeed] I will make
you into an object of renown and praise among all the peoples of the
earth when I restore your fortunes [LXX, Syr., Vulg.: captivity; Tg. Jon.:
exiles] before your eyes," says the LORD.*

This final section of the book of Zephaniah features language and
imagery of restoration well-known to the reader of the prophetic literature. It picks up the glimmer of hope for both Judah and the nations in the preceding judgment sections (Zeph. 2:3, 7, 9, 11; 3:8) and
serves to remind the reader that the Day of the LORD will not only
be a day of judgment for the wicked but also a day of deliverance for
the righteous. This section also provides an eschatological context
for the following book of Haggai. The conjunction כִּי ("For") at the
beginning of Zephaniah 3:9 connects this section with what precedes
it. The following adverb אָז ("at that time") signals to the reader that
what he or she is about to read will take place in the last days (i.e.,
the Day of the LORD).

At that time, the LORD says he will restore not merely to Judah
but to all peoples "a purified lip." Such language is reminiscent of
Genesis 11:1a, which says that all the land was "one lip" prior to
the story of the Tower of Babylon.[28] In fact, some early interpreters
understood this to be a reference to language (e.g., LXX, 4Q464).
Targum Jonathan and Ibn Ezra even suggest that this is the one
chosen and holy language of Hebrew that all the nations will use to

---

27. The LXX turns "their shame" into a verb and puts it at the beginning of
v. 20.
28. See Smith, *Micah–Malachi*, 142.

call on the name of the LORD, Yahweh (cf., Gen. 4:26; 12:8; see also Joel 3:5 [Eng., 2:32]; Mic. 4:1–5). Whether or not this is specifically a reference to Hebrew, the allusion to the unity prior to the building of the Tower of Babylon is quite plausible. In that story, the people wanted to make a "name" for themselves (Gen. 11:4). Thus, it was necessary for the LORD to disrupt their unity. But now they will call on the "name" of the LORD in order to serve/worship him with "one shoulder" (see LXX and *Pss. Sol.* 17:30). That is, as one man they will bear the responsibility of serving the LORD together.[29] They will take refuge in the "name" of the LORD (Zeph. 3:12b), and the LORD will give his people a "name" (i.e., renown) among the nations, precisely because they will truly bear his name (Zeph. 3:19–20). There is also a sense in which the purification of the people's unclean lips (Isa. 6:5; 29:13) makes them acceptable to the LORD.

Earlier in Zephaniah 2:12, the Cushites were very briefly mentioned in the context of the judgment of the nations. Now in Zephaniah 3:10, the LORD says that his supplicants will carry his offering from beyond the rivers of Cush (cf., Isa. 18:1b). This may simply be a way of describing the great distance from which they will come, but there may also be an allusion here to the boundaries of the Garden of Eden and the land of the covenant (Gen. 2:11–14; 15:18; Isa. 19:16–25). According to *Targum Jonathan*, the exiles of the LORD's people are the ones who will be brought as offerings. The supplicants are called "the daughter of my scattered ones" (> LXX, Syr.). Similar terminology appears in Zephaniah 3:14: "Daughter Zion" and "Daughter Jerusalem" (see BDB, 123). Thus, the picture in Zephaniah 3:9–10 is quite similar to that of Isa. 66:18–21.[30] The LORD is coming to gather all the nations and languages, and they will come and see his glory (Isa. 66:18). The LORD will send some of the nations to declare his glory among the nations to those who have not seen it (Isa. 66:19). Those very nations will then bring the Israelite brethren from all the nations as an "offering" (מנחה) to the LORD when these "sons of Israel" simultaneously bring themselves as this same "offering" (המנחה) in the midst of the Gentile caravan (Isa. 66:20). It is from all these nations that the kingdom of priests will be established (Isa. 66:21; cf., Exod. 19:6; Isa. 61:6; 1 Pet. 2:9; Rev. 1:6; 5:10; 20:6) in the new creation (Isa. 66:22–24; cf., Isa. 65:17–25; Rev. 21–22).

---

29. See John Calvin, *Commentaries on the Twelve Minor Prophets*, vol. 4, *Habakkuk, Zephaniah, Haggai*, trans. John Owen, Calvin's Commentaries XV (reprint, Grand Rapids: Baker, 2005), 285.

30. See Keil, *Minor Prophets*, 458–59.

In that day, the LORD says, the daughter of his scattered ones will not be ashamed of all her deeds by which she transgressed against him (Zeph. 3:11a). At first glance this appears to be at odds with Ezekiel 20:43 (see also Ezek. 36:31–32): "And you will remember there your ways and all your deeds by which you defiled yourselves. And you will loathe yourselves because of all your evils that you committed." But remembering and loathing the sins of the past are not the same as continuing to live in shame. The Ezekiel text indicates that there will be no desire to return to the former way of life. On the other hand, the Zephaniah text shows that there will be no lingering guilt. For at that time the LORD will remove "the exultant ones of your pride" (Zeph. 3:11b; cf., Isa. 13:3). That is, there will never again be any human haughtiness on God's holy mountain, Mt. Zion.

The LORD says that he will leave an afflicted and lowly people as his remnant (Zeph. 3:12a; cf., 2 Kgs. 25:12; Isa. 26:5–6). This remnant will consist of all the afflicted of the earth who seek the LORD (Zeph. 2:3, 7, 9, 11; 3:8–9; cf., Hos. 3:5; Amos 9:12). They are the ones who will take refuge in the name of the LORD (Zeph. 3:12b; cf., Nah. 1:7; Ps. 2:12b; Prov. 18:10). As for the remnant of Israel (Zeph. 3:13a; cf., Mic. 2:12; 4:7; 5:6 [Eng., 5:7]; 7:18), they will not do injustice or speak lies. A tongue of deceit will not be found in their mouth. In other words, they will display the character of God himself (see Zeph. 3:5; see also Deut. 32:4; Isa. 53:9; 1QS 9:22). For they will graze and lie down as the flock of God their shepherd (Zeph. 3:13b; cf., Ezek. 34:13–15; Mic. 2:12; 5:3 [Eng., 5:4]; 7:14; Zeph. 2:7; Ps. 23; 74:1; 79:13; 95:7; 100:3). And there will be no one to cause them to tremble (see Lev. 26:6; Deut. 28:26; Isa. 17:2; Jer. 30:10; 46:27; Ezek. 34:28; 39:26; Mic. 4:4; Job 11:19).

Verses 14–17 of Zephaniah 3 break away temporarily from the LORD's first-person discourse before the conclusion in verses 18–20. Verses 14 and 15 assume the perspective of one who has already experienced the LORD's deliverance in the last days. They summon Daughter Zion and Daughter Jerusalem (i.e., Israel) to shout/cry out and be glad/exult with all their heart because the LORD has removed the judgments against them and turned away their enemies. The LORD himself is the king of Israel in their midst (cf., Exod. 15:18). Therefore, they will never fear evil again. These verses set off an inner-textual chain reaction within the Book of the Twelve that resurfaces in Zechariah 2:14 (Eng., 2:10); 9:9a. It becomes apparent in a comparison of these three passages that Zephaniah 3:14–15 is the primary text (see also Isa. 12:6; 49:13). The Zechariah 2:14 (Eng., 2:10) text serves as an intermediary or bridge text that picks up the language of Zephaniah 3:14–15 and anticipates that of Zechariah 9:9a. The Zechariah 9:9a text shares language with both of the preceding texts but then has a lengthy expansion in Zechariah 9:9b–10. Terminology shared by Zephaniah 3:14–15 and Zechariah 2:14 (Eng., 2:10) alone includes: "shout," "be glad," "the LORD," and "in your midst" (different Hebrew phrases). Terminology shared by Zephaniah 3:14–15 and Zechariah 9:9a alone includes: "cry out," "Daughter Jerusalem," and "king." Terminology shared by Zephaniah 3:14–15 and Zechariah 2:14 (Eng., 2:10); 9:9a includes only "Daughter Zion." Terminology shared by Zechariah 2:14 (Eng., 2:10) and Zechariah 9:9a includes: "look" and "coming/comes." The divine king of Zephaniah 3:14–15 and Zechariah 2:14 (Eng., 2:10) is the Davidic king of Zechariah 9:9–10 (cf., Isa. 9:5–6 [Eng., 9:6–7]; Jer. 23:5–6; Mic. 2:13; 4:7; 5:4–5 [Eng., 5:5–6]; Zech. 12:10 [John 19:37]; Dan. 7:13–14 [cf., Isa. 19:1]; see also Ps. 2; 72; 93; 97; 99; 145).[31]

When Zephaniah 3:16 says that in that day "it will be said to Jerusalem," there is no intended referent for the speaker (cf., Jer. 4:11; 16:14). It is simply a way of saying that the people of Zion will know not to fear anymore (cf., Zeph. 3:15b). It will be communicated to them that their hands need not go slack—that is, there will be no need to be discouraged (cf., 2 Sam. 4:1; Isa. 13:7; Jer. 6:24; 50:43; Ezek. 7:17; 21:12 [Eng., 21:7]). Just as the LORD will be king in their midst (Zeph. 3:15b), so will he be a "mighty man" (i.e., a warrior) who delivers in their midst (Zeph. 3:17a; cf., Isa. 63:1). Not only will the people be glad and exult with shouts of joy (Zeph. 3:14), but also the LORD himself will exult over his people with gladness and rejoice over them with a shout (Zeph. 3:17b; cf., Deut. 30:9b; Isa. 62:5b; 65:19a; Jer. 32:41). It is usually said in the commentaries that the clause, "He will be silent (or, exhibit silence) in his love," does not fit the context of exulting

---

31. "The Old Testament books were so edited that they emerge collectively as a messianic document" (William Horbury, *Jewish Messianism and the Cult of Christ* [London: SCM, 1998], 37). "Yet the biblical literature of the Persian period also reflects an intense concentration on God as king and the kingdom of God, which can be expressed without any overt reference to a messianic figure" (ibid.). "Messianism in the Persian period has been minimized somewhat comparably in the suggestion that the lowly king of Zechariah 9:9 is God rather than a messianic king, an interpretation permitted by the vitality of the anthropomorphic depictions of the deity which have just been considered. The balance of probability seems, however, to incline the other way, in the light of the royal oracles which this passage resembles" (ibid., 43).

with gladness and rejoicing with a shout. Therefore, many translators either follow the LXX (see *BHS* apparatus and the above translation) or render the verb in an unusual transitive sense according to Job 11:3. But the MT clearly has the more difficult reading that best explains the origin of the supposed Hebrew text behind the LXX. It is apparently an expression of the great understanding displayed in the solemnity and the depth of the LORD's love even in the midst of celebration (cf., Prov. 11:12; 17:28). Thus, the celebration is by no means a superficial one.

"Those grieved from an appointed time" (Zeph. 3:18) are those who are grieved because they are unable to celebrate the festivals of Leviticus 23 (cf., Lam. 1:4). This expression resumes the LORD's discourse. He says that he has collected the grieving ones from Daughter Zion (cf., Mic. 2:12–13; Zech. 10:8–12). Their grief has been a burden to them, and this burden has become a reproach to them. But a reproach against God's people is a reproach against God's reputation. Therefore, he will act for the sake of his name (see Dan. 9:15–19). The LORD points out that he will make a complete destruction of all those who have afflicted his people at that time (Zeph. 3:19). He will deliver the limping and gather the driven out (cf., Jer. 31:8; Mic. 4:6). He will make his people into an object of praise and renown in the land where their shame once was (cf., Deut. 26:19; Zeph. 2:10). This is because he is acting for the sake of his own name, which the people bear (see Isa. 48:9–11). At that time, the LORD will bring in his people (Zeph. 3:20; cf., Isa. 43:5). He will give them renown and praise among the peoples of the earth when he restores their fortunes before their very eyes (see Zeph. 2:7).[32]

The text of Zephaniah 3:9–20 exerts a great influence on how the following book of Haggai is read. Much the same way that Ezekiel's vision of the temple in Ezekiel 40–48 serves to illustrate the eschatological restoration prophesied in Ezekiel 33–39, so the historical prophecies of Haggai with regard to the rebuilding of the temple now provide pre-figurative images of the future and final restoration envisioned by Zephaniah 3:9–20. This is the way that the author of

---

32. "But inasmuch as Zephaniah not only announces the judgment upon the whole earth, but also predicts the conversion of the heathen nations to Jehovah the living God (ch. 3:9, 10), we must not restrict the description of salvation in ch. 3:11–20 to the people of Israel who were lineally descended from Abraham, and to the remnant of them; but must also regard the Gentiles converted to the living God through Christ as included among them." (Keil, *Minor Prophets*, 463–64). This will happen at the time of the Messiah (*Mikraoth Gedoloth: The Twelve Prophets*, vol. 2, 300).

Hebrews cites from Haggai 2:6 (see Heb. 12:26). In fact, this influence comes to the book of Haggai from both directions. The following book of Zechariah picks up on the language and context of Haggai and begins with eight visions of eschatological restoration beyond the immediate historical context of the post-exilic community that returned from Babylon. It is thus clear that the composer of the Twelve does not intend the book of Haggai to be read on its own as a mere documentary of historical prophecies from the year 520 BC.

BOOK OF THE TWELVE
HAGGAI

HAGGAI 1

1:1 In the second year of Darius the king, in the sixth month, on the first day of the month, the word of the LORD [Tg. Jon.: a word of prophecy from before the LORD] came by the hand of Haggai the prophet [LXX adds: saying, "Say"] to Zerubbabel the son of Shealtiel, the governor of Judah, and to Joshua the son of Jehozadak, the great priest saying, 1:2 "Thus says the LORD of hosts saying, 'This people, they say, "It is not a time of coming, the time for the house of the LORD to be built [LXX: The time has not come to build the house of the Lord; cf., Syr.; Tg. Jon.: Until now the time for the temple of the LORD to be built has not come]."'"

1:3 And the word of the LORD came by the hand of Haggai the prophet saying, 1:4 "Is it time for you yourselves to dwell in your houses, covered/paneled ones [or, They are covered/paneled],¹ and this house is desolate? 1:5 And now, thus says the LORD of hosts, 'Set your mind to your ways. 1:6 You have sown abundantly but brought in little. You have been eating but not to satisfaction. You have been drinking but not to drunkenness. You have been putting on clothes, but there is no warmth to each of you. And the one who is hired is hired to a pouch pierced with holes [Tg. Jon.: a curse].'

---

1. The Hebrew text does not translate as "in your covered/paneled houses." In order for the passive participle to function as an attributive adjective here, it would need the definite article. This is due to the fact that the pronominal suffix on the preceding noun makes it definite.

1:7 Thus says the LORD of hosts, 'Set your mind to your ways. 1:8 Ascend the mountain [or, hill country] and bring in wood and build the house, so that I will be pleased with it and so that I will be honored [Tg. Jon.: I will be pleased to cause my Shekhinah to dwell in it with honor],' says the LORD. 1:9 'Turning toward abundance, and look [LXX: and it was], to little. And you brought [it] into the house, and I blew on it [Tg. Jon.: I sent with it a curse]. Because of what?' the prophetic utterance of the LORD of hosts. 'Because of my house, which is desolate, and you are each pleased with [LXX: pursuing; Syr., Tg. Jon.: running to] his own house. 1:10 Therefore, above you [> LXX; Tg. Jon.: because of your sins] the sky withholds dew [Tg. Jon.: rain]. And the land, it withholds its produce [Tg. Jon.: fruit]. 1:11 And I called a drought [or, desolation; LXX, Syr.: sword] over the land and over the mountains and over the grain and over the new wine and over the fresh olive oil and over [mlt Mss add: all] what the ground brings forth and over the people and over the animals and over every product of the toil of the palms of the hands.'"

1:12 And Zerubbabel the son of Shealtiel [LXX adds: from the tribe of Judah] obeyed, and Joshua the son of Jehozadak, the great priest, and all the remnant of the people the voice of the LORD their God and yielded to the words of Haggai the prophet when the LORD their God [LXX: to them] sent him. And the people feared from before the LORD. 1:13 And Haggai, the messenger of the LORD [LXX: the messenger of the Lord to the people], said in the message of the LORD to the people saying, "'I am with you,' the prophetic utterance of the LORD." 1:14 And the LORD aroused the spirit of Zerubbabel the son of Shealtiel, the governor of Judah, and the spirit of Joshua the son of Jehozadak, the great priest, and the spirit of all the remnant of the people. And they came and did the work on the house of the LORD of hosts their God 1:15a on the twenty-fourth day of the sixth month.*

The book of Haggai does not begin like other prophetic books with a superscription that stands for the book as a whole (e.g., Isa. 1:1; Hos. 1:1; etc.). Rather, the date formula in Haggai 1:1 is simply the heading for the first of four messages in the book that each begin with a similar formula (Hag. 1:1; 1:15b–2:1; 2:10, 20; cf., Zech. 1:1, 7; 7:1). The dates are all in the second year of Darius the king (520 BC) when work on the new temple started in earnest.[2] This is not the Darius of Daniel 6 but the Darius of Ezra 4:24–6:22. The historical account of the prophetic ministry of Haggai and Zechariah in the

---

2. The temple was later completed in 515 BC, according to Ezra 6:15.

book of Ezra-Nehemiah is the narrative context for the prophecies in the books that bear their names (Ezra 5:1–2; 6:14; see also 1 Esd. 6:1; 7:3). According to the story, these prophets encouraged and supported Zerubbabel and Joshua in their efforts to rebuild the temple.[3] Haggai and Zechariah are also linked in several psalm superscriptions in the early versions (e.g., LXX Pss. 145–48 [MT, Eng., 146–48]; cf., Syr., Vulg.). Zerubbabel and Joshua were the leaders of the first wave of returnees from Babylon (Ezra 2:2) who established the altar and the temple foundation (Ezra 3) before work on the temple was halted (Ezra 4:1–5, 24). Zerubbabel, the governor of Judah, was the grandson of Jehoiachin, last seen in the biblical narrative living in Babylon exile as the only surviving Davidic king (2 Kgs. 25:27–30). According to the MT of 1 Chronicles 3:19, Zerubbabel was the son of Pedaiah, but all other witnesses (including the LXX of 1 Chr. 3:19) name him as the son of Shealtiel (Hag. 1:1, 12, 14; 2:2, 23; Ezra 3:2; 5:2; Matt. 1:12). Joshua was the great or high priest descended from the line of Aaron through his father Jehozadak (Hag. 1:1, 12, 14; 2:2; Zech. 3:1; 6:11; Ezra 3:2; 5:2; 1 Chr. 5:40; 6:14 [cf., Ezra 7:1]). It was to these men that the word of the LORD came by means of the prophet (i.e., the called) Haggai on the first day of the sixth month.[4]

Haggai begins by quoting "the LORD of hosts" (Hag. 1:2, 5, 7, 9, 14; 2:4, 6, 7, 8, 9, 11, 23)[5] who is quoting the people who have returned from Babylon to Judah and Jerusalem as saying that it is not time for the house of the LORD to be built (cf., Ezek. 11:3). This sets the stage for the word of the LORD that comes by means of the prophet in Haggai 1:4–6. The rhetorical question in Haggai 1:4 obviously expects a negative answer and is intended to turn the wording of what the people are saying in Haggai 1:2 back against them. It is not time to live in paneled houses, while the house of the LORD lies in ruins. Paneling was for the temple and the king's palace (1 Kgs. 6:9; 7:3, 7). It was not for luxurious homes to be built to the neglect of the sanctuary that represented God's special presence with his people (1 Kgs. 8). There is a distinct echo here of David's concern for the ark of the covenant: "See, I am dwelling in a house of cedars, and the ark of God

---

3. This support was motivated by the vision of Ezekiel's eschatological temple in Ezekiel 40–48 (see Smith, *Micah–Malachi*, 148–49) and by the messianic expectation of the son of David who would build the temple (2 Sam. 7:13; Hag. 2:20–23; Zech. 3:8; 6:12–13).
4. This was the month of Elul: August 29, 520 BC.
5. Depending on the context, "hosts" can refer to human armies, angelic hosts, or the luminaries of the sky.

is dwelling amid the curtain" (2 Sam. 7:2). It is clear from the following context that the implication of David's words was that he desired to build a house for the LORD (2 Sam. 7:5–7). But the LORD said that he would build a house (i.e., a dynasty) for David and that one of his sons would build the temple and reign over an everlasting kingdom (2 Sam. 7:11b–13). Initially, Solomon appeared to be that son (1 Kgs. 1–10), but when his kingdom did not last (1 Kgs. 11–12), and when his temple was destroyed (2 Kgs. 25), it became clear that the prophets were to look for someone who was still to come (Zech. 6:12–13; see also Ezek. 40–48 [especially Ezek. 45–46 (cf., Ezek. 34:24)]; Rev. 21:22). David's concern is now the concern of the prophet Haggai, but it is not yet that of the people. Therefore, he urges the people to consider their ways (Hag. 1:5). They sow abundantly but bring in such a small harvest (Hag. 1:6, 9). They eat, but they are not satisfied. They drink, but not to the point of drunkenness (cf., Gen. 43:34; Zeph. 1:13). They put on clothes, but they are not warm. The hired man's pouch is full of holes when he receives his wages (cf., Zech. 8:10). That is, there is no pay for the hired man. These are the curses of the old covenant (Deut. 28:30–31; cf., Deut. 6:10–15) that the postexilic community is still experiencing even after its return from Babylon. They must look to the future hope of the new covenant and eschatological restoration in the messianic kingdom (Isa. 40–66; Zeph. 3:9–20; Hag. 2:6–9, 20–23; Zech. 1–6).

Once again, the LORD urges the people to consider their ways (Hag. 1:7), speaking through the prophet to their leaders. He commands the people to go up into the mountain or the hill country and bring in timber to build the temple (Hag. 1:8). If they do this, the LORD will be pleased with it, and he will be honored. According to Ezra 3:7, they originally paid Tyre and Sidon to bring in cedar wood from Lebanon (cf., 1 Kgs. 5:15–32 [Eng., 5:1–18]). But more importantly, the instruction in Haggai 1:8 differs considerably from what the reader finds in Haggai 2:6–9—shaking of creation and the nations, filling of the temple with glory, and greater glory than the former temple. This simply was never a historical reality for the Second Temple (see Hag. 2:3; Ezra 3:12). It was not marked at its completion by the appearance of the glory of the LORD (Ezra 6:15) as were the tabernacle (Exod. 40:34–35) and Solomon's temple (1 Kgs. 8:11; Isa. 6:3–4). According to Ezekiel 43:5, the glory of the LORD will indeed fill the eschatological temple (cf., Isa. 60; Rev. 21:22). Ezekiel's vision in Ezekiel 40–48, much like his vision of the valley of dry bones (Ezek. 37), is symbolic of realities to come in the restoration prophesied in Ezekiel 34–39. It is a priest's way of depicting the ideal (Ezek. 1:3). The Second Temple in Haggai has a similar pre-figurative function in relationship to prophecies and visions of restoration beyond the initial return from

Babylon (Isa. 56–66; Zeph. 3:9–20; Zech. 1–6). That initial return was a momentous occasion, including the reestablishment of the altar (and the sacrifices) and the laying of the temple foundation (Ezra 2–3). But it also featured an attempt to return to the terms of the old covenant, which was doomed to failure despite God's faithfulness (Neh. 9:13–14, 16–18; 10–13).[6] Already within the composition of Ezra-Nehemiah there is an indication of a shift away from this to an emphasis on the reading and exposition of the text of Scripture (Neh. 7–9) and its message of the faith of Abraham, the work of the Spirit, and the role of the prophets (Neh. 9:8, 20, 30–31; cf., Acts 7:51–53).[7]

Within Haggai's context, the people are turning to find a great harvest because of their abundant sowing, but they are finding that it has only come to little (Hag. 1:6, 9). Even what they do manage to bring into the house is blown away by the LORD (cf., Isa. 40:7). This is all because the LORD's house lies in ruins, yet the people are content with their own. Therefore, they experience the covenant curses of drought and famine (Hag. 1:10–11; see Gen. 27:28, 39; Deut. 28:23–24; 33:28; Hos. 2:11 [Eng., 2:9]; Zeph. 1:3; Zech. 8:12; 1QM [1Q33] 16:1; *1 En.* 101:2–3). This is clearly not the fulfillment of prophecies about the return from Babylon in Isaiah 40–55.

Zerubbabel, along with Joshua and all the remnant of the people, obeyed the LORD and yielded to the words of the prophet who had been sent to them (Hag. 1:12).[8] They feared the LORD. This is an indication that the remnant here is the faithful remnant (cf., Zeph. 3:13). Haggai the prophet is designated "the messenger of the LORD" who comes with the LORD's message to the people (Hag. 1:13; cf., LXX Mal. 1:1). The message is that he, the LORD, is present with his people (cf., Gen. 17:4; 26:3; 28:15; 31:3; Exod. 3:12; Deut. 31:8; Josh. 3:7; 2 Sam. 7:9; Isa. 41:10; Jer. 1:8; Hag. 2:4–5). The LORD aroused the spirit of Zerubbabel, Joshua, and all the remnant of the people (cf., Isa. 41:2, 25; Ezra 1:1, 5), and they came and worked on the temple on the twenty-fourth day of the sixth month (Hag. 1:14–15a), three weeks after the message delivered on the first day of that month (Hag. 1:1; cf., Dan. 10:1–2, 13). The LORD himself is the one who stirs the hearts of the people for action.

---

6. Much like Joshua's conquest (Josh. 1–12), the LORD was faithful to bring the people into the land (Josh. 21:43–45), but there was still much to be done (Josh. 13:1; Judg. 1:27–33; Heb. 4:9).
7. See Michael B. Shepherd, *The Textual World of the Bible* (New York: Peter Lang, 2014), 65–77.
8. See Michael B. Shepherd, "The Compound Subject in Biblical Hebrew," *HS* 52 (2011): 107–120.

HAGGAI 2

1:15b In the second year of Darius the king, 2:1 in the seventh month, on the twenty-first day of the month, the word of the LORD came by the hand of [MurXII: to] Haggai the prophet saying, 2:2 "Say to Zerubbabel the son of Shealtiel, the governor of Judah, and to Joshua the son of Jehozadak, the great priest, and to [LXX, Syr. add: all] the remnant of the people saying, 2:3 'Who is there among you who is left who saw this house in its former glory? And how do you see it now? Is it not in comparison to it as nothing in your eyes? 2:4 And now, be firm, Zerubbabel,' the prophetic utterance of the LORD, 'and be firm, Joshua the son of Jehozadak, the great priest, and be firm, all you people of the land,' the prophetic utterance of the LORD, 'and do it. For I am with you,' the prophetic utterance of the LORD of hosts, 2:5 'and my Spirit remains in your midst [Tg. Jon.: and my prophets are teaching among you]. Do not fear.[9] *2:6 For thus says the LORD of hosts, 'Still one, a little it is [LXX: Yet once; Syr.: Again one time], and I am about to cause [see GKC §116p] the sky and the land and [and > pc Mss] the sea and the dry ground to quake. 2:7 And I will cause all the nations to quake, and the desire(s) of all the nations will come.*[10] *And I will fill this house with glory,' says the LORD of hosts. 2:8 'Mine is the silver, and mine is the gold,' the prophetic utterance of the LORD of hosts. 2:9 'Greater will be the glory of this latter house than the former,' says the LORD of hosts. 'And in this place will I give peace [or, well-being],' the prophetic utterance of the LORD of hosts [LXX adds: and peace of soul for a possession to every one who builds to raise up this temple]."*

---

9. The MT has a scribal insertion at the beginning of Haggai 1:5: "the word that I cut/made with you when you went out of Egypt." This does not appear in the Old Greek. It is an attempt to link the faithfulness of God in the postexilic setting to his faithfulness to the covenant made at Sinai, which is not appropriate to a context that assumes the old covenant is broken. The insertion is marked by the definite direct object marker, which is a common way to flag either scribal or authorial comments. E.g., Gen. 4:1; 1 Sam. 2:23; Isa. 29:9–11; Ezek. 44:7; Zech. 12:10 (see Michael Fishbane, *Biblical Interpretation in Ancient Israel* [Oxford: Clarendon, 1985], 48–51). English translations often try to include this insertion by translating the object marker as "according to." But even if the object marker is interpreted as a preposition, it would mean "with" rather than "according to," and it would still be an intrusion to the syntax.
10. The LXX has a neuter plural subject and a singular verb, which is a common Greek idiom.

2:10 On the twenty-fourth day of the ninth month, in the second year of
Darius, the word of the LORD came to Haggai the prophet saying, 2:11
"Thus says the LORD of hosts, 'Ask the priests Torah [Syr.: Ask about
the law from the priests] saying, 2:12 "If [GKC §159w] a man carries
holy meat in the wing [i.e., extremity, skirt, corner, or fold] of his garment and he touches with his wing the bread or the pottage or the wine
or the olive oil or any food [see BDB, 619], will it be holy?"'" And the
priests answered and said, "No." 2:13 And Haggai said, "If a person
unclean from a corpse touches any of these, will it be unclean?" And
the priests answered and said, "It will be unclean." 2:14 And Haggai
answered and said, "'So is this people, and so is this nation before me,'
the prophetic utterance of the LORD. 'And so is all the work of their
hands. And whatever they offer there, it is unclean [LXX adds: because
of their early profits; they will be in pain because of their labor. And you
hated those who reprove in the gates (cf., Amos 5:10)]. 2:15 And now,
set your mind from this day backward, before setting stone to stone on
the temple of the LORD. 2:16 Since those days [lit., From their being;
LXX: what were you], when a person came expecting to find a heap of
twenty measures [LXX: when you threw into a grain bin twenty measures of barley], there were ten. When a person came [LXX: When you
came] to the wine vat to draw fifty measures from a press, there were
twenty. 2:17 I struck you with blight and mildew and hail, all the work
of your hands, but you[11] were not to me [LXX: you did not return to me
(cf., Amos 4:9)],' the prophetic utterance of the LORD. 2:18 'Set your
mind from this day backward. From the twenty-fourth day of the ninth
month, to the day that the temple of the LORD was founded, set your
mind. 2:19 Is the seed still in the granary? And even [BDB, 724] the
grapevine and the fig tree and the pomegranate and the olive tree, each
one has not born fruit [BDB, 671]. From this day, I will bless.'"

2:20 And the word of the LORD came a second time to Haggai on the
twenty-fourth day of the month saying, 2:21 "Say to Zerubbabel [LXX
adds: the son of Shealtiel], the governor of Judah, saying, 'I am about to
cause the sky and the land [LXX adds: and the sea and the dry ground]
to quake. 2:22 And I will overthrow the throne [LXX, Tg. Jon.: thrones]
of kingdoms, and I will destroy the strength of the kingdoms of the nations. And I will overturn chariots and their riders, and horses and
their riders will go down, each by the sword of his brother. 2:23 In that

---

11. The unusual use of the pronominal suffix with the object marker here is
apparently intended to reiterate the same grammatical form from the beginning of the verse.

day,' the prophetic utterance of the LORD of hosts, 'I will take you, Zerubbabel the son of Shealtiel, my servant,' the prophetic utterance of the LORD, 'and I will make you like a seal [or, signet-ring], for it is you whom I have chosen,' the prophetic utterance of the LORD of hosts."

The second word of the LORD that came by means of the prophet Haggai is dated to the twenty-first day of the seventh month (Hag. 1:15b–2:1; cf., Hag. 1:1),[12] almost a full month after work on the temple resumed (Hag. 1:14–15a). This is the seventh day of the Feast of Tabernacles (Lev. 23:34; Num 29:32–34), a feast that figures prominently in the stories of the postexilic community (Ezra 3; Neh. 8; see also 1 Kgs. 6:38; 8:2). The message is addressed not only to Zerubbabel and Joshua (Hag. 2:2; cf., Hag. 1:1) but also to the remnant of the people (cf., Hag. 1:12, 14).[13] Apart from Ezra 3:2, which concerns priestly duties associated with the altar, Zerubbabel is normally listed first as the primary leader of the community when he and Joshua are mentioned together (Hag. 1:1, 12, 14; 2:2, 4; Ezra 2:2; 3:8; 5:2).

The initial response to the laying of the new temple foundation was a mixed one of both weeping and rejoicing (Ezra 3:12). The older generation who had seen Solomon's temple wept because the new temple foundation did not compare to that of the former temple. Those who had not seen Solomon's temple were glad simply to have any foundation. Likewise, nearly a month after the resumption of the building project, the prophet Haggai asks those who saw Solomon's temple in its former glory how the present structure compares, suggesting that it pales in comparison to the temple that they once knew (Hag. 2:3): "Is it not in comparison as nothing in your eyes?" Of course, the new structure is not complete at this point, but the completed parts do not measure up to the corresponding features of the former temple. This is commonly understood to be a rhetorical device by which the prophet identifies with the people's initial feeling of discouragement in an effort to encourage them to complete the project (Hag. 2:4–5).[14] But this perhaps reads too much between the lines. While it is true that the prophet encourages the leadership and the people to stay firm and act

---

12. This is the month of Tishri in the second year of Darius (October 17, 520 BC).
13. The phrase "all the people of the land" in Haggai 2:4 is equivalent to "all the remnant of the people" (Hag. 1:12, 14; cf., LXX Hag. 2:2).
14. See Hinckley G. Mitchell, *A Critical and Exegetical Commentary on Haggai and Zechariah*, ICC (New York: Charles Scribner's Sons, 1912), 59–60.

(cf., Josh. 1:9; 1 Kgs. 2:2; Zech. 8:9, 13; 1 Chr. 28:10), there is also an awareness that there is much more to come beyond what the Second Temple would be (Hag. 2:6–9). It is not enough to say that Haggai expected great things in his day that never happened. This is "the word of the LORD" through Haggai. The prophecy is ultimately about what will take place in the last days. For the time being, the prophet wants the community to remember that the LORD is present with them (Hag. 2:4b; cf., Hag. 1:13b). His Spirit remains in their midst (Hag. 2:5b; cf., Exod. 31:3; Zech. 4:6).[15] Therefore, they need not fear (cf., Deut. 31:8).

Unless the reader is willing to posit extreme hyperbole for Haggai 2:6–9, it is evident that these verses look beyond the Second Temple period to the eschaton, and this has been the understanding of the text throughout much of the history of interpretation (e.g., Heb. 12:26).[16] The LORD says that he is about to cause creation to quake in a little while (Hag. 2:6; cf., Isa. 10:25; 13:13; 29:17; Joel 4:16 [Eng., 3:16]). This is tied directly to the coming of the Messiah in the new world order as prefigured by Zerubbabel (Hag. 2:20–23). The temporal expression "in a little while" (lit., "Still one, a little it is") is not necessarily intended

---

15. See the explanation of Haggai 2:5a in the note to the translation above. *Targum Jonathan* interprets the Spirit to be the Spirit of prophecy (Num. 11:29; Mic. 3:8). The NET Bible claims that it is "theologically anachronistic to understand 'spirit' here in the NT sense as a reference to the Holy Spirit, the third person of the Trinity." This is presumably because of a false identification of the Hebrew Bible with the religion of Judaism, which does not hold to a doctrine of the Trinity. But the NT authors clearly understand the Spirit in their Bible to be the same one of whom they speak (e.g., Acts 2:16–21 [Joel 3:1–5 (Eng., 2:28–32)]; Eph. 4:30 [Isa. 63:10]; 5:18 [Gen. 41:38; Dan. 4–5]).

16. See Alberto Ferreiro, ed., *Twelve Prophets*, ACCS XIV (Downers Grove, IL: InterVarsity, 2003), 224–29; *Mikraoth Gedoloth: The Twelve Prophets*, vol. 2, 310; Calvin, *Haggai*, 358–64; Keil, *Minor Prophets*, 484–91; Smith, *Micah–Malachi*, 158. "According to Heb 12:18–24, the people have not come to terrifying Sinai (the old covenant) but to Zion and the city of the living God, the heavenly Jerusalem, and to myriads of angels, and to Jesus the mediator of a new covenant. The people should take care not to reject this (Heb 12:25), because God is acting again to shake creation (Heb 12:26; a partial quote of Hag 2:6) in the sense that this creation will be removed (Heb 12:27; cf., Isa 65:17; 66:22; Zeph 1:2–3; 2 Pet 3; Rev 21:1) and only the unshakeable kingdom of the Messiah will remain (Heb 12:28–29)" (Michael B. Shepherd, *The Twelve Prophets in the New Testament* [New York: Peter Lang, 2011], 55). The contrast in Hebrews 12:26 is between the trembling of the people at Sinai (Exod. 19:16b, 18b [LXX]) and the shaking of the world in the last days. See also Isa. 65:18; Gal. 4:24–26; Rev. 21:2.

to mean that the following must take place in the near future historically. It is simply a way of lending a sense of imminence to what is
described. This is not unlike descriptions of the Day of the LORD as
"near" (e.g., Zeph. 1:7, 14). It can come at any moment. The LORD will
also cause all the nations to quake (Hag. 2:7a; cf., Ezek. 31:16). The
clause parallel to this in Haggai 2:7a is difficult because of issues with
subject-verb agreement in the original language: "and the desire(s) of
all the nations will come." The noun translated "desire" is singular
according to the vocalization in the MT, but the verb translated "will
come" is plural. It is possible that the object "all the nations" from the
first clause is the subject of the plural verb in the second clause, but
this would result in redundancy: "and they [i.e., all the nations] will
come to the desire of all the nations." Another possibility is that the
noun "desire" should be revocalized to the plural "desires" (see *BHS*
apparatus; cf., LXX). This would not require any change to the consonantal Hebrew text. The meaning would then be that the desirable things of the nations will come as a result of the LORD shaking
them. Such an understanding would work well with Haggai 2:8 in
particular. On the other hand, there is a long-standing tradition that
interprets the coming of the singular desire of the nations to be a messianic prophecy (see, e.g., Calvin). This reading is not entirely without
exegetical merit. In 1 Samuel 9:20b, Samuel says to the future King
Saul, "And for whom is the desire of Israel? Is it not for you and for all
the house of your father?" Thus, the desire of all the nations would be
the desired king of all the nations (see Isa. 11:1, 10). In order for this
reading to work in Haggai 2:7, the verb would have to be emended from
וּבָאוּ to וּבָאָה (cf., LXX).

The LORD adds that he will fill the eschatological temple with
"glory" (Hag. 2:7b). Depending on the reader's interpretation of Haggai
2:7a (see also Hag. 2:8), the "glory" here could be the wealth of all the
nations (see BDB, 458; Isa. 66:12). But the glory in Haggai 2:7a and
Haggai 2:9a could also be the glory of God that filled the tabernacle
(Exod. 40:34–35) and Solomon's temple (1 Kgs. 8:11) at their completion. As mentioned above, this glory never filled the Second Temple
(Ezra 6:15), but it will fill the eschatological temple (Ezek. 43:5; see
also Isa. 60). The silver and the gold from the nations belong to the
LORD for the construction of his temple (Hag. 2:8; cf., Zech. 14:14).
This is new exodus imagery. The Israelites plundered the silver and
gold of Egypt in the original exodus (Exod. 11:2; 12:35; cf., Gen. 12:16;
13:1–2). These were used in the construction of the tabernacle (Exod.
35:5). In the new exodus from Babylon, the returnees were supported
by those they left behind with silver and gold for the construction of

the temple (Ezra 1:4; cf., Jer. 52:19). So will it be for the eschatological temple. The glory of that temple will be greater than that of Solomon's temple or the Second Temple (Hag. 2:9; see *T. Benj.* 9:2; *T. Adam* 29:6). In this place the LORD will give peace or well-being, which is one of the hallmarks of the messianic kingdom (e.g., Isa. 9:5–6 [Eng., 9:6–7]; Mic. 5:4 [Eng., 5:5]; Zech. 9:9–10; Ps. 72:7). Of course, there was peace in Solomon's kingdom (1 Chr. 22:9), but there were also problems that will not be present in Christ's kingdom (1 Kgs. 11).

But what kind of temple will the eschatological one be? Will there be a literal temple, or is the prophetic image symbolic of eschatological restoration in general (cf., Ezek. 40–48)? Some passages appear to shun the need for a literal temple (see 2 Sam. 7:5–7; 1 Kgs. 8:27; Isa. 66:1–2; Acts 7:47–50), preferring instead to think of the whole world as the LORD's temple (Isa. 11:9; Hab. 2:14).[17] Other texts speak of a heavenly temple (Ps. 11:4; cf., Exod. 25:40; Heb. 8:5; Rev. 15:5). And yet, the LORD says that he desires to dwell among his people (Exod. 29:45–46; Zech. 2:15 [Eng., 2:11]; John 1:14; Rev. 21:3). Still other passages speak of the people of God as the temple (1 Cor. 3:16; 6:19). The final reference to the temple in the biblical canon says that God and the Lamb are the temple (Rev. 21:22). It is important to appreciate the contribution of each of these texts. It is also important not to spiritualize the temple to the point that there is no correspondence to a physical reality. Perhaps one way to sort this out is to think of the intended relationship between the original sanctuary—the Garden of Eden—and the temporary sanctuaries that followed (i.e., the tabernacle and Solomon's temple).[18] The temporary sanctuaries serve to remind the believer of the original one. They also remind the believer of the hope of a new Garden of Eden (Isa. 51:3; Ezek. 36:35)—a place every bit as real as the original.

---

17. This is not to mention the replacement of temple worship (i.e., sacrifices) by synagogue worship (i.e., Scripture). See Ezra 2–3; Neh. 7–9. The loss of the Second Temple forced Jews to rethink how they were to offer sacrifices. One solution was to consider the reading of Leviticus 1–7 to be equivalent to offering sacrifices (*b. Menaḥ.* 110a).

18. See John H. Sailhamer, *The Pentateuch as Narrative* (Grand Rapids: Zondervan, 1992), 298–300. Sailhamer outlines the similarities between the preparation of the Garden of Eden in Genesis 1–2 and the instructions for the tabernacle in Exodus 25–30 (cf., 1 Kgs. 6–7). The Garden of Eden (Gen. 2:11–14) is the land of the covenant (Gen. 15:18) in which God granted the blessing of life and dominion. This blessing will be restored by means of the covenant relationship.

The word of the LORD came to the prophet Haggai again on the twenty-fourth day of the ninth month in the second year of Darius (Hag. 2:10; cf., Hag. 1:1; 2:1, 20). This was the month of Kislev (December 18, 520 BC). The LORD said to ask the priests Torah (or, instruction) (Hag. 2:11). That is, the prophet was to request a ruling on a matter from the priests in accordance with their function as teachers of the Torah (see Deut. 17:8–13; 33:10; Ezek. 44:23; Neh. 8:1–8; 2 Chr. 17:7–9). The first question describes a situation in which someone carries holy meat (i.e., sacrificial meat [Jer. 11:15]) in the flap of his garment and then touches with that part of his garment bread, pottage, wine, olive oil, or any kind of food (Hag. 2:12). If that is the case, will the item touched be holy (i.e., set apart or consecrated)?[19] The priests respond in the negative, a response based on exegesis of Leviticus 6:20.[20] An item is holy only if it comes into direct contact with the meat. The answer to this question then sets up the second. If someone unclean or defiled (i.e., ritually impure and thus unacceptable for worship) by a corpse touches any of the items listed in Haggai 2:12, will the item touched be unclean (Hag. 2:13; see Lev. 7:19; 21:11)? The answer is yes. What does this have to do with the postexilic community? The LORD answers through the prophet that the people/nation is likewise unclean before him (Hag. 2:14). Therefore, everything that they touch is unclean and thus unacceptable to offer on the altar in the new temple. The "work of their hands" refers to the produce of the land (Hag. 2:12).[21] Their defilement of the crops explains why the expected harvest is so meager (Hag. 1:6, 9; 2:15–19).

The LORD then instructs the people to turn their minds back to the time prior to the laying of the temple foundation (Hag. 2:15; cf., Hag. 1:5, 7; see Ezra 3:8, 10). Since that time, what was expected to be a heap of twenty measures was only ten (Hag. 2:16). What was expected to be fifty measures from a wine press was only twenty. This was the result of the broken covenant relationship (Deut. 28:30–31; Hag. 1:6, 9) and the result of the defilement of the work of their hands (Hag. 2:12–14). The LORD struck the people, that is, the work of their hands, with blight and mildew and hail, but they did not repent (Hag. 2:17; cf., Deut. 28:22; 1 Kgs. 8:37). This citation of Amos 4:9 shows that

---

19. The question does not concern whether the item touched will be defiled or polluted (*contra* Rashi; see Calvin).
20. See Keil, *Minor Prophets*, 491–92; Fishbane, *Biblical Interpretation*, 296–98.
21. See Mitchell, *Haggai and Zechariah*, 68. Keil suggests that though the land is in contact with the sanctuary, it cannot communicate holiness to the crops (*Minor Prophets*, 492).

little had changed since the time of Amos's address to the northern kingdom of Israel in the eighth century. The LORD again instructs the people to turn their minds back to the founding of the temple (Hag. 2:18). This could either be another reference to the initial laying of the temple foundation (Ezra 3:8, 10) or a reference to the resumption of the work on the temple (Ezra 4:24ff; Hag. 1:14; Zech. 8:9), but the wording of Haggai 2:19 suggests the latter. The seed is not still in the granary. The grapevine and the fig tree and the pomegranate and the olive tree have not born fruit up to the present time (cf., Hab. 3:17; Hag. 1:10–11). Yet from this day the LORD will bless. That is, the present situation is not the time of blessing. That time is still to come in what Haggai 2:6–9 and Haggai 2:20–23 envision (cf., Amos 9:14; Mic. 4:4; Zech. 3:10).

The texts of Haggai 2:20–23 and Zechariah 1:1–6 form a compositional seam that connects the book of Haggai to the book of Zechariah. Both passages are discrete units. The text of Haggai 2:20–23 stands apart from what precedes it, yet it also draws upon material from earlier in the book (e.g., Hag. 2:6, 21). This is not unlike what happens in seams that occur at the end of other biblical books. For instance, the canonical seam that connects the book of Moses to the Prophets in Deuteronomy 34:5–Joshua 1:9 features reference back to Numbers 27:18 and Deuteronomy 18:15, 18 in Deuteronomy 34:9–10. Likewise, the canonical seam that connects the Prophets to the Writings in Malachi 3:22–Psalm 1 (Eng., Mal. 4:4–Ps. 1) refers to Malachi 3:1 in Malachi 3:23 (Eng., 4:5). Just as Haggai 2:20–23 stands apart from what precedes, so Zechariah 1:1–6 stands apart from what follows, namely, the eight night visions that dominate the first six chapters of the book. The book of Zechariah could easily start with the date formula in Zechariah 1:7. The dates in Haggai 2:20 and Zechariah 1:1 link the two prophets together (see also Hag. 1:1; 2:1, 10; Zech. 1:7; 7:1; Ezra 5:1–2). The message of this compositional seam is the message of the programmatic passage of the Twelve (Hos. 3:5): eschatological and messianic restoration beyond the context of the initial return from Babylon. In fact, the book of Zechariah is necessary to the interpretation of Zerubbabel in Haggai 2:23 as a prefiguration of one who is yet to come (Zech. 3:8; 6:12–13). The seam also features the composer's characteristic citation from the book of Jeremiah in Haggai 2:23 (Jer. 22:24) and Zechariah 1:4 (Jer. 25:5).

The repetition of the date from Haggai 2:10 in Haggai 2:20 suggests that Haggai 2:20–23 is an extra piece of material that is now integral to the composition of the Twelve. The message of this brief section is specifically directed to Zerubbabel (Hag. 2:21; cf., Hag. 1:1; 2:2), but the implications of the message are now preserved for the reader whose hope is in the future work of God. As in Haggai 2:6, the LORD says that he is about to cause the sky and the land to quake. But this is no mere repetition of the new exodus and new temple imagery of Haggai 2:7–9. The present text adds to the eschatology of Haggai 2:6–9 by including the overthrow of the throne of the kingdoms and the establishment the messianic kingdom as prefigured by Zerubbabel (Hag. 2:22–23; cf., Dan. 2; 7). The LORD will overturn the chariots of the nations (cf., Exod. 14:28; 15:1; Zech. 9:10; 12:4), each by the sword of his brother (cf., Judg. 7:22; 1 Sam. 14:20; Isa. 19:2; Ezek. 38:21; Zech. 14:13).

In that day (cf., Zeph. 3:11, 16), the LORD will take Zerubbabel his "servant" (Hag. 2:23). Here Zerubbabel appears to be the chosen messianic servant of the LORD from the book of Isaiah (Isa. 42:1–7; 49:1–9; 50:4–11; 52:13–53:12; 61:1–9). It remains for the book of Zechariah to clarify that Zerubbabel only prefigures the Messiah (Zech. 3:8; 6:12–13), which is the way the history of interpretation has largely understood the text.[22] Zerubbabel was a descendant of King David (1 Chr. 3:19), and messianic hopes certainly swirled about him as the leader of the return from Babylon and the temple rebuilding project in his role as governor of Judah, but he never ruled on the throne himself. The LORD will set him (i.e., the one whom Zerubbabel prefigures) as a seal or signet ring (cf., Song 8:6; Sir. 49:11; John 6:27). That is, he will bear the mark of the one to whom he belongs and the one by whom he is sent (1 Kgs. 21:8; cf., Gen. 41:42; Est. 8:8; Dan. 6:18 [Eng., 6:17]). This is quite unlike Zerubbabel's grandfather Jehoiachin who was the seal torn from the LORD's right hand (Jer. 22:24; see also Jer. 52:31–34). The text of Haggai 2:23 appears to be an intentional reversal of the downfall of the Davidic monarchy as depicted by Jeremiah 22:24. This messianic and eschatological message of the book of Haggai is highlighted by its placement between Zephaniah and Zechariah and by its contribution to the larger program of the book of the Twelve. It is this message, rather than any updated versions of Haggai's historical call to rebuild a sanctuary, that should be stressed in the teaching and preaching of the book to the new covenant community of the church.

---

22. See Ferreiro, ed., *The Twelve Prophets*, 229; *Mikraoth Gedoloth: The Twelve Prophets*, vol. 2, 316; Calvin, *Haggai*, 387; Keil, *Minor Prophets*, 498; Smith, *Micah–Malachi*, 163.

BOOK OF THE TWELVE

ZECHARIAH

ZECHARIAH 1:1–6

1:1 In the eighth month [Syr. adds: on the first day of the month], in the second year of Darius, the word of the LORD came to Zechariah, the son of Berechiah the son of Iddo, the prophet, saying, 1:2 "The LORD was angry with your fathers.[1] 1:3 And you will say to them, 'Thus says the LORD of hosts, "Return to me [Tg. Jon.: to the worship of me]," the prophetic utterance of the LORD of hosts [the prophetic utterance of the LORD of hosts > LXX], "and I will return to you [Tg. Jon.: I will return by my word to do good for you]," says the LORD of hosts [of hosts > LXX]. 1:4 "Do not be like your fathers to whom the former prophets called saying, 'Thus says the LORD of hosts, "Return from your evil ways and from your evil deeds,"' and they did not listen and they did not pay attention to me," the prophetic utterance of the LORD. 1:5 "Your fathers, where are they? And the prophets, is it forever that they will live [Tg. Jon. adds: in truth the prophets do not live forever]? 1:6 But my words and my statutes [LXX adds: you receive] that I commanded [LXX adds: by my Spirit] my servants the prophets, did they not overtake your fathers [LXX: which overtook your fathers; Syr.: your fathers remembered]?"'" And they returned and said, "Just as the LORD of

---

1. The construction "verb + cognate noun" (קָצַף . . . קֶצֶף) is not emphatic ("very angry"). See Michael B. Shepherd, "So-called Emphasis and the Lack Thereof in Biblical Hebrew," *Maarav* 19 (2012): 188–90. The same construction occurs twice in Zechariah 1:14, 15. In both cases the adjective "great" is added to the noun to yield the adverb "very" in translation. Cf., LXX Zechariah 1:2.

hosts planned to do to us according to our ways and according to our deeds, so has he done with us."

The date in Zechariah 1:1 (the month of Bul [Oct.–Nov.], 520 BC) falls between Haggai's messages in the sixth and seventh months (Hag. 1:1; 2:1) and his messages in the ninth month (Hag. 2:10, 20). See also Zech. 1:7; 7:1. Haggai and Zechariah prophesied together to encourage Zerubbabel and Joshua in their rebuilding efforts (Ezra 5:1–2; 6:14; see commentary on Haggai 1:1), but they also envisioned eschatological and messianic restoration beyond the initial return from Babylon. This Zechariah is the son of Berechiah the son of Iddo, although he is known elsewhere simply as the (grand)son of Iddo (Ezra 5:1; 6:14). He is not to be confused with the Zechariah mentioned in 2 Chronicles 24:20–22 and Matthew 23:35. Zechariah the prophet is of priestly lineage (Neh. 12:16) like the prophets Jeremiah and Ezekiel before him (Jer. 1:1; Ezek. 1:3). This explains Zechariah's ability to function as a writing prophet and as an exegete of other biblical texts (cf., Ezra 7:6, 10). As discussed in the commentary on Haggai 2:20–23, the text of Zechariah 1:1–6 forms part of a compositional seam that connects the beginning of the book of Zechariah to the end of the book of Haggai. These two pieces of text share common interests, yet together they are also distinct from their surroundings. They serve to develop the central theme of the Twelve as stated in Hosea 3:5, and they also feature the composer's calling card—citation from the book of Jeremiah. Thus, the composer of the Twelve can use material attributed to the prophets Haggai and Zechariah for his own seam work.

The word of the LORD comes to Zechariah in Zechariah 1:2: "The LORD was angry with your (pl.) fathers." This short verse has several remarkable features. First, the LORD refers to himself in the third person. Second, the pronoun "your" is plural, suggesting that Zechariah represents the people. Third, the noun קֶצֶף ("anger"), which is the cognate of the verb "was angry" in the Hebrew text, is normally reserved for divine anger in biblical usage (see BDB, 893; see also Zechariah 7:12; 8:14). The term "fathers" refers to the forefathers or ancestors who lived during the time of the prophets Jeremiah and Ezekiel in the period leading up to the Babylonian exile (see Rashi). It was a time marked by the broken covenant relationship (Jer. 11:10), the ongoing effects of the reign of Manasseh (2 Kgs. 21:10–15), and the failure of the sons of Josiah to rule with justice and righteousness (Jer. 21:1–23:4).

The LORD of hosts (cf., Hag. 1:2, 5, 6, 9, 14; 2:4, 6, 7, 8, 9, 11, 23) instructs Zechariah to say to the postexilic community that they should return to him so that he may return to them (Zech. 1:3; cf., 4Q196 [=

Tob. 13:6]). This is remarkable given the fact that the people have already returned from Babylonian captivity. But they are not experiencing the fulfillment of the prophecies in Isaiah 40–55 in this initial return. Therefore, the night visions of Zechariah 1:7–6:8 will point them to a future restoration. The LORD's return appears to depend upon that of the people in Zechariah 1:3 (cf., Mal. 3:7; 2 Chr. 30:6–7), and this is in fact the way the relationship plays out in Zechariah 1:6, 16. But there is more to this than meets the eye. In Jeremiah 31:18, the LORD says that he hears the people saying, "Cause me to return so that I may return," which presupposes the need for divine initiation of the return. Likewise, in Lamentations 5:21, the prayer is, "Cause us to return, O LORD, to you, that we may return." The LORD must give the people a heart/mind to return before they can do so (see Deut. 29:3 [Eng., 29:4]; 30:6; Jer. 4:1–4; Ezek. 11:19–20). Thus, the LORD calls on the people to return, and they must do this of their own volition, being held responsible for how they act. But they would never do this on their own without the LORD's help.[2]

---

2. Augustine: "Free will and God's grace are simultaneously commended. When God says, 'Turn to me, and I will turn to you,' one of these clauses—that which invites our return to God—evidently belongs to our will; while the other, which promises his return to us, belongs to his grace" (Ferreiro, *Twelve Prophets*, 231). "[U]nless our turning to God were itself God's gift, it would not be said to him in prayer, 'Turn us again, O God of hosts' [Ps. 80:8 (Eng., 80:7)], and, 'You, O God, will turn and quicken us' [Ps. 85:7 (Eng., 85:6; LXX 84:7)], and again, 'Turn us, O God of our salvation' [Ps. 85:5 (Eng., 85:4)]—with other passages of similar import, too numerous to mention here. For with respect to our coming to Christ, what else does it mean than our being turned to him by believing? And yet he says, 'No man can come to me, except it were given to him of my Father' [John 6:65]" (ibid., 231–32). "We must further bear in mind, that, according to the common usage of Scripture, whenever God exhorts us to repentance, he does not regard what our capacity is, but demands what is justly his right. Hence the Papists adopt what is absurd when they deduce the power of free-will from the command or exhortation to repent: God, they say, would not have commanded what is not in our power to do. It is a foolish and a most puerile mode of reasoning; for if everything which God requires were in our power, the grace of the Holy Spirit would be superfluous" (John Calvin, *Commentaries on the Twelve Minor Prophets*, vol. 5, *Zechariah and Malachi*, trans. John Owen, Calvin's Commentaries XV [reprint, Grand Rapids: Baker, 2005], 21). "[B]ut when we understand these truths—that the law works wrath—that it increases sin—that it was given that transgression might be made more evident, then the false notion—that God requires nothing but what men can perform, comes to nothing" (ibid., 22).

Through the prophet, the LORD urges the present generation not to be like the forefathers whom the former prophets exhorted to return from their evil ways and from their evil deeds (Zech. 1:4). Those forefathers did not heed the voice of the prophets in their day (2 Kgs. 17:13; Jer. 25:4), and it would be foolish for Zechariah's audience to make the same mistake by not listening to him, especially in light of the fact that the words of the former prophets were vindicated (Zech. 1:5–6). The "former prophets" (cf., Zech. 7:7, 12) are the preexilic prophets, particularly Jeremiah and Ezekiel. In fact, the phrase "former prophets" is apparently a reference to a written corpus of prophetic literature (cf., Ezek. 38:17; Dan. 9:2). The citation in Zechariah 1:4 is not an appeal to oral tradition but an appeal to the specific wording of the text of Jeremiah 25:5: "Return each man from his evil way and from the evil of your deeds" (see also Jer. 23:22). Furthermore, Zechariah 1:6 presupposes that the words of the former prophets have been preserved, presumably in writing. Thus, the prophet Zechariah comes across not so much as a preacher but as a reader and interpreter of Scripture. This is the view of the prophet reflected in the LXX of Proverbs 29:18. The MT reads, "Where there is no prophetic vision, a people is let loose; but one who keeps Torah, blessed is he." The LXX has, "A lawless nation has no exegete, but the one who keeps the law is blessed." The term "exegete" is the translation of "prophetic vision."[3]

The questions in Zechariah 1:5 are intended to set up Zechariah 1:6a. The arrangement is chiastic: (A) "Your fathers, where are they? (B) And the prophets, is it forever that they will live? (B1) But my words and my statutes that I commanded my servants the prophets, (A1) did they not overtake your fathers?" The forefathers are no longer around. The words of the former prophets about coming judgment proved to be true (Deut. 18:20–22; Jer. 1–25; Ezek. 4–24; Tob. 14:4).[4] The former prophets did not live forever, but their words live on in the books that bear their names. Thus, when postexilic prophets like Zechariah and Haggai take up their mantle (1 Kgs. 19:19; 2 Kgs. 2:13), the community of faith must do better to heed their voice. This is not

---

3. It is also possible that the LXX translates a slightly different Hebrew word חֹזֶה ("prophetic seer"). Much like John in the book of Revelation, the prophet Zechariah receives visions, but he explains them in terms drawn from his exegesis of Scripture.

4. Note how this reality had no effect on the community in Jeremiah 40–44. Despite the vindication of Jeremiah's words, the community refuses to follow the divine counsel given through him, pointing to the need for a new covenant transformation of the heart.

merely a matter of learning the lessons of the past so as not to repeat it. It is also a matter of looking beyond the initial return from Babylon to the hope of a glorious future in the messianic kingdom found in the prophetic literature (Isa. 40–66; Jer. 30–33; Ezek. 34–39; Hos. 3:5; Ps. 85; 126; Dan. 9; Ezra 9; Neh. 1). The concluding narrative in Zechariah 1:6b indicates that the faithful remnant responded to the message that came through Zechariah, paving the way for the visions of future restoration in Zechariah 1:7–6:8 (see again Zech. 1:3, 16). The people acknowledged in solidarity with the past generation that the LORD acted righteously in doing exactly what he said he would do if they broke the covenant (see Lev. 26; Deut. 28; Lam. 2:17; Dan. 9).[5]

ZECHARIAH 1:7–17

1:7 On the twenty-fourth day of the eleventh month (that is, the month of Shevat) in the second year of Darius, the word of the LORD came to Zechariah, the son of Berechiah the son of Iddo, the prophet saying, 1:8 "I saw during the night, and look, a man riding on a red horse, and he was remaining among the myrtle trees that were in the deep [LXX (cf., Syr.): between the two overshadowing mountains; Tg. Jon.: among the myrtle trees that were in Babylon], and behind him were horses, red, sorrel / ruddy, and white. 1:9 And I said, 'What are these, my lord?' And the messenger / angel who was speaking with me said, 'I am the one who will show you what these things are.' 1:10 And the man who was remaining among the myrtle trees [LXX: mountains] answered and said, 'These are the ones that the LORD sent to walk about in the land [NRSV: to patrol the earth].' 1:11 And they [i.e., the riders] answered the messenger / angel of the LORD who was remaining among the myrtle trees [LXX: mountains] and said, 'We

---

5. This understanding of Zechariah 1:6b differs considerably from most translations and commentaries. Normally the text would be interpreted as a continuation of the LORD's discourse that indicates how the forefathers returned after the words of the former prophets overtook them (see Zech. 1:4), which is difficult to reconcile with texts like Jeremiah 40–44. The above translation and commentary interprets the LORD's discourse to end with Zechariah 1:6a (see Karl Elliger's arrangement in *BHS*). The text of Zechariah 1:6b is thus the prophet's narration of how the faithful remnant of the postexilic community responded to the call to return in Zechariah 1:3, which makes way for the vision of the LORD's return in Zechariah 1:16. For other examples of current generations speaking or acting in solidarity with previous generations, see Deut. 26:5–9; Josh. 24:6–8; Hos. 12:5 [Eng., 12:4]; Rom. 4:23–24; 15:4; 1 Cor. 9:10; 10:11; 1 Pet. 1:12.

*walked about in the land, and look, all the land is dwelling quietly
[lit., living and being quiet/undisturbed].' 1:12 And the messenger/
angel of the LORD answered and said, 'O LORD of hosts, how long
will you in particular[6] not have compassion on Jerusalem and the
cities of Judah with whom you have been indignant [LXX: whom you
have overlooked; Tg. Jon.: upon whom you have brought a curse] these
seventy years [GKC §136d]?' 1:13 And the LORD answered the mes-
senger/angel who was speaking with me with good words, comforting
words [lit., words, comforts]. 1:14 And the messenger/angel who was
speaking with me said, 'Proclaim, saying, "Thus says the LORD of
hosts, 'I am jealous for Jerusalem [Tg. Jon.: I will exact the vengeance
of Jerusalem], and for Zion with great jealousy. 1:15 And I am very
angry with the nations who are at ease [LXX: who joined in an attack;
Syr.: who rage]. For as for me, I was a little angry [Tg. Jon. adds:
against my people]; but as for them, they helped to evil [BDB, 740:
with evil result; LXX: they joined in an attack for evil].' 1:16 Therefore,
thus says the LORD [Ms, Syr. add: of hosts], 'I have returned [LXX:
I will return] to Jerusalem with compassion. As for my house, it will
be built in it,' the prophetic utterance of the LORD. 'And a measuring
line [Tg. Jon.], it will be stretched over Jerusalem [LXX adds: again
(from beginning of v. 17); Tg. Jon.: over the building of the walls of
Jerusalem].'" 1:17 [LXX adds: And the messenger/angel who was
speaking with me said to me] Again [cf., LXX] proclaim, saying, "Thus
says the LORD of hosts, 'Again my cities will overflow [LXX: will be
spread abroad; Tg. Jon.: the cities of my people will be filled; cf., Syr.]
with good, and the LORD will comfort [LXX: have mercy on] Zion
again, and he will choose Jerusalem again.'"'"*

Three months later, the word of the LORD came to Zechariah again
(Zech. 1:7; cf., Zech. 1:1). It comes to the reader in the form of the
prophet recounting a vision he had during the night (Zech. 1:8; cf., Dan.
2:19; 7:2). This is the first of eight visions (Zech. 1:7–17; 2:1–4 [Eng.,
1:18–21]; 2:5–17 [Eng., 2:1–13]; 3:1–10; 4:1–14; 5:1–4; 5:5–11; 6:1–8).
The verb "I saw" (רָאִיתִי) signals the genre to the reader (cf., Ezek. 1:4;
8:2). The visions are symbolic of eschatological and messianic realities
to come beyond the immediate context of the postexilic community, and
they require an angelic guide to interpret them (cf., Dan. 7–12). The
text does not say how the visions came to Zechariah (cf., Gen. 15:12;
Jer. 31:26; Dan. 10:9).

---

6. This translation is an attempt to bring out the fronting of the independent
personal pronoun "you."

When Zechariah says, "and look, a man riding on a red horse," the word "look" (הנה) invites the reader to view the vision from the prophet's own perspective. It is like viewing a film scene through the eyes of one of the characters. Angelic messengers often appear in the Bible in the form of men (e.g., Gen. 18:2, 22; 19:1; Judg. 13:6; Dan. 10:5, 16). This one was riding on a red horse and remaining among the myrtle trees that were in the deep. The word "deep" refers to the deep sea (cf., Jon. 2:4 [Eng.., 2:3]; Ps. 107:24), not a ravine. This is not a reference to a specific, known place. It is simply the backdrop for the vision. The LXX, on the other hand, says that the man was remaining between the two overshadowing mountains. This only requires a slightly different consonantal text for the first word of the Hebrew text and a different vocalization for the third: הֶהָרִים אֲשֶׁר בַּמְּצֻלָה. Behind this rider and his horse were other horses, red, sorrel/ruddy, and white. These horses presumably had riders as well (cf., Zech. 6:1–8; Rev. 6; 7:2).

The prophet then recounts in Zech. 1:9 that he asked very respectfully, "What are these, my lord?" The one who responds to him is described as "the messenger/angel who was speaking with me." The *BHS* apparatus and many English versions do their best to keep this messenger distinct from the man riding on the red horse, but it is clear from the Hebrew text of Zechariah 1:10–11 that the messenger is the same as the one remaining among the myrtle trees in Zechariah 1:8. It is as if the character comes off the screen itself to explain what the prophet is seeing. He says, "I am the one who will show you what these things are." (Note the fronting of the pronoun "I" in the Hebrew text.) He explains that the riders and their horses were sent by the LORD to walk about in the land. The English translation "to patrol the earth" makes it sound like they were sent as police for the planet, which is not the sense of the Hebrew text. To walk about in the land means to exercise dominion in the land of the covenant (cf., Gen. 13:17; Josh. 18:4; 1 Chr. 21:4). The LORD did this by sending his angelic messengers to survey the land in order that they might give a report (Zech. 1:11; cf., Zech. 6:7; Job 1:7; 2:2). The report is not about the planet. It is primarily about the status of the land of the covenant (Zech. 1:11–17).

In Zechariah 1:11, the riders give their report to the messenger/ angel of the LORD.[7] They point out that all the land of the covenant is

---

7. "The angel of the LORD" is not a title used to designate a special angel, a theophany, or a pre-incarnate appearance of Christ in the Bible. It is simply a phrase that refers to the particular angel sent by the LORD in a given context (cf., the use of the phrase "the servant of the LORD" for Moses, Joshua, David, the Messiah, etc.). There is nothing unusual about

dwelling quietly (cf., Judg. 3:11, 30; Ezek. 38:14). This initially seems to be a positive report, but the angelic messenger of the LORD laments the situation (Zech. 1:12), "O LORD of hosts, how long will you in particular not have compassion on Jerusalem and the cities of Judah with whom you have been indignant [LXX: whom you have overlooked; Tg. Jon.: upon whom you have brought a curse] these seventy years?" The Hebrew phrase translated "how long" is common in lament psalms (e.g., Ps. 6:4 [Eng., 6:3]). Thus, although the people have returned from the seventy years of captivity in Babylon to live peacefully under Persian rule (Jer. 25:11; 29:10; Zech. 7:5), they are not currently experiencing the kind of restoration envisioned by Isaiah 40–55.[8] This is similar to what the reader finds in Isaiah 56–66, which presupposes the return from Babylon yet still views the people as in need of deliverance from captivity (e.g., Isa. 61:1–9; cf., Luke 4:16–30). It is also not unlike the interpretation of Jeremiah's prophecy of seventy years in Daniel 9:24–27, which pushes the seventy years into the future (seventy sevens).[9] Therefore, the LORD answers the messenger with good words, comforting words (Zech. 1:13; see Zech. 1:17b; cf., Isa. 40:1), which the messenger then delivers to the prophet to proclaim to the people in Zechariah 1:14–17.

BHS sets the text of Zechariah 1:14–17 as poetry. The style is somewhat heightened here, but the parallelism is not sustained consistently enough to constitute poetry. The LORD says that he is jealous (or, zealous) for Jerusalem and for Zion with great jealousy (Zech. 1:14b; see also Zech. 8:2). God is jealous in the sense that he rightly demands exclusive worship (Exod. 20:5; 34:14; Deut. 4:24; 5:9; 6:15; Josh. 24:19; Nah. 1:2). Anything less would be idolatry. He is jealous for his people (Isa. 42:13; 63:15; see also Isa. 9:6 [Eng., 9:7]; 37:32), his land (Joel 2:18), and his city (Zech. 1:14; 8:2) because they all bear his name (Deut. 12:5; Ezek. 39:25). God's primary motive for action in this world is his

---

the fact that angels often appear to be interchangeable with the LORD (e.g., Exod. 3:2, 4). Angels, not unlike the prophets, are messengers who represent the LORD and speak on his behalf. This should not be taken to mean that angels are the LORD.

8. This situation of being under foreign rule would continue under Greek rule and Roman rule. Even the modern political state of Israel is not a fulfillment of prophecy about the restoration of the full extent of the boundaries of the land of the covenant (Gen. 15:18). This will only take place in the messianic kingdom and the new creation.

9. See Michael B. Shepherd, *Daniel in the Context of the Hebrew Bible* (New York: Peter Lang, 2009), 39, 96–97; idem, *The Twelve Prophets in the New Testament* (New York: Peter Lang, 2011), 94–96.

reputation and his glory (Isa. 48:9–11; Dan. 9:15–19). The LORD also says that he is very angry with the nations who are "at ease" (Zech. 1:15). That is, he is angry with those who have become arrogant (BDB, 983). He explains that he, on the one hand, was only a little angry, but they "helped" in such a way that brought about an evil result. This could be taken to mean that the LORD was only a little angry with the nations, but they exacerbated his anger by their actions. It could also be taken to mean that the LORD was only a little angry with his people (see *Tg. Jon.*), but the nations made the situation worse by leading them into all kinds of evil practices. In the opinion of the present commentary, however, the wording of Zechariah 1:15b is most closely aligned with that of Isaiah 47:6, where the idea is that the LORD was angry with his people and gave them into the hand of the Babylonians as his instrument of judgment, but the Babylonians went beyond the bounds of their role to do even more harm to the people (cf., Isa. 10:7).

The LORD goes on to say that he has returned to Jerusalem with compassion (Zech. 1:16; see Zech. 1:3, 6, 12; 8:3). In context, this cannot mean that he has already returned to restore the city in the full eschatological and messianic sense, otherwise there would be no need for visions of future restoration. Therefore, the LXX translates this in the future tense: "I will return." The LORD's house will be built in the city of Jerusalem. As discussed in the commentary on Haggai (see Hag. 2:6–9), this is not primarily about the Second Temple in the days of Haggai and Zechariah (Ezra 3–6). The visions of restoration in the book of Zechariah look well beyond the immediate context of these prophets, as does the program of the Twelve as a whole (Hos. 3:5). Thus, Zechariah 1:16 speaks of the eschatological (Ezek. 40–48; Rev. 21:22) and messianic (2 Sam. 7:13; Zech. 6:12–13) temple. A measuring line will be stretched over Jerusalem for this purpose. This measuring line is for the city, the site of the temple (cf., Rev. 21:15). The measuring cord in Zechariah 2:5–6 (Eng., 2:1–2) is for measuring Jerusalem but also for the temple structure itself (cf., Ezek. 40:3; Rev. 11:1).

The LXX reads the adverb "again" at the beginning of Zechariah 1:17 with the last clause of Zechariah 1:16 ("and a measuring line will be stretched over Jerusalem again"), probably under the influence of the phraseology in Zechariah 1:17b ("and the LORD will comfort Zion again and choose Jerusalem again"). But it is also true that the angelic messenger is instructing Zechariah "again" to make a proclamation (cf., Zech. 1:14). This fits with the phraseology of Zechariah 1:17a: "Again my cities will overflow with good" (cf., Hos. 3:5; Zech. 1:13; 2:8 [Eng., 2:4]). The LXX translates the verb "overflow" according to its more common homonym in Hebrew "spread abroad" (see BDB, 806–807).

The LORD will comfort Zion again (cf., Isa. 12:1; 40:1; 49:13; Zech. 1:13) and choose Jerusalem again (cf., Deut. 12:5; Zech. 2:16 [Eng., 2:12]; Ps. 78:67–72).[10] This will be the restoration of the fallen booth of David in the last days (Amos 9:11–15), a return to the glory days of David and Solomon (see Zech. 3:10; cf., 1 Kgs. 5:5 [Eng., 4:25]; Mic. 4:4), only new and better in the messianic kingdom. This highlights the centrality of the Garden of Eden (i.e., the land of the covenant) and the city of David from beginning to end (Gen. 2:11–14; Gen. 15:18; 22:2, 14 [2 Chr. 3:1]; 2 Sam. 5; Isa. 2:1–5; 65:17–18; Rev. 21–22).

ZECHARIAH 2:1–17 (ENG., 1:18–2:13)

2:1 (Eng., 1:18) "And I lifted up my eyes and saw, and look, four horns [Tg. Jon.: four kingdoms]. 2:2 (Eng., 1:19) And I said to the messenger / angel who was speaking with me, 'What are these [LXX adds: lord (cf., 1:9)]?' And he said to me, 'These are the horns [Tg. Jon.: kingdoms] that scattered Judah (that is, Israel) and Jerusalem [LXX: Judah and Jerusalem; Syr.: Judah and Israel and Jerusalem].'[11] 2:3 (Eng., 1:20) And the LORD showed me four craftsmen [NET: blacksmiths]. 2:4 (Eng., 1:21) And I said, 'What are these coming to do?' And he said, 'These are the horns [Tg. Jon.: kingdoms] that scattered Judah in such proportion that [or, so that] each one did not lift up his head [see BDB, 805; cf., LXX]. And these came [RSV: have come] to cause them to tremble, to cast down the horns of the nations who lifted up a horn [Tg. Jon.: weapon] against the land of Judah to scatter it.'

---

10. The third-person reference to the LORD in Zechariah 1:17b is more palatable when the reader remembers that this is the word of the LORD as delivered through the proclamation of the prophet.

11. The combination "Judah, Israel, and Jerusalem" (with object markers in front of Judah and Israel) does not occur elsewhere. The combination "Judah and Jerusalem" does occur elsewhere (e.g., 1 Chr. 5:41; 2 Chr. 33:9; 34:3, 5). Judah and Israel are combined where Judah refers to the south and Israel to the north (e.g., 2 Sam. 24:1). Assuming that the horns/kingdoms in this verse are those of the book of Daniel (chs. 2, 7, 8, 10–12), the first kingdom would be Babylon. Thus, a separate northern kingdom of Israel is not in view, having been taken into captivity a century earlier by the Assyrians before the rise of Babylon. Thus, it appears that the LXX ("Judah and Jerusalem") preserves an earlier reading, and "Israel" is a scribal comment flagged by the object marker (cf., Hag. 2:5a) that indicates Judah is now the only "Israel" that exists. This does not exclude, however, the possibility of a reunited Judah and Israel in the future (see Jer. 3:14–18; Ezek. 37:15–28). See Keil, *Minor Prophets*, 517–18.

2:5 (Eng., 2:1) And I lifted up my eyes and saw, and look, a man, and in his hand was a cord of measure. 2:6 (Eng., 2:2) And I said [LXX adds: to him], 'Where are you going?' And he said to me, 'To measure Jerusalem to see according to what is its breadth and according to what is its length.' 2:7 (Eng., 2:3) And look, the messenger/angel who was speaking with me was going forth [LXX: stood], and another angel was going forth to meet him. 2:8 (Eng., 2:4) And he [i.e., the first angel] said to him [i.e., the other angel],[12] 'Run, speak to this young man [i.e., Zechariah (cf., Jer. 1:6)] saying, "As open regions [Tg. Jon.: As un-walled towns] Jerusalem will dwell because of an abundance of people and animals in its midst. 2:9 (Eng., 2:5) 'But as for me, I will be to it,' the prophetic utterance of the LORD, 'a city wall of fire around, and for glory will I be in its midst. 2:10 (Eng., 2:6) Ho, ho, and flee from the land of the north,' the prophetic utterance of the LORD, 'for like the four winds of the sky I have scattered you [LXX: I will gather you],' the prophetic utterance of the LORD. 2:11 (Eng., 2:7) Ho, Zion [Tg. Jon.: Proclaim to the congregation of Zion and say to it]. Escape, inhabitant of daughter Babylon [or, Ho, escape to Zion, inhabitant of daughter Babylon (cf., LXX)].'

2:12 (Eng., 2:8) For thus says the LORD of hosts"' (After glory he sent me to the nations who plundered you.), '"'Indeed, the one who touches you touches the gate [LXX: young girl; Tg. Jon.: wheel; Vulg.: pupil; KJV: apple] of my eye [Tiq soph: his eye]. 2:13 (Eng., 2:9) For look, I am about to wave my hand over them, and they will be plunder to their servants'"' (And you [m. pl.] will know that it was the LORD of hosts who sent me.). 2:14 (Eng., 2:10) '"'Shout and be glad, Daughter Zion [Tg. Jon.: congregation of Zion]. For look, I am about to come to you [Tg. Jon.: I am about to reveal myself], and I will dwell in your midst,' the prophetic utterance of the LORD. 2:15 (Eng., 2:11) 'And many nations will be joined to the LORD in that day, and they will become my

---

12. The ESV (and other English versions) assumes that the other angel speaks to the first angel here, but this is very difficult to reconcile with the context. The first angel who has guided the prophet through the first two visions is going forth to measure Jerusalem (see Rashi). Therefore, another angel must be brought in to speak to Zechariah. This explains how it is that someone else, namely the other angel, is able to show the first angel to the prophet at the beginning of the fourth vision in chapter 3 (see Zech. 3:1). After the first angel finishes the role that he plays in the fourth vision, he resumes his function as the prophet's guide in the fifth vision: "And the messenger/angel who was speaking with me returned" (Zech. 4:1a).

people [LXX, Syr.: his people], and I will dwell [LXX: they will dwell;
Syr.: he will dwell]"' (And you [f. sg.] will know that it was the LORD
of hosts who sent me to you.). 2:16 (Eng., 2:12) '"And the LORD will
inherit Judah his portion upon the holy land, and he will choose [Tg.
Jon.: be pleased with] Jerusalem again. 2:17 (Eng., 2:13) Hush [LXX:
Act reverently], all flesh, from before the LORD [Tg. Jon.: All the wicked
have perished from before the LORD], for he is aroused [Tg. Jon.: he has
revealed himself] from his holy habitation [LXX: his holy clouds]."'"

The second vision is relatively brief (Zech. 2:1–4 [Eng., 1:18–21]).
According to *Targum Jonathan*, the horns that Zechariah saw represented four kingdoms, usually understood to be the four kingdoms
known from the book of Daniel. This would seem to work well with the
interpretation in Zechariah 2:4 (Eng., 1:21), but not everyone agrees on
the identity of the four kingdoms in Daniel. The so-called traditional
or common view says that they are Babylon, Medo-Persia, Greece, and
Rome. The standard critical view says they are Babylon, Media, Persia,
and Greece. The problem with the first view is that Rome is never mentioned in the book of Daniel. The problem with the second is that Media
and Persia are never separated in the book of Daniel. Thus, a compositional view says that the book itself identifies the four kingdoms as
Babylon (Dan. 2:38), Medo-Persia (Dan. 8:20), Greece (Dan. 8:21), and a
future and final enemy known from the text behind the LXX of the book
of Jeremiah as the enemy from the north (Dan. 9:1–2, 24–27; 11:36–
45; see LXX Jer. 25:1–13; see also Ezek. 38:14–17).[13] When Zechariah
asks the angel about the horns, he simply says that they are the horns
that scattered Judah (that is, Israel) and Jerusalem (Zech. 2:2 [Eng.,
1:19]). If the identification with the kingdoms in the book of Daniel is
correct, then not only are they the kingdoms who have ruled Judah and
Jerusalem in the past and present from Zechariah's perspective, but
also, they are the kingdoms who are yet to come, even to the last days.
This is consistent with the eschatological thrust of each of the visions.

The LORD also showed the prophet four craftsmen (Zech. 2:3 [Eng.,
1:20]). The Hebrew word translated "craftsmen" can refer to those who
work with metal, wood, or stone (see BDB, 360), but it can also be used
figuratively to refer to those who are skilled to destroy (Ezek. 21:36; cf.
Isa. 54:16). When Zechariah asks what the craftsmen are coming to do
(Zech. 2:4 [Eng., 1:21]), the initial response is a repetition of the explanation of the four horns, only this time the information is added that
the four horns scattered Judah in such a way that no one lifted up his

---

13. See Shepherd, *Daniel in the Context of the Hebrew Bible*.

head (see Judg. 8:28; Ps. 83:3 [Eng., 83:2]; Job 10:15). The craftsmen came in the vision to cause the horns to tremble (cf., Judg. 8:12; Ezek. 30:9), to cast down the horns of the nations who were lifting up a horn representing strength and weaponry against Judah to scatter it (see BDB, 901–902). Thus, the message of the vision is one of deliverance from the increasing worldly opposition of the enemies of God and his people. It is not necessary at this point to go beyond what is written to identify the craftsmen any further (1 Cor. 4:6).

At the beginning of the third vision, the prophet sees a man with a cord of measure in his hand (Zech. 2:5 [Eng., 2:1]). This "man" is apparently the same man that the prophet saw riding on the red horse in the first vision (Zech. 1:8). In both instances, the man is the prophet's usual angelic guide to the meaning of the visions. The "cord of measure" is a different term in the Hebrew text from the one in Zechariah 1:16b. There it is said that a "measuring line" will be stretched over Jerusalem to measure the city to be rebuilt. Here the "cord of measure" is not only to measure the city but also to measure the new temple site within the city. It is thought to be similar to "the reed of measure" in Ezek. 40:3 (cf., Rev. 11:1; 21:15). When Zechariah asks the man where he is going, the man says that he is going to measure Jerusalem to see what its breadth and its length are (Zech. 2:6 [Eng., 2:2]). Therefore, the messenger/angel who normally speaks to the prophet must depart to fulfill this duty (Zech. 2:7a [Eng., 2:3a]). This requires another angel to come on the scene temporarily to serve as the prophet's interpretive guide (Zech. 2:7b [Eng., 2:3b]). This other angel will function in this role in chapters 2 and 3 until the first angel resumes the role at the beginning of chapter 4.

And so, the angel who normally spoke to the prophet tells the other angel in Zechariah 2:8a (Eng., 2:4a) to run and speak to "this young man." The designation of Zechariah as "this young man" is apparently intended to be an echo of the self-description of Jeremiah (Jer. 1:6), the prophet after whom Zechariah models himself (see Zech. 1:4). The message delivered to Zechariah is the result of the measurement of the city: "As open regions [or, unwalled towns] Jerusalem will dwell because of an abundance of people and animals in its midst" (Zech. 2:8b [Eng., 2:4b]). This is in stark contrast to the situation described in Nehemiah 7:4; 11:1–2 where the postexilic community could barely find enough people to inhabit the city and defend it. In the future, the LORD will bless his people and his city in such a way that the boundaries of the city will extend to the outlying regions (see Isa. 2:1–5; 49:20; Jer. 31:38–40; Zech. 10:10; 14:10). Therefore, the city wall, which was so important to Nehemiah (Neh. 1:3), will be replaced by the LORD himself (Zech. 2:9 [Eng., 2:5]). The angel reports the LORD as saying that he will be "a city wall of fire" around the newly expanded version of Jerusalem. This is reminiscent of the way that the LORD protected his people in the original exodus (Exod. 14:18–20). The LORD adds that it is for glory that he will be in the midst of the city. Just as in the tabernacle and Solomon's temple (Exod. 40:35; 1 Kgs. 8:11), the glory of the LORD will appear (Isa. 4:2; Ezek. 43:5; Hag. 2:9), and the LORD will be glorified (cf., Hag. 1:8).

The LORD's discourse, which the other angel is to report to the prophet, continues in Zechariah 2:10–11 (Eng., 2:6–7). The LORD summons the people to flee from the land of the north (cf., Isa. 48:20; 55:1; Jer. 50:3), because he has scattered them like the four winds of the sky (i.e., north, south, east, and west [cf., Zech. 6:5–8]). That is, they are still in need of restoration. The LXX has "I will gather" (BHS: = כָּנַסְתִּי?) instead of "I have scattered." Verse 11 is either addressed to the people of Zion or it is a command to escape to Zion. The people are called the inhabitant of daughter Babylon because they lived there as exiles. But the reality is that the people to whom Zechariah prophesied had already returned from Babylon, and there is no indication that this message was merely a call for more people to return from the land of Babylon under Persian rule. The language suggests that the land of the north here is the eschatological land of the north. The source for this language is likely the book of Jeremiah (see Zech. 1:4). While the MT of the book of Jeremiah consistently identifies the enemy from the north as Babylon, the LXX leaves the enemy unidentified and open to an eschatological interpretation (e.g., Jer. 25:1–13). This is the way Ezekiel reads Jeremiah's prophecy when he interprets the enemy from the north to be a future and final enemy named Gog from the land of Magog (Ezek. 38:2, 14–17). It is from that context that the people will ultimately be delivered.

There is no clear indication that the LORD's discourse that the other angel is to report stops in Zechariah 2:12–17 (Eng., 2:8–13). Therefore, statements in which the speaker claims that the LORD "sent me" must be considered parenthetical statements from the prophet (Zech. 2:12a, 13b, 15b [Eng., 2:8a, 9b, 11b]; cf., Zech. 4:9b; 6:15a; see also Exod. 3:10). All but the first of these state that the fulfillment of the prophecy will vindicate the prophet in such a way that the people will know that he is a true prophet (see Deut. 18:20–22). This is especially the concern of prophets rather than angels (e.g., Ezek. 2:5b; 13:6; 33:33). The fulfillment of historical prophecies (e.g., Jer. 34–45; Ezra 5:1–2; 6:14–15) is like a down payment on the fulfillment of eschatological prophecies (e.g., Jer. 30–33; Zech. 1–6). The first parenthetical statement in Zechariah 2:12a (Eng., 2:8a) comes between the introductory formula ("For thus says the LORD of hosts") and the reported discourse of the LORD in Zechariah 2:12b (Eng., 2:8b). The Hebrew phrase translated "After glory" only occurs one other time in the Hebrew Bible in Psalm 73:24 where it has a temporal sense, a meaning that does not suit the context of Zechariah 2:12 (Eng., 2:8) very well, unless the idea is that this is sequentially after the glory mentioned in Zechariah 2:9 (Eng., 2:5). One possibility is that the LORD has sent the prophet in pursuit of his glory (see Gen. 37:17b; 2 Kgs. 25:5a; Isa. 48:9–11). In other words, the prophet bears the message of the LORD's coming glory (Zech. 2:9 [Eng., 2:5]). When the text says that the prophet was sent to "the nations who plundered you" (cf., Zech. 14:1), it does not mean that the prophet physically went to the nations. It means that the book of Zechariah is not just for or about Judah and Jerusalem. The book has something to say to the nations—to those opposed to the people of God (Zech. 2:13 [Eng., 2:9]; 12; 14:1–15) and to those who are part of the people of God (Zech. 2:15 [Eng., 2:11]; 8:20–23; 14:16–21).

The first part of the LORD's reported discourse in Zechariah 2:12b (Eng., 2:8b) in the MT has a third-person reference to the LORD: "Indeed, the one who touches you touches the gate of his eye." The pronoun "his" is one of the *tiqqune sopherim* ("corrections of the scribes"), perhaps designed to avoid having the LORD himself use such anthropomorphic language. But the original reading is, "Indeed, the one who touches you touches the gate of my eye" (see 4Q562; cf., Deut. 32:10; Ps. 17:8). That is, the people are the apple of the LORD's eye, and he will protect them as that feature of the human face is protected (see Zech. 12:9). The LORD points out in Zechariah 2:13a (Eng., 2:9a) that he is about to demonstrate this protection by waving is hand over "them." This is apparently a way of indicating that he is about to act in some way (cf., Isa. 11:15; 19:16). The implied antecedent of the pronoun "them" is "the nations" mentioned in the parenthetical statement of Zechariah 2:12a (Eng., 2:8a). In a great act of poetic justice, the LORD will turn the tables, and those nations who plundered God's people will become plunder to the very people who served them (see Jer. 30:8–9; Hab. 2:8). When this happens, the people will acknowledge that it was truly the LORD of hosts who sent Zechariah the prophet (Zech. 2:13b [Eng., 2:9b]).

The LORD calls on Daughter Zion (i.e., the people of God) to shout and be glad, for, as he points out, he is about to come and dwell in the midst of the city (Zech. 2:14 [Eng., 2:10]; cf., Zech. 8:3). He envisions his coming to be imminent. This text picks up the language of Zephaniah 3:14–15 (see commentary), which also calls on Daughter Zion to shout and depicts the LORD as king in the midst of the people. The text of

Zechariah 9:9–10 will then follow up on both passages and picture the Davidic Messiah coming as king in the same manner as the LORD himself (cf., Isa. 9:5–6 [Eng., 9:6–7]). The resultant image of God in the flesh as the Davidic king later helps the reader with the wording of Zechariah 12:10 where the LORD refers to himself in the first person as the one "whom they pierced," yet the people will mourn for "him" (i.e., the Davidic king; see John 19:37). From the very beginning it was the LORD's purpose to dwell in the midst of his people (see *Tg. Neof.* Gen. 9:27). He brought his people out of Egypt to dwell in their midst (Exod. 29:45–46). The Word became flesh and dwelt among us (John 1:1, 14). And in the new creation God will dwell with his people (Rev. 21:3).

Following what Zechariah 2:12–13 (Eng., 2:8–9) says about the nations, the content of Zechariah 2:15 (Eng., 2:11) might be the last thing that the reader expects (cf., Isa. 14:1). But the LORD not only has enemies to be judged from the nations, he also has members of the believing remnant of the people of God from the nations. Likewise, there are both believers and unbelievers from Israel. Thus, it is important to reiterate once again that the distinctive mark of the people of God in the Hebrew Bible is faith and not ethnicity.[14] Many nations will be joined to the LORD in that day when the LORD comes (cf., Isa. 2:1–5; 25:6–8; 56:3, 6; 60:3–9; 66:18–24; Amos 9:12; Mic. 4:1–5; Zech. 8:20–23; 14:16–21). They too will be his covenant people (cf., Jer. 31:33b), and the LORD will dwell in the midst of Daughter Zion with all his people from all the nations (cf., Jer. 7:3, 7).[15] This too will confirm the validity of Zechariah's prophecy.

---

14. Both Covenant Theology and Dispensationalism stumble over this and thus create different and unnecessary solutions to the same nonexistent problem. Both assume that at one point ethnic Israel was intended to be the sole people of God with promises specifically designed for them and no one else. They then explain the church either as a replacement for ethnic Israel (Covenant Theology) or as a parenthesis (Dispensationalism). But ethnic Israel was never intended to be the sole people of God. From the beginning, the blessing and the restoration of the blessing was for all humanity (Gen. 1–11). The special role of Abraham and his descendants was to be the means of restoring the lost blessing to all the nations (Gen. 12:1–3), specifically through the Messiah (Ps. 72:17). Thus, however it goes for the believing remnant of Israel, so it goes for the believing from among the nations. Passages that appear on the surface to be specifically for Israel (e.g., Jer. 31:31–34) are always supplemented in context with passages that include the nations in the same plan (e.g., Jer. 3:14–18).

15. The LXX maintains third-person reference to the LORD ("and they will become his people, and they will dwell"). Thus, verse 15 (Eng., v. 11) is read

According to the MT, the reported discourse of the LORD ends with Zechariah 2:15 (Eng., 2:11). The last part of what the first angel tells the other angel to say to Zechariah comes in Zechariah 2:16–17 (Eng., 2:12–13; see Zech. 2:8a [Eng., 2:4a]). The LORD will inherit Judah his portion upon the holy land (cf., Deut. 32:9) and choose Jerusalem again (cf., Deut. 12:5; Zech. 1:17; Ps. 78:68). The call to "Hush" or "Be Silent" in the presence of the LORD goes out to "all flesh" (see Joel 3:1 [Eng., 2:28]; see also Habakkuk 2:20 ["all the earth"]). The specific language of showing reverence before the LORD (see LXX) recalls Habakkuk 2:20 and Zephaniah 1:7. According to Zephaniah 1:7, the reason for doing this is the imminent Day of the LORD. This is depicted in Zechariah 2:16 (Eng., 2:12) in terms of the LORD being aroused from his holy habitation (cf., Ps. 78:65), which is his holy temple according to Habakkuk 2:20 (cf., Mic. 1:2; Ps. 11:4).

ZECHARIAH 3

3:1 "And he showed me Joshua the great priest [RSV: high priest] standing before the messenger/angel of the LORD, and the adversary [LXX: the slanderer; Tg. Jon.: sin; Vulg.: Satan] was standing at his right hand to oppose him. 3:2 And the LORD [Syr.: the messenger/angel of the Lord] said to the adversary, 'May the LORD rebuke you, O adversary, and may the LORD rebuke you who chooses Jerusalem [Tg. Jon.: who is pleased to cause his Shekhinah to dwell in Jerusalem]. Is not this [NET: this man] a firebrand rescued from a fire?' 3:3 And Joshua, he was clothed in garments covered with excrement [Tg. Jon.: he had sons for whom were taken wives not proper for the priesthood] and standing before the messenger/angel. 3:4 And he [NET: the angel] answered and said to those standing [Tg. Jon.: serving] before him saying, 'Remove the garments covered with excrement from upon him [Tg. Jon.: Let him bring forth women who are not proper for the priesthood from his house].' And he said to him [NET: Joshua], 'See, I have caused to pass away from upon you your iniquity and clothed you [or, will clothe you; see GKC §113z; LXX: clothe him (pl. impv.)] with stately robes [LXX: a robe; Tg. Jon.: innocence].' 3:5 And I said, 'Let them put [Vulg.: And he said, Put] a clean turban on his head.' And they put the clean turban on his head and clothed him with garments [Tg. Jon.: caused him to take a wife proper for the priesthood], and the messenger/angel of the LORD

---

with verses 16 and 17 (Eng., vv. 12 and 13) as separate from the LORD's reported discourse. It is the last part of what the first angel tells the other angel to say to Zechariah (see Zech. 2:8a [Eng., 2:4a]).

was standing.[16] *3:6 And the messenger / angel of the LORD admonished Joshua saying, 3:7 'Thus says the LORD of hosts, "If in my ways you walk, and if my charge you keep, you will both judge my house [Tg. Jon.: those who serve in my sanctuary] and keep my courts, and I will give to you goings [BDB, 237: free access] among these standing [Tg. Jon.: and at the resurrection of the dead I will keep you alive and give you feet walking among these seraphim]. 3:8 Listen, Joshua, O great priest, you and your companions who are sitting before you, for men of wonder are they [Syr.: you (pl.)]. For look, I am about to bring [see GKC §116p] my servant Branch [LXX: Ἀνατολήν; Syr.: dawn / shining; Tg. Jon.: my servant the Messiah, and he will reveal himself; Vulg.: orientem]. 3:9 For look, the stone that I have put before Joshua. Upon one stone are seven eyes [Tg. Jon.: seven see it]. Look, I am about to engrave its engraving [LXX: dig a ditch; Syr.: open its gates; Tg. Jon.: reveal those that see it]," the prophetic utterance of the LORD of hosts, "and I will remove [LXX, Syr.: touch]*[17] *the iniquity of this land in one day. 3:10 In that day," the prophetic utterance of the LORD of hosts, "each of you will invite his friend to a place under a grapevine [Tg. Jon.: the fruit of his grapevine] and to a place under a fig tree [Tg. Jon.: the fruit of his fig tree]."'"*

Zechariah begins his account of the fourth vision by saying that the other messenger/angel from Zechariah 2:7 (Eng., 2:3) showed him Joshua the great priest (see Lev. 21:10; Num. 35:25, 28) standing before the first messenger/angel (Zech. 1:8–14; 2:2 [Zech. 1:19]). This is the same Joshua that the reader of the Twelve knows from the book of Haggai (Hag. 1:1, 12, 14; 2:2, 4; see also Ezra 2:2; 3:2; 5:2). The other angel also showed him the adversary standing at "his" right hand to oppose Joshua. The term הַשָּׂטָן ("the adversary") is not a name ("Satan") but a title for a particular angel who has the specific role or function to oppose or to accuse. The adversary also plays this role in Job 1–2, but there he is also an instigator, calling into question both the authenticity of Job's piety and whether the LORD is worth worshiping for his own sake.[18]

---

16. See Patricia Ahearne-Kroll, "LXX/OG Zechariah 1–6 and the Portrayal of Joshua Centuries after the Restoration of the Temple," in *Septuagint Research: Issues and Challenges in the Study of the Greek Jewish Scriptures*, eds. Wolfgang Kraus and R. Glenn Wooden (Atlanta: SBL, 2006), 180–83.

17. If the verb here is from מוּשׁ ("move"), it would be the only *qal* transitive use (cf., *hiphil*). The LXX interprets the verb to be from the homonym מוּשׁ ("touch") (see Isa. 6:7).

18. Some think that this same adversary is in 1 Chronicles 21:1 (see Ralph W. Klein, *1 Chronicles*, Hermeneia [Minneapolis: Fortress, 2006], 418–19),

Here the adversary simply does his job by pointing out the iniquity of the community that Joshua represents. God has every right to judge the community for this, but he will make provision for their iniquity and establish a new covenant relationship (Zech. 3:9; 8:8; 12:10; 13:1, 9). After the response to the adversary in Zechariah 3:2, he no longer appears in the vision (cf., Job 42). It is not immediately clear from the Hebrew text at whose right side the adversary stands, Joshua's or the angel's. But the wording of Psalm 109:6 suggests that the adversary stands at the right side of the one opposed, which in this case is Joshua. It is clear from the discourse in Zechariah 3:2 that it is the messenger/ angel of the LORD who responds to the adversary, so why does the MT introduce this as the LORD's discourse? This is simply because the messenger speaks on the LORD's behalf and is thus interchangeable with him (cf., Exod. 3:2, 4). The Syriac makes this explicit by introducing the discourse as that of the messenger/angel of the LORD. The angel does not take matters into his own hands. Rather, he says, "May the LORD rebuke you" (cf., Jude 9). This is not because the adversary is wrong about the iniquity of the people. It is because the LORD will choose Jerusalem again in spite of the people (Zech. 2:16 [Eng., 2:12]). The angel then uses a rhetorical question to characterize either Joshua (and the community he represents) or Jerusalem as a firebrand or burning stick rescued from a fire (cf., Amos 4:11). In other words, the LORD has already judged the people for their breaking of the old covenant. It is now time to look forward to the restoration of the remnant.

Turning to Joshua, Zechariah recounts that he was clothed in garments covered in excrement in the vision (Zech. 3:3). These are not merely filthy or dirty garments. They are utterly repulsive. According to *Targum Jonathan*, these garments represent the fact that Joshua "had sons for whom were taken wives not proper for the priesthood" (see Ezra 10:18). But this limits what the garments represent in a way that is not consistent with the context. According to Zechariah 3:4b, 9b, they represent the iniquity of the people of the land in general. The text of Zechariah 3:3b repeats the fact that Joshua was standing before the angel (see Zech. 3:1) so that the reader knows that this angel is the one who responds in Zechariah 3:4 and tells "those standing before him" to remove the garments from Joshua (cf., *Tg. Jon.*). Those standing before him are presumably other angels who are at the service and direction of the primary angel in the vision

---

but there the adversary is more than likely a foreign adversary nation (see John H. Sailhamer, *Introduction to Old Testament Theology* [Grand Rapids: Zondervan, 1995], 302–308).

(cf., Dan. 7:16). The removal of the garments represents the fact that the angel has caused Joshua's iniquity to pass away, and these garments are replaced by stately robes (cf., Isa. 3:22). But this is not just about Joshua's personal iniquity. The text of Zechariah 3:9b clarifies that this is about the removal of the iniquity of the people of the land whom Joshua represents as their high priest (cf., Lev. 16; Zech. 13:2; see also Rev. 19:8 [cf., Exod 19:6; Isa. 61:6; 1 Pet. 2:5, 9; Rev. 1:6; 5:10; 20:6]).[19] At this point the prophet jumps in and participates in the vision by suggesting that the angels complete the priestly garb by putting a clean turban on Joshua's head (Zech. 3:5; but see Vulg.; see also Isa. 3:23; 62:3; Job 29:14 [cf., Exod. 28:4, 37–39; 29:6; 39:28, 31; Lev. 8:9; 16:4; Ezek. 21:31]). The angels then do this, with the primary angel presiding.

The messenger/angel of the LORD then admonishes Joshua in the vision with words that apply not only to him but also to the Messiah, the messianic kingdom, and the people of God (Zech. 3:6–10). If Joshua "walks" in the ways of the LORD and "keeps" his charge, he will judge the LORD's temple and "keep" his courts, and the LORD will give to him "walkings" among "these standing" (Zech. 3:7). The chiastic structuring of this conditional statement highlights the reciprocal relationship between the protasis and the apodosis.[20] The last part of this refers to the angels mentioned in Zechariah 3:4 and suggests that the prophecy is not merely about priestly privileges in the Second Temple. *Targum Jonathan* interprets it to be about access to the resurrection from the dead and the afterlife: "and at the resurrection of the dead I will keep you alive and give you feet walking among these seraphim."

In Zechariah 3:8, the LORD addresses Joshua and his companions in the vision through the angelic messenger. These companions are usually thought to be Joshua's fellow priests,[21] but these companions are called "men of wonder" (אַנְשֵׁי מוֹפֵת), which is never used for priests in the Bible. It is, however, a term that could be used for prophets (see Isa. 8:18; 20:3; Ezek. 12:6, 11). Therefore, it is best to understand Joshua's companions in this context to be prophets like Zechariah and Haggai

---

19. Early church fathers understood Joshua to be a type of Christ here (see Ferreiro, ed, *The Twelve Prophets*, 240–42), but that would be more appropriate for Zechariah 6:9–15. Here Joshua represents the people as one who stands guilty among them.
20. The conditional nature of this should not remind the reader of the old covenant relationship (Lev. 26; Deut. 28). It is evident from Zechariah 3:4–5 that what the LORD establishes here is all of grace.
21. See, e.g., Keil, *Minor Prophets*, 529.

(see Ezra 5:1–2). The LORD wants Joshua and his companions to listen because he has a message about the imminent coming of the Messiah and his kingdom. He envisions ("look") that he is about to bring his servant Branch. This picks up the description of Zerubbabel in Haggai 2:23 and clarifies that Zerubbabel is only a prefiguration of one who is still to come (see *Tg. Jon.* Zech. 3:8b). This is evident from the fact that Zerubbabel is already present as a leader in the community, but the one of whom the LORD speaks here is yet to come in the future—not to mention the fact that Zerubbabel never actually reigned as king. The Branch is the messianic Branch whose family tree is of Davidic lineage (Isa. 4:2; 11:1–10) and who will reign in justice and righteousness (Jer. 23:5–6; see also Ezek. 17:22–24). The text of Zechariah 6:12–13 will develop this image even further. The Branch is also the messianic servant of the LORD (Isa. 42:1–7; 49:1–9; 50:4–11; 52:13–53:12; 61:1–9). The translation of "Branch" in the LXX as Ἀνατολήν links Zechariah 3:8 (and Jer. 23:5; Zech. 6:12) with its translation of the messianic passage in Numbers 24:17 ("a star will rise out of Jacob").

In Zechariah 3:9, the LORD points out a stone that he has put before Joshua. This appears to be a prop in the vision, but the stone clearly represents someone or something else. Stone imagery is both common and consistent in the Bible, so it is not difficult to narrow the possibilities. In some texts the stone is the Messiah (Isa. 8:14; 28:16; Ps. 118:22 [cf., Zech. 4:7, 10]; Matt. 21:42–44; Rom. 9:33). The text of 1 Peter 2:6–8 brings several of these together to say that Christ is the stone and Christians are the stones. But the stone can also be the messianic kingdom (Dan. 2:34–35, 44–45; cf., Zech. 12:3). Because the Messiah and his kingdom are somewhat inseparable, it can be difficult to distinguish between the two in a text like Zechariah 3:9, and it may very well be the case that no distinction is intended. The text says that upon one stone are seven eyes. This probably does not mean that seven eyes are attached to the surface of the stone, unless they are intended to depict the omniscience of the Messiah (cf., Rev. 4:6, 8). Rather, they are the all-knowing eyes of God that providentially and perfectly watch over the Messiah and his kingdom to bring the messianic kingdom to fruition and to sustain it (see *Tg. Jon.*; cf., Zech. 4:10b; see also Deut. 11:12; 4Q177).[22]

The LORD then says that he is about to engrave the stone (Zech. 3:9b). This calls to mind the engraving of the names of the sons of Israel on the two stones of the priestly garment (Exod. 28:9, 11, 21, 36; 39:6, 9, 30), perhaps in anticipation of the picture of the Messiah in Zechariah 6:12–13 as both priest and king. The LORD will remove

---

22. Ibid., 531.

411

the iniquity of the people of the land in one day (cf., Isa. 66:8), which is what the removal of Joshua's excrement-covered garments and their replacement with stately robes represent (Zech. 3:4–5). In that day, each person will invite his friend to a place under a grapevine and to a place under a fig tree (Zech. 3:10; cf., Hag. 2:19). This is not merely a description of abundance and well-being, it is a signal of return to the golden days of David and Solomon in the messianic kingdom: "And Judah lived, and Israel, in security, each under his grapevine and under his fig tree, from Dan to Beersheba all the days of Solomon" (1 Kgs. 5:5 [Eng., 4:25]). This text was already cited in Micah 4:4 to describe the messianic kingdom in the last days.

ZECHARIAH 4

4:1 "And the messenger / angel who was speaking with me returned and aroused me like a man who is aroused from his sleep. 4:2 And he said to me, 'What do you see?' And I said [kethiv: he said], 'I see, and look, a menorah [or, lampstand] of gold, all of it [BDB, 481–82], and its bowl [BDB, 165; GKC §91e] on its top, and its seven lamps on it, seven [lit., seven and seven; LXX: seven] pipes [lit., castings; LXX: funnels; Syr.: mouths; Tg. Jon.: that empty oil; RSV, ESV: lips] to each of the lamps that were on its top [cf., ASV, RSV; NET: fourteen pipes going to the lamps; Redak: one for each lamp], 4:3 and two olive trees by it, one on the right of the bowl and one on its left.' 4:4 And I answered and said to the messenger / angel who was speaking with me saying, 'What are these, my lord?' 4:5 And the messenger / angel who was speaking with me answered and said to me, 'Do you not know what these things are?' And I said, 'No, my lord.' 4:6 And he answered and said to me saying, 'This is the word of the LORD to Zerubbabel saying, "Not by might and not by strength but by my Spirit [Tg. Jon.: my word]," says the LORD of hosts. 4:7 Who are you, O great mountain [Tg. Jon.: foolish kingdom]? Before Zerubbabel you will become a level place [or, Who are you, O great mountain, before Zerubbabel? You will become a level place]. And he will bring forth the chief stone with noises / shouts [BDB, 996] of "Grace, grace" to it [LXX: And I will bring forth the stone of inheritance, equality of grace, grace for it (cf., Syr.); Tg. Jon.: And he will reveal his Messiah whose name has been said since long ago, and he will rule over all the kingdoms].' 4:8 And the word of the LORD came to me saying, 4:9 'As for Zerubbabel's hands, they established this house. But his hands, they will finish [lit., cut off; see BDB, 130].' And you will know that it was the LORD of hosts who sent me to you. 4:10 'For who despises a day of small things? And they will be glad and see the separated stone [ASV: the plummet; NET:

the tin tablet] in the hand of Zerubbabel. These seven are the eyes of the LORD. They are roaming through all the land.'[23] *4:11 And I answered and said to him, 'What are these two olive trees on the right of the menorah [or, lampstand] and on its left?' 4:12 And I answered a second time and said to him, 'What are these two branches [lit., ears of grain; or, flowing streams; see LXX] of the olive trees, which are beside the two golden pipes, which are emptying from upon them the golden oil [lit., the gold; Tg. Jon.: oil to the lamps of gold; NET: which are emptying out the golden oil through the two golden pipes]?' 4:13 And he said to me saying, 'Do you not know what these are?' And I said, 'No, my lord.' 4:14 And he said, 'These are the two anointed ones [lit., the two sons of fresh oil; see BDB, 121, 844; Tg. Jon.: two leaders] who are standing at the service of the Lord of all the land [see GKC §119cc].'"*

The messenger/angel who guided Zechariah through the first two visions now returns in the fifth vision (Zech. 4) after temporarily giving that responsibility to another angel for visions three and four (see Zech. 2:7–8 [Eng., 2:3–4]; 3:1). He arouses the prophet like one who is aroused from sleep (Zech. 4:1). This probably refers to the sleeplike experience of the visions (cf., Gen. 15:12; Jer. 31:26; Dan. 10:9). The question-and-answer format of the vision in Zechariah 4:2–3 is similar to what the reader finds in Jeremiah 1:11, 13; Amos 7:8; 8:2; and Zechariah 5:2. According to the *kethiv*, the messenger/angel answers his own question. This is likely due to the introduction of the prophet's discourse in Zechariah 4:4. But according to the *qere*, the prophet answers the angel's question. This suggests that the reintroduction of his discourse in Zechariah 4:4 indicates a pause after Zechariah 4:3. A comparison of the menorah or lampstand in Zechariah 4:2 to the one in Exodus 25:31–40 yields some similarities (e.g., gold, seven lamps), but for the most part the descriptions focus on different features. This is no doubt due at least in part to the fact that the one in Exodus 25:31–40 is for the construction of actual furniture for the tabernacle, while the one in Zechariah 4:2 is symbolic and thus intended to represent something else in the context of the vision and its interpretation (see Zech. 4:10b; cf., Rev. 1:20). The same is true for the two olive trees in Zechariah 4:3 (see Zech. 4:14; cf., Rev. 11:4). Perhaps the most uncertain aspect of the description in Zechariah 4:2 is the reference to "seven and seven castings," an expression variously rendered as noted in the above translation.

---

23. Or: And these seven will be glad and see the separated stone. The eyes of the LORD are roaming through all the land.

After Zechariah answers the angel's question about what he sees, he poses a question of his own in Zechariah 4:4b: "What are these, my lord?" It is apparent from the eventual response in Zechariah. 4:10 that the prophet is specifically asking about the seven lamps in Zechariah 4:2. He will wait to ask about the two olive trees until Zechariah 4:11. The other possibility is that the prophet is asking in Zechariah 4:4b about everything he sees, but the angel only tells him what the seven lamps represent, thus requiring the prophet to ask another question about the olive trees. The angel's initial response to the prophet's question seems designed to point out the obvious (Zech. 4:5; cf., Zech. 4:13): "Do you not know what these things are?" Of course, the prophet does not know. But the intent is not to humiliate Zechariah. The purpose of having the prophet make this admission is to make explicit for the reader the fact that interpretation of the vision must come by revelation and not by human ingenuity (2 Pet. 1:19–21). The reader is every bit as dependent upon the angelic guide as the prophet is. Therefore, the reader would do well not to go beyond the interpretation that the angel provides.

The explanation of the vision does not begin in Zechariah 4:6–9 (*contra* Calvin). Rather, Zechariah 4:6–9 serves as a preface to the explanation of the seven lamps in Zechariah 4:10 and the explanation of the two olive trees in Zechariah 4:11–14. The reader knows this from the pattern set by previous visions. For example, in Zechariah 1:9–10, the prophet asks, "What are these?" and the angelic messenger responds, "These are. . . ." Likewise, in Zechariah 2:4 (Eng., 1:21), the prophet asks, "What are these?" and the angelic messenger responds, "These are. . . ." In Zechariah 4:4b, the prophet asks, "What are these?" but the response, "These are . . .," does not come until Zechariah 4:10. The response that comes in Zechariah 4:6 is instead, "This is the word of the LORD to Zerubbabel." This is the same Zerubbabel that the reader of the Twelve knows from the book of Haggai (Hag. 1:1, 12, 14; 2:2, 4, 21, 23; see also Ezra 2:2; 3:2; 4:3; 5:2; 1 Chr. 3:19).

The message of the LORD of hosts/armies is, "Not by might and not by strength but by my Spirit" (cf., Mic. 3:8; Hag. 2:5; Zech. 6:8; 7:12; 12:10). That is, what the prophetic vision anticipates will not be accomplished by military might or physical strength. It will be accomplished by the work of God's Spirit. The NET Bible says without argument and without evidence that it is "premature to understand the Spirit here as the Holy Spirit." But this would only be the case if the reader were to equate the Hebrew Bible with the religion of Judaism, which is obviously not Trinitarian. Jesus and the NT authors do not equate the Hebrew Bible with Judaism (see Matt. 5 and Hebrews).

They derive their understanding of the Holy Spirit directly from the Hebrew Bible (e.g., Isa. 63:10 [Eph. 4:30]; Joel 3:1–5 [Eng., 2:28–32; Acts 2:17–21]). The wording of Zechariah 4:6 appears to draw upon the text of Hannah's prayer in 1 Samuel 2:9b: "For it is not by strength that a man prevails." This link is potentially significant, given the fact that Hannah's prayer also introduces the LORD's anointed (1 Sam. 2:10), which is the central theme of the book of Samuel. The text of Zechariah 4:14 interprets the two olive trees to be "the two anointed ones." Furthermore, there are other features of Zechariah 4:7–14 that have suggested messianic interpretation throughout history (see, e.g., *Tg. Jon.* Zech. 4:7).

The syntax of Zechariah 4:7a can be read in more than one way (see translation options above), but either way the image is that of a great mountain that becomes a level place before Zerubbabel (cf., Isa. 40:4). The word of the LORD addresses the mountain as if it were a person. The mountain is usually understood to be symbolic of a seemingly impossible obstacle to overcome (cf., Matt. 17:20), while the level place represents the removal of the obstacle. Zerubbabel is a prefiguration of the messianic king who is to come (cf., Hag. 2:20–23; Zech. 3:8; 6:12–13). The LORD will prepare the way before him (Isa. 40:3; Mal. 3:1, 23 [Eng., 4:5]). Neither the LXX or *Targum Jonathan* understands Zerubbabel to be the subject of the verb at the beginning of Zechariah 4:7b. The LXX has a first-person verb: "And I will bring forth the stone of inheritance, equality of grace, grace for it." *Targum Jonathan* has a third-person verb, but the LORD is clearly the subject, apparently under the assumption that the angel is referring to him: "And he will reveal his Messiah whose name has been said since long ago, and he will rule over all the kingdoms." This messianic reading finds its warrant in the reference to "the chief stone" (cf., Zech. 3:9; Ps. 118:22). According to such a reading, the stone in Zechariah 4:7b and the one in Zechariah 4:10a are not merely the literal chief cornerstone of the Second Temple structure and the plumb line or tin tablet. Rather, the stones are representative of something and someone much greater. The shouts of "Grace, grace" to the stone are in response to the answer to supplications for divine grace or favor by God's Spirit (see Zech. 12:10).

The word of the LORD comes to Zechariah himself in Zechariah 4:8–9: "As for Zerubbabel's hands, they established this house. But his hands, they will finish." This is usually taken to mean that Zerubbabel laid the foundation of the new temple structure (Ezra 3), and he will also complete it (Ezra 6). But the syntax ("x + *qatal* . . . *waw* + x + *yiqtol*") favors a contrast. Zerubbabel's hands laid the foundation of the Second Temple, but the hands of the Messiah will complete the eschatological temple (2 Sam. 7:12; Zech. 6:12–13). When this happens, the people will know that Zechariah was a true prophet sent by the LORD (cf., Num. 16:28; Zech. 2:13b, 15b [Eng., 2:9b, 11b]). The Leningrad Codex has "you [sg.] will know," but the Cairo Geniza, a few Masoretic manuscripts, the Syriac, *Targum Jonathan*, and the Latin Vulgate all have "you [pl.] will know."

When the angel resumes his discourse in Zechariah 4:10, his words initially explain the word of the LORD to Zerubbabel in Zechariah 4:6–7. The task ahead seems insurmountable like a great mountain, but by the Spirit of the LORD it will be accomplished. The present laying of the Second Temple foundation seems meager compared to that of Solomon's temple (see Hag. 2:3; Ezra 3:12), but the eschatological temple of the messianic kingdom will surpass all expectations. The people of God will rejoice when they see "the separated stone" (cf., Zech. 10:7b). This has traditionally been rendered as the plummet or plumb line because it is in the hand of Zerubbabel, but it is literally "the stone, that which is separated" (see BDB, 95; *HALOT* 1:110), and it has already been established that the stone represents the Messiah and his kingdom in context (Zech. 3:9; 4:7), which is separate from the kingdoms of the world (cf., Lev. 20:24). More recent attempts to render this as "the tin tablet" obscure the presence of the word "stone" in the original language (cf., Zech. 5:8b).[24] Only in context can it be determined that the thing separated is that which is separated from precious metal (see Num. 31:22; Isa. 1:25; Ezek. 22:18, 20; 27:12).

The second half of Zechariah 4:10 features the explanation of the seven lamps in Zechariah 4:2. The present translation and commentary arranges the text according to *BHS*, which puts "These seven" with what follows. Others follow the arrangement of the MT accentuation and translate "These seven" as the subject of the verbs "be glad" and "see." The problem with this second option is that there is then no clear explanation of the seven lamps according to the pattern set by Zechariah 1:9–10; 2:4 (Eng., 1:21) as mentioned above. The seven lamps in the vision represent the eyes of the LORD. That is, the light and the number seven stand for the LORD's omniscience and perfect providential oversight (cf., Zech. 3:9). The eyes of the LORD

---

24. The NET Bible claims that the word is not from the root meaning "divide" or "separate" but from a root meaning "tin." "This finds support in the ancient Near Eastern custom of placing inscriptions on tin plates in dedicatory foundation deposits." The problem with the suggestion is that it has no real basis in the context of Zechariah or in any usage within the Hebrew Bible.

are said to be roaming through all the land (cf., Zech. 1:11; Ps. 33:18; Rev. 5:6). The difficulty is that the pronoun "They" and the participle "roaming" are masculine plural, while the Hebrew noun for "eyes" is feminine. The text of 2 Chronicles 16:9, which is quite similar to that of Zechariah 4:10b, uses the feminine plural participle for "roaming." It is not immediately clear, however, that the Chronicler is borrowing from Zechariah 4:10b in his account of Asa. The story of Hanani's rebuke of Asa is not in the book of Kings (see 1 Kgs. 15:9–24), but the wording of 2 Chronicles 16:9a may have already been present in the source cited in 2 Chronicles 16:11. Thus, this source may have been common to Zechariah 4:10b and 2 Chronicles 16:9a. It is worth noting that in 2 Chronicles 16:9a the LORD is roaming the land specifically to strengthen himself with those whose heart is fully devoted to him.

Zechariah then inquires about the two olive trees from Zechariah 4:3 on the right and the left of the lampstand (Zech. 4:11). He adds a second question in Zechariah 4:12, which is perhaps separated by a brief pause (note the use of another introductory formula at the beginning of the verse, even though there is no change in speaker). What makes the second question so unusual is the fact that it is about features of the vision not noted in Zechariah 4:2–3. Furthermore, the angel basically ignores this second question and only explains the two olive trees in Zechariah 4:14. Prior to this explanation, the angel repeats his question to the prophet from Zechariah 4:5 in Zechariah 4:13. He then explains that the two olive trees are the two sons of fresh oil standing at the service of the LORD of all the land (Zech. 4:14; cf., Zech. 6:5b; see 4Q254; *b. Sanh.* 24a). This is not the usual Hebrew term for the oil of anointing, but these two are generally understood to be the two anointed leaders of the community: the high priest descended from Aaron (Exod. 29:7) and the king descended from David (1 Sam. 16:13). It is also not uncommon for commentators to take the next step and interpret this to be a reference to Joshua the high priest and Zerubbabel the descendant of David (e.g., Keil). But there are several problems with this latter move. First and foremost is the problem that Zerubbabel was never an anointed Davidic king. Moreover, it has already been shown in Zechariah 3:8b that the language about Zerubbabel in Haggai 2:23 prefigures one who is yet to come, one whose coming is perpetually imminent. It will also be shown that the picture of Joshua in Zechariah 6:11 prefigures a single individual who will occupy both the office of king and the office of priest (Zech. 6:12–13; cf., Ps. 110). Thus, it is best to understand the two anointed ones of Zechariah 4:14 to be embodied in the one messianic ruler.

ZECHARIAH 5

5:1 "And I lifted up my eyes again [see BDB, 998] and saw, and look, a flying scroll [LXX: a flying sickle]. 5:2 And he said to me, 'What do you see?' And I said, 'I see a flying scroll [LXX: a flying sickle]. Its length is twenty cubits [lit., by the cubit; i.e., thirty feet], and its width is ten cubits [lit., by the cubit; i.e., fifteen feet].' 5:3 And he said to me, 'This is the curse that goes forth over the surface of all the land. For every one who steals, on one side [see BDB, 262] according to it [i.e., the scroll or the curse], he is purged out [or, acquitted; ASV: cut off; NET: removed]. And every one who swears, on the other side according to it, he is purged out.[25] *5:4 "I bring it forth," the prophetic utterance of the LORD of hosts, "and it will come to the house of the thief and to the house of the one who swears in my name falsely, and it will lodge [see GKC §73d, 80i] in the midst of his house and destroy it [see GKC §75mm] and its woodwork [or, timber; see BDB, 781] and its stones."'*

5:5 And the angel who was speaking with me went forth and said to me, 'Lift up your eyes and see what is this that goes forth.' 5:6 And I said, 'What is it?' And he said, 'This is the ephah [or, receptacle holding an ephah] that goes forth.' And he said, 'This is their eye [or, their spring; Ms, LXX, Syr.: their iniquity (= עֲוֺנָם)] in all the land.' 5:7 And look, a round piece of lead lifted up,[26] *and here [lit., and this; LXX: and look; see GKC §136d²] was a woman sitting in the midst of the ephah.*[27] *5:8 And he said, 'This is the wickedness.' And he threw her into the midst of the ephah. And he threw the stone [BDB, 6: weight] of the lead to its mouth. 5:9 And I lifted up my eyes and saw, and look, two women going forth, and*

---

25. "And he said to me, 'This is the oath which is going out over the surface of all the land, for everyone who steals has been held innocent (i.e., acquitted) from that which is according to it [viz., the oath], and everyone who swears [falsely] has been held innocent from that which is according to it'" (Max Rogland, "Flying Scrolls and Flying Baskets in Zechariah 5: Philological Observations and Literary Implications," *JNSL* 40.1 [2014]: 97).
26. Ibid., 98–99.
27. *Tg. Jon.* Zech. 5:6–7: *"And I said, 'Who are they?' And he said, 'These are the people who were trading with false measure, and behold, they are going into exile before all the inhabitants of the earth. And behold, swift-footed peoples took them into exile in haste, and other peoples came and settled in their place because they were trading with false measure'"* (Kevin J. Cathcart and Robert P. Gordon, *The Targum of the Minor Prophets: Translated, with a Critical Introduction, Apparatus, and Notes*, The Aramaic Bible 14 [Collegeville, MN: The Liturgical Press, 1990], 196). Cf., Amos 8:5.

wind was in their wings,[28] and they had wings like the wings of a stork. And they lifted the ephah between the land and the sky. 5:10 And I said to the angel who was speaking with me, 'Where are they [see GKC §32n] taking the ephah?' 5:11 And he said to me, 'To build for her/it a house [or, temple] in the land of Shinar. And it will be established, and she/it will be deposited [LXX: they will put it] there upon her/its fixed placed.'"

The prophet Zechariah sees yet another, sixth vision in Zechariah 5:1–4. This time he sees, according to the MT, a flying scroll. But the LXX says that he sees a flying sickle. It is not difficult to trace the development of these two readings. The original text probably read עָף מִגַּל (without the use of final ף). This was read by the LXX translator as עָף מַגָּל ("flying sickle"). Since this is a masculine noun with a masculine participle, the references to its length and width in Zechariah 5:2 must be revocalized with third masculine singular pronominal suffixes (אָרְכּהֹ and רָחְבֹּה). The tradition behind the MT, however, read the original text as עָף מְגִלָּ ("flying scroll"), which then developed into the spelling עָפָה מְגִלָּה. It is interesting to note that John uses the imagery of all eight of Zechariah's visions in the book of Revelation, following the reading of the LXX here in Zechariah 5:1 (see Rev. 14). John does not use the image of the flying scroll. His scroll in Revelation 10 comes from Ezekiel 2:8–3:3.

The measurements in Zechariah 5:2 are unusually large for either a scroll or a sickle (cf., 1 Kgs. 6:3). The speaker giving the measurements and the subsequent explanation in Zechariah 5:3 is presumably the angelic messenger who normally guides the prophet through the visions (see Zech. 5:5). When he says, "This is the curse that goes forth over the surface of all the land," the demonstrative "This" is feminine, suggesting anaphoric reference to the feminine noun "scroll" in the MT. But the Greek text of the LXX also has a feminine demonstrative here, even though the expected antecedent is "sickle," which is neuter in Greek and masculine in Hebrew. It is possible that the feminine demonstrative refers in general to the preceding context of Zechariah 5:1–2 and not to a specific antecedent (cf., GKC §135p), but it is more likely that it has a deictic and cataphoric function and thus agrees with the feminine gender of the noun "curse" (cf., Zech. 5:7b). It is an explanation of the vision in Zechariah 5:1–2, but it does so by pointing to the thing that the vision represents: "Here is the curse." The language of the curse is that of the Sinai covenant (see Deut. 29:11, 13, 19, 20), suggesting that despite the Babylonian exile the postexilic community continues to

---

28. The merging of the third feminine plural suffix with the third masculine plural suffix is a feature of Late Biblical Hebrew.

struggle with failure to keep the terms of the old covenant and is therefore in need of a new, transformative covenant relationship (Deut. 30:6).

The text of Zechariah 5:3b–4 further explains the curse with reference to the thief and the one who swears falsely as representative violators of the Decalogue (Exod. 20; Deut. 5) and the covenant in general (Deut. 4:13; Jas. 2:10–11; see commentary on Hos. 4:2). The stealing of Exod. 20:15 is specifically kidnapping according to the following Covenant Code (Exod. 21:16). Swearing falsely is to take an oath in the LORD's name and give false testimony about someone in a court of law (Exod. 20:7, 16; Lev. 5:24; 19:12; Deut. 5:11, 20; 19:18; Jer. 7:9; Zech. 8:17; Mal 3:5; Ps. 24:4; see also Jer. 4:2; 5:2). Some translations of Zechariah 5:3b give the impression that the prohibition against stealing is written on one side of the flying scroll (and the thief is removed in accordance with it) and that the prohibition against swearing falsely is written on the other side (and the one who swears falsely is removed in accordance with it) (e.g., ESV; see Exod. 32:15; Num. 5:11ff; Ezek. 2:10; Rev. 5:1; see also Exod. 17:12).[29] The main difficulty with this rendering is the less-than-common translation of נקה as "cleaned out," "purged," "removed," or "cut off" (but see Isa. 3:26). Max Rogland's translation, which is given in the footnote to the translation above, addresses this difficulty and does not see reference to the two sides of the scroll. According to Rogland, the thieves and those who swear falsely have been held innocent, thus requiring their judgment in Zechariah 5:4 and the removal of wickedness in Zechariah 5:5–11.

Other possibilities come into view for Zechariah 5:3b–4 if the reader follows the LXX in Zechariah 5:1–2 ("flying sickle"). For example, this could be the sickle of judgment (Jer. 50:16; Joel 4:13 [Eng., 3:13]; Rev. 14:15, 18; 1QapGen ar XV) purging offenders on one side and on the other. Such a reading works particularly well with the LORD's reported discourse in Zechariah 5:4. He will bring forth the judgment of the curse, which is what the sickle represents. It will enter the house of the thief and that of the one who swears falsely in his name. It will lodge in that house and destroy its woodwork and its stones (cf., Lev. 14:45). Such destructive imagery is easier to associate with a sickle than with a scroll.

The text of Zechariah 5:5–11 has traditionally been read as a separate, seventh vision. Rogland, however, argues that Zechariah 5:1–4 and Zechariah 5:5–11 are two parts of one vision.[30] Most notable among

---

29. The NET renders Zechariah 5:3 with the sense of "[on the one hand] . . . on the other hand," but this is not a well-attested meaning for the construction מזה . . . מזה.

30. Rogland, "Flying Scrolls," 103–104.

his observations is the presence of the key word יָצָא ("go forth") in Zechariah 5:3 and Zechariah 5:5–6, 9 (but see also Zech. 6:1). According to this view, Zechariah 5:1–4 indicates that the guilty have thus far been held innocent, but Zechariah 5:5–11 shows that their wickedness is contained and will be removed. This would make the final vision in Zechariah 6:1–8 number seven. In response to this, it must be said that a close relationship between Zechariah 5:1–4 and Zechariah 5:5–11 does not necessarily make them one vision. There are verbal links among the other visions as well, in part because they are of the same genre and in part because they all contribute to the same message of eschatological restoration. The most important feature of the vision in Zechariah 5:1–4, the flying scroll or sickle, is nowhere to be found in Zechariah 5:5–11. Likewise, the most important feature of the vision in Zechariah 5:5–11, the ephah, is nowhere to be found in Zechariah 5:1–4. The angel's instruction to the prophet in Zechariah 5:5 to lift up his eyes and see something else suggests a shift to a new vision (cf., Zechariah 2:1, 5 [Eng., 1:18; 2:1]; 5:1; 6:1). If in response the reader objects that this criterion would make Zechariah 5:9 the beginning of a new vision, then it is only necessary to point out the continued reference in Zechariah 5:9–11 to the main feature of the vision introduced in Zechariah 5:5–8— the ephah. Thus, Zechariah 5:5–8 and Zechariah 5:9–11 are two parts of one vision. The texts of Zechariah 5:1–4 and Zechariah 5:5–11 are not.

The angelic messenger instructs Zechariah in Zechariah 5:5 to see something that goes forth. The prophet does not identify what he sees (cf., Zech. 4:2; 5:2). Rather, he asks what it is. The angel answers that it is the ephah that goes forth. In context, it becomes apparent that the ephah is metonymy for a receptacle, such as a basket, that holds an ephah, which is normally a measure of grain. He then explains what the ephah represents in the vision. The only problem is that there are at least three plausible ways to understand this explanation. The Leningrad Codex has עֵינָם, which can mean "their eye" or "their spring": "This is their eye/spring in all the land." If it means "their eye," it could be a reference to the all-seeing eye of God (i.e., their eye, which is on them) that watches over the wickedness of the people to contain it and to ensure its judgment (see Zech. 3:9; 4:10). Others (e.g., Keil) have suggested that "their eye" means "their appearance" (see Lev. 13:55; Num. 11:7; Ezek. 1:4), perhaps indicating that just as the grains of the ephah are gathered together, so will the sinners of Zechariah 5:4 be gathered together for judgment. On the other hand, Rogland argues for the meaning "their spring," a source of wickedness that must be contained.[31] This would work well if the unit of measure were a בַּת (a liquid measure), but the unit of measure is an ephah, which is normally a dry measure. The third option is to read with one Masoretic manuscript, the LXX, and the Syriac עֵינָם ("their iniquity"): "This is their iniquity in all the land." This is an attractive option until the reader realizes in Zechariah 5:7–8 that the wickedness of the people is something separable from the ephah and contained by the ephah. Thus, it is preferable to go with the reading "their eye" (i.e., the eye of God that is on them), since this has support from the context of the book (see again Zech. 3:9; 4:10).

In Zechariah 5:7, the prophet points out a round piece of lead (i.e., the lid or cover) lifted up on the one hand and a woman sitting in the midst of the ephah on the other hand. Rogland is certainly correct to note that the participle "lifted up" is not a predicate (*contra* ESV: "And behold, the leaden cover was lifted").[32] The image is not that of a removal and then a replacement of the cover in Zechariah 5:7–8. Rather, the image begins with an already lifted cover. The angel says in Zechariah 5:8 that the woman sitting in the ephah represents the wickedness of the people (see Zech. 5:3–4). This is because the Hebrew noun translated "wickedness" is grammatically feminine.[33] The fact that the angel throws the woman back into the ephah implies that he has held her up from her sitting position in Zechariah 5:7 to show that she is the one who represents the wickedness. He then casts the lid to the opening of the ephah (not to the mouth of the woman) to contain the wickedness inside. It is now ready to be transported.

In the second part of the vision, Zechariah sees two women going forth with wind in their wings, wings like those of a stork (Zech. 5:9a). These two women lift the ephah between the land and the sky (Zech. 5:9b). But when the prophet asks the angelic messenger about this part of the vision, he does not ask about the two women. He asks where the two women are taking the ephah (Zech. 5:10). In other words, the identity and explanation of the women are not important. They are simply functionaries that serve the purpose of the vision. What matters is the location to which the ephah containing the woman who represents the wickedness is taken. The answer to the prophet's question about this location is that they are taking the ephah to build for her/it a house (or, temple) in the land of Shinar. The

---

31. Ibid., 100–102.
32. Ibid., 98–99.
33. Cf., the personification of the feminine Hebrew noun translated "wisdom" as a woman in Prov. 1:20–33; 3:13–20; 8.

antecedent for the feminine pronoun "her" could be either the woman inside the ephah who represents the wickedness or the feminine noun "ephah." The house will be established, and the woman/ephah will be placed there in the land of Shinar on her/its "fixed place" (cf., 1 Kgs. 8:13). The land of Shinar is the land of Babylon (see Gen. 10:10; 11:1–9). But this cannot be a prophecy about Babylonian exile, which has already taken place, nor can it be a prophecy about another exile in Babylon, which is no longer a world power. Rather, it speaks to the ongoing prefigurative role of Babylon in biblical prophecy (see Rev. 17). Babylon foreshadows the final enemy from the north (Ezek. 38–39) because an attack on Israel from Babylon in the east would ordinarily come from the north (but see Gen. 14). Thus, to say that the wickedness will be removed to this location is to say that final judgment on this wickedness is reserved for the final battle against the last enemy before the establishment of the messianic kingdom and the new creation (Zech. 6:8; 12; 14; Rev. 16; 20–21).

ZECHARIAH 6

6:1 "And I lifted up my eyes again and saw, and look, four chariots going forth from between the two mountains, and the mountains were bronze mountains. 6:2 With the first chariot were red horses, and with the second chariot were black horses, 6:3 and with the third chariot were white horses, and with the fourth chariot were spotted horses, strong ones [4QXII^e: אמצ; LXX: dappled gray; > Syr.; NET: all of them strong (but see Keil); cf., Zech. 6:7]. 6:4 And I responded and said to the messenger/angel who was speaking with me, 'What are these, my lord?' 6:5 And the messenger/angel [LXX adds: who was speaking with me] answered and said to me, 'These are the four winds/spirits of the sky/ heaven going forth from stationing themselves at the service of the Lord of all the land [see BDB, 426], 6:6 in which the black horses are going forth to north land. And the white ones, they have gone forth to after them [NIV: toward the west; NLT: west; see BDB, 30]. And the spotted ones, they have gone forth to the land of the south. 6:7 And the strong ones, they went forth and sought to go to walk about in the land. And he [NET: the Lord] said, "Go, walk about in the land." And they [i.e., the chariots (f. pl.)] went about [f. pl.] in the land.' 6:8 And he summoned me [see BDB, 277] and spoke to me saying, 'See, the ones going forth to north land, they have caused my Spirit [BHS: the Spirit of the LORD; LXX: my wrath; see BDB, 628] to rest in north land [Tg. Jon.: Say to them: Do my will in the land of the north].'

6:9 And the word of the LORD [Tg. Jon.: the word of prophecy from before the LORD] came to me saying, 6:10 'Take [GKC §113bb] from the exiles, from Heldai [LXX: from the rulers] and from Tobijah [LXX: from its useful men] and from Jedaiah [LXX: from those who have known it]—and you will enter in that day and enter the house of Josiah the son of Zephaniah—who came [MT: pl.; LXX, Syr.: sg.] from Babylon. 6:11 And you will take silver and gold and make crowns[34] and put on the head of Joshua the son of Jehozadak, the great priest [BHS: Zerubbabel the son of Shealtiel]. 6:12 And you will say to him saying, "Thus says the LORD of hosts saying [saying > pc Mss, LXX, Syr.], 'Look, a man whose name is Branch [GKC §155e; LXX: Ἀνατολή; Tg. Jon.: the Messiah], and from his place he will sprout and build the temple of the LORD [and build the temple of the LORD > Syr.]. 6:13 And he is the one who will build the temple of the LORD [And he is the one who will build the temple of the LORD > LXX]. And he is the one who will bear royal splendor [see BDB, 217] and sit and rule on his throne. And he will be a priest on his throne [LXX: And the priest will be at his right hand], and peaceful counsel will be between the two of them. 6:14 And as for the crowns, it will be to Helem [i.e., Heldai] and to Tobijah and to Jedaiah and to Hen [Syr.: Josiah] the son of Zephaniah as a memorial in the temple of the LORD. 6:15 And people far away [Tg. Jon.: from a distant land], they will come and build in / at [BDB, 88] the temple of the LORD.'"' And you will know that the LORD of hosts was the one who sent me to you. And it will happen if you will indeed obey the voice of the LORD your God."

The eighth and final vision in Zechariah 6:1–8 returns to some of the imagery of the first vision in Zechariah 1:7–17. Zechariah sees four chariots going forth between the two bronze mountains in the vision (Zech. 6:1). Neither the vision nor its explanation makes any further reference to the two bronze mountains. They apparently serve as back-drop for the main features of the vision without any symbolic value (but see also Zech. 4:7; 14:4). The fact that there are four chariots going forth in four different directions to four lands may bear some relation-ship to the four kingdoms represented by the four horns in Zechariah

---

34. The *BHS* apparatus suggests reading the singular עֲטָרֹת ("crown") on the basis of a few Masoretic manuscripts, witnesses to the LXX, the Syriac, and *Targum Jonathan*. The LXX, Syriac, and *Targum Jonathan* also have the singular in Zechariah 6:14, where the MT has the plural. The verb is singular. It must be noted, however, that the singular absolute of this noun would nor-mally be עֲטָרָה. עֲטֶרֶת is normally the construct form (see BDB, 742).

2:1–4 (Eng., 1:18–21). The colored horses with the chariots in Zechariah 6:2–3 are reminiscent of the colored horses in Zechariah 1:8 whose riders were angels (see also Rev. 6). Presumably the drivers of the chariots here are angels. At the end of Zechariah 6:3, the designation "strong ones" is placed in apposition to the list of all the horses. Thus, Zechariah 6:7 uses this same term to refer to all the horses together.

As expected, the prophet inquires about the chariots and their horses in Zechariah 6:4. The angelic messenger responds that these are "the four winds/spirits of the sky/heaven going forth from standing at the service of the Lord of all the land" (Zech. 6:5; cf., Josh. 3:11, 13; Mic. 4:13; Zech. 4:14; Ps. 97:5). On the one hand, the winds of the sky are the four directions (north, south, east, west) in which the chariots go (cf., Zech. 2:10 [Eng., 2:6]). On the other hand, the spirits of heaven are the angels who stand at the Lord's service (see Zech. 3:4; Job 1:6; see also Ps. 104:3–4; Heb. 1:7, 14). They, like the wind, form a chariot on which the Lord rides. This is likely based on the depiction of God above the cherubim in the holy of holies (Exod. 25:22). There is also a wordplay between רכב ("ride") and כרוב ("cherub") (see 2 Sam. 22:11; Ps. 18:11 [Eng., 18:10]).

According to Zechariah 6:6, the black horses lead their chariot forth to the land of the north (i.e., to Gog in the land of Magog [Ezek. 38–39]). The white horses do not follow after them to the land of the north (*contra* NET, ESV). The assumption in Hebrew directions is that the face is always to the east. Thus, to go forward is to go east. To go to the right is to go south. To go to the left is to go north. And to go backward/after/behind is to go west. Therefore, the white horses lead their chariot forth to the west (i.e., to Greece/Rome [cf., Num. 24:24; Dan. 11:30]; see NIV, NLT). The spotted horses lead their chariot forth to the land of the south (i.e., Egypt). Conspicuously absent from this list are the red horses. By process of elimination, it becomes evident that they lead their chariot forth to the land of the east (i.e., Babylon, Medo-Persia), as noted by the *BHS* apparatus (see also Zech. 8:7). All these strong horses go forth and seek to go to walk about in the land (Zech. 6:7; cf., Zech. 1:10). Either the angelic messenger (cf., Zech. 3:4) or the LORD himself commands them to do so, and they follow orders.

The LORD then summons the prophet in Zechariah 6:8 and points out the horses going to the land of the north in particular. He says, "they have caused my Spirit to rest in the land of the north." The *BHS* apparatus suggests that רוחי ("my Spirit") is the result of a misreading of רוח י, which is an abbreviation for רוח יהוה ("the Spirit of the LORD") (cf., Jer. 6:11 MT, LXX). If this is correct, then the speaker is likely to be the angelic messenger referring to the LORD in the third person. The problem, of course, is that there is no textual evidence for the proposal. The LXX apparently understands Zechariah 6:8 in terms of Ezek. 5:13. That is, the LORD is going to appease his wrath in the land of the north. But it is perhaps more precise to think here in terms of the language about the land of the north in LXX Jeremiah 25:1–13 and Ezekiel 38 and 39 (see also Zech. 5:11). According to Ezekiel 39:29, the LORD will pour out his Spirit (LXX: wrath!) on his people after the defeat of the final enemy from the north (cf., Joel 3:1 [Eng., 2:28]; Zech. 12:10). What Zechariah 6:8 envisions is the down payment on future deliverance for the people of God, by means of God's Spirit (see Zech. 4:6; Rom. 1:4; 5:5; 2 Cor. 1:22; Eph. 1:13–14; 1 John 3:24; 4:13).

The second half of Zechariah 6 (Zech. 6:9–15) is not another vision. It is the word of the LORD that came to the prophet (Zech. 6:9). The LORD instructs Zechariah to take some of the exiles who came from Babylon—from Heldai (Helem), Tobijah, and Jedaiah—and enter the house of Josiah (Hen) the son of Zephaniah (Zech. 6:10, 14). The LXX attempts to translate the meanings of these three names, but the way that the words appear in the Hebrew text suggests that they are in fact names. There is no background information provided for these individuals, and such information appears to be irrelevant. All the reader needs to know is that these men bore witness to what was portrayed through the high priest Joshua in Zechariah 6:11–13 (cf., Isa. 8:2). Zechariah is further instructed to take silver and gold and make "crowns" (Zech. 6:11a; cf., Zech. 6:14). Some textual witnesses have the singular "crown." It seems that the Hebrew word translated "crowns" can be plural in form yet singular in meaning (see Zech. 6:14; cf., חכמות in Prov. 9:1).[35]

Why does the LORD instruct Zechariah to put a royal crown (see Ezek. 21:31–32 [Eng., 21:26–27]; Zech. 6:13a) rather than a priestly turban (see Zech. 3:5) on the head of the high priest Joshua (Zech. 6:11b)? The *BHS* apparatus suggests substituting "Zerubbabel the son of Shealtiel" here, but Zerubbabel does not rule on a throne in accordance with Zechariah 6:13a, even though he is of Davidic descent.[36] It will also

---

35. Gary Rendsburg considers רוֹ- to be a feminine singular ending in northern "Israelian" Hebrew ("Northern Hebrew through Time: From the Song of Deborah to the Mishnah," in *Diachrony in Biblical Hebrew*, eds. Cynthia Miller-Naudé and Ziony Zevit, LSAWS 8 [Winona Lake, IN: Eisenbrauns, 2012], 343). According to Keil (*Minor Prophets*, 554), the plural form translated "crowns" indicates one crown with several diadems (see Job 31:36; Rev. 19:12).

36. "[I]nterpretations that identify Shoot as Zerubbabel lack coherence on important issues (such as how the passage authenticated Zechariah as

not suffice to say that Zechariah 6:11 depicts Joshua and Zerubbabel together. Zerubbabel is nowhere to be found in Zechariah 6:9–15. And the image of a priest with a royal crown in Zechariah 6:11 is that of one man who occupies both the office of the high priest and the office of the king, which the historical Joshua did not do. Furthermore, the content of Zechariah 6:12b–13 is something that the prophet is to say "to" Joshua, not "about" Joshua. The message about the messianic king/priest is spoken to Joshua who is there simply to illustrate the prophecy.

The prophecy begins in Zechariah 6:12b, "Look, a man" (הנה איש; or, "Look, the man" [הנה האיש]). This comes at the end of a series of prophecies in the Tanakh that refer to the Messiah as "a man" or "the man" (LXX Num. 24:7a, 17b; 2 Sam. 23:1; LXX Isa. 19:20), and John likely uses Pilate's words in John 19:5 ("Look, the man") to create a link for the reader back to Zechariah 6:12–13 in order to identify Jesus as the Messiah (see also 1 Tim. 2:5).[37] The name of the man is "Branch," which was discussed in the commentary on Zechariah 3:8b (see again LXX Num. 24:17; Isa. 4:2; 11:1; 53:2; Jer. 23:5–6; Ezek. 17:22–24; Ps. 132:17). It is the name of the Messiah according to *Targum Jonathan*. He will "sprout" from his place and build the temple of the LORD in accordance with the terms of the covenant with David (2 Sam. 7:13).

Contrary to the evidence of the LXX and the Syriac (see translation above), the last clause of Zechariah 6:12b ("and build the temple of the LORD") and the first clause of Zechariah 6:13a ("And he is the one who will build the temple of the LORD") are not redundant in the MT. The clause at the beginning of Zechariah 6:13a has a fronted pronoun that specifies the coming messianic Branch, and not someone else, to be the one who will build the temple in accordance with 2 Samuel 7:13 (see also Ezek. 40–48; Hag. 2:6–9; 2 Chr. 36:23; Matt. 27:40; Rev. 21:22). Solomon built the temple (1 Kgs. 6–8), and both David and Solomon were under the impression that Solomon was the son of David anticipated in 2 Samuel 7:12–16 (see 1 Kgs. 2:1–10; 8:19–21). But the author

---

sent by Yahweh when Zerubbabel did not become king), in terms of inner-biblical exegesis they reduce the significance of the wider Davidic dynasty tradition found in other texts (Zerubbabel as *a* messiah, rather than *the* Messiah), and/or limit the intention of the passage to the audience of the prophet" (Anthony R. Petterson, "A New Form-Critical Approach to Zechariah's Crowning of the High Priest Joshua and the Identity of 'Shoot'," in *The Book of the Twelve & the New Form Criticism*, eds. Mark J. Boda, Michael H. Floyd, and Colin M. Toffelmire [Atlanta: SBL, 2015], 303).

37. See Michael B. Shepherd, *The Text in the Middle* (New York: Peter Lang, 2014), 85–88. Cf., John 11:49–51.

makes it clear that Solomon's kingdom did not last (1 Kgs. 11–18), indicating to the reader that the everlasting kingdom of 2 Samuel 7:13b is yet to come (see also 1 Chr. 17:13–14). This is precisely the way the prophets, including Zechariah, and the NT authors understand the covenant with David (e.g., Isa. 9:5–6 [Eng., 9:6–7]; Jer. 23:5–6; Ezek. 34:23; Hos. 3:5; Heb. 1:5). The terms of the covenant were reapplied conditionally to subsequent sons of David (see Ps. 89:31–33 [Eng., 89:30–32]), but the original unconditional terms remained intact for the ultimate son of David (see Ps. 89:34–38 [Eng., 89:33–37]).[38] This messianic king will bear royal splendor. He will sit and rule on his throne on the earth (cf., Dan. 7:13–14).

This king will also be a priest on his throne (Zech. 6:13b; cf., 1 Sam. 4:13). The LXX, however, translates this to mean that there will be a separate priest at the king's right hand. Such a translation is not a very natural reading of the Hebrew syntax. It is closer to what is envisioned in 1 Samuel 2:35 where the faithful priest (according to God's heart) whom God will raise up and for whom God will build an enduring house will walk before the anointed king all the days. But even the language of that text is not applied specifically to a priest like Samuel or Zadok but to the king (see 1 Sam. 10:1; 13:14; 16:7, 22b; 2 Sam. 7:11, 12, 16).[39] How then can the Davidic king also be a priest if he is from the tribe of Judah and not from the tribe of Levi (and the lineage of Aaron in the case of the high priest)? Even Moses, the messianic prototype (prophet [Deut. 18:15, 18; 34:10], priest [Exod. 6:16–27], and king [Deut. 33:5]), was from the tribe of Levi. The Qumran community tried to resolve this with a theory of two Messiahs: the Messiah of Aaron and the Messiah of Israel (see 4QD[a] 10 I, 12; 1QS 9:11; 1QSa 2:11–22). But Genesis 14 and Psalm 110 have provided a category for a Davidic king who is a priest according to a different priestly order (see also Matt. 22:41–46; Acts 2:34–35; Heb. 1:13; 5:6; 7). Melchizedek, the king of Salem (i.e., Jerusalem, the city of David [Ps. 76:3 (Eng., 76:2)]), was also priest of God Most High (see Ps. 110:4; see also Ezek. 45:17). This is why the counsel of peace (or, well-being, agreement) will be between the king and the priest according to Zechariah 6:13b2 (see Mic. 4a [Eng., 5:5a]; Zech. 9:9–10). It is not because two different individuals will be in agreement. The agreement will exist because the two offices will be held by one messianic king/priest.

---

38. See Shepherd, *The Text in the Middle*, 122–29.
39. Ibid., 26. Of course, the immediate context does anticipate a shift from the line of Ithamar to the line of Eleazar (1 Kgs. 2:26–27, 35).

The crown from the illustration in Zechariah 6:11 is entrusted to the witnesses in Zechariah 6:14 (cf., Zech. 6:10) to serve as a memorial in the temple. That is, it will serve as an ongoing reminder of the prophecy of the one who is to come in Zechariah 6:12–13. According to Zechariah 6:15a, people from far away (i.e., the nations) will come and build in or at the temple (cf., 1 Kgs. 5:15–32 [Eng., 5:1–18]; Isa. 2:1–5; Mic. 4:1–5; Zech. 2:15 [Eng., 2:11]; 8:20–23; Acts 2:39). The people of God will include believers from all the nations. This will confirm that Zechariah was a true prophet (cf., Zech. 2:13b, 15b [Eng., 2:9b, 11b]; 4:9b). And it will happen if the people obey the voice of their God (Zech. 6:15b). This is not intended to put the fulfillment of the prophecy in jeopardy, as if it were a return to the conditional terms of the old covenant. Rather, in the new covenant the Spirit of God will make possible the obedience that the people themselves could not generate on their own (see Jer. 31:31–34; Ezek. 11:19–20). The language of Zech. 6:15b is a reference back to the description of Abraham's faith (Gen. 15:6; 26:5), which is the model for new covenant faith (Rom. 4). Abraham was credited by faith the righteousness embodied by the law (Gen. 15:6). Therefore, he could be said to have kept the law (Gen. 26:5; cf., Deut. 11:1 et al.), even though he did not keep it perfectly, and even though he did not have the law.[40]

ZECHARIAH 7

7:1 And then, in the fourth year of Darius the king, the word of the LORD came to Zechariah on the fourth of the ninth month, in Kislev [Dec. 7, 518]. 7:2 And Bethel [or, the house of God] sent Saretser [or, chief of treasure] and Regem-melekh [or, friend of king] and his men to appease the face of the LORD [LXX: And Sarasar and Arbeseer the king and his men sent to Bethel (cf., Tg. Jon.) to propitiate the Lord; Syr.: And he sent to Bethel, to Saretser and Rabmag (chief soothsayer; see Jer. 39:3, 13), and the king sent, and his men, to pray for him before the Lord], 7:3 saying to the priests who were of the house of the LORD of hosts and to the prophets saying, "Should I weep in the fifth month, consecrating myself [GKC §113h; Syr.: or abstain; Tg. Jon.: withholding myself from delicacies] just as I have done this period of so many years [see BDB, 554; GKC §136d]?" 7:4 "And the word of the LORD came to me saying, 7:5 'Say to all the people of the land and to the priests saying, "When you fasted and mourned in the fifth and in the seventh and this period of seventy years, did you really fast for me in particular [see GKC §59a, 113q, 117x]? 7:6

---

40. See John H. Sailhamer, *The Pentateuch as Narrative* (Grand Rapids: Zondervan, 1992), 66–77.

And when you eat, and when you drink, are not you the ones eating [Tg. Jon. adds: to do good to yourselves], and are not you the ones drinking [Tg. Jon. adds: to do good to yourselves]?"' 7:7 Have you not heard the words that the LORD proclaimed [see GKC §117l; LXX: Are not these the words that the Lord spoke; Syr.: These are the words that the Lord proclaimed] by the hand of the former prophets when Jerusalem was dwelling quietly/at ease, and its cities around it, and the south and the lowland were inhabited?" 7:8 And the word of the LORD came to Zechariah saying, 7:9 "Thus says the LORD of hosts saying [saying > 2 Mss], 'As for true justice, do it. And as for loyalty and compassion, practice them, each with his brother. 7:10 And as for widow and orphan, resident alien and afflicted one [Syr.: widow and orphan and poor and one who turns to me], do not oppress them [Syr.: do not take advantage of them and do not oppress them]. And as for harm against one another, do not plan it in your heart [see GKC §139c].' 7:11 And they refused to pay attention, and they gave a stubborn shoulder [LXX: a senseless back]. And as for their ears, they caused them to be too heavy [i.e., dull] to hear [see BDB, 582]. 7:12 And as for their heart, they made it too hard to hear the Torah and the words that the LORD of hosts sent by his Spirit by the hand of the former prophets. And there was great anger from the LORD of hosts. 7:13 And so, just as he called [Syr.: I called], and they did not listen, so they would call, and I would not listen," says the LORD of hosts. 7:14 "And I would scatter them with a storm wind [see GKC §52n] upon all the nations that they did not know. And as for the land, it was too desolate after them for anyone to pass through or return. And they made a desirable land [LXX: chosen land] into a desolation."

The dates given in Zechariah 1:1, 7 were in the second year of Darius (520 B.C.). Here the date is in the fourth year (518 BC), on the fourth day of the ninth month, that is, the month of Kislev (Zech. 7:1; see also Neh. 1:1; 2 Macc. 10:5). What follows is not a vision, but, as in Zechariah 6:9–15, it is the word of the LORD to Zechariah. The LXX, the Syriac, and *Targum Jonathan* all render Zechariah 7:2 to say that men were sent to Bethel at this time to appease the face of the LORD, albeit in different ways (see translation above). This is a difficult rendering to accept given the status of Bethel since the time of Jeroboam I (1 Kgs. 12:28–29) and since the downfall of the northern kingdom of Israel (cf., Jer. 7:12–15). Once an honored location because of Abraham and Jacob (Gen. 12:8; 28; 35), there was now no sanctuary and no reason to send to Bethel for such a purpose. It is possible that "Bethel" here is not a place name but simply the phrase "the house of God," a reference to the newly founded temple in Jerusalem. But the reader might expect "the house of the LORD" for this, as in Zechariah 7:3. It is thus preferable to concur with modern versions that render Zechariah 7:2 to say that the people of Bethel sent men ("Saretser and Regem-melekh and his men") to appease the face of the LORD. That is, the people of Bethel sent men to Jerusalem (see Zech. 8:21–22). No further identification of the men is provided. These men were to say to the priests of the house of the LORD (such as Joshua) and to the prophets (such as Haggai and Zechariah), asking on behalf of the people of Bethel collectively, "Should I weep in the fifth month, consecrating myself just as I have done this period of so many years" (cf., Mic. 6:6–7)? The fifth month commemorated the destruction of Jerusalem and the exile at the hands of the Babylonians in the nineteenth year of Nebuchadnezzar (2 Kgs. 25:8–22). The people had mourned this event for seventy years (Zech. 1:12; 7:5), but now they wondered whether they should continue to do this in hopes of appeasing the LORD's wrath and finding full restoration beyond what they were currently experiencing as part of the post-exilic community that had returned to the land from Babylon.[41]

In Zechariah 7:4–6, the word of the LORD comes to Zechariah in response to the question. The response is directed to all the people of the land and to the priests, but it comes in the form of a question. When the people fasted and mourned in the fifth and seventh months during the seventy years of Babylonian captivity, was it really for the LORD that they fasted (Zech. 7:5b; cf., Isa. 58)? This question adds the fast of the seventh month, which commemorated the assassination by Ishmael of the Babylonian appointed governor of Judah, Gedaliah, who was supported by Jeremiah (Jer. 41:1–3). The implied answer to this rhetorical question is no. Conversely, when the people ate and drank (e.g., Ezra 3:4), were not they the ones doing the eating and the drinking (Zech. 7:6; see Ps. 50:7–15)? It was not unto the LORD that they were doing so (cf., Rom. 14:8, 17; 1 Cor. 11:17–34).

The text of Zechariah 7:7 helps to make the transition from the first word of the LORD in response to Zechariah 7:3 (Zech. 7:4–6) to the second word of the LORD (Zech. 7:8–14). The first word of the LORD in Zechariah 7:4–6 has indicated that mere fasting is not what the LORD requires. The second word of the LORD in Zechariah 7:8–14 will clarify what the LORD does in fact require and provide the context of the people's failure to meet this requirement historically. The Hebrew text of Zechariah 7:7 requires the reader to supply something in translation

---

41. Critical scholars join Zechariah 8:18–19 with Zechariah 7:1–3 (cf., Zech. 7:4–5), but despite the similarity of the material, no textual witness gives warrant for this kind of rearrangement (see *BHS* apparatus).

(see options above). Zechariah is referring by means of a rhetorical question to the message of the former prophets (e.g., Jeremiah, Ezekiel) prior to the Babylonian invasion (cf., Zech. 1:4–6). This message is then formally introduced in Zechariah 7:8–9a.[42] It is important to note the fronting (i.e., listing) of each item in the Hebrew text of Zechariah 7:9b–10: "true justice/judgment," "covenant loyalty and compassion," "widow and orphan, resident alien and afflicted one," and "harm against one another" (cf., Zech. 8:16–17). What is commanded in Zechariah 7:9b and what is prohibited in Zechariah 7:10 are frequently part of the prophetic teaching about the importance of obedience over sacrifice or religious ritual (e.g., Deut. 10:12; 1 Sam. 15:22; Isa. 1:10–17; 58; Jer. 7:21–23; Hos. 6:6; Amos 5:21–24; Mic. 6:6–8; Pss. 40:7–9 [Eng., 40:6–8]; 51:18–21 [Eng., 51:16–19]; Prov. 21:3). In this case, such obedience is preferable to mere fasting in the fifth and seventh months.

True justice according to Ezekiel 18:8 is the act of not charging interest (Lev. 25:36) and the act of withholding oneself from injustice or wrongdoing against someone else. That is, it involves not taking advantage of someone for personal gain at that person's expense. Covenant loyalty and compassion are both characteristics of God himself (Exod. 34:6–7). The people are called to be loyal or faithful to their covenant relationship with God, and part of this means that they are to have a similar kind of self-binding obligatory loyalty toward one another (Deut. 6:5; Lev. 19:18, 34). Furthermore, a compassionate people will not be an unjust or oppressive people. The prohibition against mistreatment of social outcasts—widows, orphans, resident aliens, afflicted people— is also rooted in the character of God (Deut. 10:18–19). The prohibition against planning harm against one another in the heart/mind cuts off the problem at the source and anticipates the teaching of Jesus in the Sermon on the Mount (Matt. 5:21–48), which focuses on the condition of the heart (cf., Deut. 6:5; 29:3 [Eng., 29:4]; 30:6; Jer. 31:31–34; Ezek. 11:19–20; Prov. 3:29) and not merely on the behavior.

The text of Zechariah 7:11–14 recounts the refusal of the preexilic forefathers to pay attention to the teaching of the former prophets in Zechariah 7:7–10 (cf., Zech. 1:4–6). They gave a "stubborn shoulder" (cf., Neh. 9:29) and made their ears too dull to hear (cf., Isa. 6:10). Their hearts/minds were too hard to hear both the Torah and the Prophets (Zech. 7:12). Therefore, there was great anger from the LORD (cf., Deut.

---

42. There is no textual evidence for the deletion of Zechariah 7:8–9a according to the *BHS* apparatus. It is not enough to say that Zechariah 7:7, Zechariah 7:8, and Zechariah 7:9a seem like three introductions to the same message. All three are different, and they can easily be read as complementary.

29:27 [Eng., 29:28]; Jer. 21:5; 32:37; Zech. 1:2). It is worthwhile to note that Zechariah 7:12 does not simply refer to the Torah that came by means of the prophets as is stated elsewhere (e.g., 2 Kgs. 17:13; Dan. 9:10; Ezra 9:10–11). The text refers to the Torah and "the words that the LORD of hosts sent by his Spirit by the hand of the former prophets" (cf., Num. 11:29; Joel 3:1 [Eng., 2:28]; Mic. 3:8; Neh. 9:30). This suggests a written corpus of prophetic literature that stands alongside the Torah (see Ezek. 38:17; Dan. 9:2; see also Isa. 1:10; 2:3; 8:16).[43] And so, because of the rejection of these words, just as the LORD called and the people did not listen, so would the people call and the LORD would not listen (Zech. 7:13; cf., Jer. 11:11, 14; 14:11–12). Rather, the LORD would scatter them with a metaphorical storm wind to the nations they did not know, and the once desirable land of the covenant became a desolate place (see Jer. 3:19; 4:23–29; Ps. 106:24).

ZECHARIAH 8

8:1 And the word of the LORD of hosts came [Luther, RSV add: to me] saying,

8:2 "Thus says the LORD of hosts, 'I am very jealous for Zion, and with great wrath am I jealous for her [Tg. Jon.: I am taking vengeance for Zion with great jealousy and great wrath from before me on the peoples who provoked her].'

8:3 Thus says the LORD [Mss, LXX^{Mss}, Syh, Vulg. add: of hosts], 'I have returned to Zion, and I will dwell in the midst of Jerusalem. And Jerusalem will be called "the faithful city" [lit., the city of faithfulness;

---

43. "In their commentary, C. and E. Meyers have shown great sensitivity to the scriptural force of these formulas, suggesting that 'the word and the statutes' and 'the law and the words' refer to an emergent canon. Clearly both 'torah/statutes' and 'words' are presented as twin categories of divine revelation, transmitted (in *both* cases!) through prophetic agency. The pairing suggests a more specific reference than general teaching or instruction. The Meyers see especially in the phrase 'the torah and the words' a 'connection to past usage and the invention of a new idiom which may well have a technical connotation.' Could 'the torah' here refer to the emergent Pentateuch and 'the words' to an early corpus of prophetic writings, as I have argued for the book of Jeremiah' (Stephen B. Chapman, *The Law and the Prophets: A Study in Old Testament Canon Formation*, FAT 27 [Tübingen: Mohr Siebeck, 2000], 212–13)? See also Michael B. Shepherd, *Textuality and the Bible* (Eugene, OR: Wipf & Stock, 2016), 28–32.

Syr.: the holy city; Tg. Jon., Vulg.: the city of truth], and the mountain of the LORD of hosts [will be called] "the holy mountain" [lit., the mountain of holiness].'

8:4 Thus says the LORD of hosts, 'Again old men and women will sit in the broad open places of Jerusalem, each with his staff in his hand [Tg. Jon.: each will be protected by his good works] from [or, because of] an abundance of days. 8:5 And as for the broad open places of the city, they will be filled [see GKC §145p,t,u] with boys and girls in its broad open places.'

8:6 Thus says the LORD of hosts, 'If [or, Though] it is difficult in the eyes of the remnant of this people in those days, also [4QXIIe: הגם] in my eyes is it difficult?' the prophetic utterance of the LORD of hosts.

8:7 Thus says the LORD of hosts, 'Look, I am about to deliver my people from east [lit., land of place of sunrise; Tg. Jon.: a faraway land] and from the west [lit., the land of the entering of the sun]. 8:8 And I will bring them in, and they will dwell in the midst of Jerusalem. And they will become my people, and I, I will become their God in faithfulness [Syr., Tg. Jon., Vulg.: truth] and in righteousness.'

8:9 Thus says the LORD of hosts, 'Let your hands be firm, you who are hearing in these days these words from the mouth of the prophets who were present when the house of the LORD was established in order that the temple might be built. 8:10 For before those days, the pay of man did not exist, and there was no pay for the animal [see GKC §146a]. And to the one who went out and to the one who came in there was no peace from the foe. And I would send [Vulg.: And I sent] every man each against his neighbor. 8:11 But now, not like the former days will I be to the remnant of this people,' the prophetic utterance of the LORD of hosts. 8:12 'For the seed of peace [or, well-being; LXX: But I will show peace; Syr.: Because the seed will be in peace; Tg. Jon.: For at that time the seed will be peace]: the grapevine, it will give its fruit; and the land, it will give its produce; and the sky, it will give its dew. And I will cause the remnant of this people to inherit all these things. 8:13 And so it will be, just as you were an object of a curse [BDB, 887] among the nations, O house of Judah and house of Israel, so will I deliver you, and you will be a blessing [BDB, 139]. Do not fear, let your hands be firm.'

8:14 For thus says the LORD of hosts, 'Just as I planned to harm you when your forefathers provoked me,' says the LORD of hosts, 'and I did not relent, 8:15 so have I planned again [see GKC §120g] in these days to do Jerusalem and the house of Judah good. Do not fear. 8:16 These are the things that you will do: Speak truth to one another; truth [> LXX] and judgment for peace [or, well-being] judge in your gates; 8:17 and each the harm of his neighbor [see GKC §139c] do not plan in your heart; and a false oath do not favor, for all these things are what [what > pc Mss, LXX, Syr.; see GKC §117l] I reject [or, hate],' the prophetic utterance of the LORD."

8:18 "And the word of the LORD of hosts came to me saying, 8:19 'Thus says the LORD of hosts, "The fast of the fourth and the fast of the fifth and the fast of seventh and the fast of the tenth, each will become to the house of Judah rejoicing and joy and good appointed times. And as for the truth [or, faithfulness] and the peace [or, well-being], favor [or, love] them."'"

8:20 Thus says the LORD of hosts, "Yet it will be that [see BDB, 83] peoples [2 Mss, LXX: many peoples] will come and inhabitants of many cities. 8:21 And inhabitants of one [city] will go to another saying, 'Let us go now to appease the face of the LORD and to seek [Tg. Jon.: to seek instruction from before] the LORD of hosts. Let me go also.' 8:22 And many peoples and mighty nations will come to seek [Tg. Jon.: to seek instruction from before] the LORD of hosts in Jerusalem [in Jerusalem > Ms] and to appease the face of the LORD."

8:23 Thus says the LORD of hosts, "In those days, it will be that [see BDB, 83] ten men from all the tongues [or, languages] of the nations will grasp, and they will grasp the extremity of a Judean man's garment saying, 'Let us go with you [pl.], for we have heard that God is with you.'"

There are two sections marked as "the word of the LORD" in Zechariah 8 (Zech. 8:1–17 and Zech. 8:18–23). These two sections are subdivided by the formula "Thus says the LORD of hosts" (Zech. 8:2, 3, 4, 6, 7, 9, 14 and Zech. 8:19, 20, 23). The opening statements in Zechariah 8:2 and 8:3 revisit material from Zechariah 1:14–17 (see commentary there). The LORD is very jealous for the city that bears his name (see Exod. 20:5; Deut. 12:5; Nah. 1:2) and very angry with the nations who have provoked him. He has returned to Zion in the sense that he will one day dwell in the midst of Jerusalem (see commentary on Zech. 2:14 [Eng., 2:10]; see also Jer. 7:3, 7; 12:7; Zech. 8:8). Jerusalem will be called the faithful city, and Mount Zion will be called the holy (or, set apart) mountain. This language is derived from Isaiah 1:21, 26. The once faithful city had become a harlot (Isa. 1:21), but it would be called the city of righteousness, a faithful city, again (Isa. 1:26; see also Isa. 2:1–5).

The text of Zechariah 8:4–5 envisions the old and the young inhabiting and filling the broad open places of Jerusalem (cf., Neh. 8:1–3; 1 Macc. 14:9). This is reminiscent of two other prophetic passages. The image of the new creation and the new Jerusalem (and the messianic kingdom [cf., Isa. 11:1–10]) in Isaiah 65:17–25 includes in its depiction the thought that no nursing child will live only "days," nor will an old man fail to fulfill his days (Isa. 65:20a). This is because the "youth" (ranging from boyhood to early adulthood) will "die" at the age of one hundred, and the one who does not reach that age will be considered cursed (Isa. 65:20b). The emphasis here is not on death (see Isa. 25:8). What is striking is that someone would be considered a "youth" even at the age of one hundred (see LXX), giving the sense of immortality.[44] The second passage is Joel 3:1–5 (Eng., 2:28–32), which anticipates the indiscriminate outpouring of God's Spirit on his people, including both the old and the young, in connection with the Day of the LORD and the deliverance that will take place in the city of Jerusalem. If this is too wonderful or difficult in the eyes of the remnant of God's people in those days,[45] is it thus too difficult for the LORD (Zech. 8:6; cf., Jer. 32:17, 27; Ps. 118:23)? The expected answer is no. The LORD delights in working through seemingly impossible situations in order that all may know that he alone is responsible for the results (see Judg. 7:2). He will deliver his people from east and from west (Zech. 8:7) and bring them in to dwell in the midst of Jerusalem (Zech. 8:8a), just as he will dwell in Jerusalem (Zech. 8:3).[46] They will be his people, and he will be their God, not falsely as in Jeremiah 5:2, but genuinely (Zech. 8:8b; cf., Jer. 4:2). This is the so-called covenant formula. Because the old covenant is broken, this text anticipates a new covenant relationship (see Ezek. 11:19–20; Jer. 31:31–34; Zech. 13:9).

The section in Zechariah 8:9–13 is bracketed by the exhortation, "Let your hands be firm," in Zechariah 8:9a and 8:13b. It is addressed

---

44. It is also possible that the prospect of living to the age of one hundred is given from the perspective of a youth to whom such an expectation would seem like an eternity.

45. The phrase "in those days" suggests that the remnant here is not merely the remnant of Judeans who survived Babylonian captivity to form the postexilic community in Judah and Jerusalem (Hag. 1:14; 2:2). This is the remnant of believers from all the nations in the last days (Zech. 2:15 [Eng., 2:11]; 8:11–12, 20–23).

46. Again, the people whom Zechariah addressed were already in Jerusalem. Thus, this text looks forward to a future, eschatological work of God.

to those listening "in these days" (Zech. 8:9a) as opposed to the remnant of the people "in those days" (Zech. 8:6a). They are the ones who hear the words of the prophets Haggai and Zechariah who were present at the laying of the foundation for the Second Temple (Zech. 8:9b; see Hag. 2:1–5; Zech. 1:1, 7; 7:1; Ezra 3; 5:1–2). Prior to the laying of the new foundation, the situation in the land for the postexilic community was considerably less than ideal (Zech. 8:10; cf., Hag. 2:15–19). The people were still experiencing the covenant curses (Lev. 26; Deut. 28). There was no compensation for work done by man or beast (cf., Deut. 28:30–31; Hag. 1:6; Mal. 3:5). Those who went out to war and returned from the battle (cf., Num. 27:17; 1 Sam. 18:13, 16) found no peace from the enemy (cf., Deut. 28:19; 2 Chr. 15:5). Every man would be sent even against his neighbor (cf., Judg. 7:22; 1 Sam. 14:20; Isa. 19:2; Hag. 2:22; Mic. 7:6).

But now the LORD will not be to the remnant of this people like the former days (Zech. 8:11). He will begin to sow the seeds of restoration that will ultimately come to fruition in the last days. The "seed of peace" is the seed of prosperity: the fruit of the grapevine, the produce of the land, and the dew of the sky (Zech. 8:12a; cf., Isa. 4:2; 27:6; Hos. 2:23–25 [Eng., 21–23]; 6:3–4; Amos 9:11–15; Hab. 3:17; Hag. 1:10; 2:19; Zech. 9:17; 10:1; 1 Macc. 14:8). This is the restoration of the lost blessing of life and dominion in the land of the covenant (Gen. 1:26–28; 2:10–14; 15:18). It is the hope of a real physical and spiritual existence in the messianic kingdom and the new creation (Isa. 65:17–25). It is the hope of the resurrection (Dan. 12:2). The remnant of God's people will inherit all these things and reign with Christ in his kingdom (Zech. 8:12b; Dan. 7:13–14, 27; Rom. 8:17; Gal. 4:7; Rev. 1:6; 5:10; 20:6; 22:5).

The text of Zechariah 8:13 addresses "the house of Judah and the house of Israel," which anticipates a reunited kingdom as in the days of David and Solomon (see Jer. 3:14–18; 31:31–34; Zech. 9:10, 13; 10:6). They had become the object of a curse among the nations as a consequence of the broken covenant (cf., Jer. 24:9; 25:18). But just as the LORD was faithful to judge them according to the terms of the old Sinai covenant, so will he be faithful to deliver them in a new covenant relationship. As in the covenant with Abraham (Gen. 12:1–3; 15:18), the LORD will bless the people in order to be a blessing to all the nations. That is, he will bless them in order to restore the lost blessing of life and dominion in the land to all those who believe (Gen. 15:6; 17:5; Rom. 4). This will primarily come by means of the Messiah who will be a descendant of Abraham, Judah, and David (Gen. 22:18;

27:29; 49:8–12; Num. 24:7–9; 2 Sam. 7:12–16).[47] Therefore, the true remnant need not fear (cf., Isa. 41:10).

Solidarity between generations past and the present generation allows the LORD to say in Zechariah 8:14–15 that just as he planned to harm the present generation in accordance with the covenant curses when the past generation provoked him, so has he planned to do good to Jerusalem and the house of Judah (see Jer. 29:11; see also Exod. 20:5; Deut. 24:16; Ezek. 18; Zech. 1:2; Ps. 90:15). In other words, if he was faithful to judge, then he will be faithful to deliver. He always does what he has said. Unless he has made some sort of provision (e.g., Jon. 3), he does not relent. Thus, Zechariah 8:15b reiterates Zechariah 8:13b, "Do not fear." The things that the new community is to do are clearly delineated in Zechariah 8:16–17 (see commentary on Zech. 7:8–10; see also Zech. 5:4; Mal. 3:5; Prov. 6:16–17; *T. Benj.* 10:3; *T. Dan.* 5:2; *T. Reu.* 6:9; *T. Zeb.* 8:5). The apostle Paul cites this text in his instructions for the new humanity in Christ, which consists of both Jews and Gentiles (Eph. 4:25; cf., Zech. 8:20–23).[48] This is not a social program. It is the transformative power of the gospel in the home, in the community of faith, and in the culture (Eph. 4–6).

When the word of the LORD comes to Zechariah in Zechariah 8:18, there is first a reference to the fasts of the fourth, fifth, seventh, and tenth months (Zech. 8:19; see *b. Rosh. Hash.* 18b). The fasts of the fifth and seventh months were already mentioned in Zechariah 7:5 (see 2 Kgs. 25:8; Jer. 41:1) where the LORD indicated that what he required was not the fasting but the kind of justice and faithfulness described in Zechariah 7:9–10. Now that this has been reiterated in Zechariah 8:16–17, he returns to the fasts and adds those of the fourth and tenth months, which commemorated the siege of Jerusalem in the tenth month of the ninth year of Zedekiah (2 Kgs. 25:1) and the breach of the city wall in the fourth month of the eleventh year of Zedekiah (Jer. 39:2–5). These fasts were occasions for mourning and for seeking to appease the LORD (Zech. 7:2), but they will become appointed times for celebration (cf., Ps. 30:12 [Eng., 30:11]; Est. 8:16–17; 9:29–31; Neh. 8:9–12), much like the appointed times of Leviticus 23. At that time, the people are to love or prefer truth/faithfulness and peace/well-being to injustice (see Zech. 7:8–10; 8:16–17).

The text of Zechariah 8:20–22 envisions many peoples, not merely Judah and Israel, coming to the new Jerusalem in the last days (cf.,

---

47. For further discussion, see Benjamin J. Noonan, "Abraham, Blessing, and the Nations," *HS* 51 (2010): 73–93. See also Shepherd, *Text in the Middle*, 21–24.
48. See Shepherd, *The Twelve Prophets*, 56.

Isa. 2:1–5; 66:18–25; Mic. 4:1–5; Zech. 2:15 [Eng., 2:11]). They will come to appease the face of the LORD (cf., Zech. 7:2) and to seek the LORD himself. This is in accordance with the program of the Twelve (Hos. 3:5), which anticipates that the people of God will seek the LORD and the Davidic Messiah in the last days. Throughout the Twelve, the inclusion of the nations among those who will seek the LORD has been evident (e.g., Amos 9:12). *Targum Jonathan* interprets the seeking of the LORD in Zechariah 8:21–22 to be the seeking of the LORD's instruction. This likely has its basis in Isaiah 2:3 (Mic. 4:2): "And many peoples will go and say, 'Come, and let us go up to the mountain of the LORD, to the house of the God of Jacob. And he will teach us from his ways, and we will walk in his paths.' For from Zion Torah will go forth, and the word of the LORD from Jerusalem." This joining of the believing people from the nations with the believing remnant of Judeans is vividly depicted in Zechariah 8:23. There will be ten men of every kind of linguistic group among the nations per every Judean man.[49] The ratio is startling (cf., Rev. 7). These Gentiles will take hold of the garment of a Judean man going up to Jerusalem and request to go with the Judeans because they will have heard that God is with them (cf., Gen. 26:28; Josh. 2:9–13). This highlights the central role of Abraham and his descendants in the restoration of the lost blessing to the world (see Gen. 12:1–3; see also Isa. 55:5). On the other hand, Isaiah 66:18–25 anticipates that the believing Gentiles will play a role in bringing the remnant of Israel to Jerusalem. The combined prophetic witness reveals a mutual relationship.

ZECHARIAH 9

9:1 The oracle of the word of the LORD in [Syr.: upon / concerning / against] the land of Hadrach, and Damascus is its resting place [Syr.: offering; see GKC §128a]. For an eye on mankind belongs to the LORD, and all the tribes of Israel belong to him [see GKC §128a; LXX: for the Lord watches over men and all the tribes of Israel; Syr.: for the sons of men and all the tribes of Israel are going into exile to the Lord; Tg. Jon.: for before the LORD the deeds of humanity are revealed, and he is pleased with all the tribes of Israel; NET: The eyes of all humanity, especially of the tribes of Israel, are toward the LORD], 9:2 and also Hamath, which borders it [i.e., the land of Hadrach or the city of Damascus], Tyre and

---

49. English versions tend to translate "Judean man" as "Jew." The problem with this rendering is that it gives the impression to the modern English reader that the man is an adherent of the later religion of Judaism. In this context, the term "Judean" is ethnic rather than religious.

Sidon, for [or, though] it [i.e., the land thereof] is very wise. 9:3 And Tyre built a siege-enclosure for itself and piled up silver like the dust, and gold [lit., yellow; cf., Syr.] like street mud. 9:4 Look, the Lord [mlt Mss: the LORD], he will dispossess it [i.e., the city of Tyre] and strike into the sea its strength [see LXX; Tg. Jon.: wealth]. And as for it, in / by the fire will it be consumed. 9:5 Let [the city of] Ashkelon see and be afraid [but see GKC §109k], and [let the city of] Gaza [see] and writhe greatly; and Ekron too, for its expectation is put to shame [or, dried up; lit., for he (indefinite) puts its expectation to shame]. And a king will perish from Gaza, and Ashkelon will not be inhabited. 9:6 And a bastard [LXX: foreigners] will live in Ashdod [Tg. Jon.: And the house of Israel will live in Ashdod where there were foreigners], and I will cut off the pride of the Philistines. 9:7 And I will remove his blood [BDB, 196] from his mouth [Tg. Jon.: And I will destroy those who eat blood] and his detestable things from between his teeth. And also he [i.e., the Philistine] will be left to our God [Tg. Jon.: and their army will come to an end, and foreigners who are left among them will be added, also they, to the people of God]. And he will be like a chief [ESV: clan] in Judah, and Ekron like a Jebusite. 9:8 And I will camp at my house / temple as a guard [BDB, 663; LXX: an elevated structure; Syr.: overseer] against anyone passing through or returning [Tg. Jon.: The dwelling of my glory will rest in my holy temple, and the strength of my powerful arm will be like a wall of fire around it against anyone passing through or returning (cf., Zech. 2:9 [Eng., 2:5])]. And an oppressor [LXX: someone driving away; Syr.: taskmaster; Tg. Jon.: ruler; Vulg.: exactor] will never again pass through against them, for now I have seen with my eyes.

9:9 Rejoice greatly, Daughter Zion. Cry out, Daughter Jerusalem. Look, your king, he is coming to you. Righteous and delivered [LXX, Syr., Tg. Jon., Vulg.: savior] is he. [He is] afflicted [LXX, Syr., Tg. Jon.: gentle / meek] and riding on a donkey, and on a colt, a foal [GKC §154a¹]. 9:10 And I [LXX, Syr.: he] will cut off chariots from Ephraim and horses from Jerusalem. And the battle bow will be removed, and he will speak peace to the nations. And his rule will be from sea to sea [Tg. Jon.: west], and from river [Tg. Jon.: Euphrates] to land's ends.

9:11 Also you [f. sg.; Tg. Jon.: m. pl.], in [or, because of] the blood of your covenant I sent your prisoners from a pit [Tg. Jon.: . . . I redeemed you from the servitude of the Egyptians. I supplied your needs in the desolate wilderness . . .] in which there was no water [Vulg.: in quo non est aqua]. 9:12 Return to a stronghold, O prisoners of hope [LXX: You will sit in a fortress, O prisoners of gathering]. Also today I [GKC §116s]

440

declare [LXX: and instead of one day of your sojourning] that a double portion is what I will restore to you. 9:13 For I have bent for myself Judah, a bow is what I have filled with Ephraim. And I will arouse your sons, O Zion, against your sons, O Greece [Tg. Jon.: the sons of the peoples], and I will make you like a mighty man's [or, warrior's] sword. 9:14 And the LORD, over them will he appear, and like the lightning his arrow will go forth. And the LORD [Codex L: Lord GOD], the shofar will he blast, and he will go in the storm winds of the south [LXX: in the surge of his threat]. 9:15 The LORD of hosts, he will defend them [lit., cover over them], and they will devour and subdue sling stones [LXX: with sling stones]. And they will drink his blood [read רָמוּ instead of הָמוּ (they are boisterous); LXX = הֵם (they will drink them); LXX^BWS = דָּמָם (their blood)], and they will be full like the sacrificial bowl [see BDB, 284], like corners of an altar [LXX: like bowls; Aq., Symm., Theod.: like corners]. 9:16 And the LORD their God [their God > LXX] will deliver them in that day like the flock of his people, for they are stones of a crown [BDB, 634] elevated / conspicuous [BDB, 651] over his land [LXX: holy stones are rolled upon his land]. 9:17 For how great is his goodness [or, produce (see BDB, 375)], and how great is his beauty! Grain, [it will make] choice young men [bear fruit]; and new wine, it will make virgins bear fruit [Tg. Jon.: For how good and how proper is the teaching of the Torah for the leaders, and true judgment prepared in the synagogue!].

Zechariah 9–11 is the first of three sections labeled "the oracle of the word of the LORD" (Zech. 9–11; 12–14; Mal. 1:1–3:21 [Eng., 4:3]). These are the only three sections in the entire Hebrew Bible to bear this heading. Zechariah 9–14 has been called "Second Zechariah" by critical scholarship because of its supposed discontinuity with Zechariah 1–8, but the differences are primarily due to a change in genre. The visions that dominated Zechariah 1–6 no longer play a central role in Zechariah 9–14. Nevertheless, the eschatological and messianic message of Zechariah 1–8 finds continuity in the second half of the book in other ways (e.g., Zech. 2:14 [Eng., 2:10]; 9:9–10). Following the interest in the inclusion of the nations in Zechariah 8:20–23, the first oracle in Zechariah 9–11 also shows concern for the nations, especially at the outset (Zech. 9:1–8, 9–10; cf., Joel 4:4–8 [Eng., 3:4–8]). In contrast to Zechariah 12:1 and Malachi 1:1, the oracle of the word of the LORD is not concerning Israel or to Israel but "in the land of Hadrach" (Zech. 9:1a). Its resting place is Damascus (cf., Zech. 6:8; see Isa. 17; Amos 1:3–5). The language suggests that the oracle is not simply about the northern region stretching from Aleppo in the north southward to Damascus. Rather, the word of the LORD is present and effective there.

Translations typically render Zechariah 9:1b to say either that the eye of mankind and of all the tribes of Israel is toward the LORD or that the LORD has an eye on mankind and all the tribes of Israel. But both options would normally require the word translated "eye" to be repeated in the construct state before the phrase "all the tribes of Israel." It seems rather to be the case that two phrases are coordinated here to describe what belongs to the LORD. First, he possesses a watchful eye that is on mankind (cf., Zech. 3:9; 4:10). He providentially oversees the nations not only to judge the wicked but also to deliver the righteous by faith (see Zech. 2:12–17 [Eng., 2:8–13]; 8:20–23). Second, all the tribes of Israel, not simply Judah, belong to the LORD. This anticipates the reunited kingdom envisioned by texts like Zech. 9:10, 13; 10:6 (see also Zech. 8:13; cf., Jer. 3:14–18). Verse 2 adds Hamath, which borders "it" (either the city of Damascus or the land of Hadrach), and Tyre and Sidon, two wealthy seaport cities on the coast of Phoenicia. Tyre in particular was known for its great "wisdom" or skill (Ezek. 27:8; 28:17).

The story of Tyre begins in Zechariah 9:3 with a play on words: "And Tyre (צֹר) built a siege-enclosure (מָצוֹר) for itself." The city piled up silver like dust, and gold like street mud (cf., Joel 4:5 [Eng., 3:5]). According to Job 27:16–17, the wicked who hoard their wealth in this fashion will find that the righteous will inherit it in their place. Thus, the Lord will dispossess the city of Tyre and strike its wealth into the sea (Zech. 9:4; cf., Ezek. 27:25–27)—a startling image given the location of the city. And the city itself will be judged by fire (cf., Amos 1:10). Zechariah does not limit the prophecies about Tyre found in Ezekiel 26–28, Amos 1:9–10, and Joel 4:4–8 (Eng., 3:4–8) to historical judgments (e.g., Ezek. 29:18; see also Isa. 23). The nations listed in Zechariah 9:1–6 are representative of unbelieving Gentiles who will face final judgment and defeat in the days of the coming of the Messiah (Joel 4:1–3 [Eng., 3:1–3]; Zech. 9:9–10). This is thus equally true for Philistia—a perennial enemy of Israel (Zech. 9:5–6; cf., Isa. 14:28–32; Jer. 47; Joel 4:4–8 [Eng., 3:4–8]; Amos 1:6–8; Zeph. 2:4–7; see also 1 Sam. 4–6; 17; 31; 2 Sam. 8). Four of the five major Philistine cities (1 Sam. 6:17) are listed in Zechariah 9:5–6 in the following order: Ashkelon, Gaza, Ekron, Gaza, Ashkelon, and Ashdod. Missing from this list is Gath. Ashkelon will "see" (תֵרֶא) the judgment of the LORD and "be afraid" (תִירָא). Likewise, Gaza will see and writhe greatly. Ekron's expectation of great things will either be "put to shame" (from בּוֹשׁ) or "dried up" (from יָבֵשׁ). That is, it will come to nothing. Gaza will lose its king, and Ashkelon will not be inhabited. A "bastard" (מַמְזֵר) will live in Ashdod (cf., Deut. 23:3). The LXX interprets this word to mean "foreigners"

(מְמֻזָּר = זָר מֵעַם [*"from a foreign people"*]).[50] *Targum Jonathan* takes it a step further to say that Israel will live in Ashdod where there were foreigners. In other words, Israel (foreigners to Ashdod) will live in Ashdod (foreigners to Israel). This will effectively destroy the pride of the Philistines (cf., Zech. 10:11b).

But the LORD will remove the ceremonial uncleanness of the Philistines and the Gentiles whom they represent (Zech. 9:7). The shift in the text at this point from third person to first person is unexpected and unmarked. The LORD himself says that he will remove the forbidden blood (the Hebrew plural is for blood in its unnatural state) from the mouth of the Philistines (see Gen. 9:4; Lev. 17:10–14; see also *Tg. Jon.*). He will remove this detestable food (i.e., meat with blood in it) from their teeth. This will pave the way for a remnant of Philistines (Gentiles) to be added to "our God" (cf., Zeph. 2:11; Zech. 2:15 [Eng., 2:11]; 8:20–23; see *Tg. Jon.*). According to the MT vocalization, the text says that a Philistine will be like a "chief" in Judah (see Gen. 36:15–43; Zech. 12:5–6). Many English versions, however, follow the suggestion in the *BHS* apparatus and revocalize the text to say "tribe" or "clan." Either way the Philistines will be included with equal status within the believing remnant of Judeans. The end of Zechariah 9:7 adds that Ekron (see Zech. 9:5) will be like a Jebusite, alluding to the fact that the Jebusites were the original inhabitants of the city of Jerusalem (Josh. 15:8, 63; 18:28; Judg. 1:21; 2 Sam. 5:6, 8; 1 Chr. 11:4). In context, this apparently does not mean that Ekron will be driven out of the city as the Jebusites were by David. Rather, it means that they will be genuine inhabitants of the city as the Jebusites once were, but their status in the new Jerusalem will be determined by their faith in the LORD. According to Zechariah 9:8, the LORD will camp at his eschatological temple (Ezek. 40–48; Hag. 2:6–9; Rev. 21:22) as a guard. *Targum Jonathan* interprets this to mean that the LORD's glory will dwell there and that his strength will be like a protective wall of fire around it. This rendering seems to have its basis in Zechariah 2:9 (Eng., 2:5; cf., Exod. 14:19–20). No oppressor will ever pass through the land again to come against them (cf., Isa. 9:3 [Eng., 9:4]; Hab. 1:11; Zech. 10:4b). Why? Because the LORD has now seen with his eyes (cf., Job 42:5). That is, he has looked upon the affliction and the helplessness of his people just as he did in the original exodus (Exod. 2:23–25; 3:7). Now he will act to deliver them again and to establish a new covenant relationship.

---

50. See Abraham Geiger, *Urschrift und Uebersetzungen der Bibel in ihrer Abhängigheit von der inner Entwickelung des Judenthums* (Breslau: Hainauer, 1857), 52–71.

The small unit in Zechariah 9:9–10 serves to connect what the LORD says concerning the nations in Zechariah 9:3–8 with what he says concerning Judah and Ephraim in Zechariah 9:11–17, because the LORD not only has an eye on all humanity, but also all the tribes of Israel belong to him (Zech. 9:1–2). The coming of the Messiah will affect both. The text of Zechariah 9:9–10 picks up the thread of the language in Zephaniah 3:14–15 and Zechariah 2:14 (Eng., 2:10) to say that the image of the coming of the LORD as king in those texts is to be understood in terms of God coming in the flesh as the ideal Davidic king (see commentary on Zeph. 3:14–15; Zech. 2:14 [Eng., 2:10]; see also Isa. 9:5–6 [Eng., 9:6–7]; 10:21; Zech. 12:10; 14:9; 1QM 12:13; 19:5).[51] Daughter Zion (a term of affection for the people of God who inhabit the city) is called upon to rejoice in light of what is envisioned for the coming of this king. He is the righteous king who stands in right relationship to the LORD and the people. He will bring righteousness to his kingdom (cf., Isa. 9:5–6 [Eng., 9:6–7]; 11:1–10; 53:11; 61:3; Jer. 23:5–6). He is "delivered" by the LORD (cf., Num. 24:8; 2 Sam. 22:51; Hab. 3:13; but see LXX, Syr., Tg. Jon., Vulg.: "savior" [cf., Isa. 45:21b]; see also LXX Isa. 19:20). Furthermore, Zechariah 9:9b depicts him as "afflicted" yet riding on a donkey, even on a colt, a foal. This is often translated to mean that the king is "humble" with the understanding that riding on a donkey is a picture of lowliness, but עָנִי normally describes a righteous person afflicted by the wicked (see BDB, 776–77; see also Zech. 7:10). The king will suffer as a righteous man on behalf of the people (see Isa. 53:7; Zech. 12:10). As for the donkey, it is the ride of the messianic lion king from the tribe of Judah who defeats his enemies and rules over the nations in the last days (Gen. 49:11).[52] The temporary king Absalom rides into battle on a mule (2 Sam. 18:9; see also Judg. 5:10). David himself has a she-mule on which Solomon is to

---

51. Gregory Goswell ("A Theocratic Reading of Zechariah 9:9," *BBR* 26.1 [2016]: 7–19) does not see this until Matthew 21:5 and John 12:15. He insists that evidence for the king in Zechariah 9–10 as an ideal Davidic king (although he does not deal with all the evidence) is a "reapplication of the picture of the Davidic world rule to the universal dominion of the Divine King." He does not explain why it is not more likely that the text is an application of the picture of the universal dominion of the Divine King to the Davidic world rule, which would put Matthew and John in direct continuity with Zechariah.

52. See Richard C. Steiner, "Four Inner-Biblical Interpretations of Genesis 49:10: On the Lexical and Syntactic Ambiguities of עַד as Reflected in the Prophecies of Nathan, Ahijah, Ezekiel, and Zechariah," *JBL* 132 (2013): 33–60. See also Shepherd, *Text in the Middle*, 46–49.

ride (1 Kgs. 1:33; cf., Est. 6:8). The donkey is not a symbol of humility. It is a symbol of royal and military might. The juxtaposition of affliction and royalty is what makes the image so striking.

Both Matthew (Matt. 21:5) and John (John 12:15) cite Zechariah 9:9 in their accounts of the so-called "triumphal entry" of Jesus Christ into Jerusalem (see also *b. Ber.* 56b; *b. Sanh.* 98a, 99a; *Gen. Rab.* 56:2; 75:6; 98:9; *Eccles. Rab.* 1:9).[53] They differ in their treatment of the parallelism in the verse, but they both combine their citation of Zechariah 9:9 with a citation of Psalm 118:25–26 (see the Targum of Psalm 118), albeit in a different order (see also Matt. 21:42).[54] The psalm looks forward to a new exodus (Ps. 118:14; cf., Exod. 15:2; Isa. 12:2) and the triumphal entry of the once rejected messianic "stone" (Ps. 118:22–26; cf., Isa. 28:16; Ps. 24; Dan. 2:34–35, 44, 45).[55] Both Zechariah 9:9–10 and Psalm 118 anticipate the establishment of the messianic kingdom on earth in the last days (cf., Ps. 2; 18).[56] Thus, in what sense do the accounts in Matthew and John serve to "fulfill" what is revealed in these texts given the fact that Jesus did not ride into Jerusalem to reign as king but to suffer and die? His death was necessary to make possible a people who would occupy the kingdom that his first-century entry into Jerusalem foreshadowed (Isa. 52:13–53:12; Zech. 12:10).

According to the MT, the LORD says in Zechariah 9:10, "And I will cut off chariots from Ephraim and horses from Jerusalem" (cf., Hos. 2:20 [Eng., 2:18]; Mic. 5:9 [Eng., 5:10]). This would be in continuity with the use of the first person in Zechariah 9:7–8. On the other hand, the LXX and Syriac say, "And he will cut off," referring to the king in Zechariah 9:9. This would fit with the remainder of Zechariah 9:10: "and he will speak peace to the nations" (but see Ps. 85:9 [Eng., 85:8]). One of the marks of the messianic kingdom is not only peace for Ephraim and Jerusalem/Judah but also peace between Ephraim and Jerusalem/Judah (Isa. 11:13). The Messiah will bring peace to all the nations (Isa. 2:4; 9:5 [Eng., 9:6]; 11:6–8; 52:7; Ezek. 34:24–25; Mic. 4:3; 5:4 [Eng., 5:5]; Nah. 2:1 [Eng., 1:15]; Hag. 2:9, 22; Ps. 72:3). His rule will extend from the Dead Sea to the Mediterranean Sea and from the Euphrates River to the ends of the land (see *Tg. Jon.*), corresponding to

---

53. See Shepherd, *The Twelve Prophets*, 56–58.
54. See Shepherd, *Text in the Middle*, 139; "Targums," in *Dictionary of Jesus and the Gospels*, 2d ed., ed. Joel B. Green (Downers Grove, IL: InterVarsity, 2013), 933.
55. See Shepherd, *Text in the Middle*, 62–64.
56. Each of the Torah psalms in the Psalter (Ps. 1, 19, and 119) is coupled with a messianic psalm (Ps. 2, 18, and 118).

the boundaries of the land of the covenant (see Gen. 15:18; cf., Mic. 5:3b [Eng., 5:4b]; 7:12; Pss. 22:28–29 [Eng., 22:27–28]; 72:8; Sir. 44:21). This is not intended to limit the extent of the kingdom as compared with the known world today. Rather, it is intended to highlight the central role of the land of the covenant from beginning (Gen. 2:10–14) to end (Isa. 2:1–5; 65:17–18; Rev. 21–22). The full boundaries of this land from the Euphrates to the Nile, which were never completely possessed in Israel's history (1 Kgs. 5:1 [Eng. 4:21]; 2 Chr. 9:26), constituted much of the known world for the biblical authors.

The pronoun "you" at the beginning of Zechariah 9:11 ("Also you") is feminine singular, referring to Daughter Zion/Jerusalem in Zechariah 9:9. It is in or because of the blood of the covenant that the LORD sent Zion's prisoners from a pit in which there was no water. This cannot be the blood of the Sinai covenant (Exod. 24:8). That covenant was broken (Zech. 11:10), resulting in Babylonian captivity. It must be the antici-pated blood of the new covenant (Isa. 42:6; 49:6; 61:8; Jer. 31:31–34; Ezek. 34:25; Hos. 2:20 [Eng. 2:18]; Mark 14:24). The imagery of the waterless pit comes from the stories of Joseph (Gen. 37:24; 39:20; 41:14) and Jeremiah (Jer. 38:6). The LORD has sent the captives home from Babylon, but there is a sense in which they are still prisoners in need of deliverance (Isa. 42:7; 49:9; 61:1; Luke 4:16–30). They have not experi-enced the full restoration prophesied for the future beyond Babylon (Isa. 40–66; Zech. 1–6). Therefore, the LORD calls on "the prisoners of hope" (cf., Hos. 2:17 [Eng., 2:15]) to return to a "stronghold" (בִּצָּרוֹן), which is likely a play on "Zion" (צִיּוֹן) (Zech. 9:12). Even today the LORD declares that he will restore a double portion to his people (cf., Job 42:10). Judah is the LORD's bow, and Ephraim is his arrow (Zech. 9:13; cf., Zech. 8:13; 10:4, 6; Ps. 78:9). The LORD will arouse the sons of Zion against the Greeks who represent the nonbelieving Gentiles who are the enemies of the people of God (see *Tg. Jon.*; see also Num. 24:24; Joel 4:6 [Eng., 3:6]; Dan. 8:21; 11:2). Zion will be like a warrior's sword. This battle (cf., Zech. 12; 14) will make possible the peace depicted in Zechariah 9:10 for the people of God from Judah, Israel, and all the nations.

The text shifts back to third person again without warning in Zechariah 9:14–17. The LORD will appear as in other examples of bib-lical theophany to make his people victorious against their enemies (Zech. 9:14; cf., 2 Sam. 22:8–16; Nah. 1:2–9; Hab. 3:3–15; Ps. 18:8–16 [Eng., 18:7–15]). His arrow will go forth like the lightning (cf., 2 Sam. 22:15; Hab. 3:11; Ps. 18:15 [Eng., 18:15]). He will blast the shofar as at Sinai (Exod. 19:16; cf., Jer. 4:5; 6:1) and go in the storm winds of the south (or, "Teman" [see Hab. 3:3]; see also Nah. 1:3b). The LORD of armies will defend his people (Zech. 9:15; cf., Gen. 15:1; Zech. 12:8).

And thus, his people will "devour" and "subdue" (cf., Gen. 1:28; Josh. 18:1) those who come against them with sling stones. Alternatively, this text could also mean that they will use sling stones like David to devour and subdue their enemies (see LXX; see also 1 Sam. 17:49). The people will drink the blood of the enemy like wine (cf., Num. 23:24). They will be full as when the sacrificial bowl and the corners of the altar are full with the blood of a sacrificial victim (Exod. 27:3; Lev. 1:5). This is obviously not to be understood literally (see Lev. 17:10–14; Zech. 9:7). It is a metaphor for the shed blood of those defeated in battle (see Gen. 49:11–12; Isa. 63:1–6; Ezek. 39:17–24; Rev. 14:20; 19:13).

The LORD will deliver his people as their shepherd in that eschatological day like the flock of his people that they are (Zech. 9:16; see Zech. 10:2; Pss. 74:1; 79:13; 95:7; 100:3). This is because they are conspicuous stones of a crown upon the LORD's land. Christ and his kingdom are the singular stone (Isa. 28:16; Zech. 3:9; Ps. 118:22; Dan. 2:44–45), and his followers are the stones plural (1 Pet. 2:5). Christ will reign as king (Zech. 6:12–13; Dan. 7:13–14), and his saints will reign with him (Dan. 7:27; Rev. 5:10; cf., Gen. 1:26–28). How great will the LORD's goodness be, and how great will his beauty be (cf., Isa. 4:2) when the land of the covenant brings forth its produce in the messianic kingdom and in the new creation (see Hos. 2:23–24 [Eng., 2:21–22]; Amos 9:11–15; Zech. 8:12), making the once weary young men and virgins bear fruit again (cf., Amos 8:13)! *Targum Jonathan* renders, "For how good and how proper is the teaching of the Torah for the leaders, and true judgment prepared in the synagogue!" This is perhaps prompted by the similarity to Psalm 133:1. Both Psalm 133 and Psalm 134 speak of those who serve in the temple and have the responsibility of teaching the Torah (Deut. 33:10)—a practice that ultimately transfers to the synagogue setting (see Neh. 8–9; see also Isa. 2:3). Furthermore, Psalm 133:3 refers to the blessing of eternal life and dominion in the land of the covenant commanded in Genesis 1:26–28. It is the restoration of this blessing that Zechariah 9:16–17 has in view.

ZECHARIAH 10

10:1 Ask from the LORD rain in time of latter [i.e., spring] rain, the LORD who makes thunderbolts [Syr.: sprinklings; Tg. Jon.: winds]. And rain upon rain will he give to them [Syr.: to you], to each herbage in the field.[57] 10:2 For the household idols [LXX: those who utter; Syr.:

---

57. The formatting of the text in *BHS* suggests a different arrangement of the syntax than the MT accentuation: "Ask from the LORD rain in time of

*soothsayers; Tg. Jon.: worshipers of images], they speak trouble [Tg.
Jon.: oppression]; and the diviners [i.e., those who foretell future events
by casting lots], they see [Tg. Jon.: prophesy] what is false.*[58] *And the
dreams of nothingness are what they speak [Tg. Jon.: False prophets
in their false prophecy speak what is false], in vain [or, with emptiness]
they comfort [Ms: they utter prophecy]. Therefore, they travel [Tg. Jon.:
are scattered] like sheep. What's more, they are afflicted [Tg. Jon.: gone
into exile], for there is no shepherd [LXX: healing; Tg. Jon.: king].*

*10:3 It is against the shepherds [Tg. Jon.: kings] that my anger burns,
and it is upon the he-goats [Tg. Jon.: rulers] that I will visit. For the
LORD of hosts has visited [Tg. Jon.: remembered] his flock, the house
of Judah, and he will make them like his horse of royal splendor in the
battle. 10:4 From it/him [i.e., the house of Judah; or, the LORD] will
be a corner [Tg. Jon.: the king], from it/him will be a peg [Tg. Jon.:
the Messiah], from it/him will be a battle bow. From it/him every oppressor*[59] *will depart together.*[60] *10:5 And they will be like mighty men
[i.e., warriors] trampling in [pc Mss: like] street mud in the battle. And
they will fight, for the LORD will be with them. And they will put to
shame riders [רָכְבֵי chariots?] of horses. 10:6 And I will make the house
of Judah mighty, and the house of Joseph will I deliver. And I will
settle/restore [mlt Mss, LXX: from יׁשֵב; Tg. Jon.: from שׁוּב; see GKC
§72x] them, for I will have had compassion on them. And they will be
just as if I had not rejected them, for I am the LORD their God, and I
will answer them. 10:7 And Ephraim will be like a mighty man, and
their heart will rejoice like wine [NET: as if they had drunk wine]. And
as for their sons, they will see and rejoice. Their heart will rejoice in the
LORD [or, Let their heart rejoice in the LORD]. 10:8 I will whistle to
them, and I will gather them, for I will have purchased them. And they
will increase as they increased. 10:9 And I will sow them among the*

---

latter rain, the LORD who makes thunderbolts and rain upon rain. He will
give to them, to each herbage in the field."

58. *Targum Jonathan* renders all the finite verbs in Zechariah 10:2a as par-
ticiples. Note the pattern: two *qatal* verbs (Zech. 10:2a1, 2), two *yiqtol*
verbs (Zech. 10:2a3, 4), a *qatal* verb (Zech. 10:2b1), and a *yiqtol* verb (Zech.
10:2b2).

59. English versions (e.g., NET, ESV) often render "oppressor" in a positive
sense as "ruler." But in context this word has a negative connotation (Zech.
9:8). This is the kind of tyrant that the ideal Judean king will drive out.

60. The *BHS* apparatus suggests placing the word "together" at the beginning
of Zechariah 10:5.

peoples, and in the distant places will they remember me. And they will live with their sons and return. 10:10 And I will restore them from the land of Egypt, and from Assyria I will gather them.[61] And into the land of Gilead and Lebanon [Tg. Jon.: the sanctuary (cf., Hab. 2:17)] I will bring them, and space will not be found for them [LXX: not one of them will be left]. 10:11 And he [LXX: they] will pass through a sea of distress [Tg. Jon.: And signs and mighty deeds will be done for them just as they were done for their fathers when they passed through the sea], and he [LXX: they] will strike in the sea waves, and all the depths of the Nile will show dryness [Syr.: be ashamed]. And the pride of Assyria will be brought down; and as for the scepter of Egypt, it will turn aside. 10:12 And I will make them mighty in the LORD, and in his name they will walk about [Ms, LXX: boast; see 4QXII^g; Syr.: hope; Tg. Jon.: walk redeemed (cf., Isa. 35:9)], the prophetic utterance of the LORD.

Calvin saw in the imperative of Zechariah 10:1 an implied reproof, suggesting that the people are commanded to request what they ought to have known to ask for themselves.[62] Another possibility is that this is similar to Jesus's imperative in Matthew 9:38: "Therefore, ask the Lord of the harvest to send workers into his harvest." In other words, "Ask me to do my will." The LORD seeks in Zechariah 10:1 to bless his people with the rain and produce that they were unable to attain under the old covenant for lack of obedience (see Deut. 28:12, 24; Jer. 3:3). Such abundance will be one of the marks of the new covenant relationship in the messianic kingdom (Ezek. 34:25–27; Hos. 2:20, 23–24 [Eng., 2:18, 21–22]; 6:3; Joel 2:23; Zech. 8:12, 9:17; Ps. 72:6). The people are to ask the LORD for this precisely because he is the only one who can do it (see Jer. 10:11–12). The "household idols" (see Gen. 31:19; 1 Sam. 15:23; Hos. 3:4) have nothing worthwhile to offer (Zech. 10:2; cf., Hos. 2:10 [Eng., 2:8]).[63] The "diviners" (see Num. 23:23; Deut. 18:10) see nothing but what is false. They are false prophets (see Deut. 18:20–22; Jer. 23:9–40; Ezek. 13) who speak empty dreams and comfort the people with nothingness

---

61. *Targum Jonathan* renders this as if it were a comparison between the past deliverance from Egypt and a future deliverance from Assyria.
62. Calvin, *Zechariah*, 277–78.
63. The early versions render "household idols" in various ways (LXX: "those who utter"; Syr.: "soothsayers"; *Tg. Jon.*: "worshipers of images") in order to avoid the impression that idols actually speak (Jer. 10:5; Ps. 115:4–7). But this impression is by no means a necessary conclusion to be drawn from the poetic image. It is simply a vivid way to say that idolatry causes nothing but trouble for those who practice it (cf., Hab. 2:18–19).

(see Jer. 6:14). They give the people a false sense of security for their own personal gain (see Mic. 2:6–11; 3:5–8). Therefore, the people travel like an afflicted flock of sheep without a shepherd (cf., Num. 27:17; 1 Kgs. 22:17; Matt. 9:36).[64] That is, they are still a people scattered in exile without a king, even though they have returned to the land from Babylon. The LORD is the shepherd who will deliver his flock (Zech. 9:16; cf., Ezek. 34:11–16; Mic. 2:12–13; 7:14; Ps. 78:52). The Davidic Messiah will be their king (see Jer. 3:14–18; 23:5–6; Ezek. 34:23–24; Mic. 5:3 [Eng., 5:4]; Zech. 11:4–14; 13:7; Matt. 26:15, 31; 27:9–10).

The LORD's anger burns against the bad "shepherds" (i.e., kings, leaders; Zech. 10:3; cf., Ezek. 34:1–10; Jer. 23:1–3; 25:34–36; Zech. 11:3, 15–17). He will "visit upon" (i.e., punish) the "he-goats" (i.e., rulers; see BDB, 800). This is because the LORD "visits" (i.e., cares for) his flock, namely, the house of Judah (cf., Jer. 23:4). He will make them like the horse of his royal splendor in battle (cf., Hab. 3:8b; Zech. 6:13; 12; 14). From either the house of Judah or the LORD himself (cf., Mic. 5:1 [Eng., 5:2]) will come a "corner" (Zech. 10:4), which is a term occasionally used for a leader (Judg. 20:2; 1 Sam. 14:38; Isa. 19:13). In Ps. 118:22, it is used for the chief cornerstone, the messianic stone that the builders reject (cf., Isa. 8:14; 28:16; Zech. 3:9; Dan. 2:44–45). Likewise, a "peg" will come. The term "peg" can also refer to a leader (e.g., Isa. 22:23). *Targum Jonathan* has "king" for "corner" and "Messiah" for "peg." There may be warrant for this from the usage in Psalm 118:22. The two terms together describe the messianic king. The bow of battle will come to defeat the enemy (Zech. 9:13) and to create peace (Zech. 9:10). Thus, every "oppressor" will depart. This term does not refer to the messianic ruler as do the words "corner" and "peg." It is the same term used for the "oppressor" in Zechariah 9:8. English translations that render this only as if a ruler were going forth have missed this connection.

The people of God will be like "mighty men" trampling street mud in the battle (Zech. 10:5; cf., Mic. 7:10). The root for "mighty" (גבר) runs throughout this passage as a key word (Zech. 10:5a, 6a, 7a, 12a). They will fight, for the LORD will be with them (cf., Zech. 12:5–6; 14:3), and they will put the riders (chariots?) of the enemy's horses to shame (cf., Exod. 14:23, 25; 15:1; Zech. 9:10). This language anticipates the new exodus imagery in Zechariah 10:10–11. The LORD will make the house of Judah mighty (Zech. 10:6), and he will deliver the house of Joseph (i.e., the northern kingdom of Israel). There will be a reunited kingdom in the days of the Messiah just as there was in the days of David and Solomon (cf., Zech. 8:13; 9:13). The LORD will "settle" or

---

64. See Shepherd, *Text in the Middle*, 89–90.

"restore" them because of his compassion (cf., Hos. 2:25 [Eng., 2:23]). The Leningrad Codex has a mixed form here, "settle/restore," but other witnesses have one or the other (see translation above; see also Zech. 10:10a). It will be as if the LORD had never rejected them for the broken covenant (cf., Zech. 8:14–15), for he is the God who is present with them to act for the sake of his name both in judgment and in restoration (see Exod. 3:12, 14; 7:1–7; 9:16). Once unwilling to answer his people or his prophet because of the broken covenant (see Jer. 11:14; 14:11), he will again answer them when they call (cf., Isa. 41:17; Jer. 33:3; Zech. 7:13). Ephraim (i.e., the northern kingdom of Israel), like the house of Judah, will be like a mighty man (Zech. 10:7). They will celebrate in the spoils of battle as victorious warriors (cf., Gen. 49:12; Isa. 53:12; Ps. 78:65; see also Zech. 9:15). Their children will see and be glad (cf., Zech. 4:10), so that their heart will rejoice in the LORD (see Zech. 9:9; cf., Pss. 13:6 [Eng., 13:5]; 78:6–7). Every generation of the people of God that reads this prophecy rightfully longs to take part in such a glorious occasion.

The LORD will "whistle" (cf., Isa. 7:18) for his people and gather them (cf., Zeph. 3:19–20), for he will have purchased them at that time (Zech. 10:8a; cf., Jer. 31:11). The people will increase as they once increased in the land of Egypt (Zech. 10:8b; see Exod. 1:7; Hos. 2:1 [Eng., 1:10]). They had been as numerous as the stars in the sky and as the grains of sand on the seashore in accordance with the covenant with Abraham (Gen. 15:5; 22:17), but now only a remnant remained (Isa. 10:22). In the messianic kingdom and in the new covenant relationship, however, the people of God will experience the fullness of the covenant with Abraham, the father of all who believe. The reader might expect then to find at the beginning of Zechariah 10:9 something about how the LORD will sow his people in the land of the covenant (cf., Hos. 2:25 [Eng., 2:23]). But the text says that he will sow them among the peoples, and in the distant places they will remember him. The *BHS* apparatus even suggests changing the first verb to "summon" or "scatter" to account for the apparent discrepancy, but there is no textual evidence for such a change. It appears that the text envisions Judah and Ephraim being sown among the peoples in the land of the covenant to form the believing remnant of the people of God from all the nations (cf., Isa. 2:1–5; 66:18–24; Jer. 3:17–18; Amos 9:11–15; Mic. 4:1–5; Zech. 8:20–23). It is among the peoples from distant places (metonymy; cf., Isa. 8:9) that they will remember the LORD in the land of the covenant. They will live with their children in peace and security. They will return to the land and thus return to the LORD who will restore their fortunes.

451

The return from the land of Egypt and the gathering from Assyria in Zechariah 10:10a are not merely about the return of Judeans who fled to Egypt and the gathering of northern Israelites from Assyria. The imagery in Zechariah 10:11 makes clear that this is the new exodus (cf., Isa. 11:11, 15–16). Just as God delivered his people in the original exodus, so will he deliver them from Assyrian/Babylonian captivity—a theme developed throughout the composition of the Twelve (see, e.g., commentary on Hos. 2:16–17 [Eng., 2:14–15]; 8:13; 9:3; 11:1, 5, 11).[65] The people have returned from Babylon, but there is a sense in which they are still in "Egypt" precisely because they have yet to experience the full restoration of the lost blessing. This will only happen in the messianic kingdom of the last days. The LORD will bring the people into the land of Gilead and Lebanon (Zech. 10:10b), the land of the covenant on both sides of the Jordan, but the boundaries will go far beyond the ones known in the kingdom of Solomon (1 Kgs. 5:1 [Eng., 4:21]) to the full extent described in Genesis 2:10–14; 15:18. And even then, the land will be packed to full capacity (cf., Josh. 17:16; Isa. 49:20; Zech. 2:8 [Eng., 2:4]; see also LXX).

The subject of the verbs at the beginning of Zechariah 10:11 is not immediately clear (cf., LXX). The use of first-person verbs in Zechariah 10:10, 12 might suggest that the people (singular) are the subject of the first verb, passing through the sea as they did in the original exodus (but see Hab. 3:15). *Targum Jonathan* highlights the connection to the exodus story very well. But then the striking of the sea into waves would seem to be the work of the LORD (cf., Isa. 11:16). The reader might expect next to see a reference to the drying up of the depths of the sea, but instead there is a reference to the drying up of the Nile—a poetic image of the shame and reproach brought upon Egypt in the exodus event. This will be the fate of the enemies of the people of God in the last days. The pride of "Assyria" will be brought down (cf., Zech. 9:6), and the scepter (i.e., kingship) will depart from "Egypt" (cf., Gen. 49:10). The LORD will make his people mighty in himself (Zech. 12:11; cf., Zech. 12:5), and it is in his name that they will walk—an allusion to the description of the eschatological people of God in Micah 4:5.[66]

---

65. See Michael B. Shepherd, "The New Exodus in the Composition of the Twelve," in *Text and Canon: Essays in Honor of John H. Sailhamer*, eds. Robert L. Cole and Paul J. Kissling (Eugene, OR: Pickwick, 2017), 120–36.

66. The LXX says that they will "boast" in his name (cf., Ps. 34:3).

ZECHARIAH 11

11:1 Open, O Lebanon [Tg. Jon.: peoples], your doors, so that fire may consume your cedars [Tg. Jon.: strength]. 11:2 Wail, O cypress [or, fir tree; Tg. Jon.: kings], for a cedar has fallen [Tg. Jon.: for the rulers who were rich from plundered possessions are broken], because [see LXX, ASV] majestic ones [LXX: nobles] are destroyed. Wail, O oaks of Bashan [Tg. Jon.: magistrates of the lands], for the fortified forest has come down [Tg. Jon.: the marketplace has been plundered]. 11:3 The sound of the wailing of the shepherds [Tg. Jon.: kings], for their majesty is destroyed [Tg. Jon.: for their marketplaces are plundered]. The sound of the roaring of young lions, for the pride of the Jordan [see BDB, 145] is destroyed.

11:4 Thus says the LORD my God [LXX: the Lord Almighty], "Tend the flock of slaughter [Tg. Jon.: Prophesy about the stewards appointed as stewards of the people, and they ruled over them like a flock for slaughter] 11:5 whose buyers slaughter them and are not held guilty [LXX: do not regret] and whose sellers say, 'Blessed be the LORD, and I gained riches,' and whose shepherds do not have pity on them [LXX: have not suffered anything for them]. 11:6 For I will never again have pity on the inhabitants of the land," the prophetic utterance of the LORD, "and look, I am about to deliver the people each into the hand of his neighbor and into the hand of his king, and they will crush the land, and I will not rescue from their hand." 11:7 And I tended the flock of slaughter for the merchants of the flock [cf., LXX; ASV: verily the poor of the flock]. And I took for myself two rods. To one I called "Pleasantness," and to one I called "Binders" [LXX: allotment], and I tended the flock.[67] 11:8 And I hid [LXX: removed] the three shepherds in one month, and my soul was short [i.e., I was impatient; LXX: my soul will be made heavy] with them; and also their soul, it felt a loathing against me [Tg. Jon.: my word rejected them because their soul rejected the worship of me]. 11:9 And I said, "I will not tend you. The dying will die, and the hidden will be hidden [i.e., those going to ruin will be destroyed], and the rest will devour the flesh of one another." 11:10 And I took my rod,

---

67. *Tg. Jon.*: "And I appointed the stewards over the people, and they ruled over them like a flock for sacrifice. They made my people poor and led them astray, and they were divided before me into two halves. The house of Israel was divided against the house of Judah. They loathed the kingdom of the house of David in whom was the will before me to be stewards over my people."

"Pleasantness," and I cut it in two to break my covenant [Syr.: the covenant] that I made [BHS: he made] with all the peoples [BHS: people].[68] *11:11 And it was broken on that day, and the merchants of the flock [cf., LXX; ASV: and thus the poor of the flock] who kept me [or, who watched / observed me; Tg. Jon.: who did my will] knew that it was the word of the LORD. 11:12 And I said to them, "If it is good in your eyes, give my pay [Tg. Jon.: do my will]; but if not, cease." And they weighed my pay, thirty pieces of silver. 11:13 And the LORD said to me, "Throw it to the potter [LXX: the smelting furnace; Syr.: the treasury], the magnificence of the price at which I was appraised (and dismissed) from them [see BDB, 429]."*[69] *And I took the thirty pieces of silver and threw it into the house of the LORD to the potter [LXX: the smelting furnace; Syr.: the treasury]. 11:14 And I cut in two my second rod, the one called "Binders," to break the brotherhood between Judah and Israel.*[70]

11:15 And the LORD said to me, "Again take for yourself a foolish shepherd's equipment [Tg. Jon.: Prophesy about a stupid steward; NLT: play the part of a foolish shepherd]. 11:16 For look, I am about to raise up a shepherd in the land. As for the hidden [i.e., those being destroyed], he will not pay attention to them. As for the scattered [see LXX; see also BDB, 654], he will not seek them. And as for the broken, he will not heal them. As for the one that stands on its own, he will not support it. And as for the flesh of the fat / stout, he will eat it. And as for their hooves, he will tear them apart. 11:17 Woe [or, Alas], O worthless [Syr., Tg. Jon.: foolish] shepherd who forsakes the flock [see GKC §90l]! A sword is against his arm and against his right eye. As for his arm, it will surely wither. And as for his right eye, it will surely grow dim.

Chapter divisions are not original to the text of Scripture, and they often obscure the intended arrangement of the text. If the first three verses of Zechariah 11 are read with what follows them, then the

---

68. *Tg. Jon.*: "And I brought the king of Assyria against the king of Israel and sent him into exile because they changed the covenant that was made with them not to worship idols. Then they went into exile among the peoples."

69. *Tg. Jon.*: "Write the record of their deeds with a reed pen [or, on a writing tablet] and throw it into the temple under the hand of the temple official because of the honor of the fear of me in their eyes."

70. *Tg. Jon.*: "And I brought Nebuchadnezzar the king of Babylon against Zedekiah the king of the tribe of the house of Judah and exiled him because also they of the house of Judah with their brothers the house of Israel changed the covenant."

reader will have the impression that they are words of judgment for the rulers of Israel (cf., Zech. 10:3).[71] But the connections back to the end of Zechariah 10 and the use of similar figurative language elsewhere strongly suggest that these words are directed to the enemies of the people of God who will be conquered in the last days (see *Tg. Jon.*). The text is thus designed to be a message of comfort to the faithful remnant. The three locations mentioned in these verses—Lebanon, Bashan, and the pride of the Jordan[72]—take the reader back to the reference to the land of Gilead and Lebanon in Zechariah 10:10 where the LORD says that he will restore the people in a new exodus to the land of the covenant. Therefore, the proverbial "Egypt" and "Assyria" in Zechariah 10:10–11, who in a sense still hold the people captive (because full restoration is still future) and/or currently possess the land, must be defeated and displaced. It is no coincidence then that the metaphors for rulers (i.e., nobles and shepherds [kings]) in Zechariah 11:1–3—cedars, cypress, oaks, and young lions—are elsewhere used for the rulers of Egypt (Ezek. 31:8) and Assyria (Isa. 10:33–34; Nah. 2:12–14 [Eng., 2:11–13]; see also Isa. 2:12–16). With this understanding, Lebanon is instructed to open its doors so that fire may consume its famous cedars (Zech. 11:1; see 1 Kgs. 5:20 [Eng., 5:6]; cf., Amos 1:4, 7, 10, 12, 14; 2:2, 5). As in the original conquest, the land must be conquered before it can be possessed (see Josh. 6:24; 8:28). The call to wail over the fall of a king or a nation is common to the prophets (Zech. 11:2–3; cf., Isa. 13:10; 14:12; 15:2; 16:7; 23:1, 6, 14; Jer. 25:34–38; Ezek. 27:27–36).

The LORD's command to the prophet in Zech. 11:4 to tend the flock destined for slaughter sets up a kind of parable in which the prophet plays the role of the good shepherd (cf., Jer. 23:5–6; Ezek. 34:23–24) rejected by the people and by their leadership.[73] This passage does not address a particular period in the people's history. Rather, it speaks to the nature of their relationship with the LORD in general (cf., Neh. 9). It is in this sense that it can be read as prophetic (see Matt. 26:14–16;

---

71. See Keil, *Minor Prophets*, 589–90. Keil leans toward the rulers of Israel, but he focuses more on the destruction of the land itself.
72. "referring to the green and shady banks, clothed with willows, tamarisks, and cane, in which the lions made their covert" (BDB, 145).
73. Mitchell (*Haggai and Zechariah*, 303) argues that the prophet is to personate the typical king and his brand of government, but this fails to deal well with the dismissal of the shepherd in Zechariah 11:12. It seems unlikely that the reader is to expect the typical unjust king to arrange or allow for his own dismissal like a hired hand. The willingness of the good shepherd to lay down his life in such a way is what makes him the righteous king.

27:3–10). The command itself anticipates the initial "failure" of the relationship between the good shepherd and the flock. The suffering of this righteous king will be necessary before the establishment of his kingdom on earth (see Zech. 9:9–10; 12:9–13:1, 7–9). The sheep are described in Zechariah 11:5 as those whose buyers (Rashi: foreign nations) slaughter them and get away with it. Their sellers show their wickedness by praising God for wealth acquired at the expense of the flock entrusted to them. These sellers are apparently distinct from the shepherds who do not have pity on the sheep. The shepherds are the kings who unjustly oversee such mistreatment of the people (cf., Jer. 23:1–3; Ezek. 34:1–10). And yet the people are not without guilt themselves, so the LORD explains in Zechariah 11:6 that the reason why they are destined for slaughter is that he himself will not spare the inhabitants of the land of the covenant.[74] He will be the one to deliver each into the hand of his neighbor and into the hand of his unrighteous king. They will crush the land, and the LORD will not rescue from their hand. In other words, the people and their leadership will self-destruct in their breaking of the covenant. Only after their demise will redemption come. It is into this situation that the messianic shepherd enters unrecognized as their true king (cf., John 1:11).

And so, as the story goes, the prophet plays the part and tends the flock destined for slaughter on behalf of the flock's merchants (Zech. 11:7). That is, the prophet does not come as a full-fledged ruler acknowledged by all. He is merely a shepherd who works for the sellers who work for the king (Zech. 11:5). This is a way of indicating that he is not someone whom the people or the leadership hold in high esteem (cf., Isa. 49:7; 52:15; 53:2–3). The prophet recounts that he took two rods for his task, calling one "Pleasantness" and the other "Binders." It will become apparent in what follows (Zech. 11:10, 14) that these are for a prophetic sign-act (cf., Isa. 20; Jer. 13:1–14; Ezek. 4–5; 12; 21; 24). Zechariah says that he hid (LXX: removed) three shepherds in one month (i.e., a short period of time) in his role as the hired tender of the flock (Zech. 11:8a). There is no indication that the reader is to think of three specific kings from the history of Israel or Judah who were removed within the span

---

74. Both Keil (*Minor Prophets*, 593) and Mitchell (*Haggai and Zechariah*, 304) interpret this verse to mean that the LORD will judge the inhabitants of the earth ("mankind"). But apart from the possible reference to foreign nations ("buyers") in Zechariah 11:5, this interpretation seems remarkably out of context. The passage is not about judgment of the nations. It is about the flock (the people of the land of the covenant), their leadership, and the rejection of the good shepherd whom the prophet represents.

of a single month. Rather, the idea is that the friction between the one whom the prophet represents and the leadership is such that the one represented by the prophet grows impatient with them, and the leadership feels a loathing for him (Zech. 11:8b). This results in a fracture of the relationship between the one represented by the prophet and the flock (i.e., the people). He will no longer tend them, leaving the dying to die, those going to ruin to be destroyed, and the rest to devour one another (Zech. 11:9; cf., Zech. 11:16). They are truly a flock destined for their own self-induced slaughter thanks to their corrupt leaders.

Zechariah then says that he took his rod called "Pleasantness" and cut it in two, thus breaking the covenant (Zech. 11:10). According to the MT, this was a covenant made with all the peoples. This reading is difficult, if not impossible, to reconcile with the context. The prophet had an arrangement to tend the flock (the people of the land of the covenant), not the nations. Furthermore, if the covenant here is intended to represent a divine-human covenant, then it is important to note that there is no conditional (i.e., breakable) covenant with the peoples in the Bible. The only conditional covenant is the Sinai covenant with Israel. It may be helpful to compare a similar textual problem in another passage. According to the Leningrad Codex in 2 Samuel 22:44, the text has the word עַמִּי ("my people"). A few Masoretic manuscripts, Lucian's recension of the LXX, the Syriac, the Targum, and the parallel in Psalm 18:44 (Eng., 18:43) read עַם ("people"). But a few Masoretic manuscripts, the Sebirin ("scribal suggestions"), the LXX, and some Targum manuscripts read the plural עַמִּים ("people"). Thus, it is possible, and quite likely given the context, that the original reading for Zechariah 11:10 was עַמִּי ("my people"), which was subsequently changed, perhaps accidentally, to עַמִּים ("peoples"). It was then to this latter reading that the definite article was added. The breaking of the rod called "Pleasantness" represents the breaking of the old covenant. When the breaking of the rod occurred in the parable, the merchants of the flock (i.e., the sellers; cf., 4Q163 21:7–8; CD-B 19:9) who kept the prophet as their hired hand knew that the breaking of the rod stood for the prophetic word of the LORD. It was a sign-act that declared the breaking of the covenant.

Thus, Zechariah suggested that his employers should either pay his wages and dismiss him or leave him alone to do his job—whatever was pleasing in their sight (Zech. 11:12a). They decided to dismiss him at the price of thirty pieces of silver (Zech. 11:12b; cf., Gen. 37:28; Exod. 21:32). Matthew's account of Judas's betrayal of Jesus alludes to this amount (Matt. 26:15) and cites from Zechariah 11:13 (Matt. 27:9–10). Matthew does not primarily interpret this text as a prophecy of Judas's betrayal but as a prophecy of the dismissal of the good shepherd, Jesus, by the leadership, the chief priests, on behalf of the people. Judas is simply a means to an end. In the Zechariah parable, the merchants/sellers arrange for the dismissal of the prophet as the mediating group between the flock and the ruling authorities (i.e., the shepherds). Likewise, the chief priests in Matthew's gospel mediate between the people and the ruling authorities in their day (see Matt. 27:11–14, 20).

The LORD instructs Zechariah in Zechariah 11:13 to throw his pay ("the magnificence of the price at which I was appraised")[75] to the potter. When the prophet follows this instruction, he throws the thirty pieces of silver to the potter in the house of the LORD (i.e., the temple). On the other hand, the LXX says that he threw the silver into the smelting furnace. The Syriac says that he threw it to the treasury (= הָאוֹצָר; cf., MT הַיּוֹצֵר ["the potter"]). Matthew appears to show an awareness of both the MT and the Syriac in his citation of Zechariah 11:13 (Matt. 27:9–10). His version reads "the field of the potter" rather than "the house of the LORD to the potter." According to Matthew 27:5, Judas threw the thirty pieces of silver into the temple and went out and hanged himself (cf., 2 Sam. 17:23; Acts 1:17–19). The chief priests did not consider it permissible to put the money into the treasury (cf., Syr. Zech. 11:13) because it was blood money (Matt. 27:6). Therefore, they used the money to buy the potter's field to serve as a burial place for strangers (Matt. 27:7). That field was known as the Field of Blood (Matt. 27:8). And so, the money did not go to a potter who was actually in the temple. It went into the temple, but because it could not stay in the temple treasury, it went to the potter for the purchase of a field.[76]

---

75. The NET Notes consider this a sarcastic expression for the low value placed on the prophet, what amounted to two-and-a-half years of pay.
76. Matthew cites Zechariah 11:13 as if it were from Jeremiah (Matt. 27:9), but there is really no match in the extant LXX or MT of the book of Jeremiah (see Jer. 18:1–6; 19; 32:6–9). It is possible that Matthew uses Jeremiah's name as the head of all the Prophets (see *b. B. Bat.* 14b; cf., Mark 1:2–3 where Mark uses Isaiah's name to introduce a quote from Malachi [and Exod. 23:20] followed by a quote from Isaiah), but this practice is not well attested. Another possibility is that Matthew understood Jeremiah to be the author of Zechariah 9–14 (so-called Second Zechariah). This would be analogous to the potential attribution of Isaiah 40–55 (so-called Second Isaiah) to Jeremiah in Ezra 1:1 (see Isa. 41:2; 44:28; 45:1; but see also Jer. 25:11; 29:10; 50:8; 51:11). Yet another option to explore is the possibility that either Zechariah or the composer of the Twelve is citing an oral tradition or a no-longer-extant text attributed to Jeremiah. Both authors are readers of the book of Jeremiah who cite from him elsewhere in their work. It is worth noting that this is the section of the book of Zechariah that

Zechariah concludes his role as the good shepherd in Zechariah 11:14 by breaking his second rod called "Binders," another prophetic sign-act. This time the sign indicates not the breaking of the old covenant but the breaking of the brotherhood between Judah and Israel (cf., Ezek. 37:15–28). It is a special concern of the prophecy of Zechariah's book to show that this divided kingdom will in fact be reunited in the last days (see Zech. 8:13; 9:10, 13; 10:6).

After playing the part of the good shepherd, Zechariah receives instruction to play the part of the foolish shepherd (Zech. 11:15; cf., Jer. 23:1–3; Ezek. 34:1–10; Zech. 10:3). The reason for this is that the LORD is about to raise up such an antichrist figure in the land who will not care for those going to ruin (Zech. 11:16). He will neither seek the scattered nor heal the broken. He will not provide support to the isolated. Rather, he will devour the flesh of the healthy and tear their hooves apart. Therefore, the LORD announces judgment for the worthless shepherd who forsakes the flock (Zech. 11:17). A sword will be against his arm and against his dominant eye, resulting in a withered arm (cf., 1 Kgs. 13:4) and a dim eye (cf., Gen. 27:1; see also Num. 24:7–8 [LXX]; Ezek. 39; Dan. 9:26b–27; 11:45; Rev. 20:8).[77]

ZECHARIAH 12

12:1 The oracle of the word of the LORD concerning Israel, the prophetic utterance of the LORD who stretches out sky and establishes land and fashions man's spirit within him.[78]

12:2 "Look, I am about to make Jerusalem a cup of reeling to all the peoples around. (And also against Judah will the attack be in the siege against Jerusalem.) 12:3 And so, in that day, I will make Jerusalem a stone of burden to all the peoples. All who try to carry it will be severely cut. And against it all the nations of the earth will be gathered. 12:4

---

connects to the following book of Malachi (Zech. 9:1; 12:1; Mal. 1:1). See Shepherd, *The Twelve Prophets*, 58–59.

77. Critical scholars put Zechariah 13:7–9 after Zechariah 11:17 (e.g., Mitchell, *Haggai and Zechariah*, 316–20). There is no textual evidence for this rearrangement. See commentary on Zechariah 13:7 for reasons why the shepherd in that verse is not to be identified with the foolish shepherd in Zechariah 11:15–17.

78. See Cynthia L. Miller-Naudé, "Mismatches of Definiteness within Appositional Expressions Used as Vocatives in Biblical Hebrew," *JNSL* 40/2 (2014): 97–111.

In that day," the prophetic utterance of the LORD, "I will strike every horse with confusion and its rider with madness. And upon the house of Judah I will open my eyes, but every horse of the peoples I will strike with blindness. 12:5 And the chiefs [BHS: tribes] of Judah will say in their heart, 'Strength to me are the inhabitants of Jerusalem [Ms: Strength to the inhabitants of Jerusalem; LXX: We will find for ourselves the inhabitants of Jerusalem; Tg. Jon.: Deliverance will be found for the inhabitants of Jerusalem] in the LORD of hosts their God.' 12:6 In that day, I will make the chiefs [BHS: tribes] of Judah like a pot of fire among pieces of wood and like a torch of fire in a sheaf, and they will consume on the right and on the left all the peoples around. And Jerusalem [i.e., the people of Jerusalem] will dwell again in its place, in Jerusalem [i.e., in the city of Jerusalem; > Ms, LXX]."

12:7 And the LORD will deliver the tents of Judah at first [LXX: as before (= כראשנה)] in order that the beauty of the house of David and that of the inhabitants [nonn Mss, Vrs] of Jerusalem might not be great above Judah [see 4QXII^e]. 12:8 In that day, the LORD will surround / defend the inhabitants [nonn Mss, Vrs] of Jerusalem, and the one who stumbles among them in that day will be like David, and the house of David will be like God, like the angel [or, messenger, prophet] of the LORD before them.

12:9 "And so, in that day, I will seek to destroy all the nations who come against Jerusalem. 12:10 And I will pour out on the house of David and on the inhabitants [mlt Mss, Vrs] of Jerusalem the Spirit of grace and supplication, and they will look at me whom they pierced, and they will mourn for him like mourning for the only son, and they will show bitterness for him [see GKC §113z] like showing bitterness for the firstborn. 12:11 In that day, the mourning will be great in Jerusalem like the mourning of Hadad-Rimmon [Tg. Jon.: like the mourning for Ahab the son of Omri whom Hadad the son of Tab-Rimmon killed] in the valley of Megiddo [see GKC §85v; Tg. Jon.: like the mourning of Josiah the son of Amon whom Pharaoh the Lame killed in the valley of Megiddo]. 12:12 And the land will mourn, each family alone [see GKC §123d], the family of the house of David alone and their wives alone, the family of the house of Nathan alone and their wives alone, 12:13 the family of the house of Levi alone and their wives alone, the family of the Shimeite [2 Mss, Syr., Tg. Jon.: the house of Shimei] alone and their wives alone, 12:14 and the families that remain, each alone and their wives alone."

Zechariah 12:1 begins the second of three sections labeled "the oracle of the word of the LORD" (cf., Zech. 9:1; Mal. 1:1). This oracle is "concerning Israel," but it is clear from the following context that "Israel" here does not refer to the northern kingdom of Israel or to the united kingdom of Israel and Judah but to Judah and Jerusalem in particular (cf., Zech. 2:2b [Eng., 1:19b]). The oracle is "the prophetic utterance of the LORD." A little hymn then describes the LORD as the one who stretches out sky and establishes land (cf., Isa. 42:5; Jer. 10:12; 51:15) and fashions man's spirit within him (cf., Gen. 2:7; Num. 27:16; Amos 4:13; Prov. 20:27). He is the creator. Therefore, the land belongs to him, and he gives it to whomever he pleases (see Dan. 4:14 [Eng., 4:17]). Nothing is too difficult for him (Jer. 32:17, 27; Zech. 8:6).

The LORD points out that he is about to make Jerusalem "a cup of reeling" to all the surrounding peoples (Zech. 12:2a). This is an image that the reader of prophetic literature is familiar with from elsewhere (e.g., Jer. 25:15–26; Hab. 2:16). It is the cup of judgment that the nations must drink in the LORD's defense of his city against their attack. The parenthetical comment in Zechariah 12:2b adds that the attack will also be against Judah in the siege of Jerusalem (cf., Zech. 14:14).[79] The phrase "in that day" at the beginning of Zechariah 12:3 is pervasive throughout the last three chapters of the book (see Zech. 12:4, 6, 8, 9, 11; 13:1, 2, 4; 14:1, 4, 6, 8, 9, 13, 20, 21). It is the eschatological Day of the LORD in which he will vindicate his people and defeat his enemies. The LORD will make Jerusalem "a stone of burden" to all the peoples (cf., Zech. 3:9; 4:7, 10). All who try to carry it will be cut severely (cf., Isa. 8:14–15; Dan. 2:45). And all the unbelieving from the nations of the earth will be gathered against it (see Zech. 14:2; Luke 21:20).

In that day, the LORD will strike every enemy horse with confusion and its rider with madness (Zech. 12:4a; cf., Exod. 14:24–25; Hag. 2:22; Zech. 9:10; 14:3, 15)—one of the covenant curses according to Deuteronomy 28:28 (see Gen. 12:3a). The LORD will have his eyes open, providentially watching over the house of Judah (Zech. 12:4b; cf., Zech. 3:9), but he will strike every horse of the peoples with blindness (see again Deut. 28:28). The MT of Zechariah 12:5 gives the thought of the "chiefs" of Judah in that day, but this term is normally reserved for the chiefs of Edom (Gen. 36; see also Zech. 9:7). *BHS* suggests revocalizing the consonants of the Hebrew text so that it means "tribes" or "clans"

---

79. The *BHS* apparatus suggests that Zechariah 12:2b, 3b, 4b1, 6a are additions. There is no textual evidence that these were not part of the original final form of the book. Therefore, if they appear somewhat additional or parenthetical, they must be considered authorial additions or comments.

(lit., "thousands") of Judah. According to the Leningrad Codex, the chiefs say to themselves that the inhabitants of Jerusalem are their strength in the LORD (cf., Judg. 5:2; Ps. 110:3). One Masoretic manuscript, however, reads, "Strength to the inhabitants of Jerusalem" (cf., Zech. 10:6, 12), which could be an expression of desire or fact. Both the LXX and *Targum Jonathan* read אמצה (MT: "strength") as if it were from the root מצא ("find"). The LORD will make the chiefs (or, tribes) of Judah like a pot of fire among wood and like a torch in a sheaf, consuming all the surrounding peoples on both sides (Zech. 12:6a; cf., Obad. 18). The people of Jerusalem will inhabit their city once again (Zech. 12:6b; cf., Isa. 65:18). There is no need to emend or omit the second occurrence of "Jerusalem" in Zechariah 12:6b. The name is used in two different senses: the people of Jerusalem and the city of Jerusalem.

Verses 7 and 8 of Zechariah 12 are like a parenthesis between Zechariah 12:1–6 and Zechariah 12:9–14. The LORD is not speaking in the first person. Rather, the prophet refers to the LORD in the third person. But verses 7 and 8 are certainly not unrelated to the surrounding material. They serve to comment on what is happening in context. Verse 7 identifies three groups: the tents of Judah, the house of David (primarily represented by the Davidic king), and the inhabitants of Jerusalem. The MT says that the LORD will deliver the tents of Judah "at first" (בראשנה) in order that the beauty of the house of David and that of the inhabitants of the city of David might not be greater than that of Judah. The idea seems to be that the house of David and those associated with it already have a kind of prominence. Thus, priority given to Judah in the LORD's deliverance might prevent any sort of imbalance in the relationship. It is not clear, however, what this prioritization of Judah would actually look like. On the other hand, the LXX says that the LORD will deliver the tents of Judah "as before" (= כבראשנה). A comparison with the MT shows that the difference between the two readings is the difference between the prepositions ב and כ. Because of their graphic similarity, these two prepositions were often confused accidentally in the transmission of biblical texts. The sense of the LXX is that the LORD will once again deliver the tents of Judah as in the golden age of David and Solomon in order to prevent exaltation of the royal house and city over the rest of the tribe of Judah (cf., Mic. 4:4; Zech. 3:10), for in the days of David and Solomon a victory for the king was a victory for the people (see 1 Sam. 18:16; 2 Sam. 2:4; 5:3; 8; 1 Kgs. 5:1–14 [Eng., 4:21–34]).

In the day of the deliverance of Zechariah 12:7, the LORD will surround/defend the inhabitants of Jerusalem (Zech. 12:8; cf., Zech. 2:9 [Eng., 2:5]). Even the straggler among them will be like David, a mighty warrior (cf., 1 Sam. 2:4), which is to say that there will be no one who stumbles. They are only stragglers in comparison with what the house of David will be in that day. All the people of God will be like David, but the house of David will be like God (cf., Gen. 3:5). The leader of the house of David (i.e., the Messiah) will in fact be "God with us" (Isa. 7:14), "Mighty God" in the flesh (Isa. 9:5–6 [Eng., 9:6–7]; Jer. 23:5–6). This provides an explanation for the language of the piercing of the LORD in Zechariah 12:10 and the sudden shift in pronouns there from "me" to "him." Thus, the people of God will seek the LORD and David their king in the last days (Hos. 3:5). In apposition to the phrase "like God" is the phrase "like the angel of the LORD." The house of David will be like God, that is, it will be like the angel of the LORD before the people. Readers of the narratives about David know that he is said to be "like the angel of God" several times in those stories (1 Sam. 29:9 [> LXX]; 2 Sam. 14:17 [LXX^L: "angel of the Lord"], 20; 19:28). The Davidic Messiah will be God to the people as Moses was like God to Aaron (Exod. 4:16; 7:1). He will be a messenger from the LORD before the people—a prophet (cf., "messenger" in Hag. 1:13; Mal. 3:1), priest (cf., "messenger" in Mal. 2:7), and king, leading them in a new exodus (cf., "messenger/angel" in Exod. 23:20).

The LORD's discourse resumes in Zechariah 12:9 (see Zech. 12:1–6). He says that he will seek to destroy all the nations who come against Jerusalem in that eschatological day (cf., Zech. 2:12–13 [Eng., 2:8–9]; 14:2–3). The LORD will pour out on the house of David (i.e., the messianic king) and on the inhabitants of Jerusalem (i.e., the people of God) the Spirit who gives grace and who responds to the people's supplication (Zech. 12:10). The presence or absence of the article with the word "Spirit" in the Hebrew text is not the sole determining factor in deciding whether it is a reference to a spirit or to the Spirit. The language of the Spirit (not a spirit) being on the messianic king is also in Isaiah's prophecies (Isa. 11:2; 42:1; 61:1; cf., Matt. 3:16). Furthermore, the language of outpouring (שׁפך) is used elsewhere not for outpouring of a spirit but for outpouring of the Spirit (see Ezek. 39:29; Joel 3:1–2 [Eng., 2:28–29]; Acts 2:17–18; see also Num. 11:29; Isa. 32:1, 15; Zech. 4:6; Rom. 1:4; *T. Jud.* 24:3). The LORD's grace in this context is his act of self-sacrifice that makes provision for the people's sin through the suffering and death of his Spirit-anointed Son (see Zech. 13:1). This is coupled with the outpouring of his Spirit on all his people.

The LORD adds, "and they will look at me whom they pierced." There are at least two possibilities for the presence of the definite direct object marker (את) in the Hebrew text of this clause. One is that it marks the following relative clause as a comment on the pronoun "me" (cf.,

Hag. 2:5). The other is that the *aleph* and the *taw* represent the LORD as the beginning and the end because they are the first and last letters of the Hebrew alphabet (see Isa. 41:4; 44:6; 48:12; Amos 9:12 [LXXᴬ]; Acts 15:17; Rev. 1:8, 17; 2:8; 21:6; 22:13). Either way, the LORD is saying that the people of God will see him as the pierced one. The word translated "pierced" is also used for the piercing of the false prophet in Zechariah 13:3. How is it possible to pierce the LORD? The following shift in pronouns from "me" to "him" ("and they will mourn for him") indicates that this refers to the piercing of the messianic king who is God in the flesh (cf., Isa. 50:4–11; 52:13–53:12; Zech. 9:9; Dan. 9:24–27).[80]

John refers to Zechariah 12:10 in his account of the piercing of Jesus's side (John 19:37). The form of John's text does not match the Masoretic Text or the Septuagint. It is noteworthy that John combines his quotation of Zechariah 12:10 with a quote from Exodus 12:46; Numbers 9:12 (John 19:36; cf., Ps. 34:21 [Eng., Ps. 34:20]) since there is a possible allusion to Exodus 12:46 in Psalm 22:15, 18 (Eng., 22:14, 17)—a text that portrays the suffering of the servant of the LORD not unlike the servant songs of Isaiah (e.g., Isa. 53:5).[81] John 19:24 draws upon Psalm 22:18 (Eng., 22:17), and John 19:28 alludes to Psalm 22:15 (Eng., 22:14). Psalm 22 as a whole is one of the most important texts in the passion narratives of the Gospels (Matt. 27:46; Mark 15:34).[82]

---

80. "Jews and Christians understood Zech 12:10 to be messianic in the early history of interpretation. A marginal reading to the Targum of Zech 12:10 in Codex Reuchlinianus (A.D. 1105) belongs to a no longer extant Palestinian Targum of the Prophets and refers to the Messiah son of Ephraim rather than the son of Judah or David: 'And I will let rest upon the house of David and upon the inhabitants of Jerusalem the Spirit of prophecy and true prayer. Afterwards Messiah son of Ephraim will go out to wage war with Gog, and Gog will kill him before the gate of Jerusalem. And they will look at me and ask why the peoples pierced Messiah son of Ephraim, and they will mourn over him. . . .' It is difficult to date this interpretation, but the theory of two Messiahs—of Ephraim/Joseph and David—does appear elsewhere in rabbinic literature (see Ex 40:9–11 *Tg. Ps. Jon.*; *Tg. Song* 4:5; *b. Sukkah* 52a; *b. Sanh.* 98a; cf., *b. Pesah* 118a; *4 Ezra* 7:28–29), apparently in an effort to explain why the Messiah is a king in some passages but a suffering servant in others" (Shepherd, *The Twelve Prophets*, 60–61).
81. See Ps. 22:17b (Eng., 22:16) in the Septuagint (Ps. 21:17) and 5/6ḤevPs: "They have pierced my hands and feet."
82. Shepherd, *The Twelve Prophets*, 61. The suffering figure in these texts is an individual who acts on behalf of the people according to the reading of

John's version of the text essentially collapses the first-person pronoun into the third because Jesus the Christ has already been identified as God in the flesh (John 1:1, 14).[83] The true remnant of the people of God will genuinely mourn the suffering and death of the Christ as for the only son and show bitterness as for the firstborn (cf., Amos 8:10; Jer. 6:26; see also Gen. 22:2; Prov. 8:22; 30:4; John 1:14, 18; 3:16, 18; Col. 1:15, 18). Thus, when Zechariah 12:10 is cited in conjunction with Daniel 7:13 (the coming of the Son of Man) in the NT (Matt. 24:30; Rev. 1:7), the reference to those who will be mourning at the time of Christ's coming is not a reference to unbelievers who must face judgment (*contra* NT commentators).[84] It is a reference to those who, according to Matthew 9:15, will mourn the loss of Christ from the time he is taken away until the time that he returns. At the time of his coming, Christ will find his followers faithfully awaiting his return.

According to Zechariah 12:11, the mourning in that day will be great like the mourning of Hadad-Rimmon in the valley of Megiddo. The name "Hadad-Rimmon" is not the name of a god (see BDB, 213) or a king (*contra* Tg. Jon.) in this context. It is the name of a location in the valley of Megiddo where king Josiah was killed by Pharaoh Neco (see *Tg. Jon.*; see also 2 Kgs. 23:29–30; 2 Chr. 35:20–25; Rev. 16:16).[85] Josiah was the last righteous king of the line of David before the Babylonian captivity. He died prematurely at a relatively young age. He thus became a prototype for the messianic suffering servant who would die young but also reign as a righteous Davidic king.[86] His death was mourned by the prophet Jeremiah (2 Chr. 35:25). The solemnity of the mourning in the land for the messianic king is marked by the separation of families and the separation of wives (Zech. 12:12–14). Two main groups are designated here: (1) the royal line of David traced through his son Nathan (see 2 Sam. 5:14; Luke 3:23–31) and (2) the

---

the biblical authors. This is not the only reading from antiquity, but it is an exegetically defensible one. It is no less plausible than any other.

83. See also Wm. Randolph Bynum, *The Fourth Gospel and the Scriptures: Illuminating the Form and Meaning of Scriptural Citation in John 19:37*, Supplements to Novum Testamentum 144 (Leiden: Brill, 2012). John's citations serve his overall purpose of encouraging faith in the fact that the Christ from the Hebrew Scriptures is Jesus (John 20:30–31).

84. In any case, mourning would be a very strange response to the threat of judgment. Fear would be more appropriate. Contrast, e.g., *1 En.* 62:5.

85. See R. Joseph's comment in *b. Moed Qatan* 28b: "Were it not for the Aramaic translation of this verse, we would not know what it means."

86. See Horbury, *Jewish Messianism*, 21.

priestly line of Levi traced through Shimei (see Exod. 6:16–17; Num. 3:17–18). The rest are included in Zechariah 12:14.

ZECHARIAH 13

13:1 "In that day, a fountain will be opened for the house of David [LXX: every place (= מָקוֹם) will be opened in the house of David].[87]

13:2 And so, in that day," the prophetic utterance of the LORD of hosts, "I will cut off the names of the idols [lit., shapes] from the land, and they will never be remembered again. And also the prophets [LXX, Tg. Jon.: false prophets] and the spirit of uncleanness will I remove from the land. 13:3 And so, if someone prophesies again, and his father and his mother who bore him say to him, 'You will not live, for deception is what you have spoken in the name of the LORD,' then his father and his mother who bore him will pierce [LXX, Syr., Tg. Jon.: bind] him when he prophesies. 13:4 And so, in that day, the prophets will each be ashamed when he prophesies, and they will not [not > LXX] wear a hairy garment [Tg. Jon.: prophesy falsely] in order to deceive. 13:5 And he will say, 'Not a prophet am I. A man working ground am I, for a man, he caused me to be purchased [LXX: fathered me] from my youth [Vulg.: Adam has been my example from my youth].' 13:6 And he will say to him [or, it will be said to him], 'What are these wounds between your hands?' And he will say, 'These are the ones with which I was stricken in the house of my friends.'

13:7 O sword, wake up [Tg. Jon.: be revealed] against my shepherd [LXX: my shepherds (= רֹעַי); Tg. Jon.: the king] and against the man who is my associate [Tg. Jon.: the ruler, his companion who is like him, who resembles him]," the prophetic utterance of the LORD of hosts. "Strike the shepherd [LXX: shepherds] so that the sheep may be scattered, and I will cause my hand to turn against the little ones. 13:8 And so, in all the land," the prophetic utterance of the LORD, "a portion [lit., mouth] of two in it, they will be cut off, they will expire [mlt Mss: and they will expire].

---

87. The MT adds, "and for the inhabitants of Jerusalem for sin [Syr.: sprinkling] and for impurity." This text is not in the Old Greek. Codex Sinaiticus includes it but marks it with asterisks. See also *Tg. Jon.*: "At that time the instruction of the Torah will be revealed like a spring of water to the house of David and to the inhabitants of Jerusalem; and I will forgive their sins as purified by the water of sprinkling and by the ash of the cow of sin offering." Cf., Ps. 1; Eph. 5:26.

But as for the one-third, it will be left in it. 13:9 And I will bring the one-third through the fire, and I will refine them like refining silver and test them like testing gold. As for him, he will call on my name. And as for me, I will answer him. And I will say [see LXX, Syr.], 'My people is he.' And he, he will say, 'The LORD [> pc Mss] is my God.'"

The text of Zechariah 13:1 is separated from Zechariah 12:9–14 in the MT. There is a space at the end of Zechariah 12:14 and an indentation at the beginning of the next line. *BHS* marks this with ס (סתומא ["closed paragraph"]). But *BHS* also formats the text so that Zechariah 13:1 is read with Zechariah 12:9–14. The phrase "in that day" in Zechariah 13:1 occurs in Zechariah 12:9, 11 and in Zechariah 13:2, 4. The phrases "house of David" and "inhabitants of Jerusalem" in Zechariah 13:1 (the phrase "inhabitants of Jerusalem" is in the MT but not in the Old Greek) are in Zechariah 12:7, 8, 10, 12 but not in Zechariah 13:2–6. The content of Zechariah 13:1 seems to indicate what the death of the messianic king accomplishes (Zech. 12:10). On the other hand, the language of impurity in Zechariah 13:1b (if the MT is correct) may anticipate the spirit of uncleanness in Zechariah 13:2 (see Ezek. 36:17, 25). It seems best not to see a hard break between Zechariah 12:9–14 and Zechariah 13:1–6.

According to the MT of Zechariah 13:1a, there will be a "fountain" (מקור) opened for the house of David (i.e., the house represented by the Davidic Messiah) in the future. This speaks of spiritual provision for the members of the family of the house of David who genuinely mourn the death of the Messiah and place their faith in him, a provision made possible by the death itself (see Zech. 12:10, 12; see also Isa. 53:1, 5, 11). It is possible that this is a fountain of the life-giving, cleansing water of the Spirit (see Jer. 2:13; Ezek. 36:25–26; Ps. 36:10 [Eng., 36:9]; John 3:5; 4:14; 7:37–39), but the context suggests the atoning and cleansing blood of sacrifice (see Lev. 17:11; 1 John 1:7).[88] On the other hand, the LXX reads "place" (מקום) instead of the MT's "fountain" (מקור). Unless this reading is a mistake on the part of a scribe or the translator, it looks on the surface to be the more original one. If the text originally read "place," which is very general, why not change it to something more specific like "fountain"? If the text originally read "fountain," why change it to "place"? The word "place" could refer to the place (i.e.,

---

88. See Calvin, *Zechariah*, 374–75. See also the words of the William Cowper hymn, "There Is a Fountain": "There is a fountain filled with blood, Drawn from Immanuel's veins; And sinners plunged beneath that flood, Lose all their guilty stains."

land) that God said he would give to his people in the covenant with David (2 Sam. 7:10), but apart from the reference to the house of David in Zechariah 13:1, this would seem to have little to do with the context. Another possibility is that the place is the ceremonially clean place where the ashes of a sin offering would be deposited outside the camp, as in the case of the red heifer whose ashes were used for waters of impurity (i.e., purification waters; see Num. 19:9). If this understanding of the reading behind the LXX is correct, then it is easy to see why the change to "fountain" would have been made. It is also easy to see why the remainder of the verse in the MT ("and for the inhabitants of Jerusalem for sin and for impurity"), which is not in the Old Greek, would have been added. The text expands to include all the nations who will inhabit Jerusalem in the last days (Isa. 2:1–5; 66:18–24; Mic. 4:1–5; Zech. 8:20–23). The provision made by the death of the Messiah is not only for the house of David but also for all those in the kingdom. This expansion also makes explicit that the opened "place" (or, "fountain") is for sin and impurity (cf., Lev. 12:2; Num. 8:7; 19:9). That is, the death of the Messiah is the substitutionary sin offering that satisfies God in his righteous wrath, covers the sinner, cleanses the impurity, and makes way for forgiveness and reconciliation between God and man (see Lev. 4:27–31; 2 Cor. 5:21; Col. 1:22). Thus, while the MT of Zechariah 13:1 is likely not the original text, it is a very early and accurate interpretation of the original text represented by the LXX.[89]

The LORD envisions that he will cut off the names of the idols from the land in that same eschatological day, so that they will never be remembered or mentioned again (Zech. 13:2a). Idols had names associated with the local manifestations of the false gods that they represented (e.g., Baal of Peor [Num. 25]). The LORD will also remove the false prophets (see LXX, *Tg. Jon.*) and the spirit of uncleanness from the land (Zech. 13:2b). The false prophets are the ones who prophesy by Baal (Jer. 2:8b; see also Deut. 18:20–22; Jer. 23:9–40; Ezek. 13; 1 John 4). The spirit of uncleanness in this context is the spirit of idolatry (see Ezek. 22:3). It is in contrast to the Spirit of grace and supplication in Zechariah 12:10. If someone does try to prophesy falsely again in the LORD's name, that person's parents will be the ones to confront him

---

89. The LXX itself is not entirely free of corruption. The addition of the word "every" seems to come from the translator rather than the Hebrew *Vorlage*. This addition does not reflect a very good understanding of the context of the original on the part of the translator. Nevertheless, it is the translator's source text that is of value here.

and execute him (Zech. 13:3). This is in accordance with the instruction given in Deuteronomy 13:2–12.

In that day, the false prophets will be ashamed of their fake prophetic visions (Zech. 13:4a; cf., Mic. 3:7). According to the MT, they will not wear a hairy garment in order to deceive their audience by pretending to be prophets like Elijah (see 2 Kgs. 1:8). The LXX, however, does not have the negation. It says that they will wear a hairy garment. The sense of this reading seems to be as follows: because the false prophets have lied and been exposed for it, they now must disguise themselves as Elijah-like prophets in order to continue their charade. Either way, they will no longer claim to be prophets themselves, simply in the interest of self-preservation (Zech. 13:5a). Rather, they will claim to have been purchased workers of the ground ever since their youth (Zech. 13:5b). This is not the same as Amos' denial in Amos 7:14. Amos was a true prophet. He denied being a professional prophet for hire. Therefore, he said that he made his living through another occupation. The Latin Vulgate's translation of Zechariah 13:5b2 says, "Adam has been my example from my youth." This rendering is based on reading אָדָם ("a man") as a name ("Adam"). It refers to the consequences of the fall for Adam and his offspring (Gen. 3:17–19; 9:20). When someone asks about the wounds on the chest of one of these false prophets claiming to be lifelong workers of the ground, he will say that he received them in the house of his friends (Zech. 13:6). But in reality, the wounds are from the pagan practices of the false prophets (see 1 Kgs. 18:28).

Christian commentators have historically followed the lead of Matthew 26:31 and Mark 14:27 and interpreted the shepherd in Zechariah 13:7 to be the good shepherd from Zechariah 11:4–14 (e.g., the church fathers [ACCS], Calvin, C. F. Keil, etc.). More recent commentators have favored traditional Jewish commentary (e.g., *Tg. Jon.*, Rashi) in seeing a reference to the foolish shepherd of Zechariah 11:15–17 here. In favor of the latter interpretation, the LORD refers to the foolish shepherd in Zechariah 11:17 as "my shepherd" just as he does the shepherd in the MT of Zechariah 13:7.[90] Furthermore, the LORD says that a sword will be against the foolish shepherd in Zechariah 11:17 just as he commands one to be against the shepherd in Zechariah 13:7. Thus, it is possible that the foolish shepherd is "my shepherd" to the LORD just as Cyrus (Isa. 44:28 [cf., LXX]) and just

---

90. The LXX reads the same consonantal Hebrew text as the plural ("my shepherds"). It is also possible to revocalize the same consonants to read "my friend" (רֵעִי) or "my friends" (רֵעַי) (see LXX Isa. 44:28), which would make a nice parallel with "the man who is my associate."

as Nebuchadnezzar can be "my servant" to him (Jer. 25:9; 27:6 [cf., LXX]). On the other hand, there is nothing necessary about this interpretation, and the reading of the text reflected in the NT is at least equally plausible. The parallel to "my shepherd" in Zechariah 13:7 is "the man who is my associate." The word translated "associate" only appears elsewhere in the Bible in Leviticus (Lev. 5:21; 18:20; 19:11, 15, 17; 24:19; 25:14, 15, 17). It refers to a fellow citizen without any negative connotation. Moreover, it is an essential part of the revealed divine plan to have the Messiah suffer and die to make provision for the sin of the people (see Gen. 3:15; Isa. 50:4–11; 52:13–53:12; Zech. 12:10; Ps. 22; Dan. 9:24–27).

The command to strike the shepherd in the MT of Zechariah 13:7b is a first-person singular verb in some LXX manuscripts and in Matthew 26:31; Mark 14:27 ("I will strike"). The LORD will work through the agency of others to accomplish his purposes. The flock will scatter because of the striking of the shepherd (cf., 1 Kgs. 22:17; Ezek. 34:5; Matt. 9:36; see also Num. 27:17; Zech. 10:2), and the LORD will "turn his hand against" (cf., Isa. 1:25; Amos 1:8; Ps. 81:15 [Eng., 81:14]) the "little ones" of the flock (i.e., the followers/disciples; see CD-B 19:7–11; Matt. 10:42; 18:6, 10, 14; Mark 9:42). In all the land, only a remnant (one third) of true followers will remain in the wake of the persecution following the death of the shepherd (Zech. 13:8; cf., Isa. 6:13; 10:22). The rest (two thirds) will be cut off (cf., Ezek. 5:1–4). Not only is the contrary hand of the LORD necessary to determine who the genuine disciples are, but also, he will refine the faithful remnant in fire like silver and test them like gold (Zech. 13:9a; cf., Isa. 43:2; 48:9–11; Mal. 3:2–3; Prov. 17:3). As a result, the remnant will call on the name of the LORD in faith (cf., Joel 3:5 [Eng., 2:32]), and he will answer them (Zech. 13:9b; cf., Jer. 33:3; Zech. 10:6). The LORD will say that this remnant is truly his people, and they will affirm that the LORD is their God (cf., Deut. 6:4; Jer. 31:33; Zech. 8:8; 14:9). This hearkens back to Hosea 2:25 (Eng., 2:23): "And I will say to Lo Ammi [not my people], 'You are my people.'"

ZECHARIAH 14

14:1 Look, a day is coming of the LORD [LXX: days are coming of the Lord; Syr.: the day of the Lord is coming], and your plunder will be divided in your midst [Tg. Jon.: the house of Israel will divide the possessions of the peoples in your midst, O Jerusalem]. 14:2 And I will gather all the nations to Jerusalem for the battle, and the city will be captured, and the houses will be plundered; and the women, they will be ravished [qere: will be lain (see BDB, 993)]. And half of the city will go out in the exile, and the rest of the people will not be cut off from the city. 14:3 And the LORD will go forth and fight against those nations like the day of his fighting in a day of war [Tg. Jon. adds: at the Sea of Reeds]. 14:4 And his feet will stand [Tg. Jon.: he will reveal himself in his might] in that day on the Mount of Olives, which is opposite Jerusalem eastward. And the Mount of Olives will be split from its middle eastward and westward into a very great valley [see GKC §93v, 121d, 128w¹], and half of the mountain will move northward, and half of it southward. 14:5 And you will flee through the valley of my moun- tains [pc Mss, LXX, Tg. Jon.: the valley of my (Tg. Jon.: the) mountains will be stopped up], for a valley of mountains will reach to Azal. And you will flee just as you fled from before the quake in the days of Uzziah the king of Judah. And the LORD my God [pc Mss: God; Ms: God of Israel] will come, all [mlt Mss, LXX, Syr., Tg. Jon.ᴹˢˢ, Vulg.: and all] holy ones with you [mlt Mss, Vrs: with him]. 14:6 And so, in that day, there will not be light. As for precious light sources, they will congeal [see BDB, 891].⁹¹ 14:7 And it will happen one day, it is known to the LORD, there will be no day and no night [cf., English versions]. And so, at evening time, there will be light. 14:8 And so, in that day, living water [or, running / fresh water] will go forth from Jerusalem, half of them to the eastern sea, and half of them to the western sea. In the summer and in the winter will it be. 14:9 And the LORD will become king over all the land. In that day, the LORD will be one, and his name one. 14:10 All the land will change [lit., turn; see BDB, 685] like the Arabah [or, desert plain] from Geba to Rimmon, south of Jerusalem. And it will rise up and dwell in its place from the Gate of Benjamin to the place of the First Gate to the Gate of the Corners and the Tower of Hananel [mlt Mss, Syr., Vulg.: from the Tower of Hananel] to the wine vats of the king. 14:11 And they will dwell in it; and as for divine devotion to destruction [LXX: anathema], it will never be again. And Jerusalem will dwell in security. 14:12 And this is what the plague will be with which the LORD will strike all the peoples who wage war against Jerusalem: causing each one's flesh to rot while he is standing on his feet; and as for each one's eyes, they will rot in their sockets; and as for each one's tongue, it will rot in their mouth. 14:13 And so, in that day, there will be great confusion from the LORD among them, and they will each grab the hand of his neighbor, and each one's hand will go up against the hand of his neighbor. 14:14 And also Judah will

---

91. LXX: "In that day, there will not be light and cold and frost." See *BHS* apparatus.

fight in Jerusalem, and the wealth of all the nations around will be gathered, gold and silver and clothes in very great abundance. 14:15 And thus will be the plague of the horse, the mule, the camel, and the donkey, and every animal that will be in those camps according to this plague. 14:16 And so, every one who is left from all the nations who come against Jerusalem, they will go up from year to year to prostrate themselves to a king, the LORD of hosts, and to celebrate the Feast of Tabernacles. 14:17 And so, whoever does not go up from the families of the earth to Jerusalem to prostrate themselves to a king, the LORD of hosts, not upon them will the rain be [LXX: and these will be added to those]. 14:18 And if the family of Egypt in particular does not go up and does not enter, not on them will it be [Tg. Jon.: the Nile will not come up for them].[92] The plague with which the LORD will strike the nations who do not go up to celebrate the Feast of Tabernacles will occur. 14:19 This is what the punishment for the sin of Egypt will be, and that of all the nations who do not go up to celebrate the Feast of Tabernacles. 14:20 In that day, there will be upon [pc Mss: all] the bells [LXX, Syr.: bridle; Tg. Jon.: plume] of the horses "Holiness to the LORD." And so, the pots in the house of the LORD will be like the bowls before the altar. 14:21 And so, every pot in Jerusalem and in Judah will be holiness to the LORD of hosts. And those who sacrifice will come and take from them and boil in them. And there will never again be a merchant [see Tg. Jon., Vulg.; see also LXX, Syr., Luther: Canaanite] in the house of the LORD of hosts in that day.

Zechariah 14 revisits the scene of the final eschatological battle from chapter 12 (cf., Gen. 49:11–12; Isa. 53:12; 63:1–6; Ezek. 38–39; Dan. 7:21; Rev. 16:12–16; 19:11–21; 20:7–10). Several key similarities between these two chapters will be noted in the following commentary, but there are also some important complementary differences. For instance, in chapter 12, the focus seems to be on the people of God fighting and defending themselves against the enemy nations (e.g., Zech. 12:5–6; cf., Zech. 10:5–12). In chapter 14, on the other hand, the text highlights the reality that the LORD is the one who fights for the people against the nations (e.g., Zech. 14:3; cf., Isa. 59:17). In chapter 12, the nations surround the city of Jerusalem and come against it (Zech. 12:3b, 9). But in chapter 14, the LORD is the one who brings the nations to the city for battle (Zech. 14:2; cf., Joel 4:2 [Eng., 3:2]; Luke 21:20). In chapter 12, there is no indication that the nations make any

---

92. Several witnesses (pc Mss, LXX, Syr.) read the phrase "on them" without the prior negation ("not") and with what follows: "on them will the plague be."

headway into the city of Jerusalem. In chapter 14, however, it is clear that they do capture and plunder the city before the LORD rescues it (Zech. 14:2). Finally, chapter 12 does not mention the inclusion of non-enemy nations, but chapter 14 fills this gap in accordance with what the rest of the book envisions for believing Gentiles (Zech. 14:16–19; cf., Zech. 2:15 [Eng., 2:11]; 8:20–23).

Chapter 14 sets the final battle firmly within the context of the Day of the LORD (Zech. 14:1), a theme that has been developed throughout the Twelve (see Joel 1:15; 2:1, 11; 3:4 [Eng., 2:31]; 4:14 [Eng., 3:14]; Amos 5:18; Obad. 15; Zeph. 1:7, 14; Mal. 3:23 [Eng., 4:5]). The plunder of the city of Jerusalem will be divided in its midst (note the second feminine singular pronominal suffixes). *Targum Jonathan* tries to turn this into Israel dividing the possessions of the peoples in the midst of Jerusalem, but it is evident from Zechariah 14:2 that the nations will plunder Jerusalem first (cf., Zech. 2:12–13 [Eng., 2:8–9]). The text slips rather easily from third-person reference to the LORD in Zechariah 14:1 to first-person discourse from the LORD in Zechariah 14:2 and back to third-person reference in Zechariah 14:3 and for the remainder of the chapter. The LORD himself states in Zechariah 14:2 that he will be the one to gather all the nations to Jerusalem for the battle (cf., Joel 4 [Eng., 3]). The city will in fact be captured. The houses will be plundered, and the women will be ravished (see Deut. 28:30). Half of the city's population will go into exile, and half will be left—a situation reminiscent of the Babylonian invasion (see 2 Kgs. 25:11–12). But then "the LORD will go forth and fight against those nations like the day of his fighting in a day of war" (Zech. 14:3; cf., Zech. 10:5, 12). *Targum Jonathan* understands this to be a comparison to the way the LORD fought for his people at the Sea of Reeds in the original exodus (see Exod. 14:14, 25; 15:3; 17:16; Josh. 10:42; 1 Sam. 17:47; Neh. 4:14 [Eng., 4:20]; see also Zech. 14:10–11).

In that day, the LORD's feet will stand on the Mount of Olives east of Jerusalem (Zech. 14:4; cf., Acts 1:11–12). The mountain will be split in two from east to west, forming a very great valley (cf., Exod. 14:21–22). Half of the mountain will move northward, and the other half southward. According to the Leningrad Codex, the people will flee (וְנַסְתֶּם ["And you will flee]) through the valley of mountains created by the LORD, a valley that will reach to a place called Azal (Zech. 14:5; cf., Zech. 6:1; Matt. 24:16). They will flee as they did before the earthquake in the days of Uzziah (see Amos 1:1; see also Judg. 5:4–5; Ps. 68:8–9 [Eng., 68:7–8]). But according to the LXX, the valley will be "stopped up" (= וְנִסְתַּם) as in the former days. *Targum Jonathan* forms a compromise between the two different vocalizations of the Hebrew text: the valley will be stopped up (presumably to block any pursuers), and the people will flee as in the days of Uzziah. The text of Zechariah 14:5b then appears to allude to Deuteronomy 33:2–3 (see also Hab. 3:3; Jude 14). The LORD came from Sinai, from holy myriads, and all his holy ones are in "your" hand (Deut. 33:2–3; see also Deut. 33:4; Ezra 7:14; Acts 7:53; Gal. 3:19; Heb. 2:2). These "holy ones" are angels (see LXX Deut. 33:2b; see also Dan. 7:9–10; Matt. 16:27; 24:31; 25:31; 1 Thess. 3:13; 4:17; 2 Thess. 1:7; Rev. 19:14), not saints (as in Dan. 7:18, 21, 27). The LORD will come again as he once did from Sinai, and all the angels will be with "you" (i.e., the people of the city of Jerusalem; mlt Mss, Vrs: "with him"). That is, they will be on the side of the people of God.

The reader is then faced with several possibilities for interpretation of Zechariah 14:6–7. One option is to see the imagery of Joshua 10:12–13 (see Sir. 46:4; *T. Naph.* 5:1). The precious luminaries of the sky (i.e., the sun and the moon [cf., Job 31:26]) appear to stand still to allow time for the people of God to defeat their enemies (see Josh. 10:9, 27; Hab. 3:11). Another possibility is that that Zech. 14:6–7 speaks of a reversal of the created order (Gen. 1:5) and the absence of light in the Day of the LORD (e.g., Joel 2:2; Amos 5:18; see also *b. Pesah.* 50a). But a third possibility has even stronger inner-biblical connections:

> The vision of the new creation in Isaiah 60:19–20 is that of one where there is no need for the sun or the moon because the glory of YHWH (Isa. 60:1–3) will be an everlasting source of light. The book of Revelation picks up this image in its description of the new Jerusalem (Rev. 21:23). But Revelation 22:5 adds the thought that there will be no night. This likely derives from Zechariah 14:6–7. John sees a relationship between Isaiah 60:19–20 and Zechariah 14:6–7 that forms a complete picture for him. IIe does not seem to understand Zechariah 14:6–7 to mean that day becomes night and night becomes day, in a reversal of the norm due to divine judgment. Rather, the normal light sources congeal precisely because they are no longer needed. There is no day or night (or evening) because there is only the light of God's glory (cf., Isa. 24:21–23; 30:26).[93]

Thus, Zechariah 14:6 does not speak of the absence of light. Rather, it indicates that there will be no need for the usual light sources due to the presence of God's glory (see also Isa. 9:1 [Eng., 9:2]; Mic. 7:8–9; Mal. 3:20 [Eng., 4:2]). In one day known only to the

---

93. Shepherd, *Text in the Middle*, 143.

LORD (Zech. 14:7; cf., Isa. 66:8; Acts 1:7),[94] there will be no daytime and nighttime in the ordinary sense (*contra* ESV, et al.). Even at evening time, there will be light.

In that day, water will go forth from Jerusalem (Zech. 14:8). The term "living water" is likely used in a dual sense in this context. It is the fresh water reminiscent of the original Garden of Eden (see Gen. 2:10–14), but it is also the spiritual life-giving water of Christ (Jer. 2:13; Zech. 13:1; Ps. 36:10 [Eng., 36:9]; John 4:7–15; 7:37–39). This water will run both to the Dead Sea and to the Mediterranean Sea. Since present-day Jerusalem has no such water source, it is understood that this is a feature of the new Jerusalem (see Isa. 65:18; 66:12; Ezek. 47:8–12; Ps. 46:5 [Eng., 46:4]; Rev. 22:1). It will last forever through summer and winter (cf., Gen. 8:22). "And the LORD will become king over all the land" (Zech. 14:9a; cf., 1 Sam. 8:7). The Davidic Messiah, God in the flesh (Isa. 7:14; 9:5–6 [Eng., 9:6–7]; 10:21]; Jer. 23:5–6), will reign as king (see Zeph. 3:14–15; Zech. 2:14 [Eng., 2:10]; 9:9–10; 12:10; 14:16). The LORD will be one, and his name will be one (Zech. 14:9b; cf., Mal. 2:10). This is an allusion to the *Shema* (Deut. 6:4): "Hear, O Israel, the LORD our God, the LORD is one." In context, this means the people are not to go after "other gods" (Deut. 6:12–15). They also are not to credit Yahweh's blessings to other gods (see Hos. 2:18 [Eng., 2:16]). They are to call on his name, and he will answer them; they will be his people, and he (Yahweh) will be their one true God (Zech. 13:9; see also Rom. 3:29–30; *b. Pesaḥ.* 50a).

Verse 10 describes the change to the land of the covenant from north to south in the last days. It highlights the new Jerusalem from east to west and from north to south (cf., Jer. 31:38–40). The land will rise up at that time in the sense that Mount Zion will be the most prominent of all the mountains to which the nations will come (see Isa. 2:1–5; Mic. 4:1–5). The people of God will live in it (Zech. 14:11; cf., Zech. 12:6), and never again will they or the land be devoted to destruction (cf., Isa. 43:28; Mal. 3:24 [Eng., 4:6]). The city of Jerusalem will dwell in security (cf., Jer. 23:6; Ezek. 34:25, 27; Hos. 2:20 [Eng., 2:18]). Indeed, everything in the land of Judah and Jerusalem will be set apart to the LORD (Zech. 14:20–21).

The LORD will strike all the peoples who fight against Jerusalem with a plague (Zech. 14:12; see Zech. 12:2–6, 9; 14:1–3). The covenant curses will now be against the enemies of God's people (see Deut.

---

94. The phrase "one day" refers to the beginning of the eternal state. It is "unique" (ESV) in contrast to what precedes it, but it is common to what follows it.

28:21–22; see also Exod. 7–12; Rev. 16). There will be great confusion from the LORD among the enemy nations in that day (Zech. 14:13; cf., Exod. 14:24), and they will fight against one another (cf., Judg. 7:22; 1 Sam. 14:20; Hag. 2:22; Zech. 11:6). This does not mean, however, that Judah will fight against Jerusalem (Zech. 14:14a; cf., Exod. 17:8; Judg. 1:8). Judah will fight in Jerusalem against those who attack the city (see Zech. 12:2). It is true that the nations will initially plunder the city (Zech. 14:1–2), but in the end the people of God will gather the wealth of all the surrounding nations—"gold and silver and clothes in very great abundance"—just as they did in the exodus from Egypt (Zech. 14:14b; see Exod. 11:2; 12:35; Hag. 2:8; Ezra 1:6). And the same plague that will be against the humans—rotting flesh, eyes, and tongue (Zech. 14:12)—will also be against the animals of the enemy armies (Zech. 14:15; cf., Exod. 9:3; Zech. 12:4).

Verse 16 anticipates along with the rest of the book of Zechariah, the Book of the Twelve, and the Prophets generally that there will be a believing remnant from the nations that will join the believing remnant of Israel (see Isa. 2:1–5; 66:18–24; Jer. 3:14–18; Amos 9:12; Mic. 4:1–5; Zech. 2:15 [Eng., 2:11]; 8:20–23; 9:7). They will go up to Jerusalem annually to worship the LORD as their king (cf., Zech. 14:9; Mal. 1:14) and to celebrate the Feast of Tabernacles (cf., Isa. 66:23). But why the Feast of Tabernacles? It is perhaps because of the connection to the exodus imagery in Zechariah 14:14b (see Lev. 23:42–43), but the reader might expect the Passover festival for such a connection. It could also be a way to show that the nations will be like natives of Israel (Lev. 23:42). Biblical depictions of the Feast of Tabernacles in the postexilic period highlight its role in expressions of worship that respond to key events in the life of the people of God. Thus, the people celebrate the Feast of Tabernacles in conjunction with the establishment of the new altar and the laying of the Second Temple foundation in Ezra 3. They also celebrate the Feast in response to Ezra's reading of the Torah in Nehemiah 8 (cf., Deut. 31:9–13). Whoever does not go up to Jerusalem from "the families of the earth" (cf., Gen. 12:3) to worship the LORD as king will not have any rain in accordance with the covenant curse of Deut. 28:23 (Zech. 14:17). This is not to say that worship will be forced in the last days. It is only to say that there will be consequences for those who choose not to take part in the kingdom (cf., Isa. 50:11; 66:24). Feigned allegiance will not suffice in the end (see Deut. 33:29b; Dan. 12:2b).

Verses 18 and 19 focus on Egypt in particular (cf., Isa. 19). This is in part due to the exodus imagery in Zech. 14:14b (Exod. 12:35) and the plague language of Zechariah 14:15 (see Exod. 9:3; 11:1). But these verses are also in response to a question that would naturally arise from the threat of a lack of rain in Zechariah 14:17. Egypt depends more upon the Nile than upon rainfall for its water, so how would the lack of rain be a punishment for Egypt's sin? *Targum Jonathan* interprets the clause, "not upon them will it be," at the end of Zechariah 14:18a to mean, "the Nile will not water them." Thus, while the clause seems to parallel Zechariah 14:17b ("not upon them will the rain be"), it does not actually have the word "rain" in it, leaving open the possibility of the Targum's interpretation. Other textual witnesses (pc Mss, LXX, Syr.) do not have the negation here, and they read the phrase "upon them" with what follows: "upon them will the plague be." It is uncertain, however, whether this resolves anything. The plague in this context is likely not the plague of Zechariah 14:12, 15, which is prior to the nations coming up to Jerusalem to worship the LORD (Zech. 14:16). The plague here is the lack of rainfall. Therefore, this latter reading either understands the lack of rainfall to affect Egypt indirectly or it understands the plague to be more general (lack of water). Either way, drought is the punishment for the sin of those from Egypt or from any other nation who do not go up to celebrate the Feast of Tabernacles (Zech. 14:19).

The final two verses of the book of Zechariah begin by indicating that the horses will be marked as set apart to the LORD in the last days (Zech. 14:20a; cf., Exod. 28:36; Lev. 27:9; Jer. 31:40). These horses will no longer be needed for battle (see Zech. 9:10; 12:4; 14:15). Furthermore, the pots used for common purposes in the temple will now be as sacred as the bowls used before the altar (Zech. 14:20b; see Exod. 27:3; 38:3; 1 Kgs. 7:40; Zech. 9:15). Indeed, every pot in Jerusalem and in Judah will be set apart to the LORD (Zech. 14:21a). This is a way of saying that there will be nothing profane in the land. All those who come to sacrifice (i.e., those who come to worship) will take from such pots and boil in them (see Deut. 16:7; 1 Sam. 2:13; Ezek. 46:20, 24; 2 Chr. 35:13). Here Zechariah's priestly background comes into the foreground (see Zech. 1:1; Neh. 12:16; cf., Jer. 1:1; Ezek. 1:3). In the last days, every person will be a priest (see Exod. 19:6; Isa. 61:6; 66:21; 1 Pet. 2:5, 9; Rev. 1:6; 5:10; 20:6) and every place will be the temple (see Ezek. 40–48; Hag. 2:6–9; Rev. 21:22; see also Calvin). The final clause in Zechariah 14:21b can then be read in one of two ways. One way is to say that no Canaanite will ever be in the temple again. This obviously would not mean that no one from the nations will be allowed in the kingdom (see Zech. 2:15 [Eng., 2:1]; 8:20–23; 9:7; 14:16). It is possible, however, that it would mean that no Canaanite in a religious sense (i.e., no idol worshiper) will be allowed (see, e.g.,

Deut. 7:1–6; Ezek. 16:3). The other option is to interpret the word "Canaanite" to mean "merchant" or "trader" (see Isa. 23:8, 18; Job 40:30; *b. Pesah.* 50a). There will be no commerce in violation of the Sabbath (see Jer. 17:19–27; Neh. 13:15–18; see also Isa. 56:7; Jer. 7:11; Matt. 21:12–13; Mark 11:15–17; Luke 19:45–46; John 2:13–22). Each and every day will be the long-awaited Sabbath rest (see Gen. 2:3, 15 [*Tg. Neof.*]; Heb. 4:9).

TEACHING AND PREACHING ZECHARIAH

The eschatology and messianism of the book of Zechariah may be more evident to the average Christian reader due to the way the book is cited in the Gospels and in the book of Revelation, although modern historical-critical scholarship has done its best to try to strip the book of any genuine continuity with the NT documents. It is important to recognize, however, that Zechariah is not unique among the Twelve in this regard. Each of the books of the Twelve contribute to the overall eschatological and messianic program of the composition (Hos. 3:5). The book of Zechariah is not a manual for living. This is not to say that the book is irrelevant for the Christian life (see 2 Pet. 3). It is only to say that the book is not so blunt and boorish as to publish mere lists of instructions. It is instead a grand vision of Christ and his kingdom. After all, the goal of reading Scripture is to see Christ, to treasure Christ, and to become more like Christ (see Pss. 1–2; 18–19; 118–119; John 5:39–40, 46–47; Eph. 4:11–13; see also Luke 10:38–42). It is the task of the teacher and the preacher to uphold this vision so that those who hear can also learn to proclaim Christ and be prepared to reign with him in his kingdom (Dan. 7:13–14, 18, 27; Luke 24:25–27, 44–49).

BOOK OF THE TWELVE

MALACHI

MALACHI 1:1–5

1:1 The oracle of the word of the LORD to Israel by the hand of my messenger [LXX: his messenger; or, Malachi; LXX adds: put then upon your hearts (cf., Hag. 2:15, 18; Mal. 2:2)].[1]

1:2 "I chose you," says the LORD. "And you say, 'In what way did you choose us?' Was it not a brother that Esau was to Jacob?" the prophetic utterance of the LORD. "And I chose Jacob, 1:3 and it was Esau that I rejected. And I made his mountains a desolation and gave his inheritance to wild jackals [LXX, Syr.: as wilderness dwellings]. 1:4 For [or, If] Edom says, 'We are beaten down, but we will return and build ruins [i.e., we will again build ruins into habitable places].'" Thus says the LORD of hosts, "They, on the one hand, will build, but I, on the other hand, will tear down. And they will be called a border of wickedness and the people with whom the LORD is indignant indefinitely. 1:5 And your eyes, they will see. And as for you, you will say, 'Great is the LORD [or, May the LORD be great] from upon [i.e., above or beyond] the border of Israel [Tg. Jon.: May the glory of the LORD who broadens the border of Israel be great].'"

The superscription in Malachi 1:1 includes the heading, "The oracle of the word of the LORD," which is found elsewhere only in Zechariah 9:1 and 12:1. Thus, the "book" of Malachi is a third section to Zechariah

---

1. The Targum as it appears in Rabbinic Bibles adds, "whose name was Ezra the Scribe." See also *b. B. Bat.* 15a.

9–11 and Zechariah 12–14, and yet it is also numbered among the "Twelve" (e.g., Sir. 49:10).[2] The book's unique combination of six disputations (Mal. 1:2–5; 1:6–2:9; 2:10–16; 2:17–3:5; 3:6–12; 3:13–21 [Eng., 3:13–4:3]) gives Malachi its own integrity. Nevertheless, it is now an integral part of a much larger composition. Much like Zechariah 12–14, this oracle in the book of Malachi is "to Israel" (cf., Zech. 12:1, "concerning Israel"). The oracle comes by means of "my messenger" (LXX: "his messenger"; cf., Hag. 1:13; Mal. 3:1; 2 Chr. 36:15–16). The Targum understands this prophetic messenger to be "Ezra the Scribe" either because of points of contact between the content of Malachi and that of Ezra-Nehemiah (e.g., Mal. 2:10–16; Ezra 9–10; Neh. 13:23–27) or because of the tradition about the role of Ezra and the Men of the Great Assembly in the composition of the Book of the Twelve (b. B. Bat. 15a). Later translations such as the Latin Vulgate, Luther's German translation, and most modern English versions interpret "Malachi" to be the name of the prophet. The earlier pseudepigraphal book *Lives of the Prophets* says that Malachi was named for his piety, mildness, and fair appearance. It also claims that his prophecy was repeated on the same day by an angel (i.e., a messenger).

The opening section in Malachi 1:2–5 is an exegesis of Genesis 25:23, 28. The individuals Jacob and Esau represent the nations Israel and Edom who come from them (cf., Hos. 12). The terms אהב and שנא in this context are not emotionally charged words ("love" and "hate"). Rather, they are covenant terminology designed to indicate the election of one and the rejection of another (cf., Deut. 7:7–11; Ps. 78:67–68; 1QS 1:3–4).[3] Just as Abram was chosen (Neh. 9:7), and Isaac after him (Gen. 21:12; 25:11), so the line of blessing continued through Jacob rather than Esau (Gen. 27; 35).[4] This theme of divine election versus birthright is a prominent one in Genesis (Abel and Cain, Isaac and Ishmael, Jacob and Esau, Perez and Zerah, Ephraim and Manasseh). The following is an excerpt from the present author's book, *The Twelve Prophets in the New Testament*:

---

2. See John M. P. Smith, *A Critical and Exegetical Commentary on the Book of Malachi*, ICC (New York: Charles Scribner's Sons, 1912), 4; Ralph L. Smith, *Micah–Malachi*, WBC 32 (Nashville: Thomas Nelson, 1984), 296–97. There is no witness to such a thing as the Book of the Eleven.

3. See R. Smith, *Micah–Malachi*, 305; Michael B. Shepherd, *Textuality and the Bible* (Eugene, OR: Pickwick, 2016), 94–102.

4. Nevertheless, things do turn out well for Esau (Gen. 33 and 36). There will be a remnant of believers from Edom in the kingdom of God (Amos 9:12; Obad. 19–21).

Malachi consists of six formulaic disputations each with a statement from the LORD, a question from the people, and then a response from the LORD (Mal 1:2–5; 1:6–2:9; 2:10–16; 2:17–3:5; 3:6–12; 3:13–21). These units address specific problems in the post-exilic period: God's love, the priesthood, the broken covenant, confusion of good and evil, robbing God, and the futility of serving God. The final section of the book (Mal 3:22–24 [Eng., 4:4–6]) relates more to the overall composition and eschatology of the Twelve.

The first disputation begins with the assertion from the LORD that he has loved the people (Mal 1:2; cf., Hos 9:15; 14:5 [Eng., 14:4]). There had been concern during the exilic period that the LORD had abandoned the people (Isa 40:27), but the LORD gave assurance that those who would wait on him would find strength (Isa 40:28–31). His word would not fail (Isa 40:6–8; 55:10–11). The question from the people in Mal 1:2 reflects the renewed concern of the post-exilic community: "How have you loved us?" The post-exilic period had failed to produce the kind of grandeur envisioned by Second Isaiah (Isa 40–55). According to the post-exilic perspective of Third Isaiah (Isa 56–66), this meant that the fulfillment of those prophecies was yet to come in the future.

The LORD assures the people of his love for them with a reference to his love of Jacob and hatred of Esau (Mal 1:2–3). This is first of all a reference to the two sons of Isaac in Gen 25:19–36:43. The LORD passed over the firstborn Esau in favor of Jacob—a very prevalent theme in Genesis (Cain and Abel, Ishmael and Isaac, Esau and Jacob, Zerah and Perez, Manasseh and Ephraim). This apparently did not mean that Esau would be without at least some measure of blessing (Gen 27:38–39; 33:9). The statement in Mal 1:2–3 also has corporate implications. The nation of Jacob/Israel is the object and means of God's blessing (Gen 12:1–3; 28:10–22), but the nation of Esau/Edom is the object of judgment (Num 24:18; 2 Sam 8:14; Obad 1–14). Yet there is also the possibility for inclusion of Edomites in God's kingdom (Amos 9:12; Obad 19).

Paul addresses a very similar concern about God's love for his people in Romans 9–11. Israel according to the flesh had largely rejected their Messiah in Paul's day, but that did not mean the word of God had failed (Rom 9:6). Paul makes an important contrast between the children of the flesh and the children of the promise (Rom 9:7–9; cf., Rom 4:11, 16) and points out that God's election, not birthright, is first and foremost (Rom 9:10–12). The prime example of this is the choice of Jacob over Esau (Rom 9:13). This does not make God unjust (Rom 9:14). It only elevates his mercy and grace (Rom 9:15, 19–23). There is no reason to create a false dichotomy here between individual and corporate election. Both are in view (Rom 9:16–18). God preserves the believing remnant of Israel (Rom 11:1–10) while he brings in the Gentiles (Rom 11:11–24). In the end the true Jewish-Gentile people of God will be saved (Rom 11:25–32).[5]

Thus, the opening verses of Malachi highlight God's faithfulness in spite of Israel's lack thereof. The old covenant is broken, and it is not the intent of the prophet to return to that covenant. Rather, the presentation of the LORD's rebuke of the postexilic community's continued failure to live up to the standards of that covenant points to the need for a new covenant relationship based on divine faithfulness rather than human fidelity. This sets up the hope for the future in the final verses of the book (Mal. 3:22–24 [Eng., 4:4–6]).[6]

The LORD notes that he made Edom's mountains a desolation and gave his inheritance to wild jackals (Mal. 1:3b; see Isa. 34:5–6, 13; Jer. 49:13, 17, 18; Amos 1:11–12; Obad. 18).[7] This is given as an indication that the LORD has been faithful to vindicate Israel against its enemies (see also Isa. 63:1–6 [cf., Gen. 49:8–12; Rev. 14:17–20; 19:11–16]). Even if Edom were to defy the LORD and attempt to rebuild, the LORD would tear down whatever they build (Mal. 1:4a; cf., Jer. 49:16; Obad. 4). Insofar as Edom represents the enemies of God's people, its land will be called a border characterized by wickedness, the people with whom the LORD is forever indignant (Mal. 1:4b). The true remnant of God's people will see this and acknowledge that the LORD is in fact great above and beyond Israel's border (Mal. 1;5). This remnant will ultimately include those from Edom who believe (Amos 9:12; Obad. 19–21). Thus, the LORD will dispossess Edom and include believing Edomites in his kingdom (see commentary on Obadiah).

---

5. Michael B. Shepherd, *The Twelve Prophets in the New Testament* (New York: Peter Lang, 2011), 62–63.

6. "In keeping with the trend of post-exilic thought, he sets his whole mind upon the coming of the Messiah and his kingdom. This kingdom, which is to be above all the kingdoms of the world, needs not the assistance of any earthly power to establish itself in its rightful place. Yahweh himself will bring it into its own" (J. Smith, *Malachi*, 14).

7. See also Jer. 9:10 (Eng., 9:11); 23:10; Joel 1:19, 20; 2:22; Ps. 65:13 (Eng., 65:12).

MALACHI 1:6–2:9

1:6 "A son, he honors a father, and a servant his master. But if a father is who I am, where is my honor? And if a master is who I am, where is my respect? says the LORD of hosts to you, the priests, the despisers of my name. And you say, 'In what way have we despised your name?' 1:7 You bring near upon my altar defiled food [LXX pl.]. And you say, 'In what way have we defiled you [LXX 3mp]?' When you say, 'The table of the LORD is despised' [LXX adds: and the set food is despised]. 1:8 And when you bring near a blind animal to sacrifice, is it not evil? And when you bring near a lame animal or a sick one, is it not evil? Draw it near to your governor. Will he be pleased with you [LXX, Vulg.: it]? Or will he lift up your face [i.e., show you favor]? says the LORD of hosts." 1:9 And now, appease God's face that he may be gracious to us. "It is from your hand that this has come. Will he lift up from you faces [or, Will he show favor to any of you]? says the LORD of hosts. 1:10 I wish that even one among you would shut the doors [see GKC §151a] so that they might not light up my altar for nothing. I have no delight in you, says the LORD of hosts, and a gift / offering I will not accept [or, be pleased with] from your hand. 1:11 For from the rising of the sun to its setting great is [ESV et al.: will be] my name among the nations. And in every place incense is [ESV et al.: will be] brought near to my name, and a pure gift / offering [Tg. Jon.: And at every time that you do my will I receive your prayer, and my great name is set apart upon your hands, and your prayer is like a pure offering before me]. For great is [ESV et al.: will be] my name among the nations, says the LORD of hosts. 1:12 And you are profaning it when you say, 'The table of the Lord is defiled, and its fruit is despised, its food.' 1:13 And you say, 'Look, how wearisome.' And you [LXXʷ, Syr.: I] sniff at [or, set aflame; Tg. Jon.: strangle] it [Tiq Soph for: me], says the LORD of hosts, and you bring a stolen animal and [and > mlt Mss] the lame and the sick, and you bring the gift / offering. Will I accept [or, be pleased with] it from your hand, says the LORD [pc Mss, LXX, Syr.ʷ add: of hosts]? 1:14 And cursed is a deceiver [LXX: one who is able] in whose flock is a male, and he vows and sacrifices a corrupted animal to the Lord [mlt Mss: LORD], for I am a great king, says the LORD of hosts, and my name is feared [or, respected] among the nations.

2:1 And now, to you is this command, O priests. 2:2 If you do not listen, and if you do not take it to heart [lit., set upon heart / mind] to give honor to my name, says the LORD of hosts, I will curse your blessings [LXX: blessing]. And indeed, I have cursed, for you are not taking it to heart [lit., setting upon heart / mind]. 2:3 Look, I am about to rebuke your seed /

offspring [LXX: I am separating your shoulder; Tg. Jon.: I am about to rebuke you like the produce of the land], and I will scatter offal on your faces [Tg. Jon.: I will reveal the shame of your sins on your faces], the offal of your festivals [Tg. Jon.: and I will stop the greatness of your festivals], and he will lift you up to it [Tg. Jon.: your portion will be withheld from it]. 2:4 And you will know that I sent to you this command so that my covenant might be with Levi, says the LORD of hosts. 2:5 As for my covenant, it was with him, life and well-being. And I gave them to him [Tg. Jon.: I gave to him the complete instruction of my Torah] for respect, and he respected me. And before my name he was shattered / dismayed. 2:6 Reliable instruction is what was in his mouth; and as for injustice, it was not found on his lips. In integrity and in uprightness he walked with me, and many were the ones he caused to turn from iniquity. 2:7 For a priest's lips should be the ones to keep knowledge, and instruction is what they [i.e., the people] should seek from his mouth. For the messenger of the LORD of hosts is he. 2:8 But you, you have turned aside from the way, you have caused many to stumble over the Torah. You have corrupted the covenant of Levi, says the LORD of hosts. 2:9 And also I, I have made you despised and low to all the people [mlt Mss, LXX, Vulg.: peoples] to the extent that you do not keep my ways and to the extent that you show favoritism [lit., lift up faces] in the instruction."

The second disputation is addressed to the priests (Mal. 1:6) and is easily the longest of the six disputations in the book (Mal. 1:6–2:9). In keeping with the general pattern of the disputations, the opening words from the LORD prompt a question in response (Mal. 1:6). The remainder of the disputation is the LORD's answer to the question. The opening words are based on exegesis of the Decalogue. A son should honor his father (see Exod. 20:12; Deut. 5:16; Eph. 6:1–4; Col. 3:20–21), and a servant should honor his master (e.g., Exod. 21:2–6; Eph. 6:5–9; Col. 3:22–4:1). But if the LORD is father (e.g., Deut. 32:6; Isa. 63:16; Mal. 2:10), where is the honor due to him? If he is master (i.e., Lord), where is his respect? This was especially true for the mediating class of priests under the old covenant who had the responsibility of treating the LORD as set apart (i.e., holy) when they exercised the privilege of drawing near to him (see Lev. 10:3). They were to honor him before all the people. Yet those addressed here who served as priests in the post-exilic period despised the name of the LORD. They treated it with contempt. That is, they did not represent his reputation well. Of course, this is not the way they thought of their actions. Therefore, they would have asked, "In what way have we despised your name?" The rest of this section is designed to answer that very question.

The initial response from the LORD is that the priests bring near upon his altar "defiled" food (Mal. 1:7; cf., 1 Sam. 2:17). This word translated "defiled" (מגאל) occurs in later biblical Hebrew (see BDB, 146) and is not the same word from Leviticus for the ceremonially "unclean" (טמא; see Lev. 11). It is used here somewhat interchangeably with the word translated "despised" (see Mal. 1:6, 12). The priests have "despised" the LORD's name (Mal. 1:6b) in that they have "defiled" him (Mal. 1:7a). The food that they offer is both "defiled" (Mal. 1:7a) and "despised" (Mal. 1:12b). The table of the LORD (i.e., the altar) is both "despised" (Mal. 1:7b) and "defiled" (Mal. 1:12b). The priests would have taken the accusation of offering defiled food to mean that they had defiled the LORD himself, and thus they would have asked in what way they have done this (Mal. 1:7a; but see LXX). When the LORD responds that the priests say the table of the LORD, which is the altar (cf., Ezek. 41:22; 44:16), is despised (Mal. 1:7b), he does not mean that they verbally articulate this. Rather, he means that they say this with their actions as outlined in Malachi 1:8. In violation of the Torah, they draw near blind, lame, and sick animals to sacrifice (see Lev. 22:22; Deut. 15:21). These are unacceptable offerings. The rhetorical question, "Is it not evil?" carries more force than a mere statement of fact. These priests would not make such an offering to their "governor" (see Hag. 1:1, 14; 2:2, 21; Neh. 5:14). If the governor would not be pleased with them (or their offering) or show them favor, why would the LORD?

Michael Fishbane has demonstrated that the disputation in Malachi 1:6–2:9 is in large measure an exegetical reversal of the words of the priestly blessing in Numbers 6:22–27:

> The ironic reversal of the priests' language, actions, and hopes is thus textured through a series of reworkings and plays on the liturgical language of Num. 6:23–7. In this way, the priests' cultic language is desacralized and their actions cursed. By unfolding the negative semantic range of most of the key terms used positively in the Priestly Blessing, the rotten core and consequences of the language and behaviour of the priests is echoed throughout the diatribe. And further, in so far as the prophetic speech of Malachi is presented as a divine word, Malachi's speech is revealed to be no less than a divine exegesis of the Priestly Blessing, and a divine mockery of the priests who presume to bless in his name.[8]

---

8. Michael Fishbane, *Biblical Interpretation in Ancient Israel* (Oxford: Clarendon, 1985), 333–34. See also 1QS II.

By means of the blessing in Numbers 6:24–26, the priests were to put the LORD's "name" (שֵׁם) on the children of Israel (Num. 6:27), and yet now they despise his "name" (Mal. 1:6; see also Mal. 1:11, 14; 2:2, 5). The content of the blessing was that the LORD would "bless" (בָּרַךְ) and "keep" (שָׁמַר), but now he will curse the priests' "blessings" (Mal. 2:2) because they do not "keep" the LORD's ways (Mal. 2:9). Its content was also that the LORD would "light up his face" (יָאֵר יְהוָה פָּנָיו) and "be gracious" (חָנַן), but now the priests "light up" the altar for nothing (Mal. 1:10), and the prophet must urge them to appease the LORD's "face" in order that he might "be gracious" (Mal. 1:9). And finally, the LORD was to "lift up his face" (יִשָּׂא יְהוָה פָּנָיו) and give "peace/well-being" (שָׁלוֹם) according to the blessing's content, but now not even the governor would "lift up the face" of the priests (Mal. 1:8b), and the priests have turned away from the covenant of life and "peace/well-being" that the LORD gave to them (Mal. 2:4–5, 8). Will the LORD "lift up" their "face" (Mal. 1:9b)? No, he will scatter the offal of their festival sacrifices on their "faces" and "lift" them up to it (Mal. 2:3) because they "lift up faces" (i.e., show partiality) in their teaching of the Torah (Mal. 2:9).

The prophet calls on the priests in Malachi 1:9a to appease the face of God, that he might be gracious to "us." This use of the first-person plural pronoun shows that the priests represent the people in general. The LORD's discourse resumes in Malachi 1:9b with the comment that the situation described in Malachi 1:6–8 is from the hand of the priests. Therefore, will he show favor to them? The implied answer is no. It may seem strange that the LORD refers to himself here in the third person, but Malachi 1:9b concludes with, "says the LORD of hosts." Even this clause, which also refers to the LORD in the third person, appears to be part of the LORD's discourse. Such a clause would normally be considered outside the speech of the speaker to whom it refers, but the use of it in Malachi 1:6, which requires it to be part of the discourse, colors the way it is understood throughout the passage (Mal. 1:6b, 8b, 9b, 10b, 11b, 13b, 14b; 2:2a, 4b, 8b). The LORD expresses the desire in Malachi 1:10 that someone would shut the doors of the temple so that the priests would no longer light up the altar gratuitously (cf., 2 Sam. 24:24a; 2 Chr. 28:24; see also CD-A 6:12–14; 4Q266 [= 4QD^a] 3 II). If the priests insist on despising the LORD's name in their practice, then it would be better to shut down the whole operation. The LORD has no delight in them (cf., Isa. 62:4; Hos. 8:8), and he will not accept an offering from their hand (cf., Amos 5:21–24). The LORD delights in loyalty rather than sacrifice (see Hos. 6:6; see also Deut. 10:12–22; 1 Sam. 15:22–23; Isa. 1:10–17; Jer. 7:21–23; Mic. 6:6–8; Ps. 40:7 [Eng., 40:6]; Prov. 21:3). Only when the heart is contrite will the LORD be pleased with sacrifices (Ps. 51:18–21 [Eng., 51:16–19]).

The text of Malachi 1:11 then explains that the LORD is not in need of temple worship from a people and priests who have broken his covenant.[9] He has a people for himself from all the nations among whom his name is great and not despised (cf., Ps. 86:9–10; Acts 13:46; Rom. 11).[10] It is in fact one of the great themes of the Book of the Twelve from beginning to end that the nations would seek the LORD (see, e.g., Hos. 3:5; Amos 9:12; Mic. 4:1–5; Zech. 8:20–23). Since this was not a present reality in the prophet's day, the understanding is that it would happen in the future.[11] Both Isaiah and the book of Psalms envision a day when a people from east to west will honor and respect the name of the LORD (see Isa. 45:6; 59:19; Ps. 50:1; 113:3). Incense and pure offerings will be brought to the LORD in every place. That is, there will no longer be a separate mediating class of priests for one nation but a priesthood of believers from all the nations (Exod. 19:6; Isa. 61:6; 66:21; 1 Pet. 2:9; Rev. 1:6; 5:10; 20:6).[12] On the other hand, the priests of the prophet's day treat the LORD's name as common rather than holy or set apart when they treat the altar as defiled and its fruit (i.e., its food) as despised (Mal. 1:12; cf., Mal. 1:7). Their privilege as priests has become a wearisome task to them (Mal. 1:13). They have "sniffed" at the LORD's name in contempt (NET: "You turn up your nose at it"). This is one of the *tiqqune sopherim* ("corrections of the scribes"). The reading, "you sniff at it (i.e., my name)," is in place of the more directly offensive original, "you sniff at me." The priests do this when they offer the stolen, the lame, and the sick (cf., Mal. 1:8). The LORD will by no means accept such an offering. Thus, cursed is the one who acts deceptively by vowing and sacrificing a corrupted animal to the LORD when he is fully able to offer a healthy male (Mal. 1:14). For the LORD is a great king who will receive the respect due his name from among the nations (cf., Zech. 14:16). The LORD has no interest in encouraging the priests to stay the course of the old covenant relationship. That covenant is broken, and

---

9. "But probably the thought is that Yahweh is not dependent upon the worshippers in Jerusalem for a right recognition of his place and power. He can refuse to receive them for he has other worshippers scattered throughout the world. The honour denied him in his own city is freely accorded him in foreign cities" (J. Smith, *Malachi*, 30).

10. See John Calvin, *Commentaries on the Twelve Minor Prophets*, vol. 5, *Zechariah and Malachi*, trans. John Owen, Calvin's Commentaries XV (reprint, Grand Rapids: Baker, 2005), 498.

11. Keil, *Minor Prophets*, 642; R. Smith, *Micah–Malachi*, 315.

12. See Michael B. Shepherd, *The Text in the Middle* (New York: Peter Lang, 2014), 74–75.

the postexilic community is doing no better with it than the preexilic community. Therefore, it is time to look to the future (see Mal. 3:3–4).

The reference to the command to the priests in Malachi 2:1 is not followed by an imperative, but the context of Malachi 1:6 and 2:2 suggests that the command to honor the LORD's name is implied.[13] If the priests do not pay attention to this command, the LORD says that he will send the curse against them and curse their blessing(s) (Mal. 2:2a). It is possible that this could be a general reference to the covenant curses, which are the opposite of the covenant blessings (see Lev. 26; Deut. 28), but since the address is specifically to the priests, it seems more likely that this is a removal of priestly privilege and perhaps more precisely a nullification of the priestly benediction (Num. 6:22–27). In fact, the LORD has already cursed their blessing because they do not take his command to heart (Mal. 2:2b). The LORD illustrates this by pointing out in Malachi 2:3 that he is "rebuking" (or, "cutting off"; cf., 1 Sam. 2:31; Nah. 1:14) the priests' offspring. He will scatter the fecal matter of the sacrificial victims of their festivals on their "faces" and "lift" them up to it. This is in place of, "The LORD make his face shine on you and be gracious to you. The LORD lift up his face to you and give you well-being" (Num. 6:25–26). Then they will know or acknowledge that the LORD sent this command to them for a purpose: that his covenant with Levi might remain (Mal. 2:4). But by that time, it will be too late to fulfill that purpose. The reference here is to the covenant with Phineas the son of Eleazar the son of Aaron of the tribe of Levi in the wake of the Baal Peor incident (Num. 25:12–13; see also Num. 18:19; Neh. 13:29).[14]

Verses 5 and 6 of Malachi 2 are almost like an aside designed to explain what the priestly covenant was and what it had been prior to its demise (cf., 1 Sam. 2:27–28; note the fronting of the topic "my covenant" in the Hebrew text at the beginning of Malachi 2:5). According to Numbers 25:12, this covenant was to be a covenant of "peace" or "well-being" (שלום). Thus, the LORD gave the priests "life" and "well-being"

---

13. See J. Smith, *Malachi*, 35.
14. There was no covenant with the Levites (i.e., the Levitical priesthood). There was only a covenant with the high priestly lineage of Aaron. The lengthy addition found in Jeremiah 33:14–26 of the MT of Jeremiah, but not in the Hebrew behind the LXX, attempts to leverage the wording of the covenant with David found in Jeremiah 23:5–6 to make the case for a covenant with the Levites (see Shepherd, *The Twelve Prophets*, 98–99). This was a secondary, postbiblical move designed to elevate the status of the Levites. For the rift between Aaron and the Levites, see Numbers 16. For the distinction between the two groups, see Ezekiel 44.

in order that they might respect and honor him, and they did (Mal. 2:5). But the priests of the prophet's day have failed to give the honor and respect due the LORD's name (Mal. 1:6). According to Numbers 25:12, the covenant was to be one of "an indefinite priesthood." The word translated "indefinite" (עוֹלָם) does not automatically mean "eternal" or "everlasting." Only the context can make it so. Thus, unconditional "indefinite covenants" are by definition everlasting covenants when they depend on God's faithfulness rather than man's (e.g., Gen. 9:16; 17:7; 2 Sam. 23:5; Isa. 55:3; 61:8; Jer. 32:40; Ezek. 37:26). Conditional covenants like the Sinai covenant, however, are "indefinite" (Exod. 31:16) in the sense that the time of their inevitable end is undetermined. They are temporal and finite, and the expectation of their breaking is built into them (Lev. 26; Deut. 28). The priestly covenant is inextricably tied to the Sinai covenant. There is no need for a priestly covenant apart from the Sinai covenant. Once the Sinai covenant is broken, the priestly covenant ceases to have any relevance. There was a time when the priests were to teach reliable instruction from the Torah without any injustice (Mal. 2:6a; cf., Deut. 17:8–13; 33:8–11; Neh. 8–9; 2 Chr. 17:7–9). There was a time when a priest walked with the LORD in integrity and uprightness and turned many from iniquity (Mal. 2:6b). But that time is long gone. The priests were to keep knowledge so that the people could seek instruction from them (Mal. 2:7a). A priest was to be the LORD's "messenger" (Mal. 2:7b; cf., Eccl. 5:5 [Eng., 5:6]). But now a different kind of "messenger" (Mal. 1:1), a prophet, must announce the end of the priesthood and look forward to the coming of another prophetic "messenger" (Mal. 3:1, 23 [Eng., 3:1; 4:5]) who will prepare the people for the Day of the LORD.

In contrast to the ideal priests of the covenant, the priests of the prophet's day have turned aside from the way (Mal. 2:8a). That is, they have not walked the path of integrity and uprightness intended for them (Mal. 2:6b). Rather than teaching reliable instruction from the Torah (Mal. 2:6a) in order to turn many from iniquity (Mal. 2:6b), they have caused many to stumble over the Torah (Mal. 2:8a; cf., Jer. 2:8). They have not heeded the LORD's command in order to continue in the covenant (Mal. 2:4). They have corrupted the covenant of Levi (Mal. 2:8b). Therefore, just as the priests have despised the LORD's name by despising his altar (Mal. 1:6–7), so the LORD has taken away the status of the priests by making them despised and low to all the people (Mal. 2:9a). He does this to the degree that they do not keep his ways and to the extent that they "lift up faces" (i.e., show favoritism) in their instruction (Mal. 2:9b; see Lev. 19:15). The LORD will no longer "lift up his face" (i.e., show favor) to them (Num. 6:26).

MALACHI 2:10–16

2:10 Do we not all have one father? Was he not one God who created us?[15]
Why do we act unfaithfully against one another [lit., each against his
brother; LXX: Why do you forsake one another], profaning the covenant
of our forefathers? 2:11 Judah has acted unfaithfully [LXX: has been
forsaken], and an abomination is what has been done in Israel and in
Jerusalem. For Judah has profaned the holiness of the LORD that he
loves and has married a foreign god's daughter [4QXIIᵃ: בית (house); Tg.
Jon.: they have desired to take for themselves wives from the daughters
of the peoples]. 2:12 May the LORD cut off to the man [Tg. Jon. adds:
son and grandson] who does it awake [4QXIIᵃ: עד (witness)] and an-
swering [LXX: until (= עַד) he is humbled] from the tents of Jacob and
who draws near a gift / offering to the LORD of hosts [Tg. Jon.: and if he
is a priest drawing near an offering of the temple of the LORD of hosts,
he will not have a son].

2:13 And this also [lit., second] you do [LXX: And these things, which I
hate, you were doing]: covering [LXX: you covered] with tears the altar
[Syr.: house] of the LORD with weeping [4QXIIᵃ: and with weeping] and
groaning because there is no longer turning [4QXIIᵃ: because of trouble
(מאון) is there still turning (interrogative)] to the gift / offering [BHS: the
LORD still refuses to turn to the gift / offering] and taking an acceptable
offering from your hand [LXX: Is it still worthy to pay attention to sac-
rifice and to receive an acceptable offering from your hands?]. 2:14 And
you say, "On the basis of what?" On the basis of the fact that the LORD is
the one who testifies between each one of you and the wife of your youth
against whom each one of you has acted unfaithfully [against whom
each one of you has acted unfaithfully > 4QXIIᵃ], yet she is your com-
panion and the wife of your youth. 2:15 And there is not one person who
does this who has a remnant of the Spirit [Tg. Jon.: Was not Abraham
one, a unique one from whom the world was created?]. And how did
the one seek offspring from God? Thus, you should watch yourselves
in your spirit, and against the wife of your youth let not a single man
among you act unfaithfully [nonn Mss, LXX, Tg. Jon., Vulg.: do not
act unfaithfully]. 2:16 "For I [see GKC §116s] hate / reject sending away
[or, divorce; 4QXIIᵃ: שלח שנתה אם כי; cf., LXX: But if, having hated, you
send away; Tg. Jon.: Look, if you hate / reject her, release her; see also
Vulg.]," says the LORD the God [4QXIIᵃ: אל] of Israel, "and he covers

---

15. The two rhetorical questions at the beginning of Malachi 2:10 are in the
opposite order in the LXX.

*with violence his garment [4QXII^a: they cover with violence my gar-
ment; LXX: then ungodliness will cover your thoughts; Tg. Jon.: and
do not cover with sin your garment]," says the LORD of hosts. And you
should watch yourselves in your spirit and never act unfaithfully.*

The third disputation in Malachi 2:10–16 delays the question-and-
answer pattern common to all the disputations until Malachi 2:13–16.
Thus, the opening verses of this unit are crucial to the reader's understanding of the marriage language in the latter verses. The two rhetorical questions at the beginning of Malachi 2:10 are parallel. The one
father of the postexilic community is not Adam or one of the patriarchs
as some interpreters have suggested. It has already been noted in the
previous disputation that the LORD is the father of this people to whom
honor is due (Mal. 1:6; cf., Isa. 63:16). The parallel thought to this is
that he is their one creator (cf., Deut. 32:6; Isa. 43:7). This is perhaps
why the LXX has the two clauses in Malachi 2:10a in the opposite arrangement—in order to lead with the thought of the one God as creator
and to avoid any confusion over who the referent of "one father" might
be. There are then certain implications that come from the fact that the
people have one father and one God who created them (see Deut. 6:4–9;
Zech. 14:9). They are not to worship idols or other gods in violation of
the terms of the covenant (Deut. 5:6–10; 6:12–15). And so, the prophet
asks in Malachi 2:10b, "Why do we act unfaithfully against one another,
profaning the covenant of our forefathers?" This is undoubtedly a reference to the Sinai covenant (Exod. 24:8), the one conditional/temporal
covenant that could be profaned or broken. Once again, the prophet
exposes the fact that the postexilic community is no better at living up
to the standards of that covenant than its ancestors. They must look
beyond that covenant to the hope of a new covenant based on divine
faithfulness. As it stands, those who worship idols and other gods are
acting unfaithfully toward their fellow community members, creating
an unpleasant situation for everyone (cf., Ezra 9; 1 Thess. 4:3–6).

Judah has acted unfaithfully (Mal. 2:11a). An "abomination"
(תועבה) has been committed in Israel and in Jerusalem. This word
translated "abomination" is commonly used in the Bible for idolatrous
practice (e.g., Ezek. 8:6; see BDB, 1072). This charge is laid against
Judah because the people have profaned the holiness of the LORD that
he loves with their worship of idols and other gods (Mal. 2:11b). The
"holiness" of the LORD here is not the temple but the separateness
or uniqueness of the LORD himself. Worship of idols and other gods
makes the LORD look like nothing but another common god of the
nations (cf., Mal. 1:12). The "husband" Judah has thus divorced his

"covenant" (feminine noun in Hebrew) relationship with the LORD and married "a foreign god's daughter."[16] This foreign god's daughter is not necessarily a reference to a specific female deity such as Asherah or a reference to a particular foreign people. It is likely a reference to Judah's marriage to foreign worship in general. It is not uncommon for the prophets to describe covenant infidelity in terms of the analogy of marital infidelity (e.g., Jer. 3; Ezek. 16; Hos. 1–3), although normally the LORD is the husband in the metaphor, and the people are the wife. Here Judah is the husband, and the covenant is the wife. Thus, the passage is not primarily about marriage or cohabitation with foreign women that leads to divorce of Judean wives (Mal. 2:13–16), as is commonly thought.[17] Nevertheless, the situation described in Ezra 9–10 and Nehemiah 13:23–27 is very likely the background for the imagery. In the days of Ezra and Nehemiah, Judean men were cohabitating with foreign women who could potentially lead them into the same kind of idolatry that landed them in the very Babylonian exile from which they had only recently returned (see Deut. 7:3–4; 23:4; 1 Kgs. 11:1–10; see also 2 Cor. 6:14). Therefore, there was a concerted effort to dissolve these relationships as soon as possible. The prophet expresses his desire that the LORD would cut off the offspring of any man who engages in idolatry consciously (lit., "awake and answering") from the tents of Jacob and who attempts to bring near an offering to the LORD (Mal. 2:12; cf., Mal. 1:7–14; 2:3). Such an offering will not be acceptable (see Isa. 1:10–17; Jer. 7; Amos 5:21–24).

In addition to their idolatry, the people of Judah attempt to court the LORD's favor merely by covering his altar with tears, with weeping and groaning (Mal. 2:13a). They would rather do this than forsake their idolatrous religion. This is not the weeping of divorced Judean women, as some have thought, nor is it the kind of weeping referenced in Ezekiel 8:14. It is the weeping of those whose offerings the LORD refuses to accept because they refuse to let go of their idols (Mal. 2:13b). Thus, the question comes from the people in Malachi 2:14, "On the basis of what?" Why does the LORD refuse them? It is because the LORD himself bears witness between each one of the Judean men (note the singular pronoun) and the wife of his youth, which is the old covenant (cf., Jer. 2:2; Ezek. 16:8). Of course, it is possible for the wife of a man's youth to be a literal wife married in

16. Note the use of the singular "daughter" here. It does not say "daughters of a foreign god." This is not a reference to women who worship a foreign god. See *b. Sanh.* 82a.
17. See C. C. Torrey, "The Prophecy of Malachi," *JBL* 17 (1898): 4–5, 9–10.

youth (Prov. 5:18),[18] but in this context the wife of youth is the one against whom each Judean man has acted unfaithfully. According to Malachi 2:10b, the men of Judah have acted unfaithfully against one another by profaning the covenant of their forefathers. According to Malachi 2:11, Judah has acted unfaithfully by committing an abomination (i.e., idolatry). They have profaned the LORD's holiness by marrying the daughter of a foreign god, not by divorcing or mistreating literal wives married in youth. The background accounts in Ezra 9–10 and Nehemiah 13:23–27 do not even mention such divorce or mistreatment. They do not even speak of actual marriages. Ezra's question in Ezra 9:14 mentions the potential of intermarriage but not the act itself. Rather, the texts speak of cohabitation (*hiphil* of ישׁב; see Ezra 10:2; Neh. 13:23). This is what is meant by the taking of foreign women and the mixing of the holy seed, which have led to idolatry (Ezra 9:1–2). There is no indication of the marital status of these men prior to their actions. Thus, the end of Malachi 2:14 speaks of the wife of each Judean man's youth as his companion and as the wife of his covenant. That is, she is the wife, which is the covenant (epexegetical; see GKC §128). Marriage in the Hebrew Bible is not a covenant. It is a union (Gen. 2:23–24). The other text cited in defense of marriage as covenant is Proverbs 2:17, which speaks of the adulterous woman who forsakes the friend of her youth (her husband) and forgets the covenant of her God. But that text is referring to the prohibition against adultery in the Decalogue (Exod. 20:14). It is not about the covenant of marriage. It is about the Sinai covenant. As noted above, it is not unusual for the prophets to use marital infidelity as an analogy for lack of faithfulness to the covenant with God, but that is not the same thing as saying that marriage is a covenant. When the biblical authors want to use marriage in a positive analogy, they appeal to its true nature as a union in order to depict union with Christ in the new covenant (e.g., Eph. 5:25–33). The primary thought of Malachi 2:14 then is that the LORD testifies to the fact that Judah has continued to act unfaithfully against the broken old covenant by means of idolatry.

The beginning of Malachi 2:15 is often rendered as a question (e.g., ASV) under the assumption that the word "one" refers either to Adam or to Abraham. But questions in the book of Malachi are normally made explicit by means of interrogative pronouns and interrogative

---

18. Even in Proverbs 5:18 the phrase goes beyond a mere literal reference in order to represent wisdom that leads to life, just as the adulterous woman also represents folly that leads to death (see Prov. 9).

markers (see Mal. 1:2, 6b; 2:14a, 17; 3:7b, 8a, 13b). That is not the case here. The above translation renders the text as a statement: "And there is not one person who does this who has a remnant of the Spirit." No one in whom the Spirit of God remains persists in the practice of idolatry. This is perhaps a reference to both Joseph and Daniel who had the Spirit of God (Gen. 41:38; Dan. 4:5, 6, 15 [Eng., 4:8, 9, 18]; 5:11). Joseph refused to commit literal adultery with Potiphar's wife (Gen. 39). Daniel refused to commit spiritual adultery (i.e., idolatry) in the story of the lions' den (Dan. 6; see Dan. 6:8, 11 [Eng., 6:7, 10]). The next part of Malachi 2:15 is a clearly marked question: "And how did the one seek offspring from God?" Here the word "one" has the definite article and refers specifically to Abraham in the stories of Genesis 16 and 21 (cf., Isa. 51:2b). Although Abraham initially erred in following Sarah's advice to seek offspring through Hagar, he ultimately did not divorce Sarah, nor did he abandon trust that the LORD would be faithful to the covenant by giving him offspring through Sarah. In the end, Hagar was the one whom Abraham sent away, and thereby he sent away all that was contrary to the covenant relationship (see Gal. 4). Therefore, the prophet suggests that his audience would do well to watch their own spirits and not act unfaithfully against the wife of their youth (i.e., the covenant). Once again, the design is to highlight the continued failure of the postexilic community and the need for a new covenant relationship.

The opening words of Malachi 2:16 in the text of 4QXII[a] and in the translations of the LXX and *Targum Jonathan* assume that the context speaks of literal divorce on the basis of Deuteronomy 24:1–4 (cf., Isa. 50:1; Jer. 3). That is, if a husband rejects his wife, he can divorce her—a law added because of transgression (Matt. 19:8; Gal. 3:19; see also 1 Cor. 7). But the MT is more attune to the actual context of Malachi 2:10–16 (see the above translation and GKC §116s). The LORD himself hates or rejects sending away. In other words, the LORD hates how Judah has dismissed the covenant. The people of Judah have acted unfaithfully and practiced idolatry in the same manner as their preexilic forefathers who broke the covenant. Books like Zechariah indicate the presence of a believing remnant in Judah, but such believers are only a remnant. The others have covered their garments with violence (Mal. 2:16; cf., Gen. 16:5; Ps. 73:6), the filthy garments representing the iniquity of covenant infidelity (cf., Zech. 3:4). Thus, the prophet reiterates that the people should watch themselves in their spirit and not act unfaithfully against the covenant in their practice of idolatry (Mal. 2:16b).

MALACHI 2:17–3:5

*2:17 You have wearied [LXX: you who have provoked] the LORD with
your words. And you say, "In what way have we wearied?" When you
say, "Every person who does evil is good in the eyes of the LORD, and it
is in them that he delights," or, "Where is the God of justice/judgment?"
3:1 "[4QXII*ª*: Therefore] Look, I am about to send my messenger, and he
will prepare a path before me. And suddenly he will come [4QXII*ª*: they
will come] to his temple, the Lord whom you seek. And as for the messenger of the covenant whom you desire, look, he is coming," says the
LORD of hosts. 3:2 And who can endure the day of his coming [4QXII*ª*:
endure them, they come]? And who is the one who can stand/remain
when he appears? For he [Tg. Jon.: his anger] is [LXX: comes] like a
refiner's fire and like fullers' [or, launderers'] soap. 3:3 And he will sit as
a refiner and purifier of silver, and he will purify the sons of Levi and
refine them like gold and like silver. And they will be to the LORD those
who bring near a gift/offering in righteousness.[19] 3:4 And the gift/of-
fering of Judah and Jerusalem will be sweet to the LORD like days of
old and like former years. 3:5 "And I will draw near to you for the judg-
ment/justice, and I will be a swift witness against the sorcerers and
against the adulterers and against those who swear [mlt Mss, LXX add:
in my name] falsely and against oppressors of a hired worker's pay, a
widow, and an orphan, and [against] those who turn aside a resident
foreigner [LXX: justice of a proselyte]. And they do not respect me," says
the LORD of hosts.*

The fourth disputation opens with a charge from the prophet against
the Judeans that they have wearied the LORD with their words—an
anthropopathism (Mal. 2:17; cf., Isa. 43:24b). The remainder of the disputation follows the standard question-and-answer format. The people
ask in what way have they wearied the LORD. The prophet responds
with what the people say or think, although their actions speak as
loudly if not more loudly than their words. They say that evildoers are
good in the LORD's sight, that he delights in them rather than in those

---

19. The ESV ("and they will bring offerings in righteousness to the LORD")
    assumes that the finite verb of being and the participle "bring near" form
    a periphrastic construction with "gift/offering" as the object and "to the
    LORD" as a fronted indirect object in the Hebrew text. But the word order
    and the Masoretic accentuation suggest that this clause indicates what the
    sons of Levi will be as a result of their refinement. The use of the participle
    in the construct state suggests that it likely functions as a substantive.

who do good (cf., Isa. 5:20). They also ask where the God of justice or judgment is, as if he were absent (cf., Isa. 41:23; Jer. 10:5; Zeph. 1:12). This mindset reflects the frustration of the postexilic community. They have yet to experience the glorious restoration envisioned by texts like Isaiah 40–55. It seems to them as though the LORD is unnecessarily allowing evil to persist. It is as if he were pleased with evil rather than with good. Thus, it appears vain to serve him (Mal. 3:14). Where is the God of justice who vindicates his people and judges his enemies? Just as the preexilic generation doubted whether the prophetic threat of judgment would ever come to pass (e.g., Ezek. 12:21–28), so the postexilic community doubts the prophetic message of restoration. Yet the LORD has clearly indicated that he does not delight in the current situation (Mal. 1:10). He responds in what follows to the question embedded within the prophet's answer to the people's initial inquiry. Judgment/justice is on its way (Mal. 3:5).

Commentators do not agree on the number of individuals or their identity in Malachi 3:1. There may be as many as three or as few as one. Most think that there are two. It is not uncommon for these two to be identified as a preparatory prophetic messenger and the Lord. Those who think that "the Lord" refers to the LORD must either understand the LORD to refer to himself in the third person or take the middle of Malachi 3:1 to stand outside of his discourse in some way.[20] It is also not unusual for commentators to say that the LORD and the messenger of the covenant are one and the same,[21] although this is far from clear.

The text of Malachi 3:1a—"Look, I am about to send my messenger, and he will prepare a path before me (הנני שלח מלאכי ופנה דרך לפני)"—is an exegesis of two prior texts: (1) "Look, I am about to send a messenger [Sam., LXX, Vulg.: my messenger] before you to keep/watch/protect you on the path (הנה אנכי שלח מלאך לפניך לשמרך בדרך)" (Exod. 23:20a; cf., Exod. 32:34a; 33:2a); and (2) "A voice calls, 'In the wilderness prepare the path [or, way] of the LORD' (קול קורא במדבר פנו דרך יהוה)" (Isa. 40:3a). In the first text (Exod. 23:20a), the LORD announces that he is sending an angelic messenger before Moses and the people in the wake of their departure from Egypt and as they make their way through the wilderness to the land of the covenant (see also Exod. 3:2a; 14:19). In the second text (Isa. 40:3a), the prophetic voice urges preparation of the way of the LORD in the wilderness so that he (the LORD) can prepare the way of the people (Isa. 57:14; 62:10) for a new, eschatological exodus from Babylon (Isa. 43:16–21) through the ministry of the messianic servant of

---

20. See, e.g., R. Smith, *Micah–Malachi*, 328.
21. E.g., Keil, *Minor Prophets*, 656.

the LORD (Isa. 42:1–7; 49:1–9; 50:4–11; 52:13–53:12; 61:1–9). According to the appendix (or, appendices) in Malachi 3:22–24 (Eng., 4:4–6), the messenger who prepares the way before the LORD in Malachi 3:1a is the prophetic messenger Elijah who will prepare the hearts of the people for the coming of the Day of the LORD: "Look, I am about to send to you Elijah the prophet (הנה אנכי שלח לכם את אליה הנביא)" (Mal. 3:23a [Eng., 4:5a]). Also, the remembrance of the Torah of Moses in Mal. 3:22 (Eng., 4:4) links the reader to the future hope of a messianic prophet like Moses (Deut. 18:15, 18; 34:10). Thus, Mark's gospel opens with a conflation of the two texts in Exodus 23:20a and Malachi 3:1a (Mark 1:2) and combines it with a citation of LXX Isaiah 40:3 (Mark 1:3). Mark identifies John the Baptist as the forerunner prophet like Elijah (Mark 1:4–8; cf., 2 Kgs. 1:8; see also Matt. 3:1–12; 11:10; 17:9–13; Mark 9:11–13; Luke 1:17, 76; 3:1–14; 7:27; John 1:19–28) who prepares the way for Jesus, the messianic prophet like Moses (Acts 3:22; 7:37).

The prophetic messenger will prepare the way before the LORD who is speaking in Malachi 3:1, but it is "the Lord" (האדון; not יהוה or אדני) referenced in the third person who will come suddenly (i.e., imminently) to his temple (Mal. 3:1b). It is not uncommon for the term "the Lord" to refer to God in the Bible (see BDB, 11). But since the LORD refers to "the Lord" here in the third person (cf., Ps. 110:1), it is likely that "the Lord" is the Davidic Messiah who is God in the flesh according to the previous two sections of Zechariah (Zech. 9:9; 12:10; cf., Isa. 9:5–6 [Eng. 9:6–7]).[22] He is "the Lord whom you seek." These words echo the words of the programmatic passage of the Twelve: "Afterward, the sons of Israel will return and seek the LORD their God and David their king and fear to the LORD and to his goodness at the end of the days" (Hos 3:5). When the text says that the Lord will come to his temple, it is not a reference to the Second Temple, which was not the eschatological temple according to Haggai and Zechariah (see also Ezek. 40–48; Rev. 21:22). It is a reference to the temple of the covenant with David (2 Sam. 7:13), which would not be built by Solomon (1 Kgs. 6–8) but by the messianic son of David who would reign over an everlasting kingdom (Zech. 6:12–13).

It is understandable that interpreters have identified the messenger of the covenant whom the people desire with the Lord whom the people seek. The chiastic structure of the two clauses in Malachi 3:1b

---

22. Redak interpreted the Lord to be the King Messiah (see *Mikraoth Gedoloth: The Twelve Prophets*, vol. 2, trans. A. J. Rosenberg [New York: Judaica, 1996], 413). Augustine and Cyril of Jerusalem saw references to the first and second comings of Christ in these verses (Alberto Ferreiro, *The Twelve Prophets*, ACCS XIV [Downers Grove, IL: InterVarsity, 2003], 299, 301).

is suggestive of such an identification. But in what sense is the Lord a messenger? Perhaps this is akin to the messianic herald in Nahum 2:1 (Eng., 1:15; cf., Isa. 41:27; 52:7). It is also possible that there is a connection here to Zech. 12:8b: "and the house of David will be like God, like the angel/messenger of the LORD before them." On the other hand, it is at least equally plausible that the messenger of the covenant is the same as the messenger in Malachi 3:1a. This would create a ring structure for the whole of Malachi 3:1. On balance it seems to follow the path of least resistance in this context to say that there is one messenger (rather than two) who prepares the way and one Lord for whom the way is prepared. The covenant here is not the old Sinai covenant. That covenant is broken (Jer. 11:10). This covenant that the messenger announces is the new covenant established by the Lord (Jer. 31:31–34; see also Isa. 42:6b; 49:8b; 61:8b).

The rhetorical questions in Malachi 3:2a initially give the impression that the answer to both is "no one." Who can endure the day of the coming of the Lord (i.e., the Day of the LORD; see Mal. 3:19, 23 [Eng., 3:19; 4:5]; see also Jer. 10:10)? Who can stand or remain when he appears (cf., Nah. 1:6)? No one can endure his judgment whose heart is not prepared by grace through faith (Mal. 3:24 [Eng., 4:6]). But Malachi 3:2b indicates that the Lord is coming not to annihilate but to refine—"like a refiner's fire and like fullers' soap." According to the prophet like Elijah (i.e., John the Baptist), Jesus will baptize with Holy Spirit and fire and separate the wheat from the chaff, which he will burn in inextinguishable fire (Matt. 3:11–12; cf., Isa. 66:24; Dan. 12:2; Rev. 20:11–15). He will cleanse the violence-stained garments of Mal. 2:16. Thus, the general thrust of Malachi 3:2 and the following context is not unlike that of Psalm 24. There the psalmist asks who can ascend the mountain of the LORD (i.e., Zion) and who can rise up in his holy place (Ps. 24:3; cf., Ps. 15) in preparation for the coming of the LORD as king (Ps. 24:7–10; cf., Zech. 9:9; Ps. 118:22–26). The answer would seem to be "no one," but Psalm 24:4–5 reveals that the innocent of hands and the pure of heart who have not taken the LORD's name in vain and sworn falsely will receive a blessing from the LORD. This refers to the same text of the Decalogue as Malachi 3:5a does (Exod. 20:7, 16). Such people are the generation that seeks the LORD (Ps. 24:6). They are enabled by the Spirit of the new covenant to do the will of God (Ezek. 11:19–20; Rom. 8:4).

The image of the Lord refining and purifying the eschatological remnant of his people through fire like silver and gold is a familiar one (Mal. 3:3; see, e.g., Isa. 48:9–11; Zech. 13:9; Prov. 17:3). Here the sons of Levi are the object, returning to the disputation against the priesthood in Malachi 1:6–2:9 and the unacceptable manner in which they bring near their gift or offering to the LORD. As noted in the commentary on that section, the hope for the future is not a refined priesthood for the new covenant community. The covenant with the priests is broken. The hope for the future is a return to the ideal kingdom of priests (Exod. 19:6; Isa. 61:6; 66:21; 1 Pet. 2:5, 9; Rev. 1:6; 5:10; 20:6). This new people of God will be to the LORD those who bring near a gift/offering in righteousness. They will essentially bring themselves as a pleasing gift to the LORD (cf., Isa. 66:20; Zeph. 3:10). Unlike the gifts of the recent past and present (e.g., Jer. 6:20; Hos. 9:4), this gift will be sweet to the LORD like days of old (Mal. 3:4; e.g., Mal. 2:5–6).

In response to the question at the end of Malachi 2:17 ("Where is the God of justice/judgment?"), the LORD says in Malachi 3:5 that he will indeed draw near to the people for the judgment/justice. He will be a "swift witness" (i.e., an imminent one; cf., Mal. 3:1b) against the sorcerers (see Deut. 18:9–13) and against those who break the Decalogue—adulterers (see Exod. 20:14) and those who swear falsely (see Exod. 20:7, 16; cf., Jer. 7:9; Hos. 4:2; Zech. 5:4; 8:17)—and against those who oppress a hired man's wages (see Lev. 19:13; Zech. 8:10), against oppressors of widows and orphans (see Deut. 10:18), and against those who turn aside resident foreigners (see Lev. 19:33–34; Deut. 10:19). These people will not take part in the new covenant and will thus remain under the curse of the old. They do not respect the LORD as he deserves (cf., Mal. 1:6; see also Mal. 3:20).

MALACHI 3:6–12

3:6 "Because I the LORD do not change [Tg. Jon.: have not changed my covenant from antiquity], you O sons of Jacob are not finished [LXX, Syr.: have not abstained from the unrighteousness of your fathers; Tg. Jon.: you imagine that whoever dies in this world, his judgment has ceased]. 3:7 From the days of your forefathers you have turned aside from my statutes and have not kept [them]. Return to me, and I will return to you [or, so that I may return to you]," says the LORD of hosts. "And you say [4QXIIᵃ: ואמרת], 'In what way should we return?' 3:8 Will a man rob [LXX: deceive (= היעקב); Tg. Jon.: make angry] God [Tg. Jon. the judge]? Indeed, you are robbing [LXX: deceiving (= עקבים); Tg. Jon.: making angry] me. And you say, 'In what way have we robbed you [LXX: deceived you (= עקבנון); Tg. Jon.: made you angry]?' The tithe and the contribution [LXX: because the tithes and the first fruits are with you; Syr., Tg. Jon., Vulg.: in the tithe and in the contribution]. 3:9 With the curse are you cursed [4QXIIᵃ: ראים אתם ראים ומראים (You are looking on *appearances); LXX: And you certainly turn your attention away; Vulg.: And in need you are cursed], and me you are robbing [LXX: deceiving (= עקבים); Tg. Jon.: making angry], the nation, all of it [LXX: the nation is finished]. 3:10 Bring in the whole of the tithe [4QXII^a: every tithe; LXX: all the things the earth produces], to the storehouse [LXX: storehouses] that there may be food [lit., prey, torn flesh] in my house [4QXII^a: my houses; Tg. Jon.: that there may be support for those who serve in my sanctuary]. And test me [LXX: consider] now in this," says the LORD of hosts, "if I do not open for you the windows of the sky and empty for you a blessing [4QXII^a: the blessing; LXX: my blessing] until there is not enough [Syr., Tg. Jon.: until you say, 'Enough'].*[23] *3:11 And I will rebuke for you the eater, and it will not destroy for you the fruit of the ground. And the grapevine will not show barrenness for you in the field," says the LORD of hosts. 3:12 "And all the nations will call you blessed [Tg. Jon.: praise you], for you will be a land of delight [Tg. Jon.: you will be living in the land of the house of my dwelling and doing my will in it]," says the LORD of hosts.*

The text of Malachi 3:6 can be read with Malachi 2:17–3:5 or with Malachi 3:7–12, depending on how the conjunction כִּי is interpreted at the beginning of the verse. If it is a causal conjunction that introduces an independent clause (= γάρ), then Malachi 3:6 explains why the LORD's judgment in Malachi 2:17–3:5 is a sure thing. Even though the sons of Jacob are not currently at an end, they can count on the faithfulness of the LORD to judge them. But if the conjunction introduces a fronted dependent clause (= ὅτι), then Malachi 3:6a explains why the sons of Jacob are not finished. The very existence of the postexilic community and the presence of a believing remnant for whom there is hope in the future are due to the LORD's unchanging faithfulness (see Jer. 30:11).[24] In favor of this latter option is the closure of Malachi 2:17–3:5 using the formula, "says the LORD of hosts." The disputations in Malachi 3:6–12 and 3:13–21 also conclude with the same formula. According to this reading, the text is very similar to that of Lamentations 3:22: "As for the LORD's acts of covenant loyalty,

---

23. BDB: "i.e., until my abundance can be exhausted, or, as this can never be, for ever" (191). It is possible that Malachi 3:10b should be interpreted as an oath (see GKC §149).

24. The text of Malachi 3:6 has long been cited by systematic theologians as a proof text for the unchanging nature of God in general (see, e.g., Wayne Grudem, *Systematic Theology* [Grand Rapids: Zondervan, 1994], 163). But in context this verse is about the unchanging faithfulness of the LORD.

surely they are not complete,[25] for his compassion is not finished." His loyalty and compassion are new every morning, his faithfulness is great (Lam. 3:23). The LORD is the spiritual portion of every believer (Lam. 3:24; cf., Num. 18:20), therefore, it is best to hope in him (Lam. 3:24–27).

The situation in which the postexilic community finds itself (Mal. 2:17) is not due to the LORD's lack of faithfulness. He has been faithful to judge the people according to the terms of the old covenant, and he will be faithful to vindicate his true remnant and to judge his enemies in the last days (Mal. 3:1–5). But the current majority is like the past majority, turning aside from the LORD's statutes (Mal. 3:7a; cf., Deut. 9:24; Jer. 7:25; Rom. 9–11). Therefore, the LORD says, "Return to me, and I will return to you." The same call to return appears in Zechariah 1:3 (see the commentary there). The people must take responsibility and respond, but they will not do so without the LORD's work on their heart in the new covenant (see Deut. 29:3 [Eng., 29:4]; 30:6; Ezek. 11:19–20; Jer. 31:18, 31–34; Lam. 5:21). Thus, they are said to ask the question, "In what way should we return?" (Mal. 3:7b). This sets off the question-answer pattern of the disputation, but the difference in this fifth disputation is that the initial charge of robbing God,[26] which is laid against the people in Malachi 3:8 in response to the question in Malachi 3:7b, prompts a second question, "In what way have we robbed you?"

The rhetorical question at the beginning of Malachi 3:8 about whether a person will rob God expects an answer in the negative, and yet it is precisely this unthinkable act that the people are doing. They do this with regard to the tithe and the contribution. In context, this seems to refer primarily to the provision the LORD had made for the Levites (see Lev. 27:30–34; Num. 18:21–32; Deut. 14:22–29; Neh. 13:10–13). English versions tend to give a cause-effect relationship to the two clauses in Malachi 3:9, as if the people are cursed because they rob God. But no such relationship is explicit in the syntax of the Hebrew text. It appears more likely that the sense of the text is that the people have long been cursed with the curses of the old covenant (Lev. 26:14–41; Deut. 28:15–68; Mal. 2:2), and yet the nation in general still persists in robbing God.

---

25. See the Syriac and the Targum. Codex L: "we are not complete [i.e., consumed]."
26. Robbing God is representative of the people's continued failure to live up to the standards of the old covenant, which is the focus of the six disputations. Again, the point is not to return the people to the old covenant. It is to highlight the failure of the old covenant relationship and to call the people to return to the LORD in whom there is hope for a new covenant relationship.

The exact nature of the robbing of the tithe depends upon whether the interpreter reads "the whole of the tithe" (MT) or "every tithe" (4QXII^a) in Malachi 3:10. The command is to bring the tithe to the storehouse of the temple so that there might be food for those who work there. It is obvious from this text and elsewhere (e.g., Lev. 27:30–34) that this is not a monetary contribution. It is a contribution from the produce of the land. The LORD then invites the people to test him in this (cf., Mal. 3:15). They are to bring in the tithe to see if he will open the "windows of the sky" (i.e., the clouds; see Gen. 7:11; 2 Kgs. 7:2, 19) and empty a blessing (Lev. 26:3–13; Deut. 28:1–14) "until there is not enough" (i.e., forever, because God's blessing is inexhaustible). In addition, the LORD will rebuke the "eater" (i.e., the locust) so that it no longer destroys the fruit of the ground (Mal. 3:11). Furthermore, the grapevine will no longer show barrenness in the field (cf., Hag. 1:6, 9; 2:15–19). The nations will call the people blessed (Mal. 3:12; cf., Deut. 4:6–8; Mal. 1:11, 14b; 3:15; Ps. 1:1), for they will be "a land of delight." The land will be the object of the LORD's delight, and in turn the land will be a delight to all those who see it. This refers to the restoration of the lost blessing of life and dominion in the land of the covenant (i.e., the Garden of Eden), which was not attainable under the terms of a covenant that depended upon the people's fidelity. The land will be enjoyed in the messianic kingdom and in the new creation by the members of the new covenant.

It is a blatant misuse of Malachi 3:6–12 to demand a tenth of monetary income from members of the new covenant community to support the ministry of the local church. The pattern of disobedience-curse and obedience-blessing clearly presupposes the context of the old covenant (Lev. 26; Deut. 28). The disputations of the book of Malachi are designed to highlight the continued failure of the postexilic community under the terms of the old covenant. This ultimately points beyond that covenant to the need for a new covenant relationship. The standard for giving in the new covenant is not the tithing of produce for Levites. The standard for giving in the new covenant is the sacrificial death of Jesus Christ on the cross (2 Cor. 8:1–15). In other words, the standard for giving under the old covenant is too low for the new covenant. The new covenant believer must lay down his or her entire life for the sake of the gospel. This includes not only possessions but also time, talents, abilities, spiritual gifts, etc. Such giving is voluntary giving under the guidance of the Holy Spirit (see, e.g., Exod. 35:4–36:7). Thus, pastors would do well to focus more on regenerate church membership than on specific requirements for giving. The result will be an overabundance of gospel ministry rather than a mere balanced budget.

MALACHI 3:13–21 (ENG., 3:13–4:3)

3:13 "Your words are strong against me," says the LORD. "And you say, 'How have we spoken with one another against you?' 3:14 You say, 'It is vain to serve God. And what gain is it that we have kept his charge and that we have walked in mourning [lit., in dark clothing] before the LORD of hosts? 3:15 And now, we call presumptuous people blessed. Doers of wickedness not only are built up but also they test [LXX: oppose] God and escape [see GKC §162].'"[27] *3:16 Then [LXX, Syr.: These things] those who respected the LORD spoke to one another, and the LORD paid attention and listened. And a book of remembrance was written before him for those who respected the LORD and for those who had consideration for his name. 3:17 "And they will be mine," says the LORD of hosts, "for the day that I make a special possession. And I will spare them just as a man spares his son who serves him. 3:18 And you will see again [lit., return and see] the difference between a righteous man and a wicked man, between one who serves God and one who does not serve him. 3:19 (Eng., 4:1) For look, the day is coming, burning like a furnace [LXX adds: and it will set them on fire]. And all presumptuous people and every doer [mlt Mss: all doers] of wickedness will be like chaff, and the coming day will set them on fire," says the LORD of hosts, "to whom it will not leave [LXX: will not be left] root or branch. 3:20 (Eng., 4:2) And for you who respect my name a sun of righteousness [or, vindication] will rise, and healing will be in its wings [Syr.: on its tongue]. And you will go forth and spring [or, scatter] like calves [4QXII^a: like a calf] from a stall [LXX: sent from bonds]. 3:21 (Eng., 4:3) And you will crush [4QXII^a: counsel] wicked people, for they will be ashes under the soles of your feet in the day that I am making," says the LORD of hosts.*

The sixth and final disputation of the book in Malachi 3:13–21 (Eng., 3:13–4:3) begins with the charge that the words of the people are strong against the LORD (Mal. 3:13a). As expected, the people are represented as inquiring how they have spoken with one another against the LORD (Mal. 3:13b). The LORD responds by quoting the people as saying that it is vain to serve the LORD (Mal. 3:14a). After all, if every person who does evil is good in the eyes of the LORD (Mal. 2:17b), then why bother with keeping his commands? Of course, the premise is not true. The LORD is in fact coming to judge the wicked and to vindicate

---

27. English translations typically do not reflect recognition of the "גַּם . . . גַּם" ("not only . . . but also") construction. But see Keil, *Minor Prophets*, 660.

the righteous (Mal. 3:1–5). The people also ask, "And what gain is it that we have kept his charge and that we have walked in mourning before the LORD of hosts" (Mal. 3:14b)? Here the people claim to be like Abraham (see Gen. 26:5b ["he kept my charge"]) who was reckoned the righteousness of the law by faith (Gen. 15:6). But nothing could be further from the truth. According to the LORD himself, the people have turned aside from his statutes and not kept them since the days of their forefathers (Mal. 3:7). All that they have been able to muster is the external expression of mourning for their sin (i.e., dark clothing; see also Mal. 2:13), but there is no internal change of heart (cf., Isa. 58). So now the people capitulate to what they think is the new reality, and they call presumptuous people blessed (Mal. 3:15a; cf., Mal. 3:12, 19 [Eng., 3:12; 4:1]; Ps. 1:1). Not only are doers of wickedness seemingly built up, they say, but also they test God in an uninvited way and appear to get away with it (Mal. 3:15b; cf., Mal. 3:10; Ps. 95:9).

At that time (אז), the faithful remnant of those who respected the LORD (cf., Mal. 1:6b; 3:5b, 20 [Eng., 4:2]) also spoke to one another, but the prophet does not provide the content of their words (Mal. 3:16a; see CD-B 20:17–20). What he does report is that the LORD paid attention to them and listened (Mal. 3:16b). Furthermore, a "book of remembrance" was written before the LORD for those who respected him and for those who had consideration for his name (cf., 4Q417 2, I 15–16). There are several good possibilities for the identity of this book. One is that it contains the names (and perhaps the missing words) of those who respected the LORD's name and either memorializes them (cf., Exod. 17:14) or preserves them for the day of their reward (cf., Est. 6:1). Another possibility is that this is the metaphorical book containing the names of the elect (cf., Exod. 32:32; Isa. 4:3; Dan. 12:1; Rev. 3:5; 13:8; 17:8; 20:15; 21:27). But a third very plausible option has yet to be explored fully. It is not uncommon for biblical books to conclude with a reflection on the writing of the book as a whole (e.g., Deut. 31:9–13; Jer. 25:13b; 45; Prov. 30:5–6; Dan. 12:4; John 20:30–31; 2 Pet. 3:1; 1 John 5:13; Rev. 22:18–19). Thus, it would not be out of place for the book of remembrance to be intended as a reference to the Book of the Twelve by the final composer.[28] The book serves as a reminder to the faithful that they will be vindicated in the last days. Just as Malachi 3:22 (Eng., 4:4) calls on the readers to remember the Torah of Moses and the hope of the coming prophet like Moses (Deut.

28. I would like to thank my colleague, Ched Spellman, for prompting me to think about this possibility. Augustine thought that the book of remembrance was the New Testament (Ferreiro, *The Twelve Prophets*, 306).

18:15, 18; 34:10), so the Book of the Twelve calls to mind the hope of the coming of the Messiah (Hos. 3:5).

The faithful remnant will belong to the LORD for the day that he is preparing a "special possession" (Mal. 3:17a). When Israel came to Sinai, the people were to be a "special possession" and a "kingdom of priests" (Exod. 19:5–6), but they transgressed (Exod. 19:16b; Gal. 3:19) and became a kingdom with priests (Exod. 19:22).[29] The new covenant people of God will again be a kingdom of priests (Isa. 61:6; 66:20–21; Zeph. 3:10; Mal. 1:11; 3:3–4; 1 Pet. 2:5, 9; Rev. 1:6; 5:10; 20:6). The LORD will spare them just as a father spares his son who serves him (Mal. 3:17b; cf., Ps. 103:13). As in the days of Moses, or as in the days of David and Solomon, true believers will again see the distinction between the righteous and the wicked (see Ps. 1), between those who serve God and those who do not (Mal. 3:18). No longer will evil go unpunished (Mal. 2:17). No longer will the wicked prosper while the righteous suffer unjustly. The LORD will bring justice to the world in final judgment.

How do the righteous by faith know that all will be set right in the end? They know because, as the LORD points out in Malachi 3:19 (Eng., 4:1), the Day of the LORD is coming (cf., Mal. 3:2), burning like a furnace (cf., Gen. 15:17; Isa. 31:9; Ps. 21:10 [Eng, 21:9]). All the presumptuous people whom the community calls blessed and all the doers of wickedness who are seemingly built up now and free of consequences for their actions (see Mal. 3:15) will be like chaff (cf., Isa. 13:11; Ps. 1:4). The coming day will set them ablaze (see Isa. 66:15–17, 24; Dan. 7:9–10; 2 Pet. 3; Rev. 20:11–15). It will not leave them a root or a branch (i.e., anything at all).

But for those who respect the LORD's name (Mal. 3:16), the coming day will be a day of salvation (Mal. 3:20 [Eng., 4:2]). A "sun of righteousness" will rise for them with healing in its wings (cf., Ps. 139:9). The depiction of salvation in terms of a morning sunrise is a common one in the Prophets because it helps the reader envision restoration in the new creation (Gen. 1:3; Isa. 58:8; 60:1–2; Mic. 7:8–9). The early church fathers understood the sun of righteousness in Malachi 3:20 (Eng., 4:2) to be a direct reference to Christ.[30] Others prefer to see it simply as a metaphor for salvation or vindication in general (Isa. 56:1).[31] There is, however, good evidence in favor of the messianic reading that is often

---

29. See John H. Sailhamer, *The Pentateuch as Narrative* (Grand Rapids: Zondervan, 1992), 51–57.
30. See Ferreiro, *The Twelve Prophets*, 307–311. See also Calvin, *Malachi*, 617–21.
31. E.g., Keil, *Minor Prophets*, 662.

overlooked even by those who advocate for it. Already in the LXX of Numbers 24:17b is the image of a messianic star (*Tg. Onk.*: king) rising like the sun out of Jacob. The pseudepigraphal *Testament of Judah* puts this text together with Malachi 3:20a (Eng., 4:2a): "And after these things a star will rise to you from Jacob in peace, and a man will rise from my seed as the sun of righteousness, walking with the sons of men in meekness and righteousness, and no sin will be found in him" (*T. Jud.* 24:1). The prophecy in the last words of David also anticipates that the messianic ruler will be like the light of the morning when the sun rises (2 Sam. 23:3–4; cf., Hos. 6:3a; Ps. 72:5, 17). The Davidic Messiah is the great light that those who walk in darkness will see (Isa. 9:1, 5, 6 [Eng., 9:2, 6, 7]), and the messianic servant of the LORD will be a light to the nations (Isa. 42:6; 49:6). It is through faith in the person and work of the servant of the LORD that the people will be declared righteous and bear the fruit of righteousness (Isa. 53:1, 11; 60:21; 61:3b). Thus, they will go forth from their bondage and spring like calves from a stall as they rejoice in their newfound freedom (Mal. 3:20b [Eng., 4:2b]); cf., Isa. 42:7; 49:9; 61:1; Jer. 50:11). They will crush the wicked like ashes (from the burning [Mal. 3:19 (Eng., 4:1)]) under the soles of their feet in the day that the LORD is preparing for them (Mal. 3:12 [Eng., 4:3]; cf., Gen. 3:15; Isa. 26:6; Rom. 16:20).

MALACHI 3:22–24 (ENG., 4:4–6)

3:22 (Eng., 4:4) "Remember the Torah of Moses my servant whom I commanded at Horeb concerning all Israel statutes and judgments.[32]

3:23 (Eng., 4:5) Look, I am about to send to you Elijah the prophet [LXX: the Tishbite] before the coming of the great and terrible [LXX: manifest] Day of the LORD. 3:24 (Eng., 4:6) And he will cause the heart of the fathers [LXX: father] to return to [or, in addition to] the sons [LXX: son] and the heart of the sons [LXX: a man] to [or, in addition to] their fathers [LXX: his neighbor] lest I come and strike the land with a ban [or, completely destroy the land]."

The last three verses of Malachi stand apart from the six disputations that form the main body of the book. At first glance, these verses appear to be the work of the composer of the Twelve who has consistently provided seams that connect the ends of the individual books to the

---

32. The LXX has this verse at the end of the book after Malachi 3:23–24 (Eng., 4:5–6).

beginnings of the books that follow them. But in this case the text of Malachi 3:22–24 (Eng., 4:4–6) stands at the end of the Book of the Twelve and connects the Twelve and the entire canonical division of the Prophets to the beginning of the book of Psalms, which stands at the beginning of the third and final division of the Hebrew canon according to Luke 24:44 and other witnesses. Nevertheless, the seam does meet the criteria for identification of the composer's activity. Just as Malachi 3:22–24 (Eng., 4:4–6) is distinct from the material that precedes it, so Psalms 1 and 2 are distinct from what follows them. Both psalms lack superscriptions and are intended to be read together as an introduction to the Psalter (see *b. Ber.* 9b–10a).[33] The seam also develops the program of the Book of the Twelve (Hos. 3:4–5) by means of the theme of the Day of the LORD (Mal. 3:23 [Eng., 4:5]). And thirdly, the seam features citation from the book of Jeremiah. Psalm 1 contrasts the righteous and the wicked in a manner similar to Jeremiah 17:5–8 and uses the imagery of the tree planted by water found in Jeremiah 17:7–8. According to Jeremiah 17:7–8, the person who trusts in the LORD is like a fruit-bearing tree planted by a good water source. Psalm 1 develops this idea and gives concrete expression to that trust: Torah study (Ps. 1:2).

The canonical seam in Malachi 3:22–24 (Eng., 4:4–6) and Psalms 1–2 also runs parallel to the canonical seam that connects the Torah to the Prophets (Deut. 34:5–Josh. 1:9). Both seams draw upon material in the books that precede them. According to Deuteronomy 34:9, the same Joshua who was said to have the Spirit in him in Numbers 27:18 is now said to be filled with the Spirit of wisdom. Verse 10 of Deuteronomy 34 picks up the language of the prophecy about the prophet like Moses in Deuteronomy 18:15, 18 and indicates that such a prophet never came. This reflects the perspective of someone looking back over the history of Israel's prophets—someone like Ezra (Ezra. 7:6, 10; 9:10–11; Neh. 8–9). The messianic prophet like Moses never came. Therefore, he is still to come in the future. Thus, the wise man Joshua is instructed to await his coming by "murmuring" in the book of the Torah day and night (Josh. 1:8). Likewise, Malachi 3:23 (Eng., 4:5) picks up the language of Malachi 3:1a and indicates that the messenger being sent by the LORD to prepare the way is a prophet like Elijah. According to Psalm 1, the wise person awaits his coming by "murmuring" in the Torah day and night (Ps. 1:2; see also Josh. 1:8b and Ps. 1:3b).

---

33. The two psalms share several key verbal links in the Hebrew text (e.g., Ps. 1:1a and Ps. 2:12b; Ps. 1:2b and Ps. 2:1b; Ps. 1:6b and Ps. 2:12a). See also the citation of Psalm 1:1a; 2:12b and Psalm 1:6b; 2:12a at the beginning and the end of the acrostic poem in Psalm 112:1a, 10b.

The interpreter is thus left with two main options for the identity of the person responsible for Malachi 3:22–24 (Eng., 4:4–6). Either the composer of the Twelve is also the composer of the Hebrew canon (i.e., the one responsible for the canonical seams), or the composer of the canon knew the work of the composer of the Twelve and created a canonical seam consistent with it. The first option seems less likely due to the fact that there is no citation from the book of Jeremiah in the first canonical seam. Since this is the calling card of the composer of the Twelve, the reader expects to see it wherever he is active. On the other hand, both canonical seams reflect intimate knowledge of the books to which they are attached, making it probable that the composer of the canon has fashioned the seam that connects the Prophets to the Writings after the pattern of composition in the Twelve.

The difference in the arrangement of Malachi 3:22–24 (Eng., 4:4–6) between the MT and the LXX suggests that Malachi 3:22 (Eng., 4:4) and Malachi 3:23–24 (Eng., 4:5–6) are two separate appendices that have been put together in two distinct ways. The LXX has Malachi 3:22 (Eng., 4:4) after Malachi 3:23–24 (Eng., 4:5–6). The usual explanation of this arrangement is an appeal to the Masoretic tradition that says when Isaiah, the Twelve, Ecclesiastes, and Lamentations are read in the synagogue, the next to last verse is to be repeated after the last verse in order to avoid concluding with the harshness of the final verse.[34] Another possibility is that the placement of Malachi 3:22 (Eng., 4:4) at the end shows a canonical awareness of the conclusion of the Prophets (cf., *b. Sotah* 48b) and consciousness of the position of the following book of Psalms at the beginning of the Writings. The call to remember the Torah anticipates the reference to the Torah in Psalm 1:2. Both options for the arrangement of the LXX presuppose that its order is secondary. Given the order of the MT, it is easy to see why someone might rearrange the text. But given the order of the LXX, it is not so easy to see why someone would change to the MT order. Thus, the present commentary will work under the assumption that the MT arrangement is original.

The call to remember the Torah in Malachi 3:22 (Eng., 4:4) is often read as a call to remember the law given at Sinai, the "statutes and judgments." But the "statutes and judgments" in this verse are part of a relative clause designed to describe "Moses my servant." They do not describe what is meant by "Torah." There are several clues within this verse that the reference is to Deuteronomy as a commentary (see Deut. 1:5) on the whole book of the Torah (Gen.–Deut.).

---

34. See J. Smith, *Malachi*, 83.

The designation of Moses as "my servant" (see Num. 12:7) directs the reader back to the seam that connects the Torah to the Prophets in Deuteronomy 34:5–Joshua 1:9 (see Deut. 34:5; Josh. 1:1–2). The use of "Horeb" rather than "Sinai" points to the preference for "Horeb" in Deuteronomy (e.g., Deut. 28:69 [Eng., 29:1]). The phrase "statutes and judgments" is unique to Deuteronomy (Deut. 4:5, 8, 14). The content of the six disputations in Malachi makes it clear that the prophet does not intend for the people simply to try harder at keeping the laws of the Sinai covenant. The people must look beyond that covenant to the future work of God. This ties in directly to the purpose of the composer of the Twelve. The call to remember the Torah is not a call to keep the law. It is a call to remember the hope of the messianic prophet like Moses in Deuteronomy (Deut. 18:15, 18; 34:10).[35] It is for this messianic figure that the prophet like Elijah will prepare the way. The Book of the Twelve (i.e., the "book of remembrance" [Mal. 3:16]) serves to remind its readers of this hope (Hos. 3:5).

As noted above, Malachi 3:23 (Eng., 4:5) revisits the language of Malachi 3:1 and indicates that the messenger whom the LORD is sending to prepare the way is Elijah the prophet (see *m. Sota.* 9:15). Despite the fact that Elijah never died (2 Kgs. 2:11; cf., Gen. 5:24), this text does not mean that Elijah himself will literally return (see John 1:19–28). Rather, just as there will be a prophet "like" Moses (Deut. 18:15, 18; 34:10), so there will be a prophet "like" Elijah who will come in the spirit and power of Elijah (Luke 1:17).[36] He will come before "the great and terrible Day of the LORD" (cf., Joel 2:11; 3:4 [Eng., 2:31]). This Day has been much discussed over the course of the Twelve and need not be belabored here. John the Baptist came as the prophet like Elijah to prepare the way for Jesus through his baptism of repentance. This brought about a kind of inaugurated eschatology and the establishment of a spiritual kingdom, but we still

---

35. The likelihood of this connection increases with the recognition that the composer of the canon is responsible for Deuteronomy 34:5–Joshua 1:9 and Malachi 3:22 (Eng., 4:4)–Psalm 1.

36. Elijah himself is a Moses-like prophet in 1 Kings 19 and 2 Kings 2. Moses and Elijah are together with Jesus on the Mount of Transfiguration (Matt. 17:1–13). The two witnesses in Revelation 11 are based on Moses and Elijah. The language of Malachi 3:23 (Eng., 4:5) is also comparable to references to a future David (Jer. 30:9; Ezek. 34:23–24; 37:24; Hos. 3:5), which are clearly not references to the historical David or to a resurrected David but to the Davidic Messiah. The difference, of course, is that the coming Elijah is not necessarily of Elijah's lineage.

await the tribulation and the earthly kingdom of Christ. It is not immediately clear why Elijah is chosen as the paradigm for preparatory prophetic ministry. It may very well be because of the commission Elijah receives in 1 Kings 19:15–18, which, among other things, involves the passing of the torch to Elisha who would have a double portion of Elijah's spirit (2 Kgs. 2:9).

The final verse (Mal. 3:24 [Eng., 4:6]; cf., 4Q521; Sir. 48:10; *m. Ed.* 8:7) can be read in at least two different ways. Perhaps the most common way to read it is that the prophet like Elijah will restore families—fathers to sons and sons to fathers. But this would seem to make little sense of the reading in Luke 1:17: "to restore hearts of fathers to children and the disobedient/unbelieving in the wisdom of the righteous to prepare for the Lord a ready people" (cf., Matt. 17:11; Mark 9:12). According to this interpretation, it appears that the fathers represent the righteous generation and that the sons represent the disobedient or unbelieving who need to repent in order to be ready for the coming of the Lord. Nevertheless, this is by no means a necessary way of understanding either Malachi 3:24 (Eng., 4:6) or Luke 1:17. Given the characterization of the fathers in Malachi 3:7, it is highly unlikely that the composer of the canon wants to use them as the standard of righteousness in this seam (see also Luke 11:47–48). It seems that both the fathers (the older generation) and the sons (the younger generation) need to return in preparation for the Day of the LORD. Thus, the prophet like Elijah will restore the hearts of the fathers in addition to the hearts of the sons and vice versa. Both the fathers and the sons are the disobedient/unbelieving who are in need of the wisdom of the righteous. They must respond to the call to repentance lest they face the coming of the LORD who will strike the land with a ban (cf., Zech. 14:11) and thus completely destroy it.

FINAL THOUGHTS ON TEACHING AND PREACHING THE TWELVE

One way to give a congregation a sense of the Book of the Twelve as a whole would be to do a twelve-week series, devoting one week to each of the twelve parts. The goal, however, should not be to treat each part as a self-contained unit, to trace common themes, or to address topics. The goal should be to follow the compositional strategy of the entire Book of the Twelve. Each week would then be focused on outlining the individual book at hand, explaining the compositional seam that connects it to the following book, and relating the book to the overall program of the Twelve. The summary at the end of the Introduction to this commentary can be used as a guide.[37] But it must be kept in mind that such a series would by no means do justice to the content of the Twelve. A preaching series like this needs to be supplemented by a longer, more in-depth exposition of each word of the Twelve in smaller, more interactive settings for members of the congregation who have a genuine interest in the Bible. This kind of teaching would need to be done by someone with skill and expertise in biblical languages and exegesis (i.e., textual criticism, grammar and syntax, semantics, compositional analysis, and intertextuality).

"Preaching" or "proclamation" (κήρυγμα) in the New Testament is primarily something that takes place outside the gathering of the local church.[38] When the earliest church did gather, it came together for "teaching" (διδασκαλία). It was only later that preaching became identified with the rhetorical delivery of an oral performance in the context of a worship service. Nowadays "preaching" is almost exclusively thought of as the act whereby the lead pastor "teaches" the congregation of believers. Actual teaching in smaller, more interactive settings is largely left to those with no formal training who follow a curriculum handed down to them by the staff. This leaves a massive gap in the teaching ministry of the local church. At no point does anyone with exegetical skills actually deal with the details of the text and allow for questions, comments, and clarification.[39] The communication situation of preaching necessarily leaves out detailed exposition. Such one-way communication requires the preacher to sustain the audience's attention with things other than textual details. Even the most ardent advocate of expository preaching leaves out important exegetical information in an effort not to lose his audience. This problem is alleviated in smaller settings where interaction takes off the edge and allows for treatment of finer points.

It is not the job of the preacher or the teacher simply to tell people how they should live their lives. The Bible in conjunction with the Holy

---

37. This will help to provide a macrostructural framework for understanding the lower levels of the text.
38. See C. H. Dodd, *The Apostolic Preaching and Its Development* (New York: Harper, 1964). But see also 2 Timothy 4:2. Most biblical texts, especially the Tanakh, are composed for reading and study (Ps. 1; Neh. 8–9; 1 Tim. 4:13). Of course, apostolic epistles would be read aloud at church gatherings (e.g., Col. 4:16).
39. A biblical model for this is found in Nehemiah 8–9 where Ezra, an expert (Ezra 7:6, 10), reads and expounds the text according to its own form and sequence in the context of worship, and the Levites (also experts) are disseminated among the congregation to help with explanation in smaller groups.

Spirit does that. Therefore, it is primarily the job of preachers and teachers to explain the text in the manner that it has been given and on its own terms. People do not need more to-do lists and clever outlines that fade away. They need a model for reading the Bible that teaches them to ask the right kind of exegetical questions so that they can read the Bible for themselves. They do not need a finished product (e.g., a sermon or a lesson) as much as they need to be brought into the workshop so that they too can learn the tools of the trade. A repackaged version of the Bible that caters to the concerns of the audience will not suffice. The people must be reoriented to the concerns of the biblical text. It is fine to make the text as accessible as possible, but ultimately the reader must come to it. The text of Scripture, like all things great and worthwhile, does not come to anyone on his or her own terms.

Arbitrary obsession with application has become so out of hand that all the genres of the Bible have been flattened into one: that of a manual or handbook for life. There are plenty of practical texts in the Bible—law, wisdom literature, epistles, etc.—but preachers and teachers often feel the pressure to add application even to these. When it comes to something like the Book of the Twelve, the drive to be practical causes the reader to miss the profound impact that its vision of Christ and his kingdom has on the heart and mind of the believer. The text does ultimately shape the thoughts and the actions of the believer (2 Tim. 3:16–17; 2 Pet. 3), but it does so more like pictures at an art exhibition than like commands from a drill sergeant. The history of Christian preaching has always been plagued by proof-texting and by topical approaches motivated by the practical interests of the church. The history of Christian commentary, on the other hand, has been wonderfully constrained by the requirements of the text.[40] It seems that we would do well to learn from this by using good Christian commentary not as a mere reference tool but as the primary content for our preaching and teaching, thus giving our churches the full tour of the biblical text.

---

40. "[T]he later biblical commentary literature does tend to read the biblical books *as books*, and this prominent stream within the history of interpretation provides an important counterweight to the use of isolated verses or pericopes in preaching" (Stephen B. Chapman, "A Threefold Cord Is Not Quickly Broken: Interpretation by Canonical Division in Early Judaism and Christianity," in *The Shape of the Writings*, eds. Julius Steinberg and Timothy J. Stone [Winona Lake, IN: Eisenbrauns, 2015], 303).

BIBLIOGRAPHY

Ackroyd, Peter R. "A Judgment Narrative between Kings and Chronicles? An Approach to Amos 7:9–17." In *Canon and Authority: Essays in Old Testament Religion and Theology*, eds. George W. Coats and Burke O. Long, 71–87. Philadelphia: Fortress, 1977.

Ahearne-Kroll, Patricia. "LXX/OG Zechariah 1–6 and the Portrayal of Joshua Centuries after the Restoration of the Temple." In *Septuagint Research: Issues and Challenges in the Study of the Greek Jewish Scriptures*, eds. Wolfgang Kraus and R. Glenn Wooden, 179–92. Atlanta: SBL, 2006.

Andersen, Francis I. *The Sentence in Biblical Hebrew*. The Hague: Mouton, 1974.

_____, and A. Dean Forbes. *Spelling in the Hebrew Bible*. Biblica et orientalia 41. Rome: Biblical Institute, 1986.

Anderson, Bernhard W. *Understanding the Old Testament*, 4th ed. Englewood Cliffs: Prentice-Hall, 1986.

Armerding, C. E. *Nahum*. Expositor's Bible Commentary 7. Grand Rapids: Zondervan, 1985.

Bacher, Wilhelm. *Die exegetische Terminologie der jüdischen Traditionsliteratur*. Hildesheim: Georg Olms, 1965.

Bar-Efrat, Shimon. *Narrative Art in the Bible*. London: T&T Clark, 2004.

Barr, James. *The Semantics of Biblical Language*. Oxford: Oxford University Press, 1961.

_____. *Comparative Philology and the Text of the Old Testament*, with additions and corrections. Winona Lake, IN: Eisenbrauns, 1987.

Beckwith, Roger T. "Formation of the Hebrew Bible." In *Mikra: Text, Translation, Reading & Interpretation of the Hebrew Bible in*

Ancient Judaism & Early Christianity, eds. Martin Jan Mulder and Harry Sysling, 39–88. Philadelphia: Fortress, 1988. Reprint, Peabody, MA: Hendrickson, 2004.

Ben Zvi, Ehud, and James D. Nogalski. *Two Sides of a Coin: Juxtaposing Views on Interpreting the Book of the Twelve / the Twelve Prophetic Books*. Piscataway, NJ: Gorgias, 2009.

Bewer, Julius A. *A Critical and Exegetical Commentary on Obadiah and Joel*. International Critical Commentary. New York: Charles Scribner's Sons, 1911.

Black, Matthew. *An Aramaic Approach to the Gospels and Acts*, 3d ed. Oxford: Oxford University Press, 1967. Reprint, Peabody, MA: Hendrickson, 1998.

Blau, Joshua. *Phonology and Morphology of Biblical Hebrew*. Linguistic Studies in Ancient West Semitic 2. Winona Lake, IN: Eisenbrauns, 2010.

Blenkinsopp, Joseph. *Prophecy and Canon: A Contribution to the Study of Jewish Origins*. Notre Dame, IN: Notre Dame University Press, 1977.

Blomberg, Craig L. "Matthew." In *Commentary on the New Testament Use of the Old Testament*, ed. G. K. Beale and D. A. Carson, 1–109. Grand Rapids: Baker, 2007.

Boda, Mark J. "A Deafening Call to Silence: The Rhetorical 'End' of Human Address to the Deity in the Book of the Twelve." In *The Book of the Twelve and the New Form Criticism*, eds. Mark J. Boda, Michael H. Floyd, and Colin M. Toffelmire, 183–204. Atlanta: SBL, 2015.

Brown, F., S. R. Driver, and C. A. Briggs. *A Hebrew and English Lexicon of the Old Testament*. Oxford, 1907.

Bruns, Gerald. "Midrash and Allegory." In *The Literary Guide to the Bible*, eds. Frank Kermode and Robert Alter, 625–46. Cambridge, MA: Belknap, 1987.

Budde, K. "Eine folgenschwere Redaktion des Zwölfprophetenbuchs." *Zeitschrift für die alttestamentliche Wissenschaft* 39 (1922): 218–29.

Bullinger, E. W. *Figures of Speech Used in the Bible*. London: Spottiswoode, 1898 Reprint, Grand Rapids: Baker, 1968.

Bynum, Wm. Randolph. *The Fourth Gospel and the Scriptures: Illuminating the Form and Meaning of Scriptural Citation in John 19:37*. Supplements to Novum Testamentum 144. Leiden: Brill, 2012.

Calvin, John. *Commentaries on the Twelve Minor Prophets*. Translated by John Owen. Calvin's Commentaries. Reprint, Grand Rapids: Baker, 2005.

BIBLIOGRAPHY

Cathcart, Kevin J., and Robert P. Gordon, *The Targum of the Minor Prophets: Translated, with a Critical Introduction, Apparatus, and Notes.* The Aramaic Bible 14. Collegeville, MN: Liturgical, 1989.

Chapman, Stephen B. *The Law and the Prophets: A Study in Old Testament Canon Formation.* Forschungen zum Alten Testament 27. Tübingen: Mohr Siebeck, 2000.

_____. "A Threefold Cord Is Not Quickly Broken: Interpretation by Canonical Division in Early Judaism and Christianity." In *The Shape of the Writings*, eds. Julius Steinberg and Timothy J. Stone, 281–309. Winona Lake, IN: Eisenbrauns, 2015.

Childs, Brevard S. *The Book of Exodus: A Critical, Theological Commentary.* Old Testament Library. Louisville: Westminster John Knox, 1974.

_____. *Introduction to the Old Testament as Scripture.* Philadelphia: Fortress, 1979.

_____. *Isaiah: A Commentary.* Old Testament Library. Louisville: Westminster John Knox, 2000.

Christensen, Duane L. "The Acrostic Poem of Nahum Reconsidered." *Zeitschrift für die alttestamentliche Wissenschaft* 87 (1975): 17–30.

_____. "The Acrostic of Nahum Once Again: A Prosodic Analysis of Nahum 1:1–10." *Zeitschrift für die alttestamentliche Wissenschaft* 99 (1987): 409–415.

_____. *Nahum: A New Translation with Introduction and Commentary.* The Anchor Yale Bible 24f. New Haven, CT: Yale University Press, 2009.

Clements, Ronald E. "Patterns in the Prophetic Canon." In *Canon and Authority: Essays in Old Testament Religion and Theology*, ed. George W. Coats and Burke O. Long, 42–55. Philadelphia: Fortress, 1977.

Clines, D. J. A., ed. *Dictionary of Classical Hebrew.* Sheffield: Sheffield Phoenix, 1993–2011.

Cook, Gregory. "Nahum's Shaking Cypresses." *Bulletin of Biblical Research* 26 (2016): 1–6.

Cowley, A. E. *Aramaic Papyri of the Fifth Century B.C.* Oxford: Clarendon, 1923. Reprint, Eugene, OR: Wipf & Stock, 2005.

Crenshaw, James L. *Hymnic Affirmation of Divine Justice: The Doxologies of Amos and Related Texts in the Old Testament.* Society of Biblical Literature Dissertation Series 24. Missoula, MT: Scholars, 1975.

_____. *Joel.* The Anchor Bible 24c. New York: Doubleday, 1995.

Day, John. "A Case of Inner Scriptural Interpretation: The Dependence of Isaiah XXVI.13–XXVII.11 on Hosea XIII.4–XIV.10

(Eng., 9) and Its Relevance to Some Theories of the Redaction of the 'Isaiah Apocalypse.'" *Journal of Theological Studies* NS 31 (1980): 309–319.

Dempster, Stephen. "A Wandering Moabite: Ruth—A Book in Search of a Canonical Home." In *The Shape of the Writings*, eds. Julius Steinberg and Timothy J. Stone, 87–118. Winona Lake, IN: Eisenbrauns, 2015.

Driver, S. R. *An Introduction to the Literature of the Old Testament.* New York: Charles Scribner's Sons, 1891.

Dunn, James D. G. *Romans 1–8.* Word Biblical Commentary 38A. Dallas: Word, 1988.

Eichrodt, Walther. *Theology of the Old Testament.* Vol. 2. Translated by J. A. Baker. Philadelphia: Westminster, 1967.

Eisenstein, Sergei M. *The Film Sense.* Translated and edited by Jay Leyda. San Diego: Harcourt Brace & Company, 1942.

Ellis, E. Earle. "The Old Testament Canon in the Early Church." In *Mikra: Text, Translation, Reading & Interpretation of the Hebrew Bible in Ancient Judaism & Early Christianity*, ed. Martin Jan Mulder and Harry Sysling, 653–90. Philadelphia: Fortress, 1988. Reprint, Peabody, MA: Hendrickson, 2004.

Eshel, H., and J. Strugnell. "Alphabetical Acrostics in Pre-Tannaitic Hebrew." *Catholic Biblical Quarterly* 62 (2000): 453–58.

Ferreiro, Alberto, ed. *The Twelve Prophets*, Ancient Christian Commentary on Scripture Old Testament XIV. Downers Grove, IL: InterVarsity, 2003.

Fishbane, Michael. *Biblical Interpretation in Ancient Israel.* Oxford: Clarendon, 1985.

Floyd, Michael H. "The Chimerical Acrostic of Nahum 1:2–10." *Journal of Biblical Literature* 113 (1994): 421–37.

_____. "New Form Criticism and Beyond: The Historicity of Prophetic Literature Revisited." In *The Book of the Twelve and the New Form Criticism*, eds. Mark J. Boda, Michael H. Floyd, and Colin M. Toffelmire, 17–36. Atlanta: SBL, 2015.

Frei, Hans. *The Eclipse of Biblical Narrative: A Study in Eighteenth and Nineteenth Century Hermeneutics.* New Haven, CT: Yale University Press, 1974.

Fretheim, Terence E. *Reading Hosea–Malachi: A Literary and Theological Commentary.* Macon, GA: Smyth & Helwys, 2013.

Gathercole, Simon J. "Torah, Life, and Salvation: Leviticus 18:5 in Early Judaism and the New Testament." In *From Prophecy to Testament: the Function of the Old Testament in the New*, ed. Craig A. Evans, 126–45. Peabody, MA: Hendrickson, 2004.

Geiger, Abraham. *Urschrift und Uebersetzungen der Bibel in ihrer Abhängigheit von der inner Entwickelung des Judenthums.* Breslau: Hainauer, 1857.

Goswell, Gregory. "Jonah among the Twelve Prophets." *Journal of Biblical Literature* 135 (2016): 283–99.

_____. "A Theocratic Reading of Zechariah 9:9." *Bulletin of Biblical Research* 26.1 (2016): 7–19.

Grudem, Wayne. *Systematic Theology.* Grand Rapids: Zondervan, 1994.

Gunkel, Hermann. "Nahum 1." *Zeitschrift für die alttestamentliche Wissenschaft* 11 (1893): 223–44.

_____. *Introduction to Psalms: The Genres of the Religious Lyric of Israel.* Completed by Joachim Begrich. Translated by James D. Nogalski. Macon, GA: Mercer University Press, 1998.

Hardy II, Humphrey Hill, and Benjamin D. Thomas. "Another Look at Biblical Hebrew *bama* 'High Place.'" *Vetus Testamentum* 62 (2012): 175–88.

Harper, William R. *A Critical and Exegetical Commentary on Amos and Hosea.* International Critical Commentary. New York: Charles Scribner's Sons, 1905.

Heschel, Abraham J. *The Prophets.* New York: HarperCollins, 1969. Reprint, Peabody, MA: Prince, 2001.

Holladay, William. *Jeremiah 1: A Commentary on the Book of the Prophet Jeremiah Chapters 1–25.* Hermeneia. Philadelphia: Fortress, 1986.

Holmstedt, Robert D., and Andrew R. Jones. "The Pronoun in Tripartite Verbless Clauses in Biblical Hebrew: Resumption for Left-dislocation or Pronominal Copula?" *Journal of Semitic Studies* 59 (2014): 53–89.

Holmstedt, Robert D. *The Relative Clause in Biblical Hebrew.* Linguistic Studies in Ancient West Semitic 10. Winona Lake, IN: Eisenbrauns, 2016.

Horbury, William. *Jewish Messianism and the Cult of Christ.* London: SCM, 1998.

House, Paul. *The Unity of the Twelve.* Sheffield: Almond, 1990.

Huehnergard, John. "On the Etymology of the Hebrew Relative šɛ-." In *Biblical Hebrew in Its Northwest Semitic Setting: Typological and Historical Perspectives,* ed. Steven E. Fassberg and Avi Hurvitz, 103–125. Winona Lake, IN: Eisenbrauns, 2006.

Jastrow, Marcus. *Dictionary of the Targumim, Talmud Babli, Yerushalmi and Midrashic Literature,* 2d ed. New York: Judaica, 1903.

Jenni, Ernst, and Claus Westermann, eds. *Theological Lexicon of the Old Testament.* Translated by Mark E. Biddle. Peabody, MA: Hendrickson, 1997.

Jeremias, Jörg. *The Book of Amos: A Commentary.* Translated by Douglas W. Stott. Old Testament Library. Louisville: Westminster John Knox, 1998.

Johnston, Philip S. *Shades of Sheol: Death and Afterlife in the Old Testament.* Downers Grove, IL: InterVarsity, 2002.

Jones, Barry Alan. *The Formation of the Book of the Twelve: A Study in Text and Canon.* Atlanta: Scholars Press, 1995.

Kahle, Paul E. *The Cairo Geniza,* 2d ed. New York: Praeger, 1960.

Kautzsch, E., ed. *Gesenius' Hebrew Grammar.* Translated by A. E. Cowley, 2d ed. Oxford: Clarendon, 1910.

Keil, C. F. *The Pentateuch.* Translated by James Martin. Keil & Delitzsch Commentary on the Old Testament 1. Edinburgh: T. & T. Clark, 1866–91. Reprint, Peabody. MA: Hendrickson, 2001.

_____. *The Minor Prophets.* Keil & Delitzsch Commentary on the Old Testament 10. Edinburgh: T. & T. Clark, 1866–91. Reprint, Peabody, MA: Hendrickson, 2001.

Klein, Ralph W. *1 Chronicles.* Hermeneia. Minneapolis: Fortress, 2006.

Koehler, Ludwig, and Walter Baumgartner. *The Hebrew and Aramaic Lexicon of the Old Testament.* Study Edition, 2 vols. Leiden: Brill, 2001.

Kugel, James L. *The Idea of Biblical Poetry: Parallelism and Its History.* New Haven, CT: Yale University Press, 1981. Reprint, Baltimore: Johns Hopkins University Press, 1998.

Levy, Samuel. *The Messiah: An Aramaic Interpretation, The Messianic Exegesis of the Targum.* Cincinnati: Hebrew Union College Press, 1974.

Martin, Gary D. *Multiple Originals: New Approaches to Hebrew Bible Textual Criticism.* Atlanta: SBL, 2010.

Mays, James L. *Hosea: A Commentary.* Philadelphia: Westminster, 1969.

McCartney, Dan, and Peter Enns. "Matthew and Hosea: A Response to John Sailhamer." *Westminster Theological Journal* 63 (2001): 97–105.

McLaughlin, J. *The marzēaḥ in the Prophetic Literature: References and Allusions in Light of Extra-biblical Evidence.* Vetus Testamentum Supplement 86. Leiden: Brill, 2001.

Michel, Diethelm. *Tempora und Satzstellung in den Psalmen.* Bonn: H. Bouvier u. Co., 1960.

Mikraoth Gedoloth: The Twelve Prophets. 2 Vols. Translated by A. J. Rosenberg. New York: Judaica, 1986.

BIBLIOGRAPHY

Miller-Naudé, Cynthia L. "Mismatches of Definiteness within Appositional Expressions Used as Vocatives in Biblical Hebrew." *Journal of Northwest Semitic Languages* 40/2 (2014): 97–111.

Mitchell, Hinckley G. *A Critical and Exegetical Commentary on Haggai and Zechariah.* International Critical Commentary. New York: Charles Scribner's Sons, 1912.

Moshavi, Adina. *Word Order in the Biblical Hebrew Finite Clause.* Linguistic Studies in Ancient West Semitic 4. Winona Lake, IN: Eisenbrauns, 2010.

Niccacci, Alviero. *Syntax of the Verb in Classical Hebrew Prose.* Translated by W. G. E. Watson. Sheffield: JSOT, 1990.

Nogalski, James D. *Literary Precursors to the Book of the Twelve.* Beihefte zur Zeitschrift für die alttestamentliche Wissenschaft 217. Berlin: de Gruyter, 1993.

_____. *Redactional Processes in the Book of the Twelve.* Beihefte zur Zeitschrift für die alttestamentliche Wissenschaft 218. Berlin: de Gruyter, 1993.

_____, and Marvin Sweeney, eds. *Reading and Hearing the Book of the Twelve.* Atlanta: SBL, 2000.

_____. *Hosea–Jonah* and *Micah–Malachi.* Smith & Helwys Bible Commentary. Macon, GA: Smyth & Helwys, 2011.

Noonan, Benjamin J. "Abraham, Blessing, and the Nations." *Hebrew Studies* 51 (2010): 73–93.

Pajunen, Mika S., and Hanne von Weissenberg. "The Book of Malachi, Manuscript 4Q76 (4QXII^a), and the Formation of the 'Book of the Twelve.'" *Journal of Biblical Literature* 134 (2015): 731–51.

Paul, Shalom M. *Amos.* Hermeneia. Philadelphia: Fortress, 1991.

Petterson, Anthony R. "A New Form-Critical Approach to Zechariah's Crowning of the High Priest Joshua and the Identity of 'Shoot'." In *The Book of the Twelve & the New Form Criticism*, eds. Mark J. Boda, Michael H. Floyd, and Colin M. Toffelmire, 285–304. Atlanta: SBL, 2015.

Pritchard, James B., ed. *Ancient Near Eastern Texts Relating to the Old Testament*, 3d ed. Princeton, NJ: Princeton University Press, 1969.

Raabe, Paul. *Obadiah: A New Translation with Introduction and Commentary.* Anchor Bible 24D. New York: Doubleday, 1996.

Rendsburg, Gary. "Northern Hebrew through Time: From the Song of Deborah to the Mishnah." In *Diachrony in Biblical Hebrew*, eds. Cynthia Miller-Naudé and Ziony Zevit, 339–59. Linguistic Studies in Ancient West Semitic 8. Winona Lake, IN: Eisenbrauns, 2012.

Rendtorff, Rolf. *The Old Testament: An Introduction.* Translated by John Bowden. Philadelphia: Fortress, 1986.

_____. *The Canonical Hebrew Bible: A Theology of the Old Testament.* Translated by David E. Orton. Leiden: Deo, 2005.

Roberts, J. J. M. *Nahum, Habakkuk, and Zephaniah.* Old Testament Library. Louisville: Westminster John Knox, 1991.

Rogland, Max. "Flying Scrolls and Flying Baskets in Zechariah 5: Philological Observations and Literary Implications." *Journal of Northwest Semitic Languages* 40.1 (2014): 93–107.

Sailhamer, John H. *The Pentateuch as Narrative.* Grand Rapids: Zondervan, 1992.

_____. *Introduction to Old Testament Theology: A Canonical Approach.* Grand Rapids: Zondervan, 1995.

_____. *Genesis Unbound.* Sisters, OR: Multnomah, 1996.

_____. *Biblical Prophecy.* Grand Rapids: Zondervan, 1998.

_____. "Hosea 11:1 and Matthew 2:15." *Westminster Theological Journal* 63 (2001): 87–96.

_____. *The Meaning of the Pentateuch: Revelation, Composition, and Interpretation.* Downers Grove, IL: InterVarsity, 2009.

Schart, Aaron. "Zur Redaktionsgeschichte des Zwölfprophetenbuchs." *Verkündigung und Forschung* 43 (1998): 13–33.

_____. "The Jewish and the Christian Greek Versions of Amos." In *Septuagint Research: Issues and Challenges in the Study of the Greek Jewish Scriptures*, eds. Wolfgang Kraus and R. Glenn Wooden, 157–77. Atlanta: SBL, 2005.

Schmidt, W. H. "Die deuteronomistische Redaktion des Amosbuches." *Zeitschrift für die alttestamentliche Wissenschaft* 77 (1965): 168–93.

Schmitt, Hans-Christoph. "Redaktion des Pentateuch im Geiste der Prophetie." *Vetus Testamentum* 32 (1982): 170–89.

Schneider, D. "The Unity of the Book of the Twelve." Ph.D. diss., Yale University, 1979.

Schneider, Wolfgang. *Grammar of Biblical Hebrew.* Translated by Randall L. McKinion. New York: Peter Lang, 2016.

Schniedewind, William M. *How the Bible Became a Book: The Textualization of Ancient Israel.* Cambridge: Cambridge University Press, 2004.

Schultz, Richard L. *Search for Quotation: Verbal Parallels in the Prophets.* Journal for the Study of the Old Testament Supplement 180. Sheffield: Sheffield Academic, 1999.

Seeligmann, Isac Leo. *Gesammelte Studien zur Hebräischen Bibel.* Tübingen: Mohr Siebeck, 2004.

Seitz, Christopher R. *Prophecy and Hermeneutics: Toward a New Introduction to the Prophets.* Grand Rapids: Baker, 2007.

BIBLIOGRAPHY

Seybold, K. "Vormasoretische Randnotizen in Nahum 1." *Zeitschrift für die alttestamentliche Wissenschaft* 101 (1989): 71–85.

_____. *The Goodly Fellowship of the Prophets: The Achievement of Association in Canon Formation*. Grand Rapids: Baker, 2009.

Shepherd, Michael B. "Compositional Analysis of the Twelve." *Zeitschrift für die alttestamentliche Wissenschaft* 120 (2008): 184–93.

_____. *Daniel in the Context of the Hebrew Bible*. New York: Peter Lang, 2009.

_____. "Hebrew Acrostic Poems and Their Vocabulary Stock." *Journal of Northwest Semitic Languages* 36/2 (2010): 95–108.

_____. *The Twelve Prophets in the New Testament*. New York: Peter Lang, 2011.

_____. "The Compound Subject in Biblical Hebrew." *Hebrew Studies* 52 (2011): 107–120.

_____. "So-called Emphasis and the Lack Thereof in Biblical Hebrew." *Maarav* 19 (2012): 181–95.

_____. "Targums." In *Dictionary of Jesus and the Gospels*, 2d ed., ed. Joel B. Green, 931–34. Downers Grove, IL: InterVarsity, 2013.

_____. *The Textual World of the Bible*. New York: Peter Lang, 2013.

_____. *The Text in the Middle*. New York: Peter Lang, 2014.

_____. "Is It 'To Him' or Is It 'Not'? Intentional Variation between לֹו and לֹא." *Journal for the Study of the Old Testament* 39 (2014): 121–37.

_____. *Textuality and the Bible*. Eugene, OR: Wipf & Stock, 2016.

_____. "The New Exodus in the Composition of the Twelve." In *Text and Canon: Essays in Honor of John H. Sailhamer*, eds. Robert L. Cole and Paul J. Kissling, 120–36. Eugene, OR: Pickwick, 2017.

Smith, John Merlin Powis. *A Critical and Exegetical Commentary on the Books of Micah, Nahum and Zephaniah*. International Critical Commentary. New York: Charles Scribner's Sons, 1911.

_____. *A Critical and Exegetical Commentary on the Book of Malachi*. International Critical Commentary. New York: Charles Scribner's Sons, 1912.

Smith, Ralph L. *Micah–Malachi*. Word Biblical Commentary 32. Nashville: Thomas Nelson, 1984.

Sommer, Benjamin D. *A Prophet Reads Scripture: Allusion in Isaiah 40–66*. Stanford, CA: Stanford University Press, 1998.

Staerk, W. "Der Begrauch der Wendung בְּאַחֲרִית הַיָּמִים im alttestamentliche Kanon." *Zeitschrift für die alttestamentliche Wissenschaft* 11 (1891): 247–53.

Stead, Michael. *The Intertextuality of Zechariah 1–8*. London: T&T Clark, 2009.

Steck, Odil Hannes. *The Prophetic Books and Their Theological Witness*. Translated by James D. Nogalski. St. Louis: Chalice, 2000.

Steinberg, Julius, and Timothy J. Stone. "The Historical Formation of the Writings in Antiquity." In *The Shape of the Writings*, eds. Julius Steinberg and Timothy J. Stone, 1–58. Winona Lake, IN: Eisenbrauns, 2015.

Steiner, Richard C. "Four Inner-Biblical Interpretations of Genesis 49:10: On the Lexical and Syntactic Ambiguities of עַד as Reflected in the Prophecies of Nathan, Ahijah, Ezekiel, and Zechariah." *Journal of Biblical Literature* 132 (2013): 33–60.

Sternberg, Meir. *The Poetics of Biblical Narrative: Ideological Literature and the Drama of Reading*. Bloomington: Indiana University Press, 1985.

Stuart, Douglas. *Hosea–Jonah*. Word Biblical Commentary 31. Nashville: Thomas Nelson, 1987.

Sweeney, Marvin A. *The Twelve Prophets*, 2 vols. Berit Olam. Collegeville, MN: Liturgical Press, 2000.

Sweeney, Marvin. Review of Michael Stead, *The Intertextuality of Zechariah 1–8*. London: T&T Clark, 2009. In *Journal of Semitic Studies* 56 (2011): 414–17.

Tigay, Jeffrey H. *The Evolution of the Gilgamesh Epic*. Philadelphia: University of Pennsylvania Press, 1982. Reprint, Wauconda, IL: Bolchazy-Carducci, 2002.

Timmer, D. C. "The Non-Israelite Nations in Zephaniah: Conceptual Coherence and the Relationship of the Parts to the Whole." In *The Book of the Twelve and the New Form Criticism*, eds. Mark J. Boda, Michael H. Floyd, and Colin M. Toffelmire, 245–63. Atlanta: SBL, 2015.

Torrey, C. C. "The Prophecy of Malachi." *Journal of Biblical Literature* 17 (1898): 1–15.

Tov, Emanuel. *The Greek and Hebrew Bible: Collected Essays on the Septuagint*. Leiden: Brill, 1999.

_____. *Textual Criticism of the Hebrew Bible*, 3d ed. Minneapolis: Fortress, 2012.

Ulrich, Eugene. *The Dead Scrolls and the Origins of the Bible*. Grand Rapids: Eerdmans, 1999.

VanderKam, James, and Peter Flint. *The Meaning of the Dead Sea Scrolls: Their Significance for Understanding the Bible, Judaism, Jesus, and Christianity*. New York: HarperCollins, 2002.

_____. "The Festival of Weeks and the Story of Pentecost in Acts 2." In *From Prophecy to Testament: The Function of the Old Testament in the New*, ed. C. A. Evans, 185–205. Peabody, MA: Hendrickson, 2004.

van der Merwe, Christo H. J. "The Challenge of Better Understanding Discourse Particles: The Case of לכן." *Journal of Northwest Semitic Languages* 40/2 (2014): 127–57.

_____, Jackie A. Naudé, and Jan H. Kroeze. *A Biblical Hebrew Reference Grammar*. Sheffield: Sheffield Academic, 1999.

van der Toorn, Karel. *Scribal Culture and the Making of the Hebrew Bible*. Cambridge, MA: Harvard University Press, 2007.

von Ewald, Georg H. A. *Commentary on the Prophets of the Old Testament*. Vol. 3, *Nahum, Zephaniah, Habakkuk, Zechariah 12–14, Jeremiah*. Translated by John Frederick Smith. London: Williams and Norgate, 1878.

von Rad, Gerhard. *Old Testament Theology*. Vol. 1, *The Theology of Israel's Historical Traditons*. Translated by D. M. G. Stalker. New York: Harper & Row, 1962.

Ward, William Hayes. *A Critical and Exegetical Commentary on Habakkuk*. International Critical Commentary. New York: Charles Scribner's Sons, 1911.

Watson, Wilfred G. E. *Classical Hebrew Poetry: A Guide to Its Techniques*. Sheffield: Sheffield Academic, 1984. Reprint, London: T&T Clark, 2006.

Westermann, Claus. *Basic Forms of Prophetic Speech*. Translated by Hugh Clayton White. Louisville: Westminster John Knox, 1991.

Wilson, Gerald H. "Psalms and Psalter: Paradigm for Biblical Theology." In *Biblical Theology: Retrospect and Prospect*, ed. Scott J. Hafemann, 100–110. Downers Grove, IL: InterVarsity, 2002.

Wolfe, R. E. "The Editing of the Book of the Twelve." *Zeitschrift für die alttestamentliche Wissenschaft* 53 (1935): 90–129.

Wolff, Hans Walter. *Hosea*. Translated by Gary Stansell. Hermeneia. Philadelphia: Fortress, 1974.

_____. *Obadja und Jona*. BKAT 13/4. Neukirchen: Neukirchener, 1977.

Würthwein, Ernst. *The Text of the Old Testament*, 2d ed. Translated by Erroll F. Rhodes. Grand Rapids: Eerdmans, 1994.